MY THREE SONS

MY THREE SONS

How God Separated Man, After Man (Through Satan) Separated Himself from God

Gabriel Obed David

Printed in the United States of America

ISBN 979-8-89114-095-0 (hc)
ISBN 979-8-89114-094-3 (sc)
ISBN 979-8-89114-096-7 (e)

Library of Congress Control Number: 2024912801

2026.03.17

MainSpring Books
5901 W. Century Blvd
Suite 750
Los Angeles, CA, US, 90045

www.mainspringbooks.com

"This book is dedicated to all people, that stood up for and shared God's truth – the Bible – with people around the world, throughout history and today, and sharing the truth of salvation for all mankind – all of noah's sons – through the Lord Jesus Christ – for His love and sacrifice for us all."

CONTENTS

CHAPTER 1

The Creation and Fall of Man: God, Satan, and Adam and Eve

HOW GOD SEPARATED MAN, AFTER MAN (THROUGH SATAN) SEPARATED HIMSELF FROM GOD USED KJV

When God created the heavens and the earth, everything was 'very good', including man (**gen. 1, gen. 2:1-7**) – and man_(adam and eve – **gen. 5:1-2**) had a connection to God through the Holy Spirit in man's soul, put there at creation, by Jesus (who is the Creator – **john 1:1-14; col. 1:12-20**), and He has been around forever (**heb. 13:8**), and all knew Him (Jesus) from adam on – before the flood – to noah (**gen. 3:8-10; gen. 5**), and possibly abraham and sarah (**gen 21 and 22; john 8:56-58**), maybe job (**job 19:25-27**), even moses did (**heb. 11:24-29**), and daniel's friends (**dan. 3:23-25**), and the people when He was here on earth (**matthew to john**), and ever since His death – with the Holy Spirit (in the saved – the true Christians).

And that connection (the Holy Spirit) was to go to every human that would ever be born on this earth (passed on in our soul – from adam to us), and as long as that connection (to God) was still there (obedience, no sin), we all would live forever here (**gen. 3:22**) in a loving, obedient relationship with God (and each other). And the Holy Spirit is what would keep us connected to God (with a relationship, and be holy to be with God – like in the garden of eden) so that He could help us and make the most of our life here (obeying and following Him), which would be best for all of man, then and now.

What happened? Why isn't it nice in the world?

First, we have to know none of us are good (**gen. 8:21; psalm 14; rom. 3**) – no one is – only God (**matt. 19:16-26**). Keep this in mind (it's not easy to accept) – we have to know this to understand man, this life, and world, etc. – go to Jesus to find out and change. Otherwise, we will not change or get along, etc. And we won't figure anything out here, unless we know we are evil (born that way) – and only God (Jesus) can get us to love, be nice, know truth, etc. – it (He) is the only way (**john 14:6**).

There is evil in the world and in us (an evil world of satan) and it affects us all until we go to Jesus. You have to accept this fact, then avoid the evil (and its consequences, etc.), by going to Jesus. And those consequences and punishments, etc. should get you to look into going to Jesus.

Be honest – you need to have punishment, to change, to learn, to grow, etc. – it's good for you – we need to try to help people. With God – He knows best. Only with Him, and share Him.

We all can see this evil world and man, and know what each of us think and sometimes look at – evil, so you can see who you are – who we all are, and need to go to God to change. Jesus does that – God tells us, in His word. That is why He came.

We are all born evil (sinful) – so you need to accept that, so no excuse for anyone. And you will have some behaviors or ideas, etc. (we are all born with – won't all be the same, but it will be against God and His word), and you will never get over them until you go to Jesus (truly saved – with the Holy Spirit), and not with false churches or ideas, etc. – going to church doesn't mean you are saved, etc. – you will still have your behaviors until you totally give in to

Jesus and His word, with the Holy Spirit. Need to be born again (**john 3**), spiritually, with Jesus, truth. People are going to church, etc. but not changing – having Jesus change their life with the Holy Spirit. Change you and your family, etc. – read and follow the bible (with the Holy Spirit).

All truth is to help people – and should motivate them to go to Jesus. This information is for that, and needs to be told.

You are not going to be perfect, but can be better – we all can be – we can change and go to Jesus – to really change, and be honest, otherwise we keep struggling, and blame others. And people seem to blame others or other things for their problems – nationality, color, some addiction, where they are, family, etc. – need to change and look at themselves – inside. Go to Jesus to do that.

It isn't God that abandoned us (we were created holy, as He is holy – **gen. 1 and 2**), it is man that abandoned God (and we still do through history, even today) – through satan (following him and his ways), with adam at the beginning (**gen. 3**), and we need to be holy again – and Jesus and the Holy Spirit is the only way back – through Him and His word, to be with God.

So man being separated from God (by God), causes God to reconcile with man – through Jesus (and the Holy Spirit).

And another thing you have to do, is to know something is wrong with you – then your family, nationality, etc. – leading you to know there is something wrong with man – humans, then that will lead you to Jesus – and the truth – no matter how smart or rich, etc. You know there is something wrong with this world, people, etc. – look today and in history, and know we have to change. And why God did and does what He does, and wants us to go to Him – to go to Jesus.

People are stubborn and prideful (like satan), and may not do what's best for themselves. That started at the beginning.

Adam and eve are who we all come from (**gen. 3:20**), but they sinned (disobeyed God – **gen. 3**, by listening to satan, who sinned first – **isa. 14:12-15**; **rev. 20:1-3** – and they ate of the tree of the knowledge of good and evil – which we all know the difference between the two today – no excuse) and they (adam and eve) lost the connection (the Spirit) to God, and death was the punishment (otherwise we would have lived forever here – **gen. 2:16-17**, with a loving relationship to God and each other), so they died spiritually first (since we are all connected to adam, we are all born dead spiritually – without the Holy Spirit, in our souls, from then on, and we are all born sinful – evil, disconnected, or separated, from God, and all – all of noah's sons, are destined for hell – **john 3:17-21**, until we go to Jesus), then eventually they (adam and eve – and the rest of mankind) died physically (**gen. 5**), as we all do since then (**heb. 9:27**) – so we wouldn't live forever in sin. The wages of sin is death (**rom. 6:23**).

And adam was originally a son of God when created (**luke 3:38**) – which changed after adam sinned, but we all can be sons (and daughters) of God through Jesus (and the Holy Spirit) – to be born again (**john 3:3-7**).

Ever since the beginning – the creation – adam had to believe in and follow God – he had a choice (free will – as satan, and angels. has, too), as we all do since (and today) – all of noah's sons need to go to God (through Jesus and the truth of His word). All of the evil in man and the world comes from sin (evil through satan) – we are all from adam and now from noah's sons – with satan leading man without God – Jesus. God set the world up (and cursed it – **gen. 3:14-19**), so there is punishment for sin in this world (then became more after the flood, and more with the jews). We need to choose Jesus (or satan and you, with sin). Sin has its own punishments and consequences – the way we live our lives and what we believe – so go to God and change that.

We have to go back to how it would have been if adam never sinned – to live like that – with Jesus (still connected to God – body, spirit and soul), the way man would have been today – but now only with Jesus is as close as we can get – with our spirit and soul (we will get a new body at the rapture), and live that way – the way God intended at creation – in heaven it will be that way.

Everyone – from adam on (presence of the Lord – **gen. 3:8-9; gen. 4:16**), has known of Jesus – He has been known by all men in the world, today and before (who is the Lord – **john 1:8-14; titus 2:11-15**), but not all have listened or followed, we follow satan – it's our fault – we send ourselves to hell (or have a choice to go to Jesus and heaven). No excuse. So we will live forever somewhere. Go to Jesus now to be in heaven.

So God created us to live forever (we still will, but not in this body or earth) – and we still will after this world (that God cursed, after man sinned – **gen. 3**) – in heaven or hell. And Jesus is the tree of life now for what God wanted for us.

The beginning was with one heaven, and one earth (**gen. 1:1**), and then the heaven was split up into two heavens – **gen. 1:6-10** – one for angels, near God, with stars, planets, etc., and one for the space around the earth – where angels also can and do come to – **gen. 2:1** – where eventually satan ended up (the stars were created on the fourth day near the earth – like the sun, and then spread out to their position in the universe, by God immediately, no evolution, or millions of years, etc., and so God controlled them, including the star of bethlehem, when Jesus was born in the manger – God put it in place and kept it there for two years and then took it away – it is not there now). And the creation days were twenty-four-hour days – just like we have today – 'the evening and the morning' – **gen. 1**, and why the jews next day starts at sundown, not midnight like we have (and the earth revolved around the sun – and there were about twelve hours of sunlight and about twelve hours of darkness – even in Jesus' day – **john 11:9**).

But there would be no need for more heavens (other than the third heaven that God is in, and was always there – and paul went there, **2 cor. 12:1-4**), nor would there really be any need for any earth (and the earth is a circle, as other planets, etc., even though man may not have known – God mentions it about 2500 years ago – **isa. 40:22**), if there is nothing on it – plants, animals, man, etc. (especially if satan and angels were in heaven – at least they don't need the earth, mainly since satan had not sinned yet – not until the eighth day – the day after the seventh day – the seventh day rest). So after all the creation and rest (and man hadn't sinned either) to have sin enter the creation (which is when death entered creation, not before, and even fossils, after the flood – which are caused by death – that were there and we find only after the flood, etc.).

After sin, God had to curse the creation, etc., since adam gave it to satan (**gen. 3**). If not, then the bible is not truth – we have to believe it, then see it (and we do see the evil in the world, and in ourselves – quit denying it). So the earth would be for man only (the only reason it was made) at first (even though angels can minister to man – and was their main purpose for being created – doing God's work – helping man and God's creation).

And there was no sin – by anyone – man or angels – if everything was 'very good' through the seventh day. So satan (who is a created being, as all angels are, during the creation week – **gen. 1:16; gen. 2:1; rev. 12:3-4**), didn't sin and neither did adam and eve until at least after the seventh day rest – the eighth day is the earliest – so no sin, (satan hadn't fallen, etc.) no death, etc. until after the seventh day.

It wouldn't be long after the seventh day rest, and six day creation, that satan sinned, and came to earth to tempt man (adam and eve), and man sinned (when sin – and death and evil, entered the creation) – which would probably have been on the eighth day (a new beginning), and the main reasons would be that adam and eve would have listened to God's command, and would begin to be fruitful and multiply (had sex), **gen. 1:28** – eve getting pregnant – which happens right away (how long would you take with a pretty wife, and both of you naked?). And if any amount of time had gone by, then not only would eve have been pregnant (the most amount of time would be a few months – eve had her first children after sin – **gen. 4:1-2** – both cain and abel were sinful, but both knew of God and could and did go to God – to sacrifice – **gen. 4:3-7** – so even if we go to God, we need to obey and know the truth – even today). So satan would have to have been there soon.

And also, with adam and eve (or any person), the longer they didn't eat of the tree of knowledge (and with the Lord walking and talking in the garden daily – **gen. 3:8-10**), the more of a habit and belief would set in to where they would have been used to not eating of the tree (there were many other trees – including the tree of life, that they could eat of, but didn't yet – **gen. 3:22-24**) – even eve would have followed (and satan wouldn't have been able to sway eve), and both would be set in their ways, habits, and beliefs, etc. (like people do with what they believe, even today – religions, politics, etc.), and won't be swayed to do or believe anything different (or at least very tough to do – even you). So satan would have to get there soon – and the soonest for him, would be on the eighth day (and death to start – first with the spiritual death, then physical death).

And if even a little time had passed, both adam and eve would have eaten of the tree of life (which God didn't want them to after they sinned – to live that way forever, **gen. 3:22-24** – sinful – we all would be that way forever – we are all sinful, evil – then and now). And God created us to live forever – death only came, because of sin (disobedience to God – **gen. 2:16-17**). So if they sinned, He had to keep them out of the garden – where the tree of life was (the rest of the earth was nice to live, comfortable, etc. – made for man, not like today – which can be uncomfortable, etc., after the flood). If we live forever in sin (like we do now), we would never be happy, safe, etc. – no laws, punishments, etc. – all of those are from God, we would never get away from the evil in this world, and never die – to escape this evil, satanic world. Thank God for Jesus (who is like the tree of life). So God kicked them out, and kept them out. Nothing else had changed from the creation, except we all were going to die, and the whole creation (cursed by God) would eventually come to an end.

So male (adam) and female (eve), both were created on the sixth day – **gen. 1:26-31**(and **gen. 2:16-25** is a recap of **gen. 1**, for man and woman), and both were 'very good', and there was no sin, death, etc. then. Then God rested on the seventh day.

And satan had to get adam and eve to eat of the tree of the knowledge of good and evil – to sin, before they ate of the tree of life – that would have them live forever in sin **(gen. 3:22-24)**. Know the truth.

So no later than the eighth day (and not earlier than the eighth day) – when satan had sinned and came to earth. Eight is a new beginning (seven-day week) – just like in music – eighth note is an octave – a new beginning.

So adam and eve had children – cain and abel, after sin. Even though abel followed God, cain did not, and cain killed abel (**gen. 4**), so adam's line from seth (adam and eve's son after cain and abel), cain's descendants all died in the flood, and seth continues the line that is related to noah and his sons (**gen. 5**). So we are not from cain or abel, but from adam through seth **gen. 5:3-8**) up to noah (when we looked similar) – now we are all from one of noah's three sons (**gen. 9:18-19**) – God starting over with man (but still sinful from adam) after the flood (now we all look different – about 500 years after the flood).

So evil started before the flood (with adam, through satan – **gen. 3**), but got worse after the flood (and people are not from cain, after the flood, but from noah's sons – **gen. 5:32**, and some, like today, may not go to Jesus), and even more after Jesus died – the evil all from satan – getting the evil brought out of man (even though man is capable of some 'good'), without God in our life – His Spirit (the good thing after Jesus died and rose, is that He is available to all to fight satan, and for us to be better) – but none (in the world – now and in the past) are good, and it is what God thinks and says (in His word) that matters (**rom. 3**).

Even noah was not perfect (and neither were his sons), and neither are all of us. But noah listened to God – we need to also. Be on His side, not man's (or satan's). So we are separate.

And it was all of the separations that God made in the earth and in man (through noah's sons – japheth, shem, and ham – **gen. 9**) – after the flood that helped keep satan from uniting man all against God (like before the flood – **gen. 6**, and a little after – **gen. 11**). God separating man with noah's sons.

The big issue that is not being talked about, is that we are all from one of noah's sons and are stuck and connected to them (and their abilities, talents, etc., and also our lot in life, from them – the type of evil person you are). All need to go to God individually since then (adam, now from noah's sons). And it is still that way today (stuck with man), until we go to Jesus, and get born again (get the Holy Spirit).

Before we go to Jesus we are stuck with this world – to sin, man, etc. (all of noah's sons – with the differences, etc.), but if we are with Jesus we are changed and one (**gal. 3:22-29**), and not connected to this evil world (or man anymore).

We bear the image of the earthly – man (adam, and noah's sons after the flood) – but with Jesus (and the Holy Spirit), we bear the image of the heavenly (**1 cor. 15:49**).

Before God separated man – noah's sons at the tower of babel, with the language change (**gen. 11**) – all of noah's sons were dependent on each other, and worked together (with ham, nimrod trying to lead) – even to be successful (building the tower of babel, etc.) and they (all of noah's sons) stayed together (they didn't scatter like God wanted man to do – **gen. 11:4, 9**). Once God separated man, then the differences started to show in each of noah's sons from then to now (not only their talents, abilities, etc., but their color, speech, etc.) – showing how different japheth, shem, and ham are (and still are today).

Ham – through nimrod (cush's son – **gen. 10:6-14**), was leading all of man against God (**gen. 11:1-9**) – all of noah's sons – so God had to separate man (all of the sons), and put ham in a lower position (where noah cursed canaan, including ham, and nimrod – to be a servant of servants – **gen. 9:25**), and eventually so ham would need japheth and shem someday (and they would use ham and his descendants like they do today – their lot in life) – **gen. 9:25-27**. And now we all have to live with whatever son we are from – their lot in life (just like God would do to the jews – **jer. 13:22-27**) – we are stuck with them (you, and your ancestors did) – until we go to Jesus and be one with Him (and get away from man – noah's sons, and even adam) – like we start to see the sons do in america (Jesus' land to help us all get together and go to Jesus and share Him with the world).

Why don't we all get along?– God doesn't want us to without Jesus – and satan keeps trying to make it look like we can without Jesus, but we can't – and we can see that – but we (and satan) keep trying without listening to God and going to Jesus.

We can't get away from what God did and is doing – only go to Jesus, when we finally wise up and accept this is what God wants for us – and the alternative is satan (and eventually hell).

This world is evil – so no matter what happens – your people (noah's sons) need to go to God to make things work for you. Do it. Or live with the consequences. Jesus is waiting.

The flood (especially after the tower of babel – **gen. 11**) led to everyone being separated and the reason for Jesus to come here, to unite us all – not satan uniting all against God. But it will happen again in the end times – basically today. Go to Jesus.

All sons of noah can and need to be saved by Jesus – have you done that? If not, stop complaining about your lot or place in life. God made this world, and Jesus is the only one to help or change you.

Everyone is from noah's sons – no matter what you look like, and noah was from adam when God started over (**gen. 5; gen. 9**) – after the flood – so we are from adam, too – and like adam, the food that God gave him (man) to eat (**gen. 1:29**) is still the best for our bodies (that God had man eat before the flood – fruit and vegetables) – for all of us, even today (after the flood), no matter what country you were born, or what you look like (or what diet you ate with them). People have a tough life and hurt themselves – don't take care of themselves (eat unhealthy, bad lifestyle, etc.) and still want a good life or a better one – but they can't even take care of themselves (and causing problems for others) – how would they be able to take care of anyone else. And we still need to go to Jesus, and the truth of His word.

About 400 years after the flood (after man scattered all over the world – about 100 years or so after the flood, around the time peleg was born or lived – **gen. 10:25** – because of the tower of babel – God still wanted us to scatter or divide, even though the earth was separated by water – continents, like we see today – caused by the flood – making it harder on satan to unite us all against God again) – we then all started to look different – nationality, color, etc. – new traits coming out for our appearance – about 3900 years ago (about1900 bc), and stayed that way – and all from noah's sons (helped along by the language change at the tower of babel – **gen. 11**, and the weather and geography change after the flood). Even in **gen. 10** – before the tower of babel – which caused man to scatter (**gen. 11**), God mentions that the languages will eventually change man's life (nations, and the gentiles – told to moses, in 1400bc). And it's not as long ago as you think, and it doesn't need to be – that still is a long time ago (satan, using man, wants you to think it is millions of years, so 4,000 seems ridiculous – but it is enough years for who we are – the way God made things – and satan doesn't want you to believe the bible is truth). God wanted us separated – not like before the flood.

So the earth (the creation – about 6,000 years ago) was created for man (and all that is on it) when he was created (**gen. 1,** and was 'very good'). It was created in six days (not millions, and billions of years ago) by God – Jesus (God could have done it in two seconds, but seven days is important to Him and to us).

And God uses the number seven a lot – seven day creation, joshua circling jericho for seven days, seven years for nebuchadnezzar in the wild, seventy weeks of daniel, seven year tribulation, and many more, and other numbers are important, too – three, and ten, etc., and even a thousand – no number bigger than that until modern times – like the last 700 years – using a million, billion, etc. – but there are no years that long (no evolution, etc.) – God only used a thousand (like in **rev. 9:16**). And in **gen. 24:60**, the word million (which is from the word millennium – which is for a 1,000 year reign of Jesus) is used, but shouldn't be – added later around the 1500's or so (by the english, when million was starting to be used), and should be called a 'myriad' of people (which is many – or too many to number, in hebrew – rebabah). Even the chinese and romans didn't use any number bigger than 1,000. There are only thousands of years, not millions (even though we can use it for other things – but know the truth about it).

A thousand years is like a day to God (**psalm 90:4; 2 pet. 3:8**) – it shows that God is outside of time (days are our days at creation in **gen. 1** – evening and morning is the first day, etc.) – and the end will happen at any time (**2 pet. 3:9-10**). It is even possible that God uses a day for 1,000 years (not in the creation – it is clear it is one 24-hour day), but maybe some others, like in **hosea 6:1-2**, possibly – those would be the last 2,000 years, and then after the tribulation, the 1,000 year millennium – Jesus' reign (for the jews). So we have six days creation, and will be here for 6,000 years (representing those years – showing we will be here for 6,000 years) – then God had the seventh day rest (after the six day creation), and the 1,000 year reign of Jesus will be after the tribulation (after the 6,000 years on earth are used – so 7,000 years total, like 7 day creation with the day of rest), just before eternity – heaven.

You have to first believe God created us and need to go to and obey Him – which is through Jesus – no other way. You can get to know Jesus and get saved, but you need to know Jesus believes the whole bible, and we need to know the truth of it.

So God had a process (six days – our work week – for us) He wanted to go through to create what we see – and it is the first earth (with nothing on it – it started void – **gen. 1:2** – just like man was, until the Lord God breathed the Holy Spirit into him – **gen. 2:7**) and a heaven (with nothing in it) – nothing before the creation (**gen. 1:1**). Jesus is the Creator (**john 1:1-4, 14; eph. 3:8-10; col. 1:9-20**). And God will make a new earth and heaven (**rev. 21**). And light and darkness were important for man to live here – day and night (**gen. 1:3-5**) – for sleep, time, rest, etc. (and eventually seasons, etc. – **gen. 8:22**). And only since satan (lucifer) sinned – in heaven first – after the seventh day rest – did sin enter the creation at any time. And lucifer, with the angels (created for man), were possibly created before the third day – when God set the foundation of the earth – land – **gen. 1:9-13**, which seems to be in **job 38:4-7** (but looks like angels were created on the fourth day – **gen. 1:14-19; gen. 2:1; rev. 12:3-9**) – but most of the verses in **job 38** are mostly at the flood and just after, when God remade or restored the earth – laying the new foundations of the earth (which is different like we see today – separated land – not like it was before the flood – the land and oceans being all in one place, etc.), and the mentioning of clouds, lightning, thunder, snow, hail, ice, lions eating prey, etc. – were all after the flood (**gen. 8:22; gen 9:2-4, 13-16**), not before (**gen. 1:29-30; gen. 2:5-6**). And noah and his family were hidden in the ark, until the water subsided – so the sons of God could be there to see when God did that (when all of the people were killed in the flood – no people to see it restored) – whether it was at creation or after the flood.

Regardless, satan would have come to earth no earlier than the eighth day (the day after the seventh day rest – when everything was done – and very good – **gen. 2:1-4**, including the host – angels, cherubim, etc., of heaven – who God uses for His purposes, in some cases to help us, but they can also sin, and leave God, and heaven for good) – and that is when sin entered the creation first – not before – **gen. 3** (and satan has free will, and we all do – to be with God or not).

And the rainbow is the sign that God won't destroy the earth like that (**gen. 9:8-17**) – but the world will end just after the tribulation (in the future – and should be soon), then the 1,000-year reign, and eternity forever. The earth will last until then (**gen. 8:22**). So go to Jesus now.

And satan came to earth (God allowing) and tempted man to sin (on earth, only after the six day creation, and seventh day rest), then sin would enter this world and universe (not before the creation, or during) – then they were all cursed by God (satan, man, and the earth, universe, etc. – the creation – **gen. 3**), and that is when sin entered first (not before the seven day creation – **gen. 1 and 2**) – and sin (disobedience to God) is death (**gen. 2:16-17; gen. 3**). So satan has only been here for 6,000 years – since the creation, in the garden of eden – the only amount of time that man (and the universe, etc.) has been here (and hidden in **rev. 20:2-7** – has 1,000 in each verse), and there will be one more 1,000 years – when Jesus reigns here on earth, but satan will be bound for those 1,000 years (**rev. 20:3**). So there are 7,000 years total for the life on this earth, then eternity starts – heaven. And there was nothing before that, except God, the Father, Son, and Holy Spirit (the Godhead), without time.

So there would be no need for angels to hangout or go to earth or a planet, etc. – since they can go anywhere in the universe (unlike man) – why focus here? At first there is no one here (man was created on the sixth day) – nothing before the creation – the only reason satan would come to earth is because it is important to God (with man here – who God loves – probably more than angels, and angels were to minister to man, and do God's will). Nothing before this earth or creation (**gen. 1**) – except the Godhead – the Father, Son, and Holy Spirit – no time, space, matter, etc. (nothing to prove otherwise, just like evolution is not true and no proof – even though they say they do). And God says 'us' (the Godhead) at creation in **gen. 1:26**, and also the Lord says 'us' (the Godhead) after sin in **gen. 3:22 and in gen. 11:7** after the flood at the tower of babel (and maybe even in **isa. 6:8**). And that was the first and only creation, then there will be a new heaven and new earth later (**rev. 21**) – the first earth (that we are on now – first created in **gen. l** – even after the flood changed it – **gen. 7 to 9**) – because of sin of man (and satan), and the heaven above will be gone (there will be a new one of each forever – **rev. 21** – without sin, satan, etc.).

So in this world (this planet), there is need for sleep, time, night, darkness, pain, limits, etc. – on earth (**gen. 1** – and still created perfect and very good – before sin – **gen. 3**) – and there were no need for those before this earth was created (just God, the Father, Son and the Holy Spirit), and in heaven – eternity, there is no need for those – no night, no pain, no darkness, no sleep, etc. (**rev. 21**). Nothing before the six-day creation, and nothing after the 1,000-year reign of Jesus (after satan is let loose for a while – **rev. 20** – then put in the lake of fire, with hell and those in it).

But for now, we are living in a sinful world (caused by man – through satan – **gen. 3**), so God cursed what could have been a perfect world, if satan or man had not sinned (although we have free will), but now we have to choose Jesus or not (and get to heaven, forever).

God has evil here – and satan – and an uncomfortable world to live in after the flood – so we would go to Jesus. Everyone wonders why this world is evil – sin – and it is because God separated man (after the flood), because of sin and man not going to Him (separated now – so satan couldn't unite all of man against God – like before and just a little after the flood – **gen. 6 and 11**) – and hopefully that will lead us to unite and be one with God. So everything divided can't stand (**luke 11:18**).

So satan could be in the waters (before the flood) or space above the earth after creation – in the air, so he could be there, and on the earth, until he is sent to the pit (temporarily), or lake of fire (forever). There are heavens now (mainly two that are used – one near the earth – for birds, clouds, etc., and one for outer space – for planets, stars, etc.) – **gen. 2:1-3** and there will eventually be a new heaven after the first creation is gone (**rev. 21:1**) – with no sin. God has His own heaven (the third heaven – Holy).

Was sin in heaven with God (with satan – the accuser of man, **rev. 12:10**)? Possibly, when satan (lucifer) was first created (until he sinned), and then was kicked out when sin – iniquity was found in him (**ezek. 28:15**), but he is not now in heaven (after sin – only in the heaven near the earth or in space – not God's heaven) – since the beginning (**gen. 3**). And God still uses satan (God can get rid of satan any time, but wants free choice for us to see the difference of good and evil), even though satan is sinful, evil (and leads us also – for our choice), and was kicked out of heaven, because of his sin (**isa. 14:12-15; ezek. 28:13-19; rev. 12:7-8**) – like adam and eve were kicked out of the garden of eden because of sin – not to go back (**gen. 3:22-24**) – and both **gen. 3** and **rev. 12** are similar – both have satan trying to stop man, especially Jesus (first with eve, then with israel). And satan (after he sinned – **isa. 14:12-15**) was only in the presence of the Lord – who is Jesus (**job 1:6; job 2:1**) – like man could be or not (**gen. 3:8; gen. 4:16**) – in His presence (before and after the flood), and like who (the Lord Jesus) was here on earth for a time – but it was before the flood, the Lord wasn't going to strive – with His Spirit, with man anymore (**gen. 6:3**), and just like the human Jesus (who is the Lord all throughout the bible – always has been the Lord – **heb. 13:8**) was here on earth physically (and satan tempted Him when He was here – **matt. 4:1-11** – just like satan does us today), and man (sinful, evil) could be around with Him (Jesus – who is sinless) – unlike God, the Father, who cannot be around evil, sin (satan, man, etc.), and only with holy things. But satan is not with God the Father in heaven (after satan sinned), and satan was only fighting with michael (who can come to earth), not anyone else (**jude 1:9; rev. 12:7-9**), and not in the heaven with God (**2 cor. 12:1-4**), after he sinned. And satan was not with God (in heaven) in the **book of job** (**job 1:6; job 2:1**) – only in the presence of the Lord (Jesus), not in heaven. God separated satan from heaven – from His heaven (which would be the third heaven). Angels can (as can the Holy Spirit and Jesus) be with evil – but God the Father cannot be (that's why we will get an incorruptible body – a holy one, when we get raptured and go up to Him, when Jesus comes back for the true Christians – **1 cor. 15:50-57**). And Jesus (in His incorruptible body) and the Holy Spirit are not evil and are with God, the Father, in heaven.

It's possible that God would have sent satan (lucifer) to hell or the pit, etc. forever, if adam and eve would have listened to God and not satan, and didn't eat of the tree of the knowledge of good and evil – no sin. And we would be here forever with God in paradise. And God wanted to know what man would do with satan here (follow God or satan), even though God knew what would happen. But He loves us and wants us to be with Him – but holy, not sinful. Now we all have to be with Jesus and get saved and then be with God in heaven after we die. And that is the purpose for satan – to show us the difference between good and evil (sin, etc.). Once we see the difference, then we make a choice. And should lead us to Jesus.

And God knows that satan (and his evil) will lead some people to Him – to Jesus. God uses everything for good. Even sin.

There is always separation (from God and by God) with sin.

And sin is why God made laws, punishments, etc. – there would be no need for laws, if we would listen and follow God and His commandments, etc. Laws are only for the lawless and disobedient (**1 tim. 1:8-17**). And now we need Jesus and the Holy Spirit, with His word, to guide us – to connect us to God.

Man is separated from life to death, with sin, until we go to Jesus (the Creator) to unite us back to life (salvation – with the Holy Spirit). Otherwise we are still stuck and connected to noah's sons (and adam – man) and sinful, and who they are (and why we don't get along and never will), until we go to Jesus, and become one with Him.

Sin separates us from God (**isa. 59:2**), and Jesus reconciles us to God (**rom. 5:9-11**).

God made this world (mainly after the flood) with different types of people – besides color, abilities, etc. (after the flood to the tower of babel – **gen. 9, 10 and 11**), but also size – tall, short, etc., and all can get along – but only with Jesus can this work the best (or work at all).

So the flood separated the old world – before the flood, to the new world after the flood – God making it a different world and people (a punishment and a tougher world to live in – what we live in now), but not a new creation (He used all of the original parts of creation – man – with noah and his family – like adam, and the animals, etc. – all on the ark).

This is the most important issue – God made this world to only work best for man, if (big if) we all go to Him – and get connected to Him with His Spirit (the Holy Spirit – that He originally created man – adam, with), only through Jesus (the Lord) and His word – the truth of it. Mainly because of satan's plan (especially since Jesus' death and resurrection) – to go against God and His word – all of mankind to do the same – like man – first with adam (through satan) did before the flood (**gen. 6**) and just after the flood at the tower of babel (**gen. 11**), before the language change. We all were the same, looked the same, and talked the same, etc. – but still evil – so satan could unite man easier – all together against God (and satan did that).

Things are built – including towers, pyramids, churches, etc. – all against God – satan wanting places for man to worship him (satan) – man has made them all through history – since the flood (but satan can't get all of man against God, except at the tower of babel – so the languages changing, separated man).

If there was no separation of man and God – then there would be no need for reconciliation (**rom. 5:8-11; 2 cor. 5:14-21; eph. 2:11-22; col. 1:18-29; philip. 3:17-21**) – it would not be necessary. Jesus wouldn't have to come here and die for all of us.

God created us for Him, and if we go against Him, He is the one to punish us – and also the one to help us out of anything. And He did it with Jesus. We need to go to Him and His ways – His word (and it has to be the truth), to solve our problems, and to get along with Him and each other – we are made for that. But only can with God.

God had to make laws – for man's sin, but with the Holy Spirit we have a chance (the only chance) to obey God – because of Jesus.

But if we are truly with Jesus, then we are now in grace, not law (like the jews were) – with Jesus we die to sin. Go to Him. We will follow the laws naturally with the Holy Spirit (**gal. 5:22-23**). But we still need laws in this world – for all.

Our main purpose on earth is to reconcile with God – through Jesus (**rom. 5:10; 2 cor. 5:16-21; col. 1:19-29**). And only by Jesus and only with the Holy Spirit that only Jesus (the Creator) can give you, like He gave adam and eve at creation (who lost it). Now you see why we all (all humans then and now) have to go to Jesus and to Jesus alone, or not get along like we see in the world – in the past and still see today. We can't do anything, except go to Jesus to change. If you are picky about words, meanings, etc. (and it is important in the bible) for anything in the bible – then you need to see our connection to noah and his sons – and it is not that hard (**gen. 9:18-19, 27; gen. 10:32**). And how it affects all of us today – it has not stopped since the flood – our punishment for all of mankind's sin before the flood (who we are all from – initially all from adam and eve – **gen. 1 to 5**) – and still being punish – all from sin, evil, etc.

The best way to live in this world – for all groups, is to do what God wants – in His word (and it has to be the truth), which will work best with Jesus and the Holy Spirit, when you get saved – or people (men, women, nationalities, beliefs, etc.) will not be happy no matter how hard we try to get along.

If you don't follow adam or noah's sons, then don't follow your own nationality – german, arab, jew, italian, native american, african, religions, beliefs, culture, etc. (don't look at where you are born and to who – you have no choice of that). Stop going back to your own recent ancestors – great, great, grandfather, etc. (don't stop there – for whatever problems they had, etc.), if you are not going to go all the way back to the beginning – to when God created man – adam. That's the starting point for all of us – then now through to noah's sons. We are all connected and evil for what all of us do from the beginning – sinful. We can't escape our connection to noah's sons (to man), except by going to Jesus and getting connected to God – otherwise we are stuck to man and satan and problems, hate, prejudice, evil, sin, etc.

No matter where you are born, you are free, if you go to Jesus – even if it is tough – share Jesus – God feels you can and will handle where you are born and to who, He will help you, if you go to Him (and the reason it may be tough for you). No matter what son of noah you are.

Go to God through Jesus. There are some of noah's sons not connected to them anymore (but not many), because they have gone to Jesus and changed their lives and destiny (become the sons of God, with the Holy Spirit) – for their direction in this world and after. We all are not connected to who Jesus is from – Jesus was a jew, and gentiles follow Him – because He is God and the truth – not because He is one of your own – nationality, etc. (like some nationalities do for their religion). Most people are not jews and almost all true Christians are not jews – but all believe in Jesus and the bible – that are both from the jews. Know the bible is true – not your own nationality, beliefs, family, etc.

So the jews brought us the bible and who Jesus came from, but they still need to go to Him – as we all do – all of noah's sons. That is why God had the jews developed – to follow Him (a people for Himself) and share the truth with the world – including the bible, and Jesus (and no one else can get us to God). And we know that the bible is truth – because no one writes bad, evil things about themselves, as much as the bible does about the jews. Should keep leading us to Jesus.

It is satan who makes people hate jews – all of noah's sons can, so we will hate Jesus – who is a jew – even jews don't follow Jesus. Look in the world – the religions, beliefs, etc. – they mostly follow their own people and leader, etc. – whatever son of noah. They think their belief is right because it is one of them – their nationality, culture, etc. – they have no idea. We are all from adam (from man – now from noah's sons), and sinful (because he disobeyed God), and only Jesus can change that and us – not your own leader, nationality, etc. – they are fooled and lied to by satan to start their religion, belief, etc., and have those follow them. Wake up. Be strong enough not to follow your own – whatever son of noah (nationality) you are.

Even though the jews as a whole don't believe in and follow Jesus – it is Jesus who is protecting and keeping the jews alive (especially today with america). God is doing that.

Man obviously knows there is a God (or some being – like satan, that is powerful and not seen) – with all of the religions, etc. (that satan creates), and God tries to get man to go to Him (although satan wants to be God and be worshipped, too, so he tries to fool man, if he can, and has over the years, from the beginning, and today), but we don't go the right way to get to God – the true God (and He has to show us – and we have to, and need to, know that the way is really from Him – **john 8:32; john 14:6**) and is why He comes (the Spirit, the Lord, etc.) to us since the beginning, through Jesus (especially since Jesus' death and resurrection), and only Jesus (He proved He is from God – with miracles, healings, resurrection, etc. – **john 20:30-31**, and many things not written – **john 21:24-25**). No one else has – ever (even though satan does some things over the years, that God allows him to do, being an angel – a higher one, and has power more than man – as do demons – fallen angels, but not more power than Jesus – **john 10:21; 1 john 4:4** – who is God, **john 8:58; exo. 3:13-16; col. 2:8-10**). Jesus covers our sins (and our sin nature – we are born with), and only Jesus can forgive and take our sins (satan cannot – neither can any man, religious leader, etc. – satan just makes it worse on man – to sin more, and not go to Jesus, and His truth).

If you don't have Jesus in your life – you don't have the true God in your life – you have only satan leading you. So look in the world and see who is in charge.

We have to know satan is real – but evil – against God, truth, etc., as we do know Jesus is real – to help us. Don't people want to know the truth of how we got here – all the different nationalities, languages, looks, abilities, beliefs, etc.? And satan doesn't want you to know the truth, so you won't go to the bible, or to Jesus. Most Christians are ignorant of the truth of the bible (satan leading all) – we need to keep learning then, so we can share better – all through the Holy Spirit we are saved with by Jesus. Make sure you are truly saved – too many false churches, etc.

Prove your belief, church, etc. by the truth of the bible and how you live your life, not by rituals, traditions, leaders, etc. –by being saved by Jesus and the Holy Spirit. Otherwise satan fools you (**john 8:43-59**).

You have a choice for the truth – don't believe that all go to heaven (like most religions do) – only with Jesus can we. Know the truth – we and the world are so evil – stop living in denial. God and the bible are true – read it – and go to Jesus (the way God made us to). Don't believe satan (with all of these false churches, religions, beliefs, etc.) – he is going to hell (even though he knows the truth – he still lies) – don't join him. Choose Jesus.

How does the bible know so many things, way before we know it, or it before it happens – like what's best for health, prophesies, end times, technology, etc., besides where we are going after this life. And there is no one else in the universe (just angels, and man on this earth), no matter how long we have tried to search and find that out. No evolution, etc.

And satan had man come up with evolution and millions and billions, etc. of years (so that 6,000 years will seem like a short time), so it looks like it will take time for us to change, from how man is today – evil, unhealthy, etc., and be able to change eventually with all the years left (and survival of the fittest, etc.), and along with technology, etc. to be better sometime down the road – so we don't need God, etc. to get better and be nice and get along, etc. We never will, until we go to Jesus, and the truth of His word – the bible, and why He wrote the bible, so we would see satan's lies better.

The bible has predicted many things in this world – including Jesus, and wrote of historical things, etc. – trust it, and believe it. Jesus came to us, when He didn't need to – to help us. Read it. And there are still more predictions to come (**matt. 24; book of revelation**). God cares about us and wants us with Him and to know the truth.

Many people saw Jesus (even after He died and rose – **1 cor. 15:1-8**), and knew the things He did and said – He wanted us to see Him and know Him, and you can't say that with any belief (only satan trying to copy God – and be God – tricking people to follow him and his lies – all of these false churches, religions, beliefs, etc., in all of the cultures in the world – of all of noah's sons).

Jesus came to show that God is real and that He is the Creator and made humans (and angels) and everything else (**john 1**). And God came here as a human – showing He made us (and can heal us, etc.). And to share the truth – not just satan sharing his lies. Jesus is for all of us, and He came to save us (from our sin of following satan and his lies, etc.), if we would just go to Him (get the Holy Spirit) and follow Him and His truth in His word.

Jesus told us that – all the prophesies of what He did and was going to do, are in the old testament (like **psalm 2** – tells things leading up to Jesus, and **psalm 22** – Him on the cross, **and isaiah 9:6-7** – His birth, and who He is – **isa. 53**, and as King riding on a colt – **zech. 9:9**, and many others), as well as the new testament reveals (**mark 15:34; luke 1:26-33; luke 19:28-40; john 19:24; john 20:30-31**, and many others). Go read them (there are so many things He did that the books couldn't be written – **john 21:25**). These are the main verses that show Jesus in the old testament – **gen. 3:14-15; deut. 18:15-19; dan. 9:24-27; psalm 22:1,13-18; isa. 11**, and related to the new testament – **rom. 15:8-13; heb. 11:24-26; heb. 13:8**). There are no excuses. God tells us and shows us through the Holy Spirit. God will help you understand. It's all there. Look at the world, science, history, man, etc. through the eyes of God, in the bible, with the Holy Spirit (**1 cor. 2**). He set it up for us. So we can see the lies of satan and sinful man (all of us).

There are so many predictions about Jesus coming – you read them all in the old testament (so much evidence). God coming to us.

Jesus is from God and is God (**john 1**) – and is the only begotten Son of God (**psalm 2:7; john 3:16; acts 13:32-33; rom. 1:1-6**), and died for us all – all of our sins (we need to believe that and follow Him), so we can get to God, and be with Him.

And after Jesus died and rose, there is no one else to follow (only satan trying to fool people since then, **2 cor. 11:13-15** – since satan would want to be God – **isa. 14:12-17; ezek 28:13-19**). And when satan goes to you, you think it is real and from God, when it is just satan using your pride to think you know the truth that no one else knows, etc. – like all of the different 'prophets', cultures, etc., have over the centuries.

But it is God who came to us, through Jesus, and He proved who He is (miracles, etc.), and was open about all He did, with many witnesses (especially the jews – who should have followed, but rejected Him). It is Jesus who we need to go to. You don't have to be a jew to go to Jesus – He is for all people (all of noah's sons – and make us all one, though we are different – **1 cor. 12:12-14**). He died for all of us.

It is through Jesus (**eph. 2:11-13**), that we all can be one (**gal. 3:26-29**). The only good in this world is with Jesus – people that are truly following Him.

So we can go to God through Jesus (because He paid for all sins of all of us – **2 cor. 5:14-21**), if (and a big if) we would just go to Him and believe (have faith) and follow Him (and only the truth of Him and His word). We have a choice. So go to Jesus.

People don't like to be criticized, just complemented – but we need both – being truthful – knowing what is right and wrong (even though we all have known both since adam – **gen. 2:16-17; gen. 3:1-5, 10-12**) – the truth. What is best.

So people don't always want to know the truth – we need to go to Jesus and His word and change, grow, etc. – hard for some to do.

God (Jesus) is for the best for man. No one else can help man – can't be anyone but Jesus (**acts 4:10-12**). And why God wrote the bible – and it was written for man to understand – the truth – it's plain and clear, so believe it, and what it says to all of us. To go against all of satan's lies over the years and especially today in all areas (and groups – even false churches, etc. – **2 pet. 2:1-3**) of our life. Don't follow this world (**rom. 2:12**).

If God needs to do miracles to help people to get to know Him and His power – know He is God – like Jesus did, He will. But if He doesn't do miracles or they don't help people go to Him – He won't – like

God did in egypt (why didn't the egyptians, or pharaoh, etc. believe and follow Him, when they saw how powerful He is – or any of the others throughout the bible? – because of pride, stubbornness, etc. – satan blinding them). Or some miracles that Jesus didn't do, because of unbelief (**matt. 11:20-24; luke 10:8-20**). You don't always need a miracle to believe, but if there are miracles, then why don't you believe?

Don't wait for a miracle – just go to Jesus (get the Holy Spirit) and follow His word. Getting the Holy Spirit back in us through Jesus is a miracle – salvation.

We should be walking by faith, not by sight (**2 cor. 5:7**). Go to Jesus – the truth (His word), before you or anyone dies.

We are saved by faith (**heb. 11**) – just like abraham was – he listened to and believed God (**gen. 22**), and we need to do that today – believing in and following Jesus. But the truth of God today (like abraham) – no law, no ritual, no leader, etc. – just His word – like in Jesus (then and today – **heb. 11:24-29; heb. 13:8**). Then we do good works, etc. – believe and live the way God says – by faith in Jesus and His word.

God wants us to have faith in Jesus – then and today – even though there is evidence for Jesus and what He did in the bible and the truth you see in the creation – from the beginning to now (**rom. 1:18-25**). And He says, 'blessed are they that have not seen, and yet have believed' (**john 20:29**). Through the bible and the Holy Spirit, we get when saved. So we cannot wait until we die and are in hell, before we believe (**luke 16:19-31**). We need to get saved before we die.

There isn't a lot of time in this life, sometimes – spend it doing good things – like read and learn the bible to know the truth (His truth) and what we should do in this life (use your time wisely) – so go to Jesus for help. And know where you are going after this. And share Him and His truth today.

That's why God wrote the bible – so we would know the truth – apart from satan's lies over the years (even in churches, religions, beliefs, etc.). And know the truth of Jesus.

God won't allow satan to get rid of the bible – so satan makes up lies about it, and starts false churches and religions, etc. (sometimes using the bible to throw people off the truth in these beliefs – almost to the point of being good, or working for your salvation).

So works means religion, etc. (satan leading) – trying to be good. God with the Holy Spirit – can only help you – through Jesus, then He will lead you, and connect you back to God, will do good things then that He wants you to do.

People belong to many religions, beliefs, etc., but don't really know all of what they are to believe, or know anything or why they believe, except because of their parents, family, friends, culture, etc. that believe in it. That is not good enough – know the truth and look for that in the world. And Jesus has already come here and shared that with us all, but we don't look into it, and we are driven by our sin and pride, etc. (and sometimes hatred, etc.) – just like satan (who is separating man from God, even with false churches, religions, etc.). So don't be loyal to your family, culture, etc., but to the truth. Go to Jesus, truth.

It is sin that separates man from God, and Jesus is the only way (Mediator, Savior, etc.) to get back to (with the Holy Spirit), and get right with, God (**john 14:6; 1 tim. 2:3-6**) – with His word, through Jesus. To be one with Him. And His love, as well as justice, righteousness, etc. – away from our sinful nature. We are happiest this way, and God wants us to be that way. We have to stop fighting against Him. Be with Him.

All souls are God's – He created us (**ezek. 18:4**), and wants us to be with Him (and why He created us – for Him, but we have to choose to be with Him – free will) – but it has to be the way He wants, not what we want (or what satan says) – so He tells what way that is – it is only through Jesus. Be one with Him again.

Even man and woman started as one (woman started in man – **gen. 2:18-25; gen. 5:3**), then God separated them (him), then they became one again (with marriage – only a man and woman), and separate from (or leave) their parents (but God was their parent then, so they wouldn't separate from Him – as we all should be with Him, unless with sin). So man and woman leave their parents when they get married (but married only by God, as we should be, with Jesus).

It is satan that tried to (and did – basically man doing it to himself) separate man from God (and still tries it today with us), and satan tried to separate man from woman (when satan went to eve and tempted her – and she gave in – **gen. 3**), but adam gave in to eve and stayed with eve (because he loved her, and maybe he didn't see eve die right away, physically), and in doing that adam separated both man and woman from God – all of us, even today (from what He wanted for them, for mankind – what His plan and roles for man and woman here on earth). Husband (man) or wife (woman) can separate us from God.

And if men have or want things, it is to look good, please women, etc., like adam did when he went along with eve in the garden – to get her, to stay with her, etc., which all men and women have done ever since (we are all from them). It is that way still today. Need to go to Jesus to change the way we are.

Adam and eve – the only people – humans, on earth at the time (or anywhere in the universe) became one against God (sinful, evil, etc.), until they went to the Lord God together (**gen. 3:21** – the first sacrifice, and salvation at that time, to stay with God – in His presence). So God changed their roles (even after they came to Him) for man and woman (the woman was to be a compliment to man – a help meet, **gen. 2:20-25**, and still is, but in a subordinate role, because she gave in to satan, and his lies, and went against man, and God, **gen. 3:16; 1 cor. 11:8-9; 1 tim. 2:13-15**). And when we go away from those roles (that God wants), we get in trouble (even today) – it is best for us to do what God wants (and for the other changes God made to man over the years since then – we have to obey, or man and woman, will have problems here and not be able to solve them, get along, etc., without going to Jesus and His word – but it has to be the truth). Marriage (the way God wants) can only work if both are with Jesus and following His truth – His word (otherwise why follow what He says – **luke 6:46**, if you are not with Him – truly saved? – like so many false churches, etc. out in the world – it won't work – your marriage will fail or be miserable). So satan separated man from God, and man was willing (and turned good, love, and life – to evil, hate, and death), which we all live with today – it's man's fault (just like everything that is evil in this world that man has done in history – is all man's fault – satan leading, and man following, and we all have to pay for that). Go to Jesus to change all of that – and only to Him.

So adam gave up the world for eve (woman), and plunged the world and mankind into sin (and set up the roles men and women have today in the world). And in doing so adam gave the world to satan. We need to go back to God – Jesus. And we need to sacrifice and give up things of this world (men and women). These roles are still here today.

And men and women have been the same since the garden – man followed and listened to woman (who desired the tree and it's fruit – things of this world), and has caused problems for man (and woman) ever since (all through the bible, and life) – even lot's wife, who looked back at sodom, when she was told not to by God, and turned into a pillar of salt (**gen. 19:15-26**) – she desired things of this world (and wanted them so badly) – and women still do today – and fill their life with things to make up for voids in their lives (even though man may to a point, too) – not listening or following God and the truth of His word. So don't want this world – all of us – don't look back, once you are with Jesus (**luke 9:59-62**). Go to Jesus and be filled with what you need (**matt. 6:33**). We need to trust God and what He wants, with Jesus. He will take care of the rest.

Each person or group can end their limitations, prejudices, or oppression, etc. by going to God – who put those limitations, etc. there. Go to Jesus to change our lot in life – to have what God has for us – freedom, equality, etc. And get away from man and satan.

We need the Holy Spirit to be saved (**2 cor. 5:11-21; eph. 1:3-14; eph. 4:30**), that adam lost for us – and we can only get it back from Jesus (who gave it to adam and eve at creation). We have to believe Him and ask Him. He will give it, then we are ready for heaven. He will change us. But we need to believe and follow. Keep going to His word – learn, grow, and share.

Men need women, and children do, but do what God says. Women need to listen to man who want to talk about the bible – the truth of it, and men need to know the truth, and find a woman that wants to learn. Caring about each other – but especially God – Jesus. Help each other. Learn and share.

So women are made for man – since the beginning. And God put adam and eve together in marriage – his wife. And there are many people that are married or have been married, that never were married as far as God was concerned. We need to get married with Jesus truly in your life – like God marrying you – as He did adam and eve. And no man can separate.

God allows things in this world (including satan) – letting satan do some things here – to see what people are attracted to – in their heart, then He can find out who wants to be with Him (or satan), and so man can also know what they believe and make a choice. We need to do it God's way – with Jesus, for it to work.

God will help you through things – even if you think there is a better way – do things right and truthful, and God will get you through.

All people need to know man is born evil – sinful – especially women need to know and believe it, and go to Jesus (or you will suffer the consequences of those decisions, etc.) – don't depend on evil man (and satan) to take care of you – only Jesus (and any man that is truly with Jesus – and you better know that he really is – so you know the truth of Jesus and His word), and be saved with the Holy Spirit.

We first have to admit we are sinners, no matter how 'nice' we think we, or others think we, are. And repent and go to Jesus, or we are destined for hell (**john 3:17-21**).

So you need to tell the truth about God and about people – all through history (read the bible) – those in the past needed to tell others (their family, friends, etc. – which over the years we forgot, or just didn't want to believe, led by satan, and those against God and His truth) what went on before them and at that time (we always need to share it with the next generations – the truth) – the truth of God and history (not forget God and His truth, His creation, flood, etc. – we all saw it, can all see it still here – **rom. 1 and 2** – no excuse – those that were there, saw it, and eventually shared it with others after them – to their great, great, great, etc. grandkids – especially people who lived before the flood and just a little after the flood – they lived long ages and could share truth about God, history, etc.) – and know about people today (who we really are – and why we are here), and see it – the evil (or just let it go, or didn't want to follow God) – now they have to choose – Jesus (and His truth), or satan (keep living in sin, to hell). So we have no excuse – we just choose to do evil. It is all man's fault – with satan's help.

If we don't have hardships, struggles, discipline, punishments, etc., we will never learn what to do that is right in this life. God knows what we need – go to Jesus and His word.

When we go to Jesus and His word, we separate ourselves from the world – God is separating us from sin, evil, satan, etc., by going to Jesus. And be ready for heaven with Him.

If you are not going to follow God – Jesus (after sin), then there will be problems with you and this world – punishments, etc. God wants you with Him (the reason He created man – sin separates us) – with Jesus, or you will end up in hell.

Man wants to be in charge – be God (like satan wanted to), and make the rules, etc. – satan leading man to do that against God's rules (laws, etc.), and His truth. But the only way to be right with God is to do things the way God wants done – not what we want done – so He sent Jesus to save us – pay the penalty for sin we all have. So we need to go to Jesus.

All through history, God waited, and then had to punish those that didn't follow and went against Him (and sometimes man hurting each other) – like before the flood, and after, in sodom and gomorrah, etc. Even those against the jews – the canaanites (from noah's son ham) in the land that God was going to put the jews – the promised land – israel (**exo. 23:20-33**), and those against the true Christians today – against Jesus. Or He wouldn't be a just God. And He waits (like america that has all of noah's sons together – and all of those with God, and those against Him, put together – **matt. 13:36-43**). But He will punish all nations today that don't go to Him (partly it would be people taking them over that don't treat the people very good, desolation, disasters, etc. – like He did with the jews at times) – as you see the nations struggle today (and america is going in that direction, too). But all can go to the true God – Jesus.

Even though God was here for jews only – from abraham through to the disciples (before Jesus died and rose – and a little after until 70ad), God (Jesus) still was exposed to the gentiles – and all through that time, and they saw the power of God, and some could have believed (maybe a few did – like with jonah in nineveh, etc.), but most didn't, although they should have. No excuse for anyone then or today.

God separated the jews (His people – **gen. 12 to 17**) from the gentiles (the rest of the world) – all of noah's sons. And God used the jews to tell His truth – the bible, and where Jesus came from. And people knew of the true God, from the beginning.

So all nations, and nationalities, empires, people, etc. have known of the true God – Jesus, throughout history – from adam to noah to abraham to jacob to egyptians, arabs, jews, gentiles, babylonians, persians, romans, etc. – all the way up through history to today – no excuse for anyone (**rom. 1**). They all have seen His power, etc., and heard of Him. And it is satan that wants you to not know about the true God (he doesn't mind you making up all kinds of religions, false churches, beliefs, etc. of your own – really worshipping satan – even going to church and reading the bible, but not know what the truth is and who Jesus is – **matt. 7:13-23; 2 cor. 4:1-6**) – especially today – getting close to the end times.

Even the priest melchizedek alludes to Jesus and who He is and what He would do – starting way back in genesis (**gen. 14:18-20; psalm 110; heb. 5 and 7**), all knew of Jesus since adam – He is the same always (**heb. 13:8**).

Knowledge of all history – from adam and before the flood, and through noah's sons after the flood, and all of the information that they had (living through it) – and would and could share it all with all people at that time, and we can know today. The truth. We always have needed to go to God (**psalm 2; psalm 14**). But He came to us.

All of the things God wrote in the bible are for a reason and to know – including the flood and why the world is the way it is, today since the flood (especially after the tower of babel – **gen. 9 and 10 and 11**). We need to know why this world is the way it is (and why He separated man and the world) and why we need to go to Jesus (why He came here) – because satan is here with lies, etc. (trying to always unite us all as one against God) – God did it this way for us (mainly for us to go to Him). To be one with Him. So for now we (with satan) have to be divided – all of the nations, etc. need to be, as we see today (**luke 11:18**).

If you can't believe the bible, then you can't believe any of the old books – any religion, belief, culture, etc. And Jesus proves He was God. Jesus made the whole world and wants the whole world to come to Him (**matt. 24:14; mark 16:15; john 3:17**). All for us. Following Him, for what's best for us (because we don't know what's best for us – you can see that in the world).

Think of this when you read this – all of the bible is of God and from God, but not all of it is for us today – mainly just since Jesus died and rose, but all of the bible is truth and for us to learn (**rom. 15:4**) – especially how and why God did all that He did (from **genesis to revelation**) – mainly for us to go to Him.

Even though satan does divide – mainly having people go against God and His truth (satan trying to unite all against God), but God also divides (including Jesus dividing families, etc. – **matt. 10:34-39** – bringing a sword – the truth of His word) – to keep satan from uniting man all against God and His truth (that satan has done in the past) – so God sent the flood and changed the languages at the tower of babel (**gen. 6; gen. 11**).

And we don't want to be one – hating and miserable, and no hope – have faith with love. With Jesus. Only satan makes us one and miserable – whether it's a family, culture, nationality, belief, etc. – all going against God.

People can't just agree on just anything – it has to be truth and good. God wants us to know the truth, and be one, after He separated us – but only be one with Him, with Jesus, be one with love and truth.

The bible is truth – read it and prove it (satan is the liar, and he leads man away from God and His truth – **john 8:43-47**). There is so much evidence and proof and facts in it – so we can look in the world and life and see it there (look at the world through the eyes of God's truth – the bible). Not just blind faith – there is proof enough for any honest person to see and learn (**2 tim. 3:15-17**), and is for man's learning (away from satan's lies). Since we are all born evil (without the Holy Spirit), we are all evil and need of a Savior (**john 3:16**), then that's why we have to try to be nice to each other – because we are sinners and evil – and need help – but it is only with Jesus – so go to Him and change (get the Holy Spirit), and then share Him with others. Then love the way He wants us to – the way we were created to. So open your eyes to the truth – Jesus.

We all know of **john 3:16** – we see it all of the time, everywhere, and that is nice, but we have to read after that verse (**john 3:17-21**) to know who we are here and where we are going (until we go to Jesus – truly saved with His truth) – we are sinful, evil – going to hell (born that way). We are all condemned – sinful – to hell by sin here when we are born – until we go to Jesus. We all need to be saved (**rom. 8:1-2**).

If you want to figure anything out in this world (especially anything important or good) – read the bible – but go to Jesus first – to also get to the next life.

Everyone (all of noah's sons) in this world has to deal with the same things – money, health, relationships, safety, weather, etc. – all the problems that may go with them. Jesus will help you through them, if you go to Him. And the rain falls on the good and the bad, and the sun shines on the good and the bad (**matt. 5:45**) – God makes it even for all, but we need to control what we can and live to avoid problems. And Jesus knows best for all of that (10 commandments, etc.). And they are all the same throughout history for man (with satan leading man).

History may be true, but not be good or right (for all of noah's sons) – what people believe and follow and act on or defend, etc. – find the truth of Jesus and His word (and read of the truth of the history of man – the good and the bad – mainly through the bible, from the beginning), to know the truth, and to know what to follow and believe and how to live. Don't trust yourself – just Jesus and His word.

When you look at the laws and punishments that God gave to the jews – you see He means business, to make sure what He wants done – especially obedience and His truth written – the bible – which the jews (following God – the Holy Spirit) did. Shows we are sinful, and need to know the truth and change.

You can't live any old way you want – you need to go to Jesus before you die. We all don't go to heaven (without Jesus – the Holy Spirit), so we need to keep people alive to get to know Jesus.

Following laws and rituals, etc. didn't save the jews (or false churches or religions, etc.) doing that, and won't save you either. You need to be born again (with the Holy Spirit – **john 3**), through Jesus and that's all you need. You will live right naturally (**gal. 5:22-23**), as much as you can here.

There is evil in this world, and we need to try to help people and protect people from evil – like you would yourself, family, nation, etc., and God will do that – but we need to help and share Jesus, and God will help you. And try to treat all people (all of noah's sons) well, and share Jesus and His truth to all of them, but this is still an evil world (and there are consequences for the way people live and behave) and we need to protect ourselves. But if there are any deaths, be ready to go with Jesus.

So we all (all of noah's sons – originally from adam's sin) are born now with a body and an empty soul (which should have had the Spirit in it, connecting us to God, to govern and guide us here, but our soul is void since adam and eve – who we are all from, **gen. 3:20**), so we fill that void (empty soul) with the things of this world – a world which is satan's now (selfish, desires, evil, lies, etc.), which is why people can be possessed – even today – many of the people that we put away from society (asylums – need to share Jesus with them), and give drugs to, prison, dead, commit suicide, etc., and some that are running around loose in the world (homeless, mentally ill, etc.), because our soul is empty, and it can be filled with evil – demons, etc. (possessed – and false christians and churches, etc. can't exorcize a demon from a person – satan fools them to think they can – **matt. 7:22-23; matt. 15:57-58; matt. 17:14-21**) – especially if we go to them, etc., until we go to Jesus and get the Holy Spirit in our soul (if you are saved, you have the Holy Spirit and can't get a demon in you – be possessed – **matt. 12:43-45**, so those false churches are not saved – don't have the Holy Spirit), since adam and eve sinned and gave the world to satan (**gen. 3; matt. 4:1-11; 2 cor. 4:3-4; eph. 6:11-12**), and it is cursed by God, and we have to be born again with the Spirit (**john 3**), which only Jesus can give us, and we have to go to Him – He is waiting for us each to make that decision, but we need to know the real truth first (this is a sinful world which God the Father does not come to – He is holy, and stays in heaven on the throne, but God the Son and the Holy Spirit do come here to help man, as do angels sometimes). Those three are the Godhead – God the Father, God the Son, and God the Holy Spirit (**col. 2:9; 1 john 5:7**). Jesus says we are dead (still being alive physically, but without Him in our lives, spiritually dead – **matt. 8:22; luke 9:60**), and we are all destined for hell – born condemned, **john 3:17-21** (which is another separation – because of man, heaven and now hell) until we are born again, this time spiritually (**john 3:6-7**). We need to put on the new man (**1 cor. 15:45-50; eph. 4:17-32; col. 3:5-11**) – the Holy Spirit (**acts 5:32**). So we can be with Him in heaven.

Then we can be sealed by Jesus with the Holy Spirit (**eph. 2:4-10**), because He loves us. We have to be one with God (not connected to man – culture, belief, nationality, etc.) – and only through Jesus can we be (since He can make up for and pay for our sins) – and why God created man – to be one with Him. Not one against Him – like satan led man to be in the garden, and before the flood, and at the tower of babel, and even in sodom, etc. – and ever since – even today (even america is getting away from God and His word). We need to go back to Jesus, and share His truth, and help people get saved, and be ready to go.

So we don't do it – Jesus does, with the Holy Spirit (our connection to God) – in us when we get saved. Ask Him into your life and follow Him and His truth, or satan and sin will keep leading you.

And only go to and listen to Jesus and His word – don't even listen to an angel (**gal. 1:6-10**) – like satan, to tell you anything different than Jesus (like satan has throughout history, since man has been here – **gen. 1 to 3** – with all of the lies, making religions, beliefs, etc. all over the world – especially in the last 2,000 years). And Jesus is God (**john 10:25-30**) – and has been forever (**heb. 13:8**).

Basically demons (fallen angels) possession can be false Christian leaders (as many other religions, beliefs, etc.) – liars, like satan is (truth mixed with lies). So it can be in people that say they are Christian, read the bible, go to church, etc., and may say Christian things, but are not saved – satan leading their thinking. Beware. Keep sharing the truth of Jesus and His word.

It is satan (and fallen angels) that we are fighting here (**eph. 6**), and that causes all of our evil (and we follow, and keep causing our evil to each other – **james 4**) – we need to stop, but we can't do it alone. Only Jesus can help.

So even today people can be possessed by demons today, but was more when Jesus was here because no one had or could have the Holy Spirit in them before Jesus died and rose – He sent the Comforter to the saved (some jews) after He rose and went to heaven (**acts 1 and 2**).

Jesus gives the Holy Spirit – even to adam at creation (and eve), and now to any (that go to Him to be truly saved) after He died and rose – He also casts out demons, even before He died, and casts out the demons today, we don't. And when satan came to the garden – **gen. 3** – adam and eve had the Holy Spirit in them (like the truly saved have today), so they couldn't be possessed by satan (that's why he went into the serpent – since there were no other humans around) – just bothered and tempted, like the saved are today, by satan (but God took the Holy Spirit out of adam and eve – and listening to satan caused that, for all of us). So when you get saved and get the Holy Spirit from Jesus, it will cast out demons – no exorcism (if you try, all you do is call on satan and demons). Even paul doesn't talk about casting out demons in his books (paul only mentioned once healing of evil spirits, etc. – **acts 19:11-12**) – possession, and healing, was mainly before Jesus died and rose – and if anyone would have had a demon in them – it would have been paul (saul). Saul (paul) got saved by the risen Jesus (**acts 9**) on his way to killing Christians (jews) – no demon, etc. (although he was blinded for a time) – just getting the Holy Spirit. Demons - fallen angels - mainly go to you because you go to them and satan and you go to them to their world - would be psychics, mediums, voodoo, false beliefs, etc. and by not going to Jesus and His truth.

Jesus defeated sin, satan, and death – we need to go to Him to do the same – get the Holy Spirit - form Jesus, to take the spirit of sin and satan out of you. And satan is still here, but he doesn't have to run your life. Go to Jesus and the truth of His word to keep satan away (with having the Holy Spirit in you), like Jesus did (**matt. 4:1-11**)

We are of one body (after being truly saved with the Holy Spirit) – with different gifts of the Holy Spirit (**1 cor. 12**) – no matter who you are – whatever of noah's sons, etc. If there are people who would know of discerning spirits (**1 cor. 12:10**), that would be more in paul's day – especially with the jews believing many things after Jesus died and rose – if those are 'exorcists', all are not given that gift – but paul doesn't talk about that, other than getting saved with the Holy Spirit. Basically spirits (maybe devils), would be mainly of false doctrine (**1 tim. 4:1-2**). Even the devils believe (**james 2:19**) in God and Jesus (they just don't follow Him). Being able to discern spirits would be one that could know what the spirits (and beliefs, etc.) are – mainly if someone is saved or not, lying, etc. – Jesus takes demons out of you and replaces it with the Holy Spirit – you then start to grow and become knowledgeable of the truth of His word and your life here for Him. There are really no 'exorcists', and no need of them.

The Holy Spirit casts out a demon when someone gets truly saved (and keeps it out) – the demons know who Jesus (and the Holy Spirit) is (**matt. 8:28-34; mark 5:1-20; luke 8:26-36**), and the truth of the gospel, and after a demon gets out, a person has to have it replaced with the Holy Spirit (which wasn't there in people before Jesus died and rose), or the demon will come back (**matt. 12:43-45**). If demons know who Jesus (and the truth) is, then man should know, also – and why the demon possessed act like they know the truth. Go to Him, and read and share. At that time – in Jesus' name (with the Holy Spirit today) you can cast out demons then (**luke 9:37-50**). Even after Jesus died and rose some jews tried to cast out demons and couldn't – trying in their own name (and being fakes – like some are today – false churches, religions, beliefs, etc) – exorcists (**acts 19:13-20**).

So someone you would have thought would have had a demon in them, would have been saul (paul), who killed jewish Christians, until he got saved by Jesus on the road to kill more Christians (**acts 9**). He got saved by Jesus and got the Holy Spirit, and then followed and shared the truth of Jesus, and helped Christians for the rest of his life (and suffered for it). That's what we need to do – go to Him.

People didn't get the Holy Spirit with Jesus being here (or before) – so demons stay in people until you do – mainly Jesus gets rid of them – but eventually to get the Holy Spirit in you, after Jesus died and rose – so we don't need demons and baptizing (just the Holy Spirit). Go to Jesus – get saved.

God can use satan and fallen angels (demons) to lead us to the truth of God's word – satan goes against it and man follows – look at the beliefs in the world. Then go against satan (all of the ideas that satan pushes) – look in God's word to find the truth.

And satan knows he is going to the lake of fire, and he convinced a third of the angels to follow him (**rev. 12:3-9**) – and the angels will go with satan to the lake of fire. And satan wants to convince and lead man to follow him to hell and the lake of fire. That is satan's plan. So don't follow satan, and we all do when we don't follow Jesus.

So satan knows the truth of God and Jesus, but wants to lie to help man go to hell (like he is going to – the lake of fire).

Go to Jesus and believe in Him and you will get the Holy Spirit (He casts out demons) – and it has to be the true gospel (too many false churches) – **1 cor. 15:1-6**. Even when God saved adam and eve (**gen. 3:21**), they weren't possessed by satan (they just listened and followed him). Go to Jesus. Know the truth, and be saved – Jesus will help you with satan (especially with His word of truth – and it better be the truth, and trusting Jesus).

So God gave everything to adam – then adam lost it, because of listening to satan – God took it away – it is satan's now (even Jesus knew that – **matt. 4:1-11**, using the word to fight satan), and we have it only (all that is here) with satan running our lives. There is a price to pay, but you can go to God (through Jesus), and He will give you things – what you need (**matt. 6:33**). Even job (**book of job**) lost all by satan (God allowing it), but job stayed strong (with his faith in God) to the end and God gave all (and more) back to him.

From adam and satan in the garden, up to today and eternity – heaven, is like the story of job – the **book of job** – beginning to end.

Even job talks of Jesus – the redeemer (**job 19:21-29**) – Jesus is here always (**heb. 13:8**), and His words shared in the bible. Time is short – go to Jesus, and be ready.

When you think about life on this earth – which is short compared to eternity, would you rather have three days of good times, every wish come true, etc., then after that, misery for the rest of your days (or forever), or would you want three days of pain, misery, etc., then after that, have good times, etc. for the rest of your days (or forever)? When you think of it that way, you (at least most of us) would choose the second option. Well life on this earth is like three days compared to eternity (in heaven or hell) – very short, even though it may be 80 to 100 years, but it would be worth it to have the misery here (and it could be still better with Jesus in your life here), than the misery you would have after this life (hell, forever). We have a choice – choose Jesus, not satan (and this world, etc.).

Take the focus off of you and this world and put it on Jesus and live. Don't be selfish and self-centered and think of yourself – and having others know of you – go to Jesus and learn and share and talk of Him, and His word – the truth.

This world is not worth holding onto – anything in it. This is not going to last – and is not our home, and only going to Jesus can we live in heaven. So resist satan and his world.

God can get rid of satan, but God uses him, and we have a choice (only two choices – satan or Jesus – hell or heaven – death or salvation), and with all of the evil and problems here – it should make us go to Jesus. And you can see the evil clearer with satan here and make a better choice. Know the truth.

We are connected to man – first adam (who sinned, and eventually why God sent the flood) – and satan is the ruler here now, not man (**gen. 3; 2 cor. 4:1-4**) – then after the flood we are all from noah's three sons (**gen. 9:18-19; gen. 10:32**) – and God likes threes. We are all a servant (slave) of satan and sin, since the beginning.

So satan uses God's creation (after adam's sin, and after God cursed the creation – **gen. 3**) and man to do his work in this world (using man, and his different abilities of noah's sons – who we are all from, to have all of man follow satan) – don't follow satan (or noah's sons – man) – go to Jesus and follow Him and His word (be one with Him), not this world (**rom. 12:2**).

We have to know the truth of the bible (and its effect on us) before we – man (all of us), can live our life here – first get saved through Jesus (and get the Holy Spirit).

We are all from noah's sons (adam originally) – **gen. 9:18-19, gen. 10:32**. We need to start there to understand our problems (as well as knowing that satan is leading man to evil without Jesus). And noah's three sons were born about 100 years (or less – **gen. 5:32; gen. 7:11-12**) before the flood.

It doesn't matter if you know exactly which son of noah you are – but you have a good idea (some mixtures, etc.) – we are all from man (first adam, now noah) and sinful, and need Jesus.

No matter what belief, ability, nation, etc. we all are from one of noah's sons and we have to know this, and have to all go to Jesus. Mainly japheth – intellectual (and descendants) would enlarge with shem – spiritual (and descendants), and ham – physical (descendants) would be their servants (**gen. 9:18-19, 24-27**) – around the world (basically after the tower of babel – **gen. 11**). God set it up that way. And today, america uses them all. Basically shem are the jews, and japheth and ham are gentiles (and some of shem). Obvious some are mixed.

All of the rituals, traditions, etc. – from all religions, beliefs, etc. – are gone with Jesus – faith in Him – and getting the Holy Spirit back from God, that adam and eve lost for all of us.

We can't get away from adam and noah's sons – from man – sinful, evil, etc. – without Jesus. Or get away from your nationality, culture, belief, etc. (and their lot in life – good or bad) without Jesus. The problems we have in this world (all that sin leads us), are the ones that Jesus takes care of – or the police, psychiatrists, drugs, etc. do, if you don't go to Jesus.

Troubles in this world come from not going to God – Jesus, with sin and satan here (where the problems come from).

So it won't happen without Him – no matter what things we try – it will just get worse – trying to look like we get along – without Jesus. Go to God and His word – stop going against it and Him, and you will help yourself. Stop hurting yourself.

No matter how 'nice' we are (or think we are), we are all evil (**gen. 8:21; psalm 14; rom. 3**) – even Jesus says we are (**luke 11:13**) – we need the Holy Spirit with Jesus to be righteous – to be good (as much as we can here in these bodies and on this earth – until the end).

All of the things we do on this earth – including against or with man – are against God. We need Jesus to change that.

People are trying to look for good in the world, without going to Jesus and His word. We won't find the good, until we do.

Help mean people (as much as you can and they will let you), and root for good people – mainly those truly with Jesus. Keep learning and sharing the truth and Jesus. And do the right, caring thing in this world for people – know what that is. Jesus will help.

So japheth and shem need to try to get along with ham – and ham with them, too. All of us (noah's sons – man) need to go to Jesus for it to work out between all of us.

And no matter what we believe – there are nicer and meaner people (still all born evil – and differences between noah's sons), and both need to go to Jesus – get saved. Which would be away from satan's world we live in. And one of the reasons we live to a younger age – only to 120 years or less (**gen. 6:3**) after the flood, than before the flood. We die younger and do less evil here (get older faster, etc.). Go to Jesus as soon as you can – and get ready for life after this with Him – heaven.

Man has had enough time to figure out how to get along with all the different people throughout history, but still hasn't. And we should have figured out how to live longer by now, but we haven't. God has set up everything here (after we have ruined it for people, including ourselves, here). We need to go to Him.

Don't live in the world – money, things, behavior, etc. – God will provide. So don't compromise for fame, money, things, etc. – you will be fine with Jesus (otherwise satan will lead you) – if it is the truth of Him and His word and follow (**gen. 22:8; gen. 24:1; gen. 26:12; gen. 30:30; gen. 39:5; psalm 23:4-6; matt. 6:33; matt. 25:14-30; john 10:10; 3 john 1:2; heb. 11:39-40; 3 john 1:1**). Go to Him for everything to work.

We all do things in this world (tough things, and good things) that we don't want to do, but have to. And be best for others, and sometimes best for you. Forgiving is tough, but Jesus will help with that – He forgave us, if we would just go to Him.

We all try out things in this life – new things, but they can be bad for you in this evil world. We need to know this to make it through with less problems, or even an early death, etc. – and always be ready to go with Jesus. We need to teach others – especially children – and need to be a good example (know what that is). Go to Jesus to help you through and be ready.

People fill their void (in their soul – life) with things of this world, and some God wants us to (but with Him in our life) – family, jobs, money, hobbies, sports, games, marriages, etc., or we may go to drugs, alcohol, partying, depression, etc. – for the most part, which is satan's world, instead of going to Jesus. All those things may help a little here, but they are trying to keep us from realizing how depressed and evil we really are. And when some or all of those things are gone, we either may kill ourselves (or others), or go to Jesus (hopefully to Him).

So man has sports, hobbies, etc. for outlets – hopefully keeping people from doing things that are not good for them or others. But go to Jesus (and His word) for your outlets, and how to live. Even though man uses internet, videos, tv, etc. for outlets, too (and God can, too), it is satan that wants you to use them for more temptations for sin – stop your behavior and choices with Jesus – He is the only way.

God made us all individual, different, and special (**psalm 139:13-18; matt. 10:29-33**), but it only works with God in our life through Jesus and the Holy Spirit – the way God created us (**gen. 2:7**). Go to Jesus to make it work and make you special – you don't have to show yourself off, etc. – God will for you.

Don't compare yourself with man (noah's sons, adam) – whether you are better or not than someone – only what God says about you – with Jesus or not. Get away from noah's sons – you are them, and nothing, without Jesus, or you will be still lost here. Don't depend on good works or this world, just Jesus (and His word). Don't be wise in this world (satan leading – against God's truth) – it is foolishness to God (**1 cor. 1:18-31**).

Man can be 'good', but it is only with Jesus that it can really happen – the only way to fight satan, this world, and his control of us. So any 'good' in the world that you may see or that people do – is because of Jesus – people see that and should copy that. And makes the world livable – to a point. But you need to have Jesus help you, and find out who you really are, help you to grow in a different way of life – to change to what you should and could be and what and who you can be. To change the road you are on.

When you get drunk, on drugs, etc. you become the real you – more evil (what you are born with comes out) – no excuse – you are guilty of what you do and to who you do it with. You will have less control over yourself. Go to Jesus to help you – and let Him (and the Holy Spirit) control you.

Things in this world can take your mind off of your problems (but also cause them), but Jesus is best, and He doesn't give us a Spirit of fear (**2 tim. 1:7-8**), if you are trying to forget things, etc., Jesus will help you overcome things. Go to Him.

The world will not make you happy (**luke 12:15**).

We can't afford to be a bad example – even as adults, being able to do things here, just because it is lawful – alcohol, drugs, smoke, unhealthy diet, etc. – don't use these things yourself, and try to tell children, etc. not to – any behavior that is not good (and a waste of money – no wonder you are poor and in trouble, etc.) – and it hurts you and them. Don't depend on those things to help you – they keep you from God – hopefully they will eventually get to go to Jesus and His word.

Some people don't care about their own children (by the way they act, live, example, habits, etc.) – even though they think they do (satan keeps fooling them) – going to and depending on and believing in man, and not God and the truth of His word. Go to Jesus and trust Him. And change how you live.

All children need help and guidance (as well as adults) – mainly to go to Jesus and His word – know Him and His truth, then they will be fine. All know of Jesus today in the world – need to go to Him and help others to do the same.

You don't have to try everything or anything to see if it would be bad for you – just know it, and see what it does to others – no matter how fun or not that they make it sound or look.

The things of this world should not keep us from God or believing in Him – the way God wants (not what satan wants us to). And help us to use them to share Jesus.

So satan can make people rich and look like they are doing well (not all nice people) and can fool the world (and getting away with things) into believing you don't need Jesus, etc. And make you look like you have Jesus, but you don't, and even make you think you need Him, and you may not (just need to keep going to Him and His word and learning His truth for everything in your life).

We have to do some things in this world – interests, career, family, etc., but this is not our final stop – live to be ready to go after this world. Go to Jesus. Make sure you are.

And satan may leave you alone (looking like you are fine to the world, even if you go to church, etc.), if you are not truly saved, and not going to Jesus and His word – the truth of it (or wanting to), because satan can give you things in this world (it is his world – adam gave it to him – **gen. 3**, even though God allows and limits him – **book of job**, etc.), if you give him your soul and worship him (and not to Jesus – with the Holy Spirit) – not knowing. But that comes with a price – and you will have other struggles, because if you are not following what God says (in His word) about this life and world (to live here), you will struggle (in some way – going against God), no matter what good things you have – basically from satan, just like satan tried to tempt Jesus with the riches of this world, if Jesus would only worship satan (**matt. 4:8-11**) – which people do without knowing it. This world is evil. We all are evil, but can change.

If you didn't have military, police, weapons, etc. (mainly some protection, etc.) – there would be no way to defend or protect yourself, family, society, nation, etc., and you would have ten times more evil (or more) and killing in this world than you do now, or ever. Unless you go to Jesus and change. You cannot just tell people to be nice (try that with your children, enemies, etc.), when they have no way of being nice – we are all born evil – only God (through Jesus) can change that and help you be nice (which is different than being innocent or helpless). No matter how much you discipline (even though it is needed).

There is unfairness in the world – evil, sinful, etc. – and people need to accept that. Go to Jesus and His word (and share Him) to have a chance to change that.

Citizens need to protect themselves (family, etc.) from evil of this world – including governments, criminals, etc., and why america allows that. God will protect you, too, if you go to Him.

Even though we are all born evil – we keep proving we are evil, by acting and doing crazy things, so people think you are and keep getting away with evil (don't follow satan).

Don't kill if you can (satan does) – God wants us all to get to know Jesus (while we are alive), but stop evil, and God will, and be fair – help people to live. Going to Jesus (and His truth), will only work – and if we die (we all will), we know where we are going. Help people to get to know Jesus – you first.

How does a person defend themselves? – with a weapon – the word of God is a sword – against the real and worst enemy – satan (**eph. 6:10-20**). Even Jesus used it (**matt. 4:1-11**).

Jesus died for us all, and we all are going to die, but we need to be with Jesus before we do – and even though man has died all through history – since adam – we are dead here, and death is the penalty for sin – and God has done that to us, but it is our fault – we really kill ourselves.

So God really killed only one person in the history of our existence – and that is Jesus on the cross – for us.

Jesus stood up for man – just like people have for their country – defending freedom, like in america – but Jesus did much more. Go to Jesus and live.

Be a soldier for Jesus and stop people you know from hurting others and share Jesus with them and others, but the truth.

Why isn't evil and hell enough of a deterrent in this world (**john 3:17-21** – we all are destined for hell, when we are born) to get people to go to Jesus? Why do religions, groups, etc. have to kill (because of satan, and his lies) – and still have people follow them (him)? And not just for protection, etc.

All Christians are not one – satan would like you think that they are – satan is a liar, from the beginning (**gen. 3**), in the garden with eve. And Jesus says the same – satan is the father of lies (**john 8:43-45**).

And satan (through man) does try to be 'nice' (or look nice – tolerant, etc.) in some groups, even churches, religions, etc. (like an angel of light, etc. – **2 cor. 11:13-15**), but he is just trying to get people to be nice without the real truth of Jesus (and His word) – to be god themselves, and make their own rules, etc., while still being evil and hateful in this world, and as long as you don't try to learn or share the truth, satan will keep you thinking you are 'nice' – only Jesus can help you be really nice and love – the way He made us to be (so we need to be born again – with the Holy Spirit – which satan can't give you, only enter you and hurt you, if you don't have the Holy Spirit). So don't be fooled by them (or satan). Need to keep safe in this world (and get to the next), and can only be done with Jesus.

If you are in a false church or not truly saved – you will have problems – because going to church, being good, etc. will not help you or save you (and you will still be going to hell – **matt. 7:21-23**). You need to go to Jesus to get the truth (not just a church, leader, rituals, traditions, etc.) – you won't just get the truth naturally – you have to go to Jesus and get it, and get saved with the Holy Spirit. Go to Jesus and learn the truth of His word (**1 cor. 2:13-16**). If you know the truth of anything – like knowing the bible – you will spot a false church, belief, etc. easily – and not be fooled by them (satan) – even if it is in your own family, friends, etc. – Jesus says that families will be separated by the truth (**matt. 10:34-39**) and even His own family is not His (or with Him), unless they follow and believe in Him – the truth (**matt. 12:46-50**). All (humans) have to go to Him (get saved). Learn the truth and what is right and real, and you will know what's not right when you see it or hear it (get the Holy Spirit).

God wrote the bible so mostly only the truly saved – going to Jesus and getting the Holy Spirit – would understand it (**1 cor. 2:13-15**) – so anyone (the unsaved) who would read it wouldn't always understand the words and meanings (like satan leading man to – maybe rewriting the bible – translations, etc. – or teaching lies in the world – schools, churches, etc., basically against the bible), and they wouldn't care to rewrite it (thinking it is foolishness – **1 cor. 1:18-25; 1 cor. 2:14; 1 cor. 3:19**). Even though we all can understand the ten commandments, etc. No excuse for not knowing how to live and what is best for man. We are sinful, and it is easy to live a tougher life, but not necessary – except to get us to go to Jesus and His word.

And the main part about Jesus being here and dying and being resurrected and being the Savior of all, is simple for all to understand – to go to Him and get the Holy Spirit.

Hopefully no one would try to change the words – like with a translation – to pervert the meaning (like false churches do – even with a true translation, and preaching lies – to explain the passage in their own belief – their version). And even so, God would also make sure there would be a bible with true words here in the world (the **KJV** is good) – so we can see and understand the truth. And help you to understand the truth (with the Holy Spirit).

False churches make Christianity and Jesus, even the bible, look bad. The truth needs to be told in true churches about false ones and use the bible – the truth, to prove it – satan uses them to spread his lies, to fool and blind people (**2 cor. 4:1-6**).

If some people that are against God – but think they are with Him – and are hated, persecuted, even killed, etc., like false churches do – they will think they are being hated because Jesus said it (**matt. 10:25-28**), as if they are truly with Him.

So just because you may be persecuted, disliked, etc. for your belief in a church, etc., it doesn't mean you are a true Christian – truly saved – there are many false Christians (false churches), and they need to be told the truth (that is in His word – nowhere else) – so don't think you are bearing a cross for Jesus. Even when john told Jesus that he saw someone (not of their group – those with Jesus), that was casting out demons in Jesus' name – Jesus said to john, no one can be against them, that is using Jesus' name to cast out devils (**mark 9:38-40**). But all those, at that time (before His death), that were doing anything in Jesus' name, would have to be a jew – and they know the bible (gentiles, even today, do not know the truth of the bible – not like the jews, at that time did – so anyone talking about Jesus at that time, would be doing alright – not a false belief, etc.) – because a jew going to Jesus was not easy to do then (especially when He was alive and here).

And when Jesus says that He has other sheep (**john 10:14-18**) – the other sheep are the gentiles (eventually – mainly with paul – and not what a false church claims) after the jews rejected Jesus – and died and rose. And even after that, the jews (as a nation) still rejected Jesus after He came back after His resurrection and was seen (**1 cor. 15:1-8**). He gave them a chance (mainly until the temple was destroyed in 70ad, and then the bible was completed – with the **book of revelation** to the jews). Then the risen Jesus had paul go to the gentiles (with his books that Jesus had paul write – **romans to philemon**). But know the truth.

But Christians are not sheep anymore, but jews still are until they go to Jesus. Jesus came here for jews, but after He died and rose (and the bible complete – mainly after 70ad), He went to the gentiles – mainly with paul – and paul doesn't use sheep for Christians (only in **rom. 8:36**, does paul mentions sheep – referring to an old testament verse – **psalm 44:22**, and that is it). So make sure you know the truth, and what church you go to. Don't believe everything – just the truth, and look in His word for the truth, and know why it is in there. We are not to just follow anything – because satan is out there lying and hurting, and misleading people.

So some churches, religions, etc. persecute their own people (those that leave), or are not part of their belief – so people go against you, the way you believe – including false churches, religions, etc., that hurt or kill the people for not believing their belief – it is not God doing it, but satan (and man). Know the truth – go to Jesus, and the truth of His word. A true church. Be on His side (with the truth) and let Him help you with these problems.

God talks and warns about satan fooling people (**2 cor. 11:13-15**) – saying they are saved, and they are not – most people are not saved – and are false Christians. Today's false belief, put themselves and the church above Jesus and His word (satan leading), so make sure you know the truth of the word, and who you are following.

False churches (even religions) give Christianity a bad name and mislead people – which is satan's plan against Jesus, and man follows (then shares the lies – **matt. 7:15; matt. 24:11, 24**).

False teachers could be your parents, pastors, teachers, etc. – don't just listen (and they should do the same – know the truth) – go to Jesus and His word to find the truth. There are many today and after Jesus was here (**2 pet. 2:1-3**).

These churches and beliefs change the truth – what satan does is diminish Jesus and His truth of the bible – satan wants to be God, or like a god, etc. (as do the leaders, etc. – satan led).

And satan fears, and bothers the truthful church, and the true Christians that share the truth of Jesus and His word, and people get truly saved through them, knowing the truth – and stand up in the world against lies (things against the truth of the bible and of Jesus). Know the truth, and who to be with.

And being nice doesn't mean you are right or saved – you still can be in a false church and try to love people and be unsaved (satan can turn into an angel of light – in churches, anywhere) – thinking you are doing what Jesus wants – but not following the truth of His word – and we can judge (or should) who is a Christian (**1 cor. 6**) – who to marry, and hang out with, etc. (**2 cor. 6:14-16**).

All of noah's sons have had problems from the flood to today – so don't hate or love anyone (put down or raise up people throughout history) – all people learn and grow and may get better – with Jesus we can. See if He is in their life eventually.

Just like the prodigal son in **luke 15:11-32**, the one son leaves the family, security, etc. (which is like the church), and the other son stays home (stays in the church), but one is not believing out of the church, and the other is not believing in the church – just being in church does not mean you are saved. Both sons are lost. Know you are with Jesus (and have the Holy Spirit) and know the truth of His word (**matt. 7:13-23; john 3:3-8; rom 10:8-18; 1 cor. 15:1-6**). Then live your life.

Any problem in this world is to be solved by going to God (Jesus and His word), not man (don't trust man – **jer. 17:5-18** – satan uses man), and in america should be even more.

God puts you in your family, culture, etc. (so don't complain) – grow and learn and help others – after you go to Jesus – you can help them better. And help others that go through the same things in their life.

Even though you don't have a choice of your family, culture, nationality, beliefs, etc. – you do have a choice after you are grown. Go to Jesus and to His word.

People are afraid to go against their own – they think they belong – but we all need to go away from our own – to go to Jesus (and the truth of His word) – even the jews are afraid to go against jews, family, culture, etc. – even though Jesus was a jew (you would think they would follow Him, but they all didn't). Even though all Christians are not true Christians. Know the truth and know who Jesus is (in His word) – get the Holy Spirit.

Everyone is free to go to their own god (satan behind each one) – but there is only one true God (Jesus). People have heard of Jesus and

His word, but need to hear and follow the real Jesus – not the false one that satan tells of.

Things of God and the bible don't always apply to non-believers – other than salvation (**1 cor. 1:17-31; 1 cor. 2; 1 cor. 3:18-23; 2 cor. 4:1-6**). And they have to deal with the consequences of their actions (sins) in this life (and after this life) – the punishments, etc. (even though we all do here).

People are stubborn – they would rather keep hurting themselves and others, than go to Jesus and change. People don't want to believe in God, because of all of the evil in the world – but it is caused by man (all of noah's sons) – and people kill in the name of God – false beliefs, etc. We are sinful and evil, and why we need Jesus. And some people don't want to go to believe in a God who sends people to hell – but God is a just God – and we really send ourselves to hell – we are all evil. There has to be punishment (and it is fair and just) – man is not better than God, and we have a choice to be with Him (Jesus) or not.

If a person or a people go against God and His truth (and what He wants done), let God punish or kill them – you and others will see what God wants and who He is with (those with Jesus and His truth). Like He did over the years with the flood (**gen. 6 to 8**), moses (**num. 16 and 17**), and with elijah (**2 kings 1**), and others. But don't you kill them – like false churches, and religions, etc. do (or others in this evil world). And there will be no mistake or question that God did or didn't do it – punish or kill. God's will is going to be done, and He will do it and help you do it. And obviously things happened when Jesus was here. But He wants all to go to Him – none to perish (**john 3:16**), we can and are given a chance to while we are alive. It is what is best for us and what we were created for.

Some things that happen are just consequences of the way you or others live their lives, or what they believe (apart from God – following satan). Go to Jesus and learn the truth, and live His way – let Him help you. Share Jesus with love the best you can.

If people are against what is in the bible (the truth) – their own opinion, they won't believe in the bible or Jesus or Christianity, but they are wrong, and don't know it. God knows better than we do. Those lies (satan's) are here for a reason – to see what you will believe in this world – God only wants the righteous in heaven (the rest will be in hell – to the lake of fire, separated forever in misery).

And hell is a real place – fire, heat, torment, etc. (**luke 16:22-25**) forever without Jesus (eventually in the lake of fire – **rev. 19:20; rev. 20:10**).

People know there are terrible things that happen in this world – death, etc. – we need to go to Jesus, and be ready to go. And share Him – the most loving thing you can do – but the truth.

You would like a warning for any danger in this life – bridge out, cliff coming up, shooter on the loose, a bomb, any danger, etc. – so we need to tell people of hell, a real, bad, dangerous place.

The punishment from God for sin, and not going to Jesus, has to be severe in order to get people to go to Him – the penalty is death and separation from God forever in hell – to the lake of fire (**rev. 20:11-15**). Know the truth and believe it. But He waits.

Why don't people say – why did God make it so easy to escape hell by just believing in Jesus? – but they don't – they say how evil God is for sending man to hell (but in reality, you send yourself to hell). You know the truth, and it will set you free.

Now you know we are connected to each other – before the flood (with adam and sin) and now after (through noah's sons – who are sinners) – all born into this evil world (that we – along with satan, made), and all need to be saved by Jesus (we are all sinners). We need to go all the way back to the beginning (**gen. 3**).

Most people – including some churches, pastors, leaders, etc. don't know who a real Christian is – because most people are not Christians, even if they say they are. We need to know who real Christians are (even to hang out with, to marry, etc. – **2 cor. 6:14-18**). Need to get the Holy Spirit from Jesus yourself.

And satan tries to mislead you – even with the bible (satan doesn't care if you read the bible or go to church, if you don't know the truth and are not really saved) – and he tries to tell you what a verse says (through church or leader, tradition, etc.), but it doesn't mean that – we hear it from people that say that are Christian (false churches, etc.) – then we pass it along (family, friends, etc.), traditions, etc., but it is a lie, and we still share it. We need to know the truth of His word. Look into His word, but get saved first through Jesus, with the Holy Spirit (who will help you know the truth) – and we all can believe the same – one in Christ – the mind of Christ (**1 cor. 1:10, 1 cor. 2:16; 2 cor. 4:3-5; philip. 1:27**).

There are enough people out in the world to help – and all need Jesus – mentally and physically disabled, elderly, single mothers, poor, children, etc. but all need to go to Jesus – so we need to share Him and help people (all of noah's sons) – or it is not good.

So those with Jesus should be getting you to go to Jesus and the truth of His word – not necessarily to a church, leader, etc. But churches should do a better job of telling the truth of the bible and Jesus – for this world. For people to know the truth. You don't need to be a member of a certain church to be saved.

There are not that many Christians in the world – maybe 2% - 3% of the world – not 33%. So mostly the world is evil and satan led (including most churches). So wise up and go to Jesus – make the world and you better. Only need to be saved by Jesus (**rom. 10:8-13**). Then maybe find a truthful church.

Get to know what a true Christian is and what they believe and talk about – and the way they live. Even though no one is perfect, we need to know, and try to live, the truth (and it better be the truth). Be true to the truth (**titus 1:9-16**) – know the truth (in His word), and try to live the truth, and it needs to start with Jesus (and the Holy Spirit), or we are stuck with man (now with noah's sons).

People still will have problems after they are saved – but have a way out through them with Jesus (and the Holy Spirit). Even though we may still sin once in a while (even just in your thoughts – **matt. 5:27-28; 1 john 3:15**) – you have to be grateful that it could be worse without Jesus and His word in your life (with the Holy Spirit helping – **rom. 7 and 8**).

Narrow is the way to be saved (**matt. 7:13-15**) – only through Jesus (and following and knowing and sharing the truth of His word – not lies that most churches, leaders, nations, etc. do – **matt. 7:16-20**), so not all that say they are Christian, are true Christian (**matt. 7:21-23**). Most follow satan, and why he is here – to see who wants to really follow Jesus – know the truth and know you are truly saved and going to heaven.

God can get rid of satan, fallen angels, etc., when He wants (**2 pet. 2:4; rev. 20**), and false churches. But He uses them (to show the evil, sin even more). We just need to go to God – Jesus (and get the Holy Spirit). And share Him and His word.

There is evil here in this world (even you can see that – and even in you). Always in the history of man has man had to defend and protect himself and others (family, tribe, village, nation, etc.), from other groups – man is evil. People that think that people are naturally nice (which seems nice – like liberals, etc. think, but even they are not nice, and they think there are others that are not nice – those against them – they are hypocrites) will always have problems, because God says different. No one wants to do what God says – just their own opinion and thinking. And it is what God thinks and says that matter (about anything) – His opinion matters most, not man's (or really satan's). People put man first (and man's rules, beliefs, etc. – especially their own), before God and His word – that causes all of the problems for man – letting man be God (really satan) – looking like they care – hypocrites (just like when a person goes from being homosexual to being straight, because of Jesus – they don't want you to do that, hear that, say that, etc. – Jesus can and will do anything). God and the bible are truth – once you understand that, you can help the world – go to Jesus. And we all need Him to go after this world to heaven (we all are destined for hell otherwise – **john 3:17-21**).

People (many groups) think you need to force people to do things their way – thinking their way is right, when they are not necessarily. That's not the way to get things done. Jesus knows what's right and best for man. Don't go against God. Look into it and go to Jesus – for you, and family, friends, etc.

Even some of the people that don't like war, but do like crime, hurting, killing, lying, etc., for their selfish wants and beliefs, etc. but are just hypocrites – even (maybe especially) in government, politics, etc. And even those that are against the death penalty, guns, killing, etc. – hurt and kill people for their reasons – all are evil, sinful, etc. What people accuse others of, they don't want to be accused of themselves, but are guilty, too – trying to look better than others. Not going to God (Jesus), and still trying to be 'nice' themselves (or look that way). All need to go to Jesus, and change – the only way.

And war will be here as long as this earth is here, and man doesn't go to Jesus (**james 4**). And the real war is from satan – spiritual warfare, and that causes physical warfare (which may be needed sometimes – mostly to protect and defend people from the evil in this world). Hopefully get you to go to Jesus.

We don't want to fight people, but help people from danger, and share Jesus and the truth of His word.

If you go against God and His word (which is with satan), you will be unhappy. If you go with God – Jesus and His word, you will be happy (in this life and after this life). Going against God – satan led – like before the flood (**gen. 6**) got us into the situation we are in today, since the flood – the separated, uncomfortable world we live in today. It is a punishment and should lead us to God. We can only be one with Jesus.

All of those that want equity (which is good – especially in a nation that is as diverse as america – so not as much prejudice, etc. in most other countries – not as many of noah's sons), but without God (Jesus and His word – the truth of it, and following it) – it is a waste of time – in america or anywhere. People in power, rich, celebrities, politicians, etc. – those that make an impression on us (really with satan), and want us to live and believe the way they do (no matter how unfair it is – or what God thinks, etc.) – seem to get away with too much – and are let off the hook too easily, but eventually God will punish them – those people really cause their own problems.

Go to Jesus to be one – equal – for change, there is no other way. But just be nice to each other, and the only way is with Jesus.

Some people (those that are doing wrong, lying, and hurting others, etc.) get back at, or hurt, or even kill those that try to help them change. Need to pray for and share Jesus – the best way to change anything.

People worry about offending people – even if they are trying to show things that are wrong – and those people are thinking they are prejudice, hateful, etc. – we need to do and say what is right and stop evil, no matter what color or nationality, etc. a person is. People try to get away with whatever they can, because they think they are able to say they are being singled out because of the way they look, but it is because of what they are doing and how they are behaving, etc. – we shouldn't be able to get away with evil or doing wrong things, because we can't say things to someone that might offend them, etc.

We need to be at peace with all you can in this world – as tough as that is to do sometimes in this world (**rom. 12:10-21; 1 thess. 5:12-24**). But we also need to share and to correct people – to tell the truth and they do, too, for us to get along. Hopefully that will lead people to Jesus.

Even Jesus offended people – mainly the jews, telling the truth.

So be at peace the best you can in this world, but share the truth of Jesus, and His word (and try to obey laws, etc. – **rom. 13**), and follow Him and His truth. Not politically correct, etc.

If you love God and your neighbor, you will live a better life, naturally, obey, etc. (**matt. 22:36-40; gal. 5:22-23**). You have to go to Jesus to do this – with the Holy Spirit.

We all need help – help and change with Jesus. Help each other – have to want help and change. We have to want to know the truth (not your opinion, belief, etc.) – then want to change – because it's best – through Jesus (and His word). Try it and see (**prov. 9:10**). God separated us to help us go to Him.

He's our Maker (**isa. 45:5-13**) – if you think you are nice, or that someone else is nice, you can only imagine what nice really is to God – Jesus. Only with Jesus can it change and work out for all – how to treat others. Help all that need help (and want to change, work hard, etc.) – all done with Jesus to work. Certain people can get along in the world, but not all will without Jesus – ever. Otherwise satan will keep you against each other – because of selfishness, evil, etc. – basically against God and His word (through Jesus). Don't always listen or follow those who are trying to help you – trust and listen to Jesus and His word – because satan may be trying to lead you and fool you. Need to go to Jesus. Read His word. Everything has been tried by man (**book of ecclesiastes**) – nothing will work without Jesus in our lives. Each generation goes through the same thing – all in vain – need to go to God and follow Him and the truth of His word, that is what we are here for (**eccl. 12:13-14**). Or we will continue to have problems.

The reason why we are here is because of Jesus (He's the Creator), and the reason we struggle here is because of us – man, sin (adam – **gen. 3**) – disobedience. It is our fault, your fault. God's will is the most important for man – find it and live better. Go to Jesus. We have to believe it the way God set it up and do what He says to do. Man doesn't know what's best. Go to Jesus for our best – do it God's way (**john 14:6**).

If all of the things, ideas, beliefs, etc. that are against God (Jesus and His word) – the evil, etc. like today (the evil ideas and people) don't 100% take over the world (basically satan able to convert nearly 100% of all people against God – like satan has before throughout history), then God is here through Jesus stopping it, because these evil things should have taken over by now, by everyone, because people and satan have been trying to push the same evil things – against God – for hundreds, and thousands of years (like before the flood – **gen. 6**, and just after the flood – **gen. 11**, and will happen again soon – can see it today – when the rapture takes place first – **1 cor. 15: 50-55; 1 thess. 4:13-18**, and then the tribulation starts – **matt. 24; book of revelation**). And those things of satan are not best for man, and God does not want that for us (and didn't create us for that – we will not be happy), because of sin – they are not good or right for man (and is why satan is here – so we can see the difference faster), so go to Jesus and change (the only way).

God sets up this world to have us to make decisions – free will. Man causes problems, and can avoid them, if you would go to God – why He sent Jesus – and did other things before Him, so man would go to Him. We need to decide. Then share Him.

If you, a nation, etc. put God first – Jesus and His word – the truth, we will have what we need for all (if you want all to have things) – and be and live the way He wants (**josh. 1:8-9; 2 chron. 7:13-15**) – not what man or satan says, otherwise we will all suffer. It's the only way. Heal our nation with Jesus in your life. And don't be influenced by politics, etc.

And america lets you live the way you want, for the most part, and why people came here from other countries (and still do), and if you don't hurt people, and are not selfish, follow the laws, etc., you can do things here – but go to Jesus. We started separated, since the flood – mainly after the tower of babel (**gen. 11**). Only with Jesus will we get along.

And that is why we (all of noah's sons – **gen. 9:18-19; 26-27; gen. 10:32**) are separated from each other (and the separations are needed – done by God – **acts 17:24-27**) – look in the world and in the past. Tell and teach the next generation. Go to Jesus.

Test God in all the things He says to do and not to do, and see how it turns out – you will live a better life and enjoy it – and it better be the truth (know the true bible – **kjv** is the best) and follow it. Go to Jesus and His word, then follow. You will be surprised. Then deal with life that way. What's best.

People have trouble seeing the difference between hurting someone or helping someone. When you go against God and His word – the truth, you are hurting someone – you think you are being nice, but you are not – with all of the different beliefs and agendas and ideas that people hear about and grow up with, etc., especially today in the world and even in america. Even young people hearing and growing up with and living any way you want. It will hurt people, listening to these things of man (mainly satan) – people who seem to know, but don't.

Being selfish hurts you and others – hurting you more than you think. Don't keep trying to get away with being that way.

CHAPTER 2

Jesus Christ, The Risen Lord and Saviour: Man Reconciled to God, Through His Son, Jesus Christ, Who Is Alive and Not Dead, And Reigns Forevermore

When you go away from what God wants for us (satan leading and man following), we then have problems here – He loves us, so He has to let us know what He wants – to go to Jesus to make your life better here – to avoid problems, but mainly to be with Him after this in heaven, forever.

If you are happy with your life – thank God and if you are not happy – then go to Jesus and then thank God – either way go to God. And follow the truth of His word. Help others do good.

God – Jesus, keeps His promises – do your part and go to Him to get them for you. He will help you (**matt. 6:33; rom. 8:28**).

God made the world like this (after man sinned – **gen. 3** – especially after the flood, and mainly after the tower of babel – **gen. 11**) for that purpose – so we would have to go to Him (Jesus) to have it work out for us here (and after this life).

With the world the way it is – evil – it gives man plenty of chances to help people – whatever problem it is (but people need to want to change). And to then be able to share Jesus with them (but the truth of Him and His word – not the lies that satan uses – even in some churches) – this is what God wanted after the flood and the tower of babel, and especially after Jesus died and rose.

We (that are all created – man, even angels – like satan, who chose to sin and leave God) all have a choice (free will) to decide who to follow (satan or God – Jesus) – and satan **(isa. 14:12-15; ezek. 28:13-17)** and some other angels **(gen. 6:1-2; 2 pet. 2:4; jude 1:6)** have made that decision, and have no other place that they can go (after here on earth) but hell (eventually to the lake of fire) – they (angels) were with God, and angels were all created (they don't procreate – have babies, marry, etc. – **matt. 22:23-30; mark 12:24-25**), so they were created all at once, and have been with God in heaven and made their choice to leave and to not listen and not follow God (Jesus). But man still does have a choice (free will), because we are born (procreate – to be fruitful, multiply) – have babies and each person has the choice of following God (Jesus) or not, but if we don't (by not following Jesus – to get the Holy Spirit that we are missing – the real 'missing link' – no evolution, etc.), then we will go to hell, then the lake of fire with satan (and fallen angels) – **rev. 20:10-15**.

We don't get to choose our parents, nationality, nation, beliefs, family, etc. here on earth – some or even most may have chosen differently. We can choose later – with Jesus – and where we will live forever, and choose to have God as your Father in heaven (and here while we wait to go there). Through Jesus we can get to God, the Father, and have a relationship with Him **(rom. 8:9-17; gal. 4:3-7)**. Which is what God wants with man – why He made us – He loves us (**john 17:22-23**), but we have to go to Him through Jesus.

We don't need (or sometimes want) the love of our father (or mother), but we just need the love of God, the Father, and know that He loves us, through Jesus and then love others through Him. Go to Jesus and the truth of His word to love and live, then share Him.

No matter how nice you, or your parents are, that doesn't mean what they believe is truth – go to Jesus and the truth of His word to find what and who we are. And we are to believe and follow Him (and His word) – not even a leader, church, etc.

Be a son and daughter of God, the Father, through Jesus. God loves us (**1 john 4**). Believe Him and His word.

With Jesus you can get to know God – with other beliefs and religions, etc. you don't, except to have satan lead you (thinking you are fine). Go to Jesus and have a relationship with God (**rom. 5:11; rom. 8:14-16; 2 cor. 5:18-20; gal. 4:1-7; col. 1:20-21**), the way He created us to be (**gen. 1 and 2**).

Man doesn't want to believe the bible (which just shows you how evil we are – and we are), or Jesus (God), because man wants to make up his own rules (really satan), and not be controlled or told what to do – even if it is best for man, and God would know (He made us), and why satan (by sinning – disobedience) left God (heaven – kicked out by God) and thought he was better than God, and came (sent by God – wanting to see what is really in our heart – having free will – a choice – to follow good or evil) to earth to tempt man – to have man disobey (sin) and not listen to God (we choose). And adam and eve failed (as we do – without Jesus) and gave away this world to satan. There is none good on earth (**psalm 14; rom. 3**). So satan tries to explain away the creation – what we see in the creation (teaching lies – evolution, etc. – mainly from japheth), away from seeing God, even those that have known of Him (**rom. 1**). And evolution hurts ham (believed to be lower on the evolutionary tree) more with these lies. All from satan.

Just like fake news today – evolution is fake news, knowledge, etc. (satan is a liar – and the father of lies – **john 8:44**) – a long time ago. And people (led by satan) still believe it today. Anything against God and His word – against Jesus.

People don't want to believe in Jesus and His word – so they believe in lies of man and satan – like things in history, science, evolution, etc. – almost to show off their intelligence, etc. – like japheth does. All humans need to get away from noah's sons, and get to Jesus and become one with God again (with the Holy Spirit – born again – **john 3**).

Science has its place, but God's word (the bible) is what we need to base it on and follow. Go to Jesus and learn the truth about us and this world.

All of the people in the past, but especially today, have tried to deny God and His truth when it has been shown to all men. They try to explain it away from the truth (satan leading), but they all have seen and heard – no excuse. And they cause their own problems (God allowing) in their own life and in the world (**rom. 1:26-32**).

Just like God made everything – He will take it all away. Things didn't just show up here – God created it – no big bang, evolution, etc. – no one can explain, but God in His word.

Like mount st. helens (in washington state) eruption in may of 1980, showed us that things of this world – the changes (layers, canyons, etc.) can be formed in a few days, not millions of years – just like the flood did to this world in a short time (**gen. 7 to 8**). As well as the canyons, like the grand canyon in arizona, were laid in a short time, at the flood – and you can see some of the layers on the walls of the canyon, are curved (showing it was soft at one time – the flood mud, etc.), and were laid down that way and hardened curved quickly – not rock, and layers, cut through by a river, etc. over a period of millions of years, etc.

God does this once in a while to show us the truth after man has come up with his ideas without God (to see what we will believe and if we really believe in Him and His word). This just shows the bible to be true. The creation and man have only been around for about

6,000 years – what the bible says (not what man says – really satan), **gen. 5 and 11.**

If what you do or believe does not prove the bible to be true, it's not worth anything.

Science will prove the bible to be true, but you can believe it now and get saved through Jesus and His word, the truth. How many people have to listen to lies and end up in hell?

Where do you stand on this, and Who are you going to trust for this life and after?

Jesus believes this (**matt. 19:4; mark 10:6; matt. 24:37-38; luke 17:26-27**). Do you believe Him?

Go to Jesus now (and His word, His bible).

All of these so-called smart scientists, try to tell us what happened (and they were not there), as if they are smarter than God.

And all of these well-known or popular people that have 'figured' things out – or think they have – all against God and His truth – satan leading them (to be gods, etc., like satan wants to be – and wanted man to be, against God – **gen. 3:4-5**).

All of these well-known or popular people that have 'figured' things out – or think they have – all against God and His truth – satan leading them (to be gods, etc., like satan wants to be).

Somehow people believe in aliens, astrology, witchcraft, evolution, etc. (all from satan) – and none can be proved, etc. – although satan (and fallen angels – demons) does have power (more than humans have), and shows himself with the evil he spreads to people in different ways. But people don't want to believe in the truth of the bible. So we need to go to Jesus to stop this.

The sun (and moon) was and is worshipped by many religions, people, etc. (like gods) – false beliefs – the creation is being worshipped **(rom. 1)** – through astrology, witchcraft, etc. and by the egyptians, babylonians, muslims, etc., and it controls many people around the world. Only worship the Son – Jesus.

So until we all go to Jesus we can't get away from the world's hold on us (mainly through satan) – **1 john 2:15-16**. And we won't solve our problems until then. We have to change from what we are born with (from adam's sin – through satan, and go to God through Jesus with the Holy Spirit), and get away from noah's sons.

No matter how tough satan gets on or in you – God can help you through – don't let satan win. Keep going to God, and help others that struggle and hurt. Pray for all. And share Jesus – the truth.

The spiritual (the Holy Spirit with Jesus) will change your mental and physical – desires, behavior, etc. – what you believe, etc., to the truth. Even war injuries, brain injuries, genetics, and rape and abuse problems, etc. – any mental or emotional problem, behavior, Jesus can help – go to Him, with what we are born with (we are all born evil and born with something) or get here in life, and go and read and pray to Him daily. But it has to be truth. We need to change and grow.

Like from a caterpillar (all of the different kinds of people we are today – **jer. 51:17**) to a butterfly (born again, spiritually – getting the Holy Spirit from Jesus). And when you are born again – that should be your real birthday (and even birthdays were celebrated all through history – even like 3800 years ago in egypt – right after the flood – **gen. 40:20**), and when Jesus was here **(matt. 14:6; mark 6:21)**. And we celebrate Jesus' birth (and it is good), but we should be celebrating His death, even more **(john 19:28-30; philip. 2:5-11)**, for what He did for us all (if we would just go to Him and believe and follow Him and His word). And even celebrating a person's death – as long as they are truly saved and going to heaven.

And there is going to be death and dying (tragedy, etc. – satan's world and people) with anything in this world (since adam's sin, after satan did – **gen. 3**), but you don't have to do it or cause it yourself, etc. (follow this evil world of death, etc.), so we need to go to God (Jesus – salvation – with the Holy Spirit) for anything to work out or get better, and be ready to go.

And how many deaths and births are there? There is a spiritual death – all born that way (adam started that for all of us with sin – God's Spirit is not in us anymore, and why we need to go to Jesus to get it back), there is a physical death (that we all are going suffer, and we see in the world – except when we are raptured – if we are alive then, although we will get a new body and get rid of this old one during the rapture), and possibly getting the Holy Spirit causes the death to sin (and connection to man – to adam, and noah's sons now) in your life (might be another one). There is physical birth (from our mothers), and then we have to have a spiritual birth (with the Holy Spirit, that we can only get from Jesus – **john 3**) for heaven – forever. So there are two births and two deaths, but is there a third (or fourth) death (**rev. 20:14**)? This may be called the second death (**rev. 2:11**), which may be physical (after your body dying, and your soul in hell suffering, etc. – separated from God forever – never to be satisfied).

And we all have a choice individually, even today (through Jesus), as adam and eve did – to go to God (and obey and stay with Him), or not. The Lord God saved adam and eve then (**gen. 3:21** – the first sacrifice), because they wanted to go to Him (it is a free choice, and we need to want to go to Him) – but their son cain did not (**gen. 4:16**). And there still is punishment for sin and disobedience – besides death (not living forever the way God intended – connected to Him with the Holy Spirit – the Holy Spirit in our soul – in our body He created). They also were kicked out of the garden of eden – a nicer place, holy, like heaven (**gen. 3:22-24**) – even though the world was still comfortable for man to live (until the flood) – and all of mankind has been punished since (and we need punishment on this earth for sin – or the evil we do here – to others). Our soul will live forever somewhere now (heaven – without sin, or hell – with sin, but no way to be satisfied, in torment forever).

And that is what man is rebelling against forever (since then) – against each other (and God). And it is the same today when we sin (we all can see the evil in the world and in ourselves) – there is punishment (and separation), but we have a choice to go to God (the true God) and get connected back with the Holy Spirit (that is in the truly saved – **1 cor. 6:19-20**), that only Jesus (the Creator), can give us. He is the Light of the world.

Light is good, and darkness is not bad or good, just needed (**gen. 1:2-5**) for this world. But there is light that is good, and a darkness that is evil (**john 3:19**) – a choice (and we know the difference – **gen. 2:16-17, gen. 3:11-12**).

And we are to be the light of the world – His light (truth of His word – the bible), being saved through the Holy Spirit to share Him – even though we may be dead here (and still alive physically – **matt. 8:21-22; luke 9:59-62**) – until we are born again (**john 3**) – brought back to life (from the dead), and we use His light to shine, not ours. Just like the moon is dead, and doesn't have its own light, but is using the sun's light to shine, to reflect to earth and be seen, we (being saved) are using the Son's (Jesus') light (and life) to reflect Him and the truth to the world (**matt. 5:14-16; john 1:9; john 5:19-21; john 8:12; john 9:5; john 12:46; john 15:4-5; philip. 2:13-18**).

And the moon might have been different when it was created on the fourth day (with the stars, including the sun – **gen. 1:14-19**). There was a water canopy around the earth (**gen. 1:6-8**) – protecting the earth and man (no dark skin, etc. before the flood) – to make it comfortable for man to live here (and we all looked the same) – and it was probably outside the moon. And when the flood came, the water (that flooded the earth – that canopy is not there anymore – **gen. 7:11**) bombarded the moon, on its way to earth – and made the moon look the way it does – desolate – not millions and billions of years did (and the moon didn't have much dust on it when man landed on the moon – if man really went there – maybe only an inch or so – the scientists – evolutionists, etc. thought there would be many feet of dust – because of the billions of years, and were worried about landing on the moon, so may have been afraid to really go). Don't listen to man – go to God for the truth of this world – for history, and science, etc. And now the moon just reflects light – what we see in the sky from the moon – from the sun. Just like we are to reflect the truth of Jesus – from the Son.

Jesus is light (love, etc. – **john 8:12**), compared to darkness – evil (satan, and even man). Go to the Light – Jesus (and live). People like darkness – night, underground, evil, etc. – Jesus is light – come to the Light, we all need Him. Especially to not hurt each other and to all get along – as different as we are.

We all are different and need to be nice to each other, but we are not (and the only reason that there is any peace or goodness in the world is because of Jesus – even though Jesus can bring division, because we don't know the truth – His word, and people that do know the truth – follow Him, will be separated from those that don't know the truth – **matt. 10:32-39; 2 cor. 6:14-18**). And we may try to help others, but they need to try to help themselves, too, for it to really work.

God wants us all to get along – but not without Jesus.

And people can learn from each other – and help each other – all of noah's sons – when they are together (like in america), but won't totally get along without Jesus (like we can and should in america – like it has been at times, and can be again – not just hurt each other – and be selfish and mean – evil, like the way we are born). So go to Jesus to change and away from man. Or the evil of satan (and us) will remain in our lives.

God – the Lord – Jesus (He is the Creator), creates evil – **isa. 45:7** (satan, angels, man, darkness, etc. have a choice to be evil, but they all didn't start out that way – but were disobedient to God and His word – free will – even adam did, even with the Holy Spirit – and adam was the son of God, too – **luke 3:38**). But man was created perfect at first ('very good' – **gen. 1:26-28, 31**), at the beginning, as satan (lucifer) and the angels were (**gen. 1 and 2**). Men – since adam sinned (without the Holy Spirit and God in their life – not going to Jesus) – through satan (**gen. 3**), and they like darkness (evil) better (**john 3:19**). God uses satan (God can get rid of him), to get us to go to God – to see the evil more clearly. And an example is God allowing satan to bother job (**book of job**). So God is in control – go to Jesus and make it better for you and others.

And Jesus and the Holy Spirit can be with evil – like the Lord was here before the flood (the presence of the Lord – **gen. 4:16; gen. 6:3**), and when Jesus was here before and after His death and resurrection (then sent the Holy Spirt to us to be saved – **acts 1 and 2**).

God puts powers in place – all through history, even today – just like He did when israel was taken over many times, including before Jesus was about to come here when the romans took over – because the jewish leaders didn't follow God, then He changed it back when they followed Him again. And that still happens today, when we go away from God – like america does sometimes. So God will put evil in power, because we cause Him to do that. So follow the leaders in power, because God put them there (**rom. 13**), but follow God (Jesus), and share Him and the truth of His word, and it will be better, and you will be blessed.

God will put in power over a country, whatever they deserve – even in america, so we need to go to Him (**2 chron. 7:14**).

We (true Christians, churches, etc.) need to share Jesus more and the truth of His word, to change what happens here (for a person, society, nation, etc.), because God puts the powers in place here (those who rule us), and we follow (what we deserve, if we are not following God and His word – through Jesus) – like when the romans were here with Jesus (**matt. 17:24-27; matt. 22:15-22**), even to the worst of it (**dan. 3**). Let God take care of it. Keep going to God and share the truth, and praying for all (including the rulers, your enemies – only with Jesus can you do that), then He will change the powers in charge (even in america). Or the end will come, it will soon.

Even though God (the Lord) makes all – evil included – He knows who will go to Him (He knows all) and who will not (they follow satan, and stay that way until they die), and does not force anyone to go to Him – it's our choice while we are living and seeing things in this sinful world. God put the wicked (He will eventually punish them) and good together (those that have been truly saved by Jesus – have the Holy Spirit) – **matt. 13:24-30, 36-43**. Seeing what we will follow and be attracted to (and may even like more). Leading to heaven or hell. We know the difference of right and wrong since the garden – with adam and eve eating of the tree of the knowledge of good and evil. We are all (all of mankind – up to today) connected to adam (all on the same team) – man, and sin – and are all punished because of that. Choose Jesus (and His truth) and go to heaven.

This world was simple (at creation – and was supposed to be) – until satan fell (sinned), and came here (God allowing) to tempt man (**gen. 3**), then it got complicated (even more after the flood), because of the sin of man, so blame satan, then man (ourselves) for all of the evil. God will lead us away from sin (**psalm 139:23-24**). Go to Him – to Jesus.

It's hard to tell people Jesus is the only answer to their life here (and after) – because everyone thinks it has to be something else, but it is not. With Jesus and the truth of His word we can all figure it out.

Just accept where God put you – which son of noah you are, and the limitations, and appreciate america for helping all of us to have opportunities, and especially to get to know Jesus.

No matter what son of noah you are from, or nationality you are – we are or should be one in Jesus – a son (or daughter) of God, then we can all get along – as long as it is the truth.

Why did God allow the jews to stay in egypt for 400 years (mainly as slaves – **gen. 15:12-14; exo. 12:40-41; acts 7:5-7; gal. 3:16-18**), and the evil to go on before the flood (**gen. 6**) for so long? He has His reasons (His ways are above ours – **2 chron. 2:4-6; psalm 135:5-6; isa. 55:7-9; micah 4:11-12**), and He is patient and has a plan – knowing how man is (what's needed for us to learn). Even in your life.

And God keeps secrets until He needs or wants to do something (**deut. 29:29**), and He (Jesus) has shared them in the new testament (with paul – **rom. 16:25-27**). The only secret left is when the rapture is going to happen (then the tribulation) – the last 2,000 years since Jesus died and rose and the temple destroyed. No other secrets left – except satan trying to fool man with beliefs, religions, etc. that are false and leading man the wrong way against the truth of God – and away from Jesus (like we have seen in the last 2,000 years). Just trust the truth in His word (the truth of the bible) – about Jesus, and get saved, and be ready to go.

God has these checks and balances in the world – puts people where He wants them – so no one takes over the world – only Jesus with the Holy Spirit – true Christians. And when the true Christians go (the rapture) – the anti-christ (satan – **rev. 13**) will be here leading all of man (all of noah's sons). So we stay separated for now. But if we want to be one, it is only with Jesus that we can.

And if we understand why we can't figure out this world and make it work out for us (continue to be against each other – **james 4**) – then we will start to understand we can't do it ever – not without Jesus. We need to see that we need to get away from noah's sons – man (and satan), to make it work.

The world today will get just as evil (led by satan) – like before the flood (**gen. 6; matt. 24:32-39**), before the end – when the rapture comes (and man didn't know when the flood was to come – but some of those who saw noah building the ark may have wondered) – led by satan trying to unite the world as one today, like before the flood.

People before Jesus died and rose did not get the Holy Spirit that adam lost for us - the jews sent abraham, or people before the flood and even after (with a few exceptions). The righteous were with God and His spirit before the flood (**gen. 6:3**). Even abraham did not go to heaven right away, as righteous as he was (God started abraham's bosom) – maybe enoch and the others in the presence of the Lord – God's spirit (**gen. 6:3**) – maybe noah, possibly japeth and shem. But God knows and God will be fair – but it is only through Jesus after he died and rose now, to get the Holy Spirit – jews and gentiles, for salvation and heaven.

So we don't know when the rapture is – even though we see the world changing - but the world would be worse – more evil, if Jesus told us the time He is coming back – evil people would wait until the last minute to be saved or even maybe preach – many more people would go to hell. So God did it for us (for you), because He is a loving God – wanting no one to perish and go to hell (at least not as many). Even jews (as a nation), or others, that will be in the tribulation (the last 7 years of the 490 years of **daniel 9**). Gentiles and individual jews - all of noah's son - need to be saved by Jesus that have been born from Jesus' death and after (the last 2,000 years – not sure how God will judge the jews after Jesus died and rose, that didn't go to Him – from then to now, but God will come to the save the jews - **rom. 11:25-36**), but not before His death – we know what happened before Jesus came and died – they (the righteous jews that died) were in abraham's bosom (**luke 16:19-31**) before Jesus came and died – then Jesus went down and released them after His death, and they (the righteous jews) rose with Him to heaven (**matt. 27:50-54; luke 23:29-43; john 5:25-29; eph. 4:7-10**). That's why before Jesus death and resurrection, the jews went to hell (hades – abraham's bosom), they did not stay there – Jesus went there to get the righteous jews out – so the jews would not want to stay there and prayed to God not to leave them there (**psalm 16:10**). There is no more abraham's bosom (anything like purgatory, etc. – from false churches) or anything like that anymore (since Jesus' death and resurrection).

Just after the rapture, the jews still owe God seven years (of the 490 years) – to finish the last requirement that God demanded of them in **dan. 9:24-27**, but back then the jews did not comply – to anoint the Most Holy – who is Jesus – now the jews will go through the tribulation – the wrath (true Christians will not – they will be raptured first). At least a remnant of the jews will be redeemed in the end (**rom. 11:1-6**), when Jesus comes for them in the tribulation. The jews were blinded then (and now) – mainly by satan – as others are today (**2 cor. 4:1-4**).

Trust God to do the right thing. – don't worry – you just go to Jesus and get saved. Or you won't be in heaven (but hell - forever).

If God wasn't helping here, then israel and the jews (they are still God's people) would be wiped out by now – especially today. And satan keeps trying. Go to Jesus and get saved (and share Him - to jew and gentile – all of noah's sons).

God lets satan only go so far in this world for evil – like He did with job (**book of job**) – even the empires throughout history could only go so far, but were evil – even the romans (the roman empire) in Jesus' day.

All of noah's sons – went to see Jesus after His birth – about two years after, then went back to their countries – all nationalities know of Him. Eventually the whole earth.

All of the nations around israel and europe, even asia, etc. (all of noah's sons) –the roman empire – knew of Jesus (all of the wise men that came from every nation to see Him), but all have gone away from the truth of God – and God has punished them.

God lets us see that man doesn't go to God especially when it's comfortable (like it was before the flood - but was still sinful) – so God made it tough here with flood, etc.

God had moses write the bible - the bible is God with us when it was written - like the presence of the Lord – God's Spirit - before the flood - now with Jesus and the Holy Spirit. The bible is God talking to us - and the Holy Spirit helping. We talk to God, by praying. It is the truth of God. And we are not to add or take away from the bible (**deut. 4:1-2; rev. 22:19-21**) - like false churches, religions, beliefs, etc. do.

The first 4000 years is the old testament. The last 2000 years is the new testament - up to today. Then the last thousand years – the millennium - then heaven.

Read **exodus, leviticus, numbers,** etc. and see that God is serious about the sin of man – how evil (how bad it is) – following satan, and the punishments for man because of that. The only way we will learn and understand the evil of it. It has to be really bad for some to go to Jesus.

And the law shows you your weakness (and why God wrote them) – the law doesn't help you keep it – only God can – since we are evil, so we need to go to Jesus to obey (with the Holy Spirit – that adam lost for us all that would have helped us follow what God wanted us to when He created us – to be connected to Him to follow the law, obey, etc.)

With the Holy Spirit, we can follow the law naturally and be connected to God. Before Jesus came, man didn't. Even though before the flood you can be in the presence of the Lord like enoch and the others were (**gen. 5**). That is why it is grace now. Not laws, works, etc. (**gal. 5:22-26**).

Not that we are perfect – not until heaven.

All people can change - grow and be good or better than they were. We need to go to Jesus.

God is concerned about us – if He is concerned about animals, then He certainly is about man (**luke 12:6**).

So the law should show us we are sinners – and need of a Savior, because we can't be good enough on our own – so God made laws (like the 10 commandments, etc.).

But laws were needed (and still are) to show us that we cannot live without them, or to follow them on our own very well – with Jesus we can and don't need them. Since we all don't go to Jesus (or know the truth), we need laws today for this world to be livable (showing we are evil and sinful, just like God says we are). We need something to show us how evil we are (even though deep down we know we are).

Is God evil, because of all of this? No, angels and man are (not listening to God since adam – the beginning – **gen. 3** – and there was only one law in the garden, and they still failed) – we all have free will and choose these things – evil or good things – God just gives them the choice (and the situations to make that choice – especially with satan). Man (and angels) go away from God – God (Jesus) is always waiting. And God wants to know who wants to be with Him freely and not forced – just like you don't want to force your children or spouse to love you. Free will. Hell is this earth and all of its desires and satisfactions (even if temporary), and we all get to choose where we will live for eternity (we send ourselves to hell, God doesn't), but hell will be hell – you will have all of the desires, etc. like on this earth (think of what those are, even the simplest ones – **luke 16:22-24**), but not have any way to satisfy them – ever, like you do sometimes on this earth, and you will have to do that forever (that will be hell).

Maybe you want to go to hell (like satan is going to – the lake of fire), but don't lead others there, especially when it is not good for their life (or yours), here or there. It may be tough to stand up for right, but we need to.

God doesn't want us to be separated from Him in hell – forever – He wants us to know how evil we are, and this world. He is serious – it is best for us to go to Jesus. And see the difference.

We have to see both sides (and why satan is here – so thank God for satan), to have the best chance to make the best choice (to see how evil really is and how good God is – through Jesus).

Most people follow a church, religion, belief, etc., because they tell them what they want to hear or already believe (born into, etc.) – not what the truth is. Need to know the truth.

If you are forced (or brainwashed, etc.) into believing a certain way (which is really an evil way) – that can't be right. It has to be truth and out of love (and for you to look into it and make sense of it). Go to Jesus (and His word – the truth) to know what that is (He gives you freedom). A choice – free will. There can be freedom for good or for bad things (**1 cor. 6:12; 1 cor. 10:23; 1 pet. 2:15-16**) – know the difference. Know how to control them – Jesus will help. Know the truth to choose.

But we have to be holy to be with God (in heaven) – and that can only be with Jesus (and the Holy Spirit) – true salvation.

God helps His people, like when He punished egypt to let the jews go to their (His) land, the same needs to be done in america – but the difference is america is our (His) land, and needs God to take it back (God doesn't want us to be unequally yoked – **2 cor. 6:14-18**), or He needs to take us out (like the jews out of egypt, or like noah and family out of the flood, and lot and family out of sodom and gomorrah, etc.) – which would be the rapture (**1 cor. 15:5-55; 1 thess. 4:13-18**).

It would also be like when enoch went up to God (**gen. 5:21-24**), and elijah did in the chariot (**2 kings 2:9-11**), and even those that arose with Jesus after the tomb (**matt. 27:50-53**).

After the rapture – before the seven-year tribulation – the only people left here on earth are those that are all united (by satan) against the true God (even though there will be some going to Jesus in the tribulation – then killed – **rev. 20:4**) – like it was before the flood and in sodom, etc. This is the end times.

You have to accept you are evil and the things you do are your fault – and lead you to do things in this life to make bad decisions – and you need to admit you made mistakes and go to Jesus to change. You reap what you sow (**gal. 6:7-9**).

But man will not go to God and His word – satan is leading this world. We need to know and share Jesus through these evil times – people need it and would want it more – nothing else will help people – just Jesus.

Eventually satan will get so bold in the world and society – especially america, with satan's lies, that true Christians will have to be more bold and start speaking up about the truth of Jesus and His word. And that will hopefully get more people to Jesus and getting saved before they die or this world ends.

And don't believe every spirit – satan will fool you – especially toward the end, in america, like we have seen (**1 john 4:1**).

The Holy Spirit in the true Christian is keeping this world livable, etc. – once it leaves with true Christians – the rapture (**1 thess. 4:13-18**)– this world will be worse (**2 thess. 2:1-12**) – then the end, coming soon. So the Christians' job will be done.

And when the true Christians are gone, then God will use 144,000 (12,000 from each tribe of israel) to preach in the tribulation, along with the two witnesses (probably moses and elijah) – preaching Jesus to all – especially the jews (**rev. 7**).

Christians may have to get to a point of persecution in america today (to believe the truth of God – through Jesus and His word), as those (true Christians) have in the rest of the world today, and like the jews did before – like daniel's friends did in babylon (**dan. 3**) – having faith and to stand up for the truth of God (and it better be the truth) against evil people – leaders, etc. (satan leading – people following him and not being aware), that want to turn you from the true God and the truth of His word (you see in the world today – schools, government, society, etc.) – no matter what the consequences are.

Just like the military stands up and fights for a country (like america – Jesus' land), and may die for it (like Jesus died for all of mankind and the truth on the cross), we need do the same in the world – learn and stand up for the truth of Him. It is worth doing more than even for a country, etc. Share Jesus and His truth.

So american Christians – the true ones, may have to start showing they can handle persecution, like others have around the world, and in the past. Maybe God wants to test us today. And leading to the end time with satan (the anti-christ leading, etc.). But go to Jesus and be ready. And learn and share the truth.

And the anti-christ will be a man (led by satan) and the number of man is six, and the anti-christ's number will be 666 (**rev. 13**) – like the trinity, but evil. Man was created on the sixth day (**gen. 1:26-31**) and six is an incomplete number – seven is a complete number (God's seventh day rest – **gen. 2:1-3**). It is Jesus that completes man – man is not complete by himself – especially today (even though satan wants you to think you are – fooling all of noah's sons). We need to keep sharing Jesus. Even the bible has 66 books in it – not complete without Jesus, with the Holy Spirit. And why the jews rejected Jesus, and why the jews are now having to wait to follow Jesus in the end times – then they will be complete with Jesus.

The end times will have a world that we will have to deal with persecution – even in america – because if you love Jesus and stand up for Him and the truth of His word, the world will hate you like they hated Jesus (**matt. 24:9; john 15:18-27**).

But only after the rapture of the true Christians will the anti-christ be revealed (**2 thess. 2:1-12**) – then the seven-year tribulation starts.

Man (the world, satan) going against God and His word (even in america) is going on more now, and all people are letting it happen – some Christians, included. We cause our own problems without Him (**psalm 1, rom. 1**). Like before the flood.

People, countries, beliefs, etc. want to blame other people for their problems, struggles, etc. – so they hate and kill – taking it out others, when it is they that are at fault – we all are, and we need to go to Jesus, and help others to go to Him, and His truth.

So we need to stand up for the truth of Jesus and His word.

Going against the world today and what it is teaching today in families, schools, news, on television, etc. is like what a jew did by going to Jesus when He was here – going against the jews in power, and beliefs, etc. – so the jews hated those jews that went to and followed Jesus. And the world today hates those that try to follow Jesus and have people live that way (they hated Jesus, so they will hate you – **matt. 10:21-23; mark 13:12-13; luke 21:16-18; john 15:17-19**). We need to go to God – Jesus and His truth in His word. So the world (satan led) hates you.

The schools, news, government, society, etc. need to stop going against God and His truth (as happened in the 1920's, when creation was challenged with evolution in school – which eventually did win, and as america did in the 1960's taking prayer and the bible out of public schools, etc. – which caused most of the problems we have today since then). People, especially children, grow up confused and miserable, etc. (which lead to drugs, alcohol, bad behavior, etc.). Let Jesus and His truth be taught and see the truth in the world, life, etc.

We need to keep talking about putting creation (the truth) back in schools (taking evolution out – satan's lies), and the bible and prayer back in schools for a start (but needs to be put back in all churches first). Man let this happen, so man (true Christians) needs to get it back (with Jesus and His truth).

Right now we are letting satan – and those he leads – go against God and His word (His truth) to lead this nation. Stand up against them and for Jesus and His word – let God help. But learn it first, and use it in your life and share it with others.

Help share the truth of Jesus and His word, and God will help you in this world (and help this nation go in a better direction). He will help you through it all – small or big (**isa. 43:1-3; dan. 3:19-30**), with the Holy Spirit – go to Him.

So God may also punish Christians, if they sin and go away from Him (even take us out – **1 cor. 5:1-5**) – and you may be seeing that in the world today (even for a country like america) – so with all of the sins by evil man, nations, etc. (satan leading) – God has to punish man – like the flood, and the jews being punished, and even today for all sin – that goes for all of us. We need to mend our ways and repent (like He has done with israel – and america, in the past – **2 chron. 7:13-15**), and keep praying and learning and sharing the truth of His word.

If our problems are because we went away from God – then the problems can be taken care of if we go back to God. To Jesus.

There is only about 2 to 3% of the world that is truly Christian (**matt. 7:13-23**). Maybe 250,000,000 in the world – the rest are false beliefs, religions, etc. – churches included.

Many groups – religions, fake Christians, leaders, the rich, etc. are together to hurt, kill, have power, etc. over people, nations, etc. (all of noah's sons) – all against God – as satan has done since the beginning (adam and eve were the only people on earth – the world's population – and they were both against God as one – **gen. 3**, like before the flood, and in sodom, etc. – and God had to punish them) – promoting satan's lies, beliefs, etc. in science, history, fake bibles, etc. – all wanting to be a god, and keep people from knowing the truth of God and trying to stop them from getting the truth out there (by killing, etc. throughout history – don't think that all the people die normally or naturally, that are against these satanic groups, including false religious beliefs, etc.). And these people are getting rich off lies from evolution, etc. – from teaching, books, etc. (but should change to sharing the truth of Jesus). It has been going on for years, and satan is still trying to do that today (getting ready for the end times). But go to Jesus and be saved and ready to go whenever the end is.

People try to prove they are smarter than anyone – a waste of time – they are not smarter than God. Learn the truth – go to Jesus – we all know, but satan misleads us (**rom. 1**).

Everyone is egotistical to think they are good enough – good people, even without Jesus, and think they are good enough to get to heaven, better than others in the world, etc. They are without the truth of God's word, and don't have the Holy Spirit.

Don't want to be divided or separated as Christians – believe the same as Jesus and His word says – through the Holy Spirit – not a church, leader, etc. Be one with Jesus – separated no more. Only Jesus can give you the Holy Spirit and get you to heaven.

So no matter what happens, be with Jesus to handle the things in this world (**matt. 11:28-30; john 16:33; john 17:14-19**) – any of the terrible things that people do (that satan leads man to do). Even death (**matt. 10:28**). Jesus has been through it all and will be with us (**john 17**) – defeating satan.

This is not our home – for any human – Christian or not – heaven or hell is. You choose.

Since heaven is our home once we are truly saved (**2 cor. 5; eph. 2; philip. 3:17-21**) – we don't need to stay connected to this world (or to man and his evil ways). We can be here and be one with God through Jesus. And share Him and His truth until we go (so others can go to heaven and not hell). God will deal with those that don't.

God will eventually cut off the wicked and has before (**psalm 37:28**), and still does. Pray for them and share Jesus with them. And God doesn't destroy the whole world anymore (when the whole world was one with satan) – like the flood (but will someday in the end), but for now only areas that don't follow Him in parts of the world (all with satan leading), like He did with sodom and gomorrah (God only destroyed them) – and since then, and today. God controls the weather (like Jesus calmed the storm – **matt. 8:23-27; mark 4:37-41; luke 8:22-25**), and as God sent the flood (**gen. 7 to 8**), stopped the sun (**josh. 10:12-14; isa. 38:4-8**), destroyed sodom (**gen. 19**), etc. And God knows who will go to Him – and when there are disasters, we can help them and share Jesus – for those who can be saved. And don't worry about climate change, etc.

Even though man may cause this earth to have problems – to man, animals, plants, even maybe cause weather problems, etc. – with chemtrails, other chemicals, nuclear problems, pollution, etc. – also all of the pesticides hurt plants, soil, water, etc., just to make money, but it will be God that will destroy the world, not man (**gen. 8:22; 2 pet. 3:10-12**). We need to go to God to take care of this earth, until He ends it. Be with Jesus and be ready to go.

So God is still stopping satan and the people who follow him until it is time – the end. But can use him for punishment, too (**1 cor. 5:1-5**) – and at least you won't go to hell, if you are truly saved.

God will prevail (**jer. 20:11-13**). He can help us, too. Pray. And heaven is better, if it is the end.

Take up your cross verses (**matt. 16:24; mark 8:34; luke 9:23**) were before Jesus went to the cross (before He died and rose). But no one knew of the cross, except Jesus, but He used the cross as an example of following Him – that we use today in churches, wear around our neck, etc. (after He died and rose). Wondering what people would have thought of that before He went (mainly for our benefit to read today). And the jews tried to kill Him differently (than the cross), before, but He escaped.

So the jews (and satan) were after Jesus to kill Him many times, but not able to, because God protected Him (**luke 4:28-30; john 8:58-59; john 10:38-40**) and allowed Him to escape each time (it wasn't His time yet – until He voluntarily went to the cross to die for us all – God's plan), and God can do the same for you – help you to escape temptations of this world (and may have many times in your life already – for temptations, satan's attempts, etc. – **1 cor. 10:13**) – all of man has these problems, if you would only go to Him to help you, and get saved (Holy Spirit). Keep going to Jesus and the truth of His word.

We are sinful (death is the penalty) and need to be born again (**john 3**) to not be sinful, and Jesus came here and died, and was born again. He defeated death, and so can we with Him, and follow Him (to heaven). It is easy with Him. We make it hard – when we are without Him.

When are people going to stop being babies and grow up and handle things? And the best is with Jesus and His word.

Jesus will help you be free of all of the hang ups, desires, feelings, etc. (basically sins) that you are born with and grow and develop as you get older and live in this world – whatever you were brought up with – and all of it is what satan leads you in this world, in your life – whether you know it or not – without Jesus (and the Holy Spirit), all against God – He didn't want you that way (sinful) – don't listen to people that say that – that you are fine the way you are (you are not – and that includes gender issues, etc., thinking that you should be something else – that is also evil, and sinful) – we only need the Holy Spirit to be whole, and only from Jesus. Get the truth. It's a spiritual thing, then you will change your desires, problems, etc. (doing what God wants) – satan wants you to think you are happy and doing fine (and that you need something more than Jesus), but you are not. This is an evil world (and even worse in hell).

When people fail at things – parenting, work, desires, etc., people try to say it's not your fault, things will work out – feel good about yourself, and may not take the blame, or feel they are good, and so are others – so you won't go to Jesus, since you are good. Just really saying that man is good, and they are looking for good, but it is satan wanting you to think you are good. Man is evil and born that way. Know that, and then you can solve this, with Jesus.

Most people act like they did nothing in life to cause the problems they are in. We all have choices – we all need to go to Jesus – and it better be the truth. If you go to Jesus, you can get rid of any abuse – no matter how bad and evil it was in your life. Then you can move on and help others – not hurt others or yourself anymore. Not take it out on others.

It's in man's best interest if man can't solve and figure out this world on his own (every generation from the beginning has been trying to do that) – and we for sure can't get the evil – sin, out of this world (or out of ourselves). Thank God for Jesus (and why satan is here – to show us how bad we and this world really are, and it should lead us to God and His word).

If people are not evil, and naturally good, then why is there so much evil in the world? God says we are (**gen. 8:21, psalm 14; rom. 3**). And satan is leading that evil (and us), fooling us, without Jesus. All need to go to Jesus. We have a choice (free will). Everyone comes up with something.

With all of the beliefs, cultures, nationalities, etc. in the world (from all of noah's sons) – who's right, who should lead, etc. – whose ideas are you going to believe or follow? It comes down to satan or God – man's (satan's) don't work. Especially for all. All of noah's sons go away from Jesus – all want to have power, but are satan led – it doesn't work – all want to lead, but leads us all against God. Only Jesus can bring us together the best – all of noah's sons, if we would work together for what's best, then we can live together (like america tries to) – only with Jesus (and His word) will that work. Otherwise satan will lead to destruction (like you have seen).

People, groups, beliefs, etc. can't explain how to help each person to get out of our problems on this earth as humans – to do what God says Jesus does for us – solve man's selfishness, hatefulness, evil, wanting power, desires, etc. (and after this life).

We are all the same that way to begin with – without God (the true God), and we are not perfect (while we are here) – none of us – remember that, but we can change with Jesus (and we will be perfect in heaven, with Him in our life here). So know the truth and go to Jesus, before you die (to get to heaven).

Jesus didn't care that He was going to die (except for the temporary separation from God, the Father) – He knew He would be alive again – defeating death – like He showed with the raising of lazarus (even though lazarus would die again), and like we can also be alive after death, in heaven – forever – never to die again. Jesus the creator brought lazarus back to life (not reincarnation – which is satanic). It was just Jesus – God, proving who He is – God. Even john the Baptist came in the spirit of elijah (**luke 1:13-17**). And Elijah did come back with moses and with jesus (**mark 9:2-4**). And Elijah will come back in the end before jesus comes back– **rev 11**. So lazarus coming to life again is like we being born again (**john 3**) from being dead in our sins – in this body and world (let the dead – man without Jesus and the Holy Spirit – bury the dead – **matt. 8:21-23; luke 9:59-60**), then to die and go to heaven (or the rapture) after that.

Regardless without the bible, laws, etc., man is and was still evil, sinful (dead) – after adam sinned – from satan. Laws (the bible) do help us to see it better – God wanted us not to be sinful, evil anymore, and only through Jesus can we do that.

We all are looking for something in this world – some belief – something different to explain everything – looking at everything, but God and His word – and they waste their (and others) time with misinformation, lies, etc. (from satan) – thinking they came up with the answers. Go to Jesus to know the truth – for here and after this life.

It's sad that not everyone knows the truth about things in this world – what's best, and listening to wrong information from everyone (man, through satan – from the beginning – **gen. 3**), not knowing what's best for man – what God wants (Who made us) – His truth. And it is satan that leads us (through man) toward these problems (evil, etc.), and away from Jesus and the truth (His word). The bible is to show us life here and how to live here (true science, history, etc.) – mainly with Jesus (and the Holy Spirit) and it is available to all.

The bible was written for man – to give the truth (with satan's lies in the world, as time has gone by), so eventually we needed the truth (and God gave it to moses – after the flood – to start writing the truth about 3500 years ago – and now the complete truth, the whole bible), and the whole bible is for our learning (**rom. 15:4**). All of us. For everything we need to know here and where we are going from here and how to get there – through Jesus.

The bible is to show us we can know God and be saved and be with Him in heaven – through Jesus. And why we need Him – we are evil – and satan leads that evil. And that is what we need to know.

The bible becomes more real and true, the more you look into it and into the world – it all fits and makes sense more and more – go to Jesus and get the Holy Spirit, and it will be more real.

There are reasons why God doesn't want man to be other than what He wants us to be – not sinful – it's not good for us or others (and we weren't created for that or that way). God is against all those mentioned in the bible – like sodom, and the beliefs and behaviors of those that lived there, and does that today in the world. Those going away from Him and His knowledge, and helping others to do the same (like america is getting – **rom. 1**). We need to follow Jesus and His word today, and help those in the world to do the same.

Some people in the bible listened to God and followed (and had to go back to Him sometimes and follow again) – we have to do that today – read God's word and follow what He says. He will help you, like He did those He talked to in the bible. stand up for the truth, then see things happen.

We deserve much worse – but God is fair, and we all can go to Jesus. What God did throughout history was needed. And we need to be holy, because God is, and only Jesus can help us.

God had to write the bible to tell the truth about this world – against satan's lies – like evolution, how we got here, and where we go after this life, etc. For our learning (**rom. 15:4**).

God's timetable for history is right and makes sense – we need to learn and look into it, and share it – it's truth (**gen. 5; gen 9 to 12**).

God gave man the ability to look into things of this world, but we need to find the truth by looking at the world, science, history, man, etc. through God's eyes – the bible. Then we will find answers – the truth. Go to Jesus first.

And just like we watch a replay of a game, sporting event, movie, etc. – knowing the outcome – it is just like the bible is a replay of this world, history, man, events, etc. – and we know the outcome – God wins. If God wins – we win – if we are with Him – Jesus. Go to Jesus and be ready.

We are all earthly, sinful, etc. until we go to Jesus, and become heavenly (our home after salvation – **2 cor. 5:18-21; eph. 2:19-20; philip. 3:17-21**). Until you go to Jesus, you are not alive – not really a person, a man, etc. – don't let anyone tell you different or push you into something or some way of living, etc. without Jesus – and the Holy Spirit (**matt. 8:21-22; luke 9:59-60; john 3:3-7**). We are all something with Jesus – as we are all nothing without Him (and can't do anything without Him – **john 15:5**) – all of noah's sons need Him (don't let man or satan make you think differently). Know the truth.

We need to be connected to God (through Jesus), not to man (or we die) – first with adam, now with noah and his sons.

God gave adam abilities at creation – to think, analyze, create, etc. (abilities like God – in His image – **gen. 1:26-28**) – but with God, not without Him (without His Spirit). We are now in man's (adam's) image – sinful (**gen. 5:3**), with God's abilities.

God gave man intelligence to figure out and discover things, etc., but only with God's truth will we be able to. So man discovers and figures out things in this world, but doesn't give God credit. So man is following man (and satan) – man is lost following satan. Go to God and His word.

Every son of noah can be smart (but not always interested in that), and do many things, especially if they work harder and learn, and listen (being taught and helped by their parents – especially in ameica), but japheth is the son of noah that is intelligent (and interested in it). It is always best with Jesus.

Some of the smartest people – and those that think they are – are the dumbest in the world – mainly those that don't know God (Jesus). Even though satan is smart and powerful, he leads man the wrong way in this world. We have caused our own problems following satan (he is destined for the lake of fire forever), and going against God and the truth of His word. We need to go to Him to make it right or God won't hear (**isa. 59:1-4**) – america (as the world) is going this way.

People want fame, etc. – to be smarter than God or His truth, trying to come up with how to figure this life out, etc. Only being led by satan and leading man the wrong way.

Sometimes the smarter someone is, the more they can (or try to) get away with evil – being prideful, etc. So being smart is not the best – be with Jesus to know what you should try to do and use your intelligence and abilities for Him in this world. Most think they don't need Jesus, or even want to know what the truth of His word is.

People don't want to change, because they are insecure and don't want to be wrong. And they start forcing people to think the way they do – what satan and sin does – being selfish.

So satan makes this world look attractive for the wrong things, for all, but especially the young, and they get hooked on them, then those things stay with them through their life.

So people cause their own problems – nations, etc., even homeless can (here and around the world), by not going to God – to Jesus and His word. God trying to separate His truth from satan's (which are lies). And we need to help all – share Jesus.

God did all of the separation (all the differences we see in noah's sons – in us – after the flood), because it is best for man (because of satan, and our sinful nature) – and He showed all that man did in the past – the evil (even before the flood – **gen. 6**), to have us see what and why He did it (all the changes and attempts, etc.) – and put it in the bible for us to see it. Look at the world through God's eyes – through the truth of His word, and you will see the truth. Go to Jesus to do that.

There are more true facts and history in the bible than any science or history, etc. book. And all we need to figure out man and this world. Look at the world through the eyes of the bible.

The creation (and the flood) made it look like the world and universe, and all in it changed – possibly aged a lot, but it didn't, God made it look that way (even adam and eve were created already grown). So God made it that way and man doesn't want to admit that God created anything – it just all showed up on it's own. So man doesn't have to go to Jesus.

We should use the bible – God's word, to back up true history and science. The bible has all of the answers in it – final answers for man here and beyond, and why people are afraid to look into it, and accept it, knowing they will have to change and give up all of what they believe and say they were wrong. And go to Jesus. So God wrote the bible so we would know the truth (against satan's lies – man following) and that He tried things in the past, so we would know He is truth and that we need Jesus. And eventually science, man, etc. will prove the bible to be true – so far it has. So look for clues in this world to prove the bible to be true – you will find them. So go to Jesus and His word and find out the truth. It is still tough to be a Christian in this evil, satanic, etc. world, but God will help you, if you go to Him daily – Him and His truth of His word and share Him. Even Jesus had to go through some things in this world when He was here, and always went to God the Father each day. Share Him and His word – truth.

If it wasn't for the bible, we wouldn't know much about this world or of man (at least the truth of it). As well as not know of satan, and how evil he is and how he leads man (without God) in this world to continue the lies and struggle we have here – all of noah's sons.

The truth of the bible eliminates many beliefs in this world – mainly from satan, that people follow (and worship him) – all of noah's sons do. God straightens us out with the truth – away from explanations, ideas, etc. of satan, that man follows.

This evil against the bible and its truths – all of satan's and man's lies in this world, help us read and study and understand the bible more than you realize. So you can learn and see the truth better. So satan has a purpose for being here. So study.

And the struggles and the punishments, etc. should lead us to God – to Jesus. We need to keep going to Him. We need Him.

You are not doing anything good for you or others, if you can't sacrifice and do the right and good thing – in God's word and follow – be a good example. Don't joke that you can't be strong or do things that are best for you – go to Jesus, and His word and follow. Be doers of the word (**james 1:12-27**).

This is what satan makes man do (**isa. 14:9-27**) – thinking man is better (really following satan), and screws up the world and man, thinking man knows more than God – we have all of the answers in His word, and knowing we have tried everything here and it is a waste of time to do it on our own (**eccl. 1 to 3**), especially without God – Jesus. Know the truth. We should feel good that God doesn't leave us the way we are – sinful, miserable, etc. (away from God's truth for us) – hopefully the world will get us to go to Him – He gives us a way to do that – Jesus (and His truth). And help others do that.

Don't do what the jews did when Jesus came here – they didn't listen – they thought they were fine – that they didn't need Him or what He said – and that has hurt the jews ever since (as well as others around the world, now and in the past). They didn't want to believe that He was God – the Messiah. Go to Jesus more and learn the truth of His word and share Him.

Even Christians can be to blame for problems here – for not speaking up – sharing the truth, Jesus, etc. at any time in history (even though at times they did). And it is only man that causes problems here (with our sinfulness, following satan, etc. – **james 4**) – God tries to help us solve the problems here, and He uses people He wants to follow Him (so we can see the truth – **rom. 9:10-13**). Mainly through Jesus only today (and those that truly follow Him and the truth of His word). The only reason this world is or has been any good is because of what God did, not man – we can help if we go to Jesus and follow the truth of His word. He keeps coming to us and wants us to go to Him.

He loves us (**john 3:16**).

If you are with Jesus and things don't work out as you plan or hoped for – He will lead you where you can make it – be what He wants and what's better for you. We can be one with God, doing what we are good at, and God will lead us – what is best for us. We need to move on from man – with what He wants with the Holy Spirit – just like we were created at the beginning, before sin (**gal. 5:22-26; eph. 4**).

Without Jesus, you are led by and following satan – and have a miserable life – get away from man – adam, and now noah's sons. Go to God – be with Him, through Jesus (with the Holy Spirit), to change you and this world – with the truth.

And we need to keep sharing the truth of Jesus and His word – the truth – and we know His word will not come back void – it will complete the purpose intended (**isa. 55:10-13**). Written by jews only (by God) – the old and new testaments for the whole world (gentiles included). Even though the jews – prophets, etc. didn't always know and totally understand what they were writing – they just obeyed God through the Holy Spirit – that guided them to write. But they wrote what God wanted, up to the time that Jesus came here (**matt. 11:12-14; luke 16:15-17; luke 24:44**), and after (from the risen Jesus) – that's why God set apart the jews – to write God's truth. And we need to know the truth of His word – not what leaders, churches, etc. just say (**acts 17:10-12**). Only from and to Jesus, since He died and rose (and after the bible completed) – are we to listen. Read it yourself and learn (but the Holy Spirit is who teaches you, **1 cor. 2:12-14** – you have to be truly saved) – know the bible (but the truth) – it's what God wants for us to know why we are here and why the world is the way it really is (**john 13-19; 2 tim. 2:14-16; 2 tim. 3:16-17**), so learn the word so well, that you can give an answer for why you believe (**1 pet. 3:15**) – the truth. Only from Jesus. Go to Jesus now (and His word), and get the Holy Spirit. And we can get the Holy Spirit inside of us today – but before Jesus died and rose man did not.

After Jesus was resurrected, He could then give us the Holy Spirit inside of us – how we are saved today (know you are truly saved – not by a church, leader, rituals, traditions, etc.), but also understand and believe what He was going to share with paul, and have him write (and different than Jesus earthly ministry, and what the disciples knew – even peter had a hard time with what paul wrote – **2 pet. 3:15-18**) – the mysteries (**rom. 2:16; rom. 16:25-27**) that mostly would be understood with the Holy Spirit in us, teaching us the truth (**1 cor. 2:9-16**).

Most of the time when someone doesn't understand something in the bible – is they may not be saved – not have the Holy Spirit (just being religious, church things, etc.), so they may listen to their church to explain it to them, and their church may be a false church – lying to you – satan does that, even in churches (**2 cor. 4:1-6; 2 cor. 11:13-15; gal. 1:6-10**).

The worst or maybe misfortunate people are those that think they are saved and going to heaven, and are not. And that is most people, and even those that say they are believers (**matt. 7:13-23**). Make sure you are saved by Jesus with the Holy Spirit. Believe His truth.

From adam (after sin) until the flood – to abraham, God was with man – the "presence of the Lord", and man could be with God or not – with His spirit – at and a little after the flood (**gen. 11**) – God was not going to strive with man anymore – since most of men was not going to God, even after the flood. God took His spirit away (**gen. 6:3**) – mainly when the bible was written (God with us) with moses – and moses died at 120 (**gen.6:3; deut. 34:7**), and the bible started.

We pray to God to talk to Him (but it has to be in Spirit – so we have to have His Spirit – **john 4:23-24**) and He talks to us through His word (the bible – the truth of it – so find a truthful bible, like the **kjv**), through Jesus (**1 tim. 2:3-6**) and the Holy Spirit (and only Jesus can give us the Holy Spirit – which is salvation – and that is the only prayer that God will hear of a non-believer – that you want to be saved through Jesus – whether you go to church or not, a true or false one). We don't know the truth naturally (who God is, etc., and won't from the world or false churches, religions, etc.), and is why He had moses (about 3500 years ago) write the bible (moses being the last person that God knew face to face – **deut. 34:10-12**) – to separate truth, from lies (of satan, and man), like satan has since the beginning (**gen. 3**), and ever since – especially after the flood, when God (the Lord – Jesus), was not going to be with man here on earth anymore striving with man (the presence of the Lord), like before the flood (**gen. 6:3**), and then after the flood when all of man was against God (**gen. 11**) at the tower of babel (man – the world – will again be all against God soon – which has taken over 4,000 years so far). So God wrote the bible so we (man) would know the truth (His truth), and be able to follow it, and know the difference (from satan's lies we have in this world, and man follows). Even though God talked to people in the past (through Jesus and the Holy Spirit), He uses His word today – and why He wrote it – and God will usually show us in circumstances and people for what He may want to direct you to in this world (through Jesus and the Holy Spirit). And the bible talks of salvation throughout the bible – even for the jews – at that time, was physical salvation (**exo. 12; exo. 14:13-14**). God always come to man – the only choice and way to salvation, like with Jesus today, but it is our spiritual salvation (getting the Holy Spirit). God wants us to go to Him – He helps us and comes to us. And that's the first thing He wants us all to do (get saved with the Holy Spirit through Jesus). Know the truth.

God uses the Holy Spirit all through history – from the beginning to today (especially after Jesus died and rose – salvation – the Holy Spirit in us).

God (Jesus – the Creator) put the Holy Spirit in adam at creation, then adam lost it for all of us (listening to satan) – after that the Holy

Spirit wasn't in man (with a few exceptions – and usually only for a short time – leading people, and the jews, writing the bible, etc.), until Jesus came and died and rose – saved us (Jesus gives us the Holy Spirit when truly saved).

God is fair and in control – He made us, and we need to follow Him or there are consequences for us (as the jews found out – as we see in the old testament), and we know today, being with Jesus or not – heaven or hell. And it has been that way since the beginning – God let us see that man doesn't go to God – especially when we are comfortable – so God made it tough with the flood, etc. We go to heaven or hell, before the flood, or after.

The world was (before the flood) what man wants today – what we worry and complain about in the world. Man caused (what God did) – all we complain about in the natural world (weather, disasters, global warming, no fresh water, etc.), and in us (health, appearance, etc.), etc. – all after the flood. So complain to yourself. The reason for the struggle. Make sure you to Jesus. Know the truth.

Make sure that you are saved (with the Holy Spirit) – then you can't lose it (or you really were not saved), and you will see the change in you (and in others that do), which is reading the word – the truth, praying, and learning and growing – and eventually sharing the truth of Jesus (not a church, or leader, etc.). Don't be led by satan – he can fool us. Go and pray to God and ask Him, through Jesus, and be willing to change and follow Him, and the truth of His word – He will help you.

Are you going to fully believe the truth, get saved, and get the Holy Spirit, not just look like a religious person – doing religious things, etc. (some that may be good) – going to church, charities, even bible studies, rituals, traditions, etc.? Not really knowing the truth. Have Jesus and the truth of His word in you, and change you. And you want to be with others that know the truth, and have Jesus with them.

Learn the truth of the bible – even something as simple as the manger scene with the birth of Jesus – the nativity scene, people still get that wrong (passing down traditions that are wrong – not being saved – not having the Holy Spirit, in a false church) – when they put the wise men there that came to see Jesus, but they were not there at the manger, it was almost two years later (the star leading them – that all saw) at joseph and mary's house, and Jesus was a young child (**matt. 2:10-11**). And the wise men who came to see Jesus (and king herod knew of Him, too – **matt. 2:1-8**) went back to their country and around the world to tell of Jesus being born – then it's up to the people to believe, like we do today for anything we know now or in history, and keep it in our memory, written, etc. and share it with all – especially your family, and pass it along. And we see it in the world – God's work (**rom. 1**).

Even so-called Christians don't know what the truth of the bible or the truth of Jesus is – not just the world in general that don't know. False churches, religions, etc., believe mary was a virgin after she had Jesus - joseph and mary had their own children after Jesus (**matt. 12:46-50; mark 3:31-35**). And they (Jesus's family) needed to believe in Jesus to be saved too. So don't pray to or worship mary.

It is the only truth – no excuse. And think of things that are tougher than that, and more important – like if we are married in heaven (or even have sex - we won't even feel like it or desire it) - no we won't be married (**matt. 22:28-30; mark 12:23-25**), things we get (or could get) wrong (and make you live, think and believe differently here – decisions, etc.) – go to Jesus and get the Holy Spirit (to help you) to learn the truth (**1 cor. 2:12-14**). In hell we are going to desire many things on earth, but we will not be able to do them or satisfy them – hell will be hell forever (**luke 16:22-28**). What other things have you been taught, or thought were the truth from a leader, church, religion, etc., and still being taught. Like Jesus in the grave – like jonah in the whale – for three days and three nights (**jonah 1:15-17;**

matt. 12:38-40 – which would be from thursday, day, through sunday night - night comes before day, for the jews - sunday night, then sunday, day). Even like noah didn't take 120 years to build the ark – it took maybe 70-80 years (no more than 100 years – noah was 500 years old in **gen. 5:32**, and the flood came when he was 600 years old – **gen. 7:11**) – the 120 years are the years we (man) will eventually only live to after the flood (**gen. 6:3**) – no more old ages – which if you look at the statistics you will see that today (and mainly starting with moses – **deut. 34:7** – who wasn't even dying, God took him). And God's Spirit (the presence of the Lord – **gen 6:3**) wasn't going to be with man on earth anymore (eventually the bible would be here with us, then Jesus – the Lord, who saves us – starting with moses). Because man lived a long time (in nice conditions) before the flood and that didn't help anyone go to God – only eight people (noah's family – out of millions or more, that were alive then) were with God when the flood came. And noah and shem lived after the flood at the time of abram – noah lived 350 years after the flood (950 years total – **gen. 9:28**) and shem outlived abraham (shem lived 502 years after the flood – 600 total years – **gen. 11:10-11**). And shem was alive at the same time that isaac and jacob were – they all could have talked of the past (before the flood, etc.) – the truth. Many more things to know and learn (and unlearn). Read and trust the bible. Know the truth – read and study (**2 tim. 2:14-16**) – get the Holy Spirit (let Him teach you – not lies handed down, etc.) – (through satan) and be saved and ready to go.

We may even see the correlation between the six days of creation and the 6,000 years since creation - a thousand years for each day and what happened on that day and each thousand years up to today. And the seventh day rest – and the thousand-year millennium yet to come (satan will be bound for those thousand years) – will be like the seventh day rest.

We can even see each 2000 years – from creation to abraham (start of the jews) – then from abraham to Jesus (his death and resurrection) – and then the next 2000 years from Jesus to today – the end times – Jesus will return. And you can see Jesus through it all from beginning to end – Creator, Savior and Lord.

God does all of this for a reason – all to get us to go to Him. It is only through Jesus. They are one God – Father, Son and Holy Spirit.

The world will not end until 6,000 years go by – almost here.

God gave us all of the numbers and ages to know the truth and why He did all of those things – mainly because of man (through satan's lies) not listening to God (eventually God wrote it all down for us).

timetable – from creation (BEGINNING OF TIME)

(gen. 1 and 2; gen. 5 and 11)

time (beginning – creation)		age (from creation)
0-(6,000 years ago) l **creation** adam born (created)	---------------	930 years l (930 years old) adam died
130 years l seth born	---------------	1042 years l (912 years old) seth died
235 years l (men began to call on the name of the Lord) enosh born	---------------	1140 years l (905 years old) enosh died
325 years l	---------------	1235 years l (910 years old)

cainan born		cainan died
395 years	---------------	1290 years
l		l (895 years old)
mahalaleel born		mahalaleel died

460 years	---------------	1422 years
l		l (962 years old)
jared born		jared died

622 years	------	987 years				
l		l (365 years old)				
enoch born		enoch translated (didn't die)				
687 years	------	987 years	------	1656 years		
l		l (evil got bad)		(969 years old) l (year of flood)		
methuselah born				methuselah died		
874 years	------	------	------	1651 years		
l (777 years old)				l (5 years before the flood)		
lamech born				lamech died		
		1056 years	------	1656 years	------	2006 years
		1 1		(2344 bc) 1 1		(950 years old) I (lived 350 years after the flood)
		noah born		year of flood		noah died

1558 years	--	1656 years	--	1757 years	--	2158 years
l		l (2243 bc)		l		(600 years old) l (lived 502 years after the flood)
shem born		year of flood		**tower of babel**		shem died

1916 years	--	2015 years	--	2091 years
l		I (99 years old)		I (175 years old)
abram born		**abraham (new name)**		abraham died

2016 years	--	2196 years		
l		(180 years old) 1		
isaac born		isaac died		
2076 years	--	2206 years	--	2223 years
l		**jews 1st in egypt**		l (147 years old)
jacob(israel) born		**(about 1800 bc to 1400 bc)**		jacob (israel) died
		about 3400 years ago		

The rest of the times are from moses (and the jews) at the promised land, until Jesus came here – 1400 to 1500 years later. Then 2,000 years from Jesus to today (6,000 total), and the end times, tribulation – coming soon. Then the thousand-year reign of Jesus – the millennium (**rev. 20** – and you will notice that the word thousand is used six times in six verses – **verses 2-7** – 6,000 years of satan). But satan will be bound for the thousand – year reign of Jesus. And just like after the seventh day rest (the eighth day and after), satan will be let lose for a little time (**rev. 20:2-3**) after the thousand-year reign of Jesus (after the last of the thousand years – seven thousand years total), and satan will try to pull and lead people to him (people won't be perfect in the millennium – but it will be nice then) – those that seem "very good" (but those who like darkness, evil, etc. – like satan did adam and eve – but unlike adam and eve, these will not be saved) – to lead them to hell where satan is going. God only wants those that truly want to be with him in heaven, there. Those with Jesus, and His truth. We all have a choice.

As God did with moses, God knew adam (face to face) through noah (**gen 5**), and maybe some others between noah and abraham (and job), and isaac and jacob, to moses – then God used the bible (and the Holy Spirit, and angels, at times) for people – mainly at first (and the jews), until Jesus came here.

Read the whole bible to learn (**rom. 15:4**), and the **books of proverbs** and **psalms** are good for giving some wisdom for your life. We grow and learn in Him – all our life after salvation – being sanctified through the Holy Spirit, and the truth of His word (**rom. 15:16; 1 cor. 6:11; eph. 5:26-27; 2 thess. 2:13; 1 tim. 4:4-6**). Grow with good things (**2 pet. 1:1-12**).

No compromise with the bible – it is the truth, and we have to believe it all. The jews and Christians read it, but both struggle with it – you have to be with Jesus (He wrote it all), and the Holy Spirit to understand it – if not, just accept it as truth. And keep reading, and studying and praying.

Don't just hear the word (like in churches, etc. or just read it casually) – know what it means and is saying – the truth, and study it (**acts 17:10-12**) – but be saved – with the Holy Spirit to teach you (**1 cor. 2:12-14**). You have to want to learn and know the truth – and go to Jesus for the truth (not a just a church, leader, etc. –most churches aren't saved). Get saved – get the Holy Spirit through Jesus. Then we have to follow – don't let the world (satan) drown it out (**matt. 13:21-22**). God's (Jesus') word is important (especially to be saved and after you are saved – **matt. 24:35**). Share it truthfully.

Believe the truth of the word (only the Holy Spirit will help – **1 cor. 2:10-16**). Then look in the world and see it.

Jesus says we don't know the truth of the word – the scriptures (we err – **matt. 22:29; mark 12:24**) – we are mistaken.

You want and need God's wisdom (**prov. 3**)– His word, the truth – for this world (and after), through the Holy Spirit from Jesus. Written to counter the lies of satan in this world.

Only one way – a narrow way to get to God, to heaven – through Jesus (and His truth). There are many false ways, satan's ways – false churches, religions, beliefs etc. (**matt. 7:13-23**). Go to Jesus and His truth. That's why there are not that many Christians in the world (maybe 2-3% - but way more than before the flood or sodom) - but could be and should be even more today – go to Jesus and His word, and learn the truth. God wants us all – but our choice. Only one way – through Jesus. All of the sons of noah – all people, can and need to go to Jesus to be saved. So be sure you are truly saved – not fooling yourself or others (whether you were brought up that way or not).

And just like the flood and sodom, the few were saved – the righteous, and were taken out, before the destruction – and at the rapture, the few will be taken out first, then the wrath in the tribulation. Go to Jesus and be ready to go.

God may take righteous people all through history – from creation to today (but mainly before Jesus died and rose – like enoch and elijah – **gen. 5**; **1 Kings 2**) – and they knew Jesus, as even moses did (**matt. 17:1-5**; **heb. 11:24-26**). And even noah walked with God, and knew Jesus (**gen. 6:8-9**; **gen. 7:15-16**).

The tribulation and rapture could not happen in any other time than today – in this world of technology, that wasn't here until now. Read the verses in **rev. 11** and **13**, and even **rev. 17**. God mentioned this in **dan. 12:4** – that the world will get to the way it is today – modern, knowledge, travel, etc. and possible for all the things written, to happen. Jesus will come back soon – the last 2,000 years since Jesus died and rose (and the temple destroyed in 70 ad). All that is still important, is to go to Jesus, to get saved and get the Holy Spirit, and be ready for the end or death.

And knowing about the rapture doesn't mean you do nothing – keep preaching the truth.

This world will end and a new heaven and earth will be created (**isa. 65:17-25**; **2 pet. 3:5-13**; **rev. 21**) – it hasn't happened yet. It seems like time is long, but with God, a day is like a thousand years – like the six days of creation (can be related to the last 6,000 years) and seventh day rest (the last thousand years, add up to 7,000 years) – the 6,000 years are almost done. Be ready with Jesus and His truth.

And we can't go to heaven in these bodies – just like Jesus did not have His earthly body – no blood – (He shed that for us) just flesh and bones – our soul with the Holy Spirit will be in an incorruptible body – and live forever (like we were supposed to at creation) – and what **1 cor. 15:50-58** is talking about. You don't have to fully understand the rapture to be saved (we don't know when, and may not make it being alive to the rapture for all of the future things, etc.) – it will happen when it happens. But be truly saved. Just go to Jesus before you die. Do it now. Be ready.

But it is good to keep learning and knowing the truth.

There are evil people in the world – jew and gentile – all of noah' sons – all of us – and all need to go to Jesus. Man needs to know he is, and can be, evil – whether you think you are or not. Admit it. So man is evil, and people can cause others (through satan) to be more evil. Get better yourself with Jesus and help others go to Jesus, too, and His truth – His word. He can help us all. Don't be worried about the end times, just be ready and help others to get to know Jesus and get saved. Have faith in Him and get the Holy Spirit. God is in control and will only let satan do so much, like he did with job (**book of job**). God can use all people – He will change you. We all have abilities, talents, etc (all of noah's sons) and God can use them and help us. Go to Jesus, and have Him use you and enhance your talent. Know the truth and share it. Go to Him, to Jesus.

Then the grace period (going to the risen Jesus, not laws, rituals, traditions, etc. to follow, if truly with Jesus and the Holy Spirit) will be over (with the rapture and the tribulation), that started mainly since Jesus died and rose, and Jesus also went before (**isa. 60**; **book of jonah**), and is going now (with paul – read his book) to the gentile (and any individual jews) – the grace period (the last 2,000 years). For all of us – all of noah's sons need to be saved (whatever we believe, born into, or grow up with, etc.) – we are all sinners. We don't have to wear certain outfits, clothes, jewelry, markings, etc. (but how we live – on the inside) to show what we believe, and no idols, statues, etc. (worship only God through Jesus – **exo. 20:3-6; dan. 3**) - we only need the Holy Spirit and the truth through Jesus – the truth of Jesus and His word.

God finishes what He starts and says – like the 490 years of **dan. 9** – for the jews to anoint the Most Holy – who is Jesus (we would like to blame the jews – as a nation, for the last 2,000 years – but all of men is not following God through Jesus either). But the answer is still going to Jesus for all.

Struggles for all people – all of noah's sons, the last 2,000 years (those being born during this time) – but all can go to Jesus.

But the jews rejecting Jesus would bring salvation to all – with Jesus' death (Jesus had to die) – so the jews' fall helped us all - so don't blame the jews for that (**rom. 11:11-12**). They have had enough struggles, God knows. And will come for the jews again (even though any individual jew can be and need to be saved through Jesus).

It's possible that all of the things to come would have happened just after Jesus died and rose, but it didn't. The jews (as a nation) didn't go to Jesus, before or after (at least by 70 ad) His death (and then they would have gone to the gentiles to save them back then). If they did (all since then wouldn't have been born, etc.), then we all (the truly saved) would be in heaven now (and those not with Him would be all in hell – the lake of fire, with satan). And if the jews follow Jesus after He died and rose – before 70 ad (temple destroyed, etc.) – **the book of revelation** wouldn't have had to be written – and the last 2,000 years wouldn't have happened. But since we are still here – and people are being born – we might as well share the truth about Jesus, with them, until we are not here anymore.

And if this earth is going to stay here and so are the truly saved, then why did enoch and elijah (and others that follow Jesus) – need to die or leave the earth? It will eventually be gone (**gen. 8:22; 2 pet. 3:9-13**).

God knows all this will happen the way it does – knowing satan and man – we cause what God does, we have free will (not force us), but

He wants us to go to Him – Jesus. God knows how satan (as well as man) works, (blame man – adam, and satan – all of us, for all of this), and we need to know, too, so we can see why God did what he did, and will do. A punishment from God – God allows and does these things – like the flood, etc. So God lets us know. There are consequences. Know the truth. So we will go to Him – Jesus. We always can – the way he wants us to – **jer. 29:11-13; luke 10: 27-28**.

So God wrote the bible for us, and sent Jesus here.

God loves us and is why he does all of this. Go to Jesus (and the Holy Spirit), not to satan (or other angels – no angels telling us truth, after Jesus died and rose – **gal. 1:6-12**, mainly after 70 ad – temple destroyed, the **book of revelation** written, etc. - mainly the last 2,000 years) – we have a choice and God is trying to help us.

Don't worry about the past - just learn – live today, and be ready for tomorrow. Keep learning and growing – especially in God's word, and helping others to get to know Jesus and His truth. Love others with Jesus. Jesus is always in the present – from beginning to end (**heb. 13:8**).

Even though you would like the good things in the past – that you messed up, or missed out on, or would do different, etc., to come back again or go back to – to do over, etc. – you wouldn't want the bad things to happen again, etc., either. Live today and go to Jesus and look forward to being with Him in heaven. And hope those things – the way they happened in your life, got you to go to Jesus, and His truth.

God sets it up, so we will go to Him – to Jesus, He will come for you, and help you through life (**matt. 11:28-30**), and with the Holy Spirit.

Jesus wants to be with you, just like you want to be with people you want to be with – have Him in your life.

Focus on the truth – not want you want it to be (and what satan is leading you to).

Man doesn't usually like to be told what to do – even if it is good and best (even though we are all being told by satan, and don't realize it) – know the truth and Jesus, and live better. Listen to God through Jesus and His word – through the Holy Spirit – the truth of it. Go to God – they are One – the Father, Son and Holy Spirit – the only way to God is through Jesus and get the Holy Spirit – to be one with Them (**john 10:26-30**; **john 14**; **1 tim. 2:3-6**). All of noah's sons. Once we are truly saved – through Jesus, we can't be separated from God (**rom. 8:38-39**). And we can keep growing.

People do change – so try to remember who they are today – not judge what they were in the past (just like we don't want that for ourselves) – we all can learn from our past, and mistakes – hope we do, and should – and are a better person. Go to Jesus and the truth of His word to do this.

People hurt people because they have been hurt and are hurting (and are not truly with Jesus), but it is not necessary – go to Jesus and heal and change – then help people, not hurt.

You don't have to be tough, better, go off, etc. – stop causing problems, let God be in charge – you will see a better world. Stop trying to control people – satan is using you – even if you think you are in control.

We need to treat people better – not take our struggles and problems out on others – family or friends or anyone, etc. This world is tough – and it can help.

God does all of these tough things in the world to get us to go to Him – not hurt, or be better than, people. He loves us and wants us. All of noah's sons are trying to outdo each other (mainly since the flood, and the tower of babel – **gen. 9:25-27; gen. 11**), but need to go to Jesus to do it right – His way – away from, and in spite of, this world – away from satan and his leading. Jesus will put you on top – or wherever you belong – using the talents you have. Keep working hard on the right things.

We have to change – He lets us, and helps us, with the way the word is – tough. He wants us to know all of this. So we see what life would be without Him and His original plan (to be nice, comfortable, peace, love, etc.) for us all to live with Him in this world. Only through Jesus can be get back to that – in heaven – eternity.

If we don't understand the bible and future end times – rapture, tribulation (anti-christ, etc.), etc. – why are we still here? And the end hasn't happened yet – the destruction of the earth (and heaven) and the creation of the new earth and heaven (**2 pet. 3:5-13**; **rev. 21**) – it is not here yet – we are not living on the new earth (or heaven) – it is still to come– soon. Modern technology is finally here to have the end happen as it says in **rev 11 and 13**. And Jesus will come back.

There are many verses throughout the bible talking about this end time (and the thousand-year reign of Jesus happening) – before eternity – even though it has been delayed by God (the last 2,000 years), because of the actions and behavior of man (satan led) – not going to Jesus and His truth.

Who has the most to gain, if this world never ends? – satan does.

And also – why does satan want the jews gone – wiped out, not go to Jesus, etc.? – so the world will continue (not having things completed in this world – like the 490 years of **dan. 9: 24** – for them to anoint the Most Holy – Jesus), and so will satan – not having to go to hell – the lake of fire forever, until it does end.

Who started all of the sin and evil in this world, from the beginning? – satan did (who is lucifer – thinking he is God – or at least better than

God – as we do – **isa. 14:12-15**). So satan is going to try to keep this world going the way it is, as long as it can (it should have ended 2,000 years ago).

So satan would get 2,000 more years before hell, if the jews don't follow Jesus (mainly after He died and rose) – and others that have been born since, may go to hell, too. Mainly blame satan (and ourselves) – who we all follow, when we don't follow Jesus, and His truth. Don't encourage satan. But eventually, everything will end.

If we are not one with satan or each other – only with Jesus – then this world will end. God is setting that up – all having a chance to be with Jesus. In the end, we will see who is with Jesus or not and in the end (tribulation – the last seven years – **dan. 9:24-27**) – it will mainly be the jews (along with the gentiles – all of noah's sons – and those that are not with Jesus) finally going to Jesus – then the end will come (**matt. 24; rom. 11**). Be with Jesus and be ready for it (or your death, etc.). We have a choice – heaven or hell. And help others, too.

We need to go to Jesus (the truth) before we die.

After 7,000 years – then eternity – heaven or hell, forever.

The new earth and heaven (**rev. 21**) will not happen until satan and sin are gone – and people are with Jesus (our choice) after what God started is finished – the last 7 years – the tribulation is done – and the jews with Jesus. We still are waiting – go to Jesus and His truth and share him until then.

God started this world and man to be with Him forever. God knew this was all going to happen.

God finishes what he starts. But would like us to be with Him. Our choice.

It will continue in this sinful, evil, way - until it ends the way God says – the jews going to Jesus – anointing the Most Holy (**dan. 9:24-27**).

God will keep the world going until the end.

God will end it all (**gen 8:22; 2 pet. 3:8-13**). Don't worry just go to Jesus (**philip. 4:6-7**).

Six is an incomplete number (6,000 years), and seven is a complete number (7,000 years). 6,000 years are almost over.

That's all there is – no million or billion of years – no evolution, gap theory, etc.

There is an end – tribulation (seven years), destruction, one world order (like before the flood), anti-christ (satan uniting all people against God), etc., then the thousand-year reign of Jesus (and satan will be bound), and then after that it is heaven or hell for all humans (and angels) – with the new bodies for the truly saved for heaven. The saved (with the Holy Spirit in their souls) are already with God – but there are many that are here that are not yet saved (we need to before we die) – we all have the choice. Keep learning and sharing the truth of Jesus, and His word. Go to Jesus to get the Holy Spirit.

Store treasures in heaven – people here, that need to be saved – family, friends, world, etc.

We can only be at peace with Jesus, and His truth – otherwise we will not be satisfied in this world – blaming the past, people, etc. So believe in the world, other people, etc. (satan leading) are to blame for your problems – go to Jesus and have good, right, and truthful relationship with Him – and forgive and change and grow with Jesus and share His word, with the Holy Spirit. Away from your past.

People know how it feels, but still hate and hurt people. Stop thinking of yourself. It's sad when people die throughout history – anyone – famous (celebrities, politicians, etc.) or not (hopefully they knew Jesus and His truth), but the only person that died, and is needed to be known about, is Jesus, no one else – share His story. We never know when we will end (die, etc.), so go to Jesus as soon as you can – make sure it's the truth and you are truly saved (with the Holy Spirit from Jesus – not what you do, but what He did – ask Him).

We are as bad and evil as those people – the ones we hate and that kill, etc. – destined for hell (**john 3:17-21**). Most people that die will probably go to hell – hopefully some more to heaven. But share Jesus – the truth, with those who are alive (so they can go to heaven – God wants as many as can go to heaven – but we choose) – even share with the ones you hate (only with Jesus can you), and not worry about those who have died (other than being happy, if they are in heaven). This is an evil world – things happen – death, etc. Keep people from going to hell – live with and share Jesus.

You never know when you are going to die (we are all born spiritually dead) – in this world – go to Jesus now and be ready. Only with Jesus can we change (with the Holy Spirit – born again – **john 3**), and live. He will help you.

We were created at the beginning to live forever (with God – and each other) – and now we still will, somewhere – but now it is heaven (Jesus) or hell (satan) – you decide. This isn't our home. There will be a lot of crying and misery in hell – all worse than earth - forever.

If you have problems – don't take it our on everyone else. Go to Jesus for anything.

It's usually tough to be good, and easy to be bad, in this world. Be a good example for people. The truth will make you free – through Jesus (**john 8:31-32**).

Respect what God wants – not with you, or others, or this world (really satan) wants. Follow what God says in His word about us – all of men (man or woman) after sin and after the flood (**gen. 3:16-19; gen 9:25-27; gen 11:5-9**), and we will be better, happier, etc. (as much as we could be then) – but mainly today until we are with Jesus and the Holy Spirit. Go to Him now. And we need to accept his way for us when we are saved (**1 cor. 12:12-14; 2 cor. 5:14-21; eph. 4:17-32; eph. 5:17-33; col. 3:5-11**) – only through Jesus can we get along – all are one in Jesus – through the Holy Spirit. All of noah's sons – not connected the same anymore – only one belief – in Jesus through the Holy Spirit to the true God.

People think the way they live their life and what they like and do, are good – some may be, but some aren't, and they won't give up something – thinking those things are fine to have in their life, even if it is tough to do, or not good for them – need to give those up and get away from some things. People keep doing these things, because they feel somewhat satisfied comfort in, and control of, these things – but really, it's an addiction – controlling them. Which is what satan does against the truth or what's best for us. But it really hurts us and is not good for us. And we try to defend them – beliefs, behaviors, ideas, etc. – whatever it is – and sometimes hide it. Get rid of all the things that are not good for you (behavior, health, lies, danger, etc.) – know what they are. Do what's best and right – know what that is. Jesus will help you with all of them – change. Don't be stubborn.

It is satan that is the real enemy and controlling people and evil, lies, etc. (**eph. 6:10-20**). Be better with Jesus (and the Holy Spirit).

People try to make you believe what they want you to believe, because it is best for them, and not for you. Being selfish – and their desires, etc. – and happens in all people (even you) – all of noah's sons, religions, false churches, beliefs, etc. for control – like satan wants (except through true Christianity). And you will move away from the true God – Jesus, and his truth, if you don't know the truth and are not with Jesus (having the Holy Spirit) – many think they do.

If you are around people that are not honest or doing things right – you need to tell them that or someone, turn them in, etc. – get help, and have them go through whatever consequences they need to. We need to protect ourselves in this evil world. We still need laws to govern evil – but when we go to Jesus (and have the Holy Spirit), we really shouldn't need them – we would do it – obey, naturally with Jesus (**gal. 5:22-26**). Don't make it worse, than it already is here – be honest, follow the rules – be nice, and go to Jesus. Suffer your consequences – do what we need to do to get along – go with Jesus. And share Jesus when you can – hopefully before they go too far, or before anyone dies. They (and you) need help. Jesus (and his truth) is the best help.

We don't need to worry about what all these other groups, people, etc. think – love and help them go to Jesus and His truth (**acts 5:38-39**).

Don't listen to the world, just Jesus and His truth. And share Him with the world. God will help.

It doesn't matter what you mother of father think or believe (but be nice, and try to get along), or your family, or nationality, etc. (**matt. 10:34-41**) – but what God thinks. Know the truth. Go to Jesus – love Him. You can still love your family and friends, etc., and share Jesus – the truth, but don't love them (or believe them) more than Jesus.

We need to keep praying to God, through Jesus, for all.

And don't listen to angels, etc. – any angels after the book of revelation was written (the last 2,000 years) – it is satan lying to you about anything (even about who he is – saying he is another angel, etc.) other than Jesus and His truth – satan is just fooling people – leading man away (in religion, false beliefs, etc.) from the truth of Jesus and His word. And satan all through history (from the beginning) plays on your ego – thinking you know everything, something new, etc. They are hurting people – through satan, with their lies (following some beliefs) – to your family, country, nationality, etc.

Don't let satan win, any longer, with you or anyone – go to Jesus – let Him lead you and your family, country, nationality, etc. with the truth.

Jesus defeated satan (and sin, and death) – with Jesus (and the Holy Spirit) we can, too. Know you are saved with the truth (and the Holy Spirit). Be one with Jesus – not with man (from adam, noah's sons) or satan (but he is still there trying to pull us until the end).

The end will come – Jesus coming – and will change the world – like the flood with noah – not knowing the day or hour (**matt. 24:32-39**).

This is for all of noah's son – we can't control all things about the way we look – nationality, family, etc., but we can control how we act, think, behave, believe, etc. Go to Jesus to help you. So stop looking at other people – who they are, etc. – you could have been them, and maybe are.

Remember – we all looked alike, and talked the same, etc. (no separation, differences, etc. – except you were with God or not), before and a little after the flood (**gen. 11**).

Ask God – through Jesus, to help you with His word – with the Holy Spirit (**1 cor. 2:9-16; james 1:5**), He will show you. And be one with Him (and stay that way – **rom. 8:31-39**).

The choices we make affect our (and others) lives, whatever you do – work hard, face your fears – Jesus will help you (**2 tim. 1:7-8**).

Christianity and Jesus is for forgiving those that hurt you or those you don't like, or are not like you – hate, etc. It is satan that hates, and is against the true God and true love – trying to make man the same against God (like uniting man before the flood, and now in the end times trying to unite man again) – and why we don't get along (God separating man – after the flood) – but it is getting close to where we are all going to be one again in the world – but evil - leading to the end. Let it all lead you to Jesus, before the end. Share Jesus after you get saved – get the Holy Spirit and change. Love others and forgive – change – move on – only with Jesus can you – we all can (and God wants us to – **John 3:16**). Love – **1 cor. 13; 1 john 4:7-21**. Do it now. Let Jesus change you.

And Jesus comes to all in the world and is known (**john 1:9**) – so go to Him. But know the truth. We have a choice.

And the main thing – the only choice is with Jesus – is that you can go to heaven – the only way. But for now, we have to live here – as imperfect and evil (with satan) as it is (which should help us go to Jesus and His truth – all can be good with Jesus – **rom. 8:26-28**). Go to Jesus.

Don't take advantage of people with Jesus (and His word) – like false churches do (**1 john 4:1** – then and today), and like satan does. Know the truth of Him and His word (can only with the Holy Spirit from Jesus – salvation), then share that only.

People read all kinds of books, hoping to learn, grow, etc. in life – God's word, the bible, is the best for us, and really all we need (and any book that leads you to read the truth –in the bible, and to go to Jesus). We need to study and learn and examine right and true things – the truth – which is God's word – the bible, then we will be able to spot and notice false things easier.

And no matter how many times you read or have read the bible (even from genesis to revelation – three times, four times, etc.), you may still not understand it. Only with Jesus and the Holy Spirit can you understand it (**1 cor. 2**). And the old testament will help you understand the new testament (and vice versa) – and is why the jews still struggle with the old testament, because they don't usually read the new (or have the Holy Spirit). And the nation of israel is being persecuted by different groups in the world – mainly non-christians, because they won't read or believe the new testament – the truth is there for them – they can stop the problems they have. But even individual jews can be saved, if they would not be stubborn, prideful, etc. (and some have).

All religions, churches, beliefs, etc. don't lead to God – the same God – the true God. So don't be fooled by satan – false churches, religions, beliefs, etc. Go to Jesus and His word to find out the truth. The only way to get to God (**john 14:6; 1 tim. 2:3-6**). Only Jesus leads us to the true God. And God wouldn't have made the jews – a chosen, set apart people, if that were true (if all lead to the same God) – or need to send Jesus (and is the reason people – satan, don't like the jews). So we all are not sons of God, or made in His image (but in man's, adam's after sin – **gen. 5:3**) – not until we are saved and have the Holy Spirit in us (only can get from Jesus).

Not all people, beliefs, etc. go to heaven (**1 cor. 6:9-11**) – only those truly saved with Jesus. Sharing Jesus is love – and we are not God's children until we go to Jesus. We are children of hell, without Him – no matter how nice or non-judgmental we are here to people (**john 3:17-21**). If we are truly saved, and live an evil life, God will punish us (or have satan do it – **1 cor. 5:1-5**).

We are saved from our sins – not under law – freedom in salvation, and forgiven of all our sins. We know others that are not saved are still sinners – need Jesus – so we are not like them and need to live like Christ – but we are at liberty, not law.

True Christians may sin – temptations of this world and satan (your body fighting against the Holy Spirit – **rom. 7**), but keep going back to Jesus – He is our advocate with the Father (**1 john 2:1-3**) daily – not living a life of sin (**1 cor. 6:12; 1 cor. 10:23-24**) – so you don't give in. Man is not perfect – even Christians, just forgiven and saved – truly saved (with the Holy Spirit in you from Jesus) – following Jesus and the truth of His word. And only Jesus can forgive our sins – not man (**mark 2:1-12**). Keep going to Him. God doesn't hear prayers except to be saved by Jesus, or people will continue to have problems – call on Jesus if you have problems (even after you are saved). The unsaved can only pray to be saved (or God will not hear) – nothing else, until you are truly saved. So don't listen to those false churches that say otherwise – and you can't pray to anyone else except to God the Father through Jesus only – no leader, person (dead or alive), angel, etc. (**1 tim. 2:3-6**). Go to Jesus.

So once you get saved – get the Holy Spirit – we fight our sin nature, but have a way to do it – with Jesus and His word (through the Holy Spirit). We need to keep growing in Him.

If you are not saved and need Jesus – those that are saved can tell them that they need to change and get saved – get Jesus, otherwise we might as well go to heaven right after we are saved (if we are not going to learn and grow and share Jesus and His truth) – but we are better off than the unsaved. And we need to know who to hang out with – who a true Christian is (including that we are). And really know the truth of His word. And then share with all – God will help you in your life.

Those that think they are saved, and keep praying – the only thing that might happen is that God will send a truly saved person to tell them the truth about Jesus and His word, and you may think you don't need to hear it, etc., but you do.

A true Christian talks of Jesus and the truth of His word – the whole bible, because the Holy Spirit talks of them – not a church, leader, traditions, rituals, etc. Go to Jesus and get saved and share Him.

And don't trick people into believing things that are not true about life or themselves – just so they feel good. Go to Jesus and learn the truth. You may offend, as Jesus did, but still share and do it as caring as you can. Help people know the truth.

You can't make people believe and follow God – live the way He wants us to, and understand His word (**rom. 8:5-8; 1 cor. 5:9-13**), but the world and satan will lead you in this world – with the consequences of sin – hurting others and themselves – and those struggles hopefully lead them to Jesus. And having a nation, like america, for God has helped man in this world (and why He made america – to learn of and share Jesus, to the world – but it needs to be the truth). God is still trying to get people to go to Him – especially through problems, struggles, etc. for people to change. Having true churches (many false ones, too) available to help share the truth of His word – and be a good example for truth. Get saved through Jesus, then find a true one.

And you can't be a preacher, if you can't behave (**1 tim. 3**), although man is not going to live or even think perfect, on this earth, but should be better, and continue to learn and grow and preach Jesus to all that you can (and live the life that God wants us to). God will punish a true Christian, if necessary, but we can judge and need to know who a true Christian is – even to marry, etc. (**1 cor. 6**). We need to be one with Jesus – know the truth and let Him help you grow and become like Him.

Once we are truly saved (have the Holy Spirit), we can share Jesus and His truth – basically water people to grow, but God gets the increase – share truth – and God will take care of the rest (**1 cor. 3:6-11**).

You can't lay any other foundation or belief – other than Jesus (**1 cor. 3:10-11;1 cor. 15:1-4**). Go to Jesus and His word – the truth. And be one.

The reason that God – the Father, the Son, and the Holy Spirit – are One, is because they all believe the same exact thing – the truth of the bible. And all churches need to be one, by believing what the Godhead does – the truth of the bible. Otherwise they will not be one – and is why there are so many false churches and beliefs – denominations, etc., in the world (even america). All churches (and believers) need to believe the exact same thing (not add or take away from the truth – **rev. 22:18** – since the bible is completed, since the **book of revelation** was completed – otherwise you will have problems).

Jesus (when here on earth) always prayed to God the Father to make sure they are on the same page – the same agenda for their plan for us.

One God. Jesus is God (**luke 1:47; john 1; 1 tim. 1:1; 1 tim. 2:3; 1 tim. 4:10; titus 2:13; jude 1:25**).

We are to believe the same – to be one – one in the truth of Jesus, and His word – having the gifts He gives us (**1 cor. 12:12-13; eph. 4:11-16**), if we say that we are truly saved. Even a country would be better off with being all with Jesus – not going against God and His word (like man has done since the beginning).

All churches, religions, beliefs, etc. don't lead to the same God, and all churches don't agree – so you couldn't go to all – they disagree – and some would even feel persecuted (it is only because they are not truth) – and it still would be satanic lies.

Without the true God and the truth of the bible, we have no compass for america (what's best for man) – no country would. We need to get back to being with God – not against His truth, otherwise it will lead to the end (and God may want that now). But we need to keep sharing Jesus, and be ready for the end.

Why can't we go to every and any church? – because the truth is not there – satan has made churches, denominations, etc. – all false. You need to be a true Christian (with the Holy Spirit from Jesus) and know that you are (following the truth of His word – not a church, leader, etc.) – and you know you are not a true Christian, if you are trying to be politically correct in this world – but that is all against God and His word (like before the flood, and at the tower of babel, for example), and will lead to the end – you need to help people, but help people go to Jesus and know His truth (you know it first – no matter what you were born into or grew up with, etc.). And you don't want to hangout or side with people that are against God – the truth of Him through Jesus – go to Him and find out the truth.

So satan has mixed truth with lies in churches, and religions (that's why they look good – we don't know the truth), so we need to see that and not follow or go to those churches (or get out of them), no matter how nice people seem to be. Maybe help them learn the truth.

Sometimes the people, leaders, families, etc. in false churches and religions, etc. punish (or force) their children (and followers, etc.) a certain way to live from their belief – which may not be right or truth – not what God wants. They need to be saved with Jesus (and the Holy Spirit – and so do you). So don't be a cult, and punish, etc. people for not doing your version of the truth – don't act like people that are not truly Christian – and no one needs to use drugs, alcohol, or other things, etc. to live – find out what you can do and are good at in this world and what God wants you to do.

How do churches make sense of being unequally yoked (**2 cor. 6:14-18**) with non-believers in church, or even Christians jews with non-christian jews, or jews with gentiles – like when peter wasn't sure, etc. (**gal. 2:11-14**). Just like the tares and the wheat (**matt. 13:36-43**) – are like in churches, and in false churches in america, and around the world, not just evil and good in a nation, world, etc. Should we be separate? Not mingle?

Sometimes we have to learn to let people go, if you need to. Don't stand in their way. Just share Jesus and pray for them.

We need to share Jesus (and the truth of His word) and have that be the goal anywhere. God is not a respecter of persons (**acts 10:34-35;**

col. 3:25). All of noah's sons need to know the truth. No matter what you are born into.

People are not good – so don't look for the good in man or this world – know that all are evil, sinful, destined for hell (**john 3:17-21**) – and why and who Jesus died for us all (**john 3:16**) – His enemies – evil man. We all need to go to Jesus to change – to be saved for a better life after this. Share Jesus and His truth.

And satan's love, beliefs, cults, etc. are all lies and will not be good for you – they will just have you searching for the truth (hopefully leading you to Jesus) – that you (and others) may never find with them – wasting a lot of your life (and maybe die looking – ending up in hell).

We are all different and will not get along – only with Jesus can we have a chance – share Jesus. Now you know why there are so many psychiatrists, etc. – because man is sinful – mentally and physically disturbed – there would be no need for them, if man was good – we need Jesus to go against satan here, not man to do that. Know the truth and what to look for and believe. Many things that satan leads us to that are not good – against God, that man follows.

There have been cults, false churches, etc. (some you are born into) and still are, that brainwash, using their own rules for God – selfish, desires, etc. – trying to be God – but are satanic (lies mixed with some truth – to fool people and keep them fooled and believing the lies) – using their interpretation of the bible, and to take Jesus' place (that satan leads them to – to look religious, spiritual, etc. – even think they are nice) – all in the name of God (Jesus) to sound truthful (but are evil), and at times won't let you leave them, and even kill you, if you do. Even though not all are that bad – and seem nice and the truth, but are from satan. Rather hear the truth loudly, than lies told kind and softly. Jesus and the bible talk of these (**matt. 24:4-5; mark 13:5-6; luke 21:7-8; john 5:42-44; 1 john 2:18-23**).

No matter what church it is (any of noah's sons – black, white, any nationality, culture, etc.) – it needs to share the truth. So we can't be unequally yoked with family, nationality, culture, belief, etc. – against God and the truth of His word. God separates (no equality, etc. with noah's sons) – and we can only be one (and equal) with Jesus and the truth of His word.

The whole world is starting to be like a cult – against God's truth of His word – like before the flood. All kinds of beliefs – even atheism, etc. – all led by satan today. So like a cult – religious, etc. that people feels controls people in a negative way – the world is the same, with satan leading man with all the beliefs of any issue that people follow against God (Jesus) and the truth of His word.

When we go away from God (Jesus) and the truth of His word (and don't follow it) we have problems, period. Especially putting yourself above Him (don't follow those that want to put themselves above God – Jesus, like satan did and does).

So don't push denominations, etc., but Jesus and the truth of His word – the bible. Go to Jesus and His truth, or we will continue to have punishments, like God did to people, cities, societies, etc. that go against Him and His word (mainly after the flood) – He destroys them (sodom and gomorrah, etc.). The world – even america is going that way today – following satan against God's way of life for us (His way is best for us).

All false churches claim persecution (as if they are sharing the truth of God) when they are called liars, false, etc. (with satan) – with their false preaching – and they say they are right, and just being persecuted, but they are against Jesus (and the truth of His word), and are with satan. Know you are really with Jesus and His word – don't just think you are. Know the truth.

And when you find the truth of Jesus and the bible – then you will see or spot the fakes, lies, etc. easier – study the truth – the real thing. Follow Jesus and His word.

So we need to learn the truth of the word (with the Holy Spirit) – keep growing (**heb. 5:11-14; 1 pet. 2**), and we are to rightly divide the word (the truth – **2 tim. 2:14-16**). So we can share the truth (His truth). And change. And live in this world better. And Jesus said about mary (martha's sister) that she was doing what was best and right, by just listening to Jesus share the truth (not with the busyness of this life – **luke 10:38-42**). Even though we need to do things here in this world – but always go to His word and learn and grow each day.

If you don't know the truth about Jesus and the bible, then you can't share it, or if you are trying to share your truth, you are just wasting your time (just sharing a lie – satan's way). Just living and sharing man's (satan's) made up beliefs – from nationalities, cultures, religions, etc. – all from satan. Know the truth of Jesus and His word – get the Holy Spirit – **1 cor. 2:9-16** (not satan in you or leading you).

We are different – looks, speech, experiences, etc. – but we need to be one in Jesus and His word – in belief, the same, in the truth. We need to change what we believe. There is truth.

Get help to change, but how? To Jesus (not man, religion, or even a church, leader, etc. – and those that make up their own version of the truth), who can and knows how to help us. We need to know we cannot do it (only with Him) – people want to get away with things (we are evil, we all are – **rom. 3**) that we know are wrong (partially for power, etc.). Jesus (and His word, through the Holy Spirit) is the only one that can change that thinking or any other, and He knows what we are thinking anyway, so admit and change and grow – stop holding yourself back (with satan, who hurts and leads man, without Jesus, and the truth of His word). Pray to Him now and get saved.

All of the truth today (mainly the last 2,000 years – after Jesus' death and resurrection) came from the risen Jesus (especially to paul) – not angels, man, etc. Knowing the truth, and not these lies, etc. (that satan shares, and man follows). So we can know how to be saved (with the Holy Spirit from Jesus only).

If we don't go to Jesus to become one – and follow Him and the truth of His word – then we will become or stay one with man – really satan – all against God. Go to Jesus and become one – believe the truth, and share Jesus. Live for Him.

Be a good example, not see what you can get away with. Don't let others get away with things either, especially your family or friends. Go to Jesus and change, and then share Him.

Cheating of any kind (for any reason) should disgust you (it does God – **matt. 18:23-35; luke 6:31**) – by you or anyone else, and if you don't like it done to you, then don't do it yourself (to others). We all are capable of this. We need Jesus.

People, groups, government, even some laws, etc. shouldn't make it easier for people to commit and get away with crime, evil, bribes, forcing people, using money, etc., even victims shouldn't be able to get away with things.

Just because stealing, crime, etc. is easy sometimes, or you are not suspected of doing something (hiding or clever, etc.), even with friends, etc., don't do it, just to get away with it. Hang out with other people – better people. You have to make an effort to be good and not be led down that evil road (satan really leading) – that we are born with.

Lying and threatening, etc. for gain (for all ages) is becoming normal and even encouraged in the world (depending on what you believe or think) – satan leading people easier in that direction today. And it is like a punishment if you follow Jesus.

A lot of people lie, etc. and don't mind if other people die, because of it, as long as they don't die. We have to sacrifice for truth – including about Jesus and His word – the truth. And let Him help you through things – to protect you (**john 17:15**) – and don't follow satan through your life. Jesus will help you, if you are really with Him (have the Holy Spirit from Him).

You are a real man (or woman), if you tell the truth – you are not big, strong, etc., if you lie, hide the truth, protect an evil person, criminal, liar, etc. Go to Jesus and become a really strong person. And see things work out for you. Don't lie to hide, run, etc. – face it, and let people help you, if needed.

So be moral – rich or poor, and go to Jesus and He will work things out and help you – learn from Him, and He will get you what you need in this life. So admit you're wrong (or let Him humble you), and suffer consequences, punishments, etc. – He will help you through it (keep going to Him and His word).

All the things that God wants for us, are good for us. What man (or you) wants isn't what is best for us – man does his own thing – evil, with satan leading man against man (but it is satan who we are fighting – **eph. 6**) – causing problems – selfishness. So don't let people get away with evil in this world. Be with Jesus. And be ready to go with Jesus – no matter what happens.

If a person was like this (with Jesus – have the Holy Spirit and follow Him – **gal. 5:22-26**), what kind of problems would you have? And so what if others are not this way – you go to Jesus and His word (black, white, rich, poor, man, woman, young, old, etc.) – God will help you through life.

The more you go to Jesus and His word, the more you will live apart from sin, etc. – get saved first and learn and grow, and change – and you will see the difference (and others will, too), and not have to be told (or others be told), because you will start to do things naturally that Jesus wants for us, if you follow Him.

People grow up confused in this world of satan's – and need to be taught and know the truth to know what to do and how to take care of things in this evil world – as we are all evil, too. You learn it first. Go to Jesus to know the truth.

Go through the problems (that you cause or that are in this world) you're going to go through (the consequences, etc.) – stop trying to get out of them (by hiding, running – especially from God, or ignore Him, etc.) – then change and grow with Jesus.

You run because you are guilty of something (and have been taught by people who are guilty of something, etc.) –and don't give in, because you don't want to be found out – and don't make it worse on you or them. So don't tell others to run, etc. Go to Jesus and give in. Make it easier on you.

People lie and they let it go – or don't want to get involved, etc. – man is evil, and why God has laws. It's the ninth commandment (of the 10 – **exo. 20:16**). If people wouldn't lie, we could get rid of most police, courts, lawyers, laws, punishment, etc. – otherwise we need all of those and more (**rom. 13**). With man lying, you know now why lying is one of them (the commandments) – man helping evil man. We all know better, but continue to let it go on – and it causes most of our problems. Stop complaining and understand why we are the way we are (and God says we are) – go to Jesus and change. And know that we need God and His laws. And no matter what we do – know that we need to go back to God and He will work it out (**gen. 50:15-21; rom. 8:28**).

People lie all of the time – now you know why the police and the law need to be tough – to save lives (in some cases may hurt others, or even kill some – may be necessary, because man doesn't live good lives – and do it to themselves), and try to get justice, if that is what you really want or you stand up for that. The law isn't tough enough – people (even those you know) get away with too much – continue to hurt others, and not be stopped (why would they want to stop, if they can keep getting away with things – even keep hurting you and those you love – selfishness, etc.). Go after them and stop them, if you know them, etc. and share Jesus (you get to know Him first, and His truth).

And if people were honest, then we wouldn't think we would need psychologists, psychiatrists, etc., or alcohol, drugs, etc., but we would still need Jesus – go to Jesus no matter what.

If the punishments are not strict and quick (in the home or in the world – make sure you know what they did, etc.), they are a waste of time (and why God did that in the past – and with the jews, etc.). Push people in the right direction as soon as you can – mainly away from the wrong direction, as soon as possible. Use them to get them to Jesus (and His word).

Keep trying to help people – children, etc., so when they grow up they can be better parents for their children and stop the cycle of bad homes, childhoods, etc. – share Jesus so they can live better.

There is a reason why God is against sin (and wrote the bible) – satan (and his lies) and his goal to be God (**isa. 14:12-17**) causing this to us and this world (and us to be gods, etc.), as we follow satan and his ideas. And to keep man sinful and against God and going to hell forever (following satan) – either go to satan or Jesus. Follow the truth of Jesus' word that is best for man.

We need to tell people – family, etc. the truth about this world and about Jesus – knowing He is the only way to God, and heaven – as early as you can, but the truth – know the truth of His word.

Parents usually make their own problems with their children, by their lifestyle, behavior, etc., and blame the children for misbehaving (even though they may, too). Change your life – and help them and you with Jesus. Know the truth, and share it.

You have to find out what your faults are – and be honest and how they line up to what God wants us to behave and live in this world – so you can help your children.

Just like at home (or a nation, society, etc.) – need discipline, rules, punishment, etc., to grow up properly and have peace and order in the home – you also need it in the world, society, etc. or evil will get worse and so will our lives. Don't just do things that are accepted to do in this world – just because you are an adult – if it is bad, it is bad for anyone – be a better example (do without). Go to Jesus and be safe and love. So how you treat people and live your life will be the reward – what is best for them, too.

People need to sacrifice things in this life to do right – like fun, desires, pleasures, etc. – to have it work out and not have problems (at least not as many) for you or others – like family, etc. – go to Jesus and do what He wants – then you will be happy (as much as you can be here). Because the way you live can not only put you in danger, but also others – it only takes once to be awful. Go to Jesus and follow Him, and His word – His life for you, or people may take advantage of you.

And some people let people take advantage of them – especially if they think they will help them – it's not worth it. Go to Jesus to get what you need and want – what's best for you (**matt. 6:33; matt. 21:22; john 16:24; james 4:3; 1 john 3:22**).

The law, government, etc. need to put in God's laws for a nation, and put Jesus and the bible in prisons for prisoners to be taught and learn and change (if and when they get out) – as well as for those that work there. But you also have to be smart and careful what you do and who you hang around with. Have Jesus with you. Need to do this until we all go to Jesus.

God wants to have laws and protection, etc. – police, courts, jail, etc., because we are sinners and need help and control – but done with God in mind (**rom. 13**).

Prisons are tough (and should be), but you have to do what's right – go to Jesus and share there. That's why Jesus would be taught in prison and out in the world – to make it be bearable to live here (and help those that eventually get out to live a better life).

Do things right – and know what that is, and you will get the best outcome – especially if you go to Jesus. Then don't worry.

There are many evil people in the world – including lawyers, etc. (some try to do things correctly) – they get evil, guilty people off sometimes – even though they know the truth, they are guilty – maybe tricking people, etc., with just saying they are doing their job (satan works both sides). Hopefully they will get someone off that is really not guilty – although most have done something bad in this world. Go to Jesus to straighten out what is wrong with someone (in prison or not).

But if you don't have punishments, and people not being punished at all or enough, then you won't stop any evil – wake up. And satan wins. Know the truth of man and this world – born evil, sinful. Jesus is the answer.

We still have to suffer the consequences of sin – whatever punishment, etc. that go with it (in or out of prison), but still can be forgiven. Keep going to Jesus – grow, learn, and change – to live a better life.

You might be able to forgive someone that does things to you – depending on what that is, to a point. If it is dangerous and evil and a way of life – you need to stop them and turn them in (and for whatever punishment). And hopefully share Jesus and they can change (but still there are consequences for things – punishments, even if they go to Jesus, but hopefully they will change their ways). It is hard to forgive someone for evil, but those that are truly saved should, like Jesus did for us – all of us, if we would just go to Him, then do the same for others – God will take care of it.

The best thing you can do is turn someone in – stop any bad habits, etc. that someone has from starting and getting worse – no matter how tough it is to get through – but share Jesus and have Him help them – even (and especially) your family.

Forgive – not just for money, things, etc., but for those that wrong you in other ways (**gen. 50:17-21; matt. 5:23-25; matt. 6:12; rom. 4:7-8; rom. 8:26-28**) – even though there still may be consequences for you or them. Face them. With Jesus.

You really hurt yourself if you don't forgive – even those in the past – and you just continue your frustration, problems, etc., and don't grow. Since it mostly doesn't hurt them. So move on. Forgive. and pray for, them.

And you should go to Jesus to get through your consequences and punishments of whatever you have done to others – then live a better life with Him – and maybe use those things done to you to lead you and help you grow, etc.

Learn the truth – keep going to God – get truly saved by Jesus – with the Holy Spirit – then God can use you and you will share the truth of His word, and keep reading, learning, and praying.

Jesus has all of the answers to life, problems, the truth, the bible, and after this life. Go to Jesus to get help – find out.

And Jesus will forgive you for all of your sins, when you go to Him and believe in Him (and get the Holy Spirit) and follow Him and the truth of His word (**isa. 43:25; matt. 12:31-32**). When you live for Him, and grow in Him.

Whatever direction you go in life – what belief, etc. you have, God can use you and get you to know the truth eventually, even if you didn't or don't believe the truth – just keep learning and growing with His word (with the Holy Spirit, when you truly get saved), and He will use your experiences to help others, once you are truly with Jesus, and you want to know the truth.

No matter what you were born into (we don't have a choice then, but later we do) and what they believe. Then grow up and change, then help who you can – those that were like you, etc. And God can use you.

Go to Jesus and the truth, especially if you are screwed up, etc. – no excuse, He is there. And become born again (**john 3**).

When Jesus talked about loving (and judging) – He related it to if someone bothered or hurt you (even if you are saved, and they hated you, because you believe in Jesus, etc.) – you would dislike that person and those that looked or acted like them, because they may do (or did) the same to you (**luke 6:22-49**), in the first place. We have to be honest with ourselves, but also do the right thing in this world. Only Jesus can help us do that.

Even though people are not supposed to judge – because all are sinners (**matt. 7:1-5**), and all have done something wrong – sinful, against God, whether big or small (**john 8:1-11**) – still sinful (and somethings that haven't been found out, etc.) – so somethings like the 'scarlet letter' in the past, is not good, because all have sinned. Just help them get to know Jesus and His truth and change and grow, then let God deal with them. We will be able to judge better when we get to know Jesus and His truth – get saved, with the Holy Spirit (**1 cor. 6:1-11**).

Jesus laid His life down for His enemies (all of us here on earth are sinful, evil, etc. – and separated from God), and you wouldn't lay your life down for your enemies (it is not easy, but with Jesus you may have a chance). And helping others can heal you – with Jesus and His word. Then God will help us.

It's hard to do – but you hate the sin – the way people behave, but you love the sinner, and share Jesus. And why Jesus says to love your enemies – people need to change, or this world (and you) will continue to have problems.

You (and others) have to come clean for what you do (and maybe what others do) – no matter how bad something is – God knows, and you need to tell the truth – that will help you. You will be free – go to Jesus and know the truth (**john 8:32**). Just like with cain and abel – cain killed abel, and no one knew but God – and God said that abel's blood cried out to Him (**gen. 4:9-13**) – the evil we do on this earth is all against God (as well as other people), and your sin will find you out (**num. 32:23**).

And cain was not listening to God (but knew of Him), nor did he stay in the presence of the Lord (**gen. 4:1-8, 16**) – he had a choice – he was like the jews – physical. And abel – had faith and followed God, and was spiritual, like Jesus – and the jews had Jesus killed (as cain did abel) – **matt. 23:31-39; luke 11:45-54; heb. 11:3-4; heb. 12:23-24**. And cain was also like ham – who was cursed by noah after the flood, and nimrod – were against God (**gen. 10:8-10; gen. 11:1-9**). It doesn't take much to lead you in the wrong direction. We are evil after sin – and after adam (and eve) – who we all are from (**gen. 3:20**).

So from adam and eve (after sin, and the curse – **gen. 3**), came cain and abel (and cain killed abel), and cain left the presence of the Lord (didn't want to follow Him), and those are all of the cursed (**gen. 4**) that died in the flood – only those with God went with Him – starting with seth (**gen. 5**), including noah and his sons (and wives) in the ark when the flood came (**gen. 7 to 9**). And now noah's sons are who we all come from – and those from ham are cursed more (**gen. 9:24-25**) – and he was the father of those in sodom and gomorrah (**gen. 10:19-20; gen. 19**). But more cursed, or not, than others, we all (all of noah's sons) need to go to Jesus and get saved – we all could go then, and all can go now. We all choose our destiny – heaven or hell.

God doesn't want us to live just or mostly for the flesh here – that's why He created us with His Spirit. We don't have it now (since adam sinned – **gen. 3**), and need to get it back to be with Him – and why He left us, and kicked adam and eve out of the garden (we are sinful). First when adam sinned (the Holy Spirit not in man anymore) and then just before the flood when God wasn't going to strive with man anymore with His Spirit (the presence of the Lord) – because man is also flesh (and were living that way – **gen. 6:3**). Now we can get it back with Jesus (when we believe and are saved by Him). And be with Him.

Anyone is capable of evil – under the right (or wrong) circumstances – some more evil than others. Even if they want to see what it feels like – no excuse. We need to get away from sin, man, satan, etc. – and go to Jesus and His word and follow Him.

People know what they do in this life and what they are thinking (we know right from wrong – from adam eating of the tree of good and evil in the garden – **gen. 3** – like satan says to be like God), and God does, too. And people have to live with what they do. You don't get away with it (**num. 32:23**).

Most people start small (but still bad) with some lie, crime, alcohol, drugs, etc. – things that aren't good for them, and when that doesn't satisfy them – or they don't get caught and punished or change – they will do worse eventually. You have to know that man is evil – you are. And do what is necessary to change that – especially parents as soon as possible.

If you don't want your children to do something – you don't do that (even though your parents may have, and you started when you were young with bad habits, etc.) – lie, cheat, alcohol, drugs, hurt, hate, abuse, etc. (hard to give up, but it needs to be done to help your children, and others – and don't start in the first place) – be a good example – Jesus is best and His word – don't always depend on church, leaders, etc. to change them.

People could have changed when younger, etc. – when you first heard of Jesus, but you didn't listen then, and you could have avoided many problems that happened later in your life.

Everyone needs to look back in their life and see who they hurt or harmed along the way, and it will show you why you go through problems now – there are consequences to life and will come back to hurt you (**num. 32:23; gal. 6:5-10**). Go to Jesus and repent and forgive, and then grow and change. It is what you mainly do against God that matters, that hurts other people, and then yourself.

So parents need to do the same as soon as they can – for themselves first, then their children. Stop letting things continue down the wrong road (you may have to give up some things, desires, habits, etc. – go to Jesus – truly be saved with the Holy Spirit – and following His word in your life, daily) as soon you can and be a good example. Don't help or encourage anyone to do evil – just for your miserable life, family, etc. So people – adults, need to not do things, even though they legally can – drink alcohol, drugs, sex, etc. – they need to sacrifice, so children (theirs or others) can see what is best, and don't do those things either – and get into trouble of all kinds when they are young (and carry over into their adult lives). Basically what God wants us to do and not do.

If you don't have discipline, how can your children have any – for many things in this life. And should have love and share Jesus shown in your life – so they can, too. Be responsible so others can. And if the children don't listen – they will do that the rest of their lives – so you have to make sure they stop immediately when you say to do or not to do something, or you are not doing them (or you) any good – and it will just get worse.

The underlying problem with man, is that of going against authority (just like clockwork) – first as children – with parents, teachers, etc., then people with the law, police, government, etc. – the worst is going against God – the truth of Him and His word – exactly what satan did – **isa. 14:12-17** (and is where man gets that attitude in the first place – since the beginning – from and following satan and have him lead us, instead of God). Wake up. Don't follow satan and keep having the attitude of going against the authority of God (Jesus) – and His word. Man is born that way – evil. Go to Jesus.

And God punishes us to straighten us out (**isa. 13**) – mainly to go to Him – through Jesus, to help us.

At the start – God didn't have many rules, punishment, etc. (except not to eat of the tree of the knowledge of good and evil – or they would die – **gen. 2:17** – we all would die) – then God, just after creation (mainly after adam and eve sinned – **gen. 3**) – before the flood – with having man figure out whether to be with and listening to God or not (in the presence of the Lord – with His Spirit), and having no laws, punishments, etc. (except they were going to die someday – as we all do now because of them) and having a nice comfortable earth and weather, etc. to live – and to live a long time (sometimes to 900 years or so – **gen. 5** – a short time compared to forever as we were to live) – but man was evil, and out of control (**gen. 6**) – mainly because of that comfortableness before the flood – then God sent the flood (punishment for all of the evil of mankind – and creation – **gen. 7 and 8**) – God will let evil go on for only so long. And after the flood (a tougher world to live – uncomfortable), the only law for noah and his sons was to not kill others (and the one limit God said before the flood – that man will only live to be 120 years at the most – **gen. 6:3** – for man's life after the flood – a punishment, too, but would start a little after the flood, up to today), or your punishment for killing someone would be death (**gen. 9:5-6**) – and that hasn't changed since then (so we need to put Jesus – and His word, in prisons, especially on death row – noah's covenant is still there in the world – death for death) – we are all still from one of noah's sons. And also the rainbow is still a sign, that God gave to noah, that is still a promise in effect today (man doesn't put a rainbow in the sky – God does, and it started after the flood – when it was the first time it rained on earth, **gen. 6 to 8** – about 4,300 years ago, and ever since) – we see the rainbow after it rains even today to let us know (God won't destroy the world with a flood again – but will eventually end this earth – this earth will be gone, and a new earth and heaven will be created – **rev. 21** – coming soon).

And then soon after that (within about 100 years or so after the flood) God changed the language from one to many – **gen. 11**, and scattered man all over the world. Then within a few hundred years after that, God eventually developed the jews with laws, punishments, etc. (**exodus, leviticus, deuteronomy**, etc.) – even though the gentiles (the rest of the world) would have their own punishments and rules, etc. – whatever they did in their own family, tribe, village, etc. – to follow or not – will be judged (**rom. 1:17-32; rom. 2:1-16**). Then when Jesus came here and died and rose (after the jews rejected Him) – God has put in a time of grace (without the law) – salvation for all (gentiles, and any individual jews) to go to Him – through Jesus and the Holy Spirit – those with Him (and have the Holy Spirit) – are free (for about the last 2,000 years), but not to sin (even though satan is still here tempting, and our corruptible body still fights against the Spirit – **rom. 7**) – we are forgiven for mistakes, sins, etc., and still have to keep going to Him (not man, a church, leader, etc.) for whatever evil we do here (or God may take us out of here – **1 cor. 5:1-5**). And these are still things that God doesn't like (**prov. 6:16-19**). We need to keep learning His word and growing and changing to what He wants us to do (with the Holy Spirit) – not stay with man (and satan), and evil and sin (even though it is all around us). And doing good while we are here. Only Jesus can do that for us.

Whatever energy, time, expenses, etc., you put in to doing something (criminal or otherwise) – that same energy, etc. can be put into something that is good and honest, etc. – people use excuses for working hard on evil things – like they don't have a choice, but they do – go to Jesus and follow His word, and change.

God made the world this way – separate and tough (especially after the flood), and we have to know it is Jesus that is the answer to change from the way we are (the way we are born) – go to Him and you can do more with Jesus (and His word), than you can without Him, or you will be struggling and have an uphill battle and trouble with others (and always should keep trying to help others). God has a reason for giving us all of these laws, warnings, punishments, etc. for this life here, because how we are – we are not good – none of us are (**psalm 14; rom. 3**)– we are all sinful, evil (humans made ourselves that way – from adam – **gen. 3**) – even after the flood (**gen. 8:21**) – all from noah's sons (**gen. 9:18-19**) – so He made the world this way (a tougher world after the flood – for our punishment), for us to go to Him (Jesus and His word). Even though in america you can have a chance and opportunity to change and to do things even with handicaps, disabilities, etc. (of all kinds – mental, emotional, physical, etc., even lesser abilities) – mainly physically disabled, but you have to just work harder at things than others. With Jesus.

Don't be sick or unhealthy by the way you eat or what you put in your body or what you do to your body or how you live your life, or what you believe, etc. (satan wants you that way). Quit mocking those that are really ill or disfigured or disabled (at birth or after), etc. Go to Jesus and follow His word and eat and take care of yourself that way He made us (**gen. 1:29; dan. 1**).

Take care of yourself with what is best for us.

Find out what is best for us – like we found out the hard way that smoking is not good – that should have been obvious, but man waited to see how unhealthy it is, and there are other things in this world that are not good for you. So don't go down that road – be as healthy as you can – watch what you put in your body (and the medical field doesn't necessarily know that).

You can't do good things on drugs, alcohol, bad food, etc. – change – go to Jesus first, then find what you are good at and like (your abilities, etc. from noah's sons) – stop being evil. All people have problems – we have to deal with them. Go to Jesus.

And we all have talents (from noah's sons), but it may not be good to have too many talents – if you do, you don't know what to do. Better to have one or two, and focus and work hard, whatever you do, and go to Jesus (and His word) to help you get better. Learn from God's word, and let it lead you.

Starting with the abilities and talents we get from noah's sons, we need to get saved and get the Holy Spirit to enhance what you get from God in the spirit (**1 cor. 12**), not just from noah's sons, physically. Get the most out of your talents and abilities with Jesus – don't be stuck only with noah's sons only. And do good in this world. Jesus will help you for what you need.

Don't blame God for all of your problems (it is our sinful nature, and satan) – go to God to help you through, but know the truth (of His word), so you do what He wants for you and your family, etc. – not what you want.

Love is the greatest and we can only know that from Jesus (**1 cor. 13:13**). He will help us change to heal from what we are born with – sin, etc. Then you will begin to want what He wants for you. Especially in america, with it's opportunities for all.

Heal your heart with Jesus (whatever you go through).

Jesus will help you get through the things in this life (what has happened to you – your fault or not) – even if you can't change some circumstances that happen here. We all have some problems – sometime in our life.

Just like you work out to build yourself physically (your body, skills, sports, etc.), go to Jesus and His word with the Holy Spirit to build yourself spiritually.

Some people are physically blind and would like to see, but all are spiritually blind and need to go to Jesus and see the truth – to get to heaven. And if we are truly saved, we will get a new body in the rapture for heaven (**1 cor. 15:50-54**).

The one thing we all are is spiritually disabled (need to be born again – get the Holy Spirit that adam lost for us) – and we can only go to Jesus (who is the Creator) to get that taken care of (He gave that to adam to begin with – but adam lost that, for all of us, when he listened to satan, and sinned, so we don't have it – **gen. 3**) – no other way or no one else to be able to do that. We need to be in mental health, as much as physical health, but the best is spiritual health, and that is with Jesus only, and He will help you with all. And we can help those (as well as Jesus, and His word, can) with mental and physical problems.

There are people in this world that will always need help, and always will be – we need to help them, but also have them help themselves. And to share Jesus with them, which is the most important.

And we need to keep including people that have handicaps, injuries, elderly, birth defects, etc. – physical and mentally disabled, etc., for them to be part of (and be seen in) society, etc., to participate in life – and to have people (especially the young) to develop compassion for people in this world and know there are people worse off than they are (including the homeless, needy, etc. – although some cause their own problems – need Jesus). And churches should be doing a better job of helping the homeless (and some do), and sharing the truth of Jesus, and His word. To help them, if possible (and have them help themselves, too). Wouldn't be good to give money to the homeless (give some food, water, clothes, etc. – **matt. 25:34-36**) – let shelters, churches, ministries, rescue missions, etc. deal with that (and give money to ministries that do – God wants us to use our money wisely – **matt. 25:14-30; 2 cor. 9:6-14** – or He may not bless us), and especially share Jesus – but many of the homeless, etc. don't want to change (as do those that are not homeless, etc.). So don't enable those that are not living a life that is not good for them (or anyone) – just like you wouldn't enable your family, friends, etc. (on drugs, criminal, etc.). Some (of the homeless) don't want to go to shelters, missions, etc. (except in bad weather, etc.), because they make them not only stop drugs, alcohol, etc. (using whatever money they have for those things), but also may have to be told what to do, and may have to hear about Jesus, etc. (and should) – many don't like that. So have them get to know Jesus (and His word – the truth of it) – which is the most important for anyone (homeless or not), to change their life (and to avoid other problems). They need to want to be helped (and change), too. With Jesus. Why we are all here – no matter what son of noah we are or what life we live.

And peter (jews) and paul (gentiles) gave to the poor (Christians) in their ministries (**gal. 2:6-10**). It started after Jesus died and rose – that they thought at that time that Jesus was going to come back soon, and He was going to if the jews as a nation would have all believed and followed Him as their Messiah (finishing the 490 years of daniel – to anoint the most Holy, which is Jesus – **dan. 9**) – then Jesus would have come back soon (to the mount of olives – **matt. 24; mark 13; acts 1:6-12; acts 2:16-21**) and used the jews to evangelize the world. So all of the believing jews – Christians, sold all that they had (and gave to the apostles, to give evenly to all – like communism), believing Jesus was coming soon for them (**acts 2:41-47; acts 4:31-37**). But the jews didn't all believe, so Jesus didn't come back, and the temple destroyed (by 70ad) and the jews were scattered all over the world at that time (and still are today) – and the goods and money ran out. So there were poor jewish Christians that needed help (and that is who peter and paul were going to help) – and some that need help today. Help the poor, but help them get the know Jesus and be saved. Give to true Christian ministries that do.

God takes care of the righteous – even those today that are truly with Jesus (**psalm 37:25; matt. 6:33**). We are only righteous with Jesus (**rom. 5**). And that is saved with the Holy Spirit.

We are righteous because of Jesus – not our good works, etc. – then He helps us do good works (**eph. 2:10; james 1:22**).

And all of the money, things, etc. you have – no matter how much or little it is – is God's – use it wisely for what He wants. Go to Jesus, and share Him (and help those that you can).

If you are rich or well off, etc., you can help others in need – give them jobs, or work for you, etc. – and to give a chance and reason to share Jesus with them – and why there are rich and poor people, and even setbacks or disasters, etc. in this world.

This whole world is people giving and getting from other people – like working and getting paid from those at work. And buying and giving money to others. And by helping out others that are needy, etc. Hopefully doing things right in this world.

Even though we can help others – if you don't work (and you can) – you don't eat (mainly believers), be responsible – **2 thess. 3:6-16**. And share Jesus, and help poor believers.

For some people it may be harder, but all people can be helped and change – by Jesus – your best chance (like america does – **matt. 25:35-36**). So keep sharing Jesus with the homeless (lead them to good churches – the truth of the bible), but mainly to be saved by Jesus (church or not) – and you can do more for them – especially if they are trying to change, work hard, etc. (maybe help those that are to trying change with some money – can be with a church helping). Even help those in prisons, etc.

And it is good to help people when you can – but that doesn't always change things – only going to Jesus does – for anything – including work, living, taking care of yourself, equality, health, etc.

CHAPTER 3

Sin, Evil, and Human Nature

All to be with Jesus (with the Holy Spirit), and even get a new body (like Jesus did, only flesh and bones – **luke 24:36-48**) in the rapture to come soon (**1 cor. 15:42-55**), but we have to take care of our body the best and right way we can while we are here (no matter what level of health our body is, in this life) – to be healthy as you can be (**gen. 1:29; dan. 1**) – the way God wants us to take care of it (as He wants us to do for everything with Him – it is the best for us, or we suffer consequences here). Jesus says to help, but have responsibility – especially share Him – whether homeless, your children, family, friends, etc. Go to Jesus to do this, and learn His word – the truth. We won't have perfect health here – especially after the flood, but still do the best you can with what God made for us (give yourself more time to get to know Jesus). We still will all die, but go to Jesus before you do.

Whatever the problems that hurt you or those you love (including death) – know that this is not our final home (heaven or hell) – go to Jesus through these problems and have people ready to be with Jesus in heaven.

God uses this fallen, cursed world – especially after the flood – with diseases, etc. for us to go to Him, but can try to be healthy with Him and His word.

You can kill yourself slowly or quickly, but the way you live is going to kill you – living unhealthy. Live with Jesus instead. And no matter how healthy you are (you should try to be) – you can go at any time in this evil world – so go to Jesus now – even for your health. Just because someone lives to 100 years old, by smoking, drinking, etc., doesn't make it right or good – and most that do that don't live that long – don't follow that – they usually die young (and have problems up to that point). God made our bodies for fruit and vegetables (**gen. 1:29; dan.1**). If we go away from that, we will have problems – still live, and still can go to Jesus, but live with the consequences here. Regardless be ready to go with Jesus.

Whatever mistakes you make in this world, go to Jesus and heal – don't try to deny Him and His word. Don't always trust what man does – they don't care if it works or not – they just want to make money. And people are getting hooked on and depending on drugs, etc. of all kinds. Depend on God, and the truth of His word. Jesus can heal you one way or another – from Him or His truth of His word.

Everything in the world and man is about man's creations, inventions, discoveries, etc. – not God's or His truths – including drugs, etc. Depending on them (and not on Jesus) will kill us, which is the way the world is going now (**rev. 18:23-24**).

If you go against drugs, doctors, etc. trying to do all of the healing and controlling people – you look like you don't care about people, etc. – but God's ways are best – eat healthy, and share that, and you will be doing more for others, and really showing you care about them.

Taking drugs of any kind – legal or illegal – are still one of the top killers of people in the world. Without drugs, man would live better, longer lives – coupled with eating healthy – God's food for us (**gen. 1:29**).

People keep living the way they do – which is not good for them – as long as they can go to drugs, etc. (they are available and look like the answer – according to man, really satan) that allows them to stay that way – unhealthy – otherwise they would have a chance to change, and be healthy (**3 john 1:2**).

You can't take drugs to get rid of your mental or physical problems that are caused by your behavior. Your behavior is from our sinful nature (born that way), and cannot be helped without Jesus, not man (or satan).

People will start to believe we all – humans, have problems and have nothing to do with us or God – not our fault (but we are all human, and all from adam, and we are all sinful because of that – just like you get any genetic problem from your parents, etc.), and just need to take a drug for what we got. Since it is not our fault, then drugs, etc. are the answer, not Jesus. If you keep believing this, you will struggle in this life and worse after this life.

There is starting to be a drug for every problem you have, and they want you to think that is the answer, but it is from satan. You have to wake up and stop making excuses for everyone, including you and your family, etc. It is satan we are fighting (**eph. 6**).

The world is spreading disease around, so the world can sell their drugs. No one would take drugs – legal or illegal, if they didn't think they would get or feel something from them. Go to Jesus and His word to live healthy. And avoid more problems.

And satan wants you to depend on drugs, witchcraft, technology, etc., instead of God and His word to cope with problems of this world (and will kill many people in the end – **rev. 18:23-24**). Go to Jesus, not man (or satan) in this world.

Man will come and go on this earth (as much as God loves man, especially those that go to Him), but His Word (truth) is more important and will last forever (**matt. 24:35; luke 13:31; luke 21:33; 1 pet. 1:24-25**) – and best for man, so go to Jesus and change (and get saved so that you can last forever with Him), and we can deal with this world here (and eventually life after this). If you are unhealthy, then you better be with Jesus.

God told us and showed us – what death and after is – through Jesus, so we don't have to fear that, if we go to Jesus.

The bible and everything in it, is relevant today – it always is, and has been – God is saying something to all eras and times in history (including today). Read it and understand for life today (but with the Holy Spirit from Jesus) – for God's will and His timing for things in this world – and for you (**prov. 9:10**). The whole bible is for our learning (**rom. 15:4**).

If you can't believe in the creation (**gen. 1**), the flood of noah (**gen. 6 to 9**), etc. or in the time frame – when, how long ago, etc. – 6,000 years ago, with the numbers and ages, etc. that Jesus put in there – **gen. 5** (as Jesus believes in them, and the Holy Spirit – He wrote them, and was there), then how can you believe in any of the bible?

You either are saved – believe in Jesus and the truth of His word, with the Holy Spirit, and are going to heaven, or you don't, and you are going to hell – that is punishment enough. And it is your choice – believe Jesus and the truth of His word before you die.

Even if you die right after salvation (like the thief on the cross – **luke 23:32-43**) – God knows you are truly saved – by Jesus, with the gospel (**1 cor. 15:1-4**) – with the Holy Spirit (**john 3:3-8**) – and He knows if you had a chance to, you would have read His word and believed the truth of it, like Jesus does.

No matter what era it is (we can know Him and the truth of His word), especially in modern times (mainly in the last 100 years or so) – where everyone can know what is going on in your area and around the world – where people, especially children follow trends, etc., especially prejudice, etc. – all against any of noah's sons, or try to get along without Jesus (which will not ever work). We have to go to God and believe the truth of His word. All can know of Jesus – go to Jesus and get saved.

People that want change, and it doesn't happen fast enough (for you, a person, or even in america) – you have to be patient and it has to be done right – by going to Jesus and following His truth, if not it will not be good or happen. Go to Him and see what happens.

Sometimes it's hard to be patient with people – put up with them, whether it's family or friends, etc. – Jesus will help you with that. It is all in His word. That goes for anything.

Most things you get or do right away, don't always work out or work out good for you – like trying to be healthy – change eating habits take time (and man doesn't want to wait, or do what it takes, etc. – go to God and His word, and eat the way He made us to – **gen. 1:29; dan. 1**) – that's why drugs and doctors, etc. win and are able to sell you something that will (or think it will) take care of or heal you, of what you got right away – without waiting (really won't). And by not going to God and His word first – man was healthy before the flood without drugs, meat, man-made food, etc. – even though the world is tougher now and more dangerous after the flood – but fruit and vegetables are still best for our bodies today, too (if you wait too long in your life to change, it will keep making you worse, and then you will go to the medical field, drugs, etc.). So go to God for help (to Jesus) for health, etc., too (**3 john 1:2-3**) – not just doctors, medical field, etc., or you won't make it as well (especially if you die, before you get saved, and not go to heaven) – **2 chron. 16:11-13; luke 8:43-44**. He wants you to go to Him.

The things and direction your life takes – even though you may not have done all you wanted in this life, but you were able to live and go to

Jesus – otherwise you may not have gone to Him (or even lived to have time to go to Him), without the problems, setbacks, lost opportunities, etc. in your life. Keep going to God to find out what is best for you.

We have to learn hard lessons – don't blame God – it could be best, even if man caused it, and continues to cause it (with satan's help). Going to God can straighten it out, without Him, you may continue struggling – let Him help (**rom. 8:28**).

Even if you get fired – it could be good for you – for something else in your life. Go to God – He will help you. He may be leading you elsewhere, that you wouldn't do if you didn't get fired, bad things didn't happen, etc.

We go to God for help – we may have to wait – it's on His time, but keep going to Him to get through, and to get to where He might lead you. And keep helping others get through things, when you can – sharing Jesus and His word.

And don't say anything is God's will until you are truly saved with the Holy Spirit and know the truth of His word (go to Jesus), and follow it – otherwise it is satan and false beliefs, etc. that may be leading you. Read His word.

God may have talked to those in the past – like adam, cain, noah, abraham, moses (who happened to be the last one God talked to face to face – **deut. 34**, and God had moses start to write the bible), not today. So God doesn't talk to you to do something – just the Holy Spirit leading you – if you are truly saved by Jesus and the truth of His word (and learning the word). God will open and close doors for you in this life and you have to know what to do and where to go – following His word and grow to be a better follower.

And satan is out there thinking you are hearing from God, but you are not – go to God's word and let the Holy Spirit teach you the truth of His word and lead you. Believe and live the truth.

How can you believe anything about history, people, science, empires, events, even religions, etc. in the past – the things that are written and taken for granted and accepted? – if you can, then you can believe in Jesus and the bible (**1 cor. 15:1-6**), and the people who witnessed that (mainly the jews – and is why satan wants to get rid of the jews, and the bible, and go against Him and His truth). Look at who God says we are from – all of noah's sons (**gen. 9:18-19**).

So we need to believe in God's word, like you would anything in history, and it will lead you to Jesus or you may not believe like the jews did not – learn the word (**luke 16:19-31**) – but believe and follow. People saw Jesus, but didn't believe (we believe in our history, and your own, but people still all didn't believe when they saw Him – **1 cor. 15:4-8**). We believe things today from the past (and act on it) – believe what God says.

God looks down here to us – to see if any are interested (**psalm 14:1-2**) in Him (and in His word – the truth) – what He wants, especially for us, as evil as we are (**gen. 8:21; rom. 3**).

You have to accept the fact that you are no good without Jesus, and just go to Him and stop fighting it.

Deep down people know what's going on in the world – the evil in it – even in them. Go to Jesus and know and accept the truth – Jesus will help you out of your problems.

We (and satan) can cause God to do what He does here to us – all through history – but it is best for us – especially to be with Him – He set the world up the way it is. Go to Jesus to change all of that.

It doesn't matter how smart (or rich, etc.) you are (whatever that is), but it is what you believe in that matters – what is right and best – the truth – that is what Jesus is – and how you treat people, etc. – don't be selfish, evil, etc. (the way we are born) – some grow that way worse than others, but we all have a choice. And Jesus will help us the best for all of that.

You treat people right, if you want to be treated right.

And we all have to have faith in Jesus (and His word), to get something done on this earth (and after) – but it is unbelief that keeps things from happening in this world, that we would like to change (**matt. 13:57-58**). So the problems will continue without Him. Man cannot help those by himself (at least very little). Stop being selfish – which causes most problems, which is the way we are all born. Think of others, and do what's best. Jesus helps, and keeps the peace (if there is any).

We should rather have people unhappy with us, than God unhappy with us (**acts 5:29**). Praise and follow God, not man.

So love, envy, jealousy, anger, struggles, setbacks, even money, etc. (all without God), all cause problems for man – we don't know how to deal with them (emotions, desires, etc.), but we think we can. Man can't always control these problems – addictions included, for anything in this world (his selfish desires, etc.), so let Jesus help you with them, because we can't without Him, as much as we try. God made us and knows how to deal with those traits (that are in all of us – He created us that way) and to help us to deal with those also, but we have to be connected to Him to do that (with the Holy Spirit, that adam lost for us all, and only Jesus can give us – He's the Creator). We are born evil – selfish (and have problems, because we are without His Spirit), separated, so He can't guide us and lead us (the way He wanted us to be), until we go to Jesus, so don't be greedy, covet, steal, hateful, etc. – care about people (**philip. 2:3-4**), but mainly go to Jesus to change to what He wants – and is best for you – us.

How we handle adversity, problems, etc. in this world – of our own doing or from other people's decisions, etc. – how we respond that puts us in trouble. Go to Jesus (and His word) to help you for any problems in life.

You have to keep going to God when you do things you regret – some worse than others, then change and grow and learn with Jesus and His word.

Our soul (which is empty) affects our heart – desires, choices, decisions, etc. here. But the soul can be filled with satan and this world (even demon possessed, etc.), until we go to Jesus to get saved, and get the Holy Spirit (to fill our soul – the way God had intended us to be) – until then we will keep going down this miserable, evil road.

So many problems, etc. with this world and life – and all of the names and labels, etc. man puts on them – whether mental, physical, emotional, etc., and the worry about them by everyone, as well as the drugs, therapies, stigmas, etc. that go with them – trying to solve them or make them better. Stop worrying about them, and go to Jesus for the only way to solve them, not man trying to give you something new for them. God has to know more than we do – go to Him.

For the most part, the only thing that you can control here, is going to Jesus or not – then see how your life goes. That is what we are here for – go to Jesus. Our duty here (**eccl. 12:13-14**). Going to Jesus and His word daily (the truth) can keep satan away from you (that's who we fight here – **2 cor. 4:1-6; eph. 6**) – get saved and get the Holy Spirit and you won't be possessed (**matt. 12:43-45**)– resist satan (**james 4:7**). The Holy Spirit is greater than satan (**1 john 4:4**).

To get out of (or live through) this lying and cheating, evil, etc. world – you have to go to Jesus – if you don't, you are contributing to the evil here in this world (this is not our final home). God allows this world to be this way – so you will hopefully go to Him – Jesus, and be able to go to be with Him in eternity forever – and really live your life – where we are meant to be – but only with Jesus (and the Holy Spirit) will you be able to do that.

You don't have a choice (when born) – we are all evil because of man (adam, and through noah's sons – **gen. 9** – with satan leading), so it is not your fault (all of mankind's problem since adam sinned – **gen. 3**) if you are born evil (without the Holy Spirit connected to God), but it is your fault if you stay that way while you grow – by not going to Jesus (no excuse – we all know of Him – **john 1:8-14; titus 2:11-15** – and some don't know the truth, from satan's lies) and follow Him (only need Jesus – not the world, or man, or any being, it's really satan leading this world). Only with Him (getting the Holy Spirit in your soul), the truth of His word (or you will be staying with noah's sons – man, and this evil world, until then). Your fault.

We know good and evil – from adam (in the garden – **gen. 2:16-17; gen. 3:6-11**), but without God and the Holy Spirit, we are more into evil – and even after we get the Holy Spirit from Jesus, we still have a corruptible body.

Most people have problems – but you can see why they do – like in hollywood, movies, shows, schools, etc. – which may all be against God and His truth in His word. Especially leading children down the wrong road.

When you first get saved – truly saved (with the Holy Spirit) – you will change, and people will see that in you – especially your family, friends, etc. – if there is no change – not just going to church, etc., but your behavior, etc., and wanting to read the bible and learn the truth.

We are all evil – whether we are black or white, rich or poor, lawless or lawful, heterosexual (or not – change with Jesus), man or woman, young or old, jew or gentile, servant or free, etc. – until we go to Jesus – get saved and get the Holy Spirit and change. Don't listen to man – hollywood (villains and good guys, evil doers and heroes, etc.), beliefs, etc. for who is good or not (even going to heaven or not) – being or looking or acting good is not enough – it is just with Jesus only (and the truth of His word). Movies, hollywood, tv, internet, etc. make things look good or ok to do, and seem harmless, as well as ads do – everything, but Jesus. They don't have the answers, but influencing man to live against God – satan uses ideas, and agendas, etc. to hurt man – to go against God and His word – the truth. God knows what's best and tells us in His word.

Stop trying to be cool, macho, important, etc., and don't lead others to be arrogant, evil, sinful, etc. – change who you are – don't do what others do. And fame, money, etc. is no excuse for bad behavior. Do what Jesus wants you to do – in His word – know the truth. It's all about your behavior and what and who you follow in this world.

Don't be someone you're not (cool, hip, to be liked, etc.) – other than going to Jesus and change to what He wants. Trying anything else gets you nowhere, and those that try aren't either.

Deny self – don't show off, etc. (**luke 9:23-24**). Go to Jesus and have Him lead you. And share Him.

Everyone wants to make excuses for their problems – but there is no one that is good (none are good – **gen. 8:21; psalm 14; rom. 3**), especially when you can go to Jesus and you know right from wrong (**gen. 3**), and need help to control yourself.

Someone gets hurt when you do things wrong – others and even you – it's not innocent – it's selfish, especially when you don't let Jesus help you and give you things when you need them (**matt. 6:33**) – if you would just go to Him.

And don't try to take revenge on people – just turn them in (if that is necessary) if they did something wrong to you (or others) – and make sure it's the truth. God will take care of them (and you) eventually. And if you can share Jesus, do it.

Even if someone hurts your feelings – try to understand and be aware – but share the truth – not in a mean way. It's not easy to deal with things in this world – so we need help. God made the world to have us deal with these (to lead us to Jesus).

If you don't have laws, prisons, police, etc., you will have revenge, harm, killing, etc. (we would have more today) – like before the flood – there were no laws just God there – with His spirit (if you wanted to be in the 'presence of the Lord' or not), some wanted to be with Him – most weren't, and evil reigned (**gen. 6**) – to the point that God repented that He made man (**gen. 6:6-7**). But He loves us and wants us – so He started over.

If you knew how evil man is, you would know why God does punish, and sometimes kill people over the years (they really kill themselves for their behavior, etc.) – but we should let Him do that, at all possible (sometimes we have to). All people need to be cared for in this evil, dangerous world, but especially children, women, elderly, disabled – mentally and physically, etc. Understanding satan (and demons) are here, too. We would be complaining that God didn't kill some people, but it is all for us, any problem is, for us to go to God – through Jesus.

You have to know right from wrong (we all do from adam – from the tree of good and evil – **gen. 3**), before you can teach right from wrong – we all know it (but may try to get away with things, because we are selfish, evil – born that way) – especially know it from God in the bible – you should want to know it. Go to Jesus (and His word) to learn it – and get the Holy Spirit to guide you (emotions, etc.).

Don't let your anger and hatred take you over and get the best of you – to hurt or bother others, and don't listen to or be persuaded by your family, friends, culture, etc. to hate or hurt or revenge, etc. (do only good things) – just go to Jesus and change and find out the truth. Don't have desires, lusts, habits, etc. (we are born with) that put you in a bad position in this life – that people (satan led, etc.)

can take advantage of you and hurt you and others – go to Jesus and have Him help you out of that life (and get the Holy Spirit from Him that will help you).

People that are not truly with Jesus (saved by the Holy Spirit), then they are the ones that are causing all of the problems for people here – with satan.

Jesus gives some tough advice in **matt. 5** – to deal with this evil world – but with Him it is possible. If not, we suffer the consequences here – especially without Him in our life. Go to Him and live a different and better life.

Maybe the jews and true Christians may not all take revenge, but the rest of the world may do it – so we need police, laws, prisons, etc. in this world. And we need to share Jesus.

You don't get anywhere or anything by living the life you lead (without Jesus and His word) – it will catch up to you – God (Jesus) can change that. He will show you or put things in your life to lead you.

When you are struggling, depressed, frustrated, etc. – think of people that are worse off than you – they are out there, and you have seen them. Go to Jesus to help you.

Sometimes you have to learn a lesson, etc. the hard way in life (because you don't listen, learn, control, etc.), and hopefully it leads you to Jesus (to learn, control, grow, etc.), and that you don't hurt anyone, etc. (or yourself), learning your lesson the hard way.

There are many people that have gone through what you are going through and have changed through Jesus – find out and talk to them – go to Jesus yourself, you are not the only one. They will be able to help you better, and you can help others like you better, if you have gone through a problem and then to Jesus to change. Help others.

Don't make things worse on other people – family, friends, etc., do good things. Go to Jesus and follow – don't do anything just for money, gain, etc. People cause their own problems and live any old way they want and get away with it – all trying to get away with things – not be good or have justice. This world has gotten to the point to where the rich get to do what they want – even women to a point, too, and also minorities are trying to do the same, because they all are victims, or have power – no one wants to do good or do the right thing (only in their own mind).

Women should be able to get away with crime, murder, etc. like men do, and minorities should be able to get away with crime, murder, etc., too, like others do. Then you will be equal. Is that what you want? Being equal will not get rid of our evil.

It may not happen a lot, but some people make themselves victims – so they can push their agenda, etc. and are trying to get attention. Need to give Jesus attention.

People – especially women – put themselves in danger, etc., because they want to be equal, bad behavior, etc. – a victim.

Be in the best group to be a victim with Jesus and His truth. He will help, otherwise you will continue to be a victim in this world – satan's victims, and your fault. Go to Jesus.

Jesus will make everyone equal – no matter what color, nationality, culture, male, female, etc. you are, and is the only way to do this – be equal. So stop fighting and arguing and hating, etc. – go to Jesus. Conform to what He wants for us.

All can be one – the same mind in Jesus (**1 cor. 1:10**) – what God wants for us – all of noah's sons.

Keep your eyes and mind on Jesus (and His truth – His word), like peter did, walking on water – and you can do great things – but don't take your eyes off of Jesus (and His word), or you will fail like peter **(matt. 14:29-33)**.

Both the guilty and the victim need help to get through whatever they do or happens to them – both need Jesus – the world is this way and will continue until you go to Jesus.

People use their position in life to take advantage of others – looking like they are helping, but really hurting, and just helping themselves. Go to Jesus for help.

People cover up their behavior to get whatever they can – being selfish – for things, at work, in relationships, etc. – an evil life, even if it is for just a moment.

No reason to cover for someone (especially if it is going to hurt people), people need to come forward and come clean – be honest, to help others. And always go to Jesus for your help.

Don't do things – lie, hurt, etc., just because you can, and the police will listen to, and believe you, etc. (all because you hate someone, etc. – and are in the victim category, etc.).

Don't lie or gossip about someone to make it look like it is alright to take from or hurt them – like they deserve it. There is no reason for that – it is just hate, jealousy, anger, etc. – selfish.

All of your problems may not be your fault, but some are (and sometimes most), and you need to go to Jesus to change that (we all are sinful, evil, etc.), and keep going to Him and know His truth, but don't hurt you or others. And don't hate yourself, just go to Jesus.

Even something as common as pregnancy (or periods, menopause, etc.), women sometimes take advantage of the emotional feelings, etc. – and the fact that men don't go through these things (even though they may take advantage of something else for themselves) – just for an excuse to yell, scream, be mean, even to eat unhealthy, be overweight, sick, etc. (basically let yourself go – you think you have an excuse). But at least make sure the babies are healthy – you be healthy, eat healthy, and then when they come, help the babies eat healthy, too, so go to Jesus for all you do.

God made man and woman different, but we all are evil, and need to go to Jesus and His word to change, and control what we do, and go through in this world. Don't make it worse. Just because you may be able to (or you think you have a reason).

Men also (and other women) have to be sensitive to this way that women are (or anyone), and what they are going through, as you would anyone that is struggling, etc., but talk and share what you might be going through, and how you feel, and be honest about the situation, and be as caring as you can be. Best to go to Jesus and pray and get through the tough times.

We all need to develop patience (**1 thess. 5:12-24**) – for we are not born that way – we are selfish. Go to Jesus to grow in all ways. And get along with people the best you can.

And try to reconcile with someone who hurt or offended, etc. you – but be understanding of their situation, too (**matt. 18:15**).

So be kind to each other and forgive like Jesus does us (**eph. 4:32**). We need to forgive people – understanding this is an evil world – and share Jesus with who you can and His truth. To help them change and grow.

So it is best not to say anything (but should share what is needed for the situation, even if it may upset), than to lie – hopefully you can tell the truth in love – not hatred, revenge, envy, etc. We all do things in this life – make mistakes. Just try to work it out and share Jesus (or get to know Him and His word). Keep going to Him, so we can grow, and mature.

People do need to speak up about injustices, abuse, etc. – not to let it continue to stay in families, cultures, etc. – it won't change or stop until you do – change with Jesus and His word – the only way. Or stop complaining about your life. Do what God wants, and you get the things you need, and help others.

So don't ruin or waste your abilities, or talents, etc. with bad living – hanging out with bad people or following them – family or friends, or not. Go to Jesus instead to overcome your problems.

Christians (true Christians) are not the enemy – who does that leave? – all of noah's sons – all of us, that are not with Jesus (not having the Holy Spirit) – and not connected to God (and His truth), but connected to man (adam, noah's sons).

It's a selfish thing (and ego, arrogance, pride, etc.) – what man wants (each of noah's sons today, after the flood – **gen. 9**, as man did before the flood – **gen. 6**), bothering others (go to Jesus to get along), we have to get beyond the different color and abilities (and beliefs, etc.) – and not stay with (or be connected to) noah's sons (or adam), but go to Jesus – and connect to God with the Holy Spirit.

We are all different from adam – dna, fingerprints, etc. (God created us that way from the beginning), and even more after the flood (appearance, etc.), but we are the same – human race (**acts 17:24-28**) and are all connected to man – adam and noah's sons. We wouldn't need to evolve to have fingerprints that are different (for us to survive, etc.), and we didn't find those out until recently (so evolutionists could believe their – and satan's – lies, then God showed the truth) – God made us each different – **psalm 139:13-18** (special to Him, but we are all human, born sinful, and need Jesus). We have to know the truth of Him and His word. Now they all need to believe God's word and believe Him and His truth (or be stubborn and prideful and kept living in denial).

And just knowing of God or hearing of God (or even seeing the Lord), is not enough to change or save you (like you see with judas – **matt. 26; matt. 27:1-10**), as some have found out from the beginning (**gen. 4:3-16, matt. 7:21-23, matt. 26:24-25; matt. 27:3-5; luke 22:3-6; john 6:70-71; 1 cor. 15:1-8**), but God can use these people for His purposes and examples (**acts 1:15-18; rom. 9:14-24**) – God uses who He wants, how He wants them, God says who is who, He has mercy or hardened hearts (**exo. 33:16**), servant or master, and the heathen – gentiles (**lev. 25, mal. 1:11; matt. 18:15-17; gal. 1:15-16; gal. 3:8**), etc. He doesn't force you to believe, but knows what you will decide. So be with God – to be on His side – to lead you.

So God controls and leads this world to go the way and direction He wants it to go – to help man go to Him – to Jesus.

Noah's sons can all do what they want, and God can use all of noah's sons for His purposes – but God still controls or allows, etc., and may punish if they don't follow what He wants. We still need to go to Jesus (and His word) to know the truth.

And without Jesus, man follows satan (who God allows here, because of man's sin), but God wants all to go to Him – to Jesus – to connect back to Him (that adam separated us from).

People can be smart, tough, strong, etc., but God may still not use them doing things in this world – or to be listened to, be in charge, etc. – only what God wants and says – any of noah's sons – He put them (noah's sons) and what they do (**gen. 9:25-27**) and they are all different and separated in the world (after the flood – mainly after the tower of babel – the language change – separating us – **gen. 10; gen. 11**). We are all from them today – from man (**gen. 9:18-19**). Until we go to Jesus.

We that know we are sick (sinful, etc.) are the ones that go to get well – so those will go to Jesus to heal (get saved – get the Holy

Spirit) – we all are sick (sinful – from adam – **gen. 3**), but don't all think that we are, and don't go to Jesus (**luke 5:31-32**). Go to Jesus.

Jesus blessed those that haven't seen Him (or the things He did then) – we still believe (**john 20:28-31**) and get the Holy Spirit – then learn and grow in His word. The whole world can go to Jesus – and can be saved – no matter how terrible you are.

God calls all gentiles, heathen (basically hedonistic, etc. – we all are evil, without the true God) – all of noah's sons (we still are connected to them, without Jesus), whatever ability they have, or color they are today, etc. – they are all evil. And some people and countries are worse than others, but all evil and guilty (even in america without Jesus). And you can still see how bad it is in the world today – and it gets worse the more you get away from Jesus and His word – truth, especially in america. We need God (Jesus) to change that.

If you want mercy – stop ignoring God (Jesus), and stop going against His word (His word is best for us, and for others), and having pleasure in (and associating with, and thinking it is good to live that way) those that do that (**rom. 1:32**). Don't fight for those ways of living, belief, etc. against God and His word. Give yourself a chance to live a better life – don't go against God (and His word – the truth), no matter how kind you think you are being to anyone. Only with Jesus can you do this properly. And you need to keep going back to Him, when you fall.

People can do what they want in their life – to change, grow, etc., especially in america with Jesus – which is freedom. Everyone has problems, flaws, etc. – we are not perfect – basically evil, but you don't need to think they are alright for you (or others) to do – they are against God (and His word) – so don't promote these evil things (what you think you are born with, etc.) – they are not good for anyone. So go to Jesus to find the answers, not man (or yourself).

God loves us even when we are not perfect – we just have to keep going to Him and His truth – go to Jesus.

Everyone wants to be free – but can't be without Jesus – countries and people struggle against each other throughout history and today (**james 4**) – they don't realize they won't ever be free – until they go to Jesus. We need to wise up and go to Him. Share Him and His word.

We are all connected and affect each other (initially from adam, and now from noah's sons – and God separated us, **acts 17:24-28**) – and we need to be connected to God through Jesus. He wants you to choose Him and have the free will to do that – see His truth in this world (**rom. 1**).

We have free will to go to Jesus or not – to go to heaven or hell – we choose. Basically, stay with man (noah's sons, our people, etc.) or go to God through Jesus. But God wants us all to go to heaven and be with Him forever (but He knows all won't do that). Go to Jesus and get saved. It is best for all.

God set the world up to have man make choices – to go to Him or not. God tries to not interfere too much – but enough to go to show us truth and a way out, throughout history – especially Jesus dying for us all. Things we can fight satan here with. So we need to go to Jesus for our life here – what God wants, but it is our choice – and God will show us things to tell us and help us with that choice (Jesus and His truth, or satan and his lies).

And Jesus set up a country (america) to use your God-given abilities, talents, etc., and brains to succeed and help others, too. As long as we go to Him – for everyone (all of noah's sons) to have opportunities to succeed, if you want – by working hard. The freedom to do that – like america. America is founded on true Christianity and the bible, and works because of that (even with satan and evil people in this country trying to ruin it). It is best with Jesus – like america is. Jesus is freedom.

And america shows that more than any nation – the way God wanted it – to have man (all of noah's sons) – to all have a chance to go to God – to Jesus.

America – with it's freedom, prosperity, power, etc., has influenced other countries in the world over the years – but need Jesus and the truth of His word to help the best for anyone, or any nation. And needs to stay that way to work.

God doesn't want it to be what man makes in this world to work or be right (even if you are rich and it looks like what you say or do must be correct – it isn't – even satan can make you rich – but this world is not what you want to do at all costs – the death of your soul in hell) – it is following what God wants in His word – the truth and Jesus. And God will bless a nation (and your life here – to afford your life – not necessarily rich, but live comfortably with Jesus and His truth in your life). And all are welcome to go to Jesus – which is why america is great. America is Christian – and why it is free – with Jesus and His truth. All people (all of noah's sons) can become one with Him (but it has to be the truth).

America means freedom, but mainly the u. s., but not central or south america, and canada gets benefited by the u. s.

As much as people want to be equal – men, women, nationalities, etc. – you can't be more equal (even though we are all better in america) without Jesus, and we will stay unequal without Him. Go to Him and get Him in your life (**rom. 10:8-18**), and get the Holy Spirit, that He will give you.

Without Jesus and His word – His truth – america is not free – and no one will be equal or have a chance to be. And we won't get along without Jesus – and still be stuck with man – noah's sons, and adam.

And however far equality goes, you will still have man fighting each other – women fighting each other – all of noah's sons fighting each other – because nothing will ever be good enough. Only Jesus will be best for man – whatever nationality.

Why is it that women – eve (**gen. 3:16** – and that is still in effect today), minorities – mainly ham (**gen. 9:24-27** – and that is still in effect today), and also including homosexuals, transgenders, etc. – those against God and His word (**rom. 1:18-32** – and that is still in effect today) are all trying to be equal, be heard in the world, etc.? – because those are who God cursed and put limitations on more than everyone else (and satan uses them against God). And they are all trying to be equal and get ahead, without Jesus (and His truth – His word). We all are limited and need to go to Jesus, and only then can we be one (**gal. 3:27-29**). The only way that it will ever work. And eventually be one in heaven (out of this cursed world of satan's).

And why are the laws and peoples' opinions, etc. protecting women and minorities? – because satan knows those are the ones who God cursed and are limited, and satan knows it will cause hatred, killing, etc. against God and His word, and also against those people in this world (thinking that we can or should all be equal without God – Jesus, but we can't). But it should get us to go to God and His word – through Jesus.

But treat all people good, and share Jesus and His truth with them. And america (Jesus' land) tries to do that – but only with Jesus we can, but not all go to Jesus or know the truth of His word (even churches, leaders, etc.).

So if you want to get rid of cursed mankind – especially to ham (and descendants), and women, then we all go to Jesus to get rid of them, or they still will be there. No matter how hard we try to change the world. But none of it will be truly gone, until heaven, but it will be better for you here. You go to Him.

Don't let satan change God's creation – man – by mutilating, false worship, etc. – let God help you with Jesus.

No matter what you did or what you are – or think you are, Jesus will forgive you, if you go to Him and believe Him and His word, then you will follow Him (getting saved – with the Holy Spirit) and change, before you die.

Going against what God has set up (the separations, and the limitations of some people here) – and what man has done here – is what causes all of the problems for man. Trying to fight for equality, togetherness, etc. without God (Jesus) and His word, is a waste of time. That's why Jesus came here. Go to Jesus and change.

<u>JES</u>loves**<u>US</u>**

That is God with us – that is what Emmanuel means (**matt. 1:20-25**) – God with us, which is Jesus. God came to us. We didn't go to Him. We need Him to change the way it is here. And only Jesus can do that. We tried many ways – man won't and can't do it.

If God set this world up (which He did – limited man, woman, and satan, as well as the creation – **gen. 3**) – after man sinned (and even more after the flood – **gen. 11**) – then we have to live with the unfairness, inequality, evil, separation, etc. (punishments, etc. here) that is in this world by man (our fault because of sin) – and only can be remedied by God – by going to Jesus (and the truth of His word). And all of noah's sons have to go to Jesus to change from what they are connected to (man, sin, and satan – this world) and what lot in life they have (cursed or limited, etc., by God) – we mainly have ourselves to blame. Then we need to get connected to God through Jesus and the truth of His word, with the Holy Spirit.

Why does God say don't follow certain people or marry certain people – from noah's sons – all through the bible – even the jews not to be with gentiles? God did the separating. Go to God – to Jesus, to get back together. Why He came here.

Even if there was going to be 'equality' for anyone (man's programs, efforts, protests, etc.) – for minorities (ham), women, homosexuals, transgenders, etc. – they will never be happy (they just think they will be, and find out they won't be – because it will never be enough) without Jesus and His word. Get away from man (adam, now noah's sons) and be connected to God (Jesus). And He will change you to what He wants.

No matter what person you are – any curse, limitation, nationality, what son of noah you are, healthwise, disabled, divorced, criminal, into drugs, alcohol, etc. – anyone can be saved, and we need to be – only Jesus can do that, and needs to be done before you die (we all know of Jesus – **john 1:9; rom. 1:18-22; titus 2:11-15**, no excuse). Then we can be one with Jesus.

Anyone that wants equality, etc. – go to Jesus and humble yourself and do His will (in the truth of His word) and He will raise you up (**matt. 23:11-12**). All can do this.

We are all cursed and sinful – from adam (continued through noah's sons today) – but especially women (eve) – from the beginning (**gen. 3**), and ham (and his descendants) – after the flood (**gen. 9:24-27**) – but they (and all of us) would be better off with Jesus. We need to go to Jesus to change – and if we don't, satan uses that against man in this world. We won't get along or have equality, without Jesus.

All men (women) are created equal (after sin – **gen. 3**) – all are from sinful man (adam and eve), and we need Jesus to get away from what we all are born with, like adam (**gen. 5:3**). With Jesus we can all be equal. Become new – all in Jesus and be one – equal. Jesus is the only way (**eph. 4**) – born again (**john 3**), with the Holy Spirit.

We are all cursed under the law, until you go to Jesus (**gal. 3:10-14**) – all of noah's sons (and some may be more than others – but all are sinful, and need to go to Jesus). So we will never be equal like we want here, without Jesus.

We need to know the truth of His word and this world (and why Jesus wrote the bible, and came here – **john 1**).

The closest that man would look like man was trying to grow and did change, and get used to this world, would be after the flood – when man's appearance changed, because of the difference in the world before and after the flood. And man's life span diminished (down to 120 years at the most – **gen. 6:3** – a punishment by God, along with the flood and change of our environment – the earth). So the son's of noah had to get used to the new world after the flood – especially after the tower of babel (**gen. 11**) and the language change, that separated man around the world. The flood causing all of the fossils we see and find around the world – which would make man think we evolved, etc., but we didn't (including the mutations that the fallen angels made in man, before the flood – **gen. 6:1-4**). We are all created by God – from adam (**gen. 1 and 2**), but now sinful (**gen. 3**), and separated from God (mainly by satan – by adam and eve listening to him, as we do since then, even today). And we all need to go to Jesus to change that.

And there is just one race – mankind – from adam – we only look different after the flood (especially after the tower of babel), because of the earth being destroyed by God – changing the weather, geography, climate, etc. Even though there were some different people before the flood (not like today) – helped by fallen angels (**gen. 6**) – and just after the flood (initially with noah's sons, but all looked and talked the same – **gen. 11**) – the way we look today didn't happen until after the tower of babel (about 100 years after the flood – ham leading and japheth and shem following – all against God and His truth – **gen. 11**), then we started to look different about

400 years or so after that the tower (and language change), since we lived longer at that time to engrain the traits we have (**gen. 9 and 10**). People that do things against God and His word (white or black, etc.) are racists, lawless, etc. – mainly ham – especially canaan – even japheth and shem can be if they follow man, when they don't follow Jesus. It is noah (who God put in charge – **gen. 6:8-10, 18; gen. 9:17**, for all of us – made a covenant for all of us after the flood – like God did isaac for jacob – israel, instead of esau, the elder – for the birthright – and where the jews came from – jacob, not esau – **gen. 27**) who cursed (or punished) ham (especially his son canaan), and he (and his descendants) became servants of his brothers (japheth and shem – **gen. 9:22-27**), and still are today – that hasn't changed, and we still will be until we go to Jesus (and away from man – away from all of noah's sons). So stop talking about racism, etc. – it is not a topic or word, etc. – we are all the same – one race (**acts 17:24-28**). God caused us to be different (changed colors, etc. after the flood and the tower of babel – **gen. 11** – who was led by ham – nimrod – **gen. 10:6-20** – physical people, who led all people against God, and is part of the punishment, besides to canaan), and it is God that can only change us – so we only can be one with Jesus (getting away from man – who we all still are connected to today – until we all go to Jesus). We won't get along any other way – as you can see in the world – and it has to be the truth. And canaan (ham) may have been led by satan (and with demons – fallen angels), basically after the flood (**gen. 10:6-20; num. 13**). They (ham) are the physical, and cursed – **gen. 9:20-27** (even though we all are from adam – **gen. 3:17-19**) people (but still can go to Jesus and be saved and change – away from noah's sons). All of noah's sons have problems.

Japheth and shem build, experiment, invent, etc., but not all that God wanted, especially after the jews (shem) rejected Jesus (which did eventually lead the jews all over the world, like you see today) – God may keep the jews down, but america gives all a chance and has (because of Jesus) – leading to the end times (with God allowing the jews to be in their own land again – since 1948).

But all of noah's sons can do manual labor, but all are not as good as ham is, and they even like it more (and why ham always lives simple, primitive, etc. – anywhere, but especially outside of – and before – america) – but they can learn other things (especially in america where the opportunity is there for all – because of freedom, and from Jesus). And all of the sons are needed to improve and build, technology, etc. And since people have gone all over the world – especially japheth, they have helped ham everywhere to modernize places (**gen. 9:25-27**) – like you see in america – as well as other places. We are all still from one of noah's sons, until we go to Jesus to be one (and have a chance to get along).

There are no cave man days, etc. – and the longest time ago (before the flood), and man was smart from the beginning of time (from adam and eve – **gen. 1 and 2**) – maybe even smarter than we are today. But fallen angels (demons) messed with man (**gen. 6:1-7**) and caused man to look different, and God had to destroy man (except for noah and his family – **gen. 6:8**). And why we all come from one of noah's sons (**gen. 9**). Mostly all of man was against God then, and we are getting that way now.

And all of noah's sons have helped each other with their talents and abilities throughout history (with all of the empires of the world) – starting over after the flood – and why you see the world more modern, etc. – which is more evident in america (with all of noah's sons).

And with that improvement in technology, each of noah's sons – and even each nationality wants to take credit for making the most and best, but it is God that helps this world grow and we use His talents that He gave us to do that. So don't think you are better than others, etc. – and don't try to show that – feeling we don't need God. All that does is cause problems for man and this world (and has all through history). We all (all of noah's sons) are from God (and all sinful from adam). And need to go to Him – Jesus (to be saved and get away from man – noah's sons). And find out what we can do and what God wants us to do. See the differences God made in each of us – in all of noah's sons (and God made it that way – **gen. 9:24-27**). And the only way to become one is with Jesus. So stop trying to show you are better – God made you the way you are (not yourself), and satan is trying to get man to ignore God and go to man (really satan), and think more of yourself, just like satan did (**isa. 14:12-18**).

Even though we all have certain talents – and we can learn most things (especially around each other, and in america) – we need to behave and live a good life (all of noah's sons) – with Jesus you can.

Shem helps with family, society, laws, business, etc. (mainly with God and the jews – the tents of shem – **gen. 9:27**), and helps japheth and ham keep together with those things and you can see that in the world – especially in america (and we all can take advantage of that). Even though all of noah's sons try to have family, rules, etc. in any tribe or nation throughout the years (even without any of the other sons), but may not know the true God. All after the flood (and especially after the tower of babel – **gen. 11**).

So don't blame others (of noah's sons) for your problems (even though we can be nicer to each other – and help each other) – we all are connected to the evil past in our own family, culture, nationality, etc., since the beginning – so don't just go back a couple hundred years, etc., but to the beginning – to adam and eve (**gen. 3:20-21**), and now with noah's sons (**gen. 9**). We can all go to Jesus.

It's Jesus and the truth of His word that makes it any good for any of noah's sons – especially ham – and especially in america. We are all free, because of Jesus, to have opportunities, be successful, etc. – so keep america with Jesus and with you. You have a choice.

People all have opportunities in america – all of noah's sons, and some take advantage of it – controlling parts of the country and certain businesses, ideas, trends, etc. – even shem (jews) in hollywood, pharmacies, and other businesses, etc. – sometimes hurting people and going against Jesus (Jesus wants the jews to go to Him, too). All of the sons of noah do that – japheth and ham, too. Many types of people are against God – Jesus, all of noah's sons are taking advantage of opportunities in america – not always in a good way. But also false churches, religions, beliefs, etc. are taking advantage of people, and america. Everyone is to blame – all of noah's sons. So we don't need to go after any of the sons more than the others, but need to get all to go to Jesus to have things work best in this world (especially america). And share Him with all (but the truth). The only answer. He wants them all. Then have a chance to get along.

God allows all of this evil (satan, etc.) so that man has a choice (free will), and God will see what each person is attracted to in their heart and will choose where they want to spend eternity – heaven or hell – with Jesus or not. And for Him to see how you would want to live your life here, before you go.

God wants us to go to Him – through Jesus. To choose Him – make that decision to change (before you die). Best with Him.

People that come to america (Jesus' land) from other countries, do well here – not because of their belief (whatever they believe in their own country), but because of the freedom with Jesus here (and having a chance to be free to grow, learn, etc.), and the opportunities to show their abilities (of noah's sons). All people have a chance if they would just do that, especially with Jesus. Without Jesus and His word, it won't work.

Jesus is why america is so successful and helps so many people – like God gave the jews (**josh. 1:6-9**), if we would follow Him and the truth of His word with Jesus. We need to all be for God.

All of noah's sons were working together (like america is today – bringing the sons back together, but with God) – just after the flood (by the time of the tower of babel – **gen. 11** – about 100 years or so after the flood – **gen. 10:25; gen. 11:16-19**), but it was all against God – so God separated the sons from each other from then on (even today – trying to bring them together in america – and this modern world, until we can all be together with Jesus – at least have a chance to be).

We can all be friends with any of noah's sons – especially if we grow up doing things (school, sports, work, etc.), or have similar interests. We need to try to get along, otherwise most won't, but it is best (and possible) with Jesus.

Going against God – Jesus, and His word is what causes all of the problems here for us – since the beginning (**gen. 3**), even for the jews, and for all of us today.

All of the separations that God made are man's fault – your fault, our fault, and if you want to change that (and the problems you see in the world), then go to Jesus and have others do the same (don't be stubborn, prideful, etc.). He is the only answer (we've tried and seen it all in this world, and history, with man – **eccl. 1 to 3**). And God did all of this – the separations, etc., because He loves us so much (it is best for us while we are here, to give us all a chance – more problems, and more time, and reasons, to go to Him – Jesus). And since God wants everyone to go to Him (**john 3:16**) – the world will only get along when we go to Him, otherwise it won't – all need to go to Jesus (and we all have known of Him - **john 1:9-14**). To the way it originally was, the way He created adam and eve to be – one with God. And the way it will be in heaven.

Wherever you were born – country, family, parents, nationality, beliefs, etc., you have had a chance to know of Jesus – even your parents did. God put you where you were born in this world – and knows if you will go to Jesus – all have had a choice (and still do, if you are alive). Any people have to get used to living and surviving wherever they live in this world (now and in the past) – born there or maybe want to live – no matter what the weather, geography, conditions, etc. Best is to go to Jesus and let Him help you wherever you are or go.

Try to get along with people and you will have less problems – some people have trouble with that and hurt themselves. Going to Jesus will help you with that – get away from sin and man – noah's sons. Go to Jesus.

All people (all of noah's sons) know of the true God (**titus 2:11-12**) and salvation – through Jesus (**john 1:9-12; rom. 1:18-25**) throughout history – no excuse – so we can share Jesus and that may help those go to Him – share Him, and stir things up in them. They have to choose, but may be too proud or stubborn to go to Him.

God will open doors for all people – all of noah's sons – mainly to get to know Jesus, and especially in america.

The world needs love (the love of Jesus, and the love of His word) – and only Jesus can give it the best (or at all). For all people – all of noah's sons. To have a chance to get along.

And man is not going to do what God says – including love Him and one another (**matt. 22:34-40; mark 12:28-34; luke 10:26-28; rom. 13:9-10; gal. 5:14**, and as He told the jews to do to other jews – **lev. 19:18**) – or at least have a chance to this – unless we go to Jesus and follow Him and the truth of His word – with the Holy Spirit (that we get saved with, from Jesus – **john 14:15-21; 2 cor. 1:21-22; eph. 1:12-14; eph. 4:30**).

Jesus is nothing like the other prophets, religious leaders, gods, and is not an angel, etc. – He is God, and Creator (**col. 1:12-20; col. 2:6-10**), above all of them and us (He created them and us, including satan, angels, etc. – **gen. 1; john 1,** and they have choices, too, and some have made their choice), and He is the Savior for all of us (all of man today) that go to Him (salvation from no one else – **acts 4:10-12; 1 tim. 2:3-6; titus 1:4**). And now we all have to make a choice, before we die (**heb. 9:27**) – Jesus is for salvation or judgment, you choose. Look at yourself and the world – heaven or hell. And you don't know when anyone is going to die (can happen at any time to you or others you know) – and we can't go to heaven without Jesus (no matter how nice we are, or think we are) – so you might as well share Jesus with all you can. And the churches, leaders, etc. better know the truth about Him and His word. And share where they may go, and how and why.

Angels (and satan) that sin (fallen angels, demons, etc.) would go to hell or chains, etc., if they disobeyed God (some have – **2 pet. 2:4; jude 1:6**), but God uses (and used) them to tempt man – who can be saved – man (adam) created originally in His image, and can choose. So satan, angels, man, are forever somewhere (heaven, or hell – eventually the lake of fire, **rev. 20:10, 14-15**) – satan, fallen angels have made their decision (hell – lake of fire), so man has to make his (heaven or hell). We all will be somewhere. Go to Jesus.

Demons, devils, gods, etc. are fallen angels, and God, Jesus, and the Holy Spirit are more powerful. And God (Jesus) created angels, man, etc. – everything and everyone. And satan, angels, etc. went away from God from the beginning – after creation.

We will all bow down to Jesus some day (dead or alive – **rom. 14:9-12; philip. 2:9-11**), so we need to do it before we die to be in heaven with Him forever. That's why Jesus came here. He is best for all of us – no matter what son of noah you are from.

And Jesus defeated satan, sin, death, etc. and so can we (**rom. 6**), but only with Him. Go to Him now and get away from satan, and this world – evil, sinful, man, noah's sons, etc.

God allows satan to be in this world (**book of job**), and to separate man (from God and His truth) – if man wants to, and to be attracted to lies, evil, other gods, etc. (which is really satan). And we all can go to God (through Jesus), but He will not force you – you have free will, a choice, and He gives us examples for good, and evil (with satan) in this world to make a better decision. We should be glad that God gave us (and angels) free will (to see the difference), but it has caused all of our problems (choosing not to be with Him) – brought on by us (and satan), and God didn't want us that way, but man went that way, and God has to do something (make this a tough world), because it's not good for us to be without Him.

We are not made in God's image or are sons of God until we go to Jesus and get the Holy Spirit (get born again – **john 3**) – that adam lost for us all – so we are made in man's – adam's (**gen. 5:3**), image now (all born without the Holy Spirit), and are from one of noah's sons today (**gen. 9:18-19; gen. 10 and 11** – even though it is God's image that was used to make man – adam, and continued with noah's sons, and after, with the same human – **gen. 9:6**).

And there are no new revelations since Jesus died and rose – the bible is complete – so there is nothing more to write, except leading people to Jesus and the bible to know the truth, to go to Jesus to get the Holy Spirit to be saved (and be ready to go). God the Father, the Son, and Holy Spirit came to man over the years (**acts 7**), but only the Holy Spirit now (through Jesus).

The oldest any belief (religion, etc.) could be is about 4200 – 4300 years old (just after the flood – over 100 years after the flood – after the tower of babel – **gen. 11**) – the jews (by God) started about 4,000 years ago with abraham (**gen. 17**). And anything after Jesus died and rose (and the temple destroyed, and the bible completed – anywhere from 70ad to 90ad), would be from satan (basically the last 2,000 years) – and satan is also the one who says (and man follows – being born evil) that the world (universe, etc.) is billions of years old (evolution, etc. – there is no proof of that), it is not, it is only about 6,000 years old. It is satan that keeps trying to fool man and keep man from believing the truth of the bible (with false ideas and false religions, and even churches, etc.). So there is nothing older than about 4300 years (just after the flood) – no beliefs, civilizations, etc. – just God starting over. Anything else that is believed or come up with (there is no proof), is just satan lying to man (and man follows, just so man doesn't have to believe in Jesus) – which is his goal – be against God and His truth – the bible. Go to Jesus and get the Holy Spirit. Know the truth.

Even then (before the bible was completed – first with the **four gospels – matt., mark, luke, and john**), the risen Jesus came to paul (and eventually to anyone – especially the gentiles after that, through paul's writings – that the risen Jesus, not the apostles, gave to paul – **gal. 1**), and saved him (**acts 9**) – just paul (or anyone) only going to Jesus and getting saved (getting the Holy Spirit) – no church, etc. (know it's Jesus and not satan), if you really want to change and know the truth. Now the Holy Spirit is in true believers (**1 cor. 6:19-20**). People were still being saved – like the ethiopian eunuch (by philip) with Jesus' earthly ministry (**acts 8:26-40** – and philip preached for a while more), before paul got saved (**acts 9**), and Jesus had paul start his ministry to the gentiles (that Jesus died and rose for us all – **1 cor. 15:1-4**) – mainly after peter went to a gentile's home (**acts 10 and 11**) and the gentile got saved (got the Holy Spirit, without water baptism – not like in Jesus' earthly ministry to the jews – that peter and the disciples were still doing – and that was different than what Jesus had paul do with the gentiles – and everyone being saved since, with paul's ministry). Even aquila and apollos, etc. (both jews) that preached (**acts 18 and 19**) – mainly preached what peter did (and Jesus did before He died and rose) – and peter and the disciples stayed in israel (near the temple) for the jews – the church was growing (God leading) and changing to what the risen Jesus wanted paul to do (eventually paul teaching timothy, and to us today – **rom. 2:16; rom. 16:25**). And peter (and the disciples) and paul agreed to their ministries (**gal. 1 and 2**). And eventually peter's ministry (the jews) disappeared (Jesus earthly ministry), and paul's ministry – to the world (from the risen Jesus) is what we go by to be saved.

And peter and the disciples were with Jesus on the mount of olives (or olivet), before Jesus died – and Jesus tells them the end times (**matt. 24**), and after Jesus died and rose, He came back to the mount of olives with the disciples (**acts 1:1-14**), to tell them He will give them the Holy Spirit (**acts 2**), and what to do (mainly stay in jerusalem) – until He comes back – to the mount of olives sometime soon. Even in **zech. 14** it predicts Jesus will come back to the mount of olives – now in the tribulation, and then the 1,000 year reign of Jesus.

So peter and the disciples of Jesus (Jesus' earthly ministry to the jews) were to get the nation of israel to go to Jesus (**matt. 10:5-7; matt. 15:22-24; acts 11:19**), because after Jesus died and rose, the jews could have believed, but once the disciples died (except john) that ended that possibility. Then john wrote the **book of revelation** to and for the jews (as were all of the books from **hebrews to revelation** were for the jews). And Jesus will come back for them (the nation of israel) in the tribulation.

And when Jesus was here, He didn't go against the leaders of rome (or the world) or fight them, etc. (because His kingdom is not of this world – **john 18:33-40**) – He only went against the leaders of the jews (religious, etc. – His people), who were supposed to follow God and His word – the truth, including Jesus – just like the Christians are to do today. We need to keep sharing Jesus and His truth in His word to the world – and still, His kingdom is not of this world. Keep going to His word and to Jesus and share His truth to those you know and around you. He will be back soon today.

So Jesus didn't come back soon then (and to the disciples), because the nation of israel didn't follow Jesus (even after He died and rose), so He didn't come back to the mount of olives (and would have before the temple destroyed in 70ad – He would have if the jews all were to follow Him). Jesus will come back for all who believe and follow Him – in the air with a shout for all to see (the rapture – **1 cor. 15:50-54; 1 thess. 4:13-18**) – not to the mount of olives then – since the jews rejected Him – He only would have before the temple was destroyed (He gave them 40 years for all the jews to believe and follow Him), and the disciples still alive.

And Jesus didn't want people – jews mainly, but romans, too – to know who He is, because He needed to die for us all (**matt. 16:20-21**). So He had to be put in the position of being killed here, but He did want all of us to eventually know He was God, the Messiah, and the Savior of the world – especially after He died and rose from the dead (**1 cor. 15:1-11; heb. 1**).

So israel rejected Jesus – before and after He died (as adam and eve rejected God, and brought sin to man and the world – **gen. 3**, and eventually the flood – **gen. 6** – and to noah's sons). And God was always going to have salvation for the whole world (gentiles included) – for all of us (noah's sons) to have a choice of salvation – God's plan – even the reason for the jews to be developed – so He could show us the true God and share His truth – the bible. And have Jesus come here (to die and rise first for all of man's sins), so we could all have a choice to be with God.

So God put together a group for Him – after the flood – the jews. He raised them up and help direct them (and had them write the bible). Not being run by man (or satan), but by God (even though they are still sinners – and always had to go to God to forgive their sins with sacrifices, etc.). But they didn't always stay with God (He warned them, and He punished them – **deut. 18:9-14**), and they eventually rejected Jesus when He was sent here for them (**deut. 18:15-19; dan.**

9:24-27), and God eventually went to the gentiles – who were being run by man (and satan), but are now run by Jesus (those who go to Him and follow Him and His word – true Christians).

But Jesus (risen) could have come back for the jews (as a nation) after He died and rose (before 70ad – when He destroyed the temple) – if the jews, as a nation, would have believed and followed Him – then He would have used the jews to evangelize the world (gone around the world to the gentiles – and wouldn't have needed to send paul) going with Jesus for seven years (the last seven years the jews owe God – of the 490 years – **dan. 9:24-27**) – now those seven years are still to come (so far a big 2,000 year time out) – the tribulation (is for the jews – and all non-Christians, false Christians, etc.). The end times are for the jews (like when Jesus was here – with the romans, etc.) – and is getting close today. Jesus to come back soon for them. it will be the day of the Lord for them (**zech. 14:1-9; matt 24**). Then lead to Jesus' 1,000 year reign.

So those 490 years of daniel (**dan. 9**) stopped at 483 years, and will start up with the 484th year when the tribulation starts (just after the rapture of the church – and america diminished, etc.) coming soon. And it will be for the jews, and again the roman empire (something like it – **rev. 17**) will rule the world (and you can see it getting that way now, with america going in the wrong direction, etc. – getting away from God and the truth of His word), and will pick up where it left off when Jesus was here – at His death.

Man is ruining this world (and man), by man (and satan) following man (noah's sons), instead of God and His word (and going to Jesus). Man follows opinions, political ideas, beliefs, etc. (all satanic), but not God and His word. So man makes it tough in this world.

Besides adam – who we are sinners from (along with satan) – we are also connected to one of noah's sons, and are limited or cursed by their problems – until we go to Jesus – the way God set it up to today (**gen. 9:24-27**).

This world and people have done what they believed is right in their own eyes (led by satan and his lies), not what God wants and says (**judges 21:25**) – and you see that happening today – going against and away from God's truth in His word (even in churches, etc.) – not going to Jesus, and sharing His truth.

And why we need to go to Jesus more now than ever – and He will be coming back – to end the world (mainly for the jews, but whoever is still here in the seven year tribulation, after the rapture of the TRUE believers). Be ready with Him, and share His truth with others.

Jesus came to fulfill the prophesies (many verses) written in the old testament (especially **dan. 9:24**).

Jesus came here for the jews only at first – and He has to finish the covenants and promises to the jews – that He didn't finish when He died and rose (but could have after He died and rose – but the jews – as a nation, still did not believe in Him, even though they saw Him alive after He died – **1 cor. 15:1-6** – and it could have happened before 70ad when the temple was destroyed, and since then the jews have to wait for those covenants and promises to be fulfilled in the tribulation) – God always will do what He says – no matter what man does. And He will do that in the tribulation, coming soon.

Some of the covenants and promises have been completed, and some haven't – like the sin of adam (through noah – after the flood) is still here for man until you go to Jesus, the punishment of the flood for man is still here (we were all the same until after flood, and the tower of babel – **gen. 9 and 10 and 11**), as well as God's promise with the rainbow (after the flood), and we all are from one of noah's sons (no jews until after abraham) – and stay with them and their lot in life – our limitations we have here (even today) – from whatever son we are from (**gen. 9:18-27**). And will stay that way until we truly believe in Jesus – and why you still see all of the problems (hate, prejudice, etc.) in this world still. God sent Jesus – to for a reason – help us.

Jesus could have saved Himself – like the thief on the cross asked (as others did, too) – if He is God (Messiah, the Christ). Why doesn't He save Himself (and not die – **matt. 27:40-43; mark 15:29-31; luke 23:39**)? Because He had to die for all of us (jews included, if they would just go to Him). Even that thief – was sinful man, went to heaven with Jesus, and the other thief could have, too, if he would have believed – but he didn't (**luke 23:39-43**) – we all can turn and go to Jesus. That alone should have some people believing – besides the fact that He rose from the dead, and many people saw Him (**1 cor. 15:1-8**) – but obviously they didn't want to believe He is who He said He was – the Messiah, Christ, Savior – God. And it goes on today.

Jesus lowered Himself – from His level as God, to come here to help – He didn't need to do that for Him, but for us. Now we need to lower or humble ourselves and admit we are sinners (and destined for hell – **john 3:17-21**), and go to Jesus to be saved (**john 3:16; 1 cor. 15:1-4**), and get the Holy Spirit (born again – **john 3:1-8**).

It would be like man looking at ant pile, and wondering what it would be like to be one of them, and then go down and become an ant and live with them for a while. You probably wouldn't do that, but Jesus came here in this evil world, and came to save evil man. And had to pay for our sins (and the only One that could pay for our sins), and suffer a cruel death, to give us a choice to be with God in heaven forever.

So Jesus didn't have to come here (lower, humble Himself – **heb. 2**) – God didn't need to help us, unless He loves us and wants a relationship with us – those who follow Him, and why we were created by God in the first place. And now we can be in heaven with Him forever, through Jesus.

The jews were looking for a political or power leader in the world, etc. – not the Godly leader that Jesus was – the Messiah (who might take away the religious power of the jewish leaders at the time), so they rejected Him, and killed Him (**dan. 9:24-27**). So the jews will look for that same type of person (their Messiah) in the seven year tribulation, and be fooled, and follow him – which will be the anti-christ (**rev. 13**) – all people will.

So jews see Jesus as a stumbling block, because they went away from God and were being run by man, and God went to the gentiles with Jesus – even though the gentiles thought that belief in Jesus was foolishness, since the gentiles – romans, greeks, etc. thought that all gods were all powerful – not forced or even able to die on the cross, etc. So He couldn't be God.

Just being good, and giving up the things of this world – which is tough to do – no matter how good or moral or nice, etc. you seem to be, will not get you to heaven (**matt. 19:16-26; mark 10:27; luke 18:27**) – it is impossible. With God it is possible – with Jesus only you can.

We wouldn't need police, lawyers, courts, laws, etc., if man was not evil (**gal. 5:19-21**). And only God can, through Jesus, change that (with His Spirit – **gal. 5:22-23**). Man is evil – you are evil (man caused it – since adam, who we all are from – **gen. 3**). Go to Jesus and His truth and change (**gal. 5:24-25**).

So Jesus had to die for mankind (we are connected to man – noah's sons, sinful, evil, etc.) – there was no other way to save man (to be connected and have a relationship with Him) – except to die for us all (seeing how much God loves us) – pay the price for us (that we couldn't pay). And no one since Jesus died are we supposed to listen to (no other prophets, religions, leaders, beliefs, etc. that would, and have, come since He died and rose, and the bible completed – the **book of revelation** is the last book, don't even listen to angels – only go to Jesus and the truth of His word). God moved on to the gentiles with paul.

And God had jonah go to gentiles (nineveh) to preach to (God didn't go to many gentiles before Jesus died, but a few over the years) – and they believed and repented – like Jesus going to the gentiles after He died and rose (eventually with paul) – saying He would be like jonah – being three days and three nights in the earth (**matt. 12:39-41**) – jonah was three days and three nights in the belly of the whale (**jonah 1:17**) – then jonah went to the gentiles in nineveh after that. And that was the only sign that Jesus was going to give them – and He was in the belly of the earth three days and three nights (in abraham's bosom preaching to the righteous jews that already died), and said He would rise after three days (**matt. 27:63; mark 8:31**) – so He was on the cross on thursday (and died), not friday – friday was an high day, and Jesus had to be off the cross before sundown of that day (**john 19:31-42**), and it was a jewish custom to take a man down who hanged on a tree (like Jesus was on the cross), by sundown (not just for the sabbath – **deut. 21:22-23; acts 5:30; acts 10:39-40; gal. 3:13-14**).

And God used peter first to the gentiles – to go to cornelius, a centurion for the romans. But peter didn't want to go, but did, and saw that a gentile could be saved (get the Holy Spirit), especially without water baptism (**acts 10:44-48**). And God saw that peter was not interested in going to the gentiles, so that is why Jesus (risen) went to saul (paul). So peter was like the church of laodicea – not cold or hot (**rev. 3:14-16**), so Jesus didn't use him for that (he was used for the jews) – not tough like paul, so Jesus used paul.

If you have passion for what you believe in (with God or not – hot or cold) – God can use you – once you go to Him and His truth with Jesus. Saul (paul) was that way, and paul went to Jesus after he encountered Jesus on his way to kill other Christians (**acts 9**). God used him after he was saved. So God will use anyone, especially someone that is passionate about what they believe (not lukewarm like the church of laodicea – or Jesus will spue you out – **rev. 3:14-17**). They just have to go to Jesus to be saved and believe and follow, and then use that passion for Jesus. And is what paul did with going to the gentiles – to the world (even today).

The gentiles are first now – God did that, but the jews were to be first and lead the world – with God (through Jesus), but the jews rejected Jesus – now the gentiles will rule – with Jesus (in the 1,000 year reign). So Jesus' earthly ministry to the jews (and the disciples), has changed to His risen ministry with paul – to the gentiles (and any individual jews) – the first shall be last and the last shall be first (**luke 13:23-30**). And God (Jesus) went to saul (paul) – who thought he was doing God's work (before he got saved) – he did it as much as he could, but once he found out who Jesus was – the Savior – God, then paul worked for Him, and worked as hard for God, as he did against God (when he was persecuting and killing the Christian jews). Saul (paul) was one of the strictest jews – following all jewish laws, rules, etc. and was the worst against the Christian jews – so God could use him, because even the most strict jew couldn't have anything against paul – one of the best choices to be a Christian and challenge the jews (even though they hated him now). And then God had him preach to the gentiles – and go through many hardships, etc. doing it (God knew that he could handle it – paul had the attitude, etc. to go through all he did – **2 cor. 11:16-33**). He followed (the risen) Jesus and wanted all of us to follow (individual jews included).

Churches follow peter (and disciples – who were to go to the jews only – **gal. 2:6-14**), but we all should be following paul – who the risen Jesus gave all of the mysteries to (**rom. 2:12-16; rom. 16:25-27**) – to go to the gentiles with salvation (**gal. 1 and 2**), since the jews rejected Jesus.

The older churches should be better, but they are not – they don't grow (still a baby) and learn the truth to know and share the truth, by learning the bible, but the Holy Spirit is needed to learn. They tend to stay with their own belief (mainly from satan) – traditions, rituals, works, etc., and many other beliefs added to the bible, that God doesn't say or want. They all need to follow paul, and what the risen Jesus gave to him to share with the world (**gal. 1:15-18**), with mysteries that were not told before Jesus died (**rom. 2:16; rom. 16:25**).

So we need to keep reading and learning and praying and sharing the truth – growing in Him (and His word) – being sanctified in the word – washing of the word (**john 17:9; rom. 15:15-17; 1 cor. 1:2; 1 cor. 6:11; eph. 5:25-27**), not false teachings, etc. – from satan (**2 cor. 11:13-15; 1 tim. 1:4; 1 tim. 4:1; 2 tim. 4:3-4; titus 1:13-15**), even in paul's day (**2 tim. 4:1-5**), which lead to all of these false churches, etc., no matter how old or big they are. Need to lead us to perfection in Jesus, and the truth of His word.

Even though we are not perfect (even with Jesus) here on earth, but will be in heaven (with Jesus). but we can grow with the Holy Spirit and be better, and help others do the same, before we (or they) die. And make sure you find a truthful church to go to (many false ones out there – the world and satan are influencing them).

We (jews and gentiles) are to seek God – the Lord, and live (**amos 5:4-6; rom. 10:8-18**). That is through Jesus only.

So there are no signs, visions, etc. that are going to be needed – since Jesus death and resurrection (and the bible was completed – around 70 – 90ad – the **book of revelation** completed, and the temple destroyed) – except with Jesus – all go to Jesus and His word only for what is to happen. Anything like those would always have to lead to Jesus and the truth of His word. And that is why paul wasn't supposed to say anything about what he saw, heard, and did, etc. in the third heaven (**2 cor. 12:1-13**) – because people will use anything like that to say their vision is true, etc. – but it is from satan (who would not lead you to Jesus, but maybe to a false church, belief, etc.). So don't listen to any other revelation about anything against the bible and the truth (Jesus warned us – **matt. 24; mark 13; luke 21; rev. 22:16-21**) – it would be all from satan (including all of these false churches, religions, beliefs, etc. in the world). And in paul's case God may have used satan to keep paul from boasting, etc. – go by the truth of His word, through Jesus and the Holy Spirit.

So now we all (and eventually the jews, as a nation – in the tribulation) have to go to the risen Jesus and be ready to go (if we die, or in the rapture before the tribulation – for true Christians). No one else can save us or get us to heaven (**acts 4:10-12**).

Go to and pray to Jesus (individual jews and gentiles) and get saved (with the Holy Spirit) now. And then read His word (the Holy Spirit will teach you the truth – **1 cor. 2:12-14**) and grow and share with others. And keep praying.

Like **revelation 1** shows that the risen Jesus came to john to write the **book of revelation (**mainly for the jews**)** – not any angel, etc. (even though there were some angels there, too), but it is Jesus who we go to and who comes to us to be saved (with the Holy Spirit) and to know and to learn anything – not with an angel, man, etc. – Jesus only. So no angel has gone to man to tell of anything new, just Jesus, and if any angel came after Jesus died and rose, then it is from satan (especially after john wrote the **book of revelation**, about 2,000 years ago – probably around 70ad when Jesus didn't come back by then) – no new religions (no gabriel, or any other angel, etc. to come here, etc. – it would be satan masquerading as gabriel, etc.). So no new information about Christianity, or Jesus, the bible, etc. – only that the tribulation is yet to come (but the true Christians will be gone – raptured) and Jesus will come back for the jews (a second time – after a big 2,000 year time out, and they will see it is

Him who came before – **heb. 9:28**), as a nation (**rom. 11; book of revelation**), as the two witnesses (probably moses and elijah – **matt. 17:1-3; mark 9:1-8**) will be preaching to the world – especially to the jews (**rev. 11**), the message of Jesus (so that the Christians don't have to be here anymore – that is the reason you are here after you are saved – to preach Jesus and the truth of His word).

And elijah was supposed to come before the Messiah (Jesus) was to come here to earth for the jews – and he did – it was john the baptist – who was in the spirit of elijah – **matt. 11:11-15; matt. 17:9-13; luke 1:13-17; john 1:6-36**). Now he will be before Jesus comes in the tribulation. Always pointing toward Jesus (and the truth of His word).

So we then are here for Jesus and share Him, and God will use us until we go or are gone (**rom. 10:13-21**).

God will set someone up of His – put someone in place to help His people through any problem – like He did with joseph, moses, esther, etc. – even paul – even you. Trust God – keep going to Jesus and His word. God can use all of noah's sons for His purpose (and women, too), and has throughout the years. Even if He has cursed them or put limits on them (any son).

God can and does use everyone (all man is evil), if He needs to – to get His work done here – like He did in the past – with pharaoh and his daughter (**exo. 2**), rahab (**josh.**), nebuchadnezzar (**dan. 3, 4**), cyrus (**2 chron., ezra, isa., dan.**), and many others – and they can follow God, if they want, but some don't – just like us today, to their and our destruction.

God uses things (and people) that might be thought to be evil (by evil man doing it) for good – to get things done for man here – all of noah's sons throughout history to have man go to Him – to Jesus – no matter what son. And what God accepted – especially in the past, and before Jesus died and rose – was still from evil man until He had moses write the bible and explain and share the truth of what God wanted from man, and to follow Him then – and today (what the new testament tell us – mainly after Jesus died and rose) – such as marriage (only one man and one woman), punishments (not stoning to death for every sin – even though God did that to show us what He thinks of the evil here), etc. God deals with man a little different now (after Jesus died and rose) in all of those areas (even though there are still punishments and consequences for the way we live here). But God still wanted to come to us – as evil as we were and still are – for us to have a way out of sin, and this evil world (and from satan). And to change us and connect to Him.

Man or woman need to use the bible to figure things out. Go to Jesus and the truth of His word – then follow and figure things out – not before we see what He wants – or we will get too many things wrong in all areas of life.

Then He can use you in this world after you change and know the truth to help others that may have gone through what you did before you went to Jesus. Live the life God wants you to – through Jesus.

And God puts people in different jobs and positions and places in the world today, especially america, to have people – mainly Christians – even you (true Christians) in place to do His will and go against the enemy (and his lies) – the enemy is satan – who leads man without Jesus (and His truth).

Each person is different (or special) to God physically or otherwise – even with fingerprints (even identical twins are different), dna, etc. – we are special, all different, and He made us that way, and knows us before birth (**psalm 139:13-18**), and He even knows the number of hairs on your head (**luke 12:6-7**). And we are even more separated from Him by sin (from adam), but He wants you to go to Him (to get saved through Jesus – getting the Holy Spirit, the way He intended us), and be His son or daughter (and made in His image – spiritual, with the Holy Spirit) – we are only made now in the image of man (born evil), since adam (because of sin – **gen. 5:3**) – all of us from noah's three sons (the same human as adam) – until we go to Jesus. Connect back to Him and not be connected to man (or satan) anymore. And as different (and special, etc.) as we all are, we are all the same (**acts 17**), from adam (more physically the same before the flood, and a little after the flood, but now we are more different physically, in many ways, after the flood). And He wants to use us to help others, after we go to Him, to share His truth. And be one (with Him). And try to be caring for other people, as much as we can in this world.

Segregation wouldn't be thought about, if all of us were the same (we all looked the same up to the flood and just a little after the flood up to the tower of babel, and few hundred years after that – **gen. 11**) – but all of noah's sons are different now (because of the world after the flood, especially after the tower of babel, languages, appearance, etc. – a punishment for all of mankind, even for us today – but also good to be separated, because of satan). And all of noah's sons are needed, and need to do their job to make this world work (like america) – but it can only be with Jesus and His truth (not everybody else's – man's, ideas, or satan's, etc.). One son needs the other. But to be one (to all get along) and has to be with Jesus – but the truth of His word.

God's plan for man without Him in your life – is through noah's sons – since the flood – God's punishment for all of mankind. Go to Jesus to change that. And why Jesus came here.

We can't stop the way God made this world (especially after the flood) or stop punishment from sin He gave to man – this world is the way it is, and so is man, until we go to Jesus.

Jesus is the way, truth and life to God (**john 14:6**) – go to Him.

Jesus has power over heaven and earth (**matt. 28:16-20**) – after His death and resurrection, and He is the only way that noah's sons can get along (jews included).

God made the world the way it is – so we could not fix it – only with Jesus. All through history – especially after the flood – through noah's sons. And you can see we haven't yet – and we never will – not without Him.

So don't try to solve the problems (racism, hate, killing, etc.) without Jesus and the truth of His word – and don't try to put the social problems of this world in the church – when it is Jesus that will end that in you – and the problems you have with people (and their groups – black or white) that try to push those things of the world (their issues, agendas, etc.) onto everyone (all that is against God and the truth of His word). Just go to Jesus and get saved (true salvation – with the Holy Spirit) and see how you change (then learn the truth of His word).

You can stop racism, by being lawful and being a good example for your people (and children) – all of noah's sons need to do this, and Jesus and His word would do that (but we all are being blinded by satan, thinking man can do it without Jesus).

All will be one with Jesus – all of noah's sons (**col. 3:8-11**). Go to Him – get the Holy Spirit, and pray and read and follow.

We need to get back to the truth of the bible, God, Jesus – not beliefs and political and social ideas of man today – satan has always been lying about – that only can be solved with Jesus – then they will go away, if we truly know the truth and are saved.

Those that lie about anything – especially about the truth of God and His word, are not only hurting others, but also themselves – to destruction – with and like satan, eventually to hell (lake of fire).

So man (any of noah's sons) and his problems cannot be the focus (like satan wants you to) – Jesus and the truth of His word should be the focus – go to Jesus and change. And won't be focused on you and be selfish, etc.

What we need to be aware of is that we are connected to man – noah's sons – and not to God.

People are attracted to the wrong things (satan leads us) and we need to admit it. We sometimes blame others, instead of ourselves, so we need to hate satan, then go to Jesus, or don't blame anyone, but yourself and deal with it and the consequences of that life – that you chose (and sometimes born into – don't live with that, only what Jesus says).

People can 'live' in this world without God (most people try to, and some think they are going to God – but they are not) – but not very well (and certainly not after this life), so go to Jesus to get the most out of yourselves, no matter how much or little you do in this life. Man uses whatever he can use in this world to keep himself busy and occupied (which is not usually good for them or others) – not to dwell on the problems (escape with the evil of this world, etc.), instead of doing what is needed to deal with problems and be happy, but for that to work best, we need to go to Jesus (for this life and after). Normally this life leads to misery and hell, but it doesn't have to – go to Jesus to escape.

Know that God is in control, and wants you to do well, but only with Him (Jesus) – and you have to go to Him, otherwise this world (and your life) will suffer. We are not perfect, and all start the same – evil, sinful.

There are maybe some things you can't control (like who we are born to) –but not much (God gives us free will, but we will suffer, if we do things wrong), and you should change what you can (go to Jesus, and His word, which is the best change we can make, to really have a chance), and let God help with all things and it will work out (what's best for you, and us), go to Jesus and His word and learn and grow and change. His way (**matt. 6:33**).

Whether you like it or not, God is ultimately in control (especially of where you go after this life) of this world and things in your life that are good in every way – for a person, family, society, nation, etc., if you would just go to Him – go to Jesus and follow His word – don't snub Him (Jesus or His word) or a nation will fall (because of our rebellion against His way of life for us – in His word, **rom. 1**).

God sends delusions to people who do not love the truth or retain it (**rom. 1:20-32; 2 thess. 2:8-12**). Hopefully you will go to Him, because of the problems you have in this world. Many people have heard of His truth throughout history and ignored it, and not shared it or passed the truth on to others from then to now. Go to Jesus and keep learning His word.

Might as well go to the Lord (Jesus), because He puts us in our place – especially where we are born (**prov. 22:2**) – you don't have a choice of that (and in some cases you wouldn't want to be where you end up) – so go to Him as soon as you can, as you grow, etc. The rest is up to us to go to Him – He (Jesus) is there waiting. Go to Him for your way, no matter where you start (born, family, etc.).

Love the truth – and live it – only with Jesus and His word. (**john 1; john 8:31-32; john 14:6**).

Sometimes you are given things, opportunities come up, etc., but don't expect it – and we have to know it is from God or not, because satan is tempting and out there, especially without Jesus in your life. Always go to God for the answers, and pray, whether it is no or yes, or even wait – you'll have peace about it (**philip. 4:6-9**) – you can do without.

Go to God – pray, but wait for Him to help you – read His word – the truth. Pray for everything – and for everyone to go to Jesus.

God doesn't force us into a better life, but leads us or puts things (and people) in place to help us decide – hopefully go to Him for help – through Jesus.

Your plans for your life may not be God's plans for you, so your direction in life may change from what you thought – see what God wants, be prepared to change, if need be.

Whatever job you do, or whatever lifestyle, etc. you live, you have to accept the consequences that go with that, and what it might do to others, including your family, etc. – you are responsible for harm (or not) to others in this world.

People cause problems because we didn't stop it – the evil, etc. before (in you or your family's life, etc.), so people have to pay for it today (your children, theirs, etc., until you stop it)– don't let things get worse with your family, friends, etc. – stop it early. It can be with Jesus, no matter what you go through (or how stubborn you are to change and go to Him and His truth).

And God can use any tough life experiences for good to help you and others – **rom. 8:28**, because a setback in life can be a blessing (and is possibly why you go through some things, but we have to go to Jesus and change, then He can use us), but we all (jews and gentiles – **eph. 2**) can go to Jesus (through paul's message – the gospel we are saved by, **rom. 2:16; rom. 16:25; gal. 2:6-10**, which is a bringing together of what was separated long ago, and this is the gospel – **1 cor. 15:1-4**), so there is no excuse (if you want to stay the same – don't complain, etc., but you can change for good with Jesus, and only Jesus). When you change with Jesus – the whole world changes around you (and in you), you see the world through God's eyes – His truth – His word (the bible). And then you are attracted and desire different things (and people) – better things in this world (and after).

God still hates the things He hated since the beginning – since satan and adam sinned – and man has been evil to today since the beginning and God shows that throughout the bible – man doesn't and hasn't changed – we still are sinful and evil and still need to go to God – to Jesus (and His word) to change. He did and does all of this for us, because He loves (and it is best for us – we just don't know it).

Getting the Holy Spirit is being born again (**john 3**) – Jesus gives us the Holy Spirit when we get saved (believe in and follow Him). So we can change and be connected to God, and not to sin and man (noah's sons, adam).

Even though we are under grace (with some rules) – basically not under law – because of the Holy Spirit from Jesus – if we believe and accept it and Him. But when we are saved and have the Holy Spirit, we can live a different way that would be natural to obey (**gal. 5:22-26**) – not be worldly.

And it is paul's message (and books – **romans to philemon**, from the risen Jesus, even though the whole bible is for our learning – **rom. 15:4**) we need to follow (not follow peter and the disciples, or even Jesus's earthly ministry for the jews, as a nation – that was the corn of wheat – the seed that had to die, **john 12:23-26**, and Jesus will come back for them in the tribulation, coming soon – **matt. 24; rom. 11:25-27**). So paul is for the gentiles – **rom. 15:15-16** (and any individual jew), the way the risen Jesus (who came to paul – **acts 9**) wants us to understand the truth and salvation (even peter found paul's message hard to understand – **2 pet. 3:14-18**). So the church, with paul, and the risen Jesus (and the paul's books), can grow, as it has up to today.

So Jesus separated His earthly ministry to the jews, from the spiritual ministry, after He died, to the gentiles – jews were baptized with water (they were following the law and sacrifices, etc. and knew the bible, but now needed to change and follow Jesus, and would have evangelized the world – the gentiles, with Jesus) – so then all that go to Him after He died and rose, were baptized with the Holy Spirit (for salvation today), even though initially they were baptized with water (but water is not necessary to follow Jesus anymore). Even peter was surprised when God had him preach the gospel to a gentile (a centurion) and he got saved with the Holy Spirit – without water (**acts 10 and 11**) – and it is possible that the centurion was the one that was the same one near the cross that thought Jesus was the Son of God (**matt. 27:54; mark 15:39; luke 23:47**), or even the one who's servant Jesus healed (**luke 7:10**).

Jesus says to be clean on the inside not the outside (**matt. 23:23-28**) – don't look clean or saved, when you are not – like marriage without God, etc.

So we are baptized by Jesus with the Holy Spirit (**matt. 3:11; mark 1:8; luke 3:16; john 1:32-34; 1 cor. 6:11**) – after His death and resurrection, and we get washed by the water of His word – His truth with the Holy Spirit (**eph. 5:25-27**) – not in water (know why you are getting baptized). And that goes for tongues – which was needed back then – to communicate with so many different languages (**acts 2**), that started at the tower of babel (**gen. 11**), that man hadn't been able to understand each other at that time (not like we do today – since then – we have overcome that, with travel, technology, etc. – **dan. 12:4**), and is why paul says that tongues will cease and not be necessary – and all of the gifts He gives us are not for all (**1 cor. 12:29-31; 1 cor. 13:8**) – not all speak in tongues anyway (and is fine, if it is real, and needed). So just like God changed the languages after the flood (from one to many), God also made it possible for men to understand each other – at that point (peter – **acts 2**), after Jesus died and rose, with the Holy Spirit. For all to know the truth about salvation through Jesus.

So we follow paul and the message he got from the risen Jesus – not peter (don't follow peter – he is not the rock, but a stone – it's what he said about Jesus is important, who is the rock – **matt. 16:13-23; john 1:40-42; 1 cor. 10:1-4**), and not the disciples. God is using what He needs to in today's world to share His word – but follow only the truth in His word.

With technology (internet, television, cell phones, etc.) God has been able to reach more people in the last days (today), but satan also uses it, too (all of the social media, etc.). God will win – time is short – go to Jesus. And share Him. You can see the world is getting worse – even in america (with the leaders, what is taught in schools, homes, online, etc.).

Your neighbor, or village, etc. is the whole world today (as it would be in the end times), and you don't know all of those people around the world. But in the past, like 500 years ago, you only knew the people of your own area, where you lived. You didn't always know what the people of the world were doing. We might be able to still help those around us, but not as much with the rest of the world. Though we can still pray for all, and share Jesus with those we can. You just never know what is true or not about the things you hear around the world (and even sometimes in this country – with all of noah's sons here), but you can know usually around where you live. At least we know there is evil out in the world – near or far. Pray, and help who you can.

There always has been and always will be – while man is still here – those against God and His word (but don't promote it like hollywood, advertisements, businesses, etc. do) – satan is leading everyone away from and against God, so we need to keep sharing the truth of Jesus (and His word) – speak out.

God made all – even the wicked (those without Jesus) for the day of evil (**prov. 16:4**) – the last days, so don't worry – be with Jesus (**john**

16:33) – and does use them in this world. He knows that man and the world will all get more evil at the end (**prov. 16; 2 tim. 3:1-5**). It is satan having more people believe lies, and going against God and the truth of His word. Go to Jesus to change that for you and others.

People act like they are being nice to people (that seem to be treated unfairly – wanting to believe what they want) and behaving and living against God and His word (which does not help them or man here) – they are just being led by satan – going against God, being evil (selfish, god-like, etc.).

So satan is trying to make even Christians think that you can believe whatever you want, and we all can believe in everything and anything and still be a true Christian, even that we are all created in God's image, but we are not – we are born in man's – adam's image (**gen. 5:3**), after he sinned (**gen. 3**) – we all are evil, sinful. Making people think no matter what they believe, they are fine – all to believe the same thing – all against God.

This will all eventually lead to the end times – the one world order, etc. in the tribulation – understanding each other (breaking down the barriers, etc.) and all going against God – with technology, travel, etc. (led by satan – even with different languages, etc.), and has taken over 4,000 years to get back to communicating as one (from the tower of babel – **gen. 11**) – and all against God (God knowing it would take that long). It took a long time to get through the language barrier, and even longer to get together and somewhat get along – but still today it is tough (and even in america). And all of noah's sons still struggle, until we all go to Jesus – to be one with Jesus (God's plan for us). God gave man time to be able to go to Him – first by separating man from each other (language, appearance, etc.), then through the jews, then now through Jesus, continuing to today. And man will go against God again (led by satan to unite all of man against God – like the flood, and tower of babel) – the one world order, in the tribulation – coming soon. Find the truth in the bible and when things started and stopped (like sacrifices, temple, etc.), and what is truly needed (which is Jesus and His truth) – so we can understand and know the truth.

From the first time man sinned – adam in the garden (**gen. 3**) – man has worshipped God with sacrifice (God giving the first one for adam and eve – **gen. 3:21** – partly to clothe them – cover their sin, since they knew they were naked – **gen. 2:25; gen. 3:8-11**), including cain and abel sacrificing – but it needed to be what God wanted (**gen. 4**) – before the flood (and being able to be in the presence of the Lord or not – **gen. 3:8; gen. 4:16; gen. 6:3**), and even after the flood noah sacrificed (**gen. 9**), through job (**book of job**), and the jews (eventually in the temple), then to Jesus' death and resurrection (our once and for all sacrifice). God has always been available to man – to go to Him – but what He wants, not what man wants for our needs and what's best for us – to go to the true God, not satan and his many false beliefs (churches, religions, etc.) and gods (not all beliefs lead to the true God – only Jesus – **1 tim. 2:3-6**).

People throughout the years have sacrificed, because they started out knowing that God sacrificed for adam and eve (**gen 3**), and cain and abel (**gen. 4**), and that noah sacrificed after the flood (**gen. 9**), and then God had the jews sacrifice starting with abram (**gen. 12**). Then people over the years since then have sacrificed, because they heard of the practice, but not to the true God, but sacrificed to satan (and his gods), and people even sacrificed people – babies, etc. (mainly after Jesus died and rose), which God did not want done. The only time God wanted that (any human sacrifice), is when sacrificing was finished (which was supposed to be a payment for sin) – using Jesus (who was human) to die for all of us – once for all. We don't need sacrifices since Jesus died (even though many empires, kingdoms, tribes, people, etc. did over the years since Jesus died – to satan). Go to Jesus and be saved from the law of sin.

And God started out with very few laws, etc. – to test man (especially with satan tempting) – to follow God or themselves, etc. So God had to make the world this way after sin and disobedience to God. And we don't want to live this evil way forever (like we were created to do – before sin – **gen. 3:22-24**) – so He has a way out for us all. This world is no good (miserable, tough, etc.) this way (with sinful man) – so it would make us go to Him – Jesus. And we needed laws (especially God's), and some of our own, to live here, but we need to follow them. God wanted to make a point with laws and punishments before Jesus came here to die and rise for payment of our sin (God is a just God and needs to have justice – payment, etc. for our sin). We needed to see what God tried before He gave us our way to Him – and we see that only Jesus is the answer.

And there were so many laws and rules (mainly from God) that the jews followed (maybe some they made up) – the romans must have been out of their mind dealing with them, but God had them doing that. But we don't need to worry about all of those laws, etc. with Jesus (after He died and rose, and gives us the Holy Spirit). But need most until we go to Jesus. But laws were made to help us see our sin, evil, etc. – and to protect us. Man needed to know who God was and what God wanted from us. And to help us to go to Him and change.

We are to obey the laws of the land (**rom. 13**), like in america (Jesus' land), and it is based mainly on God's laws (and His word) and those that obey include politicians, servants – like police, judges, etc., as well as the population in general (including immigrants, etc.). and that is what the country is based on (and why it is prosperous and powerful and helpful and free, etc.), and if we go away from God and His word with these laws (from God), by the politicians or others, we (they) need to be punished or change (don't let satan have you go against God and His word) – and God will punish a nation – just like He punished the jews – israel, when they didn't follow Him. We should do things legally in this country, but we should first do things that God wants us to do (and we will do things that are best for all – **gal. 5:22-25**). There are sometimes, if the laws change, that may go against God, and we need to follow God (and know it is the truth, not what you feel like doing) – and God will help you (**acts 5:12-42**). And eventually God will punish. Don't be in the world (**rom. 12:2**). Help people, but they need to follow what makes this country good – Jesus, and His word. Share Him (the truth).

So we not only let every person, culture, belief, etc. into america, but we also are letting them run the country – getting those types of beliefs into society, schools, government, etc. – really letting satan run the country. We can let people in, but to get them to know Jesus, what this country is built on – and if their country (where they came from) was with the truth of Jesus and His word, they would stay where they are, and not leave. So we should be sharing Jesus with the world more (and those that come here and find Jesus, should go back to their country and change it, with the truth).

The only way that the world will all get to know the truth of Jesus and His word, is to have the whole world go against true Christianity – which is starting to happen more (even in america – satan leading people to teach against the bible, etc.), and then people will hear about it (with all of the communication, internet, etc.) around the world and then each person (all of noah's sons) can decide what to do (even in the tribulation – **rev. 20:1-4**) – and then the world will end soon (it has taken about 4,000 years – **gen. 11**). So people will have a chance to hear the gospel, anywhere. No excuse. Keep sharing.

Anybody trying to be saved (or get to heaven) by obeying the laws and being good, won't help you – only Jesus will – then do good with Him.

We need to know that the laws are good and necessary here (**1 tim. 1:8-11**) – for the evil in us. And we need to go to Jesus and His word, to find the truth of what we need to for our evil.

If we were all truly saved by Jesus – with the Holy Spirit in us, we wouldn't need all of these laws (**gal. 5:22-23**) – God wouldn't make them, and neither would we. We have to obey God (like we were created to) – like adam and eve needed to (but they didn't – **gen. 3**). We now need to go back to God (as adam and eve eventually did) – through Jesus only – and we are in a time of grace (**rom. 5:19-21; rom. 6:1, 14-15**).

Only in Jesus can we obey or be not under law (the truth). We are under grace – with the Holy Spirit – saved by Jesus. Go to Him and follow His word (**gal. 2:19-21**). But not perfect, until heaven (and out of these mortal bodies). Keep going to Him.

The law and the prophets were taught until john (the baptist – **matt. 11:12-13; luke 16:16**), then the kingdom of God (at first for the jews) was brought in (especially after Jesus' death) – now (the risen) Jesus is available to all (**matt. 11; luke 16**).

The kingdom of God – which could be the 1,000-year reign of Jesus – would have come right after Jesus came here and the 490 years of daniel (**dan. 9**) would have been fulfilled – the promises of God to the jews (which would be the last seven years the jews owed God – the jews with Jesus preaching to the gentiles for those seven years). But it is now still to come – future (after a 2,000-year time out for the jews – and God using it to allow the gentiles to have to a chance for salvation, and hopefully some jews) – the seven year tribulation (coming soon), then the 1,000-year reign, then eternity – for us to live forever with God (if truly saved with Jesus).

The tree of life in the garden **(gen. 2:9)** was for man (adam and eve) to eat to live forever here with God (**gen. 3:22-24**), and adam sinned to separate us (lost the Holy Spirit) from God, and now with Jesus (who is the tree of life) we can be written in the book of life (after we are saved through Jesus – and get the Holy Spirit) – **philip. 4:3; rev. 3:5; rev. 13:8** – to live forever with God in heaven – or forever without Him in hell – separated forever. So the tree of life (as Jesus is) will be available in heaven again (**rev. 22:14**) as it was in the garden of eden and we will live forever with God in heaven.

So all will bow to Jesus at some time (**rom. 14:11-12; philip. 2:9-11**) – dead or alive. We can only be saved when alive. And Jesus is best for us, but we don't realize that. Get saved (and have the Holy Spirit), and be ready.

Heaven (Jesus) or hell (satan – separation even after this life forever) – your choice. And hell will be hell – worse than anything on earth. So we need to share Jesus (only His truth – learn it first) as much as we can with others while we are here.

We are like Jesus here – sharing the truth to people – like He did to the jews (who mostly didn't believe), we need to learn the truth and share it, even though all people will not believe.

Even though the disciples did some things here (**mark 6:13**), and sometimes not (**mark 9:17-19, 27-29**), but mostly after Jesus died (and still only to the jews). So while the disciples were with Jesus when He was here (before He died and rose), they did not preach (only Jesus did) – so being with Jesus didn't get the disciples to preach (or be saved), not until He died and rose (saw the empty tomb, and they eventually saw Him alive, and believed – **john 20:1-9, 19-29** – His soul went to hades, then back into His body in the tomb, risen, after three days – **matt. 27:63; mark 8:31**, but now in a resurrected body – flesh and bones – no blood, like we will have at the rapture – **luke 24:36-43; 1 cor. 15:42-54**) – and then He gave (after He ascended – sent) them the Comforter (the Holy Spirit – **acts 1 and 2**, then they were saved), just like He gives us today (so we can learn and preach His word – the real truth).

So for three years they had to learn from Jesus, and then get the Holy Spirit to learn the truth and preach – just like paul did for three years in the desert with the risen Jesus (**gal. 1:11-18**) to learn the truth before he preached. And it is the same for us – to learn the truth of His word (from the Holy Spirit after we are saved, in our soul – **1 cor. 2:12-14**), then we can preach (even just to family and friends, etc.), but only the truth of His word (learn it). It may be three years or more to learn the truth of His word (the bible) – not the truth of a church, leader, etc. – going against all of the lies satan preaches in schools, families, churches, groups, religions, etc. And churches are getting as bad as schools, politics, etc. – lying to people – against God and the truth of Jesus (His word – the truth) – the bible – so satan is going to the one world order (especially getting america to fall, and leave the truth of Jesus), and has to get the churches to be false and believing the world and the people (man – noah's sons), all of the ideas they come up with – all against God's word – in the name of tolerance, niceness, racism, love, gender, etc. (calling good, evil and evil, good – **isa. 5:20-21**) – all things that are of the world – go to Jesus to change those (and you). You can't change the truth of God, and live a good life – and you can't change yourself and your beliefs, without going to God – to Jesus. Otherwise you will stay the same in your life and those that think that way, with punishment, struggles, etc. (still connected to noah's sons) – your lot in life (**jer. 13**).

If people can talk freely in this world against God (Jesus) and His word (those listening to satan – he is the one leading this world, and man), then people should be able to talk freely about Jesus and the truth of His word (but satan, and those that follow him, don't want you to).

People still have to know that going against God is bad and leads to evil, misery, and destruction – not to mention hell forever – for you and others. Stop being selfish and following in satan. It is satan that is trying to unite the world – not some great universal being or good belief, etc. We have to get away from the world (and noah's sons – man).

Staying connected to man – adam, noah – leads to death and hell – forever. Connecting to God through Jesus leads to life and heaven – forever. We all have a choice.

All of the world is getting united by technology – internet, phones, travel, etc. – to be one with satan – one world order. Man thinks that is the way to go (but it is satan). If man does what he thinks is right, then it will lead to death (**prov. 14:12**). Go to the truth of Jesus and His word.

We need to obey God and His word (the truth) – what He wants us to do today through the risen Jesus, or God will not help us, as He has done throughout history – especially to the jews (**1 sam. 12:15**).

You can't let churches and man (or the leaders, etc.) make the rules for Christians, salvation, the truth – like churches are doing now (and have done since Jesus died) – we need to go by what Jesus and the bible says (don't follow satan, as he leads man, and the world, in the wrong direction). We have to deal with the problems and stand up for the truth of Jesus and the bible. Find a true church and go to that, and the truth of the bible – know it yourself, but get saved by Jesus and get the Holy Spirit only first, then even if only two or three gather in His name – family, friends, etc., He is there (**matt. 18:19-20**).

Problems will happen in this world – even with Jesus (with the Holy Spirit), but we need to be led in the right direction and handle them – led by the Spirit (**gal. 5:13-26**). Even after salvation – true salvation – getting the Holy Spirit, we can still sin – be tempted by satan, like Jesus (**matt. 4:1-11** – even though He did not sin). But don't give in – if we do, there are consequences and punishments in this world – so we go to Jesus and His word daily to grow and change (and forgiveness).

So the Spirit (in the soul) wars with flesh (**rom. 7 and 8**), without going to God daily and His word, we struggle – because they are separated (the body and Spirit). Our desires (since we are separated from God, born without the Spirit) get us in trouble here – satan leads, but with Jesus (and the Holy Spirit) you are a new creature – away from what we were born like – sinful (away from adam and noah) – are now connected to God, and we can fight these and satan. So become a new creature (person) with Jesus (**2 cor. 5:17**).

We should think on these things daily – and we can with Jesus and His truth (**philip. 4:4-13**).

No one is perfect, and all can be forgiven of our sins (except we have to have the Holy Spirit from Jesus – **matt.12:31-32**, and is the only sin not forgiven – **matt. 12:31-32**, and that's what we get baptized with – with the Holy Spirit, only way to be saved today, **matt. 3:11; luke 3:16; 1 cor. 1:17**– not water – that's just for jews, **john 1:33**). And we are all human and prejudice (**matt. 7:1-5**), especially without Him, but we can judge better with Him and His truth (**1 cor. 2:14-16; 1 cor. 6:1-8**). So no matter what your position in life (that God has us born into – through noah's sons), we can all change when we go to Jesus, and He will put us where we should be (or keep us where we are – **1 cor. 7:17-24**), but still learn of and share Him (and His truth), and live a different life – now connected to God and not man.

All people – all of noah's sons – need to be helped and loved, but with Jesus – not just in tragedy, etc., but before – especially before death – or it is too late. Pray and share Him and His truth.

With Jesus we are forgiven, and will live a less sinful life here (**1 john 2:1**) – keep growing and having faith until we are gone.

God is not only a loving God, but also a holy and just God – and there is hell – and Jesus is the only way to be holy and just – with love (and in heaven). We have to believe in Him and His word.

People (mainly the jews) that were helped when Jesus was here (healed, miracles, etc.) had faith in Jesus and who He was – God, and His power. So faith is what is needed today (even as abraham had), even if you don't see Him (**john 20:28-29**) – and today we get the Holy Spirit in us (which they didn't get before Jesus died – He was here for the jews only then).

The sin of unbelief is the reason we have problems we struggle with here. So we need to pray for all people (and share Him), especially in the end times – today (**2 tim. 3:1-5**), people will be even worse (satan will be influencing even more – man following).

Faith in Jesus and in His word, and God will change us – with the Holy Spirit – that adam lost for us all, and sin and death came to us. Go to Jesus and change.

So you have to believe and have faith (as all people have done throughout the bible – **heb. 11**) in Him and follow and obey Him (and get saved, like we do today with Jesus, getting the Holy Spirit, to connect us back to God – born again, and start learning and sharing Him) – Jesus has been here since the beginning – the Creator, the Lord, etc. (**gen. 3:8; gen. 4:16; gen. 6:3; job 1:12; job 2:7; dan. 3:24-25; jonah 1:3; john 1:1-5; john 8:56-58; heb. 13:8, etc.**) – all have gone to Him throughout history (but not all believed) – then He finally came here to save us all – once and for all (paying for our sins). We need to go to Him.

And Jesus knows the heart (**1 sam. 16:7; jer. 17:9-10**), not appearance or outward activities, etc. (going to church, charities, praise of men, etc. – **matt. 6:1-8; matt. 15:8-9; mark 7:1-9**), all of the things that separates us now (some people look nice, but may not be, and others are not – God knows the heart). People are naturally selfish – even as a child (born that way), and that drives everything – we need to humble ourselves and help others, not hurt (with Jesus first), and have to discipline and be tough sometimes, but care. If you don't have discipline when young (and hopefully share Jesus), you will have to do it when they are older (or the world will do it, with satan leading them in their life).

CHAPTER 4

Historical Manifestations of Sin: Sin and its Consequences on Humanity

All of the evil and hurting that man does to others (how you treated others, or how you were treated – and we all have done both), shows the reason Jesus came here (and died on the cross). Man has hurt each other throughout history, so we need to accept that – and go to Jesus (no matter what son of noah you are from).

Just thinking evil (and we all do in our heart), is bad enough (**matt. 5:27-28**). People may not be considered evil until they do something, but then it may be too late for someone that is hurt or killed, etc. – then the law, police may and can do something. We need to get people to go to Jesus and change before that – to change their thinking first. We have to know we are all evil – and need Jesus.

When Jesus was saying that there are punishments for lusting, killing, adultery, etc. when you do those – and most people know – the jews did, but now Jesus is saying even if you look, lust, hate, etc., you are guilty of all of those. He was showing us our sins – who we are (born that way – from adam), and why we need a Savior, and why He came here for us all. We all are guilty, evil, and need the same solution – Jesus.

As much as people don't want to admit it or accept it – all people go through the same things – and usually cause their own problems (black, white, all nationalities, etc.) – not just now, but in the past, too. All need to go to God – Jesus.

Man is capable of all kinds of evil, especially with satan around, but Jesus can change us all – and is the only way.

All groups – all of noah's sons – white, black, rich, poor, young, old, religious, atheists, etc. – all can be hateful, prejudice, etc. – and it only takes a few to be real evil and violent, etc., and need to go to Jesus and the truth of His word.

This life is the same for everyone – same needs, problems, etc., and only God can fulfill them best – go to Jesus.

Most people want peace and quiet – to be safe, etc. – for family, and that is only with Jesus – satan won't let you, and is why this world is hard to control ourselves. We have to all help.

It's people being nice and helpful (mainly thinking of others) that help people and this country work – Jesus helping them.

God shows and tells us that we are sinners, evil, etc. – and shows us a way out – through Jesus only (**rom. 10:13**).

No matter what son of noah you are, God can raise you up and use you for His good and purpose – with Jesus.

And people need to be helped, and in america they can, but they need to listen and want to be helped – and that is best with Jesus (and His word).

If you coddle your children – especially when they do something bad – no matter how simple or terrible it is, you will hurt their life more if you do, and the terrible life they lead will last longer and so will yours – do the right thing – best to go to Jesus and have them go to Him (and His word), too. God made the world this way (just like He made cold, heat, hunger, thirst, gravity, etc.) – you can't get out of it, no matter how hard you try – you reap what you sow – consequences for your belief, and actions, etc. And if you don't believe in Him and His truth (His word), then you will just suffer – no matter who you are, what color you are, or how rich or poor you are (some of these things delay you to going to God, thinking you are doing alright, but you are not – it will catch up to you somehow).

Just like you can't spare the rod (**prov. 13:24**) – spanking, etc. – or not discipline, punish, etc. your children (but no abuse, etc.) – we are born evil – so you need to do that, and for adults, if needed in society. It is good and needed for them (and you) – to help them grow and learn – man is born that way (sinful) to need it. You discipline your children (and yourself), or God, and the world (and satan) will, and it will be worse (**prov. 13:24; prov. 22:6**), when they grow up. Anyone can get saved now.

No one teaches children to lie, sin, etc. (or need to), they just do it on their own – born that way (from adam), selfish, evil, sinful, etc. naturally – only Jesus can change us, and get us to heaven.

Criminals, even some minorities, and even some children, etc. are telling people how to fear the police, etc. – don't listen to that, and mostly don't get into trouble and make excuses. And go to Jesus and His word and cooperate. We need protection and police here for sinful man in this world (being led by satan).

So don't teach children the destructive, prejudice, hateful, beliefs and life you have (all satan led – some taught in schools, online, etc.) – or you'll pay for it later and so will others, including them. Teach them the truth and what's best – from God – go to Jesus. And have them live a better life, and you, too.

If your son (or daughter) became a criminal, etc., then you can (or are capable) of loving a bad person (and you may be one yourself) – man can do this (even with those we marry, etc. – so bad people can – or say they can – love someone) – we are all evil – so go to Jesus and change. We can do nothing – but maybe try to love (also hope and faith in something – but may not always be good or true) in some way – but go to Jesus first, and know how to love (what love is – **1 cor. 13**) – or you will have satan lead you. Because we can love bad people – we all do. Go to Jesus to change that.

Need a safe place to live for you and your children. Your life or lifestyle should not hurt you or your family – go to Jesus and follow Him (and the truth of His word).

You should be happy that God disciplines you (as your parents, society, nations, etc. do), so you don't keep going down the wrong road. He loves you. Go to Jesus and change.

We can't keep enabling people – to continue evil – bad things to themselves and others, don't let people think differently, or helping them go down the wrong road (acting as if you care or love them, etc.) – help people get to know Jesus, and get to know Him yourself first, and keep going to Him (and His word – the truth) daily. Stop covering up for people – help them – tell on them, etc., get others to help, too – so they can go through the consequences they need to go through, and not to harm any more people along the way. And satan will grab you and hang onto you to do these evil things – may even look good doing it. No matter how smart, rich, etc. you are.

So satan and his ideas against God and His word is creeping into the world (you see it everywhere, trying to be accepted – all the people that believe and follow satan against God's word) – into society and even in america and man is letting it and the government, and even the church (and Christians) is letting it in – not standing up to it with the truth of the word of God.

We need to keep sharing Jesus and the truth of His word, and see what direction God takes us and this nation, and this world – whatever His will is.

But it is satan's ideology that is starting to run the country and world right now (not just in most churches, but also in homes, schools, hospitals, businesses, etc.). And people are following him.

Be sure you share the truth of God's word and of Jesus to the world – learn it and live it yourself first. That's who and what we should obey and share, especially in america – but it should be God's will that needs to be done – even if it is the end of the world. Keep sharing the truth of Jesus and His word with all, so people have a chance to be saved, no matter what the world is going through. We all still have a chance to be saved – to overcome sin, even if it is the end. For all of noah's sons.

Just like salvation happens in a moment (only through Jesus), so does sin and becoming evil (and doing it) happen in a moment – as satan, angels and man did. Sin doesn't take hours, years, etc. – just a moment (just like on the eighth day after creation, for satan and adam, then all is evil, and evil at once_from then on – **gen. 3**, for all of us).

You cause your own problems, especially without Jesus (**prov. 22:8**), when you have a choice. We all do – go to Jesus.

Even though man is in the predicament it is in (sinful, then and today) by adam in the garden, it is the woman that was first deceived (by satan, as we are all today), and adam followed (but he didn't have to), so it is adam's fault. But women have been punished (by God – **gen. 3:16**) ever since and are still today – and God wants them to live a certain way and role in this world (**1 cor. 14:33-35; 1 tim. 2:8-14**), compared to man (even though man was punished, too, as we all are). Just like in the bible with women – the examples are eve (**gen. 3**), jezebel (**rev. 2:20-21**), delilah (**judges 16:15-24**), etc. – even sarai, abram's wife, told abram to have sex with hagar – an egyptian – to have a son – not what God wanted (instead of waiting for God's timing), and that son (ishmael) – arabs (and descendants from ham, canann) have been enemies of the jews since then – and God does say that ishmael – arabs – will be against all and all will be against them – **gen. 16:11-12** – it is that way still today (and a man – abram, listening to a women caused all of that). There is no getting along – only Jesus can change that – go to Him – all of noah's sons, if we will ever be at peace.

And also that goes for the men who listened to or followed them (women), etc. (some men have not been good either – like adam and abram did), and even when joseph was falsely accused by a wife of his master in egypt, the husband believed her lie – so joseph was sent to prison, but God helped joseph, because he went to God and believed and trusted God, and He will help you, if you go to Him (**gen. 39**) – God can work things out, even if we don't totally trust God, treated unfairly, or are wrongly accused, etc. (**gen. 50:17-20; rom. 8:28**) – if we go to Jesus (get saved). God's word is true.

And some women (like eve) that went to God to change.

So men get influenced by women (in love, attracted, etc.), ever since adam (with eve – **gen. 3**), sometimes against God (as adam did) – that's the way men are – they need to stay with God and His truth – be with Jesus, which is God's plan – be patient for God's timing, for men and women – both to do right by God. And most women are psychics, mediums, fortune tellers, witchcraft, etc. today (which God does not want – **deut. 18:9-11; 2 kings 9:22; 1 sam. 28:7; acts 16:16-21** – a woman who men used) – satan uses and tricks them to fool others, as well as women as gods in some nations in the past (and maybe today) – worshipping them (all demons) – goddesses, and even a queen of heaven – satan knows that's not true, but keeps pushing these lies (he, and demons, knows Jesus is the One – the Son of God – **matt. 8:28-29**) – and even some women have started false churches, religions, etc. (satan leading). God knows all of this – we need to go to His word, and find out the truth.

Women tend to sway men – starting with adam (swayed by eve), and it happened all through the bible, and probably all through your life. And as the jewish wives went to other gods and God punished israel because of this – husbands following (**jer. 44, etc.**). And lot's wife is who turned back (losing things of this world), and lot's daughters sinning (**gen. 19:17-38**). Even king herod (because of a woman – **mark 6:14-29**) had john the baptist's head cut off – like satan likes to do (and still does today). It still happens with men and women today.

Although there have been some women God used – rahab (**josh. 6:23-25; heb. 11:31; james 2:25**), esther (**book of esther**), mary (**the four gospels**), etc. are good examples. As well as the woman of **prov. 31**. A good woman is better than a bad man. Both need to go to Jesus and follow the truth of His word. God can use both.

But the answer to this world is not to have women act like men – just do what God wants them to – His will for them in His word.

Women are important, and to God, and to man (and for man), and is best for man, and God made her for man (**gen. 2:18-25**), and God uses women in this world for many things – but different from man (even though we all are one, if we are with Jesus, are to be one in marriage). And need to know how God wants them to be. If God put you together – with Jesus and the truth of His word, then your marriage won't fall apart (at least not until you die) – otherwise don't expect it to work. And don't be surprised if it doesn't work. It has to be the truth of Jesus – not just a church (too many false ones).

True Christianity is the best for all – especially for women (if we follow what God wants for us) – man is still evil – so people are going to hurt others still – and satan is still leading that. Go to Jesus to be set free, and follow what He wants for us.

Just like Jesus is going to do what's best for a man, but you have to follow Him – do what He says, and a women has to do what a man says (mainly a husband, but in other things, too – **eph. 5:22-33; 1 tim. 2:8-15**). But the husband better be doing what's best and what Jesus wants, and she follows, she will be happy – he has to go to Jesus and follow Him.

So men and women have certain roles (and certain traits) that God wants them to live in this world. And believe it or not people (men and women – all of us in the world) will live a better (best) life here, if we follow God, through Jesus (and His word, with the Holy Spirit). But we all don't, and we fight it (with satan leading men and women) leading us to a miserable life here (and the problems we have with each other) for most people. We are all from adam (**gen. 3:20**), and die from him, and now need to go to Jesus (**1 cor. 15:21-22**). One man – sinful, hurt all of man, and one Man – holy, helps all of man. So go to Jesus – He is the last Adam (**1 cor. 15:44-46**), we need to be born again (spiritually) with Him, and get away from the physical, with adam (**john 3** – away from man – all of us connected to noah's three sons). Go to Jesus and change – the only way that man can.

Jesus left His place with God, the Father (in heaven), to come down here to be one of us – human (and experiencing life here, and going through pain for us) – to save us. And we need to get away from who we are from – man – noah's sons (nationality, culture, family, belief, things of this earth, etc.), to be with God. Jesus now is back with God, and we can be one with Him, too.

Jesus is the Creator of man (**gen. 1; john 1**; **col. 1**), from the beginning for life on this earth (originally with the Holy Spirit in man – that adam lost for us all – with sin – **gen. 3**), and He is also the Creator after His death and resurrection – for us to be created again (born again – **john 3**), spiritually (with the Holy Spirit) – creating us for heaven. A new creation, creature (**2 cor. 5:17**).

Jesus was born sinless – with the Holy Spirit (who came upon mary and was His father – **matt. 1:16-24; luke 1:26-35**) – like adam was created sinless – both were the sons of God (**luke 3:38**), but Jesus is the Son of God and is God (**john 1:1-5, 14**) – not created, but He came to earth as a man (still being God) – to save mankind. And adam sinned – disobeyed God (**gen. 3**), but Jesus did not (who was tempted here, by satan – **matt. 4:1-11**). We all need to be born again (**john 3**) – to connect to God through Jesus, with the Holy Spirit.

Jesus wasn't going to come here and solve everything (the physical things for everyone here – all of our needs, etc.) – even though He could have. He came here to prove who He was – God, and then die for us – pay for all of our sins – the only one that could (if we would just go to Him, and believe in Him, He will save you, too – with the Holy Spirit).

Just like one person (adam – who we are all from) can hurt and mess up many people and things (after he sinned) – you even see that in the world today – so can one person help many (Jesus – after He died and rose). So go to Jesus (**rom. 5; 1 cor. 15:20-23**). Go from physical to spiritual.

So don't make excuses for doing evil things – against someone to lure someone or to tempt someone, etc. for your pleasure, or even for theirs. At the same time, don't hurt or cause problems for others, just to help someone else (if it just hurts you – you can figure that out) – sometimes people (including you) have to go through some things to grow and learn and change (consequences of what they do) – but at least help them to get to know Jesus. We all have needs, but have them met with Jesus. No excuse to do things that are wrong or bad – no matter what the reason. Do good things to help people and share Jesus – then let Him help them, even better.

It only takes one time to mess up your (or other's) life – obey laws (especially God's) in this world – they are for your protection and benefit (**rom. 13; 1 tim. 1:8-9**). Even though we are free (mostly in america) to do what we want, but not all things are good for us (**1**

cor. 6:8-15; 1 cor. 10:22-24). Be smart, and go to Jesus and follow Him and His truth.

Don't be selfish in your actions – like even if you are late for something – don't cause 20 others to wait or be late or inconvenienced, etc., so you can be on time or get something for yourself, etc. – even if it makes you look good or feel good. You suffer, and be inconvenienced, not the many.

Regardless of what son of noah we are, we are all responsible for our actions – have to pay for them, live with them, deal with them, etc. (sometimes others have to also) – our evil, and the consequences and punishment, etc. that goes with them. We need to go to Jesus to change that. Stop being selfish.

So there has to be punishments and consequences or we will never learn or change (if we do at all). God knows. Go to Jesus.

God can stop anything bad from happening to you in your life – if He doesn't, then you better see what you are doing in your life that He doesn't want you to do – go to Jesus, and keep reading and following His word.

So live a life knowing that you will be fine – with God helping you through – going to Jesus and His word – things will work out for the best. Go to Jesus daily – prayer and His word.

Pray about everything, and without ceasing (**1 thess. 5:17**).

In this world and life, it can be who you know that helps you – and the best person to know is Jesus – He can help you with everything in this life. Jesus is who you should know (and need to know – especially for after this life).

People want to live in sin (they know deep down, it is no good) – without Jesus, because they don't want to change (so they don't go to Him), loving their life, but never going to be truly happy. We have to want to give up this life (**matt. 16:24-27**). And know the truth of Jesus, salvation.

God can save us from ourselves – living a life that hurts and is no good for us (or others). Go to Jesus and grow and change.

And when we are truly saved, we can't be separated (from His love, joy, etc. – **rom. 8:31-39**) from God (as far as salvation is concerned – sealed with the Holy Spirit – **eph. 1:12-14**), but we may sin (not a way of life) and lose blessings, happiness, suffer consequences, have punishments, etc. (but not lose salvation) in this world (and need to go back to God, and the truth of His word – not to man, leaders, etc., to be forgiven, and grow and change our whole life – however long we are here – **eph. 4:17-32**), the Spirit wars against the flesh (**rom. 7**). Don't listen to those that say you can lose your salvation (if you are truly saved), if you think that, you were really not saved. If you are not going to Jesus (don't depend on a church, leader, rituals, etc., but only on Jesus and His word – the truth of it), then you may not be saved, no matter how many good things you do (**matt. 7:13-23**). Just like the jews were punished for going away from the truth of God – to false gods, beliefs, etc., then when they repented and came back to the truth of God – God blessed them. So it is the same for Christians (and His nations, etc.) today.

You can do a million good things here on earth in your life (even though it is nice to do good things), but not still get to heaven – only with the TRUTH of Jesus and His word (with the Holy Spirit) – whether with a church or not.

We all know that man is selfish (sinful, evil, etc.) – so we can't go by what man wants to do in the world – it will and has ended badly. Go to and listen to God – the true God (through Jesus and His word) – not satan and his gods and beliefs (that man worships – are from demons – devils, etc. with satan) – any being other than the true God – Jesus. God wants to help us.

It is satan that started all of the false gods in the world – throughout history (since the beginning – **gen. 3**) – he is behind all of them (hiding like he did in the serpent, but hiding behind many things today) trying to communicate with man and have man follow and worship them (him) in all religions and beliefs, etc. – and man follows.

So God had to write the bible so we would know the truth, and since the Holy Spirit led the people to write the bible (all of the true books – 39 in the old testament, and 27 in the new testament - 66 total), we need to have the Holy Spirit – from Jesus – to understand it fully (**1 cor, 2:6-16; 2 pet. 1:19-21**).

So satan is still here, and tempting and fooling man (even Christians) all through life here (**2 cor. 11:13-15; 1 pet. 5:8-9**). So be aware of what is in the world (and creeping into america for a while) and in His word – don't be in the world, but with Him and in His word – and grow in Him and His truth (**john 17:17-19; eph. 5:26; 1 thess. 5:23**). And He will help you out of it (**1 cor. 10:12-13**), if you go to Him. No matter what temptation or sin – wherever it comes from (all born with it). It is all to get you to go to Jesus and make sure you know the truth.

And even Christians – true Christians, started to let politicians, government, officials, etc. to lead beliefs, morals, etc. – and politicians were not Christians anymore and now are still making rules without God (and His word – through Jesus). We need to teach the truth and go against the world – teach the children, etc. the truth, even in america.

God knows there are evil, sinful people in the world – we all are – but not to say it is good to be that way (**rom. 1:28-32**), and to run the world, and people to live, that way – like before the flood (**gen. 6**) and just after, in sodom and gomorrah (**gen. 19**), etc., and ever since in many times and places.

It is satan that goes around looking for those to devour – even in churches, religions, etc. (**1 pet. 5:8**). Keep you sinful.

It is sin through the father mainly (starting with adam who sinned, and then now through noah's sons – from them to us today) – and fathers may give sin – and it goes to the behavior of boys and girls (but the mother can be a good or bad example). It will take a while to get you out of your children – evil, etc., but it will be faster (if it is going to happen at all) with Jesus and His truth – and you do it first. So all need to go to Jesus to change – not stay with what you are born with. So children are sinful (having the same traits, sins, selfish, etc. – **1 kings 15:1-6; psalm 106:6; psalm 109:14; jer. 14:20; lam. 5:7; ezek. 18**), but are innocent until they are taught things (by parents or the world – living and growing in this world, and it doesn't take long – nurturing their sin) – usually by parents (so parents better be knowing and understanding truth and living a good life example – dealing with their sins, etc., but it might be their sins that produced the child in the first place), but we all can go to Jesus (whose Father was the Holy Spirit here, as a human – God – **matt. 1:18-25**), and change and help us with any problem (make something good out of something bad or tough – **rom. 8:28**). And we need to protect the children (and help them grow and learn and be disciplined and respectful) – learning and sharing God's word (**1 john 2:13-17**). We all have free will.

As long as you are alive, God will continue to help (not force) you have opportunities, experiences, etc. to go to Jesus (as long as it is the truth) – we all have chances to go to Him – we send ourselves to hell.

So how your children behave as they grow up are directly associated to you – and you may not have gotten rid of your sins, etc. – behavior (or even aware of them – or at least not admitting them), and your children are going to have to go through it. So it is best to go to Jesus (you first), then the children – knowing this is how we are born and grow in this world (all evil). All of man and all of noah's sons have to go through this. Go to Jesus as soon as you can, and change.

And children should listen to their parents, not trying to get away with things, growing up too fast – and be a good parent – Jesus is best for all of that. Be responsible – clean up your mess. Age doesn't mean you're grown up – how you change and know the truth – especially about Jesus and His word.

Not everyone will be a good parent, but could be with Jesus, no matter how you started (or grew up, etc.). Go to Jesus and change and grow daily – with the truth (His word), and change your wants and desires.

Anyone can change and go to Jesus – be saved – like saul (paul) did, and he was terrible to Christians, but Jesus came to him and saved Him (he then knew who Jesus was – **acts 9**) and he changed.

Try to make yourself better than when you were born, or even than yesterday. For you or your family, life, etc. If you want to change your life – know what you are doing wrong – read the **book of proverbs**, and God will show you how to see and be aware of your problems. But go to Jesus and have Him in your life (with the Holy Spirit) leading you.

You can believe whatever you want – but it won't help anything – won't work and it never has. Go to Jesus (and His word) to figure this world out. Then you can be smart.

Children need mothers (as much or more than fathers – but need both) – good mothers, and God has roles for each, for what is best for man (or women) to stay together (but find the right person first – both saved with Jesus, and His truth, His word). And whatever job is best for a man or a woman (man should be the leader in all ways in the family – spiritual, etc., but if women need to, because of the man is gone or won't, then women may have to, for a time – and God may use women to lead, but wants man to) – but if married (and have children), think of the children (and go to God to help you) for what is best for them.

If you have a family – especially a big one – you better have Jesus and His word in your life, which is what God had planned with man to do – with Him in our lives (**gen. 1:26-28; gen. 9:1**). Go to Jesus and get Him in your life to help you and your children. And know the truth of Him – in His word.

Be a leader for people to go to Jesus, not to follow this world (and satan). We all know right from wrong – from adam and eve (**gen. 2:16-17; gen. 3:1-11**) – no excuses.

God can use anyone, and if men won't do it, then God will use women, if necessary (but it has to be the truth). God wants men to step up – and lead, but with the truth, not what man (or satan) comes up with. Even with mistakes – keep going to Him.

Besides america (with Jesus) helps all of noah's sons, women included, but we need to do what God says about women as He says about noah's sons – all get the best with Jesus, or we struggle without Him (man or woman, nation, etc.).

Possibly mothers working when they don't need to (having both parents, etc.) is causing children to grow up undisciplined, etc. (don't live above your means, etc.) – also without fathers being there will cause problems. God set this world up for a mother and father to bring up children – so being with Him (Jesus) would make it work best.

So God can use anyone – man or woman, although it's best to do what God wants and know what that is. Go to Jesus (and His word – the truth). God wants man to take the lead, with truth of Jesus.

Not only is not having a mother or father a problem, but having a bad mother or bad father is no good. Go to Jesus – He is the only answer. Not having fathers is a big deal – but not having Jesus and His truth is even worse – have God be your Father – for your children and you.

You are never alone – God is there – if you go to Jesus and His word. And be with others that are truly with Jesus. We can have God as our Father – Abba (greek for father), as Jesus called Him (**mark 14:36**), and available to us (**rom. 8:14-16; gal. 4:1-7**). Whatever problems you have should lead you to Jesus.

Doesn't really matter if you are adopted, fatherless, motherless, etc. – all people matter to God – all can and need to go to Jesus. Go to God and have Him as your Father (**rom. 8; gal. 4:1-7**). Don't worry about the past. Look to the future and heaven.

Fathers need to go to Jesus (and His word – only His truth) and share Jesus with sons and daughters. But mothers are the best parent for children (and need to go to Jesus), and be at home (and God will help with this, if you go to Him), as much as they can (especially when they are young), fathers having a job, etc., and having Jesus and His word in your life (**prov. 22:6; eph. 6:1-4**). Even when a man dies (a father, husband, or even a divorce, etc.), then a woman can marry again (good to have two parents for the children) – same for if a woman dies. But before children are taught too much and are very young, they follow most people, and things, willingly (like they do santa claus and the easter bunny, etc., and some evil, etc.), and will follow Jesus, if you let them (and share Him – truthfully), and Jesus is the only one that is real (even though satan is, and disguises himself in many things). So it is that innocence that should help you get them to go to Jesus, who likened children to how you (all of us – no matter how old) should accept Jesus, and get saved – innocently and simply (**matt. 19:13-15; mark 10:13-16; luke 18:15-17**), and babies not born yet (but are still human – **psalm 139:13-18**) have not done anything good or evil (**rom. 9:11**), but will. But let them live, and get to know Jesus.

Love and help your children until they learn – getting to know Jesus and His truth and the way we are (born evil here until we go to Jesus). We all have to change – go to Jesus.

Babies and children are to be helped and loved – with Jesus.

God made this world so that people would care about some things – people, children, family, friends, even themselves, etc. – so we would at least be nice sometimes. And have a little understanding of what love and caring are. But Jesus is the one that will help you love the best.

People love children (for the most part), especially their own (God did that for us), and it is a good thing, because children can be tough to handle at any age, and need a lot of attention when very young (and some older) – most people wouldn't want to put up with all of that trouble normally with anyone (but will usually with their children), although it is still tough, even with your love for them – but it is always better with Jesus (and His word), and His love.

If your child does wrong and pays for it – help other parents and children learn from that – especially going to Jesus.

The best way to help your children, is to love each other (husband and wife) better, and show it in your life, marriage, etc., but that would only happen with Jesus in both of your lives – to be loving people to each other, and that will calm your children down and keep them content.

Children will be happy and behave, if they see their two parents love each other, etc., not because you give the children more attention – love and be kind to each other – and only with Jesus can you do this (sharing Him and His word).

Parents aren't necessarily grown up, or even living a good life, or knowing what a good life really is – they can't even run their own life, how can they run others (how are they going to raise children?) – why not go to Jesus, instead of ruining a life (or lives), and find the right answers and help for you and others. But it has to be the truth, or you will still be struggling.

Integrity is important and we should be a better example – especially parents, leaders, etc.

Give and show good things in life – examples of a good life, and point out and share good behavior – what God would want.

If you don't help children (or anyone) try things (no matter how tough), they will never know what they can do and overcome (even when sometimes they fail) – with Jesus it is the best.

So discipline is good for anyone (but don't abuse), especially a child (**prov. 13:24; prov. 22:6**), but man doesn't know how to do it or control it sometimes (man being evil – he may go overboard with how he punishes) – but man could do a better job (and having both parents), if he would do it the way God wants (but it would have to be with Jesus and His word in your life to do it best), because without discipline and some correction physically (out of love), children will get out of control. We have to know how we are born (selfish, evil, etc. – **james 4:5**), and being naturally evil and knowing right from wrong (good and evil – **gen. 3**), man tends to lean toward and be attracted to evil – selfish, etc. (especially if that's all anyone sees), and with satan here (**eph. 6:10-12**). And since the world is in our hearts to begin with, and as we grow (with all of its misery – and people are attracted to hate and lies and free things, sometimes lazy, depressed, etc.), not working hard as we grow up (rich or poor, black or white, etc.), so we are not to be following or listening to the world and it's ideas (which will ruin man) and need to get the world (evil) out of ourselves (only with Jesus can we do that and be free, with the

Holy Spirit and changing – **rom. 12:2; james 4; 1 john 2:15**) or we are stuck (**eccl. 3:9-15; john 3:17-21**).

You have nothing to strive for, if all is given to you without working for it (honest, fair, good work) – earning what you get, gives you reason to live, etc. We can't be equal in all things – go to Jesus to get what you need – what is best for you, and sometimes we have to wait for what is best for us, but still keep working hard to live. And competition is best for all to get better. And we can help other people along the way to make in their life, when needed. And don't let satan get a hold of you and lead you down the wrong road – to get what you need, etc.

All of noah's sons can be good fathers, mothers, friends, citizens, etc. (but struggling to make it in this world, to stay together, etc.), but there is a way to live and behave to get along, etc. – it is to go to Jesus and His word, and follow.

When you follow all the evil in you or in the world – you are following and worshipping satan – causing all of your problems. Go to Jesus to change all of it – what you are born with, and get the Holy Spirit that saves you and changes you.

All of the things that God says not to do and warns us about (in His word – the bible), are things that we all are capable of doing – so He wants us not to be of the world (**rom. 12:2**), by basically following satan. Follow Jesus and get the Holy Spirit (salvation) and be able to fight these things – the desires to have the things of the world.

If you don't have a lot of things, but you see others that do, it makes it tough in this world (even though we don't need that much), although america is that way (but we have way more than we need, than most countries – especially if we use our money wisely and don't buy useless things, otherwise you do deserve to be poor, if we waste our money on things that are not good for us – it's God's money).

God won't trust you with more, if you don't or can't do well with what you have or have been given, or even with a little (**luke 16:10-13**). Give to true churches and ministries (many false ones out there and God won't honor that).

Even churches (true or false) that accept money from people (or businesses, etc.) that don't believe or agree with the bible and the truth (they may just want to look good, etc.), will have problems and not grow or be blessed.

Don't waste things, if possible. Although God even uses wastes in this world – trying to be as efficient as possible (don't always need new things). Do your part (we all can). And share (especially Jesus), if you can. Help and give to others.

And with noah's sons you will see many things, but if you are with your own only (in a nation, etc.), you will not (like in most countries – america makes you want things, but you don't need that much). Don't let evil lead the way (or satan) or follow those that do. Do an honest day's work, and a good life (stop hiding or living in denial) – whatever that might be, and if you go to Jesus, you will be able to change whatever life you lead.

Sometimes you have to do things you don't want to do – but need to (good things, work hard). God made us to do things and work – hopefully with Him in our life. And be moral and ethical – whether you are man, woman, rich, poor, black, white, etc. – and why we need Jesus. We may be able to change some things, but certain things keep happening until we go to Jesus. Don't keep covering up things in your life – stop living in denial (without Jesus and following Him and His word).

If we have something to live for – to do right, etc., then we can live on the straight and narrow – to be good (we all know right from wrong – good and evil, **gen.3**). But some think they don't have anything to live for and are tempted to do evil (even the rich, etc.

do). We are not perfect, but can have Jesus, and have hope anywhere and anytime. So the hopes, dreams, jobs, businesses, family, homes, money, etc. keeps us happy, etc. in america, but it is Jesus (and His freedom) that gives us the opportunity for those things (and to use them right and to hang onto them – and to share). We all need Jesus especially when things fall apart – sometimes people don't try anything new unless something's not the same – out of your routine (because when setbacks happen in your life, that can be a blessing – to get you to change, when you normally wouldn't have), but go to Jesus (and His word) no matter what, and He will help you (and get the Holy Spirit), and to avoid some things in this world.

We all do something in this world that God doesn't want us to – but we have to grow and overcome things, with Jesus.

When you go through tough times in your life – and you can go to Jesus to get through them – God can use you to help others that go through what you went through, and help them. And help them with Jesus, to get through these things. Then you can do what you are capable of doing here in your life.

And you need an environment that you can use your talents and abilities – be free to succeed, not control or fear (what satan wants). That is with Jesus and His truth in your life.

And happiness comes and goes – what you are doing, what you have, or don't have, etc. – but joy is being with Jesus – a choice. We need to go to Him, and even being happy will be easier – whatever you have or don't have (your desires, etc. will change) – doing good things, better things.

When we have problems, suffer, etc., we can help others through their problems better – and God uses those people (and problems, etc.) to help others better – your family, friends, etc., and helping them go to Jesus.

Remember when you have problems – there are others out in the world that have it worse than you do, so you don't need to feel sorry for yourself for very long. And always go to Jesus.

Helping people is the best thing to do in this world – best with Jesus (but we need to straighten ourselves out first).

You can help people, but they need to help themselves in order to not need help all of the time (and grow and learn). And they need to go to Jesus, and His word.

Most people don't take a chance on things (doing good) – something great, unless they are really down and desperate, so take advantage of a struggle, etc. – don't be defeated or quit (doing right and good) – work harder and try something, and go to Jesus to help you – He will. And don't be weary of doing well (**gal. 6:5-10; 2 thess. 3:10-15**).

No matter what you do, there will be evil in this world (the way man and this world is – especially with satan here) – make it better for you with Jesus and doing what He wants. Have a better chance of making it through.

Every time a person does something bad – buy a drug, sell a drug, steal, lie, destroy, hurt, kill, etc. (which is selfishness, and jealousy, envy, pride, etc. – which is what satan does, **john 10:10**) – you hurt your own family, community, people that are like you, etc. (and hurt you, etc. – why some people are hated and not treated well, then they don't like themselves, etc.). Is that what you want? If not, do something good for others (and you) and that is what Jesus does (**john 10:10**). Change. God will help you with something better for you and others, if you would just keep going to Him and His word – don't give up (doing good – **gal. 6:9; 2 thess. 3:13**).

You never know what you are capable of – good or evil – until you are in certain situations. We all are capable – and need Jesus to help change us – go to Him and His word for guidance.

If others can be mean – so can you. And if you hate others – they can hate you. Remember who you dislike the most in your life, is who you really are – no matter how many people love you or you love. Man is that way. No one wants to admit that.

Maybe you cause the way people think of and look at you – white, black, etc. at some time over the years. So you hurt others like you, because of that – and that can last for years. Change with Jesus, and eventually forgive, and don't cause the negative reactions and attitudes toward you or others.

There is no reason for evil (even with satan here) – when you can go to Jesus (and His word – the truth).

Better to be safe, than sorry – for things in this world, and is best for you, too – for avoiding anything bad for you – any problems that may come up in this world. Best is to be with Jesus. At least be ready to go, whatever happens.

Thank God for His word – the truth of it – through Jesus and the Holy Spirit – to follow the truth of it. You will do things naturally that are good for you and others **(gal. 5:22)**. If you are truly saved with the Holy Spirit, from Jesus, you will be a good person, citizen, etc., but we won't be perfect, not until we are in heaven, even though good for here on earth – then we will start to do things of God. So get saved first, then change with Jesus.

People don't always think straight, and usually won't make good decisions when you are out of your mind – even you. You have to be honest and think of others – not just yourself. Let God and the truth of His word help you.

So don't bother people – like you can't yell fire in a crowded theater, when there is no fire, or things like that – scaring, or even terrorism – you or even politicians, etc.

Have a conscience – do the right thing – not selfish. And share Jesus – go to Him and get Him into your life.

There has to be a moral compass to what people do (fairness, consideration, etc., if not, is why there are, and have need for, laws, punishment, etc.) – and it is Jesus who helps all do better, and don't let people get away with cheating, lying, etc. (and people feel better when they do the right thing – so know what that is).

Not law, but love – of Jesus, with Jesus in your life.

Love is the reason for the laws – especially the laws of God – to do right by people, to love them (**1 john 4**), be concerned, etc. (even to love ourselves the right way) – but we need the laws, so God gave them, because we don't naturally love, care, respect, etc., so we need Him (the Holy Spirit through Jesus) to do this, otherwise we will follow satan and hate, etc., since we are born evil. We need something to govern us (our evil).

If you don't want your rights violated, then don't violate other's rights, etc. – respect, fairness, and forgiveness, but don't make it worse. Do unto others – what you would want them to do or not to do for you, and how they would treat you (**luke 6:31**). And there has to be punishment, discipline, etc. (just like in a family, etc. – growing up). And definitely go to Jesus (His truth), or it won't ever work. Jesus' love (**1 cor. 13**).

Love is sharing the truth of Jesus and His word – to keep people from the lies of satan – no matter how much it hurts or offends people (or hurts you sharing it).

Jesus forgives us – we need to forgive others and ourselves. Even though Jesus forgives us of all sin (if we go to Him and follow) – there are still consequences to sin for all (here on this earth – even for true Christians), with punishments, etc.

Even when you forgive someone or acknowledge the wrong – the person you hurt may not want that – they want to be angry. Even they may hurt someone – and not be forgiven. We need to keep going to Jesus to have a chance to get past these things.

You can't help someone and coverup things, help them do their work, cheat, etc. to help just so someone can avoid consequences, punishment, etc. – they will never learn or get better or change (especially without Jesus).

Some people even defend their evil criminal friends to their dying breath – lying, when they could go to Jesus before they die. Don't be that stubborn, and don't wait to go to Jesus.

Tell on people – turn them in – do it anonymously, if needed (be safe), but tell the truth and help them and others, and share Jesus if you can. Don't worry how people look at you – don't try to fit in, or be liked by someone who doesn't want to do the right thing – don't worry about being a snitch, etc. – you really are doing them a favor in the long run – and share Jesus with them (you go to Him). Change their life for the better.

And if you tell someone – your family, friends, co-workers, etc. that you are not going to lie or cover for them for doing evil, maybe they will not go through with it – but help them go to Jesus, not to hurt or harm others. Help to stop others from hurting others, if possible. We all have to help with this.

If you are a criminal, etc., you have no rights. Stop what you do. You need to be stopped – you know who you are – don't live in denial – what man is good at. You get what you deserve.

And if you don't have punishment – harsh in some cases (or at least harsh enough), then you won't deter or stop or even hinder crime, evil, etc., and it will get worse and people will continue to get away with murder, etc.

Man is born evil – and we need to know and understand that truth (**gen. 8:21; psalm 14; rom. 3**). Go to Jesus to change that.

If you are not with Jesus, you need laws, punishment, etc. in this world (and with Jesus – He will help you, as will the Holy Spirit, but you need to go to Jesus and His word daily to fight satan – and this evil world). Get yourself back to God.

God gives us time to grow up and see the truth, no matter where you are born (all of noah's sons), and puts us all together (especially in america today) – even those with satan now (**matt. 13:36-43**), who we all start out our life with (**john 3:17-21**) – so we can get to know Jesus and the truth, and have others share the truth with us, or we can share with them. God waits, and doesn't want any to perish in hell (**john 3:16; 2 pet. 3:9**) – but we all have a choice, He won't force you (so it is our decision to go to hell or not). He gives us a way out with Jesus.

Even in noah's day – after the flood – God had a law (before the bible was written, before jews, etc.) – not to kill others, if you did, then you should be killed – told to noah, by God (**gen. 9:1-6**). God talked to man since adam – through to moses (and others writing the bible – before Jesus died and rose, until the **book of revelation** was written – after 70ad sometime – the rest of the time – the last 2,000 years or so, is with Jesus, and His word). And if you are with God, He will (or may) help you live. But at least be ready to go with Jesus, and be able to go to heaven with Him. So God wants people to live to have a chance to repent and go to Jesus to get saved – that is why He is so patient, and it seems like He is slack, slow, etc. (**2 pet. 3:8-9**).

God says to avoid and eventually kills all evil – old and young – all of the bad seeds, etc. (like in the flood – **gen. 6**), like He did to some canaanites (son of ham – descendants, etc. – **gen. 9:25-27**), etc. – **gen. 24:3, 37; josh. 3:10; josh. 24:11**, etc., so they don't corrupt others (God didn't want His people – the jews, to be influenced by evil beliefs, etc., and doesn't want us to be today) – so God will kill all, even babies (even though they will go to heaven – trust God to be fair), etc. (and people accuse God of being mean, etc. – there has to be punishment, He is just, holy, righteous, etc. – man is not, and we need to know that He is going to do the best for us, and we all can go to Him) – God wants the evil beliefs to disappear and the people that believe and share them, but He warns and waits (wants all to go to Him and not perish – as He did before the flood and has after), and doesn't want the evil to influence people or keep hurting people (satan leading against God). We are all evil (**psalm 58:3**) – get that through your head – born that way (even though we don't have a choice of where or who we are born to – and what they believe, but we do have a choice after we are grown) – for babies and children (we need to teach them), God will judge, and wants them to be in heaven with Jesus (**isa. 7:16; matt. 18:14; matt. 19:14; mark 10:14; luke 18:16**). And God is our Maker and His ways are higher than ours (**isa. 55:6-9**) – we don't always know why He is going to do something. Just keep going to Jesus and His word, and follow Him and His truth.

If you believe that God punishes, then you better also believe He created us and this world, and we need to go to Him and follow Him – Jesus, to live forever in heaven. He loves us, and wants the best for us. We are evil (because of sin, disobedience – basically following satan) and are destined for hell (**john 3:17-21**).

God set up everything – knows when man would sin – predestination for those that are saved since then – knowing who would go to Him since the beginning (at creation), and to Jesus and be saved today. God is patient, why He sent Jesus to save us – but God can take a believer early, if they are not living a good life (**1 cor. 5:1-5**). God could get rid of all of us.

We are all going to die since adam sinned – from the beginning (**gen. 3**), and with the flood (**gen. 6 to 8**), and after (including sodom and gomorrah, and others) – with disasters, killing, evil man, etc., but God knows who will go to Him (get saved) or not – knowing the end from the beginning. God will not force you to believe or follow Him, but knows who will (no matter how long they live, or die early, that they still won't go to Jesus and get saved) – and He can use evil people (including satan) for His purposes – hopefully to get people to go to Jesus. But He has to punish for what we do (and not keep letting people get hurt from these evil people) – He is a righteous God, and when we see that evil, we should be going to Him to get saved – to Jesus. The evil (including satan) in this world should get us to go to Him and why it is evil in this world – but you don't have to be – with Jesus in your life (and the Holy Spirit) and the truth of His word.

So go to Jesus and change and be with God (the only way out) and grow with Him (and the Holy Spirit) – and then we need to be nice to others (and as peaceful as you can with all – **rom. 12:17-19**) and share the truth of Jesus and His word with them. And be ready for heaven (helping others go to heaven – before we die – and we all are going to die sometime – go to Jesus).

We really kill ourselves (sending ourselves to hell). Don't blame God – He has warned us all through history. So take the responsibility and change. Just go to Jesus – have Him and His truth lead your life and to help others. Don't let satan mislead you.

Make sure you go to God and know you hear from Him (mainly in His word, through the Holy Spirit – not necessarily talking to you), and that it is not satan talking to you (which he does a lot) – go to God through Jesus – look into His word, because satan would want to lead you astray – like he did in sodom, etc. and today, and God has to do something about it or all will be evil to each other. Wake up and go to God – to Jesus to change that.

The only way this world works the best, is with man and God in a relationship – no other way, otherwise we won't get along – it is only through Jesus (and the truth of His word), that it will work – getting the Holy Spirit from Jesus (born again – **john 3**) – go to Him now to get saved and help this world work (and be in the one after this one) – to be saved and get rid of our destiny now – sin and death (**rom. 6:23**). It is satan that corrupts the good (and we follow satan and cause our own problems, and cause what God does and has done to us in this world). God tells us and shows us, and we just don't listen – know we are evil and sinners (from adam – and now from noah's sons).

The only way to fight evil is to love – but with Jesus' love (**1 cor. 13**) – not ours (or satan's). Go to Jesus and learn to love with Him. And share Him and His love. Sharing Him is love.

And when Jesus was talking about loving your enemies (whether they were jews or gentiles), and forgiving people, He was talking to the jews – **matt. 5:44; luke 6:27-35** (and jews were not to be with gentiles). Now it would be all of noah's sons – believing in Jesus – to be able to love our enemies (not just people you know or are like you) – which can only be done with Jesus in our life. Love like Jesus, not like satan.

God separated jews and gentiles, etc., and later separated jews and Christians after Jesus died and rose, and then separated saul to paul – to go from jew to Christian (**acts 9**).

But satan will not stop trying to unite all of man and the world to go against God and His truth – like satan did in the garden, and before the flood – since noah and the tower of babel, God has tried to separate man, and keep satan from uniting us against God and His truth. So we need to go to Jesus, so we can connect with God, and get away from the connection to man (from adam, and all of noah's sons) – so leave this world, man, family, nationality, etc. and go to Jesus and be one with God through the Holy Spirit – born again (away from what you were born here on earth – **matt. 19:29** – then help those you know here get to know Jesus). Then love and help people here.

And satan (lucifer) wants to lead you (and a family, society, nation, etc.) away from a relationship with God (to reconnect man, or reconcile, with God through Jesus) – thinking you don't need it or Him (just like satan thought he didn't need God or that he was God, or at least better than God – **isa. 14:12-15**) – satan is a created being like man (**ezek. 28:15**), and if God got rid of satan (and He can any time), after he tempted eve (and adam) – to fool them and mislead them (like he does us today), and cause death to mankind (since we were created to live forever), then we (mankind) may have been separated from God forever (read **book of job** – satan used to test man) – or until He had Jesus come here and die for us (we need the payment for our sins – for all of us), and He defeated satan – death (Jesus being resurrected – alive again, and so can we). But until then we may not see the evil and separation (from God) as easily – then or today. It is satan that lets us see the real difference of good (Jesus) and evil (satan) in this world (that man chose to see also, by what adam and eve did – **gen. 3**) – and then man can make a choice, a better one – with his free will (that God gave us) to make our own decision (and have no doubt) – but we need to see the difference clearly.

Or if God got rid of satan before he tempted man (adam and eve – who had the Holy Spirit from Jesus the Creator – created in them), then man (adam and eve – or anyone after them) still could sin (disobey God) without satan (just like satan did on his own – satan didn't have anyone tempt him, just his own free will, that God created him with, like us – and He created us, and satan perfect – **isa. 14:12-15; ezek. 28:11-19**). But once Jesus died for our sins – paid the penalty for us – we now can get the Holy Spirit and never lose it (but be sure you are truly saved with Jesus and His truth – not satan's lies).

There will be a time when satan will be bound – for 1,000 years (**rev. 20**), when Jesus reigns on earth – and satan won't be able to tempt man, but will be let out to tempt them after the thousand years are up, to see who will follow him or not (so it is in us, with our free will, to be attracted to evil – which is against God and His word). We are not forced (by God, or Christians, etc.) to go to God and be saved (but God lets the evidence speak for itself, including His word – the truth, and Jesus, and also satan) – but it is the best choice you can make for yourself or others. Help people with their needs (here on this earth), and share Jesus. So share Him – and His truth. And if anyone forces us to do evil (through man – and man's bullying, violence, evil, beliefs, ideas, lies, killing, etc.), and follow him and his ways – it is satan, while trying not to look like they are evil (but they are – and satan is using them). Look in the world (even some in america, that we are seeing more and more today). They (satan and those who follow him) will be more blatant (and arrogant, evil, etc.) as time goes on, especially when they have the chance. And it will be all against God (Jesus). And don't mistake arrogance, with standing up for the right thing, and trying to help people (with what God wants – not man, or satan).

And satan does have power – to do evil – so all of his ideas and beliefs and plans can cause problems and situations that control people and have power to hurt people. Go to Jesus to fight him.

It is satan that shows us more of the evil in the things we do in this life, and we can see the good in God (Jesus) better. That is the reason we are still here – to choose to be with God or not. The only (and best) way to live – with Jesus.

And satan has been going against God (and man) since the beginning – why wouldn't he be doing it now – causing problems, for man, without God – we still see problems exist.

Even though it is not quite the same – america (Jesus' land, and the most freedom in the world, because of Him) is like that 1,000 year reign of Jesus – the millennium – coming after the tribulation. The only difference is that satan is not bound right now – and is leading man, and this world, but we can have victory over satan with Jesus (and His truth), and have a land that is helping that (the best in this evil world).

There is a best and right way to live your life – for all of us, God made us for that, but it has to be with Him (that's how and why He created man in the first place – to be with Him, a relationship) and His truth (don't be against Him, or we will struggle – and we do), learning His word, that should be taught in every church, and every school and in every home (especially in america) and then you will see the change in society and how people are treated and looked at, but until we all do that it won't (and you can't make or force people to like or respect you – even God doesn't do that, but the best possible way to do that would be to be good to people, everyone should, knowing they are evil like you). Some people can't be nice to others, and they may not try to be nice to you (and really only with Jesus will you even get close to loving at all, without Him it is next to impossible). Jesus and His word will prepare you for life, so start young, or the sorrows in the world will be in your life (**psalm 32:10-11; 1 tim. 6:3-12**). Start with the truth (of God). And again, we should not be weary of doing well (**gal. 6:9-10; 2 thess. 3:13**).

You can't hate so much that you believe lies – see the truth, and it is only with Jesus (and His word).

You can believe something so bad that you want it to be true, that you become delusional, in denial, etc. – like being in love with someone, or you think you are great, or lies that are told, or some theory, or even some political or religious beliefs, or any belief, etc. Don't believe the lies (all from satan – and man follows and teaches it) – they are lying to your face, and you don't even know it. If you can't have religions, churches, etc. (separation of church and state) be part of the government – then you can't have people (or businesses, companies, the rich, other countries, etc. – and their beliefs, etc. – or like a religion or denomination, etc.) be part of (or control, influence, etc.) the government (or nation, or its leaders, etc.). Look into it, and see who is controlling and affecting the belief (and the people) in a nation (like we see today in america – our leaders, should be put in by the people – not the few), and are cheating, lying, etc. True Christianity (and why God made this country) is what built this country (laws, society, etc.). It better be the truth – with Jesus and His word is the only way. Learn and share Him.

Government should not force things, beliefs, etc. on people – give information, truth, facts, ideas, etc. and let people decide for themselves – that's freedom (and responsibility, etc.). They wouldn't want Christianity (or anything) forced on them (even though it is the best and why any country would be good – and why america is). Make sense of what you believe and care about people, not lie, cheat, and control, etc. And share Jesus.

No matter if you are believing right, left, liberal, etc. politically, or black, white, etc., we all need Jesus and His truth, not doing things on your own – help others to get to know Jesus. It should be Jesus' agenda, not political, etc. beliefs (or at least have Jesus influence any belief) – some may be closer to Jesus, but all need to go to Him (and His truth), others are closer to satan's agenda (evil, selfishness, hate, etc.).

Some people (satan, etc.) don't like some things (laws, police, morals, right, etc.), because it hinders their selfishness, evil, etc.

If you don't think all people are bad, then don't think all police, etc. are bad (including yourself) – even if they bother you. If people are nice and kind and loving all of the time, but don't have Jesus – it is a waste of time (even though it is nice to be nice) – they are still evil (man is sinful), no matter what they do without Jesus in their life. Let the problem get you to Jesus.

Like a famous musician sang – one bad apple don't spoil the whole bunch – so if it is the same with family, nationality, etc., then it is with the police, etc., too. They can have people trying to do it right, even though we all need to go to Jesus. But some of it may be true, and all groups – both sides could change – and you don't get rid of families, nationalities, etc. – just need to follow and obey, and help others to do it, too (change how you look at yourself and people). With Jesus, and His truth.

But we are all sinful, and we are all from adam – one bad apple – so from one person – adam, we are bad, sinful, etc., but also from one person – Jesus, we can be saved and change that life and curse we have (if we believe in and follow Him, and His truth) – **rom. 5; 1 cor. 15:44-46**. And that goes for women (from eve – **gen. 3:16**), and for descendants of ham – noah's son (**gen. 9:24-25**), and any other curse God put on man (or individuals, groups, etc.) – until we go to Jesus – then we can only be one (or equal, etc.) with Him – with God (Jesus).

And it is satan that is leading you down this path in life (separating you from God) – without the truth (with false churches, religions, beliefs, etc.), and without Jesus in your life. God wants us separated (and you can see all of the separations in the world – all by God – so satan can't unite all of man against God like he did before the flood and a little after the flood – up to the tower of babel – **gen. 11**) until we go to Jesus, and the truth of His word.

If you have a country that follows Jesus and keeps sharing the truth, and going by His word (rules, laws, beliefs, etc.), then you will have better people going into any group, organization, etc., from that country – but it is still all about Jesus. And we need defending and protecting (it is good and needed) – not trying to hurt or kill, etc. So follow the laws in a country (and of God's) – and change the road you are on (and have been on, since adam and noah). Jesus can help you change, and get along – but only with Him. It's not about being good, but being with Jesus – He will help you be good (with the Holy Spirit).

And if you are trying to keep all of the laws (especially of God's), then if you break one law, then you break them all – we can't keep them all – and don't depend on being good and keeping laws only – go to Jesus (truly saved with the Holy Spirit) and you will be righteous. Know you are truly saved.

If you have satanic leaders, government, society, etc., then you have people going against God's word and Jesus (the truth), to deceive and control people – see who they are – those going against God's word, the truth – the bible (which is what this country and constitution is based on).

Free speech in america is disappearing – all against God and His word – freedom to do evil is rising and all need to go to Jesus – all because man is going against God and His truth for us. So we should speak of Jesus and the truth of His word.

There is no answer for sin, evil, etc. in this world, except Jesus – all people do evil and are evil – from adam and noah's sons, and still need laws and punishment until we all go to Jesus. And we all need love and understanding, but without Jesus, it will only go so far. And discipline and punishment are love – but best to go to Jesus – otherwise we all stay connected to man and sin. We have to tell people they are sinful, evil, bad (we all are) – especially if they do something wrong, but share Jesus. You don't want people to stay that way – sinful – share Jesus – it is the only way to change.

The only way or reason we have a chance to get along – anywhere, but especially in america, is because of Jesus. Look into it – figure it out – accept it (Jesus and the truth of His word). We haven't solved it yet, as long as man has been here.

Just know we won't get along without Jesus, and His truth, no matter what we do.

With Jesus, you will have control, freedom, and love – do what Jesus wants. And we will have what is best for man here.

Jesus used parables to share truths – things that we know (or should know) here on earth – to talk and share truth of what He wants for us – how to live, believe in, etc.

God uses sometimes nature, land, animals, etc. (like He did man) to show if you are not living right and understanding things to learn throughout the bible. Should be easy. We need to learn things, or we'll have consequences, punishments, etc. So go to Jesus and follow, and keep learning, and growing in truth.

If you won't see the truth and understand earthly things – history, science, life, humans, etc. (the truth of them – which is mainly in the bible – and can be seen in the world, if you look), then how would you learn and understand heavenly, spiritual things – in the bible – salvation, the truth about our sinfulness, etc. (**john 3:11-12**)?

People should tell the truth, if they know it – stand up for the truth, and satan will still lead the liars. You can't be afraid to tell the truth – no matter who it hurts (but do it caringly) – it will work itself out (and stop a bad cycle in someone's life, etc.) – especially if you go to Jesus and His word (it's in the bible).

Don't listen to satan's (and man's) lies – in the world, leaders, government, etc. (has some good and bad) – just what Jesus says (the truth of it). Don't waste time – yours or others, with lies, cheating, etc. – really look at the people and their lives – what they do – how they treat people, etc. (selfishness, hate, etc.). Change you.

Truth and love are two things that satan doesn't have (even though people follow him and think they do) – he only fools you, the biggest liar (**john 8:43- 44; acts 5:3; 2 cor. 11:13-15: eph. 4**), even in some churches.

Certain people don't care about you – especially some of those that sell, run for office, celebrities, etc. – they just want to attract you to get benefits for themselves, etc.

You will know them by their fruits – life, beliefs, behaviors, etc. (especially from God or not – **matt. 3; matt. 7:13-23; james 3:17**). Need to repent and change from that (basically be born again with the Holy Spirit – **john 3**). Admit it.

We cause the problems, if we don't follow God (Jesus) and His truth and do it, or we will depend on man to solve it – man will try to come up with something to solve it, which will make it worse – go to God for the problems we make, He will help us solve them.

All people have problems in this life and world (life and death for sure) – no matter who they are – the level they are used to for them – their lifestyle, upbringing, expectations, etc. – the disappointments that go with their usual life (whether you are rich or poor, black or white, etc.). So people (no matter what level they live their life) should limit their problems here – do things that are best and good for you (and hopefully for others), and the best is to go and follow Jesus and His word.

Don't follow people or nationality, etc. that do evil – work hard and follow those people that go to Jesus to make it through and follow His word – the truth (know it is truth). Follow Him.

Love and follow Jesus and not your family, nationality, culture, etc. – it's not easy to do, and try to help them to get to know Jesus and His truth (**matt. 10:32-39**). And it's not that children disobey or not agree on everything – just who and what they believe in – and still try to be at peace as much as possible.

No people are perfect in this world, but give yourself the best chance. Go to Jesus (and His word) for the truth – not man or yourself (culture, nationality, family, belief, society, etc.). You have to look into the truth – not avoid it – God's truth not man's (or really satan's), to have a chance in life. Study it – the truth.

Share Jesus – the truth, not a political view, race, equity, programs, etc. – get away from man – noah's sons (and satan).

And He will lead you in the right direction. He is the only way to change, and help man – all of us.

And if you really love someone you will want what's best for them (even if it's not you) – both have to feel this way (otherwise it's a problem away from hate or at least somewhat conditional, which may be fine for part of the relationship – to love each other, and to follow Jesus and His word). But you will never know true love without Jesus (**1 cor. 13**). In marriage - love the other person and you don't need to worry about yourself - they love you and will help you. And that is best with Jesus.

People don't like (or even love – it's not really love) you as much as you think (and it starts young), and you need to know who they are and who you are – what love is – go to Jesus to find out. Don't let the world (satan) teach you love.

People can even fake being a Christian (to fool you), if you don't know what a true Christian is – a true Christian is someone wanting to read the bible and share Jesus – know and learn the truth. That's why the bible is boring to a non-christian – God made it that way (partly to keep people from changing it, etc., and to have true Christians wanting to read and study and learn it, going to and talking of Jesus – and His truth). Know who a true Christian is (who to be with and who to marry, etc.).

Love (or maybe the lack of it, or the right kind), has a lot to do with man's problems here – with each other. Go to Jesus to change that, because we all have had some problems with who we are (and how we treat each other).

You can't love someone so much that you will do anything for them – including evil. People say they will die (selfishly), or even kill for you – it may be wrong – something is wrong with you. You become a victim when you love some desire, people, etc. of this world so much – and people can take advantage of you – and you let them. That is not love. Change with Jesus.

You may not die for anything or something – but don't let someone die for you – especially so you (or they) can get away with something evil – don't be in that position in the first place.

Besides if man kills anyone here – they only kill the body – we need to be ready in life here for death to the body, but also be with God (through Jesus), to have your soul be with Him in heaven, not in hell. So fear Him (the true God) that can kill body and soul in hell, not just kill the body (which is satan, and man) – **matt. 10:28**. Be with Jesus and be ready to go no matter what happens to you here.

Jesus loves all of us (always has – and did die for us, unselfishly) and wants us to come to Him – we make the choice. He even died in the place of barabbas (**matt. 27:15-26; mark 15:6-15; luke 23:13-34; john 18:33-40**), who was evil and guilty – just like we are. He died for us all – then and now. We are all like barabbas – who lived instead of Jesus (dying for him) – and does that for us all – all of us sinners – guilty of death. Jesus did good things and was rejected in place of an evil man – barabbas, who did bad things, just like we do. So He died in his place – like for us. Don't reject Jesus – go to Him and change. Pray to Him and ask Him to lead your life – believe in Him. And we have to get saved (with the Holy Spirit) before we die.

Grace and mercy of God is what saves us through Jesus, even though we don't deserve it. He did it for us – it is a gift, we don't do anything for it, just have faith and believe, and He will change us – with the Holy Spirit.

The Holy Spirit is our Comforter (**john 14:15-26; john 15:26-27; john 16:7-14, acts 1 and 2**).

We have to see how much God loves us – He keeps us around, even though we are evil, and He wants us to go to Him, and to be with Him, and throughout the bible He shows us that (and why He wrote the bible for us – to show us the truth and His love) – He keeps coming to us and to help us (and gets rid of evil that satan does to us and this world) – for those who want to be with Him (which is why He created man in the first place). He loves us, but there is also punishment, etc. (**heb. 12**).

Jesus wants us to be a servant of all (**mark 9:35**), even if we aren't one – help people, especially to get to know Jesus.

The tougher the childhood that you have (and we all have some struggles), the more you need to go to Jesus, and His word (that is the problem – we don't do that) – parents need to go to Jesus, don't be selfish (we all are evil from our youth, God says – **gen. 8:21**, and we will be until we go to Jesus), and don't love your children so much that you can't see they are evil (and that the world is – and we all need protection from that, satan's world – only God can change us and keeps coming to us to do that, and in the meantime we need to protect ourselves –children, nations, society, etc. from that evil). But love them with real love – Jesus' love and truth (**1 cor. 13**), or you won't really love them or help them at all. So go to Jesus and learn from Him, not the world (**rom. 12:2**).

We need to learn how to bring up children – have Jesus help you and others that have done that. It is the best way – for them and you.

People need love in this world (at any age – especially young) – true love and that only can come from God – through Jesus, and we need it to live and function and survive and grow properly here – God made us that way – we try to fill that void with the things of this world (satan is trying to take the place of God's – Jesus' love, and leads you to destruction and misery here).

So we don't do just anything, because you love someone so much – things that ae not good for them or you (or others).

Love (true love) can cover sins (**prov. 10:12; luke 7:46-48; 1 pet. 4:8** – but Jesus can only save you with the Holy Spirit and the truth of His word). Know what love is with Jesus.

Don't be wise in the world (**1 cor. 3:18-20**), or teach it – know God's word (and be wise with it) – learn through the Holy Spirit (**1 cor. 2:12-14** – that only Jesus gives us), and learn and grow in Him (**john 17:17**), and you will be wise (**psalm 111:10; prov. 1:7; prov. 9:10; prov. 15:33; isa. 11:2; isa. 33:6**) – in all of life here – science, history, man, etc. and how to see why and what they mean and understand the truth of them.

Look at the world through the eyes of God – with the truth of His word. Teach the truth. And make sure your children know (but you learn and know it first – the truth of it). Don't enable people – children, friends, etc.

Read God's word and look in the world and it will make more sense than anything. Get saved by Jesus with the Holy Spirit.

And don't compare you or your children to the rest of the world (other people), but what God says is evil (and we know, too) – even some parents don't want to say bad things about their children (the honest, caring ones do) that have died living a bad lifestyle (or in prison, etc.), but they should, so other children and parents will learn and do differently (as an example – set high moral standards, honesty, lifestyle, health, etc. for them), and care for themselves and children more and how they turn out (and maybe how they failed them), and they should go to and share Jesus to have this work.

If your life or sin, etc. doesn't eventually cause a big problem in your life (and in others), then you won't stop or change – don't wait for that – go to Jesus now – being a good example.

If you don't go to Jesus as soon as you can – to the truth, then you will hurt other people (besides yourself).

Family and upbringing affect people the most – go to God and do it His way. And people are affected the most that don't go to Jesus or forgive – you are really just hurting yourself (and then let God, or satan, take care of the other person).

Your life is the life that you are connected to your parents, family, ancestors, etc., until you go to God (Jesus), and their abilities, behaviors, etc. (hopefully you can stop the cycle). We have to learn, and have to learn from our ancestors over the years we have been on earth – about the truth of this world from adam to noah to his sons to abram to abraham to david (even the tribes, people, etc. all over the world since the flood) until Jesus came and died and rose for all of us – now we have to all share Jesus with the next generation up to today (all over the world) – we have no excuse, except our own ancestors, and grandparents, etc. to learn the truth of what happened from the beginning, the truth – and people went away from sharing the truth (with satan's help) and why we are evil and end up with these groups that have problems in the world. Go to Jesus and learn the truth and share Him. Now it's your choice.

Think of this while you read this.

People that have tough lives, and children that do, can blame the people before (their family and ancestors, etc.) and eventually themselves, by not going to Jesus – following Him and His word. We all are from adam and noah's sons, and are affected by them and their choices – we are all connected.

But eventually have to blame yourself, if you don't do things to change those things (mainly the bad from them) that control you (and may still control them), and know what they are.

We have to suffer the consequences of what your parents did (and what they believed), and what their parents did, etc. for anything (including health, etc.). So don't just blame your parents (although they had a chance to change, etc.), but we are connected to adam (and now to noah's sons), and we have a chance to change now, and that is only with Jesus (and His word – the truth of it).

God loves you – Jesus does – even if you don't think your family does – even friends, etc. Go to Jesus – to live your life.

Stop trying to trust man and being disappointed – trust Jesus (and His word), and change (to make a better world – for you and others) to the way He wants us to be.

Man goes through many things – tough problems – some the world did, some you did, but no excuse for behavior, etc. when you could go to Jesus – we all can, and all will grow and get better, He will help you.

You can't always trust people (you better know them), even if you help them – but keep sharing Jesus and He will help you and them eventually, if you keep going to God – know you are truly with Jesus, and trust Him.

Some people can be tougher (meaner, etc.) than others – this is an evil world – don't be one of them (sometimes we all can be). Get help with Jesus – be kinder, humble, etc. No matter how talented, rich, good looking, etc. you are, it's how you behave and live your life that matters – and only Jesus can help you with that. Because some so-called good people do evil things at times, for certain situations – we all are capable (**jer. 17:9-10**), some more than others. We all look for the good, but we have to know how humans are – and satan tempting man in this world. Look in the world – humans are ticking time bombs ready to go off (when are you going to diffuse yourself and others, and go to Jesus, or suffer the consequences – blow up?). This is all set up by God (differences, separations, etc.), because of man (our fault), and can only be remedied by going to Him – Jesus (and He's the reason God set all this up in the world), just surrender. So it is important that all go to Jesus as soon as they can.

We have to know and accept this fact about man. People don't always know what's best for them, but God does.

Sin – evil (through satan) is what got man into the situation we are in throughout history and today – and He has a remedy for it (what we did) – to pay for it (it needs to be paid for – our sin), and Jesus did that for us. Go to Him.

God lets satan deal with those that sin (believers, too – **1 cor. 5:1-8**), to either make sick or die (or some problem). We should help others that are not following God, but they still have to help themselves, and suffer the consequences of their behavior on their own, too (**gal. 6:1-10**).

We should help people with love, as much as we can, and share Jesus – the truth, in love (**eph. 4:11-16**).

Everyone of noah's sons can be fair, caring, learn, honest, lead, etc., but not all do – with Jesus (a good example) – all can. Don't trust yourself or man (**prov. 3:5-6**) – just God and the truth of His word – to know the truth of us and this world – through God's eyes – the bible. We can't handle being like God – knowing everything (good and evil) without Him, and being evil forever (we all still will live somewhere forever – God created us to).

He had to change something, and good thing He did – because of us, and for us (things that get us to go to Him – to Jesus).

All things were different than today (meaning that we all were the same, looked the same, etc. – not like today having so much diversity from noah's sons and the change to the earth after the flood, etc.) – before the flood, and a little after the flood (about 100 years) up to the tower of babel. And for those first 100 years after the flood, living in one area of the earth (near where the ark landed) – it was like america – all one (all of noah's sons), one speech, etc. (even though we all looked different eventually after the tower of babel – like we look today), and man back then was mainly all together against God (**gen. 11**), like before the flood (**gen. 6**) – so satan could use man all against God (and the reason God had to change us, and the earth, etc., with the flood).

We keep being sinful – evil (with or without satan), and that is no way to live forever (**gen. 3:22-24**) – God had to come to us – to change that with Jesus, and it is nice that He did (to be able to live forever in heaven – not hell, or here, and miserable).

Then God separated man (which is what God wanted in the first place – for man to scatter all around the world, **gen. 11:4-9** – with all of noah's sons) after the tower of babel and language change. Then man did scatter to around the world to what we see today (**acts 17:26-27**). Man has been able to travel around the world since after the tower of babel – about 4,000 years ago – then settled, but the real travel everywhere (and a little easier) didn't happen until the last 500 to 1,000 years or so – across the seas, etc. And man initially (after the tower of babel – 100 or so years after the flood) got to the different places around the world over land bridges, maybe even ice bridges, and maybe some small rafts (that didn't have to go too far at that time) – where the continents were separated by water (water settling and some frozen in the poles, etc.), but land close together in places (like the russian – alaskan islands, australia, etc.) – but most could get to all of the continents easily, walking, etc. over a period of time (and we lived longer for a while back then to do this). And some of ham ended up in north, central, and south america – and settled for a few thousand years. Not totally the way it looks today. And it is possible that the vikings used some boats (smaller than the big sailing ships) to go to places – like to greenland, etc. and set up roots – maybe around 1,000ad, although not as much as man did around 500 years ago, but still traveled possibly to america, but not to stay. Mainly japheth went north and south, after man started to build and have more technology, and some of ham stayed mostly centralized part of the earth – the equator – which determined the color of man.

So God separated people (including the continents, land, etc. after the flood) from being all one group following satan – at the tower of babel after the flood with noah's sons, and since then, God tries to bring us back to one group again, but with Jesus. Even though satan is still trying to unite us all again against God (satan can only do it separately so far, not as one).

And all of the names written in the list in **gen. 5**, over those years before the flood (and God gave us the numbers – ages, etc. – all plain for us to see), were all in the presence of the Lord (and enoch was translated – like being raptured, he didn't die, God took him, **gen. 5:21-24; heb. 11:5-6)**, even though God may have taken those that were with Him back then, those that were in His presence, that died, to be with Him, and even possibly all those that were with Him – the righteous before the flood, and even after the flood up until abraham (abraham's bosom) – when God started the jews (maybe even up to moses when the bible was started to be written – God's word with us, He could have taken at least moses up – even though he died – **deut.**

34:5-12 – especially since moses came back, with elijah, who was also translated to heaven – **2 kings 2:9-12** – both were on the mount of transfiguration with Jesus – **matt. 17:1-8**).

If God gave the Holy Spirit to anyone before Jesus died and rose – they may have gone to heaven then when they died before the flood and a little after – like enoch and elijah did (who were raptured – body and soul), and like the true Christians (with the Holy Spirit) do today when they die (souls to heaven).

And hell is first mentioned in **deut. 32**, just before moses died – not before the flood or before abraham, until moses (even though the grave is mentioned before).

So when any jews died (before Jesus here) – since no one had the Holy Spirit, He – the Holy Spirit, was mainly just helping them – not like we do today – He is in us today (only from the risen Jesus). For the jews, the Holy Spirit was eventually in the temple (not in the jews) – after it was built, until Jesus died (**matt. 27:51; mark 15:37-38**; **acts 1 and 2**). And only the righteous jews (no gentiles, etc.) went to abraham's bosom, **luke 16:22-26**, waiting for Jesus to come here, and then die and rise, **matt. 27:50-53; eph. 4:8-10** – part of daniel's prophecy – **dan. 9:24-27** – to anoint the most Holy – who is Jesus (which the jews, as a nation, didn't do) – and it's not called adam's bosom, or noah's bosom, etc. (it would have been, if it was there before, and it is not there now – no abraham's bosom, since Jesus died and rose – no purgatory, etc.). And the disobedient jews went to hell (**luke 16:19-31**) – always separation, even after this life – for all of us, but it is our choice (blame yourself – not God), and noah's family (wife and his three sons and wives – eight people total) were in the presence of the Lord, just before the flood (**gen. 6**).

Today (since Jesus died and rose), we (those who are truly saved with the Holy Spirit with Jesus, and believing in and following His word – the truth of it) all go to heaven when we die (our soul does – with the Holy Spirit – **2 cor. 5:5-9**).

The Holy Spirit is in you when saved – your body (really your soul) is the temple (**1 cor. 3:16-17; 1 cor. 6:19-20**) – from the temple of the jews (**luke 23:44-46; heb. 9**), to where it really belongs – in man – the way God created adam, but adam lost it for us all.

We need to have faith in Jesus – Him dying for us and needed to – for our sins, then we can get the Holy Spirit from Him for that faith and then change to what God wants and wanted us to be – sinless (our soul) – like Jesus – a son of God.

You have to be perfect to get to heaven – sinless, but none of us are or can be (**gen. 8:21; rom. 3**) – except Jesus can make us perfect (righteous – **matt. 6:33**), to get to heaven. What is possible with God, is impossible with man (**matt. 19:26; mark 10:27; luke 18:27**) – don't follow man or satan (our only alternative).

Only being saved by Jesus – having the Holy Spirit is the only thing that gets you to heaven – not the things you do – no matter how good they are, and it is good to do good things, but be sure you are saved by Jesus only (not church or religious things, laws, traditions, etc. – **1 cor. 1:17-18**). Having faith (**rom. 3:21-31; rom. 4:13-15**).

Being sinful is to go against the law (**1 john 3:3-5**), which we have to live with here while in this body – so go to Jesus.

But after you are truly saved (with the Holy Spirit), you follow Him – if you want a better life here (and avoid the consequences of sinful life here), otherwise, if you get caught up in the world (if being saved), you will still have problems, even though you will still go to heaven (**1 cor. 3**; **1 cor. 5:1-5**). But know you are truly saved – and you will follow Him and the truth of His word (not perfect, but saved – that's why you keep going to Him daily).

So to be perfectly clear – there were only two different types of people before the flood – no other differences. You (men and women) were either with the Lord (in His presence) or not (and at the time of the flood there were only eight people – noah's family – all on the ark). We were all the same – not like the diversity we see today (after the flood – especially eventually after the tower of babel) – no color, nationality, etc. (how could there be with nice conditions, the weather the same everywhere, same speech, etc.?).

Today's world really tests a true Christian's faith – to follow what Jesus says and wants to do and how to live with all of the diversity, and our differences (and satan's influence in society with his ideas against God).

And just like today, we all had to go to God individually (Jesus was here – His Spirit – **gen. 6:3**), before the flood – only eight did just before the flood (noah and his family) – not many then, and not many today (maybe 2% - 3% of the world today are truly saved – many false christians). It doesn't matter if your parents are saved, you have to get saved, too. Even noah's sons had to be saved (go to God) and their sons and daughters, too – all the way to us today. And it better be the truth – go to Jesus and ask Him into your life (and get the Holy Spirit). So the Lord's spirit was striving with man before the flood – but man didn't listen – was sinful, and there was no bible, no laws, no jews, etc. (just the presence of the Lord) – and man was evil, sinful, fleshly, etc. – and they were all the same (and most didn't go to or listen to the Lord – we have free will, like we have today, but it will lead to destruction, death, hell, etc., without Jesus).

Today with the Holy Spirit from Jesus (after He died and rose), we go to heaven when we die (our soul, **2 cor. 5:1-8** – until the rapture, then we get a new body – **1 cor. 15:42-55**) – the jews did not do that back then (they went to abraham's bosom – **luke 16:19-31**). And there were no jews before abraham (isaac, jacob) – **gen. 17**. And we are not all from abraham (just the true jews, and those that are truly saved by Jesus – adopted into God's family) – arabs are mostly from ishmael (from abram, not abraham – **gen. 16**) – even though abram is abraham (**1 chron. 1:27-28** – and he raised ishmael, mostly as abraham) – technically abraham is a new person (God changing his name, just like He did sarai to sarah – **gen. 17:3-22**) – by following, trusting God (just like Jesus is said to be the son of joseph – **luke 3:23; luke 4:22; john 1:45; john 6:42** – and raised by him – but is really the son of God the Father). And it is through isaac who the people of promise are of God – where the jews come from (**rom. 9**). And most of the arabs, etc. only read or believe the bible up through **gen. 16** (and ishmael) and usually not beyond that, even though abram's name was changed (he didn't do it – God changed it) in **gen. 17**, everyone thinks that abraham was the father of ishmael, but it was abram (who turned into abraham, as did jacob to israel, and did peter to cephas – a stone, not a rock – **john 1:40-42**, saul to paul, etc. – they became new creatures, like all true believers do in Jesus – false churches, religions, beliefs, etc. change their own names). Some arabs may read the bible farther, like in **deut. 18:15-22**, where it says there will be a Prophet – who is Jesus, but the arabs' religion thinks it is someone else – there are billions in the world that are not from abraham (but that is probably what still will unite all of the people with the anti-christ, just before, and in the tribulation – a lie from satan, like you are seeing today). And those righteous jews in abraham's bosom are with Jesus now – after He went down to preach to them and have them come back with Him (the place of abraham's bosom is not there now – only hell and torment is still there) – and abraham came back with Jesus (**matt. 27:52-53; eph. 4:8-10**).

So we need to heed truthful prophesies (**1 thess. 5:20-21**) – (only from and about Jesus and His word – His truth – mainly those that wrote the bible) – so if a prophet is real, things will come true (**deut. 18:19-22**) – but there are too many false ones.

We are not all from abraham – we need to understand that we are all from one of noah's sons today – since the flood (**gen. 9:18-19**) – and all at first from adam and eve (**gen. 3:20**).

We all would or could be connected to abraham – all can be with Jesus – so all of noah's sons through abraham, through Jesus – right now only jews are connected to abraham (initially through shem, then through isaac and jacob – **gen. 11, 12, 17; rom. 9:4-13; gal. 4**) – and any children he had after his named was changed (another marriage after sarah died). Once we go to Jesus and are truly saved – born again (with the Holy Spirit – the jews have to also), we are sons of God – adopted (**rom. 8:14-21; eph. 1**), and we are then not connected to the sons of noah (man) anymore – the past is gone – we are with Jesus – sons of God (new creatures with the Holy Spirit). God does all of this and sets it up.

So we are not all from abraham, but we are all from noah's sons (and adam), until we go to Jesus. Even before the flood, man knew and went to Jesus (the presence of the Lord – and in the end – when the flood came, only noah and his family did, and we all have to go to Him individually today, before we die – if not we go to hell). So don't try to have everyone think we are all connected to abraham (only jews, and the truly saved).

And hell may not have even been there before the flood (but the unbelievers would be destined for hell and the lake of fire then) – the first time the word hell is mentioned is in the **book of deuteronomy** (**deut. 32:22**). And most bibles don't even mention hades (or sheol – which would be considered the grave – death), only hell – and the **king james bible** doesn't mention either one – just hell (and the lake of fire – which is only in the **book of revelation**). So hades/sheol (grave) was mainly for the jews after the flood (after abraham).

So God even separated hades (sheol) for the jews – the righteous – in abraham's bosom, or the unrighteous – in hell (**luke 16:19-31**), but it (abraham's bosom) is not there anymore (and it was just for the jews only until Jesus died – for the righteous jews only, then they rose with Jesus, and then went with Jesus to heaven – **matt. 27:50-53; eph. 4:8-10**). So there is no purgatory, etc. – or anything like it – for anyone to go to (don't believe that or follow that – false churches teach that, and people follow the lies of them and satan – too many of them) – not only before the jews, but not there after Jesus died and rose – that is a lie from satan (and false churches, etc., that follows satan – it's not God's truth, not from the Holy Spirit) – only hell (and the lake of fire) is there waiting for you (where satan is going) – if you don't get truly saved by Jesus – only getting the Holy Spirit from Him.

We need to get saved before we die – get the Holy Spirit (the only way to get saved, and when we die, we go to heaven – **2 cor. 5:5-9**, if we don't have it – we go to hell) – the only sin not forgiven is refusing the Holy Spirit (**luke 12:10**) – go to Jesus now and get saved, before you die.

This world is not our final home, heaven is (or hell is, if you are not saved – don't just think you are – satan leading you, and you don't know it), if you are truly saved by Jesus (with the Holy Spirit). Know you are truly saved. Once you are truly saved by Jesus – with the Holy Spirit – you are then strangers on this earth, we are really from heaven waiting to go there (**philip. 3:20-21**). Being here to share Jesus and His truth, if not, otherwise we share satan and his lies.

This world groans, because our home is in heaven – if you are truly saved with Jesus – groaning to get home to heaven and away from this struggling earth (**rom. 7:13-25; rom. 8:26-28**).

When you become a Christian – true Christian – following Jesus (and His truth), then you can truly help people – but not before – it's all been tried before by man here on earth (**eccl. 1-12; eccl. 12:13-14; 1 cor. 2:9-16**).

If you are truly saved – have the Holy Spirit from Jesus – the truth, then you don't mind dying, knowing where you are going. Many false churches, beliefs, etc. out there trying to fool people (satan led – truth mixed with lies).

If everyone is truly with Jesus – truly saved, etc. (with the Holy Spirit), then it doesn't matter who dies – be ready to go, no matter who is trying to kill people – satan keeps trying, and is evil in the world. But you be ready with Jesus – whatever happens.

We have problems, but we don't go to God, and He waits (**psalm 86:15**). He wants all to go to Him – follow and share.

The hard part in this life, is not to get back at those that hurt you – strangers, friends, family, etc. – even those that look like they do, but to go to Jesus and let God repay for you (He will deal with them – better than you can) – just forgive and go to Jesus and let Him heal you and change you (and them – for them it may be punishment, prison, etc.), then let Him lead you to what to do in this life that is better for you. And share Jesus with them when and if you can – the truth.

People don't like to be picked on, but don't mind picking on others sometimes – or at least getting back at them, etc. (and you have to tell the truth about what happens). Look at yourself – you deserve what you get – hypocrites – forget it and move on, and go to Jesus. And if you had something done to you that was so terrible – the worst ever – and hard to overcome, and hard move on, etc. and could never find the person again that did it to you (they moved, died, etc.) – so you couldn't get back at them (or tell them, or hurt them, etc.) – what would you do to get over it? You would have to go to Jesus to do that – for anything, whether you could find them or not, and forgive and heal, and then move on. And even pray for them.

That's one of the reasons that the world is so terrible, and that man is (we all are), and man needs help and a way out – it is Jesus.

People have problems and why people that drink tell them in a bar to bartenders, etc. They shouldn't hide that, and just go to Jesus – He will hear you and help you, and change you. Hope the problems you have will lead you to Jesus.

The reason that people go to drugs, alcohol, psychiatrists, etc., because they don't go to Jesus and no matter what you do – get back at someone – hurt, kill them, etc. – you will never get better, heal, etc. – it will still be there, that's why you let God do it, with Jesus. And even if you don't feel like you got justice (they got punished, prison, etc.), just know that God avenges sometimes. Leave it up to Him – for some things. Go to Him. And eventually forgive them – like Jesus does (but there are still consequences to behavior).

If God will avenge for you – He will, so don't set out to get back at someone or get revenge – you share Jesus (that is what He is for), and if someone dies (with Jesus) they go to heaven.

Don't get involved with people that you will have regrets for any reason, for anything – or it is your fault. Get involved with Jesus (and maybe share Him with them). No matter what life you live (some are more dangerous, and more of a reason to go to Jesus, and His word).

We will all be judged (**heb. 9:27**) – but be ready with the Holy Spirit (through Jesus – salvation). All of us will be judged since adam – because we are all from and connected to man (adam – now to noah's sons).

The gentiles – from the beginning of the jews – abraham (not abram) – jacob (israel) until Jesus died and rose, are judged by their knowledge of the flood, and their own laws, rules (of their own people, life, tribe, etc.) that they obeyed or didn't obey – their conscience, etc. (**rom. 2:6-16**), and any contact with the jews, etc. (knowing or hearing of the true God – like egyptians and others have in the past – and just looking at the world, universe, etc. – **rom.**

1 – no excuse not to believe in the true God). Now all people (gentiles and jews alike) can go to Jesus to be saved – since His death and resurrection (the last 2,000 years).

Today we all have heard of Jesus (but need to know the truth) – so we need to go to Him and get saved (get the Holy Spirit).

Before the flood, there were only eight people left (noah's family, even though noah's father – lamech, had died a few years before the flood, and his grandfather – methuselah, died the year of the flood, or they would have gone on the ark, too – any of those in **gen. 5** would have, if they were alive) that were with the Lord, when the flood came. And when it did come, it rained for 40 days (and nights), and noah was on the water in the ark for 150 days (five months – 30-day months then), then it rested on mount ararat (**gen. 8:1-4**), and those were 360-day years (and it will be again in the tribulation – seven years split into two pieces – three and a half years exactly – **rev. 11:2-3; rev. 12:6**). So after the flood, it changed to 365-day years, since then to today, possibly because of all of the water weight on the earth (and some water still in the poles frozen, etc.), slowed the earth down around its orbit (and with the axis tilt). And the water continued to abate for many more days **(gen. 8:5-16**), and so noah used birds (raven and dove) to check to see if the land was dry yet – water abated. A raven sent first, then he sent out a dove, three times, and eventually that dove didn't come back (**gen. 8:8-12**), not until that dove (the Holy Spirit) came back when Jesus came here **(matt. 3:16; mark 1:10; luke 3:22; john 1:32**) and lighted on Jesus – the first and last time the dove went and came and not mentioned again – to show that Jesus was with noah, and came here from heaven from God to us and for us – from noah to Jesus (here on earth), with the Holy Spirit – to get away from man (noah's sons) and connect to God through Jesus. Born again – now spiritually (**john 3**) – that adam lost for us (**gen. 3**).

Noah and his family were sealed by the Holy Spirit (like we are) – the few then and today – shut in the ark and safe from the world and the flood. And the dove was the Holy Spirit – sent out, then came back with Jesus. And like sodom – the few saved, and will be in the rapture – the few with the Holy Spirit.

The dove (sent three times) connects noah (and adam – sin before the flood) to Jesus – we can only get away from noah (and his sons, as well as adam) by going to Jesus (and getting the Holy Spirit). And after the dove landed on Jesus, He was tempted by satan for 40 days in the wilderness (**matt. 4:1-11**) – which He overcame, and proved He was God and was sinless (like water came down from the flood for 40 days – **gen. 7:17** – and noah and the ark came through it). Then Jesus started His ministry here after the temptation, just as noah's sons' effect on man ever since – up to today – started after the flood, and does not end until we go to Jesus. Jesus came to fulfill God's plan for man (and his sin, etc.) – so we can be saved (like noah was from the flood), and get away from the punishment because of evil man before the flood (and ever since).

If you believe in God, then you believe in what He believes in, and should speak out on and share that – and that is Jesus. But know Him (get the Holy Spirit – saved) and His truth first – His word is truth.

Jesus believes the whole bible – creation, adam and eve, and even noah and the flood (**matt. 24:37-38; luke 17:26**), as well as jonah and the whale (**matt. 12:39-41; matt. 16:4; luke 11:29-32** – being three days and three nights in the earth – like a person that eventually becomes a Christian and then shares Jesus, like jonah did) etc., because He wrote it all (He is the Word, and the Creator – **john 1**), and we have to believe it all to truly believe in Jesus.

And Jesus said before He died, that the temple would be destroyed (**matt. 24:1-2**), but He didn't let it happen until 40 years after He died (70ad), and He could have come back before then (before 70ad) for the jews to still believe in and follow Him as a nation. But the jews (as a nation – the leaders, priests, etc.) didn't believe and follow Him, even after He died, and they saw Him alive (**1 cor. 15:1-6**). And the leaders were upset when stephen said he saw Jesus in heaven standing (like He was ready to come back – and Jesus would have come back then – before 70ad, to have the jews, as a nation, evangelize the world – with the last seven years of the 490 years of daniel – **dan. 9:24-27** – those seven years are now in the future) at the right hand of God (alive after His death and with God – **acts 7:55-56**). And then they killed stephen – and saul (paul) agreeing with his death. Don't be stubborn or live-in denial.

Jesus is coming back, and is now at the right hand of God, the Father, but Jesus is now sitting, waiting for the end times (**psalm 110:1; matt. 22:44; mark 12:36**).

The truth of the bible and of Jesus is there for all to see and believe. So He can change who we are to what God wants.

So we all have to go to Jesus now, and connect to Jesus, with the Holy Spirit (and not stay connected to man – adam or noah, physically, anymore) – change what we are born with (and don't let the separations, and satan, run our lives anymore). To be born again (**john 3**) – spiritually, and let Jesus change you (and become one with Him). And we will know it when He is with us – and have the Holy Spirit – we will become new.

And without Jesus (and His word and Holy Spirit in us), we all will do and speak evil – from our heart and what we are born with (**luke 6:45**). Get out of those false churches and beliefs.

Even though we are born into families, cultures, nations, and beliefs, etc. that we have no control over (all of noah's sons), we need to know satan uses these to keep you from Jesus. After you grow and learn things in this world, you can go to God – to Jesus, and His word – the truth of it. Which includes being born into many false churches – if all of the churches were true Christian, then you would be able to go to any of them and have no differences, but you can't go to them all – they don't believe the same or believe the truth (**matt. 7:13-23**), and goes for religions, beliefs, etc., too. There are separations (lies, etc.).

God separated us for a reason – we can become one with Him – with Jesus. And where or who you are born to – Christian or non-Christian – family, nation, etc., you have to go to Jesus individually to be saved. Go to Him, ask Him.

So there was a separation of man (what they believed, and how they lived), before the flood (but it was still because of man and his behavior and decisions, etc., first with adam and eve – sinning, **gen. 3** – because they followed satan – who sinned first, **isa. 14:12-15; ezek. 28:13-15**, and then the evil that man did since then – following satan, that caused God to do this, and any of the separations after that, including the flood, **gen. 6**).

People should go to God for everything, especially Christians, and follow (**luke 6:46**), follow the truth, or you will not be blessed or make it through the problems here.

Without Jesus (truly saved, with the truth – with the Holy Spirit) people are different and separated in many ways (all of noah's sons), but with Jesus we are (or can be) the same or one (**rom. 8:35-39; gal. 3:26-28**).

If you don't go to Jesus – the truth, you will never get away from man, satan, sin, this world, etc. and be separated from God and stay with man and your culture, etc. (noah's sons) – eventually forever in hell. Even some the of things that happen in america are leading away from God and His word. We need to keep learning the truth of God's word and sharing here and to the world – especially true believers, churches, etc. should be doing this.

But God will win – it takes time, and good will happen – especially in america. Just go to Jesus and wait and see – don't fight it (**acts 5:38-39**).

Underneath we are all the same – one blood – **acts 17:24-28** (under all of the differences, colors, etc. – that came after the flood, mainly after the tower of babel, **gen. 11**, and all of the traits we have, came within the first 400 years after the tower of babel) – we are all sinners, evil (separated from God) – until we go to Jesus – otherwise we are all still the same from adam and noah's sons (we were all the same – color, speech, etc., before and a little after the flood) – we need to go to Jesus to be one.

Man did not make the jews – a separate called out people (chosen) – God made them (with His truth), just like He separated everyone (**acts 17:24-28**). So then there were jews and gentiles – since abraham (isaac, jacob) – two groups separated by God – mainly until Jesus died and rose. Go to Jesus to unite (equity, equality, etc.) – the only way that we will have equality is to go to Jesus and the bible and follow Him and it, otherwise we won't have a shot at it, and stuck with any of noah's sons.

A jew is not a jew just because he is born from a jew – he is a jew, because he follows the laws of the bible (mainly the old testament) and worships God and sacrifices in their temple – but they don't follow that wherever they live in the world (even today in israel) – they are lost, since God scattered them after Jesus died and rose (and their temple destroyed in 70ad). So don't follow your own – even a jew – go to Jesus – all of noah's sons. Even Jesus was a jew – but they didn't follow Him (mostly gentiles follow Him now). God did all of this (scattered them and left their land desolate – until now) to the jews, for a punishment, etc.

So with Jesus we can get away from noah's sons – whatever nationality, belief, family, etc. we are – even the jews need to and can – they need to get away from the jews (as any nationality – blacks, hispanics, asians, whites, etc. – any and all of noah's sons – japheth, shem, and ham, need to). We are all separated (by God – after the flood) and will not get along until we do. We are one with Jesus (by God) and separated from man (sin), when we all go to Him – we all need to go to Him. God wants us to – to get away from man, even family, etc. (**matt. 10:32-39; luke 12:49-59**), and love and follow Him more.

Before Jesus came here to die, israel was backed up and protected by God through their history (if they obeyed Him – if not they were ruled by others). Since Jesus died and rose, their land was left desolate. And since they have come back to israel now (since 1948), they are backed up by america – because of Jesus.

And after Jesus died and rose, we – man – are all still from adam and noah's sons – no one else. The only way to get along and not be separate and still connected to man, is to go to Jesus. And once we are saved by Jesus – we are adopted into God's family – sons of God. Not connected to man anymore, like before the flood and a little after (**gen. 6; gen. 9 through 12**).

But at that time (before the flood – and a little after – 4,300 to 6,000 ago – since creation – our time here – existence, etc.) that was the only difference between man (in the presence of the Lord or not) – man all looked and talked the same (and no jews or gentiles – adam or noah was not a jew, man was all the same then). Man looked the same because of the nice weather, etc., because of the canopy above the earth (created on the third day of creation – **gen. 1:6-8** – where the flood waters came from) protecting man from the harshness of the sun, that would eventually darken man's skin after the flood (**song of sol. 1:5-6**) – to what we see today – from the sun (and no buffer).

We need to know the truth and learn and study it to understand why God did what He did. It needs to be talked about.

It was not like it is today – diversity – that happened only after the flood (those traits were created in us, but did not come out until after the flood – mainly after the tower of babel, about 100 or so years after the flood – **gen. 11**), so no servants, etc. (no noah's sons with different abilities, talents, etc. – **gen. 9**) – all people were the same level, and just did different things, whatever they wanted and interested them (just two types of people before the flood – those with God or those not with Him). And it was such a nice place to live (nicer than today) before the flood (even after adam and eve sinned) – from the creation (like a loving God would create for man to live), that man had everything, and even lived to old ages then – over 900 years for some (**gen. 5**), so when man has nice or comfortable conditions or things (like some people today – especially in america, and it is because of Jesus that america is great, and we need to share Him), because of the good conditions, man doesn't go (or listen) to God very much (but man was still sinful and evil and disobedient then, **gen. 6** – sound and look familiar?).

We can have things (material things, and they keep changing all of the time – when does it end?) in this world, but not love those things, especially love anything more than God, because it makes us do some evil things (evil man can have money and try to buy power, and give to evil people, and take from evil people – so just don't be controlled by evil, satan is ruling this world) – and know that the root of all evil is the love of money, and causes sorrows, etc. in life (**1 tim. 6:3-12**), and you can't love (or worship) God, and money, things, etc. (**luke 16:13**), like crime, evil, etc. – choose (but suffer the consequences of that choice – a life that leads to death, and misery in hell – without Jesus, or a life eternal in heaven – with Jesus). Depend on God, not things. Even the rich have problems (sometimes more) – all need to go to Jesus.

People grow in this life and try things and are never happy – even marriage, sports, party, work, etc., and keep trying and doing things that don't satisfy (even though some things take time to happen – hard work, etc. – and it better be on the right things), but they keep trying to do things, thinking they will be happy. All of that has been done since man has been here (**eccl. 1:8-10**). We need to know what is worth making an effort for and why we would do it – to be satisfied may not take place – so go to Jesus and have Him and His truth in your life, then see what you need to do here, then we will be happy with Him in our life and for whatever we do here. That is what we are here for (**eccl. 12:13-14**).

There are people trying to be happy in this world – to be the richest, win the super bowl or championship, academy award, olympics, anything great, marry the right person, great job, etc. (whatever you think is great) – then find they are not happy (or completely satisfied, etc.) when they do that (most of us don't get any of that, so we think we are not happy because we never did, or whatever we think would finally make us happy). Even if we do something great, then we think there has to be something more to this world – there is – Jesus (and His truth for us). Don't put your hopes and happiness in the things of this world or what others have, money, etc. – just because you didn't get things you wanted (although we need to live – but with Jesus, and He will give you what you need – **matt. 6:19-34**, especially after this life).

People – all of noah's sons (man and woman today) want more in this world – but never are satisfied – it won't make you happy – it is still having Jesus help you, no matter what level you are. There still will be people trying to get more and be equal, no matter what gets better, what they accomplish, etc. – never satisfied, even if we all are equal in this world somehow, without Jesus. Only with Jesus can we be – that is what is missing in your life (the Holy Spirit in you from Jesus). Not things of this world, etc.

You have to keep going to the world and the evil things and sin to keep happy (whatever temptations, pleasures, etc.) – though you are never satisfied (or temporarily at best, and they usually lead to trouble), and you think that's all you can do. None of them work. But there is a better way – with God and His ways (the truth), with Jesus, and then change what you desire. Be satisfied and one with Him. Don't stay with how we are born – connected to man, sin, evil, etc.

Man is not changing, the things around him, or the things he makes are changing, but man is not. No evolution, etc. – we are all the same since adam – the beginning – mainly after adam and eve sinned (**gen. 3**)– we are all sinners, and need salvation – no matter what son of noah we are (or nationality, etc.).

All are from adam (from creation, and now after sin) – one race – the human race – one blood (**acts 17:24-28**), although after the flood we look different (mainly after the tower of babel), and it looks like different races – God separated all of us (around the world – **gen. 11**) – all of us are from noah's sons. Man separated from God and connected to man – first with adam (with sin, and satan – **gen. 3**), and now with noah's sons (**gen. 9:24-27**), and their descendants (and the limitations of each son), until we go to Jesus (and be free of sin – why He died for us all, but if you go to Him and follow – get the Holy Spirit). We can be with who we want, but the best is with Jesus to change from who we are, and what we see in this world.

Even if ham (any of noah's sons) gets equality, riches, etc. he will still struggle, because he is still connected to ham (and his lot in life – to noah's sons – to man, as shem and japheth are still – whatever lot in life they are that God gave them), until he goes to Jesus. It will never change – still inequality (as it still will be with women).

Be with Jesus – workers, servants, etc. – work for the Lord (**col. 3:22-25**), and care for who you work for and they should care for you. Go to Jesus to get along. Or we will struggle.

People need to know the truth – no matter how tough it is. God wants us to know – so He came to us, with His word and Jesus.

God will change this world when He wants to – for all people (not what man wants, but what is best) – for equality, etc. for all (as He has done in america), if we go to Him and follow – which is best for all – in Jesus.

If you don't go to Jesus – you will not only go to hell (if you don't go to Him before you die), but your life here on earth will be a struggle – staying with man – noah's sons (your lot in life – the limitations, etc. each son has), and not get out of your connection to man – to noah's sons.

Don't follow the traditions of your family, culture, beliefs, etc. – be with Jesus and His truth. The whole world needs to do this.

If you don't like your lot in life – nationality (noah's sons), money, level, limitations, etc., then go to Jesus (even though america does help most people, no matter who you are, because of Jesus). Jesus will level the world for you, with God – no other way to God (**john 14:6**). Then you can live.

And use your struggles in your life to grow and to share and help others. See you deal with them with Jesus – whether now or in the past – ancestors, etc. Go to Jesus with them – He is the only answer. For any of your relatives' problems, now, from the past treatment, etc., of whatever son of noah you are from. It is not things, it is what Jesus in this life that is going to help you, so get Jesus first (and help others to do the same), no matter what problems have happened in the past to you or others like you.

And for money, most people do anything – some more than others, but it isn't always good – most are bad. Money (the love of it) is the root of all evil – satan leading us – until we go to Jesus, and then use your money wisely and for good. And get it from Him – He will help you with that. Learn to live with little or much (**philip. 4:11-12**), but with Jesus in your life. Go to Him for everything. We have plenty in america, compared to most of the world, and the opportunities to live free – if we go to Jesus (and His word).

People shouldn't like you because you have money, things, etc. – go to Jesus and have Him make you happy – for what you need to live here (**matt. 6:33**). And share it with people, if you can – especially Jesus.

And satan can control the rich – then they try to control nations (like america), people, the world, etc. Jesus is still here to help us all, if we would just go to Him.

People, businesses, celebrities, etc. (even some churches) – all promote themselves (and is fine to a point), but should be promoting Jesus and His truth. He will help give you what you need (**matt. 6:33**).

Most people that go to Jesus and read His word (the truth of it) – want to know the truth (and live truth) – not cover it up, not live in denial, etc. Change your life – with Jesus.

People usually do things as long as they can get away with it – what they think is good, fun, etc., then ruin their life or get tired of it or do worse things – it never ends. So go to Jesus.

CHAPTER 5

Salvation and Redemption: Man Forgiven in The Old Testament often by The Blood Of Lambs and Redeemed in The New Testament, once and For All, By The Blood Of The Lamb Of God, Jesus Christ

We have to be willing to give up jobs and money, etc. that work for satan – against God's truth (and way of life), and accept being poor, or just comfortable, or starting over with what God wants for you – what is a godly way of life and work, and helps others, not hurt – with the truth (and maybe even get more money, etc.). but God will provide (**gen. 22:14**) – trust Him, but know His truth (He knows what's best for us, man doesn't – **rom. 11:21-23**). Walk by faith and not by sight (**2 cor. 5:7**). Still work, and work hard – or you don't eat (**2 thess. 3:10-11**). Learn to live with whatever (**philip. 4:11-13**) – but go to Jesus and you will have what you need (**matt. 6:33**). Just like when Jesus told peter to go to the sea and get a fish – then he found money in its mouth – for what they needed for their tax (**matt. 17:24-27**). Do what is right – and only God (Jesus and His word) knows that. He will lead you – God will get you what you need – go to Jesus (and follow His word).

We can't be in the world – we didn't bring things into this world, and can't take them out (**1 tim. 6:6-7**). Just Jesus (and His word – the truth of it), and share Him (and His truth).

So God tells us not to love money – if you are poor, you are poor (**1 tim. 6:1-8**) – but go to Jesus to change – He will help you with whatever life you are in (whether you stay there or not) and america is better than any country – because of Jesus (but He has to stay here and be in your life) – we should be grateful and go to Him when we can – now (and live a different, better life). In america, we all are richer than some (or most countries in the world) – even if you are poor (you are rich living here) – and can get what you need with Jesus in your life. He is waiting – and know the truth (**matt. 7:13-23**), or you are not saved. He will give you what you need (**psalm 37:25; matt. 6:33**).

So if you are poor in this world – and there will be poor (**matt. 26:11; mark 14:7; john 12:8**) – america is the place to be (even though you want more). Help them if you can – especially to go to Jesus.

Enticements, temptations, etc. everywhere (and satan leading you) – especially in america – wanting what others have. Even a little is enough with Jesus.

Everyone wants things, no matter who you are (black, white, poor, rich, woman, man, young, old, etc.) – and no matter what nation – and people are killing, stealing, lying, controlling, etc. to get things (**james 4**). We all see that.

And satan wants you to think if you are liked and loved and popular, etc. – basically someone that is trying to fit into the world, by going against God and His word – just like before the flood, and at the tower of babel (it will happen again at the end **rev. 13**). Don't make people dislike you, but don't care if they like you or not, just care about them and share Jesus – know the truth though (in His word with the Holy Spirit).

Most politically correct people believe differently than they say or act – as long as people like them, etc. – just like most children do – to be liked, loved, etc. (what they think that is – usually satan's kind of love). Go to Jesus and change.

The world (and its things) isn't the answer (**rom. 12:2**). And satan will try to give you the world – it is his (**matt. 4:8-11; 2 cor. 4:1-4**).

Even Jesus used the bible to resist satan (**matt. 4:1-11**) – satan wanting to give Jesus the world. His word is necessary – the truth of it. And Jesus read from the bible in a synagogue in nazareth (**luke 4:16-20**), and read the verses from **isa. 61:1-2**, but it wasn't word for word, but more of an explanation of it – and it was pertaining to Him – which the people in the synagogue saw, and the demons know who He is – **luke 4:21-37** (and He stopped in the middle of a verse in **isa. 61**, to make a point – about Him, and what had not happened yet, but will in the future – read the rest of the chapter of **isa. 61**). And satan also uses the bible, but to mislead – like many false churches and religions, etc. do. God will give you what you need (especially the Holy Spirit to learn the truth of His word) in this world if you go to Him (**matt. 6:19-34**) – to Jesus. He knows and will help you – go to, and follow, Him (and the truth of His word).

Don't try to be noticed or popular or make it in this world by just being gay, lesbian, transgender, victim, pedophile, crazy, or even a woman or minority, etc. to get away with living badly, crime, murder, any sex, anything, etc. – don't go against God (because all you are hurting are yourselves, and even others). Don't get wrapped up in all of these issues in the world. Go to Jesus and follow Him and His word – then see where He leads or puts you – which will be best for you and others. We all go against God without Jesus.

Many ways seem right or good for you to live in this world, but end in death and destruction (**prov. 14:12; prov. 16:25**). For some reason we still go down that road over and over and over, thinking that is the way to go, and keep having problems continuously (it's all been done – **eccl.**

1) – ending in death and hell. Go to Jesus and His word – that is what we are here for (**eccl. 12**). And in america we have the best chance.

With Jesus and His word (the truth), america can have equal people (all in america has an equal chance to change to be better with Jesus, otherwise it won't have equal people), and will continue with the differences in man – in noah's three sons – problems from a hateful life (with sin, evil, satan, etc.).

And you shouldn't hurt or kill because no one likes you or makes fun of you. Jesus is your answer – don't be stubborn – let Him help you and change you. Then care about people more. And share Jesus and His truth with them.

Know why you should kill or harm people – still need to protect yourself and family, etc. from evil man in this evil world, being sinful, and should get you to go to Jesus.

When anyone kills someone, they all have an excuse – selfish or otherwise – anger, self-defense, etc., included – and some may be forced, but not all needed. And self-defense is one thing, but revenge is not – let God deal with it, with what He has set up in this world do its job (laws, courts, police, etc. – **rom. 13**). He will do what is right, and take care of it – you just go to Jesus, and follow Him and His word, and pray to and share Jesus. And then you will have better people and nation (**2 chron. 7:14**). If you are really with Jesus, He will protect you, and if you die, you know where you are going – so you don't mind if you die – you are ready to go. Make sure you know the truth with Jesus.

If you die with Jesus, you are the happy one (even though family and friends, etc. may miss you, and should be happy for you), but if you die without Jesus you are the sad one, as well as the ones left behind. Know you are ready, and those you know are ready – share the truth of Jesus.

Many people live in the past – but we need to live now, and mostly in the future – with Jesus, now and in heaven.

People don't mind going against God and His truth and some of His people, but those people will defend people that are against God and His word. We all need to go to Jesus and His word and change.

Going against God (and His word), we will have problems, and be selfish, etc. in this world – then you, we, all have to deal with it. Go to Jesus.

There are no good people, so don't look for the good in people – only with Jesus can we have a chance to be good. None of us are innocent – all need to go to Jesus (**psalm 14; rom. 3**) – we all have to go to Jesus and have Him change us, and to care about all – sharing Jesus.

Remember we are born in man's image after sin (adam's – **gen. 5:3**), not in God's with the Holy Spirit (like we were to be when man was created, but man sinned, and now we are not in God's image). We are all sinners – all born evil and have something against God in us (all of the issues you see in the world – we have them because of sin) – we need to go to Jesus (get the Holy Spirit – born again, **john 3**), then we can be children of God (**rom. 8:14**). Go to God and His word and follow it and share it.

God warns man about things He knows that man will do here – the evil, sin, etc. that satan will lead man to do to themselves and to others. God knows. Go to Jesus to help ourselves.

We need to protect ourselves with Jesus and the truth of His word – salvation and the Holy Spirit – with faith to fight evil here – all of God's protection (**eph. 6:10-20**).

So we need to get away from the world and the issues, etc. (and away from man – from noah's sons) and it's thinking (from satan) – and we all need to be caring and patient to live with others – but it won't work without Jesus. We try it ourselves and it never works – don't depend on the world (which is satan's world).

You learn that things in life don't work for you and are not good for you (and the consequences, etc.) – but it makes you change and find the answer in God's word. You have to go to Jesus, and when you do, the bad things that happen in this world, He will and can help them become good for you (**rom. 8:28**). Look to Him and His word.

Women (anyone, men, etc.) looking for money (in a person, etc.) are the most miserable – look for Jesus first (the truth, and someone who is really with Him) and you will get what you need (**matt. 6:33**), and what's best for you.

You can't do both – be with (follow) God and be with evil (satan, the world – **matt. 6:19-24; 1 cor. 10:20-22**).

If you believe in God, then believe God – His word – read it and follow it with Jesus.

And satan makes you think you can make it in this world – but without God – Jesus. So you keep believing and living what you think – from the world (mainly satan). Don't believe satan – go to Jesus, not this world and you (**rom. 12:2**).

Give in and give up – go to Jesus – no matter what life you lead or what problems you have (even satan hurting you – like he did job – **book of job**) – with Jesus, your suffering is better (**2 cor. 11:23-33; 2 cor. 12:7-10**).

God set the world up so we – you – would lose – after adam sinned listening to satan (wages of sin is death). Only with God can you win – go to Jesus – why He came here. Wise up, satan is here against you – doing what he can to hurt you (looking like he is helping you, and others). He (satan) is hoping you will not go to Jesus. God set it up for us to want to go to Jesus – but still our choice.

And that is for all of noah's sons – all humans – we are all equal in that regard (we are all sinful from adam – **gen. 3; gen. 5:3**).

God may make it tough on you (allowing it to – the way this world is) – to see if you can handle it, and what you do to go through it – would you go to Him? And if you want to do His work, you sometimes have to handle it (paul did the most – **2 cor. 11 and 12**).

People do all kinds of tricks, superstitions, magic, sorcery, beliefs, etc. (even false churches and rituals, traditions, ideas, etc.) to avoid problems or make decisions, etc. (which don't work) – when the problems should get you to go to Jesus (and the truth of His word) – God uses them – the problems, for your benefit.

Remember, the world is the way we caused it to be – we did it – God wanting us to go to Him – He created us for that – a relationship with Him. So this world and the problems are our fault – until we all go to Him – to Jesus. Or satan will lead us away. And you deal with it by yourself, sometimes hurting others.

Can't stress it enough – when we have it comfortable – we don't go to God (only the few do) – like before the flood (weather great everywhere, food everywhere, lived to old ages, etc.) – people just did their own selfish, lustful, etc. things with each other (after man sinned and followed satan – **gen. 3; gen. 6** – and most didn't go to be in the presence of the Lord). So God tried to have it nice and comfortable here (at the creation) – before the flood, so we could see then, and looking back today at how man reacts to it being comfortable here on earth – we don't go to God, we do our own thing – and try not to struggle. God changed all of that after the flood – to what we see today – a world that has struggles, and especially so satan can't get all people to go to him all at once, like he did before the flood and after (at the tower of babel) – but satan will do it at the end (in the tribulation) – you can see it today (with all of the ideas against God and His word going on in the world – even in america – satan leading). But God had to do something then – and He did – and it is best for man – and will be today when He ends it all. Mainly to use the problems for us to go to Jesus today. So be ready to go with Jesus.

Learning the truth through the Spirit – which is from Jesus only – go to Him and learn and understand the word, and know it is the truth from God, not from satan. Read the word (the bible) yourself, not from a church or leader, etc., but go to Jesus first.

God did and tried many things over the years – for our benefit, not His (for us to see the consequences), and He needed to punish people to get them to stop hurting themselves and others, and hopefully follow Him and not go to hell forever. And all of it was for our learning (with all humans over the years, including the jews) – to see what He tried (**rom. 15:4**) – and the truth of this world and man and being sinful. So we can see the only way is through Jesus, and to go against satan's lies – so read and believe the truth (the bible). Go to Jesus.

And having riches doesn't keep you from problems – in some cases it may make more problems. Don't trust in riches (**1 tim. 6:17-19**). Go to Jesus and let Him give you things – and a way of life that is best – and after this life.

Being wealthy can even separate people (**prov. 19:4**), no matter what color or nationality, etc. Material things, people, money, even work, etc., can be your god (satan wants you to worship the world, and all that is in it – especially him, but not the true God – Jesus, **matt. 4:1-11; 1 john 2:15-16**), and all of it leads to death, etc. Just like satan has done in the medical field (keeping people sick – the 'cure' is worse than the illness sometimes) – all to make money and not do what God says (or depend on Him), but they need to truly help and heal people (Jesus may do that instantly, or with the truth in His word). You have to live your life a certain way (God's way – with Jesus and His word) to be blessed – with anything in this life (and you have to be patient and trust God's truths for us) – but it's not being taught, although it is available and can change your life (even your health). We all are going to die of something – we all are worried about it – trying to stop it or slow it down, but there are others that don't care and live dangerously, and may speed it up (for them and others). And everyone seems to want to die for something – and there are some things worth dying for – like Jesus did – die for this world (our salvation). You know what they are for you (what you would die for? – it better be something good). Go to Jesus and have a chance here and where you are going to go after this life. Pray that all of noah's sons go to Jesus.

God will give what you need, if you go to Him, through Jesus (**matt. 6:19-34**). So don't be afraid, be at peace with Jesus (**john 14:22-31**).

Jesus will help you go through when anyone dies – have them and you know Jesus, before anyone goes.

Trust Jesus to finish what He starts in you (**heb. 12:1-3**), after you go to Him and get saved (get the Holy Spirit, and His word – know the truth) – pray to Him now.

If you want things now – can't wait, then get Jesus now, and at least be ready to go, whatever happens after that – but know it is the truth and you are really with Him.

Throughout history things were good, when all followed and obeyed God – only when people didn't truly follow Him, then there were problems – like in the past with the jews, etc.

Why do you see so much evil, etc. in the world (even in america)? – it is satan that wants to use and control people, groups, etc. against God (you can see who that is in the world) and uses money, cheating, killing, threats, terror, lying, violence, fake love, etc. to get what he wants and has over the years to lead the world to a one world government, etc. – satan (using man – those that follow him, and think they are saved) wanting all against God at one time (at the same level) – like throughout history (**gen. 6; gen. 11**), but he needs america to fall first (God's nation for Jesus and truth – that is holding back this process of satan), so he can get control all of the people without God (that's why God does so much separating), like it will be in the tribulation (**rev. 13**). We need to fight this with Jesus (and His truth) and pray and share. Don't love money (or evil) – go to Jesus and you'll get what you need (**matt. 6:33**) – and at least use it for good – what God wants (know the truth). And if it is the end then be ready to go.

If it is the end – then God says it will go that way – evil, satanic, etc. to the end, but we just keep sharing Jesus and the truth and don't follow anything else – just tell the truth, not the lies of the false churches, politics, etc. (all satan led), You even like it when people are truthful with you and not lying about you, etc. – God wouldn't like that either.

No one likes cheating – on themselves – by their wife, husband, business, for money, etc. – anything (and satan leading them) – against them, but some may do it against others – and those that do are hypocrites – doing it to others to get what they want (for a person, family, nation, etc.). Jesus is the only answer to fight these people (satan, etc.). Even against churches, pastors, etc. that lead you down the wrong road – without the bible, etc. – just leading you to worry about social ideas, race, politics, etc. – it is sickening (and doing it by hating and violence, etc.) – don't let them brainwash you. Let Jesus and His truth make us one.

Absolute power corrupts absolutely – especially with cheating, lying, money, violence, false caring and love, killing, etc. – against God and His word, for a belief, society, nation, etc. Go to Jesus (and His word) to find how we live in this world (and run a nation – **psalm 33**) – whatever abilities (and success, etc.) you have.

Any group – even politics, churches, etc. – especially the evil, cheating, etc. groups – mainly against God and His word (even being against america – Jesus' country) are really a religion – satan's (which can be against people, and for sure against God and His truth), and only Jesus (and His word) can fight it. Don't avenge for yourself – go to God – and share Him – Jesus, but protect yourself (and family, etc.) from evil, and care about people, and help people – not hurt, if possible – don't be selfish.

So don't use hate, jealousy, terrorism, killing, etc. to get things done here in the world for any change you think needs to be done here – for any justice (they may have some punishments for any guilty person, and need it). Use love, helping, caring, fairness, etc. when you can – and share Jesus (and go to Jesus), and His truth, even though you may have to protect and defend yourself and your family, etc. sometimes in this evil world.

Liars, cheaters, etc. also think that others are lying, etc., because they do (satan leads man – and we let him) – we all are evil, and the truth will never be found, unless we go to Jesus and His word. Find the truth (and justice), with Jesus, and only Jesus – His standard (the truth of His word), not ours.

What would a person give up for his soul – life (for riches, etc.) – to gain everything (no matter how you do it – evil, etc.), or do things right and good (and maybe not be rich, etc.) – like politics, power, etc. – you end up hurting yourself and others – and go to hell (**matt. 16:24-27**)? You see that in the world (and even in america) –so go to Jesus (and His truth), and lose your life (the love of this world at all costs, things you have, believe, etc.), if you have to – God will help you (and eventually give you what you need – shown as an example in the **book of job; matt. 6:33**).

We allow satan to run our lives – a person, family, society, nation, etc. (even the world), when we don't go to God and follow (Jesus and

His word) – and don't share the truth. We do it to ourselves – letting satan in (and God will allow it) and giving into satan – against God, etc. – so we need to go to Jesus.

Know what to believe in and follow, and who to be with – you can make better decisions about who to be with. Find out what Jesus wants to make your decisions. We know right from wrong.

Most people don't go by their word, so why should we listen to you, if you don't listen to others? We should listen to Jesus and His word. Words can hurt or help – get the best words from God, His word, the truth (**isa. 55:11; matt. 24:35**) and help all.

What's the purpose of cheating, lying, fraud, etc.? – it's to get things that are not yours, not good (or fair), etc. – especially without God involved, but God will get justice and you won't – eventually the truth will come out (about you and what you do). Go to Jesus now.

Why do humans believe lies, (of the world, nations, leaders, beliefs, etc.) and things that are not good – do evil (illegitimate causes, etc.)? We all are evil and misled (by satan), without Jesus. We all have potential (God made us that way) to do great (or at least better) things, but not by ourselves – with Him – you can't do anything without Him (**john 15:4-6**) – He is for us, for us to have life (**1 john 5:12**) – at least good things. Isn't that what you want to do? If not, that is your problem (our problem), and hurts us all, without Him and His truth.

Even the enemy (whoever is against Jesus and His word, the truth – mainly satan and those that follow him are automatically against Jesus – **matt. 12:30**) uses God's laws – stealing, lying, killing, etc. to hurt you or even arrest you, etc. (even though they may not follow them at all) – if you are doing something or saying something that they don't want you to believe or against their belief – they lie if they have to – to hurt, kill, etc. you – satan is the accuser – a liar (their father – **john 8:44**), but God will help you, if you go to Him – Jesus.

So if you are not with Jesus, you are automatically with satan (**matt. 12:30-32; luke 11:23-26**) – no in between (no atheists, false Christians, religions, etc. – you are with satan, and destined for hell) – like it or not. God is a just and holy God, and can't be with us in our natural sinful state, and only with Jesus can we get away from satan (and the life that leads to hell). Even you can see the evil of man in the world (and in you), but we don't have to be that way. We can change, but what Jesus wants.

Use your abilities (smart, effort, etc.) for doing good, be an example (and work hard) – we all can do something and do it right and go to God. Only Jesus will help you find what you are to do in this world and do it right and best for you and others (**philip. 4:13**). If you don't give up and keep going to Jesus and His word **(gal. 6:8-10**).

You can be lazy, don't care, etc., and say you need help – help yourself first and stop being a victim (feel the world is against you, etc.) – the only way is with Jesus, not man – then maybe someone can (or should) help you. Without Jesus you will continue to be in the same cycle of life – a failed, struggling life.

When the world is against you – you should work harder (and do things you never thought), but best to go to Jesus, and let Him help you through it – that's what He and His word are there for. Go to Him. Whoever gets the worst end of anything here, better live a better, safe, life – how you behave, and who you hang out with, etc. – and go to Jesus.

If people have something they don't want to stop – that's not good for them – not obey the laws, not live a good life – stop bad behavior (and some will cry racism, prejudice, unfairness, etc. – to justify their life) – all (black, white, etc.) don't like living a good life (we are all born evil). So stop making everything a race issue (even though it is in the world and in man), so you can get out of everything – nobody wants to do the things we all have to do in this life – stop trying to get out of things (mainly what you cause, and don't want to change to get better). It's easy to go against people that are different than you – appearance, beliefs, etc. (like in america). Only have a chance with Jesus – but it has to be the truth.

Don't use racism, etc. (or any other escape, or excuse) to get out of lifestyle, criminal, bad behavior, etc. you did (or are doing) in your life – especially those that hurt others (besides yourself).

The hatred is not just color, gender, etc. – although that may play a part and also helps you identify people quickly, but it is because we are sinful – evil and we find reasons to hate and be evil to one another – because of sin. We need to go to Jesus to change.

The one thing Christianity and the bible shows us, is that we are not mean, hate, evil, prejudice, etc., because we are treated badly (even though that still hurts), but we are mean because we are not with Jesus – we are sinful, evil, and all different from noah's sons, that causes us not to get along (without Jesus).

Let Jesus take the prejudice, hate, unfairness, barriers, etc. away – not man, because we won't be able to stop trying to do it ourselves and won't get it done, no matter how long we try or how we try (we haven't been able to do it yet). Has to be done right – living how God wants us to live (and any help that we have had in that area, has been done with God's help – especially in america – with Jesus). Better be the truth.

All of noah's sons (all of us) are evil, sinful – and all need to go to Jesus.

God loves us (**john 3:16**) and is a just holy God, and has to have punishments, payments, etc. for sin. So He sent Jesus for us. Even though God tried other ways from the beginning. We have to know we are sinners – evil – we all can see it in the world and ourselves. Wake up. We all know of Jesus (**john 1:9; rom. 1:18-21; titus**

2:11-15), but follow satan instead. God wants us to go to Him – but it is only with Jesus that we can.

God is the one who made us (all of noah's sons) – separated and unequal, etc. (especially women – **gen. 3:15-16**, and ham – minorities, etc. – **gen. 9:24-27**), and only God can bring us together (God even separated the jews – **gen. 17:19, 21**), and that is with Jesus – who satan is trying to get us not to go to. We all (all of noah's sons, including jews) need to go to Jesus.

We need to get away from man (**isa. 2**) – away from noah's sons, and go to Jesus (**1 cor. 15:44-58**).

Only in Jesus (with the Holy Spirit) will we be equal (**1 cor. 12:13**). Though in america it is close – only because of Jesus, but we need to go to Him to be one – with His truth (and the Holy Spirit). It takes time.

You don't do things at all costs, just to get your way (selfish – how we are born) – you may be wrong.

You need to do things right – not just get things, or even just get them over with, etc. You get better, work harder, if you have to. And it is not always easy to do. So go to Jesus.

Work hard and trust God and His word – not money, things, people, etc. at all costs (and don't try to keep getting it for free – hopefully we can help each other). If you have it, use it for good (and only Jesus will help you do that). Getting things any way you can isn't the goal – doing it the right way, doing it yourself, work hard (for your growth, self-esteem, confidence, etc.) – like even getting good grades in school is no good, if you cheated, or basically had someone else do it. And do without if you have to – but do things right (work hard). Focus on doing things and living your life the right way (no matter what it is – or God has you do), and don't worry about the outcome – it will happen best. But do it with Jesus and His word. And if we go to Him (Jesus), and listen (learn His word), He will bless us (**matt. 6:33; john 10:10**), get what we need and maybe more (and put us in the right place), otherwise don't want or love those things (and you won't waste it either when you have some things, etc.). Don't make deals with the devil – you will lose (eventually). Prove that you're trying to be good, not evil – work hard and show you're good at something, and don't quit, don't take the easy way out – to do evil, because you quit things (stop doing things right), eventually it will get better, with Him (and still work hard at whatever you do, with Jesus in your life). Keep praying to God through Jesus (**1 thess. 5:17**). He may sometimes lead you in a different direction (or see if you really want to do something, with some obstacles). Go to Him.

Besides money, etc., God can bless you with time, good marriage, relationships, family, health, peace, safety, love, etc. – go to Jesus, because satan (which is the alternative) can't give that to you (it will just look like it, even if you are rich, etc. – because of satan). God wants to bless you with abundance (**john 10:10**), but with Him – Jesus (following Him and the truth of His word).

Appreciate what you have in this life. Help who you can. It is best to go to Jesus (and His word). Especially in america.

Many people need to help (in the world and america) and many people can help – especially in america, and with Jesus it is the best – help and share. Then all can get what they need – but need to share Jesus. The only reason anything has changed (for good) for any group, people, etc. in this country (or world) is because of Jesus. For all of noah's sons.

America is way more than fair, dealing with crime, etc. – you have to really try to be caught, and be in the wrong place – living a wrong life. There is evil in this world – don't be giving into it and we still need to fight crime. God will do that and want us to do that. Hopefully it will lead us to Jesus.

And God will have mercy on who He will and harden hearts, etc. (**rom. 9:14-18**) – He knows who will be saved and who won't be (but He doesn't make you either way – you choose, and anyone can be saved), but if you are with Jesus (it has to be the truth), and follow Him (and His word), you will be helped, and blessed. It's not what you do, but who you are with and Who is with you – Jesus (salvation – with the Holy Spirit) – then do what He wants. And it should be that way – why should it be any other way?

Have faith, and trust Jesus can heal, and turn a little into a lot (**matt. 14; matt. 15; mark 6; luke 9; john 6**) – don't need to steal, beg, etc. (**psalm 37:25; matt. 6:33**), especially if you change (become righteous with Jesus only – not works, etc.), but you have to go to Him and do as He says (and if you don't want to, then it is your fault you struggle – not man's evil in your life, because God can go around man's restrictions here – especially noah's three sons, satan, etc. – if you go to Him and follow). Don't do things you think you need to do, to be saved – only faith in Jesus dying on the cross and rising – no rituals, works, etc. (**gal. 2:15-21**) – or it is a waste of time (**rom. 3:21-28; 1 cor. 1:17; eph. 2:8-10**). Know the truth with Jesus (and His word) – then you will have a chance to do the right things – things in this life (and after).

Have Jesus work in you for good, with the Holy Spirit (**eph. 3:14-21**). And then have the love of God (**1 john 4:7-17**).

You can only be righteous with Jesus, and if you are righteous (truly saved with the Holy Spirit) and following Him and His word – the truth (daily) – you won't have to beg, etc. for anything. Live the way He wants you to live.

So we don't have to live a tougher life (**psalm 37:25**), He will provide (and we need to give to true Christian churches and ministries only, with your tithes and offerings, and you better know which ones are, or you will not be blessed – it is His money, don't rob God, **mal.**

3:8-12) just go to Him and learn His truth (those that truly teach it) and then follow. Learn the truth – know it, or you will be spinning your wheels. And it is only from Jesus and the Holy Spirit, that only He can give.

God will give you money, things, etc., that you need to live on the earth, in this life here, if you go to Him (**matt. 6:33**) – Jesus (and the truth of His word) and give to true Christian groups, churches, ministries, etc. – and the churches should not take money from businesses of fake Christians and groups (or even people – non-Christians, etc.) – to worry about what they can preach, etc., from the word – the truth. We should preach and warn all about the truth of the word (bible) – all true wisdom to make sure people are truly saved (**col. 1:28**).

Even in this world, we have insurance for many things – but they have to be honest, etc. (some may be), and so do you. No matter what happens to you – go to Jesus, whether things are good or bad – better insurance for all (all of noah's sons).

Jesus died for all – and all are dead – in sin – all of noah's sons, and all can live (**2 cor. 5:14-15; eph. 2**). Share that.

And don't make satan rich (and those that follow him), by giving to religions, cults, beliefs, businesses, products, people, charities, etc. – no matter what they say or lie about – since they can't do all the things they say they do – and they don't do it themselves. Know who you are giving to. Don't be fooled.

And be thankful – don't lie, cheat, etc., but love, no matter which of noah's sons you are (what we are born with) – be in Christ (**col. 3**). If nothing else Jesus will let you like yourself – He will change you inside and out (and not have to be stuck with what evil you are born with – be born again – **john 3**), even though we will never be perfect – not until heaven (with Jesus only – with the Holy Spirit in us). Life is only worth living with Jesus (**1 john 5:12**), even until we go.

Go to Jesus to escape the evil of this world (**2 pet. 1:4**) – that's led by satan. Man could have since the beginning.

So man didn't go to God before the flood (but God still loves us, not sure why, except for the ones that go to Him, then and now, although He made man for Him – for a relationship, to freely go to Him and love Him, not to be forced to, we have a choice, and to obey, we have to know the truth, but with His Spirit, for a better life here, and after), even as nice as God made it to live then (before the flood) for man (nice weather, food everywhere, comfortable for man's body, etc.), and we only ate plants (plants everywhere, and good weather all year – man ate no meat, animals all got along with man and other animals, no food chain, etc., just like the animal lovers like it) before the flood (**gen. 1:29**), and part of the reason why man was so healthy (even though man still may need to till the ground – **gen. 3:23**, especially after the flood). And God had not caused it to rain on the earth before the flood (just a mist – **gen. 2:4-6**), not until the flood (when He opened the windows of heaven, **gen. 7:11-12** – the water, that He put up there at creation, **gen. 1:6-8**, a covering, or a canopy of water, above the earth and making it nice all of the time, another reason why man lived so long). And the word cloud isn't mentioned until after the flood (**gen. 9:13**).

So there would be no need for electricity, etc. before the flood (but could have been), and people could sleep outside, walk across the world, not get hungry – enough food, plants, etc. – even sleep safe (except for evil man) – no animals, etc. to attack, eat, etc. you (and you didn't eat them).

And fire would not have been needed before the flood (and may not have been possible without rain, lightning, etc., that was not there before the flood). The only thing that looks like they may have had something like that would be to make some things with brass and iron – some technology, etc. (**gen. 4:22**), but may have done it another way.

So it more than likely came after the flood – when it was needed and may have come from the lightning to begin with – which came from weather, which was not there before the flood. And certainly didn't need it for heat, etc., since the weather was nice everywhere (for man's body), all year round (night or day), or needed to cook anything, including animals, etc. – we didn't eat them then (not until later – after the flood – **gen. 9:2-4**).

God didn't start out killing animals (or needing to eat them) – He created us to all get along – but with Him in our lives.

But all of that was about to change.

After the flood many things happened – God really separated man then, mainly to what we see today in man, and it started in **gen. 9**, just after the flood. We all are from adam and eve, and after the flood, God started over with man (same humans as adam and eve – which noah was), after man had been mutated (giants, etc.) by the sons of God (**gen. 6:1-5**), who are fallen angels (demons), before (and even a little after) the flood (**2 pet. 2:4-5; jude 1:6**). Before the flood it was easy for satan (or angels – who are all male – when they are visible on earth) to get to and in evil man (and with women), over those years, since most (probably millions, or more, people living then) were not in the presence of the Lord (and only eight were – noah's family, at the time of the flood), and man was allowing these sons of God (who are fallen angels, leaving heaven, and God, on their own – free will) to do what they wanted to man (and women – **gen. 6:1-5**) on earth (since most of man was not going to God, or being with God). Angels are all male in the bible (but don't look for them today – mainly demons – fallen angels will be known, and want to be known to man – to fool them) – even though man may call a beautiful, nice woman an angel here on earth.

So satan and angels mutated man before the flood (**gen. 6**), and satan uses man to mutate man today (away from what God wants) – with drugs, procedures, vaccines, beliefs, experiments (today and in the past – like the russians in the early 1900's – like the 1920's tried to mate man and apes, and others, etc. – evolutional thinking), etc. – the world will end again – Jesus will come back. God knows this was going to happen (**rev. 18:23-24**). And this time the world will end.

And satan (angels) is more powerful than man, and can harm and mislead us, etc. (even today – like ufos, aliens, etc. – all false beliefs of satan – who makes you think you were with aliens, etc.), but God – Jesus (and the Holy Spirit), is more powerful than all (man or angel) – greater is in you (if you are truly saved) than in the world (**1 john 4:1-4**), but you have to go to Jesus, or satan will run your life – Jesus can make something good out of something bad, even if you have been letting satan run your life (**matt. 19:26; luke 1:37; luke 18:27; mark 10:27; rom. 8:28**) – go to Jesus now. He is the Creator.

Even with sorcerers, magicians, etc., in egypt, when moses and aaron went to pharaoh, the satan filled egyptians had power (from satan through them – even those that try to do that today), made serpents out of rods – just like God did through moses and aaron, but those from moses were more powerful (**exo. 7:8-13**). And that is what is tried by people (through satan) today.

So satan (demons) has power – and why God says not to do anything with witchcraft, psychics, voodoo, sorcerers, magic, etc. (**2 chron. 33:1-6; gal. 5:19-21**) – all from satan against God (using man to have power). You are not only hurting yourself, but others.

And satan has had all of these people over the years go to and worship the creation (which is really worshipping satan, and not the true God) – all of the religions, beliefs, etc. worshipped the stars, planets, etc. (some worshipped many gods) – from the egyptians, greeks, romans, to the arabs today – from the sun to the moon, but not the true God – just the creation, creatures, etc. (**rom. 1:18-25**). But all have seen and known of, basically were exposed to, the true God, and didn't go to Him.

Idolatry is anything that we may follow or believe in, other than the true God in your life – beliefs, things, ideas, etc. – natural or spiritual. We should only believe and follow the truth of Jesus and His word. Over the years (from the beginning), God has shown His power to all people (all of noah's sons), but people still won't believe, or stay with Him.

Don't go to these idols (the things we put power and hope in) in this world (satanic worldly things) – there is power, but God is more powerful. We have a choice in this world – Jesus or satan.

Even with modern medicine, technology, etc. – now man (satan leading), can do things to man – to mutate humans, like the sons of God (fallen angels – demons) did before the flood (**gen. 6**) – against God's creation – mainly hurting man. All of the modern things are not all necessary for man to live, and definitely, not live better, healthier, etc. – man causes most of the problems he has, without going to God (and the truth of His word).

And God doesn't love us more today (with all of the modern 'discoveries', etc.), than He did people 500 – 2500 years ago. We all need to go to, and know how God made us (and take care of our bodies, each other, etc.) and don't listen to satan, and all that he leads man to do in this evil world – go to what God wants for us (**rom. 12:2; 1 cor. 3:18-21**). God sees the beginning to the end all at the same time, and was always available to man (even sending Jesus at the right time). Knowing what we are going to do and how we react – He wants to see what and who we will follow. Go to Jesus, and find out the truth, and be ready to go to be with Him, after this life.

People, groups, etc. do experiments (now and in the past), drugs, procedures, etc. on the human body in the guise of 'cures', progress, etc., but it is just satanic experiments, mutations, etc. on God's creation – mainly man. And man stops going to God and His word to do what's best – only to the evil of man.

Mutations by demons (fallen angels, like satan) – like before the flood (most was before the flood and one of the reasons God sent the flood), as some did a little after the flood – and also after that (**gen. 6:4**).

It is satan that looks into and changes man to see how God created everything – especially man, and to ruin and mislead man in the process – with all of his lies – trying to be God and lead man away from the truth of God's word.

If these mutations, etc. happen in this world (a cursed world), and they do – conjoined twins, limbs missing, etc. – but not very often (even like giants – goliath, and others, and those with six fingers, toes, etc. – **2 sam. 21:19-22; 1 chron. 20:5-8**) – not as many, like before the flood. But we don't need to do them to ourselves (with satan leading). Try to be healthy, with God.

So satan wants to mess with and destroy God's creation (and man – adam, gave it to satan – **gen. 3**) – especially destroy man (we have to live here) – to mutate – hurt humans (like before the flood – **gen. 6**, and since), with procedures, drugs, possessions, manipulations, bestiality, transgender, mutilations, for entertainment – freaks, hallucinations, hypnotisms, ufo's, etc., like in today's world – and we are letting him do that (and not know it – letting satan run them and this world – **2 cor. 4:3-4**). It's sad people are given drugs (even pesticides, etc.) that cause other ailments, sickness, diseases, etc., that make people take more drugs – and the pharmacy, medical field, etc. make more money (satan's ways) – having man sick and speed up death – not God's plan, so we need to go to Jesus. It is that drugs have gotten so bad that they give drugs to counter drugs you have been given, etc. The world depends on them (and man – satan) more than God. Go to God first to live healthy. Drug, etc. companies can pay people a lot of money to lie, etc. – hurting, killing people. So the pharmaceuticals, drugs, etc. (companies, medical, etc. – sorcery) are trying to run the world – satan led (which will be part of the reason man is controlled and eliminated, and the world will end – through sorcery – drugs – **rev. 18:23-24**). Doctors come up with whatever sin there is, and call it a disease, and if it is, only Jesus is going to get rid of it (whether is it physical, mental, emotional, etc.). Don't listen to those who say you need a drug to fix yourself – it's just the way we are born – evil, sinful – go to Jesus to get healed (do it His way). Blame yourself, if not. Choose Jesus and change and get away from the power of this world (and satan) on us – all of noah's sons need to.

The medical field tells you to take drugs, etc. and if you get worse or die, they say your disease, illness, condition, etc. killed you – but the drugs, behavior, addictions, and bad diet, etc. is what killed you. So go to God – to Jesus, not man to change and get better in all parts of your life (and be ready to go when you die).

Don't eat (or put things in your body) that are not good for you – that God didn't create for our bodies (what's best for it) – cookies, cakes, ice cream, pies, pizzas, hamburgers, sugary foods or drinks, coffee, alcohol, drugs, smoking anything, etc. in order to cope with this world and your problems (even from you or your family, etc.). Go to Jesus or you will continue to struggle and have bad health, too. Try to avoid them all (or passing them on to your children, etc.), by eating the way God made our bodies (**gen. 1:29; dan. 1**), and to heal – at least go to God (Jesus), and His word first.

We mainly get our preference and taste for food, bad habits, etc. from our family, nationality, culture, etc. – our parents got them from their parents, and they got it from their parents (your grandparents), etc. – all the way back, etc. So a son that ate what his mom cooked, liked it, and wanted his wife to cook the same for him – then their children ate that same food, and it keeps being passed on to the next generation, etc. (any bad habit, etc.) – and it may not be good for you, and cause problems at birth, etc. and hurt the children as they grow. Stop the cycle and eat healthy, and get rid of bad, unhealthy habits, etc. – so your children don't have to suffer, struggle – the more unhealthy you are, the more you have to eat healthy. And change the bad health cycle in your family.

Anybody can be healthy – at least healthier – there is no excuse, no matter what age – just do what God wants and how He made us. It takes time and faith and trust – especially to put good things in your body (and in america there is plenty of that). And if you don't think so, then that is why you are unhealthy.

People hurt themselves and others trying to buy cheap things – if they are not good for you (like food, drugs, etc.), or are stolen and sold cheaper, etc. – do what's right, honest, etc., and what is best for you – and you will be better in the long run. Go to God and His word – to Jesus, or do without (**philip. 4:11-13**).

People die more by eating bad (man-made food, etc.) and by being overweight, by drugs, etc., than by starvation – mainly in america (but other places in the world, too). Eat healthy, the way God made us to (**gen. 1:29; dan. 1**), no matter what nationality or culture, etc. you were brought up in – even though it may not be easy to change to – and it will take time, but worth it. And drugs of any kind – legal or illegal – alter people, especially children – mentally and physically, etc. – satan pushing them in that direction (and man gets hooked – and depends on them, instead of change to what is best for us from God). They are not good for man – many people are drug pushers – it's not innocent or safe, etc. – the little good that may help (with supervision, etc.), is barely worth it. Go to God and live the way He wants us to for the body He made to get the best help, or we are just causing a problem we can't overcome by ourselves. Not only do the pharmacies have a lot of drugs, etc. and sell them, but they have a lot of money to advertise them, etc. (things that harm and kill you – **rev. 18:23-24**). Go to Jesus (and His word) instead – at least see what He can do first.

People get hooked on drugs – legal – from doctors, and then people get used to it and keep taking drugs, etc. (and their side effects) to get healthy, etc. (and seems normal) – then it starts to change humans, to continue to be unhealthy, depending on them (some may be needed, but don't depend on them). Eventually killing all who depend on them (and man). Depend on God, and what He made us for – go to Jesus, and be concerned about where you are going after this life.

The reason man is sick, weak, dying, etc. – young or old, is that man has gone away from God and His word (His food is best for our bodies – **gen. 1:29**). Now we need to go to Jesus (and His word), not man and his answers for the sick, weak, and dying, etc. Man isn't going to live forever here anyway.

The doctors don't always know the answers or the best answer to your health problems and may make it worse, hurt you or even kill you (and is one of the top killers of man – malpractice). Go to Jesus and His word first.

Although God may use a doctor sometimes – especially if it gets people to go to Jesus. But go to Jesus first, and see.

Most people shouldn't worry about death, sickness, etc., but make sure you go to Jesus and believe the truth – be saved and ready to go (before you die) – then see what to do in your life.

And satan (and fallen angels – demons) likes to look into man and his body, etc. – satan uses ufos, and hallucinations (even the look of an alien, space being, etc. – that we all seem to accept – big eyes, no nose or mouth, and bald, all one uniform color, etc., that might be brought up by hypnotism, is because in the last 100 years, or less, babies were being born while the doctors were wearing masks, caps, and uniform, etc. and with bright lights – that's the first things babies see coming out of the womb – just a body with eyes only), fake abductions (like a possession), hallucinations, etc. to fool people so they think they have been taken, because satan (demons) wants to know about humans, etc., and always has since creation (and tempts man with all kinds of evil) – basically he's jealous, because God loves us so much – and how and why He created us (**1 pet. 1:12, 1 pet. 5:8-9**). And satan (demons) is also behind body mutilations – transgender, even cosmetic surgery, etc. and has been since the beginning (**gen. 6:1-4**). Stop believing in what man believes or what you believe (satan leading), but what Jesus says, and the truth of the bible (and why God wrote it – for us to see the difference in truth and lies, etc.). We need to go to Jesus to stop this and share Him, and to help others. And satan (and his lies) is more involved than you think, and affecting man.

Maybe doctors can try to diagnose your problem, but don't try to solve it. Go to God and His ways (His word) to get healthy – mentally and physically, but especially spiritually.

Just like what you put in your body causes health problems – get rid of what is not good for you to eat, etc. – for good health – the same with other things in your life – sin of mankind (adam, and all of noah's sons) – satan leading you – get rid of sin for life to get better health – the things you desire, think, strive for, etc. – that lead you to a miserable life. Be healthy spiritually, too. You need to go to Jesus to do this. And why Jesus came here – for us.

If you do things in this world the way God wants it to be – in His word and with Jesus, you will be better off.

Most of the problems that people have in this life are caused by themselves (with sin and this sinful world) – change with Jesus – especially be ready to go, if (and when) you die – to heaven.

Being seriously sick, disabled, even an accident of some kind, etc. can and should get you to think of your life (and death) and get you to go to Jesus, while you are alive. And are really what these things – tough times in your life are for – to get you to finally go to Jesus and have Him in your life and learn the truth of His word.

So all of the people and things you see in this world that deal with death (for the most part), has a lot to do with satan (and demons – fallen angels) – who come here to steal, kill, and destroy (**john 10:9-11**). All the ways man comes up with to hurt people – mainly for selfish reasons – man is evil. So we need to change that by going to Jesus – get away from man (noah's sons – being led by satan).

Human trafficking, sex crimes, mutilations, drugs, experiments, etc. (now and in the past) – are happening all around the world (even in america) – especially by people of fame, rich, celebrity, politics, in power, etc. (involving many other kinds of people sometimes) – taking advantage of others (especially women and children and poor, etc.). More evil in the world by man (through satan) than you think – making money, power, control, etc. God will and is punishing man (just like He did in the past – even for the flood, **gen. 6**) for how man lives (as a person, nation, and a world) – all of the evil we do (with satan's help – **psalm 5:3-6; psalm 7:8-11; psalm 9:3-8, 15-18; psalm 10, etc.**) and not going to Him (Jesus) to change (and repent – the true Christians need to speak out even more today – but about the truth of Jesus and His word).

Even people given addictive drugs, etc. by the medical field, pharmaceutical companies, groups, etc. – those that eventually change them (and control them) and cause them hurt and kill themselves and others. And those that don't die continue to make the medical field, pharmacies, etc. richer. All satan led.

So satan uses man to do all of these things (to control, etc.) and keep people from God (Jesus and the truth) – and man tries to see how much he can get away with – hurting people – sometimes people know about it (and maybe get paid to do it, and sometimes not), and people (scientists, politicians, companies, the rich, etc.) use man – especially the poor, etc. (mostly to have power, control, and for money, etc.), and we follow.

You don't know all of the evil and the level of it, in this world – it is worse than you think or know – God knows and wants us to go to Jesus and His word – to know the truth, trust Him and go to Him, and change who we are (getting away from satan and his lies, ways, etc.) and share God (Jesus) and His word – this is what we need to speak up about.

So God had to kill all of those types of man (those out of the presence of the Lord, or mutated, etc. – from the sons of God – angels – **gen. 6**) before the flood (all of man, those without God, and as He would and should today – and He does sometime – but you basically do that to yourself), and He wanted to start over (without creating again) with the same humans (and earth, etc.) – that noah and his family were (and those who were in the presence of the Lord – following Him) – the same humans as He created at the beginning – adam and eve (**gen. 1 and 2**). Starting over with noah and his three sons (and their wives) who we all come from (**gen. 9:18-19; gen. 10:32**), as we all did originally from adam and eve (not mutated, etc.).

The blood of adam (and noah's sons) to us from creation is still in us (life is in the blood – **gen. 9:4-6; lev. 17:11**) and needs certain things to be healthy, and connects all of man, and it is also what kills us, if we lose it or sacrifice it – like Jesus did – shed His blood for us, and so do we – die, to connect to God (if we have Jesus). So healthy blood is good for life here (but don't need it for life after this), but not to be eaten – from animals or anything (**lev. 17:10-12**) – that's how diseases start and spread (and death). Man and animals only ate plants, etc. before the flood – created that way (**gen. 1:29- 30**). Only after sin – and only after the flood – did God have man eat animals (and other animals to eat animals – **gen. 9:2-3**) – a punishment (sinful and not following and listening to God – **gen. 6**) – it is man's fault (all of our fault) that we kill and eat animals. Blame yourself – even animal lovers – all of man. Go to Jesus if you want to change and to be in heaven after this world is done (which may have animals – at least in the 1,000 year reign of Jesus there will be animals like before the flood – **isa. 65:17-25**).

Today healthy food can be grown all year round now and shipped (in refrigerated trucks, etc.) around the country and world, but animals are still needed, and were needed in the past, and some today. So we can be healthier today.

So don't put animals above people – God loves people (even more than angels) – **matt. 6:25-26, 28-34; matt. 19:29-31; luke 12:4-7**. God made animals and takes care of them, but they are for the benefit of people (and we should do the best we can for them, too, but they are for us) – **gen. 1:26-28; gen. 2:18-20; gen. 9:2-3**. And man needs to go to Jesus to become the people God created us to be.

So you have to believe the bible and what it says – from beginning to end – including that we are all from adam and eve – and have the same body as they had and made for the same food – plants, herbs, etc. (**gen. 1:29; dan. 1**) – basically, fruits and vegetables, etc. – best for our bodies today to be healthy. For every nationality, etc. – even though we all look different and live in different areas of the world – mainly after the flood and the tower of babel – **gen. 11**.

All nations (and nationalities) today, are from noah and his three sons (**gen. 9:18-19; gen. 9:27; gen. 10:32**) – and we are all one race (**gen. 11; acts 17:24-27**). We need to know this.

Life is in the blood (**gen. 9:4-5** – God told noah, before the jews) – and the medical field, etc. started to follow what God's word said about cleanliness and blood in the bible (**lev. 17:10-16; deut. 12:22-28**), and has helped some. Don't mess with blood – be clean, or people get sick and die (like we see in the world today, with viruses, epidemics, etc. – man causing them at times). So we all are related to each other by blood – from adam, and now from one of noah's sons (after the flood).

Man being careless and sloppy with blood – man or animals, is not good or safe or healthy – or if you use blood on purpose in the wrong way – causing illness and sickness in man. And man finding that out in the last 200 to 300 years or so (in the medical field, etc.). And seeing how it has hurt (or controlled) man, even today.

The longer that man has gotten away from God's word and what is best for man, the more man has become sicker and unhealthier, etc., over the years – especially today (and especially in america).

Depending on man (and technology, etc.) only, instead of God and the truth of His word, has only hurt man. Go to Jesus and His word for everything.

Before the flood, man (physically – nothing to change the look of man, like after the flood) was the same (and sinful, evil) and all from adam, but after the flood (especially after the tower of babel), man was eventually different (the way we look today – different ability, appearance, etc., but still sinful) until Jesus came here and died (so now we can all go to Him, no matter how different we are). We all are from adam (and noah). And when you go to Jesus and get saved (get the Holy Spirit) – then those with Jesus (and the truth in His word) are not with adam (or noah) anymore, or in their image (**1 cor. 15:21-22, 45-47**), all are one with Jesus (spiritual), and in His image (born again – **john 3**), and the rest of the world (without Jesus and the Holy Spirit) are still with adam and noah (still earthly, sinful, evil, and still different – in adam's – man's – image, **gen. 5:3**).

Throughout the time with the jews (from abraham to Jesus), the Holy Spirit wasn't given to them – with a few exceptions (only to lead them, help them write the bible, etc.), but only given to people after

Jesus died and rose – to today – who truly believe Him and follow Him (**acts 1 and 2**). And there is a vail over the jews (and those that don't have the Holy Spirit – all of Noah's sons) to understand all of the bible (**2 cor. 3:12-18**) – the old and new testaments (and the god of this world – satan – blinds man – **2 cor. 4:1-6**). It is satan (and his angels) who we are really fighting here (**eph. 6:10-20**) – leading man against God and His truth – don't be fooled (**2 cor. 11:13-15; gal. 1:1-10**).

God uses the Holy Spirit to teach man the truth – like He did from the beginning – before the flood (no bible, just God with us, if we wanted to go to Him – the presence of the Lord), but after the flood, and mainly after the jews (writing the bible, etc. – God talking to us), God uses the Holy Spirit to teach us (**1 cor. 2:9-16**) – given only from Jesus. Learn the truth – going to God, through Jesus (and the truth of His word) – not satan, angels, man, etc. And before the flood His Spirit was here on earth (the presence of the Lord – basically Jesus). and God wasn't going to strive with man anymore (**gen. 6:3**), because man was evil, wouldn't go to Him (very few did – **gen. 5**), even when the flood came – only eight – noah's family on the ark saved – because they did go to the presence of the Lord (**gen. 7 to 9**). The few then, and even the few today, that go to Jesus. Go to Him now. Don't miss out.

So only after Jesus died and rose (the last 2,000 years) can we be different than the way we are born (sinful, from adam, noah, etc.) – to be able to be one with Jesus (with the Holy Spirit), not separate (or different) from each other (which is from adam and then noah's sons). Before that (Jesus' death and resurrection) man was always from adam and noah's sons – even the jews.

Now, since Jesus died and rose, we can get away from man – noah's sons. And can be healthier, if we follow Him and His word – but be with Him, so that no matter when, or what you die of, you will be ready to go. We need to do the best we can, with helping people get to know Jesus and the truth of His word.

But even one rising from the dead will not change everyone's mind (**luke 16:27-31**). Even with that, all the jews did not believe (even those that saw Him). We keep trying, though.

And Jesus was seen by many people (in His new body) after He was resurrected (by over 500 people – **1 cor. 15:1-6**), but some still didn't believe, Jesus says blessed are they that have never seen Him, but yet believe (**john 20:29**) – that is us today. You would think that more people would have believed after that, but they did not – there were only 120 believers (jews) in **acts 1:15; acts 2:1-12**, when they got the Holy Spirit (and they were from many nations, and were only jews, and they understood each other – even in different languages – and why speaking in other tongues were needed then, but not needed now – **1 cor. 13:8**). We need to believe His word (and Him in you – the Holy Spirit) – true faith, and we need it (true faith) in Jesus to live and to be saved. And share Him with your children and their children, etc., so we won't forget the truth, like people could have done since adam, and after the flood with noah (but you can see that they didn't even make it 100 years or so, after the flood – at the tower of babel – where God had to change the language and scatter man around the world – **gen. 11**). And it has gotten worse since then – but at least satan cannot cause all of man to go against Him at the same time, anymore – at least not until the end (which is coming soon).

No matter how bad it gets here on earth – disasters, accidents, evil people killing, wars, etc. – all can and could have gone to Jesus to be saved (be ready to go, no matter what evil things happen here – now and in the past) – you don't know when or how you are going to die (but you know you are). No excuse. Even before the flood.

So with the presence of the Lord before the flood (and those that were with Him), God had His Spirit with them (with the Lord's presence physically, not in them), but He was not going to keep striving with man with His presence or Spirit anymore (the Spirit wasn't in man, just there – the Lord's – Jesus, presence), because man was so evil all of the time (not many with Him – only eight at the end), and with the humans that were changed, etc., He needed to start again (**gen. 6:3**). So He repented that He made man and was going to start over (**gen. 6:5-7, 11-13**) – still wanting a relationship with us, the reason He created us (in His image). And before the flood, people started to call on the name of the Lord when enos was born – 235 years after the creation (**gen. 4:26**). God still came to us since adam. God was still loving us – giving us a chance to be with Him, no matter how sinful we are (starting with adam).

So there really is no excuse for any culture, nationality, etc. – all of noah's sons knew of the flood – even after the languages came at the tower of babel (and man scattered all over the world – they all knew what happened, wherever they eventually lived – like we see today) – because noah knew all but adam – but noah's father (lamech – died five years before the flood) and his grandfather (methuselah – died the year of the flood) were alive when adam was, and they would have talked about the creation, sin in the garden, satan, etc., just like noah and his sons, etc. would have talked about life before the flood and the flood itself (to all of their children and children's children, etc.). Noah and his sons lived to abraham's time – so they could talk and share, etc. everything (all from creation). So there is no excuse for not knowing the truth of the past (from our ancestors – they just didn't want to believe, or even share the truth, etc. – even today – and just like stephen shared with the jews – **acts 7**, and that the wise men eventually went back and shared with their countries, when they found the star and saw that Jesus was born – **matt. 2:1-2**). God has done this all through history (with many people that He uses, but all through Jesus since He died and rose – no one else – for the last 2,000 years). So God started over and eventually wrote the bible – with all of the truth (so no one has an excuse to not know the truth about man and this world, etc. – and who the true God is). And there are some versions of the flood passed down in different cultures, etc., but the truth is in the bible (**gen. 6 to gen. 9**).

God starting over, but with a few changes (after the flood came – **gen. 7 and 8**).

God made the languages at the tower of babel (**gen. 11**) – to separate man (because of satan, man against God), and God can bring man together with people sharing Jesus in their language.

So God started over with a changed earth, flooded with water from heaven and from the deep (**gen. 7:11-12**) – and that water is still here around the world (the seas, oceans, etc., that now separate the land, after the flood), including frozen in the poles – from the one and only ice age – about 4,000 years ago (but the earth is still beautiful after being destroyed – even when God destroys something, it is still beautiful, as we see today), and God will keep it going until He is done with it (**gen. 8:22; rev. 21**), no need to worry about climate change, global warming, etc. (although it is warming since then to today, the last 4,000 years – the ice, etc. melting), He will destroy it in His time (**2 pet. 3:8-13**), man will not, so He is in control (we just need to go to Him, and be ready for whatever He will do – but we can help, too, by taking care of what we can here, especially trusting Him, and keep going to Him), and with all of noah's three sons (although man is still born evil, **gen. 8:21**, without the Holy Spirit – all from adam, continuing from noah's three sons), so we still need to go to God (as they did then) today. So we all need to go to Jesus – and be ready. And share Him (Jesus) – the truth.

So don't try to find eden, etc. – it's covered by the flood (but maybe in some area in the earth – covered). Anything before the flood is gone, changed (and the look of the earth happened quickly – not years, etc.).

So the 360-day years at the beginning that God started with (12 – 30-day months – **gen. 7:11, 24; gen. 8:3-4**, and will end the world with it, in the seven-year tribulation – **rev. 11:2-3; rev. 12:6, 14; rev. 13:5**), turned into 365-day years after the flood, because of the weight of the water – the windows of heaven – the canopy of water protection came down (and now also frozen water on earth) slowed the orbit of the earth down (as also the tilt of the earth that the flood caused, or God did – that started the seasons – **gen. 8:22**) – just like running laps around a track (like a mile), then having to do it with a weighted backpack on – slowing you down. And having it go back to 360-day years may happen because of the rapture (all of the weight of the bodies leaving the earth at one time – and/or somehow the ice and water evaporated, etc. by some catastrophic event) – like taking off a backpack, etc., speeding it up, or God will just do that (including the possibility of the axis of the earth back to the way it was – and all of the earth will have good climate – getting ready for the 1,000-year reign of Jesus – just like before the flood).

If the snow and ice frozen in the poles were to melt – it would flood the world – as the bible says of the flood waters (that are still here) – **gen. 7:17-20**. The flood waters came all at once and flooded the earth (**gen. 7:11**), flooding above the high hills (and the mountains that were made by the flood), and separated the land and making deep oceans for the water – all we see today.

The waters were high on the earth and God had the ark land on the mountains of ararat (**gen. 8:4:13-14** – and the ark is probably still there, under the snow, that came after the flood), but the water dried enough to allow noah to get out of the ark, but not all of the whole earth – only around the ark, but eventually most of the earth became dryer, with the water frozen in the poles (after the one and only 'ice age'), like we see today, as well as in the deep oceans.

God made the world this way, because of man's sin – and Jesus' truth is the solution – no matter what man comes up with to solve them – man won't and hasn't, as much as he tries. We are spinning our wheels here – don't listen to man's solutions, that he keeps coming up with. Go to Jesus and His truth.

But however it was, the climate changed after the flood – and is part of the punishment for man.

So God brought the flood, because man was all against God – if we have problems now, including climate, etc., it is because of man (especially america today) not going to God (and His truth), so in that sense, it is man's fault. And that includes tornadoes, earthquakes, fires, hurricanes, etc. – punishments after the flood by God – and some are for renewing and cleansing. So it is all man's fault. Go to God – Jesus now.

So no matter what man comes up with to destroy the world or a country, etc. (especially america), God will not let it happen, if He doesn't want it (He is in control – but lets us decide – a choice, free will – even satan, angels, have free will), but when it is the end times, God will do it, and if He does it, we can't stop it (**acts 5:38-39**).

Man has been predicting the world will end or be destroyed (even by man), etc. for many years – especially recently – God knows only and will do it – giving man time to get saved by Jesus. He will end the world (**gen. 8:22; 2 pet. 3:8-13; rev. 21:1-8**), not man. So be ready to go with Jesus, no matter how, or what happens to this world (or you). Be with Him (Jesus).

God created us a certain way – our bodies are not invincible like you think they would be (should be like armor by now – at least like the toughest dinosaurs, or alligator, rhino, etc., if we evolved from all of the animals that came before us – if evolution is true, supposedly), because man is so evil to each other and have been over the years, but it (our body) isn't tough, just useful, and versatile, but vulnerable (and easy to kill, hurt, etc. – you can do that with a pencil, etc.), like God made us to be (man or woman) – so that we would understand how each of us can be hurt or killed so easily (we should have eyes in the back of our head by now, to be safe, if evolution was true), and that we would be kind to each other, etc. God made this world tough (especially after the flood) and our bodies fragile, so we would have reason, at times, to go to and need Him to make it in this world safely, healthy, etc. And that can only be with God in our lives, through Jesus – the way God intended man to be, connected to Him and to be guided by Him and love each other, etc. (with the Holy Spirit and His word), not evil or mean. But without Him (and the Holy Spirit) we are evil and mean, so we need to go to Jesus to get the Holy Spirit back (born again) to be the way He made us originally.

Without God (Jesus and the Holy Spirit), man may act like animals. Man, people – are not from animals – don't act like one – that's what satan does – evil – leading us that way (and why people think man came from animals – because of satan – and man following him, and not God – Jesus, and His truth). Look at the world (even in america), and in the past, you can see how evil man is – those same people try to run a nation (which is starting to happen in america – showing the evil of man, and of those people – from the way they believe – hateful, spiteful, selfish, etc.). They only care about themselves (and their beliefs, selfishness, etc., no matter if they are bad, hateful, etc.), and not others. And that leads to hate and death (satan's plan for man). We all need Jesus.

God created us vulnerable and limited, so when man sinned, man could be a little easier subdued, etc. – God knows we can, and need to, protect and defend ourselves.

Only God's (Jesus') ways and truth is good for man – test Him out, and soon.

There are many ways to die in this evil world (tough world after the flood) – for many reasons (mostly from satan through man) – all the more to go to Jesus now, and be ready to go, and have a better life here, and after this one. God made it tough (after the flood), so we would go to Him.

We have things in this tough world to show us to be an example of living right with God – God shows us and helps us. The world is tough and evil and with temptations. So we need to have the tough things to show us how to live – and who to go to – to Jesus. It works with Jesus, and the truth of His word.

This world is not as good or comfortable, like before the flood – we don't live as long, and it should get you to go to Jesus, and long for heaven. It's the evil in this world that gets us to go to God – that's why satan is still here – you have to make the choice to go to Jesus – our free will. So the evil should do that.

There are tough, harsh things (natural laws – physically) in this world, like gravity (you can't jump off a bridge and live, or at least not get hurt), cold, heat, pain, thirst, hunger, sleep, breathe, etc., along with health of our bodies with the right foods (not manmade) for us, etc. (He created best for our bodies – plants – fruits and vegetables – **gen. 1:29**) – that God put all of these here (physical laws, etc.), that we have to live with and help each other with (but He wants us to go to Him for the help). We have to do things and live the way He wants us to and then keep going to Him more. Eating and drinking (plants and water) is needed here – by God, so we need to go to Him (Jesus) for that – to know what is best for us (and what is not). Just like all of the other things God put here that we all have to deal with to live. We should have evolved (if evolution was true) to not eat or even sleep (we are most vulnerable sleeping – anyone can kill or hurt you, etc.), by now, because it is not good or safe for us, or maybe not even go to the bathroom (a nuisance and depending on what one you are doing – might be vulnerable, etc. – for man or woman), and also not to have such a delicate spine, body, etc. – not evolved to have any of those, but God made us that way to be careful and care for each other (maybe need Him more). There are limitations here and we need to be aware of that. God did make this world at creation for man – and to be comfortable – that's why we have the bodies we do, and the needs we have. All of the things that are not good for us, and see today – mainly after the flood, were not there before the flood. We can be without food and even water for a while, but without air for only a short time – why?

Everything is set up for us to die – mainly after man sinned (and so we would need God and go to Him – to do it His way, not ours, for everything – to live the best we can here) – why didn't we evolve to not do any of those things that would hurt us or kill us faster, etc.? But also the hardships are for us to help each other, and care for each other's wellbeing – knowing how tough this life is (and then be able to share Jesus with others – that's why Christians are still here after we get saved – to share Jesus). And because God knows what is best for us, better than we do.

The one question would be – why would we not get rid of this sinful body, after we are saved (with the Holy Spirit in our soul – connected to God now)? We still have temptations – especially from satan – resist him and he will flee (**james 4:6-8**). We can be strong with Jesus, but not perfect, until this body dies. We still all will die (except if you are here for the rapture – when all true believers will get a new incorruptible holy body) – but we are still here (in this sinful body) to preach Jesus and His truth. And God knows this about our situation here – so go to Him. But all are going to go somewhere after this world.

So stop denying that you are going to die, and find out where you are going after this life (evolution will not help – only lead to hell – misery forever). Man is evil and we need to know all of this and understand why God made it all this way – to go to and need Him. He made the world so we would need Him to function the best, and to get the most out of this life, and especially after this life (we have to go to Him). Everything is set up for us to go to Jesus (especially after the flood – all punishment for all of man, which is actually a blessing).

One of the differences after the flood to the earth is the weather (natural disasters, etc. – tornadoes, earthquakes, hurricanes, etc., which were not there before the flood), and also the cold (snow, etc.) and the heat (deserts, etc.), which our bodies do not fit – and we still have the same body temperature as adam (anywhere from 98 to 99 degrees) – we are all from adam (**gen. 3:20**), and we can't go up or down with our body temperature too much, or we will get sick and eventually die (no evolution – or this world would be more comfortable by now for us).

So before the flood the temperature was probably about 60 degrees to 85 degrees all over the earth and all year long – to fit our body temperature that we were created with. And the people before the flood were outside all of the time (with nature, animals, etc.) – they didn't need to go inside (didn't have to worry about animals, etc. – all got along), but may have had tents, etc. (privacy, sleep, etc.) – the weather was perfect for our bodies. The only thing man did have to worry about is sinful man (just like today), that were evil to each other (**gen. 4 and 6**). Even though man could be in the presence of the Lord before the flood (but man didn't – it was too nice at that time – didn't need to go to God), and it was evil times (man doing whatever he felt like – all against God, and man) – and God decided He wasn't going to strive with man here (with His Spirit), any more (**gen. 6:3**), and all of man was destroyed at the flood, because of that (a punishment for all of us today – after the flood – a harsh, tough world to live in – in many ways).

The canopy above the earth, put there at creation, by God (**gen. 1:6-8**), protected man (skin, body, etc.) and kept the world comfortable (like a greenhouse) – no problems, no harsh weather, etc. But after the flood – no more canopy (where the water came from for the flood) to protect man. The weather after the flood (which God made) for people to bond together and be concerned about each other – and fear against the same enemy or problem, disasters, etc. (to go to Him) – and to forget the differences, etc. between us for a while – to help each other in need. And God sends and uses these disasters –punishments – all after the flood (He controls them – sets them in motion, etc.) sometimes – but let God take care of it, you just go to Him and help each other through it (but be with Jesus and be ready to go whatever happens) – this life here is short. So get to Jesus now. Get away from noah's sons – all going to hell without Jesus.

So God controls the weather to help or punish nations, or areas, etc. in the world. Go to God and His word and share His truth, and why we are here. That's how you can help you and all. God will end the world (**gen. 8:22; 2 pet. 3:9-13**), so don't listen to people that talk about how the weather is proof that we need to change things – except to go to Jesus and His word.

God wants to make sure that all can (or do) go to Him – so He made the world the way He did – uncomfortable (after the flood), so those that really want to go to Him, will. Go to Jesus. God tried it with man being in a comfortable world before the flood – it didn't get people to God, but being in a tough world will or should, and you may die young, etc.

Death isn't the worst here, death (even life) without Jesus is.

And after the flood, the world has about 98% or more of salt water (which man cannot drink, or will get sick and eventually die), otherwise we would have evolved to drink that by now (if evolution was true), but before the flood there was mostly fresh water (the fresh water is now in the rivers and lakes, etc. today, with snow run off, rain, etc., but it is mostly underground, and hard to get at after the flood covered it – another punishment, look around the world). And man only ate plants (**gen. 1:29**, which is still the best for us to fight and get rid of all of these diseases, birth defects, etc., we have today – we also need to eat healthy when pregnant – and be healthy before pregnancy – giving a child a chance – not just eat what you want or feel like – not drugs, vaccines, etc., **dan. 1** – doctors, scientists, man, etc., don't know more than God), but after the flood God said we could eat meat, and the fear of man (only after the flood – today) will be in animals now – separating some animals from man (prey and predator for man and animals now – they can eat each other, etc., **gen. 9:2-6** – but before the flood it wasn't that way, the way God created man and animals – an example is like how a giraffe is – tall to eat leaves, etc., but hard to drink water – which is needed more than food – and they have to get in a vulnerable position to drink and can be attacked and killed easily this way – they wouldn't evolve to do that). And even though meat isn't as good for us (and you can't eat the blood – causes some of our diseases, etc., **gen. 9:4; deut. 12:22-28**), and not meant for our bodies (hard on it), and why we can't live to the 120 years we are able to live after the flood (**gen. 6:3**), we don't always make it that long (we die young) – even back in the past – **psalm 90:7-12** (but with the weather change after the flood, God had to give us something to eat (meat to eat – and why He had dietary laws for the jews – certain animals to eat and not eat – so He had noah bring also clean animals on the ark – **gen. 7**) – since we can't always grow plants – in snow, cold, etc. – and the seasons started, **gen. 8:22**, not like before the flood with good weather all of the time. And we also needed to be warm when it was cold, so we needed animal skin (fur) for clothes (not sure what they all wore before the flood – with good weather they didn't need clothes, but most probably did, and could have made clothing without killing animals – sheep, etc. – even though before the flood there was a sacrifice – **gen. 3:21** – by God for adam and eve, and an offering by abel – **gen. 4:4**, and just after the flood by noah, the first mention of a burnt offering sacrifice – **gen. 8:20** – but were mainly after the flood).

So because of the weather change we needed homes, buildings, shelter, etc., after the flood (and God even recycles – wastes, decay, death, etc. for the soil, crops, etc., and the carbon dioxide from man to help plants, and oxygen from plants to help man, etc., as well as germs, bacteria, viruses, etc. and can all be good, working together, but we have to be healthy and eat the way God says for our bodies – **gen. 1:29**, and we will be healthy – and fight off diseases, etc., unless God sent it to man, as He has done in the past), and He also uses insects and animals to work together with plants, etc. for good. So just go to Him and His word (and trust Him). The healthier you are, the better to fight off other diseases (and recover, etc.) that go around – eat the way God made for our bodies to have the best chance. That includes healthy blood, because life is in the blood (**gen. 9:4**) – all from adam at creation, physically – same blood, and now sinful, including from noah's sons – Jesus shed that blood. If you lose your blood – enough of it – you will die, or if you have bad, sick blood, you will die – with some disease, etc. – so eat healthy – fruit and vegetables (**gen. 1:29**), and get your blood back to health, and be able to function better.

We all get sick, because we don't eat good – the way God created us for, and we use blood in a sick producing way over the years, and still do today – God making it that way (**lev. 17:10-16**), mainly after the flood (a punishment). So we don't need vaccines, drugs, etc., if we eat healthy. Be healthy, with God.

The diet that man had before the flood was fruit and vegetables (**gen. 1:29**) – and man probably had type A blood, but after the flood, God said man could eat meat (**gen. 9:2-3**) – we needed to eat something, since the world changed (snow, cold, desert, weather, disasters, etc.) – so today (after the flood) the majority of man has type O blood – mainly meat, but some people today have all of the types of blood – A, B, O, AB, etc. across the world, and throughout history. A study for all of this led to finding that man had a cell protector – called neu5Ac (man named), now man doesn't (after the flood – by eating meat, etc.) – and we have something that doesn't protect our cells anymore – neu5Gc (and it started in man after the flood – God knows that), and causes our diseases (some animals have neu5Ac, and they don't get the same diseases, etc.). Some people still try to eat healthy – but we need to know why that is best for us. God knows best (in His word) – about blood and about our diet – He created us that way (and we are still that way today).

So all of noah's sons have different blood (even though we are all from one blood – **acts 17:24-28**) – after the flood. And all have diseases, etc. And some live longer (but none past 120 years today – **gen. 6:3**), but it is best with what God created for our bodies – plants (fruit and vegetables, etc. – **gen. 1:29; dan. 1**). All are punishments for man's evil from sin that happened before the flood (**gen. 3; gen. 6**), given after the flood.

And don't think that just because you are alive at an old age, that you are doing things right – but we all should be able to live to be 120 years old (and no one hardly ever makes it, but give yourself a chance). So you need to take care of yourself – do good things, and eat healthy, etc., and to live long enough to go to Jesus before you die. Go to Jesus and His word soon.

Even though God said it was fine to eat meat after the flood (**gen. 9**) – to kill animals, eating fruit and vegetables are still best for us – what our bodies were created for (**gen. 1:29; dan. 1**). And most people today don't kill the meat that they eat – so it makes it easier for most to eat it.

We all should be as healthy as we can be here (we all are different, but all can be healthier) – knowing the best way to be healthy, and not accept being unhealthy as a way of life (or the need to take drugs, etc.) – and help others to be healthier.

Although the main thing here is not to live as long and as healthy as you can (even though we can try), but to get to know Jesus and be saved, before you die – but it would be nicer to live here comfortably as long as you can – mainly to help others, and sharing Jesus. Hope these problems and diseases, etc. will get us to go to Jesus. But follow God and His word for our life here, for everything – including to eat what is best for our bodies.

We won't have blood in our heavenly bodies (**1 cor. 15:50**) – like Jesus didn't have blood after He died and rose (He shed that for us) – He had just flesh and bones, and did eat (**luke 24:36-43**). So keep your blood healthy (in this life) by eating what is best for it, which is not man-made food, meat, drugs, etc.

Most of the animals are for man to eat, if need be – after the flood (**gen. 9:2-6**), but plants are best for man (**gen. 1:29; dan. 1**). And using animals for different products, etc. may not be necessary to kill for, especially today. We just need plants, if we can get them to all – but maybe the meat of fish, chicken, cattle, etc. – especially in the past (but bad conditions, drugs are used, etc. for them now today – which is not good for man), if we need meat (and some do around the world) – but mostly people struggle all around the world (for water, plants, etc.) – land becomes desolate, because they don't go to Jesus (**prov. 14:34; isa. 6:10-12; isa. 13:9; jer. 6:7-8; jer. 44:5-7; jer. 51:62, etc.**) – and it has to be the truth. If we would all go to Jesus, there wouldn't be as much hunger in this world – in america, or around the world. Jesus will give you what you need to live here, if you go to Him (**matt. 6:33**). We need to be safe and live in this world, doing things right and best for man to be healthy. Following God and His word. And the different viruses, flu, etc. (epidemics, etc.) just show how unhealthy man is here – in how he eats and how he tries to take care of or 'cure' – fight, diseases, etc. – that for the most part, man causes, and makes worse (they say they help) with drugs, chemo, procedures, vaccines, etc. (even though doctors, etc., are needed in this evil world for some things). But satan is leading man away from the truth and from God. And satan always likes to mutilate and destroy and modify God's creation – especially man – including transgenders, tattoos, body modifications – freaks, etc., including using drugs. Even for some animals, too. It wouldn't be so bad, if God hadn't given us the answers, but He did – in His word (and Christians should be the healthiest, but they are not – that is a problem, since churches, etc. don't all share the truth of His word and how He made us, or follow it themselves – **gen. 1:29; dan. 1**).

Not all of the technology, etc. is good that man makes – we can't just make or buy anything, at least be careful what we develop. Some of the things, products, etc. that man makes aren't all good for man or the world, and we have to be careful – many artificial, fake, etc. things – not healthy for man. God made natural things for man and what is best for us. Go to God (and His word) first.

There are more tragedies, etc. (along with evil) after the flood, than before the flood – more ways to die, etc. – reasons to go to God. Even though man lived longer before (and healthier) – there could have been evil in this world even more at that time (**gen. 6**), but they didn't go to God. Today (even though we live shorter lives), we still can have our bodies have problems – hopefully to get us to go to Jesus.

No matter what we have done to our body or what happens to us (how terrible – done by us or others – in this modern world, etc.) – our lives, bodies, desires, etc. can change when you go to Jesus and get saved – and when the rapture comes, and we will get a new body (**1 cor. 15:42-54**) – if you are with Jesus.

Whether it is artificial legs, arms, knees, hips, even pacemakers, etc. – all may help someone stay alive, function, etc. – but it should get people to get to know Jesus.

The doctors, medical field, drugs, procedures, etc. are good for disasters, injuries, accidents, crime, hate, killing, wars, etc. (which happened mainly after the flood), but they shouldn't be for our day-to-day health (which is where they make the most money) – God made us for a healthy diet, etc. (**gen 1:29**), and to go to Him first for everything. And the end of the world will lead to more disease and drugs, etc. (mainly by man – satan) – killing many (**rev. 18:23-24**). So we do most of the things to ourselves (including taking all of these drugs in the world), but also this world after the flood is set up for a tough life, so that we would go to Him (to Jesus to be saved), and His word.

All of the health problems we have today, were not there before the flood – no UV rays – no sunburn, chapped lips, eye problems, skin problems, cancers, obesity, diabetes, didn't need glasses, etc. (because of the canopy protecting the earth, and man – **gen. 1:6-8**, that was there until the flood – the water from heaven that came down – **gen. 7:10-12**, and that protective canopy is not there anymore for man), and because of eating plants only – **gen. 1:29** (not animals, and now today with man-made, synthetic food etc.). All of the changes after the flood – bad today (harsh world, eating meat, etc. – **gen. 9**) is the punishment for all of mankind since then – even for us today. And we have to suffer these problems (mainly because of our lifestyle, diet, etc.) and we all want relief. Even the drugs, etc. cause more problems for our bodies.

It is nice to be healthy – or have the medical field come up with some help to keep us alive or healthy, 'cures' etc. (even for your heart – one of the biggest killers) – with drugs, surgeries, procedures, etc. And as much as we can try to be healthy – we should try (for what God made us for our body – **gen. 1:29**), but we are still all going to die – so we need to know where we are going first after this life (and know the truth). Trust Jesus.

Any good that the medical field does (emergencies, accidents, etc.) – is overshadowed by the bad or evil they do (and we follow – satan led) – keep the good and get rid of the bad. Go to God and His word and depend on Him and it.

Even the advertisements on television, etc. make it look like taking drugs, etc. is normal – even look good and healthy for everyone (looking healthy, and good looking, actors, good food, etc.), and everything that happens to man. What a lie – from satan – and man falls for it – just to make money and control man, and have power, etc., (especially for satan) and lead man away from God and His truth.

No one likes pain of any kind – physical, emotional, mental, etc. – just want to stop it, and why painkillers (and other drugs) are so popular (and cause more problems) – and why these advertisements seem to work – immediate satisfaction, gratification, pain relief, etc. People wouldn't have to be so susceptible to these diseases, viruses, etc., like we see today, and needless people die (with or without vaccines, etc.).

If people believed in evolution and survival of the fittest, etc., then why give drugs, etc.? – just let all diseases run their course and kill those who can't make it – like it was supposedly in the past (thousands and millions of years ago), and the ones that survived are the powerful, stronger, etc. new species (even though not true – no evolution). And in the past, any plague, virus, etc. would only affect people in a small area, tribe, village, etc., and take a long time to spread, etc. if it ever would, but in today's world it is fast with travel, technology, etc. So we (all in the world) need to be careful and healthy – the way we eat, etc. (the way God created us), and always should – like before the flood.

Everyone wants to stay alive, and live as long as you can – however they can do that – but you may live a life that may kill you at any time, as it is possible here (including how you think you are going to be healthy, or not care) – in this evil, tough world. But we will die sometime, so be ready with Jesus, and live. Get saved before you die (can happen at any time).

You can't do whatever you want to do and not have consequences for it – there is a way to live and behave here (and how to be healthy) – and God says it – in His word. Go to Jesus and know.

And with all of the weather disasters – hurricanes, earthquakes, etc. (after the flood) – many people die at once (as God has done all through history – including the flood), we can all know of and see these things – go to Jesus now, and be ready. And these things will get worse at the end (**matt. 24**).

The world before the flood was comfortable, healthier, etc. – no disasters (weather – tornadoes, hurricanes, earthquakes, rain, cold, snow, etc.), no disease, lived longer, etc., but man was sinful and evil (although living in a nice comfortable earth – for our bodies, etc.), so God had to do something about the evil that man was doing to themselves and to and with each other (**gen. 6**) – so God sent the flood to punish man, and the world was not comfortable anymore – harsh, etc., and that is for all of mankind from then to today. Just like the world has been different since the flood – so has man (the way we look, etc., but still sinful), with noah's sons since then. Man is not the answer (and doesn't have all of the answers).

So God made it different after the flood – as a punishment for man, and we need to go to Him (Jesus) to overcome that, and even Jesus can heal you of what you have, if it is His will. But we need to do what we can to be healthy and safe – what God says to do – especially with Jesus in our life – and follow. Like we can't pray to get rid of something – like for healing of lungs, cancer, etc., if you don't stop smoking, and it is the same for eating bad food, or putting bad things in your body, etc. – praying to heal your body – stop eating bad food, putting bad things in your body. People that smoke don't care about others – not even themselves. You don't deserve help, if you don't stop your habits, etc. – you suffer the consequences, punishments, etc. – that goes for anything. Pray to stop doing bad things, and then change, to heal your body. We know better about smoking – like when everyone smoked (even doctors did) in the 1940's, 50's, 60's, then we find it causes cancer, etc. – people still do, and the same for fast food – finding out later how bad it is – and same for alcohol, now for drugs, etc. Make sense, and learn God's word – the truth – go to Jesus to be saved, and His word (and be healed), so if you die, you at least you know where you are going – but it has to be the truth.

All of the separations that God did after the flood (especially after the tower of babel – **gen. 11**) were for man's benefit – to have to go to Him (which man did not do before the flood – and why the flood was sent). If we want to stop our problems here – go to Jesus and change – then live your life.

God not only separated man (and God wants and lets you to stay with your own until you go to Jesus – then all of us to become one and get along – so we stay separated and disconnected from God until then – all of noah's sons – know the truth – go to Jesus) – separated more after the flood, than before, but He also separated animals from man (some more than others), and even separated animals from each other – to what we see today.

So animals are separated from humans (from the way we are created – **1 cor. 15:39**), and now (after the flood) God separated us more from some of the animals (**gen. 9:2**) – as He did the animals – which are prey and predator now, but not before the flood. And it will all go back to the way it was (all together – getting along – man and animals) someday (**isa. 11; isa. 65:12-25**) – in the 1,000-year reign of Jesus (and this time satan will be bound for those 1,000 years – **rev. 20**).

Animals (or man) didn't evolve – God changed them. You would think animal activists would be upset with other animals that kill animals – but only with man that kill animals (but not needlessly, etc.) – but God allowed both (**gen. 9:2-4**), after the flood (so man could have food – with the weather change, etc.), and even the animal activists could survive back then (and some today), by eating meat. Be thankful. God knows what He is doing.

So animal lovers don't need to love animals more than humans – God loves man and wants all to go to Jesus. So don't hurt, or maybe kill people who are not doing what you think is right – God gave us animals for many things, and especially to eat after the flood (**gen. 9:1-4**) – a punishment for man for what we did before the flood. And those that were not with God (in the presence of the Lord) before the flood, didn't make it through the flood (only noah and family). Even animal lovers will go to hell, if they are not with Jesus (saved with the Holy Spirit). Share Jesus.

All of the animals got along before the flood (even with man), but not after the flood (**gen. 9:1-5**). And ate only plants before. After the flood we could eat meat. And even dinosaurs (if satan didn't mutate animals – maybe dinosaurs) didn't eat meat before the flood (but may have after, if they survived after the flood – if there are true dinosaur tracks anywhere in the world – then they made it through the flood – on the ark, but didn't survive). All (man and animal) got along (even though man is evil then and now) before the flood – that would only be 4,000 years ago (just after the flood), not millions of years. But it is all our punishment (uncomfortable, tough, etc. world) today for our evil done before the flood – so we would go to God. So go to Jesus.

God had put traits in man and animals (from creation) to be able to adapt to the world after the flood (you can see the many animals – breeds, appearances, etc. today that may not all have been on the ark, just their kind). So after the flood, and especially after the tower of babel (100 years after the flood – with the language change), all of the changes and traits in man started to develop (color of skin, nationalities, etc.), because of the difference and change in geography and weather, etc. after the flood – and because man scattered all around the world then – within a few hundred years. Not evolution.

Man is evil – to man or even to animals, even though we need to treat people better. And we need to not take out our problems on animals, as some have done. Go to Jesus for your problems – not to man and animals.

Animals can be friendly, if brought up right or started with them when they were young – fed and loved (no matter how wild or ferocious they are today – any animal, but they still need to go into the wild eventually to be happiest). It is the way God created them at first – friendly – and the way they were before the flood, only after the flood did God put the fear of man into the animals – **gen. 9:1-3** (and will be friendly again in the end).

So man can love most animals, and the animals can love you – especially if you bring them up, and help and love them.

And God controls the animals for the most part (and man can sometimes to a point – good or bad), like God did leading them to the ark, and then leading them around the world after the flood (so they were there before man got to the rest of the world – continents, etc., as we see today). Even some animals may have been brought to isolated places on earth – like islands, etc. – by man at times, and some God had to lead to the places, by land or ice bridges, etc. or even through the water, right after the flood. God takes care of animals (and uses them), and man should be more concerned about man, more than for animals (even though some is needed – not to be mistreated, etc.), and for sure God is concerned more about man (**matt. 6:26-34**), especially if we would go to Him – to Jesus. There are some humans starving, too, besides some animals (stray dogs, cats, etc.) that people try to help (and maybe there should be some punishment for mistreatment of animals) – but try to help man first (his needs, but mainly to get to heaven – with Jesus). It's nice to help animals (but don't you be God to do it for others in a hurtful manner, etc.), but people are more important to help – mainly to get to know Jesus (even you) – animals already do know Him (and God will take care of them). And man at that time (just after the flood) was told not to kill (each other) or there would be a punishment – the first law after the flood, **gen. 9:5-6** (no bible yet – God – the Lord, still talked to some men then).

After the flood man and some animals started to hunt (but God didn't create us to do that in the beginning, but after sin of man – which includes you – then after the flood, God had to do that). And it will be God who ends this world – for man, animals, etc. (**gen. 8:22**). And God puts it all in the bible for us to know how it really happened, and that it was necessary.

So help animals that need it, but help man (being with Jesus will help them treat animals better). Man is sinful. Share Jesus and His truth with all (and start with you – know the truth).

God wrote the bible eventually (with moses) to share the truth of history, science, etc. – things man stinks at (with false beliefs) – especially how we got here and how old things are (satan leads man with lies – and man follows, through evolutional ideas, etc.) – building man's ego, etc. to seem intelligent, powerful, etc. – like a god – like satan wants to be.

So animals were necessary for man after the flood, even more than before the flood. God wanted us to use animals skins – fur, for clothes, etc., to be warm, right after the flood (but not as necessary today – especially the last few hundred years) – but needed after the flood (but not needed before, with nice weather, etc. – even though man used something to cover themselves – God started it with adam and eve – with the first sacrifice, **gen. 3:21**), because of the snow, cold, climate, etc. that was to come after the flood. And that was one of the reasons they (the animals – clean and unclean) were on the ark (to start over like it was before the flood), as well as for food (**gen. 9:2-3**), also for our life – to coexist and help each other (along with plants, etc.) on earth for man from then on (the creation plan – to keep going even after the flood), and it still is today, until this earth is gone (**gen. 8:22**). God will keep this earth livable until it is the end (when Jesus comes back). You don't have to be ready for the end of the world – like survival groups, etc. So don't worry about global warming or climate change, etc. (even though it may change some) – God is in control. You just go to Jesus – be ready with Him.

God set the time for the planet to go – since the flood (and knew that all that would happen on this earth would happen within about 4,000 years or so, then the tribulation, then the 1,000 year reign of Jesus), and when His eternal kingdom is to come – go to Jesus and be ready when that is – He wants us all to – as many that want to. It is soon.

There is no mother nature – God created it all (Jesus did – **john 1; col. 1:9-20**).

God controls the weather sometimes, comets, etc. (and even the stars – like the star at Jesus' birth), like the flood, plagues of egypt, sodom, jonah on a ship, Jesus on a boat on the sea, etc., but mostly it is just part of this world after the flood – man's punishment for evil before the flood (and since).

Eventually God will make a new heaven and new earth and start over – not with a flood, etc. – a new earth that will last forever, like we will – God's original intent for man (and the first and only earth – this one, will be gone, **rev. 21:1-5**) – so we don't need to go into outer space and look for planets to live, for resources, etc. (like in the superman story – a planet destroyed, and there no other people or beings in the universe) – it is a waste of time, money, etc. – we have what we need here (this one is, and still will be, the best for humans, until God destroys it – **book of revelation**). We can live better on a faulty, polluted, semi-destroyed planet earth (similar to after the flood), than on another planet or the moon – they are not made for man to breathe, eat, survive, etc. – we can build on this planet and live (and make more sense, cheaper, etc.), than build on (or even try to go to) another planet millions of miles away (need to make sense). Not just do what we feel like doing (and satan leading man to believe things like this). Be ready – God will end this planet – with Jesus.

God gave us rocks, trees, etc. to build with, and eventually metals, that we figured out how make, use, etc. – all from God. Any time when animal, earth, outer space, etc. lovers (calling it nature or mother nature) talk about how great it all is – they are really talking about how great God is, but they don't say that – it all is, including discoveries, etc. that man finds (even though man doesn't always know what they found, how old, how it got there, etc.). So admit it and give Him the glory and praise, not yourselves. And we can do some things to help or hurt the planet (and ourselves). But talk about Jesus and His word – know the truth – how it really got here originally – creation (**gen. 1 and 2**), and how it was changed by God, because of man and his evil, sin, etc. – the flood (**gen. 6 to 11**).

God made this planet the way it is after the flood (through to today) – to make it tough on man, and we can't change it – it will eventually end – God doing it). And we can take care of it the best we can for all (to a point) – but go to Jesus to do anything. And be ready to go after this (heaven – only with Jesus and the truth, with Him giving you the Holy Spirit).

And the earth is round – just like the sun and the moon are – and like the other planets, etc. – the bible says so – it's a circle (**isa. 40:21-23**) and it hangs on nothing (**job 26:7**) in space. And we can see that they are, and God created them instantly (**gen. 1:14-19**), and put them in their place – not millions of years, etc. (like man and satan, says – **john 8:44-47; 1 tim. 6:20-21**) – no evolution. And earth and man are the center of life (the only place in the universe like that) – what God created, in the universe. We know it is from God. And why Jesus came here for us.

No matter how smart you are – you are dumb, if you don't believe in God's truth and His creation (in His word), and God made us smart, but not to go against Him (**1 cor. 1:17-31**). You are smart with Him (or you are following satan to destruction).

And once this planet is gone (God will do it – **gen. 8:22**) – God will build a new one and the animals will go back to the way it was before the flood – all getting along with man, and all animals, during the 1,000-year reign of Jesus (**isa. 11; isa. 65:17-25**), and people – basically the jews (the jews, as a nation, need to and will go to Jesus – they could now, but won't – not until the end) – will be living on the earth (true Christians will be ruling with Jesus – **rev. 20:4**), and will live to maybe 800 to 900 years old again (**isa. 65:20**) – just like before the flood (**gen. 5**). Then when that (the 1,000 years) is over (satan, after being bound – for those 1,000 years, will be loosed a little to deceive people – **rev. 20**) – then eternity starts (which on that new earth, will include a city from heaven – **rev. 21**, that is 1500 miles wide, tall, etc. – about half the size of the u.s. – which is 12,000 furlongs – eight furlongs make a mile).

But remember all of what happened at the flood and after (even today), was a punishment for all of mankind (which we are – all connected to each other from adam – what one does, we all get punished) – what man did before the flood (the evil, violence, not being with God, etc. – **gen. 6**), and since we are all of mankind – connected to each other (so whatever they did, we get punished – just like we are all from adam and eve, and are sinful, separated from God, because of them, and we pass it on to our children, etc., and they may get punished, etc. – we are on the same team – like sports – one person messes up and all are punished) – there are consequences for what we do or don't do (being separated from

God – now with noah's sons). Man (or animals) were not created to have power over others, even though we see it today (after the flood) in the world – God was to rule us, the way He originally created us. We all have to go to God (Jesus) to make it right (Jesus did it for us – died, if we would just go to Him and believe), until we die, or until this world is gone (then He'll make a new one – **rev. 21:1-8**, for those who are His).

Until then, we are all connected to man (adam, noah, etc.), not to God – only with Jesus can we connect with God (getting the Holy Spirit). We are all in the same boat in this world – born into it **(col. 1:13)**, and the problems – and need to change. Reconcile to God. With Jesus **(col. 1:9-20)**. So we need to get away from man – noah's sons, and each individual person has to make that choice and go to Jesus to get salvation, because we all owe the penalty of sin – all would have to pay individually (death and hell), or go to Jesus, who paid the price for the penalty of sin for us all.

You have to work out your own salvation with Jesus yourself and the truth of His word, with the Holy Spirit – not what a church, etc. may say – go to the truth, to Jesus **(philip. 2:12-18)**. Then find a truthful church – not the many false ones.

Jesus is the bridge to God **(john 14:6; 1 tim. 2:3-6)** – and His life for you – to get away from man and go to God.

Deny yourself to follow Jesus **(matt. 16:24)** – your evil, sin, etc. – and connection to man (adam, noah's sons), and then connect to God through Jesus and the truth of His word – daily. To live the life that is best for you, and God wanted for us.

Most people cause their own problems in this world (with satan), because people don't go to Jesus and follow Him in their life and His word – the truth.

Part of the punishment after the flood, was more separation of man, and it didn't take man long to go against God after the flood – at the tower of babel (**gen. 11**), so God had to separate us again (this time not destroying the world or man, since He said He wouldn't then – **gen. 9:8-17**, at least yet), but God has to do something to control man and keep man from getting evil all at the same time, (which is all of man going to satan the same way –same level, same belief, etc., and all at the same time against God) – satan being able to control all of man at the same level – like before the flood (eventually man hurting others, and not going to God – God is the reason we are here) – so He has to separate man, and this time He did it when the son of ham – nimrod, came into power at the tower of babel (**gen. 11**). And it will be that same level (same belief – all against God and His word) in the end times (even more evil, like now, you can see it – **2 tim. 3:1-5**) – in the tribulation (after the rapture of all of the true Christians), and that is what will be left on earth – satan leading evil man at the same time and same level (**matt. 24; 2 tim. 3:1-5; book of revelation**), all against God again.

It's not a mistake that nimrod – son of ham (who is mainly against the true God), was ruling at the tower of babel – just after the flood – all against God – he was physical, strong and in power over man (all of noah's sons).

Today you see some whites, etc. (mainly japheth, and some of shem), trying to copy or follow blacks, minorities, etc. (ham and descendants) – especially in america (and the young, etc.), because japheth and shem followed ham – nimrod, at the tower of babel (**gen. 10:6-20; gen. 11**). And it will be the same at the end – like just after the flood started. Go to Jesus and change. Don't stay with noah's sons – sinful man.

So if ham (whole or part) – physical, etc. (and japheth and shem going along – **gen. 9:27**) runs the world (or america) again (which is what people in charge are trying to do – especially in america) – it will be destroyed (it will be the end) – like at the tower (and why God changed the language and scattered, or separated man all around the world – **gen. 11**) – basically with satan running it in the tribulation (anti-christ, beast, etc. – **rev. 13**) – all without God (Jesus), and all against God (even japheth or shem shouldn't run the world – mainly without God – even though God put them in a position of power, and even with ham doing great things working together – all using the three sons' abilities and talents – like america). But we do have to be careful of ham (it is still in him to be in control – nimrod, and eventually led to sodom and gomorrah, etc. – **gen. 10:19-20**) and his descendants (and those that follow them, especially canaan – **gen. 9:25-27**) – we are all that way – connected to noah's sons still (with their evil, sin, etc.), until we go to Jesus.

This world (or country) won't work without Jesus (and His truth). All need to go to Jesus. So either God will intervene (punish, etc.) and change the direction (like He has in the past) and it will be good again here – in america (because this is God's country), or it will be the end and the rapture will happen – either way it will be good for Christians (true Christians) – go to Jesus and be ready, then don't worry – knowing God is in control.

All of the modern-day nimrods – groups trying to change and lead the world (and america) – all against God (at the same time – led by satan, which is his goal again, using man to do it), like before the flood and just after the flood (**gen. 11**). You can see it around the world and in america. No men – people (noah's sons), should try to elevate themselves above another (at least without God – Jesus) – all need to go to Jesus to change (and become one), and to lead correctly.

Even though the anti-christ will probably come from the roman empire that will come back like it was when Jesus was here the first time (**rev. 17**) – from false churches and religions, and those that follow and join them – all of the religions of the world coming together (all of noah's sons) – and we are seeing that now, but it will be mainly after the rapture of the true Christians. Go to Jesus now and know His truth.

It's not all of the nations, cultures, beliefs, etc. that have to be worked on, but noah's sons in those nations individually (like america) – have to be able to get along and be one with Jesus (the truth of His word), and then that will change the nation. God separated man (**gen. 9:27; gen. 11**) – so only God can bring them back together – His way – through Jesus. Then the nations will develop to what God wants.

God knows what son of noah you are and put you in your place in this world (and your lot in life – nationality, poor, servant, etc.) – God will help you out of whatever you were born in, if you go to Jesus (and follow His truth). God even knows what jewish tribe that the jews are from (of the 12 tribes) to make up the 144,000 that are in the tribulation (**rev. 7:1-8; rev. 14:1-3**). So we need to get away from man – go to Jesus to change and be who He wants you to be – one with God.

So God had to separate man to help man (and those wanting to go with Him), and to hurt satan (and people that follow him) and his plan to unite all against God – one world order – to get all of noah's sons to be one against God – beliefs, etc. Read in **gen. 9 and 10** about how man will be separated after the flood (and still are today – **acts 17:24-28**), then more in **gen. 11**. All about noah's sons (japheth, shem and ham). Japheth and shem need to help (not hurt) ham (and ham needs to want to be helped), but all need to go to Jesus for it to have a chance to work. All sons need to go to Jesus, and follow His word.

The canaanites were always taken over, and not to be hanging out with, etc. (especially for the jews). Why is that? Because God said it – or any of noah's sons – it never works trying to be better than others, without God – God stopped that all through history – no nazis (aryan race, nation, white supremacists, etc.). All of man is evil (all of noah's sons) – but God did put some limits and restrictions on some. But with america (because of Jesus) we can all have a chance to live a better life and have freedom to do better in this world.

In **gen. 9**, right after the flood, God separates man (from noah's three sons, who we are all from – **gen. 9:18-19; gen. 10:32**) even more (to what it is in today's world). God (through noah) says that ham (especially canaan) will be the servants to and for his two brothers – japheth and shem (**gen. 9:25**, ham is also, and all of his descendants – a punishment for ham, **gen. 9:22**), and all of their descendants – even us today (we look different – color, etc.) – still holds true (**gen. 9:25-27**), until we go to Jesus. This separation and these different types of people (with the different abilities and interests in each person, and even color, etc.), that didn't happen before the flood – just after the flood (with noah's three sons – God starting over after the flood, just like we were after adam and eve sinned – especially after the tower of babel). Even the descendants of shem – jacob and esau (who are brothers) were separated (God separated them – **rom. 9:10-18**), and esau (also marrying those of canaan – God didn't want him or anyone to marry them, **gen. 24**, again separating) became a servant to jacob (**gen. 25:19-28; gen. 26:34-35; gen. 27:29, 37-40; gen. 28:6-9**) and jacob (israel) was the father to all of the tribes (twelve) of the jews. God will bless who He will bless, but we all can go to Him (no excuse – **john 1:9-14**), no matter what we are born into, and can change and be blessed, with Jesus in our life – go to Him now. So with jacob and esau – one will serve the other (**gen. 25:23-28**) – separation (God favors, because He knows them – **mal. 1:1-6,** hating esau, God knowing what he will become – He knows all, but not God making him do that – **rom. 9:10-24**, we all have a choice – free will – and God knows who will choose Him, but will not make or force you). All need to go to Jesus to overcome (**john 16:33**) what we are born with (all from adam, and then from noah's three sons – all originally caused by satan, who we all follow when we don't follow Jesus, and His word, truth). God can use the ungodly, as well as the godly, to get His plans done. Best to be with Jesus in this life. We (all of noah's sons) have a choice.

God directs man and who He favors or leads over others – like isaac (**gen. 17:19-22**), and as God did with japheth and shem (**gen. 9:27**), and the jews (a chosen people) – even the seed of david. But all of us can go to God (through Jesus today) – He isn't a respecter of persons – all through history man could go to God or not – before or after the flood, it's just that we don't choose to, even today. We are where we are until we go to Jesus, no matter what son of noah we are.

So servants in this world are a part of life – the way God made it (**gen. 9:27**), so we should all go to Him (all of noah's sons) – we don't have to stay the way we are (our lot in life from noah's sons) – the only way out is to go to Jesus – or you will keep seeing the problems you see in the world (even in america) and in you, continue to happen. And not get along until you go to Jesus, and it better be the truth, or we still will have problems – and still not get along.

God knows who will go to Him and follow Him – then and today (with Jesus only now), but all can go to Him and be saved (we just all don't – our fault, not God's – God just reacts to our sin and behavior and thinking, etc., our evil and satan's). So there is a separation in this world (also with all of the false churches). So God has to punish man – and wants what's best for us, because we don't know.

You can see that God started what looks like a caste system (and what really looks like only one system, because of the evil of man, born that way – we are all on that same level – all against God and His word), but not in every country (some countries do it on their own – the caste system, and separate people, more, by what they believe – religions, including false churches, etc. – really following satan), it is only those that have all of noah's three sons in them – real diversity (like america – which has the most), will have what looks like a caste system (God's separation – starting after the flood, with the sons of noah – **gen. 9:25-27**), and it is still that way today, until we all go to Jesus (we are free in Jesus – the truth of Him and His word – and can be equal). Not going to Jesus keeps the caste system in place – so go to Jesus or suffer what you get. The caste system is really noah's sons, and the differences we have from them – until we all go to Jesus, and change. Go to Jesus to be one together, if you are for equality, etc.

Any growth or good (to get along, be equal, etc.) that we have had in america, has come from Jesus, over the years, not man (even though it has taken time – because we try to do it ourselves, and not relying on Jesus and His word). We need to go to Him, and His word to have anything good happen (and last), and stay with Him and His word always.

We need to trust God and what He wants and when – don't rush it or it won't work. We all need to go to and trust Jesus – He will change it the right way. In His time, not our way or time – or we will slow the process down, and may hurt people in the process – just like abram and sarai did waiting for God to have their son – they got impatient and did it their way, and in their time and it was wrong, and it has hurt the jews ever since (**gen. 16**). We need to know what God did and wants. His way.

All of noah's sons have not been nice to each other over the years (that means you haven't been, or your family, or culture, etc.) – even up to today. We need to go to Jesus to change that.

The caste system is without Jesus, and with noah's three sons – japheth, shem, and ham – all different, and each son is a different level and ability, etc. (**gen. 9:18-19, 25-27**), who we are all from – with their different talents, abilities, etc. and our lot in life – one son over the other – all are needed. Some countries do it worse (separating people by class, family, etc.). Only in america (Jesus' land) gives anyone (all of noah's sons) a chance to change or get better than the rest of the world (as we have seen) – but problems, struggles, prejudice, inequality, hatred, etc. will not go away completely until we all go to Jesus – let Him lead you, and give you what you need – no laws, man's effort, etc. will change that.

CHAPTER 6

Living In a Fallen World: Challenges and Responsibilities of The Christian Living in A Fallen World

The things that happened to man after the flood hasn't changed – **gen. 9:27**, it hasn't changed until Jesus came here (and rose) and is the only One that can change that. We are all from noah's sons until we go to Jesus.

You take God and the bible – His truth, out of the country, you will have a caste system with all of noah's sons. Jesus, and His word, is freedom (but it has to be the truth).

People – all of noah's sons – have a chance to be more equal in america, because of Jesus and His word – the truth, if you go to Him and share Him. Go to Jesus to help and love.

Not your fault to begin with (but we are all human from adam and noah's sons) – where and who we are born to, although after you are born and grow up, it is your fault – go to Jesus. All of the problems that people have, comes into their life without Jesus – to get you to go to Him, hopefully.

We can't blame others – we have to blame ourselves (white, black, etc.) – we all (all of noah's sons) make situations that hurt others, etc. over the years – we all have a chance, and can go to Jesus and His truth.

Even though it looks like a caste system in the world, even in america – the opportunities are available in america to move up, etc., if you don't live a criminal or ungodly life (why slaves, prisons, etc. started, sold, etc. in any country, now or in the past, and God even had rules, etc. – **exo. 21:1-2**). Go to Jesus, and obey His word – laws, etc. – best would be to get saved and get the Holy Spirit. America uses the abilities, talents, etc. of noah's sons the best, because of Jesus, when they come to this country (however they got here).

When people go to another country, you don't want it to be worse than what you came from or just as bad for them – man is still evil, sinful, etc., and need to have protection – satan is everywhere. And we need to go to Jesus.

People have ignored God over the years – when they could have gone to Jesus sooner – all of noah's sons.

It's how we treat people before we truly go to Jesus that matters – during this time we don't get along, or are not fair to each other, or helping each other – we are selfish (and why all of these things we fight for, complain about, prejudices, etc. happen in this life and throughout history to all of noah's sons), and we need to change and grow and help. So we need to go to Jesus to change all of this – and we all have to go to Him individually to get saved, then share Him with all of noah's sons – family, nationalities, beliefs, etc. in this world.

Don't fight it (or each other), like we see in today's world (and we need to protect each other, by not hurting each other, but when we do, we need a nation that will have protection, safety – to protect, not hurt – and people that will listen and follow that – especially what God says – through Jesus). We wouldn't need any laws or anyone telling anyone what to do, if we would all go to Jesus (with the Holy Spirit) – Him telling us and following Him – so know the truth and share Him.

Throughout history man has killed many people – different nations, etc. – man is evil. All of noah's sons would have done that to everyone – to each other, it is not just one group or son, like we all think today. All of us don't get along without Jesus.

Japheth has done much of the killing over the years (being enlarged – **gen. 9:27**), as has shem – some to others, and their own, but all of the sons have done that – to their own. All are evil, and guilty – and are stuck in their lot in life – until they go to Jesus (but it has to be the truth). We need to help others to get to know Jesus, before any die.

But people have to protect themselves from the hate from each other – we all are wrong, sinful – man is, and have caused the need for protection here **(james 4**).

You have to stop people from doing evil things, or they keep doing it, and maybe getting away with it until they get turned in – prison, etc. – or possibly fired (if at a job, etc.) – no matter how important or high up a person is – all need to go to Jesus (even the ones that are fired or in prison). We have to try to do right – not to let it happen to others. Think of others that way to help.

We know we are all going to die (and are dead in sins here).

Many people do things that are not good for you in this world, and some get hurt or die from it, and all deserve death, but all don't die. So we need to go to Jesus as soon as you can.

We all have to work really hard to get along – all of noah's sons are mainly without Jesus, so make it easier with Jesus. Help people get to know Jesus (and His truth) – you first.

No matter how important or how great a man (or woman) was in history – and maybe someone we would think did great things (what man would think is good), if they (or you) are not with Jesus when they die, they are in hell, and really a waste of time. So have people focus on Jesus for their life.

Since God set the world up and how we are made and live here – the abilities, etc. we have – God is responsible for any good that happens here. Man should not brag – go to Jesus and His word. We all have free will – just like satan chose to go away from God – so did man (**gen. 3**) – we still all have that choice today – we have to believe, then follow what we believe (doing good or bad) – to where we end up – heaven or hell (with Jesus or like satan).

Don't honor men – any (especially criminals, lawless, ungodly, even religious, etc.) – don't promote man, but honor Jesus (**2 cor. 10:17-18; gal. 1:10**), and let Jesus help you, then you will succeed, and have a chance to be equal.

The thing about being equal is, is being able to have the opportunity to succeed – move ahead, etc. You have to work hard, and not cheat others, etc. to prosper – and not all will be rich, but able to live with Jesus – God will give what you need to live here (**matt. 6:33**). And if you don't work (especially believers), you don't eat (**2 thess. 3**) – and help those that struggle, but are still trying, and especially share Jesus and His truth with them.

Anything that gets you to go to Jesus is good – troubles, etc., that's why the struggles after the flood (our punishment) is better than the comfortableness before the flood. Count it all joy, rejoice and go to Jesus, whatever leads you there (**james 1**).

Jesus said that the poor will always be with you (with us in this world), because the disciples were upset that something was not used to feed the poor – they were being proud, etc. (**matt. 26:6-13; mark 14:3-9; john 12:1-8**). We can always help them and share Jesus to them (in this cursed, sinful world) – that's why we are still here – to get with Jesus and help others to that, too. So that problem (of the poor) will never be solved, but going to Jesus will be the answer to a life you can have here – poor or not (He is the most important), and being in america you are richer (even if you are poor) than most people in the world – with everyone helping and giving to each other. Without Jesus it will be more of a struggle (here and after this life). Just go to Him (and follow) and let Him work your life out.

Honor righteousness – not the poor or rich, etc. (**lev. 19:15**) – which is hard in this evil world – but Jesus will help you. In this world – when you do evil – it is against people – you hurt someone, and that needs to be punished (so don't be selfish).

And it seems like most of the time, the poor rob the poor, etc. – they should understand and not take from them (or anyone) – but work harder and show it can be done, and go to Jesus for help (not all are robin hood types – and shouldn't be that either). And those that can, should try to help others (but they need to want to help themselves, too).

And we need to work at whatever job we can to make a living – an honest one, and sometimes that means doing jobs (or two) that you may not like (but still good, honest, etc.) as well to earn enough in this world. But go to Jesus and let Him help you through that (and let Him find what is best for you) – no matter what son of noah you are.

We all are human and imperfect, but we need to try to have all of noah's sons get along, and obey God's (and the nation's) laws – help others to do that (especially your family and friends). And Jesus is the answer to all of our needs (the reason for the needs, problems, and separations in the first place – even for the existence of satan, demons – who God allows to be here), but with Jesus we can be one and together, and not until we all are with Him (at least those that are, can live a different, better life together). Only with the truth.

All the religions, cultures, beliefs, false churches, etc., all still are connected to all of noah's sons (originally with adam, and so still with satan, sin, etc.), and cause all of the problems in the world – all against God and His word – the truth. Go to Jesus – the only answer.

Do what's best for your family – no matter what others do – go to and serve the Lord (**josh. 24:14-15**).

All of noah's sons mislead people against God's truth. You can see the problems out there in the world – you are not blind – stop being in denial.

Look at japheth (intellectuals – scientists, academics, technology, etc.) and shem (beliefs, religions, philosophies, societies, laws, family, etc.) – how without God (Jesus and His word) they mislead people, from the truth of God, and hurt people (through satan). You see that even in america.

There's more to this life than intellectual, philosophical, or physical abilities and talents (and whatever success you have – money, fame, etc.) – it is knowing and being connected to God – the true God – to Jesus (with the Holy Spirit), and His truth. We are all trying to do these things (abilities, etc.) without God in our life, and that is causing all of the division and hate in the world. Get away from man – noah's sons, and hate, prejudice, etc., and connect to God – through Jesus, and have a chance to get along and help others.

We don't know what people are thinking – but if you did (if they said what they thought), you would say that all are prejudice ('racist', etc.) – black, white, etc. – some can be worse than others (don't accuse, or make yourself a victim, etc.) – we all are evil – even you (a group or nationality, etc.) – no matter what color or belief. Look at yourself. Just go to Jesus to change that – change you. You will have things (what you need), if you go to Jesus (**matt. 6:33**). Don't waste your things or use your money unwisely, or you will struggle – Christian or not.

And people that don't acknowledge Jesus as God, put themselves as gods (as some false churches do), with satan, and cause problems to themselves and others until they do. And send people to hell, as well as yourself – which is satan's plan.

Children are racist (mainly being taught not to be racist) from at least high school through college, and beyond – but try to act like they are not (black and white, etc. – all of noah's sons) – to look like they are leading the world – but are not. And not until they go to Jesus (and the truth of His word), will they know the truth about all of noah's sons (and why the differences are there), and the evil all of them have done – going away from God (Jesus and His word).

Jesus can help you get rid of prejudice, hate, etc., and help your own do the same – no matter what happens to you.

No one wants to admit they are bad or evil, etc. (sinful – born that way – from adam, and continued through noah's sons) – we all are, and only Jesus can change you – from what you are born with. Go to Him (not drugs, psychiatry, etc.).

All groups, nationalities, nations, etc. say they are the greatest people, good people, nice people, etc. – say that they are not bad – but they (we) all are bad (born that way), including jews (God's people), and they (through God) admit it – God wrote the bible, the truth, and you can see, by the jews (who wrote the bible), that the bible is the truth (and why some people, groups, etc., through satan, want to get rid of them). No group (nationality, etc.) ever writes bad things about themselves – and the bible does, about the jews, so it shows that it (the bible) is true – for all of us – to learn the truth of man and of this world.

God had to separate the jews (they are from shem) from the rest of the world – the rest of noah's sons (gentiles – japheth, ham, and some of shem), so they could learn the truth of who man is – sinners – and learn the truth of God – eventually to Jesus (a son of shem – which is sem, **luke 3:36** – where the word semite comes from) – God wants us to know. We all are still from one of noah's sons, and we need to talk about and learn about that and how that affects us all still. We are from noah's sons (**gen. 10:32**).

God wrote the bible (with all laws and punishments, etc.) – He had to – because of the lies of satan in this world – and man following satan's lies. So God, using the jews (who were His people, and following Him, for the most part) – first with moses (through the Holy Spirit – **2 pet. 1:19-21**)– to show His power and truth. Now we all (jews included) need to go to Jesus (and get the Holy Spirit to get connected to God). God shows us the truth for us to know what He wants and to go to Him.

Don't get away from what is written – by following what man says (**1 cor. 4:6**) – but the truth with Jesus in your life – the Holy Spirit, then share the truth of His word and show it to all.

And none of noah's sons should be in charge (**2 kings 21:2-9; isa. 1:1-20; jer. 18:7-10; jer. 25:29-33**), without God (even though some nations have mostly one son – one nationality in that nation), and they certainly should not be in control of the world (especially in america), without God (Jesus) – as the jews tried to do (they tried to live without God – just laws, having power, etc.) and were punished (as well as rejected Jesus) – otherwise satan will be in control, like before (God destroyed the world) and a little after the flood (God created all of the languages to separate man – **gen. 11**). Only God is good (**mark 10:18; rom. 3:9-12**), and knows what is right and best for us. Follow the truth of His word – with Jesus.

All the people who have ever led a country or had any impact on being in a position of power, have been evil, as have the ones being ruled over. And why we need laws, police, etc. – to keep evil from getting out of hand for those that rule, as those that are being ruled.

But with man being evil – especially with all of noah's sons – in america, it has been needed more.

Most of europe has a combination of many of noah's sons – mainly japheth – crossing borders, etc., but not always the other sons (not like america) – and eventually the jews scattering to many nations (after Jesus death and resurrection – especially after the temple was destroyed in 70ad), as they are today.

The romans used what they got (gold, etc.) from destroying the jews temple in jerusalem to build the colosseum – satan's temple, and used the jews to build it.

And the temple being destroyed by titus (the son of the emperor of rome – vespasian) – and by 80ad, titus built the colosseum in rome (satan's temple – to replace the temple in jerusalem) – almost 2,000 years ago – that was used for killing, even killing true Christians at one time (as the church there kept killing Christians even after that, everywhere – even today). And like the tower of babel was a temple that was evil and trying to replace God and worship satan (and man) – 4,000 years ago (**gen. 11**).

Even in the tribulation when the anti-christ is ruling the world, he will allow the temple to be built in jerusalem again (maybe just before the rapture), and he will eventually take it over, and try to be God (**dan. 9:27; matt. 24:15-22**).

Every person, nation, group, etc. – since the beginning, but also since just after the flood (all of noah's sons), think they are best, or better – they all can't be. Go to Jesus to have a chance. Any country that would go to Jesus – His truth only – would become a better nation – not perfect, but better – for all of noah's sons, and have a chance like america has and can. There are many false beliefs, and evil people in this world.

There is no master or superior race (we all are the human race – just one, **acts 17:24-28** – just looking different – mainly after the flood, after the tower of babel) – we always have one of noah's sons trying to rule – trying to be God – but can't (at least not very well) without the true God – Jesus. So don't try to rule the world without God (Jesus) – and His truth, not lies that satan wants you to think the bible says (as some false churches do). Start thinking this way and read the truth of the bible. Even though God says japheth will enlarge – be in most of the countries, as well as shem – so they are somewhat in charge, but to get along and to be with God. Look in the world and you will see that japheth and shem will live together (and in some countries – mainly america, they will be more together) – they will more than likely rule this world (**gen. 9:25-27**) – although all of noah's sons should be working together (even with ham) – but that would all work out only with Jesus and His truth.

The power that man has, is given by God (as it is given to satan) – all of noah's sons are put where God put them (including america), and their power (**acts 17:24-32**) – and why Jesus was killed, and needed to be for us. Man has a choice.

So God says that japheth will enlarge (europeans, etc. – he has all over the world) and dwell in the tents (mainly jews – family, society, laws, morals, etc.) of shem (**gen. 9:27**), still to this day – after the flood – mainly after the tower of babel (**gen. 11**). You can see that he has – and God set it up that way – japheth always has enlarged over the years in many empires, but the most of his enlargement happened in the last 500 years or so, including america today – until the end times. Go to Jesus to be one and the same – not with man trying to by himself.

And man cannot live together very well without shem – family, laws, society, etc. – america does better than most with all of noah's sons (and God's word). Shem (mainly jews – bible) holds japheth and ham together (like america). Get away from man (noah's sons, adam, your ancestors, etc.), and go to God (Jesus), and get the Holy Spirit back that man (adam) lost.

Don't follow nationality, culture, family, etc. – just Jesus and the truth of His word.

If the jews would have accepted Jesus (after He died and rose, and before 70ad – when the temple was destroyed) – the world as we know it, would be gone (never would have developed) – and we would be in heaven by now. But since they didn't, the jews have caused all of the problems they have (and the world continuing) – with satan leading their enemies (and all of the world's) – without God, and not being in their land for almost 2,000 years – until 1948 they came back, but God has america (Jesus) help them today – even though they still have enemies and struggle at times. Jesus will come back for them, and they will be saved (**rom. 11:25-32**). Giving us all a chance.

And japheth did enlarge – that happened at different times – many empires – throughout history since the tower of babel (since about 4,000 years ago – right after the flood – **gen. 10 and 11**). Most recently (the last 400 – 500 years) england went all over the world (the sun never sets on the british empire, etc.) – there were many others – like the roman empire, etc. (and the jews – shem, went everywhere japheth went).

Why do you think whites (and men), mostly, are in power (if you think that's true)? – God put them there (you can't fight God – **acts 5:38-39**) – or you will lose (like we have been even today) – all from noah's sons (**gen. 9:27**) – and that still stands today (along with the language change that God did at the tower of babel – 4,000 years ago, that eventually made us all look different – color, nationality, etc. – **gen. 11**), and we can't get away from that (noah's sons, etc.) in this world until we all go to Jesus – so share Jesus with all people (white, black, etc.), so Jesus can lead. God set it up that way, and we have to live with it – no matter what nationality we are – until we go to Jesus, and His word (and we have to learn it spiritually – going to Jesus to get the Holy Spirit – **1 cor. 2:14**). We are coming to the end of the language barrier that God set up – all separating man in this world – so satan couldn't have man all go against God at the same time – like man did before (**gen. 6; gen. 11**). It happens to be that way – color, nationality, etc. (only after the flood, and tower of babel) differences in the world, but it really is the differences in noah's three sons, that needs to be looked at and talked about. So don't fight it anymore – give in and just go to Jesus, and His word.

Don't overlook this part of the bible that still affects us today (especially **gen. 1 to gen. 12**) – there were no jews, no bible, etc. (mainly before the flood and through abraham) – and man was all the same – looks, speech, etc. (except not all going to God).

Don't depend on man to make you or your group, nationality, people, etc. somebody in this world – go to Jesus and His word to be somebody important in this world – having salvation and going to heaven and helping others do the same. Who cares what we look like now – going to Jesus is still the answer. And satan keeps you hating, etc. – so don't stay with him (and man).

Don't be connected to color, culture, nationality, etc., or this world (and man, satan) – be a citizen of heaven with Jesus (**2 cor. 5:16-21; philip. 3:20-21; eph. 2:19-22**), while you are here – get away from man – noah's sons.

Not only do people (all of noah's sons) do things that are not good – lie, hurt others, hate others (hate even the law, police, etc. that try to help do good), but it is all against God and His word (since adam, from satan). Need to follow Jesus – His truth (not man's – even those that God put in power – government, police, laws, etc.) – we all need to follow Him.

You play the game – things that are not good for you, but may get you something, somewhere, etc. – then things go wrong – not as planned, or get worse, etc. You have to pay for that – your fault. Don't be willing to do anything to get things in this world (and don't think you are owed anything) – do good things – go to Jesus and let Him help you with what you need – what's best for you. Some things are not worth it, and you really don't need the things you think you do. Or suffer the consequences, etc. Come to Jesus.

We follow laws and obey God when we are with Jesus – sin makes us do evil, and not obey.

All that do evil and love evil (all from satan), don't come to the Light – Jesus – and follow Him – like they come to darkness (**john 3:20-21**), and they don't want anyone to stop them.

It's what kind of person you are inside – not the outside – color, nationality, etc. – Jesus will change your inside (**1 sam. 16:7; matt. 23:28**). People, nationalities, etc. should be trying to humble themselves – not trying to stand out, show off, etc.

Just like voting, etc. – regardless of how you believe or think – and it's been said, but people don't do it – judge people by the content of their character – not the color of their skin or nationality, etc. – are they honest, fair, moral, humble, etc. (especially following what God wants in His word)? And that needs to happen today. And Jesus will help you with that.

Let God raise you up – not man, this world, or satan (don't try to be a god like satan). Go to Jesus – humble yourself – He will raise you up to do His work in this world.

So don't be a proud person (white, black, man, woman, etc.) – a proud black man, hispanic, italian, irish, native american, german, indian, asian, etc. or any traits, behavior, etc. that seem to be related to you (any of noah's sons – we were all similar before the flood – appearance, etc., and a little after, but still didn't go to God – **gen. 6; gen. 11**) – we all need to go to Jesus (the truth only) and change all of our problems and the world's (if we want to get along). Not to be connected to man anymore – culture, nationality, beliefs, color, etc. The separations, differences today – after the flood and tower of babel (all of noah's sons – are different), can make it hard to get along (and try to be better than others). But if you want to be proud – be proud of doing good things – things that are right – obeying the law, love, etc. not criminal, trying to get away with things, against others, hate, etc. – go to Jesus (and His word), and get away from noah's sons – man. And God will give you what you need (**matt. 6:33**), and the humble will be exalted (**matt. 23:12; luke 14:11; luke 18:14**). Be one with Christ (**rom. 12:16; rom. 15:6; 1 cor. 12:13; 2 cor. 13:11; gal. 3:28; gal. 6:8; philip. 1:27; philip. 2:2; col. 3:11**) to get along. And it better be the truth, and all believe in and follow as one – with Jesus, not what you (family, nationality, group, belief, etc.) think – like the world (**rev. 17:12-14**), which may be against Jesus.

People need to go overboard to do the right thing and help people get over prejudice, hate, etc. (to others that are not like them – including the police, etc.) – do what you can to get along and don't make things harder on people than it has to be. You be the example (for showing those like you) of getting along and not making it worse. We can help others and try to live in peace with them, but that may not always work – but try – and you can share Jesus with them all. God will work things out for all – go to Him (and His word). May take time.

God will punish and restore things – if you go back to Him – like israel was able to go back to their land in 1948 – God did that, not man – after almost 2,000 years.

God gave us all of our abilities, talents, etc. (whatever level they are or are not) – to what we see that is any good or needed in this world – technology, laws, work, etc., and satan hinders or hurts some things, and tries to help things go his way and to follow him (and the world), and not God's way (and have people complain, etc.). But we should have freedom to find what is best – with Jesus (and the truth of His word), we can, especially in america. The world is a better and safer place with america and Jesus – as long as we keep following Him and His word – but the truth.

And all of noah's sons should be free in america – with Jesus – we started that way (and has grown and got better).

All of the nations around the world are evil – none have Jesus or the truth of Him and His word. America is heading that way – need to go to Jesus (and not against God's word – bible).

People in america (or elsewhere) that have some things (food, clothes, shelter, jobs, etc.), and can live comfortably in this world, no matter what son of noah you are, but still can have some problems without Jesus. And as overweight as america is, (black, white, young, old, man, woman, etc.) – there are too many people that are starving – use your money wisely, and not be poor – go to Jesus and follow His word – He will give you what you need (**psalm 37:25; matt. 6:33**).

Jesus gives us the freedom in america and all of noah's sons can have a voice – to change things – point things out, etc., but in the end, it has to be what God says, and only with Jesus (the truth) will it work out for us all.

If you want to end racism, etc. – go to Jesus – but the truth of Him and his word, be truly saved (with the Holy Spirit) – not trust man (**jer. 17:5-10**).

Even though God has the abilities He gave us to separate us here, and there are those that are going to have the ability to develop and take over parts of the world (mainly japheth – europeans, etc., as God says – **gen. 9:27**, and are mostly white). So blame God for what looks like to you inequality, prejudice, 'racism', etc. – God set it up, but the best and only answer is to go to Jesus and His truth. And why God did this in the first place – the reason is for us to go to Him – knowing the truth.

Accept the fact that God made the world this way (especially after the flood) – and He gave us a way out – Jesus, which is the best fact of all.

God had noah have three sons, so God could separate them throughout history, to the differences we see today (after the flood) – so satan can't unite all of man together (as he keeps trying to do) – we should only be one with Jesus. Get away from noah's sons (man), and the reason God keeps coming here – get us to go to Him.

All 'races' or nationalities (all of noah's sons) want to be thought of as the best, all through history – recently (like the nazis – aryan race, etc. – whites) – including blacks – they are starting (and have through the years) with wanting to be equal, but want to be more than that, and are trying to prove it – all of noah's sons do that (satan leading – with ego, arrogance, etc.) to be higher, to be God, etc. (even though it is about equality now), but really trying to be in charge – like ham (nimrod) was in charge before – at the tower of babel (**gen. 11**). God is who limits man (all of noah's sons) here for now – until they go to Jesus and become one with Him. Like america gives us.

If you have a problem with prejudice – go to Jesus, if you have a problem with unfairness, inequality – go to Jesus, if you have a problem with the way you look – go to Jesus, you have a problem with anything – go to Jesus – that's what the problems are for – to go to Jesus. Anything you can think of. He will make us one, but not any other way – we can't do it.

People, groups, etc. don't want to be equal, they want to be above (that's how satan starts with his ideas – just wanting to be heard, then wants to take over, like he has so many times before – like with evolution in schools – taking the bible and creation out), but these groups start by wanting to be equal first, then satan wants them to be above – following him and his ideas, and not God's word – His truth with Jesus. It needs to be what God says, not what man (really satan) says or wants. All of noah's sons need to go to God and get away from what God had them (all of man today) be at first (**gen. 9:18-19; gen. 9:24-27**).

Even in america (that God started), life expectancy and life quality went up for the people who were in america, and who came to america – especially today – as america grew with Jesus and His word. And the main thing is after this life. So go to Jesus – that is why He is the Savior. Not following man (or really satan).

And there should be no white supremacists (japheth – like the germans did, maybe in other countries, now and in the past – or can be in america, but there are going to be people like that in all of noah's sons – prejudice on both sides, since we all are evil, and guilty, and even hate – satan leading, until we truly all go to Jesus – and His truth). But some blacks (ham, and others in the world) can be the most prejudice (partly due to the punishment of ham, and they don't like it), because they are from ham, and struggle the most in this world – but that prejudice is not helping them, it is just causing hatred and dislike (and problems, poverty, etc., including prejudice, and holding you down) from the other two sons of noah (japheth and shem, mainly whites, etc. – who should be nicer to them – to ham, and go to Jesus to do that – especially in america), but the arabs (half shem and half ham) may be the worst of the world, according to God (**gen. 16:11-12**), although even they can go to Jesus (and all can and should), if they want, but their stubbornness (and belief) is holding them back, as it is for many people – white or black, etc. Go to Jesus to be one, fair, equal, etc.

Any of the groups in the world – even in america, are trying to have a voice and be heard and move up in the world (**rom. 1:23-32**) – to run the world with their ideas (whether it is gay, transgender, no gender, no truth, etc.) – any of the people that feel outside the normal (but all of us are sinners), but they can go to Jesus and change – not to continue sharing satan's ideas against God and His truth. Don't defend satan and support his ideas.

Even homosexuals cheat on each other – hurting each other, etc. – as if the only bad things that happen to them only comes from those that don't like or hate them. We all are evil. And need to change. With Jesus.

No matter who someone is or what they believe – they still have to be nice. Go to Jesus to have a chance to. The only way.

Everyone feels that they are the persecuted ones – need to know what to be persecuted for. All people are sinners, and need to change. Only with Jesus (and His word) can that happen. Not this world and it's efforts, programs, etc. (man, satan, etc.). All people have been persecuted here (believing in God or not) – we should be for what God wants – believing in and following Him – the truth of Jesus and His word. Don't have God go against you – follow His word.

We all need to go to Jesus – no matter what life we lead or what we believe. Help people to do that and know the truth. Hope and help all go to Jesus. Jesus will change us to what He wants.

Going against God (Jesus) and His word is causing all of the problems here for man. We need to know the truth.

The way some people live today, hurts other people and themselves – like the way people lived before the flood (**gen. 6**), and in sodom and gomorrah (**gen. 19**), after the flood (the way some do today) – all against God – with satan.

Man makes it tougher in this world (men, women, rich, poor, black, white, etc.), by following man and his ideas (and hanging out with the wrong people, etc. – including drugs, alcohol, etc.) – away from God and His truth. don't put yourself in bad situations.

What God wants for us, is best for us, we just need to go to Jesus (and the truth of His word) and find that out. Not what we believe living here or are born into, etc. See how you change.

Don't fall into the wrath of God – we all are sinners – from a baby, person, family, society, nation, etc. – the world (because of satan). He will change us from what we believe here.

God still punishes His own, and those that are not His (not with Jesus). We should be glad God disciplines us. He punishes the world, but He waits, so we all have a chance to go to Jesus (**2 pet. 3:9**). But He will wait only so long, so we need to go to Jesus now – not keep following satan and this world.

We go through struggles to keep going to God and His word – and it better be the truth and from God (and help you go to Him), because the infirmities or weaknesses we go through, help us depend on God (Jesus) more, and He can work through us, and makes us strong (**2 cor. 12:8-12**).

But satan and his ideas are starting to lead the world more – especially in america – and man is following satan (thinking it is man's ideas), and standing up for his beliefs, like Christians should for God's word. Which how it will be like in the end times. And satan is trying to get the world together – to be nice, get along, etc. with anyone and everything (believing in what satan believes) – mainly against God and His word – Jesus. Just like satan did before the flood. We need to get people to Jesus and the truth of His word. So satan wants to keep you going to hell – with him. Go to Jesus to change and be saved – to get the Holy Spirit (and go to heaven). Don't stand against God and His word or you follow satan (stop speaking up for satan – **rom. 12:2; 2 cor. 4:3-4; eph. 6:10-20; james 4:1-10**).

God comes to us – to help us. Go to Jesus. He is waiting.

People live lives that hurts or kills them – don't live that way – and others won't get in trouble for doing evil to you. Change your life with Jesus or you may cause others to do evil.

If you really care about someone, you won't let them keep living the way they do in this world – trying to say anything and everything is fine. Share Jesus. A nation, family, person, etc. should be one with Jesus and the truth of His word – otherwise it won't work here.

Most of the problems we have come from our decisions (and who we hang out with – **prov. 13:20**) – no matter how good you think they are. So we are not innocent always for our problems. Go to Jesus and let Him help lead you and others.

Both sides of beliefs, ideas, cultures, etc., may want to force those to believe what they believe – both may be wrong, and not true Christians, but false christians.

Do what you do – caring about other people and be fair. God knows best – go to Him and His word. Go to Jesus – be helped and help others to do that.

People live with their own rules – and want others to live by them, too, sometimes – but we need to live by God's rules, which are the best for man to live by. So if you don't like people breaking your rules, then don't break God's.

You don't hurt or force, etc. – you help them to get to know Jesus – not their own beliefs without Jesus. Share and pray for them, then what is best for man and nation will happen. But you should protect yourself and others, if you need to.

If you harm someone for whatever reason – you have to suffer the consequences that come from that – someone defending themselves – hurting you, or prison, etc. Killing can't be the answer, if you don't get your way or your own belief or agenda is not turning out the way you wanted.

No criminals like the law – any restriction of their life, even if they hurt or bother others, etc. to get what they want (but don't want anyone bothering them – hypocrites) – and their behavior is always against God (satan leading). People feel like they have a reason to hurt others (even revenge, etc.), since they struggle (but usually it is their own fault – or how they grew up, etc. – and choices they made). Go to Jesus – don't let satan run your life. And satan always uses what he can to hurt others.

If you believe in what you are doing is right – then admit it – and suffer the consequences, punishments, etc. Don't lie and try to get out of it (or deep down you know it is wrong – we all do). Otherwise, don't do those things. Best to go to Jesus.

Look at the world today – even your world – and history – evil has been here and is still here. You are not going to change that, so go to Jesus and tell others to do the same – satan is still here.

And satan used whatever he wanted to use in the past to make man do evil things (or man chooses to do) and satan uses what he can now – technology, etc. to do his evil – all against God (and His word), which can be against and hurt man. And with technology you can have more evil, and get away with more, but also technology can stop or hinder the evil, too. Have to keep up with evil changes throughout history. Hopefully finding the right person, etc. that is doing the evil. Going to Jesus would help you in your life, no matter what happens, and not give in to satan and evil. We all have a choice.

In today's world, the rich, as well as the poor, can make a case for getting or being given things in this world – since the rich pay more taxes and feel they should be given more things – for them and their family – and the same for the poor – they feel they are owed things, because they are poor and the rich somehow took it from them. Stop blaming others, and trying to get things – work hard on the right things – and go to Jesus to get these attitudes out of you – always someone owes you something or dislikes you, etc. Jesus is the answer, not hating or getting back at people, etc.

Going to Jesus and getting saved is not just a good thing to do, but good for all – to help people get their problems solved – all of the issues, etc., in this world.

We are all prejudice to a point – all of noah's sons, and is why we need to get to Jesus and be born again, and get away from being connected to man (noah's sons, adam, our family, ancestors, etc.), and get connected back to God (with the Holy Spirit) – through Jesus. He does not give us Spirit of fear (**2 tim. 1:6-14**)– do what God wants and says, etc., and He will protect you (**john 16:33; john 17:13-23**). Go to Jesus and share Him and His truth – learn it (His word).

Nobody likes a world where nobody gets along – go to Jesus – and we all can – otherwise we won't – no matter what we try to do. This world is going to continue to be miserable and so will man until the end (with all of the technology, etc. – that satan will use – **rev. 13**). We all need to go to Jesus, and the reasons we go to Him is because of our struggles.

If you don't have Jesus bring us together – who are you going to have do it (He made us)? We are all different and satan has us going at each other. Once we are saved you are separate from man – from the world (and satan) – with Jesus – away from noah's sons. So separate from this world and help others do that, too.

Otherwise all we do is keep knocking our heads together – no matter what you believe – God knows. Go to Jesus – His truth.

So all need to be humble and go to Jesus. And be truly free (**john 8:31-36**).

And as long as there are really terrible people in the world, most people don't seem so bad, but all people are bad – don't compare with man, but to what God says man is (**rom. 3**).

You have to stop people to keep them from hurting others, not just you – stand up for right. If you can do something wrong, then you can do something right – don't make excuses. Jesus will help you know in His word, right from wrong.

Don't get upset with what God says in His word, that you are not doing. Just believe it and start doing it and stop making excuses or doing your own thing.

People hate God for making the world the way it is – but we need to go to Him, because of it – man caused it to be this way (having God do these things for our benefit). God gave us the answer – Jesus is the answer. Then things will change. A country (like america) won't get better or change, without going to God (through Jesus) and following His word (**2 chron. 7:13-16**).

If you want to save people from pain of this world – including yourself, family, etc., then go to Jesus.

Don't try to make yourself, world, etc. perfect – go to Jesus to make this world better and be able to go to Him after this world. To keep people from evil, have them go to Jesus, not to kill others, or themselves.

Not until we get to heaven is everything going to be alright. We have to go to Jesus first. Then do what we can here.

Man cannot love or help or get along with people very well or properly until they all go to Jesus. But we need to get along – all of noah's sons. Share Jesus and His truth – the most loving thing you can do is share with people about Jesus – His truth, and God's word doesn't come back void – read it and share it to others (**isa. 55:11**).

Whites don't get along with all whites, blacks don't get along with all blacks, and the same for any nationality, etc. – it's the way man is – won't change without going to God (Jesus). You see this in most countries – mostly the same people (nationality, etc.) live there – and they still may hate each other – it's just more visible in a country like america (more diverse, etc.).

Fortunately, not all blacks or whites, etc. (all of noah's sons) are this way. But there will be many, many 'nice' people in hell – following satan's lies. All of noah's sons (everybody) need to go to Jesus, no matter how 'good' you are (or think you are, or others think you are)– if you want to go to heaven. And only with Jesus (get Holy Spirit) can you do that – for this life or after. Just like the most loving thing you can do is share Jesus, the most evil thing you can do is not to share Jesus (the truth).

Not forgetting the past (and not forgiving) keeps all the bad going, especially not changing – which can only be done with Jesus – to be better and to get along. There have been improvements – as much as evil man can do, but mostly when Jesus is part of it, and america grows and learns and changes, just like a person does with Jesus.

With Him we can all bond – as long it is the truth. Make sure it is the truth – this is what we should be talking about.

All can go to God (through Jesus) and God can use all people (color, nationality, etc.) – all of noah's sons (and women) for His purpose – and all can go to Jesus and He will use them – man, woman, black, white, any nationality, etc.

God wants all of noah's sons to work together (and treat each other nice – but we have to live a good life – in this world of selfishness, undiscipline, etc. – change who you are – like all have a chance in america), and all go to Jesus – otherwise we have to live with what we are born with (from man – noah's sons) – selfish, and not get along and stay separate, trying to do it ourselves (and mistreating each other, etc. – shouldn't make it worse – or like the government makes it worse), but no matter who is in power (but God put japheth, with shem, in power – **gen. 9:27**). But we have to understand there is a difference and a separation between us. And it is God-made (and can't fight it – **acts 5:38-39; acts 17:24-31** – and if you do – you, we, are going to lose), and the answer is Jesus and only Jesus – to get the Holy Spirit.

Even with the Holy Spirit, we struggle here on earth, against satan and this corruptible body (the flesh – **rom. 7**), but can overcome by going to Jesus each day (and truly being saved – knowing the truth of His word), and follow Him and His word (not a church, leader, etc.). Find a good church with Jesus and the truth, so you can be with true Christians, etc.

We are all born to do evil (with sin, satan), and we need help to avoid problems – need to go to Jesus and share Him and His truth, to grow up in this world (to not be selfish). You are born a certain way – color, family, belief, etc., but you don't have to stay that way or connected to that (the problems that come from those) – no matter what color you are, etc. (what you learn, who you are, believe, follow, etc.) as you grow – and only with Jesus can you change, and make a difference. God put those barriers and separations (color, culture, belief, etc.) to see what you will follow and believe in (Him or this world).

You're poor, struggling, etc., because God put you there (born, etc.), or you (or your family, etc.) put yourself there (satan helping) – leading others there, and only Jesus can get us out of that – we all need to go to Jesus (as we grow – no matter where or who we are from), which the struggles help (or should) lead you to go to Him – all need to go to Jesus, and share Him. And He wants to help us all, if we would go to Him (the truth of His word).

God allows the evil that may lead to the good – to make the changes in this world, but we can avoid the evil, if we go to God and keep following Him (Jesus) and His word. Since we are not perfect, some evil will still be here in our lives. But go to Jesus, because of the evil (satan, man) – to help us change.

We all can make a difference (all of noah's sons), if we do good things – best to get to know Jesus (but the truth) – to do good things, and have a good life. And going to Jesus and sharing Him (learn the truth of His word), we can help the next generation.

Man is still evil – even after Jesus died and rose – that hasn't changed, and man needs to be punished. We have to get along and not hurt each other, and if anyone hurts others, they should be punished – and all need to go to Jesus to change, and live here with each other.

All of noah's sons learn and find a way to survive in this world – with a little or a lot – sometimes helping others, but too many hurt others, being selfish, etc. You don't or won't, if you go to Jesus and follow Him and the truth of His word. Eventually caring more about others, than you do yourself – but help everyone go to Jesus.

Don't worry or want things or people of this world, and you won't be bothered or bother others, because you don't have those things. Don't let satan lead you to do or want evil of the world – do without things, and go to Jesus to change and feel at peace with that (just what you need for you and your family – **matt. 6:33**).

Every problem stems from wanting things (evil – and you don't know it), etc. from this world – growing up wanting that and hanging around that and those people. Don't be attracted to or want those things (satan makes them look attractive).

So stop trying to justify the things you do – evil, etc., satan controlled – all against God and His word – Jesus' truth.

To even the playing field, over the years – those that are intelligent (japheth), can (and have) develop weapons, protections, technology, etc. to counter the strength – physical – of man – ham (who was in charge of all of man – nimrod – at the tower of babel – **gen. 11**, all against God, before all of these changes – color, etc. in man happened) that is physically stronger (**num. 13:30-31**) – although we all can use these weapons – as we have seen throughout history. Also there has been interbreeding over the years, between the sons – more with some, than others.

Intermarrying was more difficult before the first 500 to 1,000 years after the flood (God separating man around the world, after the tower of babel), and the jews and gentiles being separate later – then little by little it has happened more and more in the last 1500 to 2,000 years, especially today – the last 500 years (with travel around the world – and with america).

If you spend energy and time (and maybe money, etc.) looking into your past – ancestry, etc. – to see how good or bad you are, or how you were treated, etc. – your family, nationality, culture, etc. – then spend time looking into Jesus and the bible, which is better and truth – for our history and who we really are.

So everyone is worried about who and where they come from – ancestry, history, etc., and everyone wants to know why they are the way they are – interests, beliefs, nationality, etc. – we all come from adam (at creation), and noah's sons (now from them after the flood – **gen. 9:18-19; gen. 10:32**). Your father is adam and noah – all from one of noah's sons – after the flood – japheth, shem, or ham, and your other ancestors after them to you – and you are stuck with them and their lot in life and abilities, etc., until we go to Jesus – like america tries to do. Go to Jesus – not away from Him, or satan will use you, and you will struggle, etc. – you and your descendants (as your ancestors did). That is important to know – we are all from man, and need to go to God (and that is only with Jesus – we are separated now – with noah's sons). Have God as your Father.

So don't worry about all of these past family connections (**1 tim. 1:3-4**) – we all are evil, but get connected to God through Jesus and the Holy Spirit. And change who you and your family are.

Whatever son you are from – japheth, shem, or ham – that's how you will behave until you go to Jesus. That's all of our ancestors – and we can't get away from them and their lot in life, and evil ways – until we go to Jesus. We are from one (or more – sometimes) of noah's sons (and initially all from adam).

If you go to some books of the bible, you can see the genealogy of all of us (all of noah's sons – **gen. 9, 10 and 11**), including jews, Jesus, etc. (**matt. 1:1-16; luke 3:23-38**), and nations, etc. (the **chapters in 1 chron.** – for the genealogy from adam through noah's sons, as well as **gen. 5**), and who followed God and who did not – and some people in all of the descendants had bad people – some more than others (even yours – whatever of noah's sons). Even the people of esau (edom) – who married the daughters of canaanites (**gen. 36**) – all from ham – **gen. 10:6-20** (and God didn't want esau, or any jews to do that – **gen. 24:2-4, 37; gen. 28:1, 6-9**), and God made their land desolate, etc. (**mal. 1:1-5**). God did that throughout the years, and today for all people – so go to Him and follow. And that still happens in today's world (even in the last 500 years for all of us) – look around the world. Go to Jesus to get away from man.

So, **luke 3:23-38**, shows from Jesus (in the line of joseph – husband of mary, Jesus' mother) back to adam (which is the beginning of time) – including noah's son shem (**luke 3:36**) – not millions of years, etc. His word is true and we need to believe it all – not man's lies (from satan). God doesn't mention or even allude to anything like evolution – it's just a lie from satan. How can we believe anything like that? – then we don't believe in God (or His word – would we believe any of it?).

We are evil and don't want to admit it (following satan).

We have to understand this to know we have to go to Jesus to change it – our evil self (satan doesn't want us to know that, so he can control all of us – going against the bible, and God).

Don't be proud of your ability, family, etc. – your position in life (good or bad), but find out where it came from – all the people before you – all the way to one of noah's sons, and their knowledge and truth. Go to Jesus and the bible – the truth.

Don't rely on your nationality, family, etc. – get away from that and go to Jesus, if not, you want to stay with satan and man.

You don't have control of what family you are born into (no one does – only God does), or nationality, country, color, belief, wealth, etc., but you do after you grow – to what you want to believe in and what the truth is, which is to go to Jesus and His word to find the truth. And what God wants you to go through.

The best example is from Jesus – to how much we need to love and follow Jesus (and not man) is what He says about Him and family (**matt. 10:34-39; matt. 12:46-50; mark 3:31-35; luke 14:25-27**). And then share Jesus with them.

Family, and even friends, etc. may not believe the truth – and may belong to a false church, religion, etc. – so you need to know the truth, and eventually be separate from them (even if it is your grandmother, etc.) – and keep following Jesus and the truth of His word. Help, and pray for them as much as you can. Keep sharing Him and His truth.

So you can't keep following your family, culture, belief, etc. (if it is not the truth of Jesus) – every person is related and controlled by their family, and belief (that they got from their family – which goes all of the way back to one of noah's sons), and by what son of noah you are from – you have to go to Jesus, then share Him to them – the truth. Get away from man that is destined for hell (**john 3:17-21**).

You want to go to heaven, even if they don't – follow Jesus (and His truth) and help others do the same (**luke 9:59-62**).

You can still love your family, just not more than Jesus. Hopefully you grew up in a family that knows the truth of Jesus and His word (not a false church, belief, etc. – there are many).

People worry about what people think of them (people to vote for you, buy from you, love you, watch you, even your nationality, etc., any area of life) – and we should be worried about what God thinks – and whether you believe in God or not – don't be so consumed with yourself (selfish, etc.). Then see where God puts you. Keep learning His word and sharing Him.

Don't worry if you offend man, but whether you offend God or not – with your behavior and belief (like if you worry about being true to your boyfriend or girlfriend – cheating, sex, etc., you need to be more concerned if you bother God – disobeying Him in your behavior). So if you are not married – just dating, but you're true to each other – not cheating on them with someone else – you feel you are a good person – and the one you are dating feels the same – you are good. But if you are not married – you are cheating on God – and what He wants or doesn't want you to do (and you are not a good person – only Jesus and His word can help you change to what He wants for us here). And what would you do (or how would you react), if your husband or boyfriend cheated on you? Would you kill if they do – the man or the woman, or both (or even yourself)? Or would you forgive? Even though God would forgive them, would you? If this happened in your life, it might be what you need to go to Jesus – possibly leading to prison, or eventually death for someone – you need to think of where you are going and what you need to do in your life (and after this life) to get through something like this. All of man has to think of these things. And then do the right and best thing – use it to go to Jesus (and the truth of His word).

Find out what God's word says and follow it and Jesus – then change your behavior and belief, etc. – then share the truth – and live it, and share Jesus. It's not always easy, but you will be happier when you do. Don't worry if your ancestors were treated right, etc. – still being connected to noah's sons. You be the one who changes your family, etc. And connect to God (through Jesus) – not stay connected to man anymore. And do what God wants you to do and believe, and change to what He wants you to be (with the truth of His word).

We can't clean our self up – by ourselves – only Jesus (and His word) can get that straight **(eph. 5:25-27)**, with the Holy Spirit. Man is evil (sinful), and evil to each other, even when all looked alike and were the same before the flood – so stop using our differences as an excuse. Be one in Jesus.

All people have the same needs and problems here – all of noah's sons do (man, woman, black, white, young, old, etc) – and only God is going to help us with those needs. Go to Jesus.

The world is getting more and more connected – as one (but it is against God and His word) – all of noah's sons – to where all of noah's sons are getting closer, but are still separated and evil (and don't always get along – no matter what man does), because they are not with Jesus (and His truth in His word).

Man – all of noah's sons – have to work through all of the differences we can – and only with Jesus can we do that.

And satan uses man's abilities and talents that God gave man – originally from adam, and now from noah's sons – and the desires, needs, wants, pleasures, etc. of this world against man – to go against

God (and the way He made us) through sin of man (and satan). So satan doesn't do good things for people – only evil – and it is always against God and His word. Go to Jesus if you want good things (and know the truth). America (and the world) needs God for all of noah's sons.

And all of the things in america to today, from the beginning, have been good for all – all of noah's sons – and america has grown (using all of noah's sons together), because of Jesus. And satan is still around trying to tear it down – and he (and those with him) will do evil, lies, unfair, unwarranted, etc. things to make a point and force people to think the way they do – against God and true love (which is with Jesus and His word). As evil and bad as satan is (and God allows satan to be here) in this world – no matter how bad they are – are to get you to go to Jesus and His word. Hopefully you will.

Get to know the truth of what we need to do and why we are here. To get away from man – noah's sons (and satan, and sin) and go to God, and the truth of His word – through Jesus.

It's good to know the truth about anything – even about our roots (adam, and noah's sons) – not just our recent ancestors, etc. – and God has that information (in His word) – we just need to learn it and accept it, (our differences and where they came from – and what you can and cannot do without Jesus) for everyone. Then go to Jesus to change that (how and where you are born, etc.) – the only way that you can, or we will all still struggle.

We are all immigrants to every nation – even to america – since the flood – God had us come here (His country for Jesus). All land is God's. And for His plans. He separated us all, since the flood (and especially after the tower of babel – **gen. 11**).

And what reason would you have to come to this country (america), if you believe what you believe (religion, etc.) is correct (not Christianity)? And that your country isn't good to live in (what you and they believe should make your country good, and you would stay there). This country is good because of Jesus (as long as we follow Him and His truth of His word).

This country is free for all to come here – so that people can learn of Jesus, no matter what you believe, but this country has to preach and share Jesus and the truth of His word (the reason it is so good and prosperous, powerful, etc. – at least to other countries), and it needs to stay with Jesus to keep being good (and to follow laws, get along, prosper, happy, etc. – most of that would work only with Jesus). We have to learn and teach the truth of God's word and Jesus to those that come here. And those that come here, need to learn of this – not take advantage of this country (and the people), and possibly make it as bad as the country they are coming from (what satan wants to do – having false churches, politics, even some rich, etc.).

Letting anyone and everyone into the country without knowing them (the right way) – and they need to become a citizen, obey, etc., and if they get out of hand (as it is starting to), it will lead to having the government needing to keep an eye on everyone (in an evil, bad way) and control and limit all people, which eventually may lead to a cashless society, control, less freedom, etc. – leading to a one world order (if this is what God wants, at least be ready to go with Jesus). The government can speed this up with bad decisions, lack of law abiding and lack of punishment – so have it done fairly, and for everyone (not just certain people – leaders included), and not letting it get out of control, etc. (as well as not following Jesus and the truth of His word in society, schools, etc.). Be responsible (leaders, too) – even if you punish yourself, or turn yourself in – admit you did wrong, etc. Share Jesus and the truth of His word – have that lead our country – which it was founded on. And have those that do lead our country. And live a better life yourself here.

And whatever country you came from – now or in the past, america is better, and will be as long as Jesus is still here and we go to Him (and the truth of His word) – otherwise go back to your old country, if you don't like it here (see how that would be). Jesus is better, and so is america (as would any country be, that truly has Him and His truth in it – even your old country). As long as it is true Christianity – not false – like so many in the world (and even some in america).

Just like you report a crime, etc., and who did it, to solve it, and know the truth – help those that have been hurt, and may still be hurting, and being taken advantage of – they need to be stopped, arrested, etc. Tell the truth (and it better be the truth). It needs to be done. So tell the truth about false churches. No matter if they hate you (**gal. 1:6-12**). God will help you.

If we stay and share Jesus (His truth), and pray to the true God, then the nation will be blessed (**2 chron. 7:14; psalm 33:12; jer. 18:8; prov. 14:34; acts 10:34-36**). A nation needs to stand up and follow Jesus (and His truth) or fail.

Be as good as you can be and do what you are capable of doing in this world – and that is only possible with Jesus. Even if only praying for truth and salvation for others, but learn His word and truth – and share it.

But God has us where He put us (**acts 17:24-28**) – until we go to Him (Jesus). Knowing right from wrong (**gen. 3** – like adam and eve did) – be on the same page – know right from wrong, with Jesus (and His word) in your life.

It's not always easy to live the life Jesus wants you to, but He will help you – keep going to Him and His word, and grow – it will get better, if you believe and follow. Jesus loved, but He also offended – telling the truth. Learn and share the truth, with love (**eph. 4:12-32**) – accept the truth.

In this world, some people don't like to be told what to do – most follow lies, selfish, etc. (and they make their life tougher, not following laws, etc.). But you need to listen to God through Jesus and His word – the truth. And it may be tough, but you need it – we all do. Jesus will make it easier for you.

It is through japheth and shem (God at times leading) that we have technology and civilization, etc., but not perfect or best or always right, but just here – the world today, and still with evil of man (satan leading) – and we need to go to Jesus to change that. And ham (who stayed near the equator and are darker – man gets dark in the sun after the flood – we see that no matter what son of noah we are – and not all of ham's descendants are of color, but most would be – whatever nationality) eventually was brought together with the other of noah's sons (especially in america), and helped, or were used to help each other.

People copy people – all of noah's sons copy each other (and use each other's way of life, inventions, etc.), if they can – from the tower of babel on – towers, building, etc. (**gen. 11**). But the technology we have today took time. And also since the tower of babel with separations of noah's sons – and all are needed.

God put us where and how we are in this world (**gen. 9:27; acts 17:24-28**). All separated, until we go to Jesus, and His truth.

Ham (blacks, and some whites, maybe asians, and others, especially the son of ham's son, cush – nimrod, and canaan – **gen. 10:6-20**) keep fighting the place they are in their life and taking it out on others. People need to stand up to evil, and don't help or participate in it, and go to God. Stand up peacefully and with the truth – not like the cowards that lie and cheat (and bully, like some leaders, etc. do – in the world, and even in the churches) to get their way, because cheating and lying (like satan does) doesn't work – at least for long. The best is with Jesus and His truth. Let Him rule – all of our lives, no matter what son of noah we are from (and have to live with).

Lose your life – this world, your history, ancestry, etc., to stand up for His – Jesus (**matt. 18:24-28**).

Man (all of noah's sons) has caused all of the evil things in this world (with satan – **gen. 3**) – so we have no one to blame, but ourselves for this life. We should try to help each other, and be nicer, if possible. But only with Jesus will we be able to.

You can cheat, lie, etc. here on earth and be successful sometimes here (for all of the sons of noah) – satan doesn't care, but you can't cheat and lie your way to heaven. Only can get there with the truth of Jesus (and the Holy Spirit). Until then it is tough on all of the sons of noah.

God gave us a way out – Jesus (and the truth of His word).

Why is it still so tough for minorities – especially blacks, to move up and be where they think they should be, after all of these centuries (even with the struggles in their own country in the past – before they came here)? It's the sons of noah and what God separated (the punishment for all mankind after the flood, and to ham's son – **gen. 9**), and will stay that way (our lot in life), until we all go to Jesus. All of us (man – all of noah's sons) are evil. People are naturally selfish, evil – born that way, until they go to Jesus (and get the Holy Spirit) and learn the truth, and grow and change – and start helping people – share Jesus. There will still be a tough life – rich or poor, etc., until we do.

Even the arabs, from ishmael (from ham – **gen. 9:24-27**), struggle in this world – God says they will and they will not be liked (**gen. 16:11-12**). The only way that this world will work and be better for people is with Jesus and the truth of His word – then we all have a chance, otherwise we won't – stop wasting our time.

God is doing what is happening to people – no matter what son of noah – and no matter what color, nationality, etc. – all need to go to

God. Don't blame whites, rich, etc. for your struggles, etc. – go to Jesus to change, and be helped.

People need to get used to being around people that are different than themselves (not like before the flood, and a little after – we were all the same). Noah's sons are here to be able to do that – but naturally selfish and want power, etc. – need to change. And the jews are still separated today – from the world – but are in almost every nation. And Jesus is the one that can help us get along – no other way. And why america is here, no matter who you are. To share Jesus with all.

We all need help sometimes, but don't force people to help you – go to Jesus and you will help and get help.

Some groups get along – many of noah's sons (especially in america) – more if you know them or grow up with them or do things together (what God wanted to do with america, and to share Jesus and His truth).

And at least in america it is possible to change and grow with opportunities and freedom, etc. (all can be prosperous – black, white, etc.) – because of Jesus and is why we see some change, but it will disappear, if Jesus does – in our life and country. It may not with all of noah's sons that are without Jesus – God separated us, and then put us together (in america) to see if we will need Him and go to Him. And see it get better.

But we have to know what the truth is about everything, otherwise don't join in (just because of color, or nationality, or family, nation, opinion, etc.). We have to go to God (and His word) to know what that is – only through Jesus – for freedom (especially in america – it is God who made it – and satan wants to destroy it, any way he can, without God and His word – the truth). So satan can start his one world order (**book of revelation**) – all against God and His word (His truth).

You can't like everything, and you can't dislike everything – you have to have an opinion about something – and stand up for it. It might as well be truth and good and real.

You have to want to know the truth – learn and grow – not just live. Once you are born again – saved by Jesus, with the Holy Spirit – then you have to grow, change – not stay a baby – go to His word, but the truth – grow (**1 cor. 3; heb. 5:12-14**).

Even though not all of ham's people (of whatever color, etc.) are as bad (we all are at different levels, depending on our life – we need to be taught and disciplined with good parents and beliefs to get along and behave, etc.), nor are all whites are as bad, or asians, hispanics, men, women, any nations, police, groups, etc. (but we all are still evil – it's what God says that matters) – God separated the levels of evil in people, so that satan can't get all of us against God at the same level of evil (especially after the flood, and mainly since the tower of babel – **gen. 11**). Mainly to give us a chance to go to Jesus before we die. Look in the world and see that – none that are good (**psalm 14; rom. 3**). Go to Jesus, if you don't like things.

The separations make it hard to have satan have a one world order – all against God, but it will happen. But whatever the differences are in noah's sons, and problems they cause (and they all have problems), we have to go to Jesus to be better, and to get along.

No matter what sin(s) you have, or that you've done, or haven't done, or what you believe, etc. without Jesus you are going to have a miserable life (your sin will find you out – **num. 32:23; gal. 6:6-8**). Admit what you do and who you are (no matter what son of noah you are), and change your life. Go to Jesus.

We all make choices we have to live with – and our family, friends, too – choose to go to Jesus. Avoid some problems – bring children up with Jesus – you first (**eph. 6:4**).

It's not that people are not different and may not like each other, or get along (for a variety of reasons – some we teach, some we experience, etc.), but it is going to only be with Jesus, that we can come together and get along, no matter what side you are on or color, belief, etc. you are. The good (mainly from Jesus) in the world, force the others (mainly from satan – leading man) to hide, cover up, hurt, kill, etc. – to make it in this world, but if good (Jesus – the truth of Him and His word) wasn't here trying to stop evil – the evil would be way worse. They know they are wrong and evil. God made us that way (separated us – mainly from the tower of babel, **gen. 11**), so we would eventually go to Him (Jesus) to make everything work here in this world. We are all evil (from adam originally, and now from noah's sons) until we do. But it better be the truth of His word – many false churches.

And man will all be evil against God at the end (after the rapture of the true Christians) – in the tribulation (**matt. 24; book of revelation**). So God has a place like america. You see it coming now – that is what is happening in the world today.

The rapture before the tribulation is the only way to stop america – having all of the Christians (true ones) gone, then america will not be here – Jesus and the Holy Spirit gone in the nation and the people. Then the nations (satan) can go against israel. The end is near – Jesus is coming back. Only God can change that – sharing Jesus.

People can get the most out of themselves with all of noah's sons – like america is (we are all needed here, but mainly Jesus is – people have the opportunity to have that, with Him, and why it works). As long as america lasts – only with Jesus.

All of noah's sons need each other (like america has and can be again) – all nationalities, etc., but is only going to work out best with Jesus (or worse with satan – like we see).

People can be kind and caring to each other – even if they, themselves, are struggling – and Jesus helps you through, and why you can tell who and what we should believe in (in Jesus and the truth of His word) – look around the world.

Even people of the same nationality, color, etc. don't all get along around the world – it's just harder with different nationalities, color, etc. – like america, but we do get along for the most part – because of Jesus (and His word – His truth).

And none of noah's sons (all of us alive today) should be trying to run the world without God (whatever son you are – japheth, shem, or ham) – even though God separated us, and we have different abilities, talents, preferences, desires, cultures, appearances, etc. (and some may have more power over others – like japheth and shem do in the world, but we still need God, or we will change the world in a negative way).

Regardless of what son of noah or what color you are, etc. – all need to go to Jesus – or you will never get through this life or get along. Go beyond who you are from here – we are all from God, and need Him. Go to Him.

We need to know we can't change these differences we have (all of noah's sons), only God can – through Jesus.

Whatever excuse or rationale, etc. (political, belief, etc.), that you are using to live the life you do, or the decisions you make in life – it is not going to be better than Jesus and His word. Go to Him and His word and follow and share Him. It is why we are here (**eccl. 12:13**).

Separation of church and state is a good idea, but not separation of God (Jesus and His word) and state (or people) – america's foundation is with God (and it is Jesus who gives us our freedom, etc.), so no church (most are false) should be running it (nor groups, businesses, companies, nations, the rich, etc. – trying to run it – separate them, too). People in power need to go to God and His word for the answer and truth to run a country – to Jesus (and His word), or it will fail (and hurt people, etc.). Even that separation by man (and satan) – trying to keep God out, hasn't stopped Jesus (and those that believe) – keep praying and sharing Him. We do not run the world (or run other people – even though we have power over them – japheth or shem over ham, **gen. 9:27**) without Jesus (which is why america is so powerful – but not all go to Him, and we need to make sure we stay with Him and His truth to stay that way, treating people right), and help others get to know Him, too (then we all can have His power and be one with Him – Him ruling all of us), that's what america is for, sharing Jesus (and getting to heaven). But it has to be the truth. Then all of noah's sons can get along better – as america has seen – best as evil man can do here, as long as we are here.

And we should live for Jesus, not for ourselves (**2 cor. 5:14-15**).

You can change to what God wants (and says in His word), but you are stubborn with your own ideas, behavior, belief, etc., that is not good for man, and you find out the hard way and are fooling yourself and trying to get others to follow you, and not Jesus and His truth. God knows best – change and find out.

We are all evil (more for some than others – not all at the same level) and we will all be judged for this life (**2 cor. 5:10**).

And we should all be of one mind, but it is only with Jesus that we can be (**rom. 15:4-7; 1 cor. 1:10**), and only with Jesus can we love each other, with His kind of love – **1 cor. 13** (His love covers all sins – **prov. 10:12**, like loving your enemies, **luke 6:27-38** – which is hard to do – impossible without Jesus, **rom. 12:16-21; rom 15:4-7; 2 cor. 13:11; 1 pet. 3:8**). Don't do things to be hated (although the truth of Jesus and His word offends people – do it lovingly and truthfully), but do it to be loved (don't do it to be selfish) – loved by Jesus. And don't get out of control – because man's love (really satan's) is very close (an emotion or event away) to hate (and harm and even death – possibly to you or others). But we all have to try to live a better life (and want to), and don't let the way we are born (the differences, evil, etc.) lead us (with satan) to stay the way we are – they should and are supposed to lead us to Jesus – and away from man – noah's sons (man naturally wants to be better than others, causing problems). Let God control you (and His love).

Share the truth – it's not easy, but even to your enemies – even if you only pray for them – for them to be saved – a loving thing to do. If paul can be saved (and changed – **acts 9**) – then anyone can be. Jesus is waiting, and is there for all.

Being nice or to love someone, forgiving, etc. (even your enemies, etc.) does not mean they have to be in your life, home, car, etc. – but share Jesus, when you can. See what God does.

Stop people from hurting others – don't let them hurt others or worse – but turn them in, no matter what they need to stop doing in their life – whatever that may be that is not good for them or others. That is love.

Forgive others and have Jesus in your life – but forgive yourself, too. Go to Jesus to do that.

God loves you and you can know Him through Jesus, the Holy Spirit and His word – the truth. Go to Jesus.

People are afraid to be disliked – so they follow things (and people) that are not good – even if they are against God and His word. The best is to be loved by Jesus (doing His will for your life – read His word and follow). And hopefully share Him.

Man doesn't know what love is – it's not good by man's sin and insecurities, etc. – to hurt, smother, ignore, lies, etc. Jesus will help you – but you need the Holy Spirit (from Jesus) and let Him guide you (**1 cor. 13**).

Love of and from Jesus is the love we need (we all want love) and not man's or the world's (satan's) love to give and show others. We can only love this way with Jesus – with the Holy Spirit, and only then can we follow His word (what it tells of love and marriage, etc.) – the truth, for anything here for man.

And once you are saved and have Jesus in your life, nothing can separate you from the love of Jesus (**rom. 8:35-39**) – the truth.

This life can be frustrating, evil, etc. – don't make it worse without Jesus' truth – have hope. Man's life here is to see truth and lies – and know the difference – God verses satan.

People try to rationalize what they do – prideful, stubborn, etc. (satan traits) – not always right, even though people know right from wrong – trying to do things selfishly to have power, control, etc. – to be God – which is from satan (**gen. 3:5**) – not God. Go to Jesus and His word to change, and know that man is not bigger or better than God.

Trust and love are important – know how to be that way – have it in your life (especially with Jesus – the best way), but you need to know how it feels (if it is not in your life), and not take it out on others (selfishly, etc.), treating others the same way – knowing how it feels (being done to you), and why Jesus is the best for that to get through it, and change.

Find out what God's plan for your life (get saved early in your life, and be ready to go to heaven – **matt. 20:1-16**) – the reason we are here – go to Jesus to find out. No matter how tough that may be – even before you have been saved, He has been in your life (helping and waiting). Those that don't want to believe in God – Jesus and His word, are those that want to keep doing evil – and keep getting away with it – and have their own power, control (like satan wants you to have) – God did not create us that way – He created us to be with and have Him help us in our life. He doesn't want us to want this world (of satan's).

And find out what you are good at and work hard – God gave us all abilities, etc. from noah's sons – focus on that and go to Jesus to get the most out of it and you.

God wants to separate us from this world (of death, hate, and satan, etc. – that all started with adam and eve's sin – **gen. 3**) to go to Jesus for life and truth (**john 8:32; john14:6**), but we are all made differently (mainly after the flood – through noah's three sons – **gen. 9**).

Don't let the differences keep us from God, but lead us to Him.

This world led by satan – and all of the temptations, is to lead you away from Jesus and His word – the truth – even though satan (and demons) knows that truth of God's word, and who Jesus is – the Son of God (**matt. 8:28-29**), but won't tell you.

And we see the differences today in the world (some of the poor, workers, physical, etc. people in the world – mainly from ham, in every country – not hard to figure out who they are, in the past and today – see **gen. 10**), and we cannot change that (no matter what we do today), unless we go to Jesus (and the reason God did it that way), and why america is so good (america can get the most out of you – no matter what son of noah you are – as long we keep going to Jesus). And those physical people (ham), that have gone to other countries of japheth (mainly europe, etc.), would be similar with some opportunities, but not the same as america (it is bigger and more diverse).

And why do you think anyone would want a servant worker (or even a slave)? – to work, to build, etc., to do those physical things needed in this world (not only today, but in the past, were needed even more), so there better be people that can do that – and some that even like it, but the main thing is the treatment of these people (any people – all of noah's sons) is what matters most, and should matter – all people should be treated well, but without Jesus, man is not going to do that very well, because all of man is evil (including servants, etc.), and wants to rule over, be better, etc. But you can go to Jesus, even if others don't. Then be compassionate and help others.

Everyone knows what's wrong to do in this world, but don't seem to stop it – we are born evil – especially in the world today – what is on tv, movies, online, etc. is attractive, and filling people, especially children, with lies, because that looks real or acceptable, truth, good, fun, cool, etc., but are not – just satan leading them. All the evil that man can do in this world will never fill the void we have in this life from sin – not having the Holy Spirit from Jesus. So we come up with all kinds of beliefs, religions, lies, etc. (even about the bible and true Christianity), and follow them (really satan). No one seems to know what's right, to behave, truth, etc. Just how to simply live and deal with people.

But if you want to be treated right, then you treat others right – and that goes for your family, neighbors, the world, etc. God knows what goes on and will also punish, too, but go to Him – Jesus and change, it's the only way. Whatever you want others to do – you have to do, too (even politics, etc.). If you want people to treat you right – not look at you different, then you treat others right and not look at others different – you don't harm other people, that's justice. But we won't be that way without Jesus. But people (nations, etc.) have to treat their people right or those nations or leaders, etc., may not be treated right (and suffer) – you reap what you sow, consequences, etc. God will deal with you. And it will for sure after this world, without Jesus. So go to Jesus.

As much as you want to help equality for all people (and it is better in america), it won't happen without Jesus in your life – and being able to go to heaven (where all will be equal). But we still can be nice to all people here – as much as we can.

As bad as some people, groups, nationalities, etc. are treated, it won't get better until all go to Jesus – those that are mistreated, or those doing the mistreatment. So don't expect it to end otherwise – stop complaining until you go to Jesus and share Him.

You may not be any better than some of the people you don't like (including nationalities, cultures, the police, etc.), those you dislike, or you are trying to fool, and hide from – you deserve what you get, and you know it. Stop trying to cover up your own evil and lies. And stop standing up for your own kind – nationality, family, culture, politics, etc., if they are not living right, and not going to Jesus and His truth – they get what they deserve. You can at least pray for them.

Worry about yourself first and how you are behaving, etc. (and don't think that no matter what you do is alright), then you can worry about others – especially your family, friends, etc. – so don't complain. Go to Jesus to change and live right (you know what that is, but we all want to be selfish). You have to have laws to live with others and make right choices – best for all with Jesus – and is best for all of noah's sons, and the evil in this world. We all have to go to Jesus individually – no matter if your parents did or ancestors did, etc., we each need to do that or the world will keep being more evil, etc.

If you make the right decision, even though it hurts you – you are doing the right thing, and Jesus will help you through it. Go to Him.

If people want to think that they are better, or at least as good as others (any nationality, etc.), then why not raise up and help your own? If you don't date or marry your own, you are not helping your kind – saying your kind are not good enough. So don't say other people don't respect your kind (or are prejudice, etc.), when you don't even do that yourself. You can't win without Jesus – no matter what you try to do or ideas you push or think of in this life. Man cannot do it. Make sense of what you do – to help others. If you're not sinning, then you don't need or worry about the law, and only Jesus can help us do that. Go to Him – get the Holy Spirit, be saved and live a better life. But we all need to get along – but only with Jesus we can do that.

Children learn from what you believe and talk about with each other – and argue about, so try to get along, and it will work better with Jesus leading (and His word, and Him in your life leading you) and your children will be at ease – seeing you getting along, helping, loving, etc. Keep growing with Jesus.

Do what's best for many people, not just for you. What's safe, good and helpful, etc. – what Jesus does. Help someone and maybe they will help someone, too – for good. Not trying to get away with something – any bad behavior you feel like.

The world should be where someone doesn't do things to bother many – just to please one person (or themselves) – not to be selfish in your life and what you do. And we have to know what is right – if we are doing what God wants, then others will be helped. No matter which of noah's sons you are or who you belong to, etc., or what color or nationality, etc. you are.

People may know who to trust – family, friends, etc., and also if it is your own nationality, color, etc., especially minorities, but white people also get bothered by all. All (all of noah's sons) need to go to Jesus, and know who to trust.

People try to bring people down, because they are miserable and hurt them – instead of building them up – with Jesus and truth, then you will like yourself and others better.

You want people to do right by you and you want people to do their job better – you do better, and be better – you live right and you won't be bothered (at least as much). Need to go to Jesus, and help your own people to do the same. If someone had someone hurt them – their family, upbringing, neighborhood, etc., then someone should have helped your family or parents when they were young and they would have treated you better, and a better upbringing, etc. – so help, not hurt people. Stop the cycle, etc. Best with Jesus.

Don't take revenge – or your pain, out on others (since you know how it feels) – be honest and tell them what they did and how you feel – so they know – then forgive, go to Jesus and heal, or you will cause more problems, especially for yourself. We all need to learn things from each other – especially to go to Jesus. Get your family (even friends, etc.) saved before death comes.

You can either kill or want to kill those that hurt you, or you can pray for them, if they have done something to you – at least prison for them and they can go to Jesus there. For anything we do. God will deal with them somehow, somewhere.

And don't think the things you do, or even do to yourself, don't hurt others, too. Don't do things that will lead people to copy what you do that isn't good for you or others, and they then have problems, too. Why don't you have them see Jesus in you and copy that?

And don't set people up, just because you don't like them or the way they believe or live – mainly living an amoral way of life (let God deal with them), unless they have truly done something (or selfish, hateful, etc.) to hurt someone. And if you are accused of something wrongly, then go to God and then change to the way He wants you to be – to deal with (and avoid the problems) of this world – at least some of them. And still suffer the consequences, punishment, etc., if need be, of your actions.

No matter what crime, etc. someone has done and are convicted of (or not), the answer is still Jesus. Lives are still hurt – on both sides, punishments, etc. – but go to Jesus.

People are going to hell, if they don't go to Jesus and change - so if someone does evil to you – you need to share Jesus after you turn them in – to change their ways (and the prisons should have Him to be shared there, too). So they are not getting away with anything. We all need to go to Jesus before you die.

Whether you were right or wrong, if you die (it is still sad), you better be with Jesus – but there is still evil in this world (and people) – whatever you die from – for something or nothing (at least good), and if you die wrongfully – you had a chance to be with Jesus, and that is all you need (and then it isn't sad).

And don't be the evil in this world – go to Jesus and His truth. Help people and at least keep people alive to get to know Jesus, because there are many ways to die in this world besides people killing each other (accidents, disasters, etc.).

Even though everyone is going to die (except when the rapture comes) – most or all people don't want to die. So if you can get people to think that dying is great (like some beliefs try to – a lie from satan about the afterlife) – you will have problems with those people thinking they are doing something great. Know the truth (about Jesus and heaven, etc.) and stay here and share Him and the truth about Him and His word.

Some people are trying, but don't know the truth (needing Jesus).

Help those trying to be good people especially, but all that are in need, if you can, and at least don't hurt good people (and even though we are all born bad, we need to help who we can). And if you are a bad person, as you grow up (and you would know that), then people may not help you (at least to keep doing evil, bad things in this world to yourself or others). Helping is what we should be doing – but doing what is right and good (you know what that is). And change yourself.

So go to God – the One who would think you matter the most is God – to Jesus, don't try to get people to think you matter (and don't look for the praise of man), because God already does, and God wants you to go to Him (Jesus).

You have no choice of whose son of noah you are, or what color of skin, etc. – God put you there and you have to deal with it. We all can go to Jesus – so do it and change – or it is your fault.

Servants (ham or other people) have to accept who they are until they go to Jesus (even though in america we all have better chances for anyone, because of Jesus, and can rise above that, and should be treated well – but not all in america go to Jesus, so we don't treat each other very well with our differences).

If people would go to Jesus and not satan (especially ham, and descendants), then slavery wouldn't be looked at as evil – evil, sinful man makes slavery and those who mistreat or take advantage of them look worse. Man is evil and satan led. Go to Jesus to change that – the only way it will be good for anyone.

You don't seem to mind being a slave to satan (we all start out that way here), but not want to be a slave to man (we fight that – cry racism, inequality, hate, hurt, kill, etc.) – satan is worse, and you have a choice – go to Jesus, and be His servant. Stop fooling yourself.

Go to Jesus to change your life and problems – not to man or the government, or crime, etc. – trying to avenge yourself – let God change and help you – go to Jesus (and the truth of His word) for any changes here, that is best for man.

Put on the new man – and become one with Jesus – not stay with noah's sons anymore (**col. 3**). Now we can be one in Jesus.

Choose to be a servant – to Jesus (and follow Him) – then you are a servant to all, and sharing Him (**mark 9:35**), and His word – the truth. And we will not just be His servants, but also His friends (**john 15:13-15**). Otherwise, we are a slave to satan, sin, evil, etc. (which you don't seem to mind – yell at satan – better yet, go to Jesus).

God made the world this way (connected to man – to noah's sons, whatever your lot in life is – **gen. 9:25-27**) – so stop trying to go around it, etc. – suffer if you don't change. And go to Jesus, and stop being prideful, stubborn, etc. Don't be overconfident for anything – you will usually regret it – make sure what you are doing is right and best. Jesus (and His word) will help.

We all have to pay for our mistakes (including before the flood, and after – we – all of mankind – because are all connected to all mankind – from adam, and also now to noah and his three sons, as separated as we are, and all are punished for that), so what we do in life (especially bad) is going to find us out and eventually hurt us (**gen. 4:8-13; num. 32:23; rom. 1:18-32; gal. 6:5-10**), and as bad as that can get, that should get us to stop and go to Jesus, but we all don't –so blame yourself (and satan), not others (for your life and your misery). So stop trying to get away with something (**col. 3:25** – God is not a respecter of persons – **acts 10:34-35**). We can be nice (but aren't naturally that way, and most people are nice if they want something – money, fit in, join their group, buy, sell, love, vote, etc.), but hopefully are brought up trying to be nice, and help people (especially after we go to Jesus), and people being kind (as opposed to mean and forcing and rioting, crime, etc.) to each other can maybe change some things (like we see some things have, especially in america over the years, although still not be the best or right), but in reality we will still be the same (connected to man) until we all go to Jesus, and do it His way with Him, and His word (and is why the problems are still here – some even worse), no matter what belief you have now – religion, etc. – it is not going to help you.

Do you want to be judged by who you were in the past, or who you are right now? – do the same for a nation – growing to get better (growing pains, etc.) – same as for you. But a person, nation, etc. need to start with Jesus and the truth of His word – Jesus will help the best for growth and where you end up.

So in america people can grow and change (and all help each other – all of noah's sons, with all of our differences) – and america has grown and changed and has freedom to do that – to be better since the beginning, but it is only with Jesus that we can, or have, just like a person grows and learns, so does america (it wasn't perfect, etc. at first, and neither were you or your family, nationality, etc.) Most people know what it is like to be hated – some more than others, but we can't go on hating each other. With Jesus we can change that – only with Him. Go outside yourself (man). Learn to love, but can only be with Jesus (**1 cor. 13**).

We all know when we do things wrong or bad (especially when others do them), whether we are young or old, we know we need to change, but don't – we are stubborn, selfish, etc. – no excuse, we certainly know what we don't like. Go to Jesus to straighten everything out.

So stop living the life you're living – stop making it harder on you and others. Go to Jesus to change that.

Even if man makes mistakes, God may use things in this world – that man does – to help, but more to lead you to Him and follow Him and His word. Go to Jesus and change.

So no matter who you are, what you believe, or where you came from (and how your ancestors came here) – you are better off in america (because of Jesus, even if you don't believe in Him now), and is the reason people come here (Jesus – God's plan for america, He knows what He's doing) and we don't always know it at first, but you will still have problems (maybe not as bad) until you go to Him (as you would if you were in another country – the one you came from – now or in the past). And why america (no matter how you got here – ancestors, etc.) is better than other countries we come from (as long as we go to and listen to and follow Jesus and His word), don't try to change america, and it be like other countries in the world (like some people seem to be trying to do – satan leading) – going against God and His word. We need to get the other countries to go to Jesus – the truth of His word, not the lies – and they will have a good country to live and stay in.

So if we let people into this country – america, then we need to share Jesus and His word (who and what america is founded on) – why this country is as great as it is. But it won't be for long, if we keep going away from Him and the truth of His word – it will be worse and fall.

So being in america, and freedom, and opportunities, and especially Jesus is the reward for all – better than what people had before, for all of noah's sons – no matter where or how you live, God knows best for all and has a plan for us all, we just have to go to Him to find out. And the problems (especially physical ones, but spiritual, too) are here to give people a chance to help and to share Jesus and know the truth.

And we need Him more than ever now.

Anything that is good and best has come from God – in the world or america – for any group, etc. And remember God has to use and deal with imperfect and evil, sinful humans to do things here (caused by satan and ourselves). We all need to go to Jesus.

We all have free will – God made us this way and wanted us to choose to be with Him and His ways forever from the beginning.

Because we (man) cannot change (what God separated) without Jesus (and satan is trying to make you think differently) – stop going after each other (evil, hating, etc.) and go to Jesus.

If you want to help and have the means – do it – especially to a true church (too many false ones), but can help other true Christians in this world. But first go to Jesus and His word.

So if you're rich, (especially in america – you can help others since you are) you might think you're fine – you don't need Jesus, and even if you're white (atheists, etc.), you may think you don't need Him either (may think you don't struggle, etc., but are still sinful), but if you're poor, minority (blacks, hispanics, etc.) – most struggle, etc. (as some go to crime, evil, etc. – satan leading), then there is no excuse, with your struggling in life – you need Jesus – go to Him. And if you think whites love Jesus more, don't avoid Jesus because of that – go to Him – He wants (and made) all of us (we all were the same looking before the flood – we have to understand that) – we have to choose. Don't try to solve your problems or others, by going to man or depending on yourself, or those like you (or the government, etc.) – or trying to solve things anyway you can (violence, hate, force, etc.) – knowing you are just as evil as those you are against. Go to Jesus (and His word). The only way we can get along or change. Loving and forgiving, but sharing Jesus – go to Him yourself first.

Even atheists try to be nice, but are people that think they can be good without God (but they cannot) – they need Jesus (and His word – the truth) in their life, although they even get the benefit of living in america (started by God to share Jesus, and still does), and all of the freedom and opportunities here (even without following God – but they will still have problems). No matter where you come from or what you believe (it's easier here in america – but not for long, if we go away from God and His word – the truth). And most of them are trying to be good to get something (and hold on to something – for them, and their family, businesses, homes, etc.), and the rest don't try too much or don't care – maybe like false christians, etc. are. And people are born in these families, but you can choose different as you grow, and get older, learn, etc. – to go to Jesus. But if (as a nation or a person) we get away from Jesus (and His word – the truth) they will see the difference in their life and what they have, etc. – still a struggle, and how and what the country becomes.

So those that have been in or grew up (born into) in a false church, may not be satisfied with their life and belief, and they search for other religions or beliefs (even atheist) to get satisfied – satan leading them. We need to know it is the truth and with Jesus (and having the Holy Spirit). Don't be fooled.

No matter what son of noah we are from – we can all be nice to each other and try to help each other. But you see that doesn't work in this separated, sinful world (all of noah's sons – nationalities, cultures, etc.) – so you need Jesus to do that in your life and this world. So being nice may not happen or be real (especially with satan leading man).

Some people try to be nicer than others, but really are not, and they are trying to be nice, but without Jesus and the truth of His word, and without the Holy Spirit.

Some try to be even 'nicer' than God, or think they are, by being nicer to some in the world (gays, gender, even animals, and the planet, and even heaven or hell, etc.) – the liberals, etc., but they are against God and those that follow Him – Christians. And against Jesus and His word, so they don't care about everyone, like they say. God wants them (all of us) to go to Him, because we all are sinners, and are against the behavior and ideas of man here. We all are born evil and sinful (and God will lead man, if man rejects the truth of God, to live a life against God – **rom. 1:19-32**). But we all can still go to Jesus, and be changed. Don't call God a liar – satan is the liar (and is why man leads these evil lives in this world – following satan).

Humans are actors – some better than others (look at hollywood, the movies – academy awards, etc.) – we all can act to a point, especially to get what we want, etc. (for good or evil – selfish), and following people to be loved, popular, wanted – for any issue – whatever they believe (even some that want to look like Christians, religious, etc.). Some people act 'nice' to get away with some things – then mean when they get caught.

Some people do anything – good or bad (sometimes to feel sorry for them) – for attention. Being with God and connecting to Him is what our life should be here – not all about us, and what we think – not attention to us. Jesus is who helps us do that. Give Him attention, and He will help you, change you.

Evil, meanness, etc. is in us and done to us (mainly from satan through people, etc.) through our life – that only Jesus can help, but man thinks he can do it – and he can't, but He – Jesus can.

People don't usually do one bad thing – they will do it again, if they keep getting away with things (or seem to handle the consequences, if not that bad). If they don't change, you can forgive (if done to you), but they still need to have punishment, and hopefully that will lead them to Jesus – and He will change you.

If you do something wrong – you should pay for that. People that cry about equality and justice – really wouldn't want it – it would be worse on them (unless something bad was done to them, then they would want justice). Quit trying to get away with things.

So stop seeing how far you can go or get away with something – just do things right. Go to Jesus and change.

We are not here to make it miserable for people – we are just to go to Jesus – then share Him and His truth.

Once you have faith to believe Jesus and get the Holy Spirit (and His word), you will see it is all true for yourself, and others.

Be smart about being nice to people – and doing nice things (and hopefully they are trying to help themselves to change, too). So help others to grow and change – for a person, or family, or a nation, etc.

So even america will have problems (even more), if we don't go to Jesus – but right now (especially politically, covering up the real issues – which is man being against God and His word is destroying man) america is fighting Jesus (and His word – the truth in all areas of life) and following satan (and all of his masks he wears in these many groups – in schools, online, families, businesses, movies, government, etc. – against God and His word, that man follows, in the world – politically correct, worldly, sinful, lies, etc., that God is against, all that they believe and defend – **rom. 1:18-32; rom. 12:2; 2 tim. 3:1-5; james 4**).

Man always wars, fights, hates, etc., because of sinful man, and will keep doing that until the end (**matt. 24:3-14; james 4:1-10**). We need to go to Jesus (and His word), and get away from man (noah's sons). And be ready for heaven.

People, nations, etc. take over or make changes in the world (with wars, etc.), but what God allows here – no matter what, people still don't get along. Going to Jesus is the only answer.

So we need to get away from man (our nationality, etc.) – even the jews and arabs need to get away from those sons of noah, their beliefs, people, leaders, etc., and all need to go to Jesus – we all do. To stop all of this evil that goes on between man in this world – we won't get along until we do.

This goes for everyone and everything here.

Which side are you on, there is no in-between (**matt. 12:30**)? And it doesn't matter what it is for – man or woman (and marriage is for a man and a woman – the way God wanted it, with the roles given to us by God, that are best, but man separates that, too, with beliefs, opinions, etc., even divorce – even though God allows it, **matt. 5:32; matt. 19:9**, then being unhappy, etc., but it does not have to be that way, or have a miserable life). So you need to find the right person to marry, with Jesus – the truth. Know who a real Christian is – we can judge and know (**1 cor. 6:1-6; 2 cor. 6:14-15**) – knowing the truth (and having the Holy Spirit). If we don't do what God says that men and women should do here (the roles He gives for each of us – and only if we both do those roles will we know how happy we can be, in Jesus, **gen. 3:16; prov. 31:10-31; 1 cor. 11:8-9; 2 cor. 6:14-18; eph. 5:22-33; 1 tim. 2:13-14**), then women (women are guilty, too – their behavior, what they are attracted to, the way they think and believe, and God made them a certain way – as He did men, and they need to live that way – God's way – to be happy, but women and children are victims too much) and men – both will get away with what the politically correct way of thinking is at the time in the world (no matter what the truth is) – but try to care, and be honest, etc. – especially in america, because man will believe and be on the side of whatever trend it is going on – behavior, belief, etc. – maybe it will be hate, evil, etc.

Hopefully people treat their family well – don't abuse, etc. in any way, but however you grow up, if treated badly, people should know how it feels to be hurt, so don't hurt others, but especially go to Jesus to heal and change – it doesn't always make sense – you got abused, so you are going to take it out on someone else, knowing how it feels, no matter what area of life that may be.

All of these groups and businesses and companies, etc. trying to attract people – especially children – whether it is good for them or not.

Don't cause your own problems, by the choices you make – make good ones, and know what that is – with Jesus (and His word – the truth), you'll get what you need (**matt. 6:33**). And don't put yourself in a position to hurt yourself or others – and don't blame anyone, but yourself. That goes for anyone. What God says – the truth of His word, which is best for us, even though we don't think so or agree. Trust Him and find out.

You are not going to help some people by yourself, mainly without God – go to Jesus, then try to help people the right way (with the truth) – so they can change – otherwise you will have trouble.

There is a reason why God doesn't want women in charge – because of eve (**gen. 3; 1 cor. 11:1-12; 1 tim. 2:8-15**), and satan running or leading their life – God made them emotional (influenced, etc.) – which can be good, but they need God, and need a man (just like men need God – Jesus, to control them, not satan controlling them) that is following Jesus and His word, truthfully (that God says women are to do, **1 tim. 2:11-15** – women, and children do) – women may get caught up in the world of things to comfort themselves and to fill voids in their life – pleasant to the eyes (**gen. 3:6-7**). So all go to Jesus – as man should, otherwise you can't control women (or men, or even yourselves), and we have problems like we do in the world. Not that women can't do anything – God can use them. And man and woman will be happy – we just don't try it, or do it the way God wants, so we won't find out until we do follow Him, the right way – or just keep failing, like we see in the world.

Anyone – whoever wants to, can stop the cycle of evil that is in your family, culture, etc., but only by going to Jesus (and His word) – so do it yourself, if they didn't – but the truth, and live. And you may have to sacrifice some things in your life to do it.

God made women this way especially after sin (**gen. 3:16; 1 cor. 11:3, 8-9; eph. 5:22-33; 1 tim. 2:8-15**) and even after salvation, and women are happiest (and can live) this way (or would be), but they don't do it, because they don't try to be this way (and don't realize how much better it would be), especially in today's world (with all of world's ideas – from satan – man and woman following). And men need to do their part – part of it is men's fault – not going to Jesus (and His word), and knowing the truth, and part is also women's fault for not going to Jesus, and not being with true Godly men (even dating them, etc.) – don't say yes to them (**2 cor. 6:14-18**). Just like abram and sarai – she obeyed her husband, even if he might be wrong – God will work it out (**gen. 12:10-20**), and she called him lord (**1 pet. 3:1-7**). If abram was dead then sarai would probably be dead – because of pharaoh killing abram (which is what abram thought the pharaoh would do – and probably would have, if he knew that sarai was abram's wife). God will work it out for His plans. Both have to truly be with Jesus (and trust Him) – if not, that is much of the problem. Look at the world (**rom. 12:2**) and see the problem. Women still have to do what God wants – follow their husband (you better find the right one).

So **gen. 3:16**, is for women today as well as back then – pain in birth is still here, as is the second part of the verse – woman's desire is to their husband and he is to rule over her – with Jesus, and His truth (**eph. 5:22-33**). Even birth wouldn't be painful, but we caused that (eve did) – and we wouldn't evolve to have that (and possibly women's periods, may not have been needed). And man better love his wife properly (as Jesus does) – so women need to learn and choose wisely, and definitely know Jesus and His word – the truth. Both woman and man (all of noah's sons) have some limits on their roles in this world.

Adam told eve (his wife) about the tree (the tree of the knowledge of good and evil – **gen. 2:16-18, 21-25; gen. 3:1-3**) – she didn't listen and follow – she listened to satan (serpent – **gen. 3**). Adam (and man) was punished by God, because adam listened to eve (a woman) – his wife (**gen. 3:17**). Husband and wife both need to go to and listen to God to be one – go to Jesus. So we are all sinful from adam (he followed her – after eve ate of the tree), but eve was deceived by satan (**gen. 3:4-6**).

When eve sinned – ate of the tree in the garden, she had the Holy Spirit in her – she was still to listen to God and to adam, but she didn't – she listened to satan instead (as did adam, mainly because eve did). Those (man and woman) – the truly saved today through Jesus, have the Holy Spirit, like adam and eve did before they sinned (created that way by God – **gen. 1 and 2**), and women still need to submit to man (especially to their husband – and their husband better be a true believer – **eph. 5**) – even in a church, etc. (**1 tim. 2:11-13**). We all need God, and submit to Him (and get saved – go to Jesus), and follow Him and His word.

So eve (women – **gen. 3; 1 tim. 2:9-15**) and even nimrod (ham – **gen. 9 and 10 and 11** – and those from him – especially canaan), are who God puts limits on in this world. They, as well as all of us (noah's sons), are sinners, and need to go to Jesus and His word – His truth (no matter what limitations we have in this life). Go to Jesus (and His word) and find out what we are to do. Maybe we have to do more for ham (and descendants) and women (or they have to speak up more), because God limited them. But help all get to know Jesus, and His truth.

We need to know who are struggling on earth (because of their actions – cursed) – by God – to know who to help (which has been best in america – Jesus' land) – all need to go to Jesus (and the truth of His word) – ham (descendants) and women (eve) need help more. We all need to go to Jesus to change how we are on this earth – connected to man (starting with adam and eve – now through noah's sons). We need to know the truth about us and how to change from that.

The risen Jesus gave all of His truth to paul (he didn't get his word from man or disciples – **gal. 1 and 2**) – and we have to try to do what it says in His word to paul in his letters (**romans to philemon**) – and accept things we may not agree with – any limitation, etc. to anyone in this world, and the whole bible is for learning (**rom. 15:4; 2 tim. 3:16-17**). Things written from **genesis** on still apply today for man – just like adam's sin, and the destruction and change of the flood, etc. – the things in the past that man did, and God did (punishments for man) – still affect us today. God did it, and had to – He is just.

All of man (and woman) is sinful – and Jesus died for our sin debt – all of mankind, but we have to accept it – not reject it. Don't reject Jesus – get saved – get the Holy Spirit from Jesus – to help others do the same. Then do what He says for us to do – no matter what son of noah (from man) you are from. And God puts us in our place in this world, and we need to see that (in His word).

And if women don't want men to tell them what to do, then women shouldn't try or want to be in a position to tell men what to do (other than parents doing that when they are young) – the same thing for all equal issues. People just want to be in charge (like gods, like satan – **isa. 14:12-14**) – not equal (women, black, gender issues, etc.) – all cause problems (they are not totally innocent) – so tell the truth (it is satan leading us away from God's word for us). So satan uses the 'victims' (and those that God may have put limits on, or are against God's word) to push his (satan's) ideas and have their voices heard – but it is against God's word – although we may feel sorry for them, or think we are being nice to let them do what they want – allowing satan to sneak into this world with his ideas (using man). Just let God tell us (Jesus and His word) what we should do – but man (or woman) doesn't want to do what God says – they don't like it. And men should be protecting women, not taking advantage of them (even if the women want them to).

Man (satan) has always thrown in bible talk (slightly referring to faith, etc.) into movies, shows, tv, books, etc., over the years as well as Christian holidays with worldly, secular, etc. ideas – blending them together (satan mixing lies with some truth), to get it to be taken as all you need to know (with all of the worldly things against God, and Jesus and His word – the truth). Basically fooling people in believing that is good enough (and man can do and believe what he wants).

God wrote all in the bible against what satan would say about gender, lifestyle, women's roles, lawlessness, noah's sons, etc. – the evil of man in this world (satan leading) – which really hurts man (and women) going against what God says in the bible. We can do all of what God says (in a loving way, if possible), we have to follow His truth for us – to live the best way, and happiest way here, if we would just follow it (we think we know better – as well as satan tempting, etc.). It may look unfair (unequal, etc.), but it is not. Just give into Jesus and His word – but the truth of it. God controls things – He will you. But if you don't keep Him in mind and go to Him and His word – you may be led to do unnatural things (**rom. 1**) when you go away from Him and ignore Him. So it is your fault. Go to Jesus and know the truth. Man won't do it. People are trying to solve problems without going to Jesus – with themselves or with others – it won't work – at least not very well.

Women have many rights in america, because of Jesus, but also have and want things of the world – that leads their life – like eve did – pleasing to the eye, etc. (**gen. 3:6**) – and is not good.

Women trying to change with women's rights, women's equality, etc. is why they are not happy and struggling, etc. – because those things don't work or make you happy (it just looks like it does). No matter what women (or men) do or accomplish, they will never be satisfied – they will always want more – it will never end. Jesus (and the truth of His word) is the only thing that will satisfy us. Or you will still see the struggles in all people trying to be equal, etc. – God put limits on them, and they don't like it. Do what God wants in His word, and you will be happy.

Instead of influencing girls to be equal – you should influence them to go to Jesus and His truth (to the way God wants them to be), and then find out what is best for them and you (in His word) – the earlier, the better – if they don't, their problems are theirs (and yours). And women's lib, feminists, etc. are there because men don't always do what God says – love your wife, but women need to respect man, too. But both should be with Jesus, or it won't work. Don't want the praise of man (or woman), just from God – do what He says, and you will be happy, satisfied, etc. – not pulled by the ideas, beliefs, etc. of this world (really of satan).

Women don't always help (or treat well) other women either – they can be worse on them than men sometimes. Women hurt women in certain businesses (keeping them down – competition, etc.) – there is no one or type of person that is not guilty (man, woman, black, white, etc.) – we all need to go to Jesus, and help people.

And women do need to be treated well (by men and women) – which is what God wants, too – do what God wants, and see how your life is – and people cause their own problems.

Women usually get the brunt of the problems in this world – mainly because the men are not that great. All need to go to Jesus, and His word to change anything that can be good. And men could learn some things from women – and why God has them here – to the help men – the world would be miserable without women. But it has to be the truth of God's word, and what He wants.

The world thinks there are certain jobs that are better with women, but believe it or not, single men (and some married) cook, clean, do dishes, sew, laundry, etc., and some like it, some are good at it, etc. but do it if needed. However long they need to do it. Some women even like it more (and see that it is necessary to live, etc.). Some things in life you have to do – God will help you through it.

Most single women (and maybe divorced, etc.) are trying to be men, in charge, etc. (and may still want to be with men sometimes). God didn't make women to do that, although God can use women for His purposes – mainly those that go to Jesus, and grow and learn His truth (and live it and share it).

Not that women shouldn't do things and see what they are capable of, but trying to be equal and raise up in the world, has hurt them and made their life more miserable, at times – as well as for men. We all need each other, but with Jesus, and His word.

And you can't want to be liked or loved so much that you will just go out with and be attracted to any idiot, evil, etc. person – who looks and may act nice, etc. – or to the things of this world. Most people hang out (and are attracted to) with the wrong people, especially when young, and may carry that into being an adult – know who you are hanging out with and to hang out with. Don't help to cause your own problems. Don't be with people that have problems (or not nice), or you will continue to have problems along with them – move on or you are guilty as well for what happens to you. Go to Jesus to find out what and who to be attracted to and who to be with.

CHAPTER 7

End Times and Judgment: Prophetic Fulfillment of God's Eternal Plan: Eternal Lake of Fire in Hell for The Unsaved, And Eternal Perfect Life in Heaven for The Saved (Through Faith in Jesus Christ)

Girls can be foolish sometimes – getting into trouble, putting themselves in danger, hanging out with the wrong people and places, etc. – it's always worse for girls and women (trying to be more powerful, braver, etc., with women's groups, etc. leading them with ideas, etc. – but not always for good things), with parties, alcohol, drugs, etc. (as well as what men are doing) – shouldn't be for their desires, etc., or they will just cause their own problems – especially with men (and be your fault to a point) – and they need better women examples, etc. – be smart, careful, behave, safer, etc. – be with Jesus – the truth of His word. All it takes is one idiot guy to ruin things – be in a better place (sacrifice things in your life – do without) – don't try to be liked, etc. Don't put yourself in a position to be raped, violated, hurt, killed, etc. – drinking, drugs, parties, just the wrong people, etc. And don't follow man (woman), the world (satan), and make bad decisions, choices, etc. – women seem to be hurt worse, with these ideas. And men better be aware of this (everyone should) – so they don't have problems (at least less of them). Some things can lead to good, but also to bad things. God is here to help us – so we are to go to Jesus (and the truth of His word) which we need to have lead us and know the difference. If you can help others, do that, but you do what's right and is best – go to Jesus.

And why it is necessary to have laws, police, etc. in the world – to protect all from this evil world (especially helping women, but they need to help themselves also).

Even if you are not raped, or had sex, an accident, etc. – drugs, alcohol, etc. are not good for you or whoever you hang out with, so don't put yourself (or anyone else) in a bad situation to be hurt. Don't make it worse. It's how you live that matters – with the evil in this world. Go to Jesus to change and grow.

So don't hurt yourself more (especially young girls, women), by following women's lib, feminist's groups, etc., and not following God and His word. He will help you more than even some women will.

Sometimes women can talk to women better for certain problems in life – and need to be available for that in all areas and occupations in life (so be a better example, etc.), but sometimes women in a man's world is not good in this evil world (of satan's). Be careful. Go to Jesus (and His word), not man (or woman), for all of your help and needs.

Women shouldn't act (or try to act) like men who they seem to dislike. They put themselves in danger, become criminals, killers, even death, etc. – not worth trying to be someone, etc. (like men). A lot of what women (as men do also) have problems in this world (and why women's lib, feminists, etc. start), is because of the way women live their life – and want wrong things – at least trying to get them without Jesus (and His word). And men are not that great (not what God wants) for women to want to be equal to – just as there aren't any nationality, etc. to be equal to, etc., so don't try to be equal with men – you'll hurt yourself. Just with Jesus – be with Him (and His word – the truth). Strive for that – and what He wants for us. This world (and man) is evil, and we need to know that, and know why it is – we go against what God created us for – what He wants for us and what is best, then this world would be better. And women need to be cared for by man (**1 pet. 3**) – especially by Jesus. Go to Him. But when we go against God (and His word), and it hurts yourself, and others – this world. You may not see the evil in the situation or in the person, but God can (through Jesus and the Holy Spirit).

And men follow evil women away from God, like adam did with eve (**gen. 3**), all through history and today, following and listening to satan. Go to Jesus and follow Him and His truth – His word (and those that do). And change who we are.

People need to get to know people – who they are, what they believe, etc. – how they treat other people, how they behave – don't just like them or hang out with them – if they are not good. Don't be with them – or you are not nice either, and are causing problems with them. You have to wonder why there is evil in this world, and where it comes from. Be with Jesus. And share Him and His word. Go back to God.

If you don't have rape, molesting, abuse, bias, etc., then you don't need women's rights (or any rights), equality, etc. – black or white, etc., but as long as there is evil in this world, we will have different groups speak up (all of noah's sons). So change all of that in your life (or at least help it have a better chance), by going to Jesus and His word to lead you and others to be in a better place in life (and be satisfied in that). Because what you believe is what is going to put you in harm's way or not in your life and the decisions you make to do something or not. Get away from man – noah's sons, and go to Jesus to be one, and get along – with the truth of Him and His word.

Women don't help women get better in this world, if they go against God and His word. Women going against God and the truth of His word, mainly hurts women the most, and they are doing it to themselves, because this world is evil, since we don't follow God and His word – go to Jesus and change, and help yourselves the best. Some women politicians, etc. are worse than some men. Stop trying to change what God says is best. Basically, don't listen to satan, like eve did in the garden. And adam followed – mainly because he loved eve, or he didn't see her die physically, but she died spiritually, and so did adam (losing the Holy Spirit, and why we need the Holy Spirit, to live best here – and we can only get it from Jesus). Adam didn't have to follow eve, but did, and went against God – adam knew better, as we do, and is the reason we all are in sin – from adam. Don't follow women to sin – follow God and His word to change (with Jesus).

Just like transgenders don't help women's rights, etc. – they hurt them more (competing, etc. – being unfair). You need to stand up for fairness – not satanic beliefs at all costs. Go to Jesus and His word and change with Him.

It is satan that is leading without following God (and the truth of His word) for what man and woman should be doing here (and the roles they play that are best – the way God says we are). And it is satan that always sets it up to look like someone is being mistreated (women, minorities, etc.) and they want to get back at them, but it is because we are not doing what God wants in the first place (man is not following God, but satan – and noah's sons). Try that (God's way with Jesus) and see how it works (but it will take a while to work – to get the old ways out of you). We have gotten so far from what God wants for us – satan has us arguing and not getting along very well (especially if we don't get our way – selfish, etc.) – and being from (connected to) adam and noah's sons – all people since then, without God – and are who satan controls. Go to Jesus and change – connect to God. Get with the right people. That is why God sent Jesus here (for our sins – salvation – getting the Holy Spirit). God created us – man (who sinned – **gen. 3**), to have a relationship with Him forever (and loves us) – that's why we are here – and why God keeps coming to us to help us – and why He gives us a choice (free will) to be with Him, but it will only be good and best with Him – now and in heaven – doing what He says (in His word) – which is going to Jesus. Go to Him as soon as you can, help others do it, too. And get saved (getting the Holy Spirit).

Help yourself first, then you can help other people (just like on an airplane – when we need to put on an oxygen mask – you first, then you can help others) – children, family, friends, etc., or you will pass on habits, and hurt yourself and others.

Go to Jesus to find the truth for us in this life, and how to live together – knowing how to live and what to do for yourself, then know how to help others (**matt. 7:1-5**).

God is a loving God, but also a just, holy God, and needs to punish and have people be holy and have free will to choose. We have to go to Jesus – and His payment for us – for our sin. And God made everything in our lives to be controlled by Him (with the Holy Spirit), when we were created – even sex (and the desire, etc.), women (how to treat them) – to be controlled (originally with Him in our lives, and before sin) and in the way He wants us to do (mainly in marriage – so when we have sex and children, we will be responsible, and love and raise them right), not the way man (or satan) does (irresponsible – without God and His truth) – and God made satan (but not to follow, even though he may tempt us – with desires, etc., without God's truth), for us to see the difference, the outcomes of an evil life – that man brought on himself (and herself) from adam and eve on (up to today – **gen. 3**) – we are now separated from God and are connected to them – man (we are made in man's – adam's image now – after sin – **gen. 5:3**, without the Holy Spirit), and they listened to satan and they (man) made satan ruler (**matt. 4:11-15**) here (when God wanted man to rule, but man gave it up), because we are all from them (**gen. 3:20**). And now we are all connected to noah's sons (who are still made like adam – who was first in God's image – the same kind of human – **gen. 9:6**) – after the flood (**gen. 9:18; gen. 10:32**). And all of us sin.

God didn't make man and woman equal – especially after sin (**gen. 3**), and all men are not equal (except with Jesus – **2 cor. 5:16-18**), especially after the flood (**gen. 9:27**) – all different from noah's sons. Man does not want to believe this – that is the problem (then and today). And satan is still tempting, too. And he is real – don't give in to him, give in to Jesus.

We need to follow God and see what He wants us to do (in His word, with Jesus) for a good outcome in our life (for anything, including sex and marriage and children and family). Man was made first, but with the woman in him (**gen. 5:1-3**). And she was made for man (**1 cor. 11:8-9**) – not man made for woman – so we need to go to God and His word to know the truth on how to act, behave, love, etc., each other. Especially after we have made mistakes (but hopefully before we make these serious ones).

People don't like to read this or hear this – or think it doesn't matter, but it does, and why we still have problems – not following or understanding it. God wrote the whole bible for our learning (**rom. 15:4**) – and for us to know what He wants for us (not what satan may say).

And God didn't even have any woman write any of the bible – not even mary (Jesus' mother) – but did write of ruth, esther and rahab in the **books of ruth**, **esther**, and **joshua**, for example. God put people in their places and we have to accept it and deal with it – any of noah's sons, man or women, etc. The only thing is to go to Jesus, then see where God puts you.

Men and women may not get along in this world – but do what God says and go to Jesus and the truth of His word and do what it says – then you will have a chance.

Marriage and sex is between a man and a woman (animals are male and female also – the way God made them and us – **gen. 1 and 2**) – or there will be punishment (as all sins do – but can be forgiven, if you repent and live a life for Jesus), even for your health, but also satan possessing you, etc., and you need Jesus to change you (by getting the Holy Spirit). God may even let you (turn you over to) go to these evil ways (satan leading), because you don't go to God and believe Him and retain the knowledge of Him (**rom. 1:20-32**) – another way God separates man (always man's fault).

There are some things that God gave us that we can have (but with Him) – family, love, marriage, wife, husband, sex, work, etc. – we want these, but it has to be the way God wants them to be for you – His way with Jesus (and the Holy Spirit) and His word.

God did give the jews laws, punishments, etc. to deal with the problems that sex may bring – outside or inside of marriage (**deut. 22:12-30; deut. 24:1-5; mark 10:6-12**).

God gave us sex (a sex drive, etc.), and we need to feel that way about a person (if you are going to think about marriage) – attracted to them, etc., but it can't just be the main thing you are interested in that person – you need to have the same belief – in Jesus and His word (God in your relationship – He made marriage – man and a woman – He is to help control that in us, but satan also tempts man). He made man and woman for that. And is why we need to marry if we can't contain or control ourselves (**1 cor. 7:8-9**). So if you feel like having sex – get married – who you are with and in love with, but not just with anyone. Just going to God alone isn't always the answer to this – He gave us the sex drive (and we have to deal with that, along with all of the other physical things He gave us here on earth – which will not be in heaven), so we have to live with that while we are here (and have that for who you will marry), and God wanted us to marry (and have more children – humans, for heaven), but this world is tough and evil, because of man (not the way He intended man to live in). But not have sex a way of life, without marriage. So go to Jesus and feel attracted to who you want to be with. With Him in your life. Otherwise you will struggle with that part of your life. God knows you will, so let God control and lead you, not satan. Get Jesus, and the Holy Spirit and be led by that.

The answer to marriage is Jesus – sex in marriage here on earth – no sex in heaven or hell, but in hell you will still want to, but not get it – in heaven you won't feel like it, God won't let you feel that way – you will be content in heaven (no marriage in heaven – **matt. 22:23-33; mark 12:24-25; luke 20:34-36**), but miserable in hell forever (for wanting all of your desires, etc., but not being able to do anything about them, even the simplest ones – **luke 16:24-25**). Don't listen to those beliefs, religions, false churches, etc. that think they know what heaven is like. We are going to hell if we believe those lies about heaven from other beliefs, religions, etc. But just know it is real, and how to get there – with Jesus only.

And people can use sex, etc. to get what they want and to get used for what others want – bribes, prostitution, crime, human trafficking, power, control, etc., even though God gave us sex – but with sin and without God (Jesus) in our life (after adam sinned), we don't know how to use or control it (sex) properly, and it is dangerous for us (don't use it for evil –to be selfish, satisfaction, sleep around, etc.) – we need Jesus (the Holy Spirit) to protect us from ourselves (satan) and sin (evil), that we all have in us. Need to get married for that.

God wants marriage (two parents – a father and mother) for family – that's why He says it's best to have sex in marriage – for it is best for children, best for man here (that's a problem – no fathers around – at least good ones). Go to Jesus and His word and solve your (our) problems – no matter what you have done in your life.

Sex can be forgiven (as other things in life), but can have consequences – you have to go to Jesus for that.

So God made man and woman for marriage (and to be fruitful and multiply, but with God in our lives), but man doesn't always do what God wants. And sex is for marriage (and not to be held back – **1 cor. 7:1-6**) – to become one – **gen. 2:24-25** (and is why someone is married – as far as God is concerned, like jacob and leah, no ceremony, etc., just a feast, and just sex in the marriage bed, **gen. 29:20-26; heb. 13:4**), but man separates, and does it before, during, and after marriage (which is one of few acts you can do on this earth, that can be sin or not – unlike the ten commandments), so someone is either a fornicator or an adulterer – sex for both. Whether you are married or divorced (**matt. 5:32; matt. 19:9**) – sex causes both. And we don't live without God very well (we need Jesus to have a chance to live this life well). Be true to your wife (and to your husband).

And it is the same concept if you don't believe in the true God (Jesus) – you are a fornicator, and you are an adulterer if you believe in God and follow other gods, religions, idols, lusts, etc. (**jer. 3; ezek. 23:36-39, etc.**).

God is against fleshly desires (especially that lead you away from what He wants for us – don't let them run your life), even though He created us that way, but with Him in our lives – we all need to listen to Him (**psalm 32:8-9**), mainly His word (with Jesus and the Holy Spirit). And God says if you burn (**1 cor. 7:8-9**) – want sex (with who you are in love with) – get married (what God made for sex – have a wife – to be fruitful and multiply – **gen. 1:28; gen. 9:1** – and hopefully the people will go to Jesus). And keep going back to Him, every time you fail, or sin, etc.

Go to Jesus to help. People need to be in different places in their life so they won't be in the wrong place at the wrong time (the wrong life), and get into trouble or have some problems (or even die or hurt others), and the consequences of sex – besides pregnancy, also diseases, hurtful, hate, jealousy, anger, etc. (maybe even murder) – so change your life and be in a different life (Jesus will do that for you), and different place. Jesus can help us to get through these things and change how we live. Men need to change in this world and live better – going to Jesus. It's hard for a woman to find a good man – don't settle. And women need to change, too.

And it is sad that women go into prostitution (or other lifestyles) – since you wouldn't like yourself very much, even hate themselves (some even think that prostitution limits rape, etc. – shouldn't do it for that – go to Jesus, man is sinful). And women need help – not to be beaten or taken advantage of sexually, etc. (in the world, or in a marriage, etc.), but they also need to stop being evil, too – so women better behave properly and make good choices (and not being in bad places, etc.) and be careful (especially young girls) – be right about what they think about (**prov. 31**) and who they are with. Not what the world thinks (satan's world – what fun might be, etc.), but what God thinks (the truth) – go to Jesus to change your life and tell others to do the same, showing you can change and live a better, different life (in a better place, and with good people).

So do without, if you have to (**philip. 4:11-13**).

We will all make mistakes – and God knows that. So change the road you are on – and can only be done with Jesus, to get rid of all of your desires that lead you astray (even ones you think are fine, but are not). Jesus will give you a second chance and more. Go to Jesus and be forgiven (only He can forgive us of sins – no man, leader, church, angel, etc.). Keep going back to Him (and His word), no matter what mistakes you make in your life – He will help you and you will get better. And you will even like the new you with Jesus – better than before.

And God wants you to know who is saved (a true Christian – with the Holy Spirit from Jesus, and the truth of His word), and who is not – who to marry (and date, etc.), and who not to marry. Not to be unequally yoked with a non-believer (**2 cor. 6:14-18**), and not even to hang out with those that are living a non-Christian life (which we all are guilty of – **rom. 3:9-31; 1 cor. 5**). Separated. So we have to know who a true Christian is, and that you are truly saved, and we can know. We have to be able to judge, but hard to do without Jesus – knowing we are truly with Him (have the Holy Spirit), even to marry, hang out with, etc. And we are to judge, and can judge, and need to, with Jesus we can (**1 cor. 2:15-16; 1 cor. 6**), we can't without Him (**matt. 7:1-3; luke 6:36-38; john 5:30; john 7:24; john 8:16**). And if it is in your family, you have to handle it, until you can leave, etc. (but we have to live or work with all people, but not hang out with them – or we would have to leave this world – **1 cor. 5:9-11**). Care about people, even though we are different, but it is only with Jesus that we can do this.

And God separates again for our sake.

Don't let people fool you in love (people are actors, etc. – with satan, who blinds you – **2 cor. 4:1-4**) – know who people are and what love is from Jesus. And they are truly with Jesus.

If we don't go to God (Jesus), then we will continue to be separated and not get along.

Love – the world's love (led by satan) – does terrible things to you – we all have and want love (we think we do), but we cannot control it – and it isn't good for you. Go to Jesus (and His word) and find out (**1 cor. 13**).

So who you marry, go out with, etc. is your fault – whatever problems or evil that happens – go to Jesus as soon as you can and make better decisions for your life.

People get attracted to each other for the wrong things – partying, drinking, drugs, movies, sex, music, etc. – all think they like the same things (those aren't good things to have in common for a relationship to last) – which aren't good for you, or will not last – not for true love. And when those things you think you have in common, are not there anymore (and not liked by one of you) – the other one may continue to live that ugly life, and add marriage, children to your life, etc. – the relationship will fall apart and start to be mean to each other, etc. You have to grow up sometime, and see what is best. Go to Jesus and change. Be with someone for the right reasons.

Don't marry for money (man or woman), but for God (Jesus) and truth – He will provide for you, if you go to Him (and His word). Have Jesus in your life (**matt. 6:33**). It will be the best. So whether you marry for money or not – you need Jesus for a better life.

Even when adam had the whole world (at creation), and all in it (**gen. 2**) – all material things – he was sad – because he had no one, then God made eve (to complete him – help meet). Be with God – He knows best – and we can be happy. But you have to stay with God and listen and obey – because adam listened to eve (and satan), and gave the whole world away to satan (**gen. 3**).

If the man is not truly saved (which is having the Holy Spirit from Jesus and follows Him and His word – the truth of it), then a woman (who should be truly saved) should not marry or listen to him (and basically things that God says in His word don't apply to those that don't follow Jesus and His word – you are on your own with satan – and have problems) – don't fall in love, or you will struggle (because it will not work without Jesus, and His word), because satan is using you and him (even if one believes and the other does not). Man needs to go to Jesus, and so does the woman – know the truth. Hopefully you both will go to Jesus after you are married (but the truth), if you make a mistake. Man needs to do the same – find a godly woman (**prov. 31**).

Man, not doing his job and trusting God and leading family, marriage, etc. spiritually – may cause women to act out – fight back, etc. (even lead spiritually, etc.), maybe without God, and it is especially happening in the world today.

When you marry, you should be happier (and more in love) five to ten years and beyond, after your wedding, and that can only have a chance to happen with Jesus in your life. And you both should love each other the same (attraction, caring, etc.) – and you need to know that about each other.

Don't love someone so much that you can't see the truth about them (and when you see it, if it's bad, and still wanting to be with them) – that's not love (just an image that satan gave you throughout your life – for other things than true love), just let them go, and you go to God (Jesus) and hope they do, too. Jesus will find someone – the right one, for you (and you keep growing with Jesus and His truth until then), and for the right time. Be patient for the best – for anything – what God wants.

Take a good look at yourself – would you want someone to be with you?

Since God made men and women different – in order to be happy here, we need to know what that is, so we can be happy, but not perfect (and treat each other best). And since everyone is not following this, we are all are affected (leading to problems, struggles, hurting, death, etc.), and in trouble when that happens – so follow God (and His word), not man (or woman). And men are supposed to protect women, children, etc., and that is best with Jesus. Then you will see how to solve problems; and all can be happy (at least better than we are) – now we know why we don't get along and are not happy. But understand the differences in all of us (man, woman, black, white, etc.), and how they got there and the only answer to get along, with these separations that God put here (and in us), is through Jesus and His word.

Love your wife and follow Jesus and you will have a good relationship **(eph. 5)**. Leave mother and father and cleave to husband and wife – and love more like Jesus. And have Him in your life to be one.

God made us function better if we follow what He says for men and women – He knows best for us, so don't fight God (and His word), or you will be unhappy.

Non-christians cannot do what God wants and are enemies of God and are not subject to God's laws **(rom. 8:7-8)** – still connected to adam and noah – man, and not to God (Jesus).

So the submission of women is mainly in marriage (but those that are not truly Christian will not be able to do this, and usually have a miserable marriage – maybe treating women badly), but also in the world to a point (in the church, etc.) – but men cannot take advantage of that (how God doesn't want women treated) – go to Jesus and get saved, then He will help you to accept this and get through the things in this world.

And women can use sex for power – equality, etc. – people cause their own problems (men do, too) – and all need Jesus.

Some women don't like men (because of the experiences they have had), just like some people don't like certain nationalities, etc., (for the same reason), but Jesus can change that and help you. To do what Jesus wants for all of us – we all do.

Women have to accept this, and men have to do a better job of treating women (with Jesus in their life) – there are too many people, religions, beliefs, etc. that treat women badly – some using the bible to do it (but not following it truly themselves) – but it is satan influencing people (through the world, even churches, religions, etc.). Do what Jesus wants – love your wife, as yourself **(eph. 5:25-30)** – become one **(eph. 5:31-33)**, and you will have a better relationship, and give women a better view of themselves, etc.

And women can do certain jobs (and need to, if they don't get married, or they get divorced, etc., but it is best to be married, and take care of children, etc. – that is an important job – and God wants that done), and they can be good at certain jobs (sometimes better than a man), and learn anything in school, etc. (working hard enough, as all should do), but learn the truth (especially God's). But we need to make sense for what people can do in the right job – women may not be as good or be as safe for some jobs – since women are the weaker vessel and need to be protected (**1 pet. 3:5-7**). And if they don't go to God (or at least don't get married, or hopefully to the right person – with Jesus), they may try to do some things that are not good for anyone to do (just like men do), and may struggle with what ability they get from noah's three sons. But if we would go to Jesus (and His word), we (man or woman, any of noah's sons) will find what we are good at and do the best at it (and what He wants for us), and with God's timing for things in this life, and how we treat others.

And love others, but the way God wants you to (**1 cor. 13**) – go to Jesus and His word to know.

Each individual person matters (we didn't evolve – with dna and fingerprints – God put them there in man, for man – we are different and special – especially to God), but we have to want to change (from what we are born with) and go to Jesus yourself (**phililp. 2:12**). Be born again (**john 3**).

God loves us the most (not satan, or man, do) – He made us and is jealous, is holy, and we have to be holy (at least our soul) and have His Spirit (and we do, if we go to and accept Jesus). God is no respecter of persons, so do what He says (**acts 10:33-45**), or we suffer consequences – all of us do – the world is made the same for all (**matt. 5:45**) – with needs that all of noah's sons (and daughters) have – and hopefully not lead you to a tough life, but if it is, it will lead you to Jesus (hopefully, to be a son or daughter of God). The ugly life you may lead (satan leading), should lead you to Jesus – the only choice, hopefully (before too long) you will go to Him earlier in your life. The workers parable (**matt. 20:1-16**), is a good illustration of why we need to get saved earlier, but also no matter when we all get saved, we all go to heaven (the same reward), and be sure you get saved before you die.

We all need to go to Jesus – noah's sons, man and woman, even Jesus' mother, mary had to be saved (and His family – **matt. 12:46-50; mark 3:31-35; luke 11:27-28**)– believe in Jesus and who He is – like everyone else, to go to heaven.

Why make your life tougher – the sooner you go to Jesus and His word (and get away from satan's hold on you) – the better your life will be – what is best for you, and what you are to do here – why wait? Go to Jesus now. People go around the law and threaten if they have been guilty and try to find a way out by knowing people – in politics, business, criminals, even those in the law, etc. – man is evil – satan controls them (us) without Jesus (and His truth).

And satan knows God's laws and dangers (fears, etc.) for man, and will use man to hurt and kill man, using them and disobeying God. And satan is a liar and the father of it (**john 8:43-47**) – because he knows the truth of the bible, and will lead man that way (to more lies – so don't follow him, but when you don't follow Jesus and His truth, you follow satan, whether you know it or not – **matt. 12:30; luke 11:23**), making our lives miserable. And man loves the praise of men (from satan – who can be a separator, separating man from God and His word, but also satan binds – unites, all of those people against God and His word, with false churches, religions, beliefs, groups, politics, governments, etc., to go against how God made us after the flood, as he has over the years since adam and eve sinned), getting us to think we are all the same (good without God) and deserve something, other than Jesus, who is the true answer, but satan wants you to think you are better than you are (he blinds us – **2 cor. 4:1-6**), without God and His word, and he is not of God (**matt.16:22-23; john 12:42-50; 2 cor. 4:1-6**). We can only be one (and equal, etc. – man or woman) with Jesus in our life, not without Him, and following His word (of one mind with Jesus – **rom. 15:4-7; 1 cor. 1:27-1:10; 1 cor. 2:9-16; philip 30; 1 pet. 1:13-17**) – so we can be at peace with Him in this evil world (**john 17:13-23; philip. 4:4-13**) – and it has to be the truth – the same. Like america is trying to do (especially at the beginning – all equal under God – the true God, not without Him). But if we are not, as a nation, going to and following God and His word – the truth with Jesus, then we will be just like the jews when they didn't follow God and His truth – God had satanic nations rule israel – and will do the same for any nation today – including america (with the wrong leaders, etc., without God and His truth and laws, etc.). The government can't get away from God and His word – with Jesus, or the nation will fall – no more freedom. Jesus is freedom – don't let noah's sons, without Jesus run a nation – america. Or it will be just evil. We need to go back to Jesus and His truth (not these false christians – leaders, etc. leading this country) – which is freedom, just like the jews did and God freed them from their satanic rulers, etc. Having us be one – working all together (**rom. 12:4-5**). We all need Him (and the truth of His word). But He has to be in our life, nation, etc. to have freedom (and good things) happen. Go back to Him. True Christians have to pray and share Jesus – His truth. God will bless a nation who goes back to Him and His truth (**2 chron. 7:13-16; psalm 33:10-15**). Even america has to change. Have Jesus with you and us.

Everyone is looking for success and you can find it with Jesus – not like the world – but a life worth living here and in the next life. And america throws people off – thinking they are being successful here (from themselves, etc.), but don't realize it is because this country is from Jesus (and to share Jesus). So go to Him to be one and get what you need here (**matt. 6:33**). Or it will end (which will be fine for true Christians).

We are all brethren (one), when we are all in Jesus (the truth of Him and His word) – be with Him to all get along – of one mind (**mark 10:28-31; rom. 12:16; rom. 15:6; 2 cor. 13:11; philip. 1:27; philip. 2:2; james 1:2-3; 1 john 3:1-3; 1 pet. 3:8**). When we are not with Him, we are all one against Him and evil – the real battle, starting today (being led by and following satan – like in the end – **rev. 17:12-14**, and like before the flood, **gen. 6**, and just after – **gen. 11**, and we don't realize it – just like satan wants) – still connected to man – noah's sons.

Be happy in the Lord – know who He is and what He wants for us and you – He will then give you the desires of your heart (**psalm 37:4**) – what would be best for you – and be happy (and at least happier). You start to know what to pray for – what God wants for you.

All people matter to God (so we need to go to Him, not go to or trust man to solve problems), but all don't go to Him (Jesus) – they want man to think they matter – a big mistake.

If you are evil (without Jesus), you have no peace – only drugs, alcohol, desires, etc. to soothe you for a time, then do it all over again, and eventually gets worse. Peer pressure has lots of power – don't let peer pressure lead you to do bad things – that aren't good for you or others (and we know what that is), just to 'fit' in (which is to be liked or even loved – but Jesus loves, likes, you best) – whether it's your family, friends, nationality, culture, belief, etc. (don't want the praise of men, at least not more than of God – **matt. 16:22-23; john 12:42-43**) and don't do things that are not good for you or others (or hang out with them) – it can't be 'cool' to see someone kill, rape, hurt, steal, or beat others (so live a good life, and you won't have these problems in your life – not from man, but from going to God) – and think of others before yourself, so don't side with what's not right (even some churches, as well as religions, don't follow God's truth – only their own rules, lies, etc., because satan can turn into an angel of light and fool us with churches, religions, ministries, etc., that are not truth – go to Jesus and get the Holy Spirit – born again, with the truth, not satan's lies mixed with truth – **2 cor. 11:13-15**), and even family pressure can separate people, so train up a child the way he should go (**prov. 22:6**), God's way and truth (and Jesus may separate people, family, with the truth – **matt. 10:34-39; luke 12:51-53**). Most children don't listen to parents at some point – why would they listen to God? So help them to – you, too.

And that is why you don't hear this in the church much, because pastors are married (and should be if they want to have a church – **1 tim. 3**) and have children – so they won't say that their children may not believe them, and Jesus says He will put daughter against mother and son against father, separate family, etc. So we really need to go to Jesus and know the truth of His word and share it – not all the lies of satan, in so many churches.

Many false christians sharing satans lies – saying it is the truth of Jesus and the bible, but are not (**titus 1**). People are interested in religions, beliefs, false churches, etc. (some born into them), because they want to hate or kill or go against the true God – Jesus.

And people need to be alive to be saved by Jesus, and God wants all to be saved – so there are laws, protection, punishments, etc., but once you are saved with the Holy Spirit and grow, you will obey naturally eventually (**gal. 5:22-26**) to what is right (if you believe the truth and go to Jesus and His word daily), especially if you know that all of the commandments are in these two commands – love God with all of you and your neighbor as yourself (**jer. 29:11-13; matt. 22:36-40; mark 12:28-31**).

So all people that have died in the past – no matter how they died – hope they got saved by Jesus (the truth of Him and His word), and had the Holy Spirit. But they are gone, and we need to go to and help and focus on the people that are alive today to get saved, before they die.

So when Jesus came to the jews, He was going to have them follow and believe in Him (not all of the laws of the old testament) like we are in today – a time of grace (giving a chance for all to be saved – and need to be alive to do that). There would be no more need for all of the punishments back then (mainly death – except maybe if you killed someone – God still gave noah a command of death, if you kill – **gen. 9:5-6**) – so we just need to go to Jesus and get truly saved – and you can only do that if you are alive. So all of these people, false churches, beliefs, religions, etc. that want to kill, hate, etc. cannot be right – just love them (and pray for them) and get them to go to Jesus (especially in america). Even the jews – with saul (paul) – killed those jews going against the traditional jewish belief – those jewish Christians (mainly their own people – jews) following Jesus. Just like religions today that hate jews and other religions (all of noah's sons have done that). Some will die, and God may do it, but you should try to keep people alive (satan doesn't care) to get to know Jesus (and you never know when you are going to die, so get to Jesus now), even in prisons, etc. This world is evil, so we have to be ready.

God punishes – not just those that are not with Him (He waits, so they can be saved today – **2 pet. 3:9**), but He punishes those that are with Him – like He did the jews (and the Christians today). Keep going to Jesus and His word and share Him – He will forgive you, but make sure you are truly saved (**matt. 7:13-23**). But He will not just keep waiting (so you keep on being as evil and hurtful to people) – go to Him as soon as you can, and pray for forgiveness and for salvation (getting the Holy Spirit).

And the belief you have (the truth of Jesus) may have you go against your family, friends, culture, belief, etc. – to do the right thing. So go to Jesus and help them to go to Him also. You stay alive and help others stay alive, if possible (don't put yourself in a dangerous position in life, etc. – if you are saved, although sometimes you may be in this evil world) – sometimes you may be protecting yourself, and trust and follow God – Jesus. The truth of Him and His word.

People – children included, do stupid things to get noticed or join a group, etc. (even hazing, etc.) – most things you don't want to do, but do them anyway. Doing all those things, but won't try to get to know Jesus and the truth of the bible.

Whatever you do in your life, you don't want your family, friends, nationality, culture, etc. to not like you, and want them to think you are doing fine in this world – but it is what God thinks of what you do, that is important – know the truth, know Jesus and His word and go to and follow Him. Let Him think you are doing and living well. That may separate you, but connect you to God (and hopefully they will all follow, too).

So don't follow or join these evil false beliefs, groups, etc.

And who cares if anyone likes you – do the right thing – what God says is (read His word) – you can love or like them, and share Jesus. Stop the peer pressure from family, friends, color, nationality, culture, belief, etc. – trying to look 'cool', etc. is just labeling groups, etc. Peer pressure can be good sometimes – if it is in a positive way – good things for your life – if it's what God wants (His word – the truth) – they have to know it themselves – by being a good example. Go to Jesus and do what He wants (need to look at ourselves) – and you will know. We know right from wrong (**gen. 3**), especially with God and His word. Do things that are good (and know what that is) for you, and hang out with people that are good for you – those that may be your friends (or you want them to be), may not really care about you or be your friends (or even want what's best for you). People label themselves when they try to 'act' black, hispanic, asian, italian, etc. (any nationality), continuing stereotypes, etc. Get away from noah's sons and be connected to and labeled with Jesus. Don't care what we look like – go to Jesus to be one.

People don't mind a compliment – even if it is a lie, and don't want to be criticized – even if it is the truth. Look at yourself. Only be concerned about right and truth (and no one wants to go to the truth today). Go to Jesus to get the truth and to change.

There are some people that don't act like or associate with their nationality, family, culture, etc. in the world, but most do.

Be strong and show you don't need to be like everyone and do the things they do to fit in or be cool or be like celebrities, etc. – causing your own problems, etc. Do what God wants, and find the truth of what that is. Don't be like a fireman that is also an arsonist, and has pleasure in the evil, but looks like the hero in putting out the fire – trying to draw attention to yourself, etc. (or not caring altogether).

Pretty much what you do all your life without Jesus is a waste of time (even though when you finally go to Him, He will use those problems in your life to help others). Go to Jesus to get things done with Him. Stop trying to bring attention to yourself, especially by being arrogant, egotistical, etc. against God, etc. – go to Jesus and humble yourself. And promote Jesus, not you (otherwise all you do is really promote satan and his evil ways).

People need attention – but from God – that's what we are missing and need, and we look elsewhere – to man, the world, and satan. We have a choice – without Jesus (and the truth of His word) we go down the wrong road.

People like to draw attention to themselves – to be somebody – be liked (especially in the day of social media, etc.), which causes problems to them and to others – put attention to Jesus and what He wants for you and how He cares about you.

You keep looking for people, things, etc. in this world, because you don't have Jesus in your life – depending on Him daily and His word. Be at peace with Jesus and know where you belong – who to be with and what to have.

Who cares how 'good' you are, as far as people are concerned – the coolest, neatest, bravest, strongest, sexiest, most popular, best looking, etc. (what the world is trying to tell you is good – and is satan led)? – who cares – only what God thinks – be best in Jesus. Don't try to be someone in the world – a need to be liked, loved, known, etc. by people – it's a sickness (born that way) – even though we can have love from people, but try to be known to God – the true God (which we are missing in our life), through Jesus – get to know Jesus (with His love), and be known by Him and follow Him. He loves you better. Be humble (**psalm 113; isa.2:11-12; prov. 16:17-20; prov. 29:23; matt. 23:11-12; james 4; 1 pet. 5:5-7**), then He will lift you up and will love you, and have someone and something for you, that's best. All in His time.

But you have to trust Him (Jesus) and His word.

Keep growing and changing after you become a true Christian through Jesus and His truth – His word – daily, with prayers (**philip. 2:12-18; heb. 12**). You want His attention.

God will set things up for you (including in His word), but you have to do it and take advantage of it (trust Him – and know it is from Him) or it may be gone (or not work out or help), but He will bring something else (and maybe His timing is different for you) – but you still have to do your part – to work hard on the right things to get it done (or the result that is best), and be willing – learn the truth (of His word), and then do it. And keep going to Him, daily, for whatever you need, or if you didn't follow in the first place, etc. – giving you a second chance and a good life, no matter how old.

And help people, but don't enable them (or you're just helping satan) – and change yourself, too, with Jesus (if you're not with Jesus, then you suffer the law of the land, the world, and are with satan). You can't change someone, if they don't want to change, no matter how miserable a person's life is. They have to want to go to Jesus to change – you just share Him (and His truth). Some people that go to a shelter or rescue mission don't want to go or at least stay long, because they have to give up drinking, drugs, etc. and listen to things about Jesus. They hurt themselves and cause their own problems – they don't want help (true help), or sometimes even want to work. Just try to live your life the best you can and help them when they want.

We have to know that drinking (and other things you put in your body) lead to problems, bad decisions, etc. (**isa. 28:7-8**).

God says drinking, partying, even drugs, etc. are bad for you (**prov. 20:1; luke 1:14-16; rom. 13:13; gal. 5:19-21**) – and it is – man keeps trying to go around that. We know it's true, but still do it. Even when Jesus changed water into wine (**john 2:1-11**), it was not fermented, drunk inducing wine (not the health and life hurting wine) – new wine (they had bad addicting wine then, and we do today, that causes problems for man) – for a new beginning for the way wine should be (and for Jesus' miracles here) – basically grape juice, and what paul wanted timothy to drink to get some healing (**1 tim. 5:23**).

Some people stop drinking, drugs, etc., because they had an accident, etc. – you hurt yourself, or someone else, or even worse, etc., it bothered you and don't want that to happen again – then you stop drinking, drugs for a while, as if you are not going to drink or take drugs anymore – then two weeks later you are taking them again. There isn't something bad enough to stop you from living this way (satan has a hold of you) – and sometimes those problems you had, make you want to drink more, etc. you are weak (and sinful – we all are) – and man gets addicted to it, and struggle. Need to just get to the point that you don't want to live that way – change from your sinful life. Something has to change in your life. Has to be with Jesus for anything to help you change.

Don't do things in the world that cause danger to yourself or others (fun or not) – if you get hurt or killed – someone accidently does that to you, but it is not their fault (because of your mistake), they still have to live with that all of their life.

So stop causing your own (or others) problems by the way you live – you can change – go to Jesus. Want to change from who we all are – sinners, evil, etc. (and satan leads us), and we know it.

Don't sin – know what that is, and what causes it (the best you can do is with Jesus and His word, with the Holy Spirit, even though you won't live perfect, but better, if you keep going to Him) – sin is what satan wants (sin separates God and man, and man and man, we are born that way) – don't go against God to get your needs met, desires, etc., as tough as it is in this world (satan and sin destroys man – we need to do what God wants to live best here, and after this life), and God will help you. And it is satan (and things of this world – **rom. 12:2; james 4:1-4**), that separates you from God. You will never be satisfied in this world (with satan), trying to be happy, following your desires – only with Jesus will you find satisfaction and peace. So only Jesus can help you with sin – reconciling us back to God (**rom. 5:10; 2 cor. 5:18-20; eph. 2; col. 1:19-21**), and away from noah's sons. And be content in all things – with a lot or a little, with Jesus (**philip. 4:11-13**).

People can look back on their life and see they did somethings wrong – and may have learned from them and changed – and you have to know others have (and are doing that, too) – you have to look at them – like you are – trying to change and will be better down the road. So help them, and yourself. We all have to try, and we all can grow and change. The best is with Jesus and His word. Some can be a big change.

Paul went through many tough things (before Jesus changed him – but especially after) and still was content (**2 cor. 6; 2 cor. 11**) – Jesus got Him through. We should only be one with Jesus, not man – noah's sons. Connect to God, away from man.

And sin is what we are all attracted to – which gets us all in trouble, and need to lead us to Jesus (hopefully) and be attracted to Him (and what He wants that is best for us) – with the Holy Spirit.

Walk in the Spirit, not the flesh (**gal. 5:16-18**) – which is connected to man (sin) – walking in the flesh – man does evil naturally (**gal. 5:19-21**), so walk in the Spirit with Jesus (having the Holy Spirit in you) – to live a better life naturally as you grow (**gal. 5:22-26**) with Jesus daily, and one with Him, and you will not worry about laws, because you will not need them, if you follow the Spirit (and not satan). Follow Jesus and behave and do the laws naturally (**matt. 22:36-40; mark 12:28-31; gal. 5:22-23**), and care about others.

And satan is trying to unite all of those that are against God – like before the flood and just after the flood – the tower of babel (**gen. 11**), but has trouble since God has separated man (all the differences you see in each other) so much over the years (until we go to Jesus) – mainly after the tower of babel – through noah's sons – up to today.

And satan has been here since the beginning (creation) – after he sinned (just after the creation – the 8th day – **gen. 3**), but mainly has been here doing the most damage (or is trying to) just before Jesus came here, with many angels – demons (**rev. 12**), and ever since. Don't pray to or call on angels. So no angel will say anything new – only to go to Jesus and His word – the bible – the truth of it (**gal. 1:6-10**), since His death and resurrection (especially since the bible completed, and the temple was destroyed – in 70ad) – for about the last 2,000 years.

And satan is mentioned – as the devil, only in the new testament – 58 times (only the word 'devils' is mentioned 4 times in the old testament – mainly fallen angels, demons – and sons of God in **gen. 6**), and as satan – the word, is mentioned only 15 times in the old testament (11 are in the **book of job**) – 34 are mentioned in the new testament (God separating the old and new testaments). So satan (or devil) is used mainly in the new testament (92 times for both names) – trying to stop Jesus (and His work and His truth), with man (as satan does today – **matt. 2:13, 19-20**). And satan is still here today (trying to stop the truth of the bible and of Jesus – and keep people from being saved, with lies, etc.) – and we have to be aware of that (which most are not – even Christians). So satan is real – and against God (and His word), and is evil, etc. – leading man. But Jesus defeated satan and death, so we can too, if we go to Jesus (and the truth of His word).

We need to use the word of God to fight satan and the evil in this world (**eph. 6:10-20**), like Jesus did (**matt. 4:1-11**).

And satan is called many things in the bible (**rev. 20**) – dragon, serpent, roaring lion, maybe leviathan, etc. All of these animals are not evil when created, but can be dangerous now, after sin **(gen. 3)** and after the flood, etc. (**gen. 9:2**). God wants you to know what kind of force you are dealing with in satan.

And satan is not going to heaven – he has made his decision, not to be with God, even though satan is here now (for us to see the difference in satan and God and truth – to choose freely), God is going to send him to hell (satan really sends himself there, as we all do – send ourselves, by not believing in Jesus) – to the lake of fire, and satan wants to take as many people with him to hell as he can (and has already – even people you know in your family, friends, etc., don't let him take you – know the truth and be saved with the Holy Spirit, while you are still alive – not a church, etc. –you go to and ask Jesus). Wise up and go to Jesus (and His word – the truth).

And satan and his ways – evil, etc. is who really gets us to go to God – to Jesus. So thank God for satan – it is God who allows satan to be here – to have problems and struggles, etc., so we will go to

Jesus and get saved (and learn His truth in His word) – so we can be with Him forever in heaven.

People in hell (people that know you, that are there) want someone to go tell people on earth and who are still alive (and can be saved) to know about hell (**luke 16:19-31**) – don't wait – go to Jesus and His word. Jesus came back (and is alive and waiting for you) – that should be enough to get you to believe and go to Him. And then share Him with others – the truth of His word.

No one wants to think they are evil (and condemned to hell – **john 3:17-21**), but they are – hiding from God (**gen. 3:8-10**), and even each other, even Jesus says we are evil (**matt. 7:11; matt. 12:34; luke 11:13**). You have to look at yourself, when you look at others – know we are born evil. Try to see things in this world – you see the evil in it and people (even you). Know the truth (don't always trust a church – many are false – go to Jesus yourself – then find a true church – not just what you are born into), or it is satan that is leading you.

It is satan that separates man from the truth of God – from Jesus and His word, and always has, with ideas, etc. (in false churches, religions, beliefs, etc.), that are evil, apart from God's truth and people follow him, which causes all of the problems here, but hopefully that will get us to go to Jesus.

Just like the flood (which was the whole world against God) – God will destroy people in parts of the world, against Him – like He did sodom and gomorrah, etc., after the flood (**2 pet. 2:4-22**). Nations and countries, cities, etc. go against God and only the few will survive (He will help them get out), and eventually like the rapture before the tribulation (all with satan, against God) – the righteous will be the minority (not a nationality, culture, color, etc.), and eventually the wicked will be punished – and the few (true Christians) will be taken out – saved. So it is the true Christians that are the minority in the world. Go to Jesus and His word and share Him and stand strong until the end.

Try to keep these out of the church – running it (**1 cor. 6:9-10**) and you keep going to Jesus to behave (and share Jesus with them, if you can), but believe the truth of the bible and don't agree with or promote these beliefs, etc. (**rom. 1:18-32**), saying they are ok, etc., or God will punish (and people will be left behind).

And it is satan that works both sides of an issue or problem (in both people and sides – with some evil we are born with) that man has in this world – both groups that are involved in an issue or prejudice, etc. (satan is on both sides – the 'good' and the bad), having one group hate another and then the other hating them back – like black, white, even beliefs like homosexual, religions, view of the world, nations, culture, politics, etc. – so we all have free will, but satan uses that against us, and it is mainly against God (and His word). The reason sodom was destroyed by God, was because they were living against God (His truth and word for us) – like we are today – evil living, etc. (all were that way – but they were all at the same time that way – satan had the whole city, and all were doing the same evil, against God). It was ham's people (mainly canaan) that lived in sodom and gomorrah (**gen. 10:19-20; gen. 13:10-13; gen. 18:16-33; gen. 19**) – going against God. The whole world (even america – and when the rapture comes, and true Christians are gone – america will be like before the flood, and sodom, etc.) and is getting like sodom now (as it will in the end times – **2 tim. 3:1-5**) – leading to the end – the one world order. So satan keeps you believing something (or living a life) that is not right or good for you (mainly against God), and has the other side hate you for it (even though they may not be living a good life either – what God thinks – **rom. 1:18-32**), and it goes on (and has since the beginning – **gen. 3**). Both sides are evil – until you go to Jesus and follow Him and believe His word, and live your life His way – then we can be one. It is satan that leads both sides to the wrong life and wants you to think it is fine (how you are living – rationalizing, etc.) – he wants you to think you are living (and thinking, etc.) properly (with ego, stubbornness, pride, etc.), and doesn't want you to change – to go to Jesus. So again satan (whether you believe in him or not) is real – and he lies against God and the truth of His word (and Jesus), in some way. And the people who follow satan and go against God's word. God lets us know and allows him to be here, so beware – go to Jesus – choose Him. Just like He allows satan to be here, He allows man to do evil (eventually will punish) – anything that man tries to do even if it's evil or looks right to man, etc. Nothing matters except to go to Jesus.

Don't cut people down to make you look good – only compare you to what God wants for us.

You have to know that satan works both sides of the street, causing problems with man. But Jesus can change you and make a better life for you (no matter what it is). Go to Jesus' side – it is fair and truth.

All people have memories, feeling, etc. of bad things in their past and have to deal with them – Jesus can help you move on and heal.

All need to go to Jesus (and get satan out of your life – by getting the Holy Spirit – salvation, from Jesus only) and then when you do – go to Him (and His word) daily (with the truth). It's up to you. Or satan will continue to make it miserable (and lie to you – using the world to do that). This is a war against satan (**eph. 6:10-20**) and needs all people of all ages to fight it – do your part, even if you are not liked – first go to Jesus now and His word.

What makes you do the things you do – what you are attracted to (mainly the bad things – what God thinks is)? It is the evil in you, when you are born (and then you nurture that as you grow, if you don't change or sometimes taught or helped). You have to try to figure that out in you and in others, because we all do evil. But you have to know it is Jesus that will change you to do the right and best things (and away from what you are born with – living apart from God and His word, how He made us, and what He made us for, at creation) – but you have to have Him in your life (saved with the Holy Spirit), not just know about Him, not just go to church, rituals, traditions, etc. Know the truth in His word. And have Him in your life (and inside you – the Holy Spirit – go to Jesus).

All of man is still born evil today (without the Holy Spirit, and against God and His word – truth, since adam sinned – **gen. 3**, through adam, even though we all come from women, it is through the father that we are sinners, even though women are also – but Jesus came through the Holy Spirit, **matt. 1:18-20** – through God, the Father), and we need to understand that – the separations we have in man since noah's flood (**gen. 9:25-27**) are still here today (and we are all from noah's three sons now, with their differences). We have to live with these separations, until we go to Jesus – He will change us and help us get along, not man doing it (any changes that have been good have been done by God, especially in america, but most of us keep fighting Him, and His truth – His word).

With all of the hurts, pain, etc. you went through in your life, and in other's lives – try to help others when you can and go to Jesus and share Him – it is worth it and have to forgive to do that.

People in society should want to be helped and accept it, and work hard to move ahead – doing things right, not run, or hide things, etc. but if they don't want to, then they should suffer the consequences of what they decide (it probably won't be good for them or others), and others shouldn't have to suffer just because people don't want to do the right thing or work hard and care about others, live right with others – you have to change and admit how you live, what you did, etc. and turn yourself in, and go to Jesus, it will be easier for you – (don't be so selfish – which is how we are born, but don't have to be brought up that way or stay that way – go to Jesus). None of noah's sons has to, when they can all go to Jesus. Otherwise these differences in us will hurt us all.

The differences (separations) between noah's three sons are: japheth (intellectual), shem (spiritual), and ham (physical). And you can see where they are today (**gen. 9:27; gen. 10**) – look around the world. And we are all connected to satan without Jesus. All of the sons of noah are – all nationalities, jews included, etc. – and all can be one with Jesus – with the Holy Spirit (**1 cor. 12:13; gal. 3:27-28**).

If you have a problem and God is against it – go to Jesus and change – stop fighting it and even more important, stop defending it and others doing it (**rom. 1:20-32**). Get away from man and satan.

We are not made in the image of God anymore (after sin – **gen. 3**) – without the Holy Spirit, but in man's (adam's) image (**gen. 5:3**), and now from noah's sons (the same human as adam – the original man in God's image, not mutated, but sinful, etc., – **gen. 9:6**) – and we are all born evil – sinful (and destined for hell – **john 3:17-21**). So we all have to go to Jesus individually to change that – to be in God's image again (with the Holy Spirit – to be born again – **john 3:1-8**).

And satan comes to steal, kill, and destroy (**john 10:9-10**) – either outwardly or hiding it (all through our life here) – but all evil (and leads you to hell). Look who dies in the world that Jesus gives love to and to prosper – and He will also come as a thief (not knowing when) in the night – at the end times – the day of the Lord (**2 pet. 3:10-11**). So be ready (before you die, and no matter when you die) – go to Him (He will lead you to heaven).

And there may be levels of hell (how bad you really are – without Jesus), and the bible seems to hint of that – **deut. 32:22; psalm 86:13; prov. 7:27; isa. 14:15; ezek. 31:16-18; ezek. 32:21, 27; matt. 5:25-30; matt. 11:23-24; matt. 16:18; luke 10:14-15.** But hell will be thrown into the lake of fire – separated from God forever in misery and torment (**luke 16:23-28; rev. 20:10**) – so the levels you are at first won't or may not matter then (**rev. 20:10-15**). It will be terrible separated from God forever. So once you are in hell (have died without Jesus), you can't get out – forever.

So satan is on both sides of what is going on in this world – the evil part of all people – black, white (any nationality, etc.) – causing problems – hate, etc. All of us are evil. All of noah's sons need to go to Jesus to stop this – and it better be the truth.

All of this is part of a fallen, cursed world – by God, especially after the flood, since man would not go to God before the flood (**gen. 6:3**). All of noah's sons have suffered in this world – over the years – since the flood mainly – go to Jesus now, or you will continue to suffer (and will be in hell forever, if you don't go to Jesus before you die).

Shem is who the jews (still God's people, but didn't always follow Him and rejected Jesus) are from (and most spiritual people are from shem – even though all of those people are not with the true God, through Jesus – like the arabs, even india, and asia, etc., are not, and have hurt themselves and others over the years, by what they believe). God uses shem for family, laws, society, behaviors, etc. (tents of shem – **gen. 9:27**). And besides being spiritual – the jews, they are also intelligent, because of the bible, and the study of it – we all should study (the truth), and is best to have Jesus with you, to lead and protect you.

The whole bible is for truth and learning (**rom. 15:4**). Read the new testament to understand the old testament and the old to understand the new – the jews would understand the old testament, if they would read the new (a few do). They need to go to Jesus (and some do). You are not going to know everything about the bible (after being saved – especially how long you live, etc.), but you can know what you can while you are here – and it better be the truth – and share it and help people.

Japheth is who all of the europeans are from (and some others) and has gone (enlarged – **gen. 9:27**) all over the world and is why there is all of the technology, etc. (and not all of it is bad) in the world (but also false science and ideas, **1 tim. 6:20-21** – evolution, evil rulers, even medicine – including abortions, etc., which has caused many problems in the world, and hurting others – sometimes their own choice, now and in the past, as many countries and people have done). Don't depend on technology (and man – satan), but on God (like people had to in the past, or should have, because they didn't have as much technology as today). And without God, those nations and empires will fall, or struggle (and america would without Jesus), and they have, that japheth (as well as shem and ham) was, or is, in, even today – we should be for life and not death, and with Jesus we can be (life starts in the womb – **psalm 139:13-18; luke 1:34-45**). And those false science and ideas (that japheth has come up with, but all of noah's sons come up with things against God today), mainly evolution (people making money – teaching lies, writing books, etc., against God and His word – the truth, sending some to hell), has hurt all people throughout history (especially to those that are more physical – ham – thinking man came from animals, and that the africans were the closest to animals, etc. – so they seem like animals – having people treat them badly, etc. – even today). So satan (through evolution) caused man to hate more, because of man's difference after the flood – the differences in noah's sons. There is a difference between man and animals, etc. – **1 cor. 15:39**, God created them differently – **gen. 1:24-25** – we are all human (black, white, etc.) and created that way by God (**gen. 1 and 2**), not evolved (if whites hurt blacks, it was in this area that did the most damage – lies of evolution). Man was similar at first (looks, etc.), before the flood – man still sinful from adam, then man was separated (especially after the flood, now all from noah's sons – all looking different after the flood, after the tower of babel). And man is not out of africa (like animals, etc.) – we are from where the ark landed, after the water subsided after the flood (over 4,000 years ago) – on the mountains of ararat (**gen. 8:4**) – near armenia (and near the tower of babel) – then God scattered man (fully human – created by God) around the world (with the separated land – continents like we see today). So japheth is wrong – we are not evolved.

And the only things that evolve are things man makes – machines, vehicles, weapons, ideas, etc. (man doesn't make things perfect first, like God does). Don't depend on technology (at least use it for good), but depend on God (and His word). And japheth always has had the edge in technology, and will go against God to figure things out.

The jews, from shem, were probably the most mistreated in history (even close to the beginning in egypt) – although God allowed that (israel being ruled by others), because the jews' disobedience to God – and when they went back to Him, then God helped them again. And especially in the last 2,000 years the jews are hated (even Christians are, but sometimes caused by themselves). They, like we all, need to go to Jesus.

And most of the harm to people – from the different sons of noah, happened in the last 500 years or so, when travel became more common (otherwise most of noah's sons were separated, and hurt their own – own nationality). Even though there has been traveling and conquering, etc. all through history – especially after the flood (because of our differences) – man trying to rule, etc.

Ham (the youngest – **gen. 9:24**) is who all of the mainly physical people (live off the land, live simply, etc., and they usually liked that way of living – and still do in some countries, and remote parts of the world today, but still can work hard, and learn things, if exposed to it – like in america – all of noah's sons together, especially with Jesus). They are from ham (and who would be considered servant, workers, even athletes or some entertainers, etc. today – including africans, hispanics – like south and central americans, native americans, etc.) in the world (now and in the past, and some have been against God over the years), so we all need to go to God (Jesus), and change, or we suffer the consequences of that (and we are seeing that). Even though we can all learn (especially with Jesus in our life), and in america. God separated us all.

And hispanics, latinos, etc. – are japheth and ham – those that mainly live in central and south america (some in the u. s., and maybe spain, etc.) – even though all of noah's sons do, as well as jews – shem, are everywhere. And all need to go to the truth of Jesus and His word. God made man and the world this way (no matter what man does evil in this world), for all of us to go to Jesus. We need to see that, and learn of that, and know we need to go to Jesus to be one. Otherwise we are separate for now.

And satan tries to take advantage of man's separation (to be evil to each other) – all things against God (lies, etc. that send people to hell, like satan) – that's why we are separated until we go to Jesus (because of satan's main goal of uniting all against God again).

Man can do great things – God made us that way, but it is best with Him in our lives (and His word – **prov. 16:9, 16-21**). If left by ourselves (man) to do what we think is right, our abilities can and will lead to death (**prov. 14:12**). We need God's wisdom (the bible, with Jesus, and get the Holy Spirit) to do what's best, not the world's wisdom – not man's or satan's (**james 3:14-16**).

All of the sons (of noah) can do (or capable of doing) most things in this world (and some have to work harder, etc.) – having what is needed and available (like in america), and helping each other (and some interbreeding over the centuries), but those abilities are still in some more than others (and if there are enough jobs, etc. – we all can work). There should be enough – God will provide, if you go to Him, but if you don't work (if you are with Him), you don't eat (**2 thess. 3:6-12**).

All people can work hard and make it (black, white, man, woman, etc.), especially in america, and better with Jesus – no excuse – people just give up and may have bad role models. Don't take the easy way out and give up, listening to those that are giving up and having a miserable life. Go to Jesus.

Even being a mother and wife is working (one of the best jobs) – taking care of a family, and is what God would want women to do, especially with Jesus in your life.

When you are with Jesus, all of your talents, abilities, etc. will be better – the good ones.

Some people may not be able to make or invent certain things, but we should all be able to use these things (and do) – tvs, cars, computers, phones, appliances, etc. All people can learn (especially about God and His word – which will help you with anything you want to learn) – some more than others, and some have to work harder to learn things (talents, abilities, etc.) in this life (and that should not stop you or bother you – don't be lazy, etc.). And help people – those that want to be helped.

Other people can copy things that others have made or done (things or behavior, etc.) – all of noah's sons can with their abilities like you see in the world – especially in america – people can learn and imitate, etc. (but some can be good or bad). Be a good example (you'll have a better chance with Jesus – in your life to do that).

Being disciplined (and spiritual) can help you do well, and can be intelligence, because of discipline, and hard work, etc. (like some asians do – maybe a combination of ham and shem, but asians could also be from japheth) – so anyone can do that – work hard (any of noah's sons), especially with Jesus (and be even better). Being spiritual with Jesus (and His word – the truth), will get all to our highest level (to do well or your best), and being honest and caring at the same time.

That's why america is great – giving all a chance – freedom with Jesus – changing us. Changing from an evil, ugly life to a good, godly life is what Jesus does and shows the change in your life and then share Jesus to help others change to a better life, otherwise we have problems and struggle.

People can do more than they think they can, especially with God (and His word). Man tries everything, but doesn't go to God and His word – as if man would know more, but man doesn't. Look at the world through the eyes of God (through His word – the bible), then try to figure everything out – you will get the right or best answer, and it is through Jesus.

Follow God and His word, through Jesus, not man (or any of noah's sons), because man is fooled (especially by satan), but God makes the truth available, and man disregards it, or trips over it (**1 cor. 1:18-31**). So we all can be who God wants us to be. Whether it's history, science, way of life, etc. – anything – go to Jesus and His word – the truth.

People try to go against God and the bible (like false churches, etc. trying to fool you – following satan) to look like they know it all – like gods – are against the true God – like satan does (he leads them). You have to know the truth of His word (and Jesus).

People that are intellectual (japheth, even others) think they are smarter than God, and people that are spiritual (shem, even others) think they are kinder and deeper than God, and those that are physical (ham, even others) think they are stronger and don't need God – but all are following satan, if they are not following Jesus and His word, which is the truth (once you look into it, and go to Him). People in the world think they are better, more popular, etc., than Jesus (and don't need Him, etc.) – like a musical band has, etc. – none of us are, but satan would like you to think you are – like satan did (**isa. 14:12-17**). Share Jesus and His truth of His word, and know who He is.

If you go to Jesus – you will turn the lights on (and open your eyes) to understand the truth of the bible (of man and this world), with the Holy Spirit (**1 cor. 2:12-16**).

Evolution (scientists, etc. – japheth) is not true – God made us who we are, and we now are separated from Him (because of sin of adam – from satan) and also separated by Him from each other (after the flood – **gen. 9:25-28**), and stuck in our place in life (through man – noah's sons, and his ideas) until we go to God (Jesus) – connect back to God, not man (who we are in the image of now – **gen. 5:3**). We can only be the son of God (and in His image) with the Holy Spirit again – which only Jesus can give us. Know He is your Maker and go to Him and become His offspring (like we were supposed to be) again – all one (**acts 17:24-31**), but only with Jesus (getting back the Holy Spirit – lost by adam for all of us). Know the truth, and then grow and live.

Don't escape into your intellectual world – or ignore the problems of your life – how you grew up, etc. – need to learn who you really are. All of us need to – go to God and His word. Go to Jesus now, and follow what is best and right.

And all people (noah's sons) are lawless (for sure against God's laws) – some more than others (unless you go to the true God, Jesus). And His word (truth – the bible) should be taught and let people decide, but most people think they shouldn't (because they are afraid they will find out what they, through satan, have been teaching is wrong all of these years – and that goes for false churches, religions, schools, families, cultures, etc.). It affects all of us (especially children, growing to struggle in this world). Learn it truthfully, and then teach it.

The media, news, schools, government, etc. all going against God and His word – the truth (satan is leading man and america down that road). Need the bible and go to Jesus.

And parents need to be part of their children's education, and have good teachers – have the best teachers teach, not just hire anyone. Sharing Jesus and learning the bible helps the most for education and learning.

Don't go against whites or blacks, etc. – just against evil – be just (and fair, etc.) in your decisions – best person for the job. And have them learn and be taught properly, etc. – it will be best for children – the bible and Jesus.

And man has some of each of these abilities – intellectual, spiritual, physical (but most have one dominant ability) over the years (and you can see it in the different nationalities, etc.), as man has travelled over the world, especially in the last 1,000 years or so (interbreeding at times) – even though God separated people, some not to be together, or some not to marry, etc. in the past, and we still do that today (the jews don't marry many gentiles, and blacks don't marry many whites, and maybe arabs don't – still separation, even though europeans marry each other (nations near each other and similar – and may get along, do cross borders, but are still one of noah's sons – not a mixture of sons – like europe – japheth), and some asians marry others sometimes, etc., and other reasons keep people separate). And many babies get aborted, so there may not be as many interbred babies as there could be. And the separation of land (at the flood) and language (which was about 100 years or so after the flood – the last 4,000 years) - made it more difficult.

And satan wants you to think differently than that – not know the truth (thinking that everyone can be a god and have power, etc. – **gen. 3**). Some people don't want to work or do certain jobs (the interest is not there), so there won't be many asked to work some types of jobs, and others may not want them – they would rather do nothing (leading to laziness, boredom, privilege, depression, suicide, homeless, alcohol, drugs, crime, divorces, single mothers, etc.), especially when they see others in the world (mainly in america, making so much money and having things, etc. – but even they are not always happy, and some lose it all, and others are not happy when they finally get some, and think there has to be more to life, and there is – Jesus). Also partying, drinking, drugs, peer pressure, wanting to be loved, etc. all contribute to problems in this world – go to Jesus and change – at least you, if not, the world leads (get away from satan and his ideas). So all that people have to do is to take drugs, alcohol, be abused, bad childhood, be injured, etc. and will be an excuse to get away with murder, etc. – not their fault. But there is no excuse – go to Jesus and teach and change.

And even though there are all kinds of temptations and conditions in the world to get you do evil, you still don't have to do the evil or be in the places of evil – to be tempted in the first place, etc. – don't make more problems for yourself.

God can make something for you out of all these problems (something good out of something bad) – if you would just go to Him and follow (His word – the truth – **rom. 8:28**). We don't need much to live here – just Jesus (He will provide – trust Him, **psalm 37:25; matt. 6:33**), and work hard. The main reason why people – children included, are trying to escape life, struggles, etc. (through drugs, alcohol, even like some political views – socialism, communism, etc. – which possibly could work with Jesus involved, but freedom, etc. is best with Jesus), all because this world is evil (man is) – why do you think this world is evil? – satan leading it and man (without Jesus in our life or country, etc.), and most are miserable (and God made it that way, because of sinfulness, and not going to Him), so we need Jesus, and is why we need to (or suffer the consequences of what we do) – to solve this mess we have made (by following satan).

And why we go to psychologists, psychiatry, drugs, etc. – like using a drug is going to solve your problem (satan wanting you to believe and do this) – instead of Jesus (and the Holy Spirit) and the truth of His word. People need to be moral – only with Jesus. Go to Jesus (and His word) to solve your problems.

And if ever communism, socialism, etc. could work, it would be if the rich (many have enough – with true churches helping) in a country (because of capitalism and democracy and freedom, etc.) helping those that need it and deserve it (those that try to make something of themselves – the right way, with hard work, etc.) – not the government doing it, other than just helping a little, and by keeping truth and justice in the nation, and the politicians, leaders, etc. don't get the money (or tell people who to give it to, or who deserves it – other than those that are trying, and show it, and have hardship for a time – not the lazy, criminal, etc.). But do things to help yourself and others (what's best for them). And the only way that (or anything) could ever work out is with Jesus, and sharing Him. But freedom is the best with democracy and capitalism to get the most out of people (all of noah's sons) – work hard, competition, etc. (and fairly and morally – with Jesus), and they can help others that need it and share Jesus (and His word).

And communism comes from the bible (it was a temporary thing back then, thinking Jesus was coming back soon, and the world would end – in **acts 4:32-37**), where all of the jews that believed in Jesus, would sell all of their goods and help each other live and have enough, etc. (and gave them to the disciples to divide up to all Christian jews evenly), but only until Jesus would come back (which would have been soon – before 70 ad – when the temple was destroyed), if the nation of israel would have all believed in and followed Jesus (who needs things, if the world is going to end?), and since they didn't all believe, Jesus did not come back, and those Christian jews that sold things (gave money, etc. – and even ananias and sapphira died – God doing it, for lying and holding back money – **acts 5:1-11**, because Jesus could have come back then, if the jews all would have believed – but that doesn't happen today, because we are in grace – God may let you live, even if you sin – church age, after paul's ministry started) became poor. So the jews (believing ones) gave all they had to the disciples, then they had nothing and were poor – no more assets, income, etc., so peter (jews) and paul (gentiles) both gave to the poor (believers – mainly poor jews) in their ministries (**gal. 2:6-10**). So basically communism leads to being poor, because the leaders may use it all, and eventually is gone – and the leaders are rich – so it certainly cannot work without Jesus, even for a short time.

God allows all evil from man in the world, and lets nations develop, but God puts those in power over them – for their belief – even though it may be against God, and following satan. And God will let it happen in the end.

Nations over the years have tried to control people (really satan) – and keep an eye on them, etc. – like it will be in the tribulation, but it was only here and there (certain nations throughout history) – not the whole world (like before the flood). And not until now, is it possible (with the technology, etc.), in today's world for satan to do that (and who we really are fighting – **eph. 6**). So eventually satan will be able to rule all like before the flood – mainly in the tribulation, but you can see it coming.

So capitalism (and true democracy) is best with all of our talents, etc. and get worth out of life. But only good, fair, moral, honest work. Many more people have a chance, if they work hard, and can help others (more jobs, etc.). Competition (being able to find the best and keep people honest – have choices) is good if done right – especially with Jesus. And why america works.

And america was made and developed by Jesus, and God had the Holy Spirit lead paul in that direction, and away from asia, etc. (**acts 16:4-7**), by going to europe (japheth) to eventually get them to go to america, with true Christians (although satan always follows where man goes, and tries to destroy what God does – man has to make a choice). So japheth was to enlarge (**gen. 9:27**) and God used them to go to a land for Him – america. Sharing Jesus, even today. We have to know the truth.

But many that have come to america and taken advantage of the opportunities, are not necessarily with God (or Jesus). And even when they get things, may still not be happy – only with Jesus can you be. America does help people prosper, etc., even though satan leads people down the wrong road – and some of those businesses don't really help people, but people buy, get hooked on things, etc.

It's strange that those that cause the problems (by their business, or what they sell, etc.) are trying to help (or look like they are helping those in need – because they make money) – so those businesses are causing your problem, then have you pay for them to fix it (they are like criminals, etc. – basically satan) – have a conscience – stop doing what you are doing (to cause the problems for others) and change what you believe in and how you live (and quit your job, etc., if need be). And stop buying from and supporting those businesses (at least cigarettes say they are bad on the packages – even though people still buy them). Don't get hooked, support, keep working there, etc. go with Jesus, and change. Jesus is the best to help you with that. And God will help you with another business, etc. – trust Him.

We are all capable of evil, etc., but we don't need to give in to evil, etc. – and we need to be protected from that evil. Jesus (and His word) is the best, but we need to also do something ourselves – work hard on the right things.

Every country would or could be like america, if they would go to Jesus and follow His truth (be blessed), and share Him (along with helping israel), and having the people run it. And we don't have to be poor – being 'poor' in america is still better than most other countries. Go to Jesus.

Having a country that is run by the government too much (especially an evil one, selfish, no freedom, etc.) – lockdown, etc. is worse than what some people think of the police force, etc. (in a free country) – make sense of what is going on, and take care of yourself and do the right thing – and only Jesus will help you (or a nation) with that (freedom, etc.).

People try to control with violence, fear, etc. – as criminals, governments, etc. do – so they will keep people from resisting or fighting them, but want you to join them – basically what satan does – use violence, death, destruction, fear, etc. to get his way. Not help. Don't let your interests only from noah's sons limit you, especially in america (trying to look nice – then control you). Be with Jesus here helping you – go to Him and succeed. With His freedom for us – Jesus doesn't give us a spirit of fear (**2 tim. 1:7-14**). You don't have to wait for man to do justice (you will be waiting a long time) – just go to Jesus and get justice.

In this world, every trait or ability can be good, but bad, too, including ego, ambition, stubborn, pride, etc. (with Jesus they can be good or changed or you can get rid of them). Why do you have energy to commit crime, hurt, party, drink, etc. (basically to do evil), but no energy to do good (for you or others)? – go to God. Think differently about what is fun, etc. – God (Jesus and His word) will help you with that. If you want justice (evil man deserves death, we all do – that's you), then change the road you are on or don't complain about justice (or injustice) – go to Jesus, the only way to justice. Bad things happen to you when you (or a country, etc. – like God did with the jews and israel at times) do things against God, and good things happen when you do what God wants (He made us that way – stop believing man, scientists, doctors, teachers, and evolution, etc.). Whatever the problems are in the world, it gives people a chance to help others – any of noah's sons, especially with Jesus, and because of Him. So if you have a great life or a not so great life, it is better with Jesus (keep going to Him and His word). Everyone wants to be heard, but no Jesus, then no justice, and if you know Jesus, then you can know justice. You can't fix this evil world – only Jesus can, and only if you go to Him, including children (this world is satan's – **matt. 4:1-11; 2 cor. 4:1-4; 1 john 2:15-16**), so nothing else will work. How can people that have no money make it in this world? – but they do (especially in america) – working hard, do it right, etc. – and the best chance is with Jesus, and anyone can go to Him – no excuses – change your life. Not until then (so stop complaining) – Jesus can change anything (and help you with anything – **philip. 4:13**), and help you get the most out of your life and abilities (and change those barriers that separate man now, and may limit you), but you have to choose Him. Wouldn't it be easier to go to Jesus (and change)? Whatever Jesus changes you to or puts in your life (all in His word – not against it), you will like (maybe not at first, but you will). And keep going to Him. Stop the struggle. We can rest in Jesus (**matt. 11:28-30**). So being drunk, depressed, on drugs, etc. is not an excuse for behavior or getting you out of any punishment, etc. Change with Jesus (with the Holy Spirit).

You want justice – even as a human (even you), so God is that way even more – so Jesus had to come to give justice for man's evil (for all of us that go to Him, and accept it) – it is the only way, so go to Him.

When you want to do the right thing, and have justice (truth), you don't (or shouldn't) care about color, sex, nationality, belief, etc. – or what people think of you (including your own) – just what is right (and truth – God's truth). And there should be punishment (consequences) for what wrong you do (to protect others from you – with laws, police, prisons, etc.).

Both failing and success can help you get ahead and make in this life. Go to and stay with Jesus to make it work and get where you are going. Without Him it won't work.

We are separated in different ways, but the solution is the same – Jesus. All have the opportunity to go to Jesus – japheth, shem, and ham, as different as they are, then they can be one.

Break down all barriers of man – culture, nationality, beliefs, etc. to be one in Jesus (**col. 3:10-11**). And we all can become one (although we are separated now), one in Jesus (**eph. 2**), and that is the only way it (being one – get along, equal, etc.) will work – we can't do it ourselves, even though we keep trying (and fail). Look at the past – our history. For now (since the tower of babel – **gen. 11**), God wants us to be separated (until we go to Jesus). Or we will be one with satan, with those consequences.

God has us and our life planned out with Him – if we just will go to Jesus and start (**eph. 2:10**).

All can be one in Jesus – no matter what son (or daughter) of noah you are (**gal. 3:28**) – so go to Jesus and change your lot or position in life (what you are born as – from noah's sons), and don't let satan keep a hold on you or lead you, and keep you from Jesus – who is the only One that can change you (and help you become what He wants you to be). Otherwise we are all different – even to know there are slave types (servants – bond) and free, jew or gentile, etc. – these are all part of life here on earth (all from noah's sons) – God made it that way, until we all go to Jesus (**gal. 3:26-28**) to be one again (the way God intended us to be when He first created us – **gen. 1 and 2**), and even in heaven we are all the same – no male and female, etc. – like the angels – maybe just male (**matt. 22:29-30**) – and why adam was created alone – God made female out of adam (male).

Jesus sets us free (all of noah's sons – not to be connected to man, whatever son of noah you are, and the limitations that are put on a son that you may be connected to – bond or free – the people from noah – even through abraham – **gen. 21:1-21; gen. 28:6-9; gen. 37:28; gen. 39:1; gal. 4:23**). Jesus does that.

So we are all one, if we are with Jesus – true salvation (with Holy Spirit), here and in heaven. People kind of have to look at life as if they won't be happy without Jesus – don't look elsewhere, even with all of our differences.

And we are (or were) all the same – from adam and noah – not black, white, etc. before the flood (even up to the tower of babel – **gen. 11**). We have to be separated, until we go to God, so satan can't unite man as one. So we are different – for now.

Stop looking on the outside (we didn't use to look like that) – Jesus will change the inside (which is the problem – get the Holy Spirit – get saved, and away from satan, and man).

All of man (jews and gentiles) knows right from wrong (good and evil – from adam – **gen. 2 and 3**) – we are all from adam (jews and gentiles) – we have no excuse (**rom. 1 to 3**). We are now all sinners from noah (and his sons – **gen. 9:18-19**).

God always came to us in many ways, even though man may not go to Him – satan wants you to think you are God, as well as satan wanting to be God – many gods. We are to all go to Him (**eccl. 12:13**) and follow – the reason we are here.

God tried many ways to reconcile man to Him over the years – since adam, but had to keep separating man from each other – so satan can't unite us as one against God, at the same time.

If God didn't keep trying to come to man – through Jesus, then this world would be worse – it's bad enough. We need to go to Him – Jesus (and His truth) – follow Him. That's how much He loves us – who are not that lovable. All of us. And it was man's (adam's) decision to disobey God – and why we are in this situation in the first place. Our – man's, fault.

The love of God – when we are saved with Jesus – means we are no more servants or enemies (and are sons of God), and friends with Jesus (**john 15:9-17**), and one. Not connected to noah's sons anymore.

Love your enemies (which can be all of noah's sons) – only Jesus wants you to and is the only one that can help you do that – what is best for all people (all of noah's sons). Be one with Jesus, then get along with noah's sons – the enemies (which is really satan leading them and you). Loving your enemies is not easy – but the most loving thing you can do is share Jesus with them – or at least pray for them to get to know Jesus.

We are all equal, especially in america, but not until we all go to God, through Jesus. We are separated with noah's sons, but equal in freedom – go to Jesus. You should feel blessed you live in america, no matter what level you are on in society.

Japheth (noah's oldest son and has intellectual talents), goes away from God (it's not just shem or ham) – like man might know more than God, especially what man can see and thinks he knows, what might be right or true – much of what is now in schools, etc., and being taught today – history, science, in a society, even morals, etc. (mostly lies, etc.). All three of noah's sons think they know more than the true God (satan leading them). Don't go away from God – go to Jesus and learn the truth – and live a better life. And none of the sons can rule (at least not very well) without God – Jesus and His word.

In america all have opportunities to use their abilities (Jesus and His freedom), even though the history of america has slaves, as do most countries (including africa, etc. – and at first all man was separated from each other, only with their own kind – a few hundred years after the flood). Whether it is today or in the past – like egypt (in africa – africans and arabs are the first mentioned in the bible selling and buying slaves – about 3700 years ago – joseph's brothers giving him to the arabs – ishmaelites, to bring to egypt – **gen. 37:23-36**) enslaved the jews (shem) – God brought them to egypt – **gen. 15:13-14; gen. 46 to 47** (even though people try to say they didn't, but it did help egypt, and the jews, that they were there, and probably helped them build the pyramids, etc.), about 3600 years ago or so (and the jews were welcomed at first because of joseph – joseph even bought land from the egyptians for the pharaoh – **gen. 47** – but eventually the jews were enslaved) – for some reason there are problems with that even today, so it is possible that a mistake that was made in the past is now hurting us today (or any group or country) – we all (black, white, etc.) have to pay for our mistakes sometime in our life – even slaves and servants do (and not because they became slaves or servants, because there are servants in the world – from ham – **gen. 9:27**). God set all of this up – even for the jews.

And slaves (no matter what country – africa, etc.) were prisoners (with no prisons, etc.) or going to be put to death, etc. – punishment of some kind and were sold to many countries (by africans, etc.) – better to be a slave than put to death. But it's how some people treated them, that was, and maybe still is the problem, (and sometimes how they – the servants, may have treated others, too – we all are guilty) – all of man (including servants sometimes) is this way (and sometimes all of noah's sons may have been enslaved at one time or another in the past) – the jews have been enslaved more than any group of noah's sons – shem (sometimes their own doing) – so stop complaining, crying, etc. But also they (and all of us) should try to forgive and try to fix those problems (which some have been done to a point), but we still have problems, and it's because we don't go to Jesus – all of us (to fight satan, but only with Jesus – **eph. 6:5-13**), servants included. Since blacks (and others from noah's son, ham – even native americans) are put in a struggling position in this world (by God), all of the rest (japheth, shem and others of ham) should try to understand (only sharing Jesus is the answer), but the problem is that not all (of noah's sons) go to Jesus to be understanding – so go to Jesus, and be free (not to satan, who enslaves man – who is who we go to when we don't go to Jesus). Then (and only then) we can have a chance to get along. We are all (all of noah's sons) are supposed to go to Jesus, but will not all be equal – even in america, if we don't. For the world in general, but especially america – it took time to have all of noah's sons to get use to each other – minorities, etc. America wants to have all equal, but had to grow to be that way – like a person grows (like you – you are not perfect) – but just like a person, a nation needs Jesus to work best – go to Jesus and see the change – like we have at times in america. And america became a nation, even with the evil of man (and not all going to or doing what God wanted), because God wanted it. Go to Him and make it an easier (and in some cases, a faster) time of doing things – for you and others. By going to God – Jesus and His word.

Everyone is stuck with noah's sons, and whatever life they or their people live, or how they are treated – there is no escaping that, except with Jesus. So stop trying it any other way – even though america helps all of noah's sons to do that in this world.

We will never solve the hate, crime – 'racism', etc. without Jesus – all of noah's son against each other, because we stay connected to them – staying sinful, and separate, until we get away from man.

Why would people – groups, nationalities, etc. (especially those from noah's son, ham) resort to uncivilized, violent, etc. ways to deal with things in their life (even in their home, america, etc.), when they fall apart – getting rid of any control of society, government, etc. – instead of building back up to be civilized again, etc.? But all of noah's sons are to blame.

People don't care about right or wrong – just hate. Get away from noah's sons (man) and beliefs and connections, etc. that those people and cultures, etc. believe. Go to Jesus and change to what God wants for you – for us. Then care about all and get them to all go to Jesus and the truth of His word. Otherwise we all have to suffer the consequences that are here in this world, if we don't.

Talk to each other about noah's three sons (after the flood, and still about adam, and creation and man's fall – to sin – **gen. 3**) – then we will solve and find the answer – not until then – and churches (Christians) should start that – then teach it in schools, etc. It all leads to Jesus. God did it for that reason.

People are and were still evil to each other, before the flood (when everyone looked the same). and after the flood – even today in countries where most people look the same – so it's the not color, etc. that people are, that makes problems (although prejudice, etc. is real, and makes it stand out more), but it is our sinfulness that causes it (always has and always will – and satan will always use that) – and is more prevalent with noah's sons today (when our appearances changed). Go to Jesus to change that – to get over that and become one – equal, etc.

People, groups, etc. need to go to God (Jesus and His word) to make changes in the world, nation, society, family, etc., not man trying to do it – or it will go wrong or out of control, like you have seen in america. We need to wait on God's timing, but it has to be with Him making the changes, with us going to Him. And then it will happen faster, if it is what we should be doing, but God has to be a part of it, not just man or groups, agenda, beliefs, etc. Go to Jesus. Or we continue to struggle, like we have seen.

We are still all from noah's three sons (that hasn't changed, just like we are all sinful from adam), and struggling now, as we have in the past (because we didn't learn from before the flood). Only Jesus will change that. The other countries religions, cultures, etc. are evil and don't treat people properly, because Jesus is not there with them – america tries to treat people right – people hurt themselves without Jesus and suffer consequences, evil, etc.

So God has limited satan (mainly after the flood and tower of babel – separating us) – and has Jesus available for all (all of noah's sons) – so today we all have a chance, if we would just go to Jesus (and learn and believe His word).

And we all (everyone in the world) has had a chance to go to Jesus (slaves or not) for the last 2,000 years – no excuse for any one or any country, etc. So go now, if you haven't and change.

God put some limits on nimrod (ham – **gen. 9 and 10 and 11**) – and those from him. So ham is the servant of japheth and shem, but canaan is the servant of all – it says a servant (canaan) of servants – ham (**gen. 9:22-25**) – and at that time we all looked the same – skin color, etc. And that includes blacks, native americans, arabs, maybe asians, and others, etc. around the world – now and in the past. And we can't get away from being connected to noah's sons, except by going to Jesus – the way He set it up. That (all of noah's sons) is the ancestry you need to find out about.

Even the native americans have to get over what they went through when america changed – God did this, and they need to go to Jesus and will get through it – otherwise it will continue to be tough – all of noah's sons will suffer until they go to Jesus. And this isn't our final home on this earth – heaven or hell is – you choose. Go to Jesus and be in heaven and help us all.

Jesus reaches many nations – especially today – through america – with all of noah's sons, going back to all countries to preach the truth of Jesus. But we need to follow Him and share Him while we can. And eventually in the end times all can and will know who Jesus is in terrible times (**ezek. 38**). But we have to know where we came from and know how come this world (and people) are the way they are here today.

Ham (blacks – but only became darker skin after the tower of babel, about 400 years or so later – and look like we do today) is the majority of africa (**gen. 10**) – having some diversity (some of japheth and shem – some through slavery), but back then – right after the flood and the tower of babel – the physical part (of man – there were differences in noah's sons) was powerful then (just up to and a little after the tower of babel – then God balanced it out, and had japheth and shem have more power, etc. – **gen. 9:27** – with technology, etc.). We all (noah's sons) have been separated since (**gen. 11**). We still are today, and suffer from that – but it is best until we go to Jesus, because of satan and sin.

And all of noah's sons have hurt each other (none are innocent – that means you) – but God's will has to be done (not our will) – don't fight Him or those with Him and His plans.

Prisoners, criminals, rapists, killers, etc. need to be punished – even 400 to 500 years ago – but most nations may not have had prisons, so they enslaved them – even africa, etc. – and sold them, and made money, trade, etc. to all nations. Man is (all of noah's sons are) this way.

Africa (as other countries, including the americas, etc.), was not a great place to live, and still isn't in most places – God knows what He is doing. If it wasn't for slavery, etc., there would be no blacks – africans, etc. in america (africa wasn't great back then, and neither was america yet, as the rest of the world wasn't) – at least not many blacks (and that saved some of their lives then – they were meant for death if they stayed there – in africa, etc.), and would have not come here until recently (to get the benefits of freedom, opportunities, etc. here, that they wouldn't get in africa, the world, etc. – especially to get to know Jesus – for the native americans, too) – and america would look different today, in more ways than one (and the same with the jews in egypt, then to israel, but they have to obey God – Jesus, in both israel and america) – all of noah's sons working together, and to all get to know Jesus (and His truth) to make america great. They (minorities, etc.) should be thankful, as we all should be (including native americans – they have it better today or could if they wanted to – all now can go to Jesus, and need to – but it has to be the truth, not lies of these false churches, etc. from satan). And even in america, 10% of the people owned 90% of the slaves – most people – black or white, struggled here. There were some bad and nice slave owners, and good and bad slaves – Jesus will help you be nice and work hard. Not all are nice in the world either – slaves, owners, etc. – anyone (including you). Don't make it worse (**eph. 6:5-9; col. 3:22-25;1 tim. 6:1-2; titus 2:9-15; 1 pet. 2:18-25**). Noah's sons had to get use to each other, and to the way God made us different (all from noah's sons – **gen. 9:27**) – and the fact that america wanted all to be equal, but with Jesus, not without Him (it wouldn't work without Him). We have to have the servants and owners be Christian and work hard – both with Jesus, and stay where you are in life – but now with Jesus in your life – if you can go free – go free (**1 cor. 7:20-24**), but be with Jesus – and be His servant.

God sets everything up in the world and has sinful man to do it, so He has to get us to go to Him, as He sets everything up here.

God even talks of slaves, servants, etc. (He knew man would do that – because of how He made noah's sons, and their lot in life – we can't get away from that, with evil here, until we go to Jesus). So slaves, servants, etc. in israel would work for six years and be free in the seventh year – God gave rules for them (**exo. 21:1-6**) – people try to do what's best in this life – but man is still evil here (and all need to go to Jesus).

It is satan that mistreats slaves, servants, etc. – get mad at him and go to Jesus, but God separated man – noah's sons – so we all need to go to God (and His word) for our benefit.

In the past (and even today) in the world, africans used to go against africans, native americans against native americans, hispanics against hispanics, asians against asians, whites against whites, etc. – man as a whole does that – not just one group (and happened in all countries over the years). So no one or group is innocent, now or in the past (today all of the nations are evil, even without diversity, they go against each other – as we also saw before the flood – **gen. 6** – when we all looked and talked the same). And we all need to go to Jesus (and the truth of His word), for us all to change. So it is not white against black, etc. – it is man against man (satan leading – **eph. 6:10-20**) – we are all evil, sinful, etc., until we all go to Jesus.

And people are owed nothing and shouldn't be (thinking you should be, just holds you back) – just work and be thankful you are in america, but go to Jesus – all could in the last 2,000 years – He will give you what you need and change things for good (**matt. 6:33**). Go to Jesus and help others that need Him, too.

If you think that people owe you (minorities, etc.), and you resort to stealing, crime, hate, disrespect, hurting others, etc. (all satanic), then you are no better than some slave owners, and are racist, etc. – don't make things worse, even on yourself. Go to Jesus and change yourself, and others. Make things better.

All of the world is God's, and He wants to put His people in places (to counter satan and his plans against God) – like jews in israel and now Christians in america – there is enough land, etc. for all – to give man a chance to go to Jesus.

Man is so evil – his hatred, selfishness, etc. – doesn't let him think straight or make sense. Look at yourself and stop getting back at others. Make sense – go to Jesus and the truth of His word.

For jews or gentiles – all of noah's sons – are punished to third and fourth generations (**exo. 20:3-6**), without God – the true God. Knowing how slaves are treated and live, gives us an understanding of what sin does to us – it enslaves us – we all are slaves to satan, false beliefs (rich, poor, white, black, etc.).

Japheth started most false churches (in the past and today) – all of noah's sons are led by satan – starting with ham – at the tower of babel (**gen. 11**). We all need to know the truth and go to Jesus ourselves to get away from noah's sons – away from man (who tries to be a god, like satan – **isa. 14:12-17**). Don't follow man or satan. We are not perfect, so go to the Lord Jesus Christ. We need to make that choice to make things better here – while we are still here. And then be ready to go with Him.

Not all people that came to america at the beginning were Christian (at least true Christians – satan always follows God to destroy with lies, evil, etc.). False churches, beliefs, etc. – like (at the start in the 1600's), as many as other so-called Christians (different denominations, etc.), came from europe at the beginning of america, as well as true Christians trying to get away from evil, satanic false church (controlling all of europe, and now tries to control the whole world still today – killing true Christians, and others against that church) – which the black plague (sent by God) diminished that church for a while (1300's to 1700's) – and they are not true Christians (even though some churches that came here had some good things, but witch hunts, killing, etc. – like puritans, etc., were and are not necessary, since we all are evil, and need to keep going to Jesus and His word to grow, change, etc., and anyone can become saved, no matter how evil we are, or for how long – as long as we are still alive). Let God take care of most of these people. Not all americans are Christians – true Christians, so there are evil people (noah's sons) – slaves, or owners (black or white) and people mistreat people (satan leading), but regardless – you go to Jesus (but the truth), and change yourself and attitude. America had to grow and learn as a person does with God – while still dealing with the evil of noah's sons. Even the pilgrims that first got here had problems with the native americans and were killed, etc. – so the natives (the same as all of us) – were not as caring as you think (some just protecting, defending, etc., and others controlling, hating, etc.) – even to each other (one tribe against another in their own country, land, etc. since they got here – after the flood, mainly after the tower of babel – about 4,000 years ago). But God still wanted this country to grow, and eventually share Jesus. And He had to deal with evil man (all of noah's sons).

God uses what man builds, etc. – even if it is not initially for God – eventually God will take over there and use what was made to reach the world – even from those that don't follow Him, and has used them throughout history – like europe, americas, etc. – even like the promise land for the jews – israel, was occupied by others at first (**exo. 23; num. 13 to 15**).

Even the building of america, at the beginning – starting with the original thirteen colonies – and the flag that shows that still on it – the thirteen stripes, are all related to Jesus (america is Jesus' land) in a way, when He was here on earth – with the twelve disciples. If you add the twelve disciples and Jesus together you get thirteen (even though one was judas, and betrayed Jesus – but they picked another disciple after judas killed himself and Jesus died and rose – **acts 1**). So america comes out of the bible and Jesus and the jews. God wanted america to be here in the end times to share Jesus and the His truth to the world. All land is God's – even with evil man. All God's plan throughout the bible to show His truth for us.

Any group or people going to any country (maybe trying to take over, or just wanting to live there, and get along) is not going to be welcomed – by the natives, etc. (even the natives weren't nice to each other). Man is evil to each other. Jesus is who you should share with any country, if you can, and eventually make it work (and why america works, when it does). And anyone coming to this country today.

Those that came to america at the beginning, did have an influence on belief here – but we need to know the truth – go to Jesus and go to His word. And be aware of satan, and continue to follow Jesus. Know the truth and go to Jesus yourself – and get the Holy Spirit to be saved – we all can be saved, and God wants us to be (**john 3:16**). And help others to learn and grow and get to know Jesus – including those in america – natives or otherwise.

All of us are evil before we go to Jesus – and until we do, we go to, and are led by satan – but we can only go to Jesus and be forgiven and saved, before we die – no matter what we have done or how evil we are. There should be no hate for others, just share Jesus and help them know the truth and get saved, too. And God will do what is necessary for people – punishment, etc. – but wants all to go to Jesus and be saved – it is satan and those that follow him (even if they look like they are Christian) that may kill someone. It is satan that wants to destroy, kill, etc. (no witch hunts, etc. – just tell the truth). We need to be alive to be saved – but man is evil, and death happens, so be ready, with Jesus.

God doesn't want to force people (anyone) to go to Jesus – slave or owner – all of noah's sons, but if you have a miserable life, then you go to Jesus, and if not, you are guilty. Anyone (God knows) at any time can go to Jesus – pray to Him now. God will keep you alive to go to Jesus – God knowing you will (no matter how long or how many struggles you have), but also God knows who will never go to Him – and those may die some how (and some that you may know). Help those alive, including yourself. Go to Jesus now.

If you don't think that man is (or that america is) connected to the people who came before us (adam, noah's sons, etc., besides your ancestors), and all have responsibility for their actions, etc., then why does any group (blacks, native americans, etc.) want payment (or retribution, etc.) for past injustices, etc. (by others, whites, etc.)? – we all (blacks, native americans, etc. included) are guilty for what man (including them) did before to anyone – even their own (and also for today). And if so, why doesn't central and south america feel that way about the spaniards (who took over and interbred with the natives)? Or the jews – slaves in egypt (africa), or even more recent with germany (to the jews and others) in world war II. So we have to go way back in time for our behavior (all of us – even for the evil your grandfather did, etc.), not just a few hundred years ago (but back to adam, noah, etc. – all of man – black or white, etc.). No one is owed anything – all of noah's sons would be owed then – it's even, so move on – and go to Jesus, and His word to keep finding His truth. The bible is truth, whether you believe it or not.

And all can go to Jesus – take that as your payment.

We are all connected to the past (all the way to adam).

Even Jesus is considered (connected as) the Son of david – and mary (**matt. 1:1, 16; matt. 9:27,** and other verses) – even though joseph (who is also considered the son of david – **matt. 1:20**) is His earthy father (but not by blood – it was the Holy Spirit, God the Father, for Jesus). God put Jesus' ancestry in the bible all the way back to noah's son, shem, and to adam (**luke 3:23-38** – and adam was the son of God when he was created – before his sin).

Even in **acts 6 and 7**, stephen talks of moses, jews, and Jesus – the truth of history leading up to Jesus – including that a Prophet will come from the jews – Jesus (**deut. 18:18**) – the Messiah that they were supposed to anoint (the most Holy – **dan. 9:24**) – which the jews didn't – they rejected and killed Jesus. And peter mentions that same Prophet in **acts 3:11-26**. We have to know the truth of all of this – it is in His word. And know where we come from and go to Jesus to change that.

Stop being connected to noah's sons (or adam). Break down all of the barriers with Jesus.

Jesus came to change all of that – the last Adam (**1 cor. 1:44-49**). So we can be free.

Anyone can be a slave, servant, etc. (all of noah's sons have) – or made to be a servant, etc., because man is evil – led by satan. Still being connected to noah's sons (all were at one time). Who are you a slave to? Stop it with Jesus (**rom. 6:16**).

Jesus abolishes slavery – the truth of Him (and His word) does. So no excuse for anyone, in the past or today. The reason blacks got free in america at all – is because of Jesus – people were fighting Jesus. Jesus is freedom – satan enslaves.

Blacks (ham, or anyone – any of noah's sons) will keep getting punished by God (and even by satan, and those that follow him – even some black churches, etc.) until they go to Jesus (and His word – the truth of it), and stop living and thinking the way they do (being a victim, oppressed, etc. – and thinking man is the answer to the problem they have). Even though in america, it is better for minorities, etc., than the rest of the world. Go to Jesus, if you don't want to be oppressed, etc. We all are still connected to noah's sons, and all of the problems, until we go to Jesus – no matter where you live or what you try (stop living in darkness).

The answer is still Jesus (and His word – the truth) for the solution (not man) – for any problem here in this world – now or in the past. To get away from the connection to man – connected to adam, and to noah's sons. And not think you have any chance, because of who and where you are born. Be born again with Jesus (**john 3**). Then you will see the change in your life, and others (even a nation, etc.).

A new life, new creature, new creation (**2 cor. 5:16-21**), and away from man – noah's sons.

And if we are one with Jesus – no difference, then there is a difference to begin with – all from noah's sons.

If you are going to be enslaved, then be enslaved by Jesus, not man, the world, satan, etc. – america (Jesus' land) needs to go to Jesus – God will win and so will you (and america), if you do go to Him (but the truth). You are not going to have good results helping people – minorities, etc. (even all of noah's sons) without Jesus (and the truth of His word) – because all you have is evil man (and satan) making or not making deals with them. Go to Jesus first and have them go to Him, too. And why america has had some good changes.

You have to get connected to God – the true God, to get His blessing in this life, for anything, and that is only through Jesus – with the Holy Spirit, that only He can give us – then follow Him (and the truth of His word) – and is what makes america great (as much as we can be in this evil world – evil, because man follows satan).

Life here is for God – it is short (**eccl. 12:13-14; james 4:14**) – we just have to go to Jesus and know the truth.

God can only fulfill your needs here best (He made us), through Jesus – love, life, work, relationships, needs, etc. – so don't waste time doing it yourself – go to Jesus, and get the Holy Spirit, and learn and change and grow. Otherwise we are stuck being connected to man (adam first, and now noah's sons), and the problems they (we) keep having. You go to Him now – pray to Jesus.

No human knows who they are until they go to Jesus (God) and follow. We are all lost here (all of noah's sons) – fooling ourselves and others.

Even in the ten commandments – if you are not with God (the truth), it hurts you, and your children, grand kids, and beyond – to the third and fourth generations (**exo. 20:3-6**) – you do it to yourself and your descendants – without Jesus.

So ham, shem, and japheth (all of us) all need to go to Jesus (then we can be one, and not separated, but not until then). We should all be thankful we are in america to get to follow Jesus (and His word), or the problems will never be solved. People want to come to america and stay here – freedom – that is with Jesus, like Jesus dying for this country (like He has for all). This country is better for all people (those before, too, as hard as it might have been), but they have to try, and go to Jesus, then they will see, so let the past go, and go to Jesus (native americans, as well as africans have it better here – more opportunities, freedom, etc., but especially can have Jesus).

Anything good that happened in america (or for us, or the world, etc.) is from Jesus (**john 15:4-6**). It won't happen without Him (in each of our lives or nation, etc.). But we have to go to Him and keep following Him and His word – faith in Him and His ways and timing.

Being in america is the best for anyone – blacks, minorities, etc. included, then anywhere in the world (no matter how you got here). Like in the 1950's in america, blacks were doing well (not all were, just like not all whites, etc. were), and not perfect, but doing well (better) – possibly america was blessed for all, since the jews were able to go back to their land (israel) again, in 1948 (being helped and freed from being captive and persecuted in world war II – **gen. 12:2-3**). And israel tries to help others around the world when they can, since they became a nation in 1948 (but they still need to defend themselves – God gave them that land, just like america is for Jesus, and needs to be defended). Man keeps struggling with this – but you can't fight God (**acts 5:38-39**).

CHAPTER 8

Christian Living: Practical Applications of Christian Living According to The Word of God, The Bible - The Truth of It

There are still primitive people (ham) around the world (in jungles of south america and elsewhere – even native americans would still be living primitively here in america, if japheth – the europeans, didn't show up until recently – like last year, etc.), but only ham (still living simply, etc. – and they like that way of life) would be living simply, not japheth or shem (although they do struggle, too) – we need all of us together (all three sons of noah) to get the most out of man (using all of noah's sons' abilities, talents, etc.), especially with Jesus, like america is (and will only be good as long as we go to Jesus and His word). And america is because Jesus helped the true Christians have a place to live – and why it is so good (compared to other nations, etc.).

There are civilized people and uncivilized people in the world (all from noah's sons), but both are evil, and need to go to Jesus to change – no matter what son of noah you are from and limitations that God has put on you. We can all be saved. All of noah's sons can help each other, and need each other – with their talents and abilities, etc. Then there will be change.

A good example of a change to a land is australia – when the english sent their prisoners to australia to be punished, survive, etc. When they got there and were dropped off, they had to make it work for themselves in a primitive land – just the natives (aborigines, etc. – ham) were there (for about close to 4,000 years – after they scattered to there – God wanting man to – after the tower of babel, about 100 – 500 years after the flood – overspread the whole earth – **gen. 9:18-19; gen. 10; gen. 11**), and it still was primitive around the 1700's when the prisoners were put there. But from then to now, the english (japheth) built up that country to what it is today (just like america was when people came here around 1500's to 1700's). It is better today.

Are blacks, minorities, etc. better off (especially in america) than they were 400 years ago, 200 years ago, 100 years, 50 years, 10 years, etc.? – yes – do we still have 'racism'? – yes. Man cannot change that (no matter how many programs, etc. – good or bad, that we come up with – we will still be separated) – but God can (since He is the one that separated us in the first place), and it is through Jesus (and the truth of His word), to become one (and only through God – Jesus can we become one – away from noah's sons). All problems through noah's three sons – still are separated and man will not be able to change that, and some, like the son ham (and descendants), will struggle. Even true black Christians have to be leery of ham coming to power again – just like after the flood at the tower of babel – nimrod (the son of ham, but there were no differences in color of skin yet, back then – **gen. 10 and 11**). It's not blacks, it's just the descendants of ham (especially canaan) that is the issue (**gen. 9:27**) – who eventually had their skin change after the tower of babel and the language change (because of the climate, weather, geography, etc. change about 400 – 500 years after the flood – some of the descendants of noah's sons stayed in the warmth of the heat of the sun – near the equator – ham, and others migrated farther north and south – japheth and shem, and all became darker or lighter, etc.) that scattered man all over the world – so some of noah's son ham, stayed near the equator – still there today.

Jesus made any good changes for minorities, or anyone, in america (or in the world) over the years. Man can't do it.

Those same people (mainly from ham) – that have certain abilities, like in sports (in america), most of the athletes are black (african, etc. – from ham), especially in professional sports (even though most people participate at all levels), where there is a lot of money to be made (and they can use a lot of that money to help others that are struggling – staying out of drugs and crime, etc., and those that could use help by starting businesses, and to help those that are honest and in need in this nation, and some athletes do – by not just buying many things for themselves, and losing their money, etc.), and they are some of the richest people in america (and that wouldn't happen for them if they still were in africa – and why God made america, so all people – all of noah's sons, could rise to their potential, talents, etc. – only in a country for Jesus) – they should be grateful. And the percentage of blacks in sports is about 70-75% (not in all sports, but the main ones, and most popular in america, and even though golf is popular, for example, it doesn't always appeal to an athlete, not physical enough, etc. – but more whites and asians play and are good, and also some sports take more money than others to play, like golf, etc., although others play later in life), and the percentage for blacks in america is about 15% (those sports don't represent the country percentages, if that is important in all types of work) – is that job discrimination (like the harlem globetrotters – who are not from harlem, are all black – not even one or two whites, hispanics, asians, etc.)? These groups are fine, as long as they don't hurt people or cause people to be hurt. And there is a difference between brute strength or natural ability, and working hard on techniques, etc. (which all can do to be better). All (black, white, etc.) should have a chance to use their abilities, talents, etc. to live, and be fair to all (the hardest workers, should get the best chance, not the lazy or rich, etc.).

When you do have things, and given things and opportunities, freedoms, etc., like in america, you also have responsibility to be a good example – as a parent, citizen, celebrity, politician, athlete, etc. – go to Jesus and His word to be able to do this.

Even rich black people are having people to pay too much – for sports, entertainment, things that go with it, etc., when they should be saving money for food, family, etc. Everyone is guilty. But we need to be smart with our money, and maybe not do some things.

An example of japheth helping ham (especially in america) is sports (**gen. 9:22-27**), like basketball – japheth came up with it, but ham excelled at it – and making a living, etc. today. All can make money from it. America is for all of noah's sons – and God made america for all – especially to get to know and share Jesus. So eventually we would not be separated anymore – one in Christ. But not all go to Jesus, although we all have the opportunity to – so we stay separated (and don't get along) until we do.

People can't help it if they are black or white, etc. (where and what we are born into), but can all eventually go to Jesus and learn the truth of His word and follow it – even if it looks like it is against them – go to Jesus and change your attitude, etc.

America has most of noah's sons – most diversity and the biggest (all of noah's sons) – and why america does well in sports – olympics, etc. in the world.

Even though we are all born evil (without the Holy Spirit) we also all have talents and need to work hard – but need to thank God for them, just like for school, arts, music, etc., and for sports (most sports – like basketball, volleyball, even football, etc.). You can improve your abilities (including strength, muscles, etc.), but know that God gave them to you, including your size (or height), etc. – but you can't change that, and have nothing to do with that (**matt. 6:27; luke 12:25**), as other things God has given us, and will give us, if we go to Him. And man has taken advantage of what God gave us (all of noah's sons) – so we need to go to Him, and be appreciative of that.

No matter what son of noah you are, you can work harder, if you need to – to be good at something, you may not be as natural at (goes for anything). Like in sports, japheth may have to work harder on techniques (not just brute strength or natural athletic ability), but ham could be even better, if they worked on techniques, etc., and not just rely on natural ability, etc.

Most people can do manual labor and need to, but most don't like it, or are not as good at it, even though Ham might be. Also, some women may like doing certain things more than men, but men may do them too and vice versa. But all of noah's sons - japeth and shem and ham, want to be comfortable and relaxed (like before the flood).

In the world, and especially in the america, there are many opportunities for all.

Since there are so many high schools and colleges in america, that many whites (and any other nationalities, etc. – all of noah's sons) are needed to play all sports (and many are good) – and shows that all should go into any area of work, because you may find you're better than you think, especially if you work hard (and in america) – for any talent or line of work (and sometimes you have to do what you need to do to work and pay bills, etc. – be grateful and don't complain nor be tempted to go to crime, etc.). And if you are with Jesus, He will help you with your talents, and give you what you need (**matt. 6:33**), and lead you where to go in life. And don't waste your money on things that are not good for you, or God will not bless you.

All of the things we do and enjoy in this world should not come first – God and His word should. Learn and share Jesus and His word – the truth. All of noah's sons – then see where God leads you – the answer would be to help and love people, too. But God wants us to change - get saved and let the Holy Spirit change us - go to Jesus to do that. We need to do things right. Like when moses and the israelites were leaving egypt and were at the red sea - God said, be still and He would help them and He did by parting the red sea (**exo. 14:10-22; psalm 46:10**). We also need to listen to God and see what He has for us.

Keep going to and praying to Jesus, and reading the truth of His word to get through this world.

Have to live the life God wants and says to, not just hear (**james 1:19-27**), or just go to church, etc., or you will live a miserable life. Go to Jesus – God will help you.

Be with people in the victories, and the defeats – to help people through whatever they go through, and to get better.

Even laughing and crying is a part of life – God allowing and giving us those to help us get through this evil world – but go to Jesus and heal and change to a better life – no matter what.

All of noah's sons can be nice and friendly – growing up with people, no matter who they are, but it only takes a few to ruin things. We all need to be changing and growing – with Jesus is the best – the only way for all to get along. And things in this world can help us to be friendly to others – doing the same things we do.

And hobbies, sports, activities, etc. – relaxing things, to help us mentally, and can bring people together – and meet new people, etc. (maybe different people) – but don't use them instead of Jesus (and His word) – we can learn most things – we (all of noah's sons) all have abilities, etc.

So some people get along (all of noah's sons) – grow up together (mainly in america) – school, sports, neighborhoods, work, etc. – but even those don't always keep people together – only with Jesus will it work.

The last 250 years has helped all of noah's sons – because of america – mainly because of Jesus – giving all of noah's sons a chance to grow and improve, and live a better life – but with Jesus, and go around the world to share Him. God made it that way. The world is available to all – talents, etc. – as is Jesus.

There are many things to do in this world – people can even learn things like juggling, magic tricks, acrobatics, etc. – it's not easy or even natural, but people have to work hard and learn them (take time) a certain way (as most things are and should be) – a right and best way to do them. Find out about yourself from Jesus. Even music, art, poems, writing, etc. – expressions of man's struggle (and love, success, etc.), and to help others along with the ability to cry, laugh, etc. – all that God gave us, so we can deal with this tough life here (**psalm 126:2**), but it is Jesus that does it, go to Him and He will help you through it all (**matt. 11:28-30**). But all music or art, etc. is not godly or good.

It is good to have things for everyone, if possible, in all areas of life (we are all different, with abilities – all of noah's sons), like america has, and tries to – but you have to try and work hard, but the best is with Jesus. And try to help each other.

One person can study for ten minutes and get an 'A' on a test, and another person has to study for three days to get an 'A' – they both got an 'A', but one had to study more. So work harder – it may not be natural. Each of noah's sons have talents (different), but all can do most things, but need to work harder on some, since it may not be natural for them. But stop complaining, just work harder, if you have to. Plus you will get better at something if you keep working and don't give up. God made us that way after the flood – so it is best to go to Him – to Jesus.

Most minorities that don't want tests for schools, jobs, etc. (because they feel it's 'racist', etc. – but don't mind tests in sports, etc. that they may be good at), and think it is a demeaning process itself (all should move ahead with ability, fairness, etc.), and should make them learn and work harder (not easier, or not try, etc.). And it shows that they – the minorities, are 'racist' themselves – not just other groups, etc. doing it. Even commercials, ads, etc. are 'racist', labeling, etc. – trying to attract a certain group, or nationality, etc. with how they portray them in the ad – behavior, lifestyle, etc. And minorities don't always treat each other correctly, kind, etc., and get away with all kinds of 'racist' behavior with each other (as other of noah's sons do) – we all do.

It's your character that has to change and grow. Just work hard and learn and grow, don't let satan (or man, nationality, the world) run your life. Go to Jesus, if you want to level the playing field. We can all learn, but have different abilities. But stop blaming others – look at yourself (and your own, etc.).

Why would they need anything like affirmative action, if everyone has the same interests and abilities and are good at them? But we don't – and if not, we all need to work harder at what we may not be as good at (if we wanted to be fair to everyone). There is a difference in people (and there should be the right and best person for the job – black, white, woman, etc.) – God made us that way (from noah's three sons – **gen. 9**), separating us (from satan's control of us – all being the same evil all at the same time). God set this all up (who we are – because of sin, adam, and now noah's sons) and Jesus will help you best, and give you what you need in this world, if you would just go to Him and follow Him (**matt. 6:33**).

Whoever is best for a job – not an agenda, etc. (like girls in boys sports, etc. – just to make a point) – the best players should be playing (don't punish someone else), or even transgender issues, etc. – girl or boy, is not good for man and not what God wants. Don't fight God and His truth (like satan did and does).

People have had opportunities of all kinds – especially in america – no matter who you are – white, black, rich, poor, man, woman, etc. – any of noah's sons. But they may not be living right in their life to take advantage of these things, and have hurt their chances – their own fault. Go to Jesus first.

All of noah's sons' abilities, talents, etc. are useful, but not more than you can get with God's word – the truth. Go to Jesus and His word and learn the truth to help you through this world.

Just because people – certain ones of noah's sons – struggle here, doesn't mean we can't treat them right – be nice to, help, etc. – especially share Jesus. Then we can all be one in Jesus.

It's nice that people (groups, etc.) stand up for themselves (and others), but it has to be peaceful and right, and it won't work, or be good, without God (Jesus) – no matter how loud you yell, etc. (or how many years you try – the problems are still here). Go to Jesus (and His word) for it to work – for anything to work here. Use your talents, or improve yourself in other areas. Change to what He wants for us.

People speak up in this world about everything – for rights, justice, treatment, etc., but all is not good, and all is not what God wants. So help people, and make an effort to do good things, but not against God (or those that are with God – Jesus), and don't side with those that are against God and the truth of His word – know that you are with Him, we all have had a chance to know Him (**rom. 1:18-32**) – go to Jesus, or God will not help you. And satan's lies will lead you to destruction, sticking up for the wrong things.

We can stand up for things, but all are not good – don't picket or protest, etc. things of this world, that are against God and His word, picket and stand up for Jesus and the truth of His word. We will being going against God and what He wants for man and this world, and will struggle.

So watch what you believe and stand up for – you may be going against God and His plans and beliefs (**acts 5:38-39**). And be kind to people – help and care (the best you can – and they need to help themselves, too), but know the truth – share Jesus, but His truth. Be persecuted for truth, not lies (of this world, satan, man, etc.) – wherever you share in this world, make sure it is the truth of His word, and truly Jesus. To all of noah's sons.

Suffer here for Christ's sake – not for crime, evil, etc. (**1 pet. 4:12-16**).

Let God fight for your rights – whatever talents, etc., and whoever you are and what's best for you – not what you or the world says or wants. Go to Jesus and the truth of His word. Any of noah's sons (and daughters) can work hard.

All of noah's sons can learn things, but must put the time and effort in, and work hard (depending on the career, etc.) – like you see in america (showing all of the abilities of noah's sons, and seeing the possibilities), but most of ham, especially canaan, may not care about some things, if they are by themselves – being more physical, simple life, etc. – the way God made them (**gen. 9:27**), after the flood.

But when you get a good job, move up in the world, get your wishes met, get the world to help you and your struggle, etc., then you have to handle responsibility, etc. Be a good example – know what that is, and then help others, too.

Before the flood, all of man – from adam (given by God) had abilities to live and grow and build and move ahead, and all people were similar (**gen. 4**) – so probably before the flood, people had all abilities, talents, etc. and decided what they were interested in, if it was necessary, etc. – but after the flood, God separated the abilities, so man – noah's sons, all had different abilities (especially after the tower of babel – **gen. 11**), but some were physical, and liked the simple life (and some still do today – mainly ham).

We make things, invent, and discover things, etc. – by God's abilities, that He gave us (and today after the flood, is mostly through japheth). And we even look at His creation and make things – like birds, and we made planes, etc. Things man makes evolve, not God's things (no evolution – just satan's lies, to get you away from God and His truth – in His word, God created).

Don't listen to your own – noah's sons (satan leading), listen to Jesus and the truth of His word. Do what's best and right – and grow – quit taking short cuts. Work hard with family, etc. to help them. There are things that are more interesting to each of noah's sons, than to the other – just the way we are made (by God) – until we go to Jesus – like in america, giving all of the sons a chance to succeed, (and to see the possibilities, etc.). So stop brainwashing each other to do evil, feel like you are deserved or owed something, a victim, etc. – living any way you want. Quit feeling sorry for yourself – if you do, go to Jesus and His word. God made you that way (**gen. 9; rom. 9**), and is the only way you can get out of it – is with Jesus, otherwise satan is leading you with your connection still to noah's sons (and their abilities, and lot in life). Stop fighting it or each other.

Staying with man – noah's sons – doesn't move man ahead or to be better (we are basically devolving) – just seems that way, especially with technology, travel, knowledge (even though most is false, etc.) – man's things evolve – ideas, beliefs, lies, etc., not God's. Go to Jesus and the truth of His word to change, or you will keep spinning your wheels, with yourself and with others.

Man will never solve the world's problems – go to God and His word.

One group or belief, etc. that starts up seems to cause another group to start up, etc. (radical or not) – against each other – that's the way man (and satan) is (and always has been since adam sinned), but it is all against God (the true God) and His word eventually. That is caused by God separating man – after the flood (appearance, language, nationality, culture, ability, etc.), so that satan can't control all of man (all of noah's sons) at the same time and for the same reason (even though they are usually always against God – but not together like before as one – **gen. 6; gen.11**). Have to go to Jesus (and His word) to solve all of this.

Growing into a man or woman that is best for you and others is with Jesus, and His word (the truth of it). We try to find many other ways and they don't work out.

God is looking down, wondering why we don't go to Him – go to Jesus. Just like when all of noah's sons, led by ham – nimrod, all as one – built the tower of babel – eventually they all split (scattered like God wanted) up after that around the world, with their many talents, languages, etc. – mainly separated and not working together – so satan couldn't bring them together all against God like before (**gen. 6; gen. 11**). Now having all (of noah's sons) together in america – but this time with Jesus (the only way for all of us to have a chance to get along). God did all of that for a reason.

No matter what you do or try, you are going to hurt or hinder or offend someone or some group (of noah's sons) – find out what God wants – go to Jesus. Otherwise it is one of satan's teams – and he has many (and none good).

Women against men, men against women, black against white, white against black, liberals against conservatives, atheists against religious, many groups and beliefs, here and around the world, nation against nation, etc. – all start up and fight, etc. – be on the best team or group – be with Jesus.

Some people switch teams and are the enemy to their last team – you don't want to hurt those on your own team, so be on the team that you can help all (Jesus'), but you have to believe and follow His truth. Put on Jesus' uniform (**eph. 6:9-20**).

Both sides of each of the groups are evil (satan's teams – even some false churches, religions, etc.), and people not living the way they believe, etc. maybe trying to fool others, but really themselves. Even to the point you don't know who you are listening to (or really voting for – wolves in sheep's clothing – one political view trying to fool people by saying they are the other political view, especially in a state that is opposite of them). And don't vote for nationality, color of skin, etc. – but what they truly believe and live it – best with Jesus. Don't be fooled – know who they are – know them by their fruits (behavior, actions, etc.). So go to Jesus and be on the best and right team to get along (and make sure it is the truth).

This is an evil world and Jesus says it is, but we can have peace with Him (**john 17:13-21**), in this evil world (because we all are evil), and only with Him can we have peace.

No one wants to think they are evil, but you are – we all are, and we need to accept that – try to keep from doing evil – stop living in denial (look at yourself – not others). We need to go to Jesus, and His word, and find out what God thinks of us and wants us to do and how to live – not comparing to man.

With all of the evil and people against God – high places, etc. in this world – pray to God to step in and reveal the truth – all of those that are against God. Go to Jesus and His word to uncover the evil and the fake – satanic in this world.

We need to give up things of this world to follow Jesus – anything that holds you back – connected to man (**matt. 19:29; mark 10:29-30**). If connected to man (adam, noah's sons), it better be with what Jesus wants for you (change with what He wants you to be). Can't be with God, and mammon – things of this world (**matt. 6:23-25; luke 16:12-13**). That's why you need to go to Jesus and His word every day.

Know that this world will pass away and the things in it (**1 john 2:17**) – so go for things that are forever – eternal. Go to Jesus, you may die young (**luke 12:13-21**), struggle, etc. – have Him and share Him, and be ready.

Businesses, government, politicians, people, celebrities, etc. don't want or like you, but want your money, attention, etc., so they cater and kiss up, etc. to you – even if it is bad for you, or against God's word – truth. Go to Jesus (and the truth of His word), and not man or this world.

As long as businesses, people, etc. are honest about what they believe – people can make better decisions about who to buy from, vote for, etc. People have to know what is truth, and best. Trust Jesus and His word, not the world.

Don't love this world (**rom. 12:2**), or people more than you love God – and you will be able to when you go to Jesus – follow Him and His word (be born again – with the Holy Spirit) – then you will be also better for people here – your family, the world, etc. (and satan won't be able to hurt you as much then). We need to not be controlled by our wants, desires, habits, etc. (**1 john 2:15-17**).

So you may have to give up your family, friends, nationalities, etc. to be with Jesus (**matt. 10:34-39; 2 cor. 6:14-18**), to get away from man – adam, noah's three sons, ancestors, etc.– to be born again (**john 3:3-7**) – to Jesus and connected to God again – with the Holy Spirit (**matt. 16:23-27; mark 8:33-38; mark 10:23-31; luke 9:23-26; luke 12:49-53**). Basically, we need to love Jesus more than our family, etc., and it's not that we don't love our family (or anyone), but that we love Jesus that much more – like Jesus loves us (which may look like hate when compared – **luke 14:25-27**). Jesus wants you to go to and love and believe Him, more than your family, people, nationality, etc. – any of noah's sons (separate from them), then you can love them better and share Jesus and the truth. It's not easy to do or even think about. But try to share Jesus with all, but if they don't want to believe, then move on (if you can) – don't bother them, but loving them and praying for them and help them and share Him again sometime (while you grow and learn His word – the truth). But it has to be the truth.

Fortunately, some people grow up in good homes and some people are true Christians to have some people behave and have good lives – we all should. God controls some things and leads events and opportunities for people to go to Him – but it is still all free will and our choice – we need to go to Jesus and follow Him (His truth).

So we are all from adam (and now from one of noah's sons – after the flood) – all on the same team – and all sinful (and evil) and punished together, because of what one man (adam – through satan) did – we all are penalized (like a team in sports – in a game). And the problems we all get from one person – like adam (sin, evil, etc.), or ham (or any of noah's sons), or from you – you cause bad things for your family, nationality, etc. – they did for all of us, and One Person can help to get us away from that – only Jesus. But all can be made righteous, because of One – Jesus, if we join His team – don't stay with team, man.

Be united with Jesus, not man (or satan). On His team (His truth – His word). Trying to help people to get to know Jesus and His truth, not their own, etc. Once you are with Jesus, with the Holy Spirit in you – true salvation – and truly following His word – the truth, then you are a saint (you, me, etc.) – what God says, not man (or church, leader, etc.).

All the things that God wrote about people before the flood, and after the flood – to noah and his sons – to the jews and today with

Christians – after Jesus died and rose, has had an impact on all of us today, and it all leads to Jesus (and even the end times, coming soon). Go to Jesus, and read it.

Most people think they are helping people – so liberals, socialists, even communists, etc. think they are including and helping people, etc. – by thinking they are being nice, tolerant, helping, etc., but are really going against God and His word (how He doesn't want people to be – it's not the way He made man) – but it's how satan is – it looks nice, but is evil (and really excluding people, like some do Christians), and won't work and it never has (actually causes more problems – always going against how God wants us to be – look in His word – **rom. 1:18-32**). Don't allow and help evil to get worse – and help people to stay that way. Go to Jesus and know the truth and change. Be on His side (all should be, and He wants us to be). But you can still help those that are against God and His word – sharing Jesus and His truth, that best you can (you keep going to Him).

You can't keep getting away with things (evil and against God, and the truth of His word), no matter what you think (or what position you have in this world, etc.) – you have to deal with them. Have Jesus help.

And satan will use evil, killing, etc. (and people to do it – mass shootings, etc.), even in america, to push and prove his agenda – whatever it is that may not be best for man – and lead to the end times – you can see it today – and those that satan put in power – those against God – to help push this world to the end. We have to be ready for when God does end this, and you will see the people that satan put in power running the world (and especially in america – to use what satan is doing to go against what God would want in this world – basically saying good is evil and evil is good – **isa. 5:20-21**, and having a form of godliness, but not real – **2 tim. 3:1-5**) – but we need to go to Jesus and share Him and His truth until the end.

Man – through satan – tries to scare people – control by fear, lies, etc. – know the truth of Jesus and His word.

Jesus (and the truth of His word) is the best for all of us (we just all don't know it). Get the Holy Spirit and be saved and learn the truth.

We – all of noah's sons – are all together in the world – especially in the same country (like america) – to try to get along and God shows it only will happen with Jesus. Only Jesus can bring all to God (**2 cor. 5:14-21**).

God keeps going to you all of your life, and is available to you – God can use anything. Go to Jesus and then share your experiences with others. We can all end up friends – any of noah's sons – especially in america – but hope all go to Jesus. Or we will still have the problems we see in the world (and the country).

There is no master race, or church, or religion etc. – only people that truly go to Jesus and follow the truth of His word – which are very few (**matt. 7:13-23**). Stop promoting what God is against – then your people, life, nation, etc. will get better. Certain white people and their evil beliefs against God and His word through Jesus are making whites look bad – look at who promotes ideas against God and His word in the world – all of noah's sons can be like this – hurting people.

Don't rule (nation, etc.) without Jesus – if you want it to work and be the best. God will bless it then (**psalm 33**). As america needs to continue to do. All can be equal in america – as much as possible – as separated as noah's sons are – so it took a while to get there – like a person grows and changes and learns and gets better, so does america – only best with Jesus.

Some groups, beliefs, activities, etc. exclude people, other groups let everyone in (like some religions, etc.), but are hateful (and can be hurtful, etc. – without the true God, or God's truth, in their life), and satan leads them all – no matter what good intentions, if any, some of these groups may have had at the start (black or white, etc.). Even God separated the jews (who God made to further Him and His truth – with the bible and Jesus), from the gentiles – not to associate with them (those that were without the true God), and if the jews didn't obey God – He punished them (and that goes for any group – Christians, etc. – even today). There are many groups that separate themselves (black and white, etc.), but are not with God (the true God – Jesus).

Be concerned about others and not just yourself – what God wants you to do – and go to Him first to do that, and share Him (**matt. 22:36-40**).

We all are guilty and why Jesus came – and God used the jews to show us the truth (mainly in His word) – we all need to go to Jesus, and need Jesus.

No group should take advantage of any other – and try to help, but know we won't get along or even be as fair as we can be, without Jesus. Or we will be stuck with man (and noah's sons – white, black, etc.), until we do. And all of the unfairness.

Be one with Jesus – the only way. Try to get away from all the groups we are in (noah's sons – man) – that separate us and go to Jesus. We can't all belong to all of these groups and get along and agree.

Should a black person (ham) be able to join a white supremacists' (japheth) group (the ku klux klan, nazis, etc. – if they wanted to, and most whites don't even like these types of groups), or a white person (although some may have) join the black panthers – or groups like that (blacks seem to like these groups, violent or otherwise – feel they have to, and there are others over the years and today)? But they don't first go to Jesus and His truth – know the truth.

Some of these can be peaceful or violent, but not necessary. Even though we shouldn't have such groups (black or white, gangs of any kind, etc.), it is the separation of noah's three sons that causes them to start up (we all should be one – together, but only with Jesus can we be – **acts 17:24-43**). Just like within the different sons of noah – like ham – may have those against each other – like the different tribes of native americans, etc. and others like japheth - europeans against each other, etc., and even shem – the jews and arabs against each other. No one gets along. We need to go to Jesus. That's what He came here for – for our good – for salvation – from sin, satan, and death.

No one wants to feel they are an inferior group – but there are in this world (even with the differences – we are all evil), as far as God is concerned (otherwise we wouldn't be considered separate now – then to be able to be one with Jesus – because we are not equal or one now, without Him) – but we all can be the same with Jesus (**gal. 3:22-29; col. 3:1-17**), not having to stay the way we are now (from the abilities, and lot in life from noah's sons – still connected to man). Accept this world the way it is (no matter where you are in this world – rich, poor, black, white, man, woman, etc.), and become one with Jesus – the only way.

Regardless of what punishment or differences there are in noah's sons – we all have to go to Jesus to change – and become one – the way God intended when He created us. And all of noah's sons can do great things – but only with Jesus.

Since we haven't solved the problem of the differences (and we won't with man – still connected to adam and noah's sons), and since we haven't all gone to Jesus, they will continue to show up and have problems (if you don't like any of those groups – different 'races', etc., then help out by going to Jesus and His word, and sharing Him – the truth of Him).

Stop crying racism, equity, etc. – just go to Jesus (and help others to) – but it better be the truth – not like false Christians.

And all of these groups start up, because of some other group, etc. (or some perceived prejudice, etc.), and it continues, but is all a waste without Jesus (and His word). He will give us all what we need (**matt. 6:33**), if we would just go to Him (and His truth).

It is why God made this world tough – the way it is – with satan – so man would go to God – Jesus – He is the only answer. He wants us all to go to Him. That's how much He loves us, even though most people think that may not be true. The only way.

We need to wake up to the lies of this world, leaders, beliefs, ideas, etc. (of satan) – go to Jesus and His word – the truth of it – share Jesus (only the truth).

You know that all people are bad (from noah's sons) – white, black, etc. – so stop pointing fingers to take the blame off of you – back and forth, etc. over the years. Go to Jesus to change.

And defending and protecting are good and needed – not trying to kill for killing's sake – yourself or others for your beliefs, etc. (like some religions, nations, cultures, etc. do, and have over the years) – saying it is godly, etc. Man is evil and will continue to hurt, kill, steal, etc. unless they are stopped – arrested, in prison, etc. – and why God made laws – like the ten commandments, etc. (and man makes laws). But they have to be followed and enforced for our benefit.

The most evil, violent, strongest, hateful, etc. groups take over (satan leading, without people knowing) when God (the true God) is not involved – in a people, city, nation, community, etc. (just like ham did after the flood – **gen. 10:8-10; gen. 11**), and sometimes there is no protection from these types of groups (especially today in america – where all of noah's sons are, and why we need and share

Jesus), and is why we need protection, etc., and God put protection (police, government, military, laws, etc.) in where people want to help and get along (mainly with Him – **rom. 13**), like america should and can be. The world is evil. Even criminals like it when they are saved or helped by the police – the law, etc. Most people seem to think that referees, umpires, etc. are good (for the most part) for a fair game (not leaving it up to the players, etc.) – just like police are needed – but those that cheat, are selfish, etc. (criminals, etc.), don't care about rules, laws, etc. – people that are not fair, etc. – to win at all costs, etc. We need rules, not haters, etc. So criminals don't think the police are fair – mistreat, etc., but the criminals mistreat everyone they deal with – hypocrites – don't feel sorry for them (black, white, etc.). Just pray and help them to Jesus.

So when people don't like a call in a game, if there is a penalty on their team – whether it is right or wrong, the team and the fans, etc. (all that are connected to that team – nationality, etc.) are going to be upset. Man is the same in real life – even if it is the right call – get the penalty (arrested and put in prison, etc.). We need to deal with this evil in the world, and accept when someone gets in trouble for their mistakes or behavior. And accept the consequences or follow the rules (laws, etc. – especially God's). But it has to be fair to punish or help all – not just some. Man doesn't seem to be good at that (selfish).

And if in a game, something illegal – penalty (or someone did something wrong to you) happens – you would want the referee (or police) to do something, etc. – don't be a hypocrite – this world (or sports, games, etc.) is evil and would be worse without the rules, laws, and punishments, etc. And make sure the punishment fits the crime (and when it is illegal, you have to stop breaking the law or it will be worse – your fault). And we all can go to Jesus and change. We all want justice and everything to work our way. But this world is not perfect – trying to get along. Only Jesus can do that.

And it goes both ways – you don't care what color a person is who scores the winning touchdown, basket, homerun, etc., but they might care if you fumble, airball, strikeout, etc. – sports are like that, and sometimes life. And accept the outcome (and consequences of your life and lifestyle) – which may not be good (depending on what you are doing). But Jesus cares either way – go to Him, so life can turn out best for you – all of us.

We can all help and care for each other. We don't have to hate people, just straighten them out (and you live it) – care about them, and we all can do a better job – go to Jesus – and share the truth. Preach the truth.

Whether you believe in Jesus, or not – you are stuck with noah's sons, mainly on this earth – and you can't get away from them without Jesus (to head in the right direction) – you are stuck in your life and place with them then. And for the most part we will have trouble getting along and need protection, etc.

You certainly don't take the law into your own hands, but without the law, police, etc. (no matter how bad you think that is), you will do that. Whatever you are dealing with – God will get you through it, if you go to Him. Otherwise, all you end up with is street warfare, if you don't have police, laws, etc. (**james 4**) – gangs and other groups (of all of noah's sons going against each other) fighting for what? That's what man does (hate, fight, kill, be selfish, etc.) for his answer to the differences in each other (all through history) – but it won't work and never has (if it ever did, it was only for a short, and sometimes miserable time), without God (or not continuing to follow God and His word). And there's always collateral damage (other deaths, or harm, etc.) when you live an evil life – don't live that way, and you will end needless deaths – including your own family, friends, etc. (and hopefully go to Jesus). People feel like they need to counter each other – all of noah's sons do, and they don't go to God (Jesus) to solve these problems.

Some people make bad behavior look good – including criminals, killers, etc. (even robin hood) – almost to the point that they are heroes, etc. – especially hollywood, internet, social media, etc. (and the world follows).

Even though there may be police that are not perfect, it's not an excuse for people to get away with evil – always blaming the police, and even blaming their own up bringing (including prejudice, etc.) for the way they live. We all can go to Jesus and change.

The people that are afraid of the police, is mainly because of what their family and friends, etc. say (and do or have done) – even in the past, but today – movies, news, websites, cell phones, shows, cameras, etc. influence even more – and they keep their prejudices for the police, laws, etc. But they are needed in this evil world, because of man trying to get away with things, etc. (with our evil, sinful nature) – and not going to God, and His truth.

The police have seen it all and have to be careful – you would be worse, if you had to deal with you and others like you – don't make it worse. Police risk their lives for all – black, white, rich, poor, man, woman, etc. – help them out and stop being a criminal, etc. (or acting like one – even to impress your friends, etc.) – somebody has to do this in this evil world – you won't. Don't make it worse. People think it is 'cool', etc. to run from the police and it has been going on for centuries, and now even more today, to fit in – and don't listen to or obey the law, etc. Police live a dangerous life – keep an eye on them, but leave them alone to do their job. And you behave – go to Jesus. And don't make it worse.

Better to be safe than sorry in this life – that should work with the police department, too. They should stop people and keep them from hurting people (they have gone soft on crime) – man is still evil (and it is getting worse, and still need to be punished, etc.). So you are the problem. And all need to go to Jesus. And the punishment may help you go to Jesus. Use it.

Disliking the police is not a recent modern thing – they weren't treated right, even back in the recent past –like the 1920's (gangsters, etc.), and like the 1960's, and since (maybe even 1,000 years ago) – nothing has changed, just excuses (man is still evil), no matter what changes or how many programs, attempts, etc. to have people get along or stop hurting each other or stop being selfish and criminal, etc. – no one wants to do right. Even the unrest, etc. of the 1960's with all of its violence, destruction (satan's traits) – and all of man's lives that were hurt, was not necessary, as the unrest in today's world is not necessary either – nothing has changed (**eccl. 1 to 3**) – and never will – the evil in man (with satan leading – all of noah's sons) is going to continue (no matter who you think deserves it). Wake up, and go to Jesus – the only answer to change that.

People are living in satan's fantasy land – evil world, in the dark – leading to hell. Live with Jesus (**john 12:42-47**).

Man loves evil – the darkness – Jesus says that (**john 3:17-21**) – man doesn't want to come to the light (which is Jesus) – man likes to hide from God (and has since the beginning, after sin – **gen. 3:8-10**), and stay in darkness and misery (knowing you are doing evil). The whole world does.

Other countries get used to having crime and stealing, taking over others, etc., because they are poor (but it happens a lot in america, because we are rich – this country is blessed and others take advantage of that) – there is no Jesus, and His truth, in those countries, and they don't have the same opportunities as america – and some leaders are rich in other nations, but not the people, and why they want to come to america, and continue crime (even though some have come here and worked hard). So without Jesus this world (and country) will have more problems. Jesus is still the answer for all of us (all of noah's sons).

You want liars, cheaters, and killers, etc. running your life, the nation, the world? No (even you don't – can't have family, home, safety, etc.). And the government, politicians, etc. need to be accountable for their actions, too – no double standard, etc. Jesus is the only answer. All going to Jesus and the truth of His word. And don't say you are a Christian, if you are not – just to have people vote, etc. for you. You have to know the truth and live that way – not lying or a form of godliness (**2 tim. 3:1-5**) – and still going against God and His word – the truth.

Don't be doing things that you owe someone (**prov. 22:7; rom 13:8**) – or they have something on you, etc. Go to God for what you need and trust Him – to Jesus (**matt. 6:33**) – if you don't, you don't need it. Don't owe man anything (**rom. 13:7-9**) – don't be beholden to anyone – to be bribed, etc. to do evil or let others to get away with evil. Tough it out – go to Jesus.

Stop running and hiding – come clean and admit it – change and work hard for what you do and get – and go to Jesus to help you through the tough things in this life. Don't try to keep people quiet – man or woman – don't hold something over someone – it will come back to you worse. (**num. 32:23; gal. 6:6-8**).

We should all treat each other the way we want to be treated – like you would the person you love the most (and care about doing things right) in this world and they do the same – work toward that, and all should, or it won't work, and we are wasting time. But with Jesus (only with His truth) we can have a chance to do that (**luke 6:31-32**).

You may live a struggling life today, or before. Don't be tempted to do evil (or really give into it). Not everything was great for everyone all of the time (now or in the past) – for any of noah's sons (and they all didn't do things right either – we all are that way).

All people have struggled over the years and should help others that struggle, too, if you can – but we all have to work hard, and help ourselves. With Jesus it is best.

Even when whites were mostly playing professional sports (a long time ago), the owners didn't give them much money (might have been a job they liked, etc.), but without Jesus, all of noah's sons struggle in some way – at some time in this world.

And so what if whites helped some blacks get ahead – they still have to work hard (and hopefully appreciate it – not think they are owed anything, etc.) when they get opportunities, etc. (we all should), and not fight what is going to help them the most – all getting along, but it can't be without Jesus. God even may set these things up (and made them happen) and see how we are going to react and handle things (good or bad) – for whatever good changes have been made in history or in america. We can help each other, but you need to want to be helped – but the help will not be as good without Jesus and His truth. It doesn't work with different people wanting power, etc. (and the evil in all of us – we are all the same that way, as there are gangs, drug cartels, neighborhoods, even countries, religions, etc., that exclude others, too, and hate and hurt as well – we are all guilty), but it is that way in the world today (especially after the flood) so that we would go to God (and His word – Jesus), to get along. No other way (**john 14:5-6**). And we are all guilty of not being good, and not going to God (**rom. 3**).

America is better because we go to Jesus, if not, it won't be.

There will always be groups like that in the world, not only in this country (it's sad – but don't let them grow and take over, or have anyone you know join them – black or white, rich or poor, etc.), because man is evil and people don't get along (all of noah's sons), and only Jesus can fix that – not man (other than you not participating, and going to Jesus). Those groups (and any like them) are definitely not the answer – but they are there today, and man keeps going to them (although we have seen how it doesn't work – even over the last hundred years or more, at least not very well). So blacks should straighten out blacks, italians – italians, hispanics – hispanics, asians – asians, etc., if need be. So people wouldn't be as prejudice as much at any group – seeing they do the right thing. But the problem is that they all want more, and power, etc. – without God (like satan did and does).

We have to accept all of noah's sons – whether we like it or not – try to get along. God put us in our place – until we go to Jesus. We are all guilty. All of noah's sons were not nice to each other – all of man is sinful since adam – you have to expect that from all people – black, white, etc., until you go to Jesus. You can try to be nice, as much as you can.

You feel sorry for some people in this world (poor, minorities, elderly, disabled, etc.), but all can go to Jesus – so help them and share Him. Getting to know Him (and His truth) yourself first. Help people get the most out of life with Jesus – His truth.

Even though being separated (by God) is good (so satan can't unite all), and even some of the false churches and religions (besides the different nationalities, cultures, etc. there are) may keep some people (separate groups, etc.) under control – trying to follow rules, laws, etc., or this world could be worse – but it is still evil and all are going against the true God (Jesus), and going to hell. And these false beliefs in the world may seem to keep some people under control a little bit (and separated), but not sinless or saved – although may act a little better – there are some groups, beliefs, etc. that are even worse than most beliefs – really evil, etc., and nothing will help any of them, but Jesus.

People see or hear of certain groups – say they are Christian, but are not, and people won't be sold or impressed with their behavior, etc., since they aren't true Christians (and we have seen those groups over the years that are evil – really satan led.

Jesus is trying to get you away from any group (black or white, etc.) that satan is leading – which is all that is against God (Jesus and His word – the truth) – even ones that look like Christians, or say they are – like the ku klux klan, etc. (as well as all of the false churches, religions, groups, etc. today in the world) – today or in the past. God wants to see what is in your heart and what you are going to believe and follow. Jesus in power, and truth.

We all will have problems in this world – and it's nice to know where to go to get over those problems. Although God made the world that way – to have problems to get to go to Jesus (and do it daily – the truth), so thank Him for the problems.

You can get persecuted for things in this life you believe in or stand up for, and man does try to (many do for many things), but will waste their time, if it's not Jesus and the truth of His word that you believe in and stand up for – at least not be as good (or won't last, etc.), or as much of a reward (**matt. 5:11-12; 2 tim. 3:10-17**). Don't fear man (or satan) – the worst they can do is kill your body (**matt. 10:27-28**) – so stand up to evil (and what is right), with Jesus (save your soul), and what He wants. The world will end, and/or we die – where will you go? Think of that.

If you are stubborn and prideful, and don't want to change and give in – you will be miserable, and you can't go around it – go to Jesus, and live.

It is satan that leads you to do things for and against man (and those he can influence – all that are not with Jesus), and he hates and persecutes the jews (the whole bible – 66 books, is from the jews, by God, and so satan and some people, would like to wipe out the jews), and satan hates true Christians – he hates israel and america, specifically – and some people hate jews and Jesus and Christians, some jews hate jews (hated Jesus), and some blacks hate blacks and some whites hate whites, etc. God used the jews to write the bible – men of God, through the Holy Spirit – the truth (**2 pet. 1:19-21**) – and satan hates them for that. No matter whom it is, satan is trying to influence them to go against God – if you are not with Jesus, you are against Him – with satan (no in between – **matt. 12:30**). You can follow satan, and don't know it (without Jesus you are), no matter how good a life you think you are leading. In this world, it may be (or can be) who you know, but that especially goes for knowing Jesus (for everyone, jews included, having a better life here) – and to get to heaven – eternal life there. Bible is true – believe it. Even God separated people like jews early (**lev. 20:24; deut. 7:6**).

And that is why God used man to share the truth of salvation (and Jesus) with other men – not angels, etc., to preach and share the gospel and the truth of the bible, because man is influenced by satan (angels), and satan has and does share lies with man (and has for many false beliefs), and has started all of the false churches, and religions, and beliefs, in the world – away from God and the truth of Jesus and His word. Man shares – plants, waters, etc. with the truth of God's word – to help share and prove the bible (and all can go into the bible to see that, especially with the Holy Spirit after you are truly saved by Jesus – **rom. 10:8-17; 1 cor. 15:1-4**), and God does the saving (the increase) through Jesus (**1 cor. 3**). Don't trust angels, etc. Man shares, God saves. Know it is the truth.

So satan hates jews (and true Christians), and wants them gone – so you don't know (or believe) the truth of the bible and the jews. And wants to have people, religions, false churches to say that they replace them, etc. No group, etc. has taken the place of the jews – they would be liars – false christians, churches, etc. The jews are still here and God's people – but will wait (as a nation) until the end times to believe in Jesus (**rom. 11:25-36**) – individual jews can be saved today. We are all sinful and guilty until we go to Jesus.

Stop fighting the way God created this world at the beginning – sinless and not cursed, but after satan and man (adam and eve) sinned, then the world is evil and tough – especially after the flood – and we are all separated by God, with noah's sons, etc.

It is satan who is against Jesus and His word, leading man in many groups – even separated now in the world (by God for now), but will all be one against God together some day **(matt. 24),** like before (**gen. 6; gen. 11**) – just after the rapture of the true Christians (better know the truth) – all that will be left are people (false Christians, religions, atheists, etc.) that are against the truth of God – as well as the jews (who the seven year tribulation is for – **dan. 9:24-27**), that satan can and will use to go against God all at one time, even the jews (as one group – one world order) – led by the anti-christ (**book of revelation**). But there will be a remnant of true believing jews at the end.

And satan knows the bible – the truth, (even maybe as much as God) more than even man does (and knows God – Jesus – and even satan, and demons, know that Jesus is God – **matt. 4:1-11; luke 4:41** – but don't want you to know), and satan does not want to follow His word or Jesus, all he does is make lies (the father of them – **john 8:43-47**), hate, evil, death, etc., and wants to lie (mixing in a little truth) and share that with man – and if you lie long enough people start to believe it (and share it and stand up for it) – including leaders, politicians, nations, people, etc. And you see that in the world today – even america. And satan wants you to think it is man, groups, etc. that hate and kill others – it is satan – who man follows (**eph. 6:1-20**). God eventually punishes who goes against Him, His word, but giving you a chance to change.

And since satan knows the bible (and has supernatural powers, etc. – trying to copy Jesus, and the Holy Spirit) – to fool people (even Christians – especially false ones, and others) at the rapture – he knows that there is a rapture – but satan will fake it or say it is ufo, etc. abduction – satan is preparing for that (and why there are so many sightings, etc. and secrecy around ufos, aliens, etc. – even though it is just satan and demons, etc.). So people think it is aliens – not from God – not the rapture, and not Christians – so the anti-christ can say it is ufos that abducted Christians, so people will follow the anti-christ. Who wouldn't say that isn't the truth, when they are still on earth, and those other people are gone? All will believe in the anti-christ. It will be some story like that. Whatever they (and satan) can get the people to believe.

Don't listen to those that say there is no truth – God's word is truth – Jesus is truth.

There are many things that you would lie for, but don't like done to you – so don't do it to others.

People (even news, leaders, nations, politicians, etc.) that lie, cheat, etc. try to prove or accuse others (to show something is true – that is evil and really about them), always covering up the evil they do (all against God – and why people don't always see it and are blinded by satan), but when they (or those like them) are accused, they try to downplay it, and say it isn't a true story, etc. (or say nothing about it). But it has to be the truth – not what man (or satan) thinks and is trying to shove down people's throat – don't follow them. Wake up. To Jesus' truth.

And God doesn't want us to help those (people, nations, leaders, etc.) that are against Him, especially against israel (and america – inside or outside of america) – that do not go to Him (and want to do harm to them – look in the world and see who that is) – only to share Jesus with them (if they will listen). God curses (or doesn't bless) those that curse (or don't bless) israel (**gen. 12:1-3** – and this is still in effect from God today – just like we are all still from noah's sons and separated – **gen. 9:18-19; gen. 10 32**). Until we go to Jesus. We don't have to do harm to anyone (and can help some, especially if they want to go to Jesus), just because they don't follow Jesus, but we have to protect those that do follow Jesus (as God will, too), and those that are still His (like israel) and protect america. And some that will go to Him.

And God developed america to share Jesus, and to make this world bearable to live in – so america is here to help those that need it, and want it (so satan doesn't lead all to evil at the same time – like before the flood, **gen. 6**, and a little after at the tower of babel, **gen. 11**), and have a chance to get to know Jesus – especially in the end times. Pray – turn from our wicked ways (**2 chron. 17:13-15**).

No matter how many people you help in need of some kind, they are going to die eventually. So if you help someone (and God is the one who gave us opportunities to help others, with this world) – poor, criminal, sick, desolate, etc. (here, or even around the world, like america does), and they die two weeks later anyway, because of the way they think and believe and live their life (lifestyle, choices, desires, tough conditions, etc., even in their nation) – what good is that? Share Jesus (and His word, and help them), and that lasts forever (even if they die), and can be in heaven (if they get saved). That's the best help you can give.

It is still nice to help people with whatever problems they have, but best with Jesus. So don't just love (and help) people, but share Jesus (with the truth) – or the help is a waste.

Don't stay the way you are – change with Jesus, and don't expect others to change – you change, too.

God can have people and nations struggle so that they can be helped and have Jesus shared with them.

America tries to help others in the world (and protect, etc.), and all countries need help, but don't always want it (only when their people are struggling, and even then, sometimes they don't, because of what they believe). Eventually this world will be one, but with satan (after the rapture, during the tribulation – **book of revelation**). All against God and the truth of His word.

Even a country like south korea (which is small), that would be taken over easily by any other country, will be protected by america – so the country looks small, but is backed up by a bigger nation. Just like north korea could be taken over by most countries but is backed up by a bigger nation – china (and even they are kept at bay, because of america, really Jesus). So they are protected, but one is evil (satan's), and the other is not (at least not as evil as this world is – no matter what you think). And the same with israel – a small nation, but backed by america. God made america for that – to protect and share Jesus and the truth of His word – and why it is so powerful and prosperous (like He did with the jews – **josh. 1:8-9**). All separate for a reason. And we do have to defend and protect people sometimes against evil, hateful groups, etc. And God had america in place and powerful before God made israel a country again in 1948.

God is in charge, and we need to go to Him to have Him help us (and know who He is). And if any country (even america) goes away from Jesus and His truth (which would not be beneficial to any of noah's sons), then God will punish them (and has even today), just like He has in the past (letting satan in some cases do that or just this dangerous, evil world do it – the consequences of man's thinking and behavior). All of the countries that say they are Christian, are not.

God has punished america – like the civil war, the 1930's depression, or the 1960's unrest, etc. (to name a few) and beyond – just like He punished other countries – famines, desolations, bad government, etc. (**lev. 26:21-23; job 15:28; job 30:3; psalm 34:21-22; psalm 69:25; psalm 109:9-11; isa. 1:7; isa. 3:24-26; isa. 13:9; jer. 4:7; etc.**).

One of the main things that hurt america recently (in the last 70 years or so), is the taking prayer and the bible out of the public schools, etc. (early 1960's). And we can see all of the problems we have had since then – but God is still here, and we need to keep going to Him and sharing the truth of Him. Or we will suffer more.

None of us are good – from birth – any of us in the world, and things happen in this world to all of us (and satan leads the world) – from all of us going and staying away from God. The world will have problems – even america – like what happened on sept. 11, 2001 (mainly that america is a Christian nation and will have people in the world against it – God will protect, if we keep going to Him). So we need to keep going to God and His word through Jesus. And share Him to the world (His truth).

The world (or nation, etc.) is not going to work without God (Jesus), no matter how you think you are going to be fair for everyone (or how you separate noah's three sons – or even try to bring them together) – this is a tough world and life (besides evil, especially without Jesus and His truth). We have to do tough things and make tough decisions (and you may be disliked even by your own kind) – but we are better with Jesus helping and in our life, knowing the truth (and it better be truth or it is no good) on how to deal with and take care of them and us, no matter who you may go against (or against you), Jesus will protect (from the world, and evil, so don't be in the world – hating, etc.), if you do His will and are His (**john 17:13-23** – follow His truth). It will continue to be a tough world, and you have to go to Him daily. Don't take the easy way out (it's really not easy – except with Jesus).

Man does not want pain or discomfort and will do whatever to be comfortable – it was comfortable before the flood (even though man was still evil, and did not go to God), but not after the flood – it is uncomfortable.

Man tries to make things comfortable – easy, because man was created for ease (the way God made the world for man – comfortable – before the flood, even after adam sinned, but since the flood, we now have it tough – all of man's punishment for sin, because having it easy, doesn't get man to go to God) – before the flood it was comfortable (weather, food, etc.) and man had everything to live (didn't need homes, or heat or air conditioning, or refrigerators, etc. didn't really need clothes, but did), and man didn't think he needed God, or to go to God either (even though all we have is from Him – Jesus, the Creator). So naturally man likes to relax (if he can), even today, as much as he can, and so he finds things (and invents things – everything we ever invented is to make life easier and fun since the flood) that he can do when he relaxed – and part of that was games and sports (soccer in most of the world, and some go back a long ways, even to greece – japheth, with the olympics, track and field, etc., but probably before that with some other games, mostly physical ones, like wrestling, etc.), and we enjoy playing them, and watching them (and it is a battle without war – although in roman times they had some sports to the death, even against Christians, and maybe similarly in central america, and other places, etc. – man is still evil), so man eventually found ways to make money with them, like we do today – sometimes lots of money (opportunities here in america for many).

Most sports are made up by japheth (whites) but are usually played better by ham (africans, etc.) – physical, but all can try (and work hard) – that's the way life should be – to help others. In this case it is a good way to spend time and sometimes relax, etc. (which man likes to do – like before the flood), but found a way to make money in the process (like man tries to do, also). And most people should and do play sports for fun and exercise – but also can be somewhat competitive, which can be fun, too – and most like watching sports. It's not necessary for all to play or try to play professionally – be competitive, but without being hurtful, etc.

(which man has in him), and not need war to prove everything (like we use the olympics today).

Jesus can use everything to help all – with all of noah's sons. It has taken a while for all of noah's sons to be good at most things and have the opportunities to do it – but it has in america (which God gave to us all – and we should feel grateful to be here, but we have to be with Him for it to work). All of the years since the flood has made some people good at these jobs, talents, abilities – to what you do today well (or could do well, if you try). So today in america all of the jobs (and activities, etc.) are there for all of noah's sons – and can bring them together.

It's just the way God made us from noah's three sons – we all have an ability that is dominant (but always better with Jesus in your life to reach the highest level – no matter what son of noah you are from), but not all countries give people with all abilities a chance to make money (some make money that are running the country, etc. – and the people are poor) – sometimes a lot (and not that you need a lot of money to survive). But don't take things for granted and live any old way you want – people (even children) are watching you, be a good example (rich or poor, black or white, man or woman, etc.), some people live a miserable life, because they see other's lifestyle, and follow (and people can lose all of their money, eventually, because of the life and behavior they have) – so use your money wisely. Besides the reality of everyone wanting to play professionally is slim (and if they don't make it, some may fall into drugs, crime, other evil, etc., so most don't make it in the pros, or life – and some of the greatest athletes are either on drugs, in prison, or dead, and they don't need to be – but they choose, we all do), and is why you need an education – learn something (the best is to learn the bible – the truth), do something (but most that want to play don't care about an education – man follows and idolizes the wrong people – and want things easy, hurting and hindering themselves, etc.), but all can learn, and may have to work harder (basically grow up – rich or poor, black or white, man or woman), or be stuck with jobs that people don't want, but are good at, if not, some may resort to crime, laziness, homeless, etc. (which leads to the government helping you and controlling you – through schools, programs, prison, even some rich people controlling, etc.) – especially what you think and do (takes away your freedom to think, etc.) – there is better out there (**prov. 14:11-12**) – Jesus' truth in His word.

The easier things are, the less appreciative you become – for work, life, etc. So work hard (and you will appreciate it more) and use your money wisely and do things the right way – get better. Know right from wrong – and follow right – know better with Jesus.

Don't give in and follow them – work and be free with Jesus and the truth. And all need Jesus. So you are fortunate that you are in america for either option (and you can succeed in something that you like or are good at, no matter how you got here). So be thankful and appreciative that you have the ability and opportunity (from God) to do what good you have in your life, and not be self-righteous, or selfish, etc., but going to Jesus and know that He made this country – could it be better? – yes, could you be better? – yes, but only with Jesus can it work, if you haven't gone to Jesus then stop arguing and protesting (at least violent, loudly, etc., but most lead to that). He is here and works for all (so go to Him). Going to Jesus and sharing Him gets you out of your problems, etc., not protests, riots, crime, hate, etc. – change you first. But if you have a lot – share it with others – as you do Jesus. If poor, you live simple and still be happy, love, family, etc., working hard, but it is best with Jesus (and His truth). Either way you can still be happy with a lot or a little, especially with Jesus – with too much you can still be sad – when things are tough, you still need others.

Remember you can do all things through Jesus who strengthens you (**philip. 4: 10-13**).

Just like you can help a person become better and change (especially with Jesus), you can also make a neighborhood better, and a city, state, nation, etc. – don't leave – stay and make it better – help out, through Jesus and His word.

Everyone can change from what they have and who they are – no matter what it is, if they go to Jesus – and save you from many problems, trust Him. Even the worst of us can, and Jesus wants to help you – otherwise it becomes selfish. Some people don't want to live in their own neighborhood – not safe, etc., so they try to work their way out, but what made that neighborhood so bad in the first place? – usually the people who live there. And people won't admit who is bad, but you don't even like them (usually your own kind), but you are stuck, because you are them and through peer pressure, etc. Although people can make things nice (or nicer) in their own home or neighborhood, by cleaning up, fixing things, working hard, etc. (and some do), but help each other. Usually people make their own mess and then hope someone else cleans it up or they may take or steal from others to make up for things. Why can't people be good at cleaning up, fixing, helping, etc. – especially for what they do, or cause, etc.? – they have energy for other things (some that are bad). And people just don't know that God will help you, if you go to Him, but people don't (keep going to Him, and His word).

And blacks need to help blacks (nationalities of all kinds should help each other) – and use the money they make wisely (especially the rich blacks – and some do, being blessed in this country) for any type of charity or program for jobs, or education, etc. or start one. Some blacks, minorities, etc., are trying, and some may need help, but it's each of us doing the right things and working harder – and mainly going to Jesus that will help the most. All nationalities have some nice people and try (and there are many that struggle, etc., in whatever land they live in), but all need Jesus, otherwise we will fail, eventually (no matter how it looks at the start).

No matter how honorable your cause is – you don't steal, lie, etc. – don't do any crime or shady way of keeping something going – do it right.

Everyone of noah's sons has to change (all of us do) – and change to Jesus to help us out of our problems (some we are born with, and some we cause – and satan leads you – go away from satan to Jesus).

And churches, ministries, and missions, etc. (here and around the world) do help (and should do more) and could – even though we all (rich, black, white, etc.) should help all people (especially help your own), but all need to go to Jesus to be equal – no other way (not man). And we need to give (tithes, offerings, etc.) to true Christian churches and ministries, etc., and when we do, God will give (bless) you with what you need to live (more than you gave away), and if you give Him time (read, learn, grow, help, share, etc., Jesus and His word – the truth of it), He will give you more time (especially to study His word and share Jesus). And it has to be the truth of Jesus and His word, otherwise you won't be blessed – if it's a false church, ministry, etc. (and there are many), you will get nothing, but problems (and satan) until you do. All need to go to Jesus and His word and know the truth – for any type of work or occupation, etc.

If you are poor, most of the time it is your fault (parents, etc.) – go to Jesus and change – use your money wisely and He will help. Do things on God's time – don't rush and go against God's word – the truth.

If you hold back or hurt others, etc. (selfish, etc.), you will have problems and be needy in some way, or you can give and help, and you will be helped and have what you need (**prov. 11:24-25**). Use what God gave you – whoever you are – do what you are good at, etc. Buy good things for yourself, not bad – use your money wisely. Even if it is just one person. Be an example. Don't pass on bad habits, etc. to hurt others (or yourself).

God has more for you and will give you more (of what's best), if you would just go to Him – Jesus – basically you can do nothing (worthwhile or good) without Him (**john 15:5**).

Even though man has a combination of abilities, you don't find many jews (shem – spiritual) in sports (and don't think they mind) – mostly in law, business, family, etc. (from bible studying, etc. – reading the bible and knowing the truth is the best for learning anything for anyone, from God), but they use the ability they have (and can create work for others – of noah's sons, especially in america), and there is work for them and their ability (but if they wanted to play sports, at least some of them, they would have to work harder to do that, as japheth may have to also, and maybe the interest wouldn't be there for most).

Even though most people can study, learn, etc., the europeans (japheth), maybe india – possibly a combination of japheth and shem (even though india's belief system holds them back, and isn't good for their country or people that follow that – they hurt themselves and people, by what they believe – and why they are all starving, sick, etc., and some other countries do similar things), maybe asia (same thing), and as does russia's, etc. (for the most part all that are in those nations like studying, learning, etc.) have the ability to learn and use the world for building, technology, business, etc. (although some like sports, and are good at them) and there is work for them all (but again they are limited in those nations by what they believe, government, etc.), and they can make work for others, too (all of noah's sons – which america has them all, trying to be with Jesus). And is why they come to america – and they do well. But some just fall apart (even though the potential is there), like russia, north korea, venezuela, etc., because of how they live (selfish, etc.) and believe (and treat their people), without the truth of Jesus. Don't depend on man and philosophy, politics, etc. (or even just yourself).

Depend on Jesus and the truth of His word – if those countries did, they would do well, too.

Leaders, even in satanic nations – without Jesus (His truth), have leaders they deserve – and God puts them in place, for what they believe (and He will in america, too). They need to go to Jesus and follow Him, to get the most out of themselves, for their people.

Man is creative like God – many talents and interests – like art, music (which was here before the flood – **gen. 4:21**), science, math, sports, building, inventing, repairing, etc. (some have all or some of these), and all are from God (from noah's three sons) – and are needed and used in this world. They all are something we all can enjoy or even perform, if we work at it (and stay with it). There are so many subjects to choose from – you have to like and be good at one (america gives you that opportunity), no matter what son of noah you are from. So you can see the differences and the interests of all sons of noah (hopefully we all can work together to get something done for everyone – not want what others have, other than working hard for it, and helping others, and see that God made us all different, but at the same time accept our limitations until we go to Jesus). Especially in america – all of noah's sons help or can help each other – especially with Jesus. Change with Him.

Change your life or stop bothering people – that's why you don't get anything in your life. Go to Jesus. If we don't, we will cause problems for each other and not get along – and then bigger problems come up (no matter what color you are – rich or poor). Because we are naturally selfish, evil – born that way, and people cause problems for themselves – but doesn't have to be.

Looking at the percentages of what is in america, the blacks that are in prison don't match the percentages in america (more percent in prison, than their percent in america, but that usually is their own fault – whoever is in prison, from what they believe or do). If anyone can get off from breaking the law it is not right (don't be bothered by that – if you are in prison – they should be in prison, too, as you are – if you are guilty, you are where you belong, and God will deal with them). Man may let man off the hook – get away with things (and if you go to prison for something you didn't do – you did something in your life that you got away with – none are innocent – and should lead you to Jesus), but God won't always let you get away with things, as you have seen in the past (**num. 32:23**). And you should try to stop people you know from living that life – don't join them or you do belong in prison. Change yourself – Jesus will. So don't live that kind of life or let anyone you know do that (at least not hang around them), but the main thing is to get them to Jesus (and His word – the truth) and help others do the same. Don't follow them, or you are guilty.

Even if the laws get you off when you're guilty, or say you're guilty when you may not be – at least not the one thing you got caught for – your sins will still find you out.

At times some people don't get caught for everything they do (or have done), but God will eventually avenge – and if you pray for them, they will eventually face it and God will lead them and have a change for Jesus – or if not, they will get what they get – more misery, struggles, etc.

We all have done something we need to be punished for (some more, and worse than others) – just like man before the flood (and since) – we all need to go to Jesus.

We all are proven guilty by Jesus (**john 3:17-21**) – no one likes that. And we are only righteous because of Jesus (**matt. 6:33**) – saved through Him (no matter how nice we think we are).

Reading the truth of the bible is like looking in a mirror and not liking what you see (especially about yourself).

People do anything (usually bad) for money – don't give into them – they are just led by satan, and it leads to destruction and death, and not worth it, whether it is a business, crime, trying to get ahead or push ideas, etc., even if they seem legitimate. Don't put yourself in a desperate position, if you do, go to Jesus and His truth. Find out what God wants (through Jesus and His word). Or no matter who you are (black, white, etc.) you will and should be punished – it's not money that is evil, it is the love of it (**1 tim. 6:6-10**). Follow what is good, and look for that (Jesus only).

So there are whites (as well as asians, etc., and hispanics – can be considered white) in prison and they go there (and should) if they don't follow the laws (especially if they are hurting others, and don't care, selfish, etc. – and that goes for anyone, black or white, etc.). We are all evil – in prison or not. But it is better to be in prison, then dead – you can still go to Jesus, and the only way you can – before you die (**2 cor. 5:5-11; heb. 9:27**), so don't make trouble, if you do something wrong – admit it, and suffer your consequences, if need be (then just go to Jesus and change), quit hiding and running from God (with your lifestyle, friends, beliefs, etc. – **gen. 3:8-13**) – and you may have gotten away with something in your life before and didn't get caught – you're guilty, too. Jesus can change the past – your past (be a different person today – repent and be forgiven, humble yourself with Jesus), all of our pasts (give us a better future), but we can't keep going to man (or ourselves) to solve these things, or keep hurting others to solve them.

And God will put you in these positions, because you are guilty of something and may want you to go through some struggle – even if you seem innocent – mainly to have you go to Him more, and change and grow and learn – especially His word. People try to get better at some things in this life – it would be best to get better at God's word and His life for you – and He may put you in a position to see that. Do things right with God (and you hope that others learn from their mistakes – some they might have done to you).

Just like sports have rules (laws) and penalties (punishments), etc. when you do something wrong or make mistakes against the rules, you have to accept them (and you want it to be enforced, especially when something wrong is done to you) and move on (the world is a little more dangerous, so you better live a better life, or there are worse punishments), so play within the rules – or be punished, and learn from that in life (especially at a young age) – don't cheat. And those rules (penalties) in sports will punish the whole team (people like you and look like you), not just the offending player – and those players are on the same team and colors and uniform, etc., and all will be punished, just like man is punished (and others that are like him in the world). Just like we are all punished, because of what adam did – and the people before the flood (and noah's sons) – until we all go to Jesus (stop being stubborn, prideful, etc., and go to Him).

Don't hurt others (especially your own), by what you do.

People cause their own problems and why people dislike them, and those that look and act like them. If we all do this (all of noah's sons – man), then we all have to change – go to Jesus.

Think, and be aware, of you who represent (your family, nationality, etc.) and affected by what you do (how you behave). All can be bad – all of noah's sons are.

And as bad as it is in some sports – even with referees, rules, etc., it would be worse without them (like a pickup game at a playground, etc.) – just like with the police, laws, etc., they are needed for you (and those you love) and because of you and others (and more important than sports, etc.). It would be worse in this world without them – police, laws, etc. We still need to go to Jesus in this world – because it will never change until we do – for a person, people, nation, etc., and it has to be the truth (as many in the world are not following the truth, even though they say they do – even in america). We can't be lawless (or live that way), and have a world (society, etc.) to live, if we ever want to be happy (and not everyone will be the same – but the best chance you have is with Jesus and His word). Laws are here by God for the lawless (**1 tim. 1:9**).

The law (from God or otherwise) does not save you – all the law does is show you are evil (like a mirror). Jesus saves – go to Him.

And this is satan's world – adam gave it to satan (**gen. 3** – listening to satan, and not God), and you see all of the evil in charge of the world in most places (and why God separated man – all of noah's sons). You can see that satan and false churches and religions have killed many people – not just the regular evil people in the world have killed people. But we can go to God – to Jesus and get through this, and be with Him, to live (and be saved), and be ready when you die. Jesus did it for all of us (**1 john 1**).

And it doesn't matter who is or has been in charge in this world, over the years – it is satan and evil. But God can help you, and you can be with Jesus, and live with Him and have Him in charge of you and your life in this world.

No matter how nice you are, or think you are, or how nice others think you are – give to charities, go to church, help the homeless, animals, etc. (and those are good things), you are still going to hell without Jesus. Man is evil – don't think you can save yourself, or be good enough. Don't be selfish – thinking of and focusing on yourself and all the problems you have or had in your life. Think of Jesus and go to Him and His word and change. And share Him and His truth – have people hear and see that in you. Then help and give to who you want so they can know of Jesus, too.

Man is that way – trying to build ourselves up – we all are. Humble yourself to Jesus (and His word – the truth of it), and change (don't stay with noah's sons, adam – man – **james 4:5-10**). What you do or don't do, may not only affect you, but others, too. Think about it – you are to blame for how people look at you and others like you in the world – if the police are looking for you and you are black, and broke the law, then they will be looking for blacks – and they – blacks, will be bothered, because of you. You are responsible for prejudice, hate, oppression – stop living that way – go to Jesus. Turn yourself in – stop blaming other people. If you don't want 'racism', prejudice, etc., then live a good, honest life – no matter how other people live – or suffer. Or you are to blame for the way other blacks, hispanics, asians, etc. are treated – be a better example for your own (stop being selfish). And help them with Jesus and His word.

You don't want hating, prejudice, etc., but you also don't want those that are hated to get away with murder, etc.

What's wrong with behaving better than other people? – don't follow bad behavior, etc. Help yourself and others like you. with Jesus it is best and possible. So you can get through these problems, struggles, etc. in this world.

If a black person hurt you (or your family) – are you going to like blacks, etc., or just like if a mexican hurt you (or your family), are you going to like mexicans, etc.? You have to know what it does when you hurt others – you really are just hurting yourself, and those like you – causing the prejudice, hate, etc. in the world to continue. Quit trying to blame it on racism, etc., and change yourself. And this goes for any type of person (black, white, etc.) – stop yourself first. Stop those that are like you or look like you (start with you and your family first), to help this problem. Blame them first. And go to Jesus to change (and forgive, if necessary). Otherwise, it won't change, no matter how much you yell or protest, etc. (that only delays it for a short time – then it happens again – go to Jesus, and stay with Him).

Even men and women are prejudice of each other – behavior, etc. – the way they look at each other – all on each other's 'team' (humans – nationalities, any of noah's sons, etc.), and people have views and prejudice of God (and His word). The reason we all are here on earth, and whatever problems happen here – is to get you to go to and know Jesus (and His word). God separates all – so we will go to Him (Jesus), because of these struggles we have with each other (that we won't ever solve without Him, and His word – even though we try). Make a change and help solve the problem, not make it worse.

And it's not always people that are against you that bothers your life (that don't look or believe the way you do, etc.) and makes you struggle – so don't always blame other people – blacks, whites, police, etc. – blame you (and satan – using your sinful nature) – it's you going against God and His ways (Jesus and His word – the truth) that makes you struggle – with satan leading you away from God.

People, political parties, etc. (maybe even government, justice department, etc.) are unfair, like some people see referees, umpires, etc. call something that looks unfair in a game, and people don't like it. So like in a game where the home team got a call go against their team – one of their own players – even if it is the right call – all of the players, fans, etc. boo, and yell, and hate the referee. And the player thinks he is innocent – just like in real life, if they are caught in a crime, etc. by the police – all of the people like them (his team) will be upset – even if it is the right call (and replay helps and usually is right – but just like in life, it may not always be clear or easy to tell – but we have to accept these things, and move on and be better and change). People don't mind it going against the other team (fair or not). No one is satisfied. Fight for right, not wrong (or color, or nationality, etc.). And keep yourself from being in those places in life.

We all need to stand up and fight against evil in this world – protect ourselves and others. We better know what is evil or wrong, and what is correct and good – and if it is – accept it, deal with it, and get better. And being a better example for your team – your own – who look like you, etc., and that is done with Jesus and His word. And suffer the consequences of what happens – then improve yourself in all areas. And also if you don't want to promote things that are not good – a way to do that is don't do business or frequent companies, buy things from, etc. that go against God's word – His truth, and Jesus.

There are all kinds of ways to make money in this world (the love of money is evil) – some not as good for you (like prostitution, drugs, human trafficking, bribes, extortion, blackmail, crimes of all types, etc.), but not necessary, and won't be needed, if you go to God and lead a different life. Until then (going to Jesus – the truth) we will have all kinds of evil done to people in the world (with satan leading – and you don't realize it). It is because of man (and his evil) that we (you) have all of these problems, and will continue. All following and believing what they want to believe. So believe Jesus and His word – and change. And we need to learn to do without much in our life sometimes – only Jesus can stop them and help them. Share Him – to all of noah's sons – to all you know.

Some people think they are better than the law and don't care about following anything, but satan leads them (like a god themselves), and only Jesus can stop them. Think of the consequences for you and others.

Everyone represents someone – family, nationality (appearance, color, etc.), beliefs, etc. – so you better behave and be a good example, etc. or you will cause harm (maybe death, etc.) to those that look like you. Because there are consequences to behavior and beliefs, likes and dislikes, etc. Take responsibility, change with Jesus. If you don't it's your fault, and others that do the same. Help others, don't go along with their evil.

If you are really guilty, then you should not let someone else be accused and be punished, and if you care that you are accused and looked at because of 'race' – don't let your lies, etc. hurt another like you, when you are guilty. Don't be selfish, and hurt others. You are to blame for the problems in this world, for you and others (not the police, laws, other 'races', etc. – but you).

How can you expect justice in this world and for your people, if you don't own up to your mistakes, evil, etc.? You are passing it on to someone else – no justice – you cause injustice (the real source of injustice is you). Stop blaming and crying a victim.

So looking the same as others (nationality, color, etc.) can hurt you, because any of those that do something that is evil (and they are looking for them) – they will look for someone like you (because they look like you) – so they are going to have to stop innocent people to find the suspect, etc.

One example that is in history that is related to this, that happens in this world – was in world war II, when america interned many asians, because the japanese bombed pearl harbor (dec. 7, 1941), which was evil (they could have interned others, too, but may have been a little harder to do). But it just didn't hurt japan (and those there), it hurt all of those that looked like them – in america (land for all of noah's sons – Jesus' land) – and hopefully some of them went to Jesus at that time. Even though america didn't have to intern them, it was a safety measure and may have been needed to secure the country, and made sense. Those asians that were interned, should have been mad at japan and other asians, etc., not america (and america needs to keep going to Jesus or the nation will fall apart). The point is that if someone looks like you, does something wrong or against the law or hurts someone, etc., and that suspect or enemy looks like you, then they are going to look for and bother you (and others like you). And that happens in the world and in america all of the time. You be better and obey the law and live right and don't make it hard on your own people, or even your family, etc. it is your fault then, if you do those evil things, if that hurts your own people. Go to Jesus to change, and whatever happens, if you did do something bad, accept the consequences of that behavior. Hopefully turn yourself in, so it won't bother other people that look like you, and deal with the punishment – and also turn someone in, that you know committed a crime, and help them suffer the consequences and hopefully get to know Jesus someday. This story just shows you how evil this world is (of satan's) – and why we need to go to Jesus (all of noah's sons).

Don't put yourself in a position to get out of or help someone get away with something. Go to Jesus and share Him.

So don't try to move up in this world to help people get off from evil, lies, etc. – only help for the truth, even if you lose, etc., it is truth and justice that matters, even for you. Tell the truth. It is satan that is the liar – don't follow him – he will make it sound like it is someone else's fault and not yours.

Man believes a certain way and problems still are there, and man tries some other belief (or some superstition, programs, etc.) to get rid of it, but it or something else comes up. Go to Jesus, not satan's ways.

People want to use excuses – why they fail, etc. – because they are black, woman, poor, etc., but it is mostly because they accept that and believe and live a certain way (without Jesus in their life), but Jesus will help anyone of noah's sons (or daughters), if you go to Him. You're punishing yourself (and others), and this world will (with satan) keep doing that to you, us, until you go to Jesus. Get away from noah's sons. Even gangs have colors, etc., and is the same problem – causing problems for others and yourself – being prideful, etc.

Even a policeman that wears the same uniform (and they are in the lime light – visible) – they need to do their job correctly (and most of the time they do), so they don't hurt other policemen (and they are held to a higher standard – even though we all should be) – but they are needed and do have a tough job and are trying to help and protect people – even you, and your family (because man is evil), so help them do their job (you couldn't handle what they do or deal with each day), and you need to live a good life, and help others live a good life. Most people – criminals, etc. would treat people worse, if they were policeman – they couldn't handle it – to have control or to be nice, etc. for doing that job. So stop making it tougher on them. All going to Jesus will help – we all need to do better, and but all (of noah's sons) are needed, but it will only work with Jesus and His word. We all need to be one in Jesus, not our own people, nationality, belief, etc.

And that is why people that look (do things, believe, live, lifestyle, etc.) alike (blacks, hispanics, asians, red hair, tattoos, politicians, young, families, long hair, musicians, democrats, irish, women, gangs, republicans, men, good looking, prostitutes, communists, fat, socialists, criminals, rich, jews, poor, athletes, movie stars, police, bosses, germans, fighters, italians, english, doctors, columbians, etc. – you name it), may all be punished (especially if it happens frequently) – since they are all on the same team (same jersey, colors, etc.), so you need to be aware of that, and how you behave and live your life, so you don't hurt others (that look like you) by your selfish actions (because when one makes a mistake – all get punished – like in a sport, and from adam, etc.), we should learn from this. Don't have your mistake be taken out on those that look like you. You cause the prejudice, etc.

Now that we are all different – from noah's sons, then we are on different teams, etc. And only Jesus can change that.

One mistake can hurt you in this world – for you or a policeman – you have to be careful – and don't make things worse for others by the way you live (for others or a policeman). Go to Jesus to direct your steps – **prov. 16:9; jer. 10:23-24** (or satan will). Otherwise you are as prejudice as anyone else.

People, groups, nationalities, etc. have to know that they do wrong – don't judge when you know you are bad, too. America is getting more and more that way now. Go to Jesus (and get the Holy Spirit), and learn His word – the truth (the bible), to know what is really bad, or not. Don't follow satan – don't be against God. Or you will continue to be against each other.

And it is where prejudice comes from (you are representing your team, community, nationality, color, culture, family, etc.), and you all act the same and look the same (so you better be aware and be good – not selfish, evil, etc.). Do the right thing (and know what that is – don't be hurtful, etc.). Think of whom you represent – your family, community, nationality, country, etc. – think of your children – help them and teach them (and you be a good, or better, example). So get after those that behave that way (evil, disrespectful, hateful, etc.), or it's your fault, too. And if you don't want to be looked at the same and judged (and don't like to be judged that way), then don't look at others the same (police, nationalities, cultures, beliefs, etc.), who are all on the same team and wear their 'colors', etc. So basically; look at yourself and change (hopefully others will do the same) – don't be a hypocrite. See if they do good or not (especially with the truth with Jesus). Not all blacks (whites, etc.) are bad and not all police (politicians, etc.) are bad (letting their evil get the best of them). But if you are – you get what you deserve. Stop trying to get out of what you do. Blame yourself. Help people the best you can, until they get to know Jesus, and keep sharing Him. And you need to look at yourself, too. All go to Jesus.

If you don't like what someone is doing – because they may be doing something bad for themself or others – maybe against what God wants (sometimes against the law, etc.) – don't try to fix it yourself – maybe say something (turn them in, etc.), but don't hurt someone, etc. to make a point. Do what you need to do to, so they would get the proper punishment (whatever that is) for what they did (what they might deserve). And share Jesus with them, and pray for them.

We can only get along with Jesus (and His word – the truth of it), and help others do the same, that's what we should be doing in this life. Maybe you can change and help solve the problem – go to Jesus, and share Him.

And sometimes people change and grow and, change teams (just like in sports, etc.) – basically learn the truth (best is Jesus' truth) and grow up. Know that change is real.

The best uniform to put on is from Jesus in **eph. 6:10-20; col. 3**. Know that you are saved with the Holy Spirit and know the truth.

Don't be fooled by people wanting to look like they are on a 'team' – acting, wearing the same, etc., but are not – just trying to make those others look bad by their behavior, remarks, etc. – look at the fruit (result, etc.) of their behavior. People can be wolves in sheep's clothing (like so many in the world – beliefs, politics, rich, even poor, man, woman, etc.) – **matt. 7:15-17**.

We still have to know man is sinful, and need to know the truth to change, but you can see how someone lives and believes, and still need to know if it is the truth, and not fool you.

Most people only agree (at least most of the time, there are times that they all don't), with their own kind (blacks, whites, cultures, etc.) – right or wrong (some more than others), partly because of peer pressure, etc., and that is not right or best for man. It should be what is best – the truth, and Jesus (the truth of His word).

In reality, all that seem to be on the same team (even americans, young, blondes, greeks, whites, Christians, blacks, even jews, etc.), may not all think the same – knowing that life is not good, and it comes down to believing in truth – right or wrong – in God (in Jesus), or not. And seeing how the world really is (controlled by satan and evil), not just black and white, rich and poor, etc., and many other people, beliefs, etc. – many, many false Christians.

Then there are the jews – for the most part believe the same (on the same team), and people that are against them (they try to stay to themselves for the most part and not bother people) – and they (as a nation) still need to believe in Jesus – and will someday (but individual jews can and do go to Jesus), and they have struggled over the years because of that (rejection of Jesus) – as most people do. And when God hardens hearts of man, it is because they are hardened and lost already – not wanting to go to God – like cain, pharaoh, etc., and the jews at times (even today without Jesus). But God (Jesus) will go to the jews again, and they will be His people (**hosea 1:6-11; isa. 10:20-23; rom. 9:19-33**) – mainly in the tribulation (**rom. 11:25-36**). As God will keep going to you to go to Jesus your whole life, but go to Him while He can be found (**isa. 55:6**) – do it now (and while you are still alive).

So there are really two types of people today (just like before the flood – in the presence of the Lord or not) – those that believe in the truth (Jesus, and His word), and those that don't (everything else – mainly satan's lies, that leads man away from God, and His word). It is satan that makes all of these different groups and levels of evil, but it is God that separates us all – to protect us (from satan's plan), and for some punishment that we may have deserved. Don't follow the world (**rom. 12:2**) – satan is the ruler of this world (**2 cor. 4:1-4**). Follow Jesus' word – not the world – get the 'L' out of there.

So God puts the wicked (unsaved) with the good (saved) together (**matt. 13:36-43**) in the world today (hopefully to get the wicked to change and go to Jesus) – but evil is here, so go to Jesus to get through this life.

And we all have to suffer the consequences of the life we live (and how others live – we affect each other – and will until we all go to Jesus), and what we believe. Find out what God wants (in His word). And He tells us and tries to help us – warn us (with Jesus and His word). And if bad things happen to you or others, it is because you're not with Jesus (and His word – the truth), and don't keep going to Him and following Him and His word.

The true God is a God of second chances (for many things – including health, relationships, finance, behavior, etc.) – and gives all a chance to go to Him, all through our life – go to Jesus now. And learn the truth of His word – the bible.

Study it and divide it rightly **(2 tim. 2:15-16)** to find the truth of who we are and why we are here and why and how God set it up this way. Get saved – the Holy Spirit – and let it teach you the truth of His word (**1 cor. 2:12-14**) – for these many things.

We are all different (separated by God), because God doesn't want satan to have all of mankind go against God all at the same time and level (like before the flood and a little after, when man was the same – speech, color, belief, etc.). But being different now, can cause prejudices and hatred, especially without Jesus (and the truth) – the world the way it is, is here, and suppose to get us all to go to Jesus. Let those evil things help you go to Jesus.

The best thing to do is to go to Jesus (and His word) and you will be on the right side (team) and live your life the way you should (and the way He wants you to). He is in charge (and will take care of you), no matter what you believe and how you behave, and you will suffer the consequences, until you go to Him and change (get saved and get the Holy Spirit). The Holy Spirit is your color (or should be – all of us). Have people see that in you.

God looks at humans that way – if you are human (no matter what color you are or belief you have, etc.), you are evil (born sinful and without the Holy Spirit), because we are all from the same team (at first from adam, and now from noah and his sons).

But when we go to Jesus and are truly saved (with the Holy Spirit), He will not see the evil, sin, etc. – covered by Jesus (His color – the red of His blood shed for us all – **rom. 4:6-8**).

Until then, we deserve what we get in life from what we do (and from our parents, etc.), because of man – sin. We are all related to each other from adam and noah's sons (black, white, rich, poor, man, woman, etc.), and all are evil (until we go to Jesus).

All people need to be nicer to each other (and all of us are prejudice to a point – some more than others), but won't truly be nice without Jesus. Jesus can raise up any of noah's sons (black, white, etc.), if we humble ourselves to go to Him and give into Him and follow the truth of His word.

Whatever mistakes and choices you make in your life can be forgiven by God, if you go to Jesus – then He will change you.

So go to Jesus to change that (the only way you can do it), and thank God for Jesus and His sacrifice for us all – but you have to go to Him individually (and get saved – get the Holy Spirit) and follow Him (and His word – believe what He believes, and live that way). Get on His team. Or you will just see your team struggle, suffer, in prison, die, etc.

Whites may not be as represented percentagewise in prisons (having opportunities and taking advantage of them – not depending on ways of life, or people, even sports, etc. to live a good life, and not listening to the negative about making it in this world, or seeing bad examples and giving up), but anyone can live a miserable life, if they want to (especially without Jesus), they don't have to – don't limit yourself. And depending on what you label as white in the world – anywhere from 40 to 50% (possibly less, because some of those countries are not having as many babies, etc.) is white in the world – mostly european (japheth – including spain – central, south america can be, too, but a mixture). People of color (medium to dark) represent close to 50% of the world (with asians possibly being the biggest group – maybe being a combination of japheth and ham), and they may be from canaan, mostly.

Anyone can have children – no matter how bad a person they are, and not take care of them, or themselves. Go to Jesus first.

When you have sex, and that person gets pregnant, it is your responsibility, and you are guilty (as well as the woman), whether it is your child or not (you still had sex, and then accept the consequences of those decisions).

And not having babies is fine, if you are not having sex, but if any are (including raping and killing – and many are guilty of this), they are separating babies from life – babies are important (just like you are), more than animals (but people seem to protect animals, more than humans, though animals can and should be protected, too). And all nationalities have sex trafficking, crime, etc. (whatever form that takes) – none any worse, but all are evil, etc. Jesus will forgive all – you just have to go to Him (repent – want to change your ways) and follow (Him and His word – the truth), and then let Him change your life.

And even adoption is an answer and is good and needed in the world – some may not be able to have children – use this option – God would want it. And Jesus will help you.

Try to love and help people – one person matters. Go to Jesus and share Him and His word – truth. Use your struggles to learn and help others.

All lives matter (even black lives, but it seems more black babies are killed by choice), and satan is for death (don't follow him), and Jesus is for life (especially to get saved, before you die), and all need to go to Him, and He will help you if you want to do what's right, because of Him, and Him in your life. Especially in america. Go to Jesus, He will help you with what you need.

Stand up for this country (america) – even more for God (Jesus) and His word (but the truth), and it will be good for you.

Whites are not perfect – none of us are, and we all need to be better (and better to each other), but all have to go to Jesus to do that. We all have things in our past that aren't good, as a person, and a nation, or nationality, or family ancestors, etc. Go to Jesus and change that. Don't judge who someone is in the past (person or nation, etc.), but what they are now (and it better be true). And go to Jesus to help you.

That's what this world is for, and why we are still here – going to Jesus – especially america – for all of noah's sons.

Don't keep thinking that it will work out any other way in this world – without Him (but it has to be the truth – many false churches, etc., too, out there – here and in the world).

It's what God thinks of us that matters, not what we think of ourselves. We need to live up to God's standards and what Jesus is for (some of us may be 'nicer' – at least we always think we are), but it is short of what God wants for us (otherwise satan is getting a hold of you). And this only can be possible with Jesus. For any of noah's sons (as diverse as they all are).

All people – man, woman, young, old, black, white, etc. – all of noah's sons – especially the true believers should do what God says (**titus 2**).

Noah's son japheth is many colors (even north, central, and south america, all maybe considered white), but japheth (the most in the world – **gen. 9:27**) is mostly white. We have to work it out so that we can get along – but it is with Jesus only that it can happen. So don't hurt each other – change – with Jesus.

And are there really almost two murders an hour (death, any way it happens – sickness, accidents, etc., is over 300 people an hour) of every day (more, if you count abortions, etc.) in america (some from defending themselves, others by choice, also those that just kill)? The rest of the world may be worse.

Just like the blood of abel cried out to God after cain killed him, so does the blood of those that were unjustly killed – God will punish. Go to Jesus and repent and change.

If you think about the abortions – people lost, not here – maybe 60 million or more, even in the last 50 years, at least in america – and the children that they would have had – there maybe would have been 150 million more people in the world today, having a chance to get to know and share Jesus. So maybe God is punishing america (and others places) because of the abortions, and God's answer is with immigrants that don't come here properly (and maybe hurting people here), until we go to Jesus and His word. So we need to share Jesus with the immigrants, too (with everyone). What america is for – why God made it – to share Jesus (especially in the end time). It is getting close to the end, and we need to all go to Jesus – as many as we can in this evil world today, and keep people alive, if possible – even the hurting immigrants (the abuse, taken advantage of, sex trafficking, drugs, etc.). So they still need to be controlled, for their sake, as well as americans.

Besides the evil – murders, rapes, etc. in the world, that happen daily, and in america – there are about 250,000 cold cases in the u. s., which is adding about 6,000 more a year – some states worse than others. America may solve about 30 cases a year – even with technology, etc., but the only way is with the truth (which comes from you – that's how evil man is – wake up). The world is more evil – man is evil (born that way), unless we go to Jesus (and really learn His truth of His word), and follow Him daily. And share Him.

This world and people are more evil than you think – man is. Thank God for Jesus and the Holy Spirit – true Christians in the world, or this world would be worse.

Crime of all kinds (any evil, etc.) is by all people – like before the flood, even though all of man was the same then (color, speech, etc. – **gen. 11**), and satan could control us all at the same time then – **gen. 6** (because man is evil, then and today – especially without Jesus), and we need protection from all evil in this world, so every country needs police, etc. (but with what God wants, not man – **rom. 13**) – if you are not doing anything wrong, who cares if a policeman stops you (not all police are perfect – neither are you, or some may need another job)? You don't want the police to stop arresting white people, do you? Including criminals, killers, rapists, etc. that are against black or white, etc. You just don't want them done to you. The problem is most of the time you don't want to stop doing these evil things in your life (your lifestyle, who you hang out with, etc.) that are not good for you or others (and usually against God, and the nation) – there is no other reason, we all do evil (you have to suffer the consequences of that lifestyle, etc. – we all do, if we live that life), so stop the complaints (we need the police, etc. to protect, all of us, and for the most part they do a good job), and they can continue to get better (like we all can). Quit bothering others with your life (especially in a harmful, evil way – for your selfish desires, etc.). And God may use a policeman to stop you (black or white, etc.) to shake you up – to change the road you are going down, use that for change, and even should be thankful, and then change, but you have to go to Jesus then (repent, and change your life). God can and does use the mistakes we make to learn and to help others, but doesn't want us to make them in the first place – either way – go to Jesus to grow and change and use them for good (**rom. 8:28**). Helping others get to know Jesus can cover many sins (**james 5:20**) – share Jesus.

Most people, including criminals, etc. couldn't handle being a policeman – they would not be able to control themselves and do a good job. Let the police do their job – and you stop making it hard for them and others in this world. We have to all change.

And when a policeman stops you – cooperate, be nice, etc. – surprise them – don't let blacks get off, by defunding the police, etc., because you will help whitey get off, too (who may be hurting you).

Be humble in all that you do – to people, law, elders, police, etc. – and tell the truth – especially going to God. He will help you through what you think is unfair, etc.

Regardless of what we are born with (including family, class, nationality, even things like astrology, beliefs, gender problems – all against God, etc.) – how we are brought up, etc. – who we are from (from noah's sons, and parents are responsible, too) – we all are evil (all against God) and responsible for what we do – behavior, etc., especially since we all can go to Jesus and change. Do it now. And don't teach people things against God and the truth of His word – go to Jesus.

Non-christians, including false Christians, etc. (white or black, any nationality, etc.), mostly use violence and threats, hatred, etc. to go against who they don't like – threatening terrorism, etc. – to those they hate. All can be saved, if you truly go to Jesus and follow Him and His word (get the Holy Spirit).

And the same person that mainly persecuted, killed, and scattered the jewish Christians out of israel, was eventually used by Jesus to save people – to become Christians – mainly gentiles – saul (paul – **acts 7 to 9, 26**). Anyone can be saved. Go to Him.

It's not just what the way you live does to you, but to others – living in fear of this world and people (just because of your selfishness, etc. – that we all are born with). And terror in any form is bad – by anyone or group (and some do that no matter what). All have done evil – and terror comes in many forms (Jesus will get rid of the need for any of that for a person, family, society, city, nation, belief, culture, etc., if you just go to Him for the answers and follow).

What is stopping anyone from going to Jesus and have Him in our lives (in this evil world)? And He will protect us here (**john 17**), but not do the evil ourselves, really following satan, and not knowing it (you know who you are – and who others are). And if God is doing it (the punishment) to you (for the way you live your lives) – how do you stop it then (**acts 5:38-39**)? Go to Jesus.

We all are evil – talking evil to evil – all are evil without Jesus, so don't look at others, but yourself, and go to Jesus (and His word) – He is the Judge and Savior (use that as your guide) – what will it be for you? He put laws, police, and prisons here for all of us – to protect us from the evil, from ourselves (all of noah's sons), and from satan (but man follows) – so you have to obey and listen or you will have problems, which lead to death and destruction (which is from satan) – so if you are doing that then you are following satan, these things – laws, police, etc., are put in place by God (**rom. 13**) to protect those that want to do right and live a good life with Him. Stop breaking the law (those of God and of the nation), and hurting others (and don't be around those that do – you know it's not right), if not, accept the consequences of your life (prison, death, etc.). The evil is real and so is satan.

Jesus can protect you and keep you safe (**john 17:13-21**) – if you would only go to Him, and follow and change your life. He loves you and is waiting (**rev. 3:20**).

And is the only way that love (**1 cor. 13**) will ever come out is with Jesus and His word – and we follow what He wants (even to love your enemies – all of noah's sons, which is tough to do – especially without Jesus). Wanting all to go to Jesus, if possible. And we are even to abstain from any appearance of evil (**1 thess. 5:12-24**) – which is tough to do (and we are not perfect), and not even think evil (**matt. 5:27-28**) – so we need to keep going to Jesus and the truth of His word. Only Jesus can help us do any of these things, and Jesus can save us – give the Holy Spirit. Our only hope.

You should do things that God would want you to do – not what you or someone else would want – it is hard to live this way, and only with Jesus (and the Holy Spirit) can you do this.

Take the weight of the world off your shoulders and give it to Jesus (**matt. 11:28-30**).

Because we are all doing it (the punishing, and the hate, etc.) to ourselves. We are all born evil – with different problems (so don't say you're fine, because you are born with something – something evil – whatever sin it is – basically against God, and His word), and we can only deal with (and change) these problems by going to Jesus (getting the Holy Spirit – being born again, **john 3**). So we need to go to Jesus as young as we can or we will suffer with more problems (especially after this life) – some worse than others. And people that are disliked shouldn't be able to get away with evil, murder, etc. (because people feel sorry for them or they were only getting back at people) – go to Jesus if you are disliked (or even dislike yourself – some people even like to hurt themselves, so they may not care about others either), since we are all born evil, we may feel that way sometimes, and have to accept that (otherwise go to Jesus and be changed). And don't kill yourself (or others) – Jesus has the answers and will help you want to live – have something better for you (and you will like), and have a good life, and when you do die, you will go to a better place – heaven, because of Jesus in your life – so live a good life here before then. There are no excuses for what we go through (only if Jesus is not there – but He is, it's just you don't go to Him, and stay with Him, and His word). And america gives you a chance to go to Jesus. He is the answer for everything – for all of our struggles with each other, including too much hate and killing.

In america (and mostly around the world), whites mostly kill whites, and blacks mostly kill blacks, etc., but they kill each other, too, and whites being the most killed. And blacks kill more blacks sometimes than whites kill whites – but the percentage of whites killed compared to blacks don't match nationality statistics of america (whites – hispanics included, are close to 75% of the u.s. and blacks may be close to 15% of the u.s., and some are a mixture of many groups), and blacks that are killed (mainly by blacks – so stop killing anyone – but especially each other) is about 40% – compared to their percentage in the u. s. (which is about 15%). It doesn't need to happen – hate, anger, etc. – when you can go to Jesus.

If the same people, family, etc. kill each other, it's still not good (it doesn't make it right or ok) – humans are humans (we are all the same from adam, but look different after the flood – mainly after the tower of babel), but all (noah's sons) are evil. Don't harm each other (protect, defend, if necessary, but do what is right). We don't have to look different to hate or kill (we are all sinners, etc.), and it (the evil) happened when we didn't have anyone, but those that looked like us around.

Don't do that to anyone, but especially, don't do it to yourself – it just shows how people are (evil in the world, mainly without Jesus). Why not go to Jesus? – if not, you like killing each other (satan does). Get away from our differences – get away from noah's sons – killing each other, and go to Jesus. And be one. Wouldn't you like the person to get Jesus first (be saved), instead of killing your family, friends, etc.? Share Jesus and you be ready with Jesus.

CHAPTER 9

Conclusion: Summary of Main Themes and Final Call to Repentance and Faith Alone in Jesus Christ

Live a different life (with Jesus, and His word – only the truth of it), and stop all of the evil (especially get away from noah's sons, and go to Jesus to do that). Look in the world and see killings, death, etc. – wouldn't it be good, if they all – those that died, were saved – in heaven or the killer got saved before and didn't do any of this? Go to Jesus and share Him.

Most of the countries that have most of the murders (for population) are mostly hispanic, and the least amount of murders are mostly asians (mainly because they have stricter punishments, etc., or not reported properly, etc.). So the countries that have the least amount of murders are those that are usually the least diverse (not many different people to hate, or prejudice, etc. – not many of the three sons of noah – but they still kill each other – man is evil), and/or they may also have the strictest punishment (and there are a few countries that are smaller and less populated, etc.) – if any statistics are true (or even history is – maybe all that you know and see and believe and are taught by family, school, culture, etc., mainly by man, is wrong, for any culture, belief, nationality, etc.), the best is to go to God and His word for any answers (for whatever problem it is – man, science, history, truth, etc.). Go to Jesus to know the truth – and to live a better life – the only way. God has something for you – a better life – go to Jesus (**1 cor. 2:9**).

So america (which has the most diversity, more different people, etc. and is the biggest, and not as strict punishment, etc. – but fair for the most part), should have the most murders (for population), but it doesn't because of Jesus (and with protection we have). And now you see why some people come to america (since america is in the middle of the world in this category, but is the one of the biggest and most diverse of all of the countries – many of each of noah's three sons – more to hate). But it is Jesus that helps america (or it would be worse, and still could get worse, if we go away from Him – like we are starting to). If not, God could bring (or allow) a plague to all of us (like He has in the past, and today) – look to Him for the answers, like we should anyway. And people may have tried to kill people in many ways – like wars, bombs, viruses, etc. – but God may have stopped some of them – others He let go. So there is less prejudice – like blacks can say what they want about other blacks, asians to asians, hispanics to hispanics, etc., with less diversity in most other countries – but they are still evil (and kill). At least america has Jesus in it (for now), no matter how evil some people are here now, but better than the other nations (even ones that say they have Jesus – even though they may not – and not have the truth – or know, follow, learn, or share it), who are definitely evil, and america cannot trust them (they are not with Jesus – even though they may say they are, and many hate us and others – through satan), and we should not help them to cause more problems in the world (but should help them to get to know Jesus – the truth, if possible), and whoever comes here should live for what america stands for – freedom (and the truth of God), and agree to that. Which Jesus makes possible – live a better life.

Even though we feel sorry for people living in other countries, and some trying to come into america – they need to believe the way we should believe and help the country – believe in Jesus and His truth eventually – not false beliefs, and not help america or the people here (and really not help themselves). Make it a better country than they came here from – or they wouldn't come here, if they don't want to live in the country they came from. Don't make it as bad as their country. Change who you are, not just your location, etc. With Jesus and the truth of His word.

But we have trouble getting people to live a better life, and how america should be, because man is selfish and stubborn (sinful and separated from God). Jesus makes it bearable here.

You can see it the world – no matter how nice you are, we have to deal with people in this world – just like when you are driving. No one cares – driving wild and fast – causing others to have problems (sometimes causing you to drive wild) and not really getting anywhere. We have to deal with that from people in everyday life sometime.

If you are not very nice (living any selfish way you want, etc. – you are not innocent, really none of us are, but some more than others), but you want everyone else to be nice to you, including the police, or even other criminals, like you (they all won't, and in some cases shouldn't be nice to you) – you have to change (with Jesus, and don't be evil anymore – we all do). Not just following the nation's laws, but especially God's laws. You know how you are – look at yourself. Then go to Jesus – the only answer. And this world could be worse, but people have been sharing Jesus with people – and they got saved and didn't kill someone, because they got saved first (we will know sometime about this – in heaven). Even if it hurts one person – God doesn't want us to sin – so He shares His laws in His word – and being with Jesus and the Holy Spirit we will be good (**gal. 5:22-26**).

If you want the evil out of the world – get it out of you first – go to Jesus and get the Holy Spirit (and keep satan away – don't listen to him or man, and go to God and His word).

There should be something for those who do the right things in life, but that should be a normal thing to do (be nice), but it isn't, although God will reward those that go to Jesus. We can't follow and obey God's laws (that shows us our sin), at least very easily, but with Jesus we can connect back to God (with the Holy Spirit), and have a chance to follow naturally the laws God has (**matt. 22:36-40; mark 12:28-34; luke 10:25-28; rom. 13:10; gal. 5:13-26**), to get through this evil sinful way that we are, or keep being evil to each other. You choose.

It doesn't matter how many people die, get killed, etc. (don't kill needlessly), in this evil world (it is going to happen in this world) – if you go to Jesus and get truly saved and are ready to go. We are all going to die sometime, some way. But try to live as long as you can and help others to do the same – and help them to get to know Jesus.

So we need the police, fireman, prison, even doctors (to a point) and lawyers, etc., because of evil people (like man is – even you), and why we need Jesus more than ever. You don't want to see anyone get hurt or killed needlessly, but you have to live a good life and help yourself out – don't put yourself in a bad situation, eventually you will have serious problems (even death) – go to Jesus before you do. If you don't want the police, government, etc., then all of us have to go to Jesus and that is the only answer, otherwise we do – need police, etc., because of people like you.

The police, courts, prisons, etc. are way worse (tougher – and maybe unfair) around the world (try going to russia, turkey, north korea, cuba, venezuela, china, japan, etc.), it's better in america (but fair, forgiving, etc. for the most part) – if you plan on living an evil lifestyle, etc. (and why some people come here), but don't do that – go to Jesus (who gives you freedom here in america). If you don't go to Jesus, then stop complaining (it's your fault what happens to you, and to those you love, or at least say you do). Jesus is what makes everything that is good work in this world (and especially in this country), whether you know it or not. So go to Him and live a better life – follow Him daily (and you better know His truth – in His word). And at least have you (and your loved ones), be ready to go, if something does happen.

God separates people, even in america, so that the worst people (with satan) can't get all of the power, (like it did in europe, etc. in the middle ages – false church, beliefs, etc. – God sent a plague, and even before and since then) and run the country (especially away from God and His word through Jesus – the truth).

And the reason Jesus can be taught and learned (the truth of His word) better in some countries is because they only have mostly one son of noah and look and talk alike, etc. – not as diverse. So america is the toughest mission field in the world – we have all of noah's sons (and many false churches, religions, beliefs, families, languages, etc. – being brainwashed with lies of satan). We can't just go to church, be good, etc. to be saved (just like the jews cannot do that – they need to go to Jesus).

We need to be balanced and see the truth (against all of the lies and evil of this world of satan – even in america) – with Jesus and His word, with the truth and look at things fairly and just. Both sides need to be looked at, and see what people believe and not be one sided in prejudice (we all are) – and be hypocrites (like you see in america today – even from the leaders, etc. – who are mostly against God and His word – the truth of it – and Jesus).

At times, this country has been ruled by those against God – especially in recent years – and evil (satan) tries to keep people from going against them, by punishing, basically good people, unfairly, and getting away with it – then letting everyone know about it – how bad it will be if you go against them. That is what satan has done in this world since the beginning. We have to stop that by going to Jesus.

Mainly look at yourself, and criticize yourself, because it's you that doesn't want to know the truth and see it. Even though we are not perfect – we need to go toward that – we only can with Jesus and the truth of His word. Care about all people – with Jesus, you can help them.

No one cares about white people (that live a bad life) – like blacks, etc. do – that are not treated fairly (and some are not), etc. – they just get what they get – what they deserve.

When are you going to see a black person stand up (protest, riot, etc.) for a white person?

And no one cares (even if it was an accident, or seems unfair) if a white person dies, or goes to prison (except maybe their family), just like anyone else (they just feel they deserve it, because they lived that kind of life) – it's how you live your life, and that it has consequences (keep living that way and it will catch up to you – black or white, rich or poor, man or woman, etc.) – so if a white person (or even a policeman, etc.) gets killed, most people think, it was the way they lived their life, or even an accident, etc., that happens in this evil world, it is accepted by all, but there are no riots, protests, etc. for whites (non-blacks, or policeman, etc.) that live a life that leads to death (by a black, or a white, or a policeman – black or white, etc.), although if it is a black person – it is considered prejudice (racism, etc.), but in reality, it's because of the way they live their life – and those like them (their parents, grandparents, family, etc. need to work harder, and do it right, to have a better life for all – and all need to go to Jesus) – those are the consequences (even if it's the first time you do something that's not good for you – it doesn't have to be a way of life yet to kill or hurt you, and don't let it become a way of life) for anyone it is the same (black or white, rich or poor, man or woman, etc. – anyone, and don't hang around with anyone like that, where they go, etc. – or it's your fault what happens to you, or others) that lives that life, or even being around those that do. And either God will allow you to die – or eventually your behavior will, but He wants you to go to Him first, and He will avenge for you, if you are with Him (vengeance is the Lord's – **heb. 10:30-31**) – get to know Jesus before you die, and you have a choice, free will, don't wait. But stop living your life that way (and change – only with Jesus can you). Even if it is an accident that you die, or even get hurt, etc. (because you put yourself in that position with your lifestyle, etc., then anything can happen – live a different life and not a dangerous, evil one, and get saved, with Jesus, then if you die you know where you are going). And it is satan that we are really fighting, not man (**eph. 6:10-13**).

We need to change with Jesus (and His truth), otherwise, you take your chances, and don't complain. People don't care if they are right or wrong (or hurt others) – they just want their own selfish desires, wants, needs, etc. met – and it all affects others. There are no guarantees in this life – but you have choices – choose Jesus. Have Him go with you wherever you go, and better yet, have Him lead you (Him and His word).

People and groups, and their ideas, fuel racism and prejudice, etc. White groups or black groups are all the same – kkk, black lives matter, etc. just hate, and try to have power (and get people to do evil) – satanic and against the true God. Share Jesus and His truth – use your time wisely.

People want weapons, drugs, money, etc. to live in this world – but we need Jesus and the truth of His word to have a chance. At least go to Him first. Then use what He gives us to live.

And Jesus can do a better job than you to fight it. Go to Jesus or go to hell – that's the choice for man here. It's that simple.

Some people preach or share Jesus with compassion and others with fear (**jude 1:22-23**) – both can work, depending on what each person needs. God will help you. But it has to be the truth.

You have to clean up your own (own family, culture, etc.), don't let it go and get worse – your hatred, prejudice, thinking etc., and don't let anyone do what they want – stop it before it gets worse. There has to be discipline and punishment (even God uses them), and responsibility for your life and actions (and for others) – you can't just do what you want and think it is fine (you're born that way, but don't have to stay that way). And especially go to Jesus. He will work it out for you. You know right from wrong from adam (**gen. 2 and 3**).

All of noah's sons (all nationalities, etc.) want to show who they are, and if society, people, power, etc. keep them down, they will eventually want to move up in the world, and people still won't get along. Have to change and go to Jesus – share Him.

You honor someone that shares Jesus (the truth of Him and His word), and you honor someone by sharing Jesus (the truth of Him and His word). But it is all for Jesus – honor Him.

Don't raise you up (any leader or group, religious, etc.) to change – raise Jesus up – follow Him.

Man can't go against God and have problems, then put that person up on a pedestal and be honored, when they should be honoring Jesus and know He helps people back to make it out of problems, and to help them live, etc. – then they should say don't honor me, etc., but honor Jesus, not men.

And you don't believe in Jesus, just because of other people, but believe because of who Jesus is – He is God, through His word, and what He did, and is doing (giving us the Holy Spirit). All having a chance to be saved now, with Him.

So don't honor evil, sin, etc. – be ashamed of it (even if it is your family, etc.) for any group or types of people (no matter who it is – man, family, culture, nationality, etc.) – they should not be honored (until you, and they, go to Jesus), but learn from it and share it with your family, etc., knowing how not to live (we don't have to be that way), because man is evil – although some do try to do good things (maybe for selfish reasons), but only with Jesus (He can be honored, or no one should) can it be good (He tells you how to live your life, if you really want to know), or it is a waste of time. We need to go to Jesus and live an honest life – you should care that they try to or do get away with things (don't let them – it will only end up hurting them or others, including you). That is what man is the same at – evil, but we are different, too.

Have integrity, honesty, etc. (how you want to be treated) – basically how you live when no one is watching – but God is. Live a good life – and only with Jesus do you have a chance to.

Jesus is a way of life – not a religion, etc., and He will lead you and help you live a better life, now and after this one, forever.

God will not honor (or bless) a person, city, people, or nation, etc., if you don't go to Him (and His word) for the answers for everything (**deut. 30:1-3; psalm 33; psalm 72; jer. 4:2; gal. 3:8**), and all can be blessed if they go to Him – to Jesus (and His word) – and start sharing and talking about Him (the truth of it – not all of these lies, from satan, that some churches and religions, etc. talk about) for our answers. That is the real issue. So go now – talk about it, for everyone and everything, but it better be the truth. With Jesus only to get to God (**john 14:6; 1 tim. 2:3-6**), since He died and rose (the temple destroyed, and the bible was completed – **book of revelation**), basically for the last 2,000 years. No one else you can go to since Jesus died and rose – no man (dead or alive), angel, leader, church, etc. – just Jesus.

So there is a separation of abilities (and hopefully work for all) – from noah's sons (there is a separation, but we can be one with Jesus), and there may be some limitations, and not all are represented in all walks of life – but it also means people need to work harder (three times harder, if needed, and sacrifice things, if needed – like fun, desires, etc. – don't give up or be lazy, drop out, and just be given things, etc. – it's family, sometimes – especially in this country, and having money, that spoils people, etc.) – so keep working, if they want to get to another level, and do certain jobs in the world (especially with the opportunities in america – take advantage of them, and why america is the best, but can even be better). In america you can find out abilities you didn't know you have – use them and the opportunities for them, God made it that way.

We can all create things (and learn things) – some more than others, God made us that way (mainly from adam), and possible under certain conditions (like the opportunities we have in america with all of the different types of people around – all of the sons of noah). God will help you do well, with talents – God made us for good things (**psalm 139:13-14**), if we go to Him (the truth, not lies, that some false churches, groups, etc. share), otherwise we will do evil (and waste what we have).

Rich or poor you need Jesus and the truth of His word and follow Him, to be able to make it in this world – to not hurt others or yourself.

When all of the brothers share and work (noah's sons), like in america, we all benefit and get better, but only with God. It doesn't go well, when it is against God – like we did in the past (as we even see today), without His word, laws, etc. and especially Jesus, because without God in a country, then man (without God – Jesus, and His word – really satan) is in charge (**gen. 11**), and that does not solve anything or help people (**psalm 33:12; prov.14:34**).

We are not sons (or daughters) of God, until we are saved by Jesus and get the Holy Spirit, then we can become a brother (and be one) with Jesus (if you want to call someone your brother). Otherwise we are still sons (or daughters) of adam and eve, and noah and his sons, without Jesus. And stay evil, sinful.

And we can help others to get better, too (they have to want to get better and be helped, and work hard). But we all need to go to Jesus first (and His word – He will help you find what is best); otherwise, it is a waste of time.

It is our fault (especially in america – since we can know Jesus), no matter what has happened to us in our life (our childhood, family, limitations, poverty, nationality, obstacles, choices, etc.) – the answer to change, and to get something, is with Jesus (and His word), He is available to all – and we all can go to Him. And even though none of us are perfect, we all need to share Him and live our life that way as an example (go to Him and teach others). Help others with what you can, and Jesus will help you. Search God with all of your heart, mind, soul, and He will give you a good life, not an evil one (Jesus can – **jer. 29:11-13**).

And the reason we still have much of the separation (of these abilities) still in us today (mainly not going to Jesus), is that God separated us even more with the change of languages (**gen. 11**), when all of man started to go against Him again at the tower of babel (with nimrod, a hunter, warrior – ham's son, physical, leading a rebellion against God, and ham may do it again today, even though nimrod was lighter, medium skin – no color change yet of man, today many of the physical, ham, are darker skin), and then God scattered man all over the world (which is what God wanted man to do in the first place – **gen. 11:8-9**, but man didn't – most stayed near the equator, and got darker – and are still there today), eventually to have different abilities (and skin color change, etc.), from all of noah's three sons.

The flood (by God) caused separation of land – continents (all at once – **gen. 7 and 8**, not over millions of years) – to what we see today. Before the flood the land was all in one place (one big mass – no islands, etc, as were the seas, in one area – **gen. 1:9-10**), and man could get around easier (and had some technology, too – **gen. 4**, but not like it is today, and we really need it today, more than before the flood), and now today we can get around easier (and communicate, etc.), because of all of the technology, phones, travel, vehicles, etc. (**dan. 12:4**), and also possible to eventually do evil all at once (just like before the flood, and a little after – all be against God, **gen. 6; gen. 11**).

Man may have been smarter before the flood. If it's true that man doesn't use 100% of their brain – or use even very little – then God caused it, so we don't do more evil in this world, or live longer doing it (like before the flood – **gen. 5 and 6**) – or that satan can't take advantage of that. Go to God to use more, but for good.

Man has been able to build things, etc. (God created man with all of these abilities – but after the flood separated them with noah's sons). Noah built the ark (before the flood) – which was huge (**gen. 6:14-16**). And the tower of babel was built by all about 100 years after the flood. And then man (all of noah's sons – mainly japheth and shem) built many things since then (after the tower of babel man separated). The jews (shem)– building their temple, and city, and romans (japheth) building the known world then, and the europeans (japheth) building throughout europe, then all over the world, eventually. As japheth enlarged (**gen. 9:27**), and shem went with them, as ham helped to do what they wanted (any of the physical work – even though all of noah's sons have done physical work over the years).

The earth was divided (the language change and man scattered – **gen. 11:8-9**) about 100 years after the flood (when peleg was born – **gen. 10:25**) – after the tower of babel, and man scattered first to the warm part of the earth then (because of the ice age starting) – to the equator (and how man got darker – man is the darkest along the equator still today), others eventually went farther north as the ice age warmed, and those got lighter (all within about 400 to 500 years after the flood, and man lived little longer then, too – about 400 to 500 years old (**gen. 11:10-17**), to ingrain these traits, appearances, etc., and eventually went down to the age of what we are today – no more than 120 years – and noah did not preach and build the ark for 120 years – maybe for 70 years, **gen. 6:3**, so we are stuck with how we look). Ham and his descendants – which would be considered mostly darker skin, because of the sun – because of the weather after the flood (we all get darker in the sun), and the canopy was gone that protected the earth and man from the effects of sun, before the flood (**gen. 1:6-8**), and where the flood waters came from (**gen. 7:11-12**).

So just after the flood it started – **job 30:30; song of solomon 1:5-6** – we can see the palms and bottom of all of our feet are light, and the skin condition that people with dark skin get – vitiligo, seeing the lighter skin under the surface, all traits that God put there – went near the equator, they are even there today (maybe some of shem, too), and eventually to the americas (native americans in north, central, and south, and since it all started – the scattering, or the separation of man around the world, at the tower of babel – about 100 years after the flood, over 4,000 years ago – and why some people had an idea of how to build towers, pyramids, etc., and why you see them all over the world, as well as our buildings, etc. today), and japheth (which would be considered mostly white, not all – but lighter, and who most of the whites come from – mainly europeans) went farther north (**gen. 10:4-5; isa. 60:9**), then eventually spread all over the world, that you see today (enlarged – **gen. 9:27**), even to the americas (where the spanish – japheth, interbred with the natives, mostly in central and south america, and are a mix breed – a little of japheth, intellectual, and ham, physical – some darker skin, and why they have countries that are fairly successful, having a little of both, but only the way they believe would hurt them – without the truth of Jesus). And there are still native americans (ham – and can be darker) today (mainly in north america) that didn't breed with anyone in america (still mostly pure), but still get benefitted by this country (but not all go to Jesus and so they suffer). All three of noah's sons have had the chance to go to Jesus in america – having an easy life or a hard life (native americans, africans, europeans, jews, arabs, etc.), some are rich and others a little less (but all of noah's sons are better off than what they used to be – being here, than where they were from – they are all richer, and free, than the rest of the world, because they are living in america), and have a life they can use all of their abilities and grow to what they can achieve (if they would work hard and take advantage of the opportunities) – but going to Jesus is the main thing (and living a life that is not selfish, evil, etc.). Then you can get what you need and be fulfilled. Help others, and maybe go back to your old country and share Jesus.

And not all of the sons of noah were nice to each other at first here (and some still have trouble with that) – man is evil. And we all still need Jesus. Go to Him and His word daily.

Shem (which would be considered somewhat dark or medium color) – jews, and arabs, too (a mixture of shem and ham mostly) seemed to stay in the middle east (**gen. 16:11-12**), like today – where God put them (just like He eventually made america, and put us here – all land is God's – He puts us where He wants us), and finishing what He started (**gen. 9:27**), as we see today. Even though adam gave the earth – all that is in it (and its land, etc.) to satan (**gen. 3; matt. 4:1-11; 2 cor. 4:3-4; 1 john 4:4**), by sinning – listening to satan, but the earth is still God's, and God can give land to whoever He wants (or take it away) – which He has with america – today to share Jesus and His word, and before with the jews, with israel (and did take it away, and gave it back).

Jesus left israel (as He has done other countries) desolate (for almost 2,000 years, until 1948 – God's plan) – **matt. 23:38**, after the jews rejected Him, and Jesus won't return until the tribulation – **matt.**

24, and these are prophesies to and for the jews (as are the books of **hebrews to revelation** – in the bible – mainly for jews). Having the jews have some influence on the country they scattered to (which is what Jesus would have done with the jews – after His resurrection, if the jews – as a nation, would have followed Him – to evangelize the world – in seven years – before the temple was destroyed – which are now in the future – the tribulation).

And God did scatter the Christian jews (using saul – paul), but even more after they rejected Jesus and the temple was destroyed (scattering most all the jews) – about 70ad (by God – using man, and it won't be rebuilt until the tribulation – **dan. 9:27; matt. 24:14-16**, and Jesus will come back for them as a nation, for prophesy to be fulfilled, that wasn't fulfilled when He was here the first time, and the world will be like it was when Jesus was here the first time – with the world being run like the roman empire, **rev. 17:9-14** – and all of the empires before that – **dan. 2:19-45** – that you can see is starting to happen – by satan). Then the jews went all over the world to most countries (and some jews are still there today – even in america – and there is some prejudice against them in those countries – like you saw in germany, etc., and still in iran, and others, etc.), in the last 2,000 years (a big time out, like man does for sports, is now for the jews) – God even separates time – He created time, so now for the jews, the clock has stopped for 2,000 years – and will start up again with the seven year tribulation (seven years left of the 490 years that the jews owe God – **dan. 9:24-27**), and also their land (israel) was left desolate by God (over the years He has done it to other empires, lands, countries, etc. – those that mainly don't go to Him – going to Him is best for all) until He had the jews come back (in 1948) – part of the end time prophesy (then when the seven-year tribulation is over, the 1,000 year reign of Jesus will start – **rev. 20:4-8**, and Christians will reign with Jesus in the 1,000 year millennium – **1 thess. 4:16-17; 2 tim. 2:11-12**). And satan being bound for those 1,000 years (**rev. 20**). Even without satan, we are still sinful.

All prophesy, and bible, is from the Holy Spirit (**2 pet. 1:16-21**) – the truth, not from angels, man, etc. – the lies are from satan. Get the truth – Jesus giving the Holy Spirit to save and to learn truth.

In the garden, satan came in the form (in it) of the serpent, and first came to man (to adam and eve) after the creation (when satan was created, too – **gen. 2:1-3**), satan came to them on the eighth day, since there were no other humans to possess (and adam being created by God from the earth – how did moses know man's make up of his body is similar to the soil, 3500 years ago – when we just recently found that out?). So satan came in a serpent (and it is possible that animals could talk then, since eve didn't seem surprised that the serpent spoke to her). But satan will come as a man (the anti-christ) in the tribulation. All satan does is go to costume balls and halloween – always wears a mask, etc., to have people not know who he is (behind all of these evil groups – religions, false churches, politicians, nations, leaders, beliefs, programs, movements, people, governments, etc.), so he can hide, and fool man – know the truth, go to Jesus and His word, and don't be fooled anymore.

In the end times, satan will first go against the u.s.a. (just before the rapture, which will complete the destruction of america – like it looks today it is starting to), and then have different nations and people that satan controls work together (one world order, etc.), nations that normally don't always work together today (and it will progressively get worse – especially since the rapture just happened and caused chaos in the world, and someone – anti-christ – needs to lead them through it), and satan controls those people (but God allows this and has His timing for events, etc., just like He did with sodom, job, and other things in the past – to see what people will follow – Him or satan), and satan will use these groups and nations and beliefs, etc., together, leading to the end times and the tribulation (especially in **rev. 13**).

Eventually God knew that every country would try to help or take over another (travelling all around the world, technology, etc. – **dan. 12:4**), and that Jesus would be able to be shared – especially by america during the end times (what we are in now), and that satan will try to have all go against God (like satan did at the tower of babel, just after the flood – **gen. 11**).

All it takes is a few evil people to ruin things and lead people to destroy – there has to be justice for any evil, no matter how small, etc., or people will (or should) rise up to right the wrong (and we better know what right and wrong is – deep down we do – **gen. 2:9, 16-17; gen. 3:1-11** – and what God wants). And satan will take advantage of anything – no matter how good the intentions are to do something.

Maybe God will, or is, blinding the evil ones in america – those in power against Him. We need to keep praying and sharing.

And only Jesus can help us against satan – who we are fighting here **(eph. 6)**, and leads us to evil. Christians, while we are still here, can preach, pray, etc. the truth, and God may change the direction the world (and nation) is going, for a time.

We all want justice – but only Jesus can do that.

A country, family, etc. divided won't stand (and shouldn't without God) – but a world divided is fine – as long as satan can't unite the world (or hopefully even a nation) against God – and the world (satan) won't be united as long as america is with Jesus and His word. Jesus will help for what is best to unite man. Otherwise, separation is best (to keep satan from controlling all). With all of noah's sons going around the world – having japheth be in control for now.

All of the countries over the years have been exposed to technology – mainly japheth and shem, but needed all of noah's sons (using ham to do some physical work) to build up these countries over thousands of years – and some later on.

God wanted people on every continent, after the flood – separated for now (there were no continents before the flood – just one big piece of land on the planet), but eventually man was to (and will) come together and affect and impact each other – all of noah's sons – and building more modern (last 500 years or so) – but also led by satan (who continues to try to get all of man to go against God, all at the same time and level together, like he did before the flood). God made it harder for satan to do this, but it is coming again. All of the world and continents, cultures, people, etc., all starting to become modern – technology, travel (planes, cars, etc.), communication, etc. (as God said – dan. 12:1-4) – satan leading, to make the world one – all of noah's sons.

God knew it would take this long – about 4,000 years, to get to the end – to where we are today in the world.

Besides noah building the ark before the flood – about 2500 b.c. – with God's help (and others alive with God at that time helping – including noah's father and grandfather and family), but after the flood, and the building of the tower of babel – which took all of noah's sons – led by nimrod (son of ham – **gen. 11**) – and was before the change of language, and scattering of man around the world. Then God made noah's sons separate, and with different abilities and talents, etc.

So people scattered, by God, all over the world, after the tower of babel, about 4,000 years ago – then they all settled down and didn't travel as much, until many years later (after each country developed and grew – mainly in europe for japheth).

So the language change (along with geography, weather, etc.) caused people to look alike within their group (nationality, etc.) – germans look alike, so do italians, africans, chinese, spaniards, etc. – that's why we look like our parents – and it keeps going. Eventually technology, travel, etc. got people together – leading to some interbreeding (some within one of noah's sons, but also some with the other sons – nationalities, etc.) – with God leading this change, and can be good, especially if we go to Him. But still keeping us separate for a while.

The meaning of japheth being enlarged (**gen. 9:27**), is seen through the example of the british, and the traveling they did throughout history – mainly from the 1500's to the 1700's and changing and influencing some lands and countries of the world (maybe not always the right way), but they travelled to india, africa, canada, australia (where england sent their convicts, criminals, etc. – then they developed that country), etc., as did the spanish to north, central, and south america, and a few others – like russia, and asia (and possibly the vikings did earlier than that) all have some influence in the world. And when they got to these countries, they mainly found primitive (simple, physical, etc.) people living there (ham) – like in the americas, australia, etc. – then they started to develop the land – modernize it (whatever technology was at that time). And God set all of this up (how man behaved was up to himself – God hoping all would go to Him, and connect back to Him through Jesus and the Holy Spirit), and He made the borders and countries the way they are today from the time (that man scattered) right after the flood (**gen. 10 and 11; acts 17:24-28**) to what we see today (especially america) – the last 4,000 years (since the tower of babel right after the flood – **gen.11**). Japheth is who develops all of the world with shem being part of it – and ham being used to work. The jewish temple was built a few hundred years b.c. or more (and destroyed in 70ad), and the colosseum in rome was built by 80ad. And the building of things started early with japheth and shem, but the tower of babel, was being built before 2,000 b.c. – all of noah's sons (mainly japheth and shem) knew how to build towers, etc. since then (as you see around the world).

God owns all of the land and it is His to give, etc. – mainly to those that go to Him, or to take away, etc. – to those that don't. So go to God and His word and share Jesus. When you look in history, you see people have taken over others, nations, etc. – God allows that, if it happens. Go to Him (or go back to Him).

Even God had america start up and wanted it to share Jesus for all of man (all of noah's sons – in the last days – end times). And america isn't just having people against it today, or have to defend it over the years – there were those that didn't want it to start from the beginning and were against it – and caused problems for people living here and coming here (man is evil). But God wanted it and had to deal with those against it (and against Him) – led by satan, and imperfect (evil) humans, and it (america) is still here (and prosperous, free, etc.), because of Jesus, and will be as long as Jesus (with true Christians with the Holy Spirit) is still here. America is still growing, as a person grows (all of their life), and learns, but with Jesus in its life, but if not, it will stagnate – and satan will prosper.

God separated true Christians from the world (as He did the jews) and separated america from the world (especially from britain at the time – evil powers, and the false church of europe at the time – from satan, and it is still in the world) – and satan's control, but satan has crept in little by little over the years (and it tried to stop america from developing – and the truth) – and america has to preach Jesus and truth of His word (and pray) more, to fight this evil, until Jesus comes back – the rapture. Keep praying.

And true Christianity is not a religion – it's the way God created us to be at the beginning – before adam sinned, and also before the flood and noah's sons, etc. Having the Holy Spirit – being connected to God.

With so much interbreeding for some nationalities – so a little of each of noah's sons, talents, beliefs, etc., but still separate – color, beliefs, etc. Many, many, many people take advantage of america (and live here), but don't want to learn or believe in why it is great or why they can succeed or be happy here – it is Jesus (and His word) – following Him and His truth. He is how the government was formed and led by – God's laws (mainly the ten commandments) – but the whole bible.

People come to america to get something, sometimes to get away from something – need Jesus and need to know that. And we need to share Him – have Him in our lives and society. Learn (His word – the truth) and share Him.

So people need to know why they come here and know the truth of why america is, and will be successful, etc. With Jesus.

There is not enough true Christianity shared – the truth of His word, in the world, society, television, online, schools, homes, family, churches, etc. (even though God uses these, too), and it hurts people – little by little people, society, families, etc. are going down to ruin – satan led.

Man (without God) wants power – to be a god – satan helping (**gen. 3:1-7**), and Jesus takes your power (sinful) away (and He should – like He was with the jews that were in power, but they didn't want Him to – the jews have suffered since), so He can run your life (and a nation – like america). But without God (and with satan) we are evil – all of us are trying to have power over each other, so God separated us (for our own good). This (separation and abilities, etc., from noah's sons, and language change – **gen. 9 through 11**) also seems to give power to some men (whatever ability or power they have over others – but the sad thing is they think they are that way, because of themselves and not the way that God made them and the world), and this power (abilities, etc.) makes them want to do things on their own (whatever ability or talent, etc. they have), and we know that there is something bigger than we are (we know God, but went away from Him and His knowledge), throughout history (**rom. 1**), and we want to be a god (like satan would lead us – **gen. 3**), and many people had gods, like the babylonians, persians, even romans (when Jesus was here) and the greeks, had many gods, as well as the people in india, and still do, also the arabs had many, then settled on one (the moon god), and asians, etc., all had and have gods they made up (so they could be gods and rule the people with them), even the jews (who had the true God – Who came to them, and no one else), went to worship other strange gods that God didn't want them to (and He punished the jews for that – all through the old testament), and all of these people don't want to go to the true God (Jesus and His word) today – although all of these groups, etc., seem to know about God (or at least have heard of Him – mainly through the jews, and some of them have even seen His power at times), and all have heard of Jesus today (and refuse Him, like the jews did) – and all of sons of noah (as separate as they are) need to go to Him (and God made the world this way – **acts 17:24-27** – after the flood), but since we don't go to Him – it is the reason why we are stuck the way we are in this world. God is a jealous God (the true God – through Jesus) – only worship Him or there are problems – and there should be (**exo. 20:1-7**). He made us.

All of the fighting and hurt, hatred, etc. between groups, nationalities, etc. did nothing to help people move up or ahead, etc. – it just made matters worse, and even in america, and we haven't overcome the differences yet – and won't, until we go to Jesus. But it is best we stay separated until then, so satan can't unite us all against God (even though he will in the end). But you be ready to go with Jesus, no matter what happens. Listen to God – through Jesus and His word.

Why is man trying to tell us who we are and what to believe – and what is truth? It is really satan. Go to Jesus and not your own beliefs, and power, etc. (or satan's).

If you think the world is going in the right direction without Jesus, then man will start to think we don't need Him – even for heaven. It won't happen, because satan is still here lying to and leading man – and God won't let that happen – He will keep showing us which direction to go – which is to Jesus and His word. And we all need to know how to get to heaven (and not go to hell) – with Jesus only (getting the Holy Spirit in us).

So since man tries to have power, who are you going to listen to? Using man to decide – which one of noah's sons are you going to listen to and follow (like man did at the tower of babel – following nimrod – ham, **gen. 11**)? You saw what happened then. So we need someone outside of man, not humans, to find the truth and answers to lead us, and we have to know it is God – we all know the only alternative is satan (and he masquerades as many gods, and beliefs, etc. in many people and nations) – so it can't be satan.

Jesus – God, had to come here as a man (like us) – to take our place – to die for us – for our sins – a payment that a just and holy God would accept, since none of us could pay for that. Go to Jesus and His word.

Go to Jesus now, or keep suffering the consequences of this world (of satan's). Man will not solve these problems.

We (our behavior) cause God to do things (like separate us – since the flood – even bring the flood or plagues, disasters, etc.). We need to go to Him – to the true God (Jesus), and straighten it out. He's patient, but can only let people hurt each other for only so long. God knows what's best for us – He made us – and loves us, if we would just go to Him and find out – have to do it His way for it to work. Through Jesus. He wants a relationship with those He created – like parents want with their children, etc. But those children have to listen and obey – behave, etc. – there has to be punishment. To change from the way we are all born. They choose to obey or not.

God waits, before He will punish, or even kill – so that as many people can go to Him as can be saved – we all have a choice, but He has to do it sometime, so we stop killing people here (because we are sinners, evil, etc.).

Although God will destroy groups, people, etc. here and there (after the flood), if all are really bad – like sodom and gomorrah (**gen. 19**) – we see in the world today sometimes, with disasters, etc., but not all of man yet. Just separating them – giving us all a chance to go to Him – whatever generation it is – hoping people will eventually go to Him (possibly these disasters, etc. will get you to go to Jesus).

So all have chances to go to Jesus – and know the truth, but we don't and it keeps hurting the next generation – still evil, and is wrong, the way they are living – we need to tell the world about Jesus – the truth. Be understanding with people - you may do the same as they have - but help them.

The people that we don't want to listen to (or hang out with, etc.) are those that think Jesus doesn't matter. Whether they are gentiles, jews (whatever nationalities, beliefs, etc.), but we can still try to help them know the truth (and it better be the truth), if you can, if they will listen at all.

God did all of this separating and scattering, etc., because of man (it's our fault, your fault, all from man, because we don't go to Him). And those separations are still here today – with the borders (that God set up – **acts 17:24-28**) and language differences, nationalities, abilities, etc., but with technology, travel, etc., man is getting to communicate together a little easier (end times – **dan. 12:4**), and also all go against God like at the tower of babel (and a one world order, etc.) – it has taken over 4,000 years to get back to being one again against God (and God knew it would take that long), and the end will come after that (and satan is pushing that, even though he wants to stay around longer – satan loves power, even more than life – just like he leads man) – we all need to go to Jesus and be ready for whatever happens, and learn the truth, His truth. Jesus is coming back (we, not knowing the day or hour, like before the flood – **matt. 24:36-39** – the rapture first) – for the jews (that the world will start to all be against them – the jews, in the tribulation – **matt. 24:3-28; rev. 11**) – but not at first. There will be peace and safety, then be ready (**1 thess.5**). The end will happen. It doesn't matter when Jesus comes back – get saved as soon as you can, so if you die before He comes back, you will go to heaven – He comes when He comes.

God knew the way the world would go and how man would decide, etc. – fitting what has happened – the last 6,000 years (6 and 7 are numbers that are important to Him), here on earth since creation – and that the jews would not believe in Jesus, etc. – we needed to know that God tried all of these things and we didn't go to Him – Jesus is the only way.

God has given us all of this time to go to Him – to Jesus, to get saved and connect back with Him – so all can be saved – to go to heaven. He's patient and loves us – go to Him. It is our choice, but we have to know the truth about the choices.

The common denominator will be all nations against God, but specifically against israel here on earth (all of the true Christians will be gone – raptured) – all of the religions (nations, false churches, etc.) uniting against the jews (mainly led by satan) – as some already do today. All of the empires from babylon to the roman empire – and similar ones – have been here, and the roman empire (like it was in Jesus' time) will come back then (**dan. 2, 7, and 8; rev. 17:7-14**) in the tribulation – a continuation after a 2,000 year time out for the jews (since Jesus' death and resurrection) – God is in control, and God will let satan rule (anti-christ, etc.) in the tribulation. These groups are all separated right now (by different things – language, borders, cultures, beliefs, etc.), but will get together (after all of those barriers are broken down – that God put there – which has taken

4,000 years since the tower of babel – **gen. 11**, for man, and satan, to do that). Especially after the true Christians are raptured – taken up, before the wrath (**1 thess. 5:8-10**). And some people will remember what some true Christians told them about the rapture, and go to Jesus during the tribulation (and be saved), and will be beheaded for their belief (**rev. 20:4**).

Even though there are differences and separations from each other (by God, because of us – man), no one should mistreat anyone – black, white, rich, poor, man, woman, children, etc. (look inside yourself for your own prejudices, and hatred, etc. – our evil). And we should have more compassion and love (what Jesus gives you), to be able to help others, and more understanding of the truth and why people live their lives this way, and die doing it. Solve the problem with Jesus, not man.

So we need to understand (the truth for) these differences (including the way we look, etc., and how and why that came about after the flood – **gen. 11** – starting at this point), but all the way God wanted it, so man would hopefully have problems (in our life, and sometimes with each other) with those many differences (unlike before the flood – when it was easier – and we were all the same) and go to Him (Jesus). Don't go against your Maker and complain (**isa. 45:5-13**) – go to Him, Jesus now, and make a difference and do something about these things for good. Jesus will help you (**eph. 2:10**). But there still will be consequences and punishment for your actions and behavior in this world (by man – satan, or God), but use them to get us going to Jesus.

This world is all set up so we will all go to Jesus and His word – so we need to all do that now, as soon as we can, if we want to make any difference, but the truth of it (not all of the lies that man, really satan – through schools, religion, false churches, etc., comes up with about us, and about the bible, about God, Jesus, etc. – be sure it is the truth). We need to know the truth.

People are restricted for what they can do on this earth and in life, by God (some do that to themselves, and worse, by what they believe – what man does, and all is not good for man and is not the truth), without Him in our life to govern man (in our separated positions in life) until we go to Him (and His word – the truth), to be one with God. People can do what they want (even Christians, etc.), but not all is good for us (**1 cor. 6:12; 1 cor. 10:23; gal. 5:13**) – we are in liberty with Jesus, with His Spirit – like in america (**2 cor. 3:2-3**). But we all reap what we sow (**gal. 6:1-10**).

And there is truth in this world and it is from Jesus – so don't make up what you want – following satan.

So don't listen to man (people on the news, science, schools, ideas, beliefs, medical, health, etc.), but the truth in His word (bible).

All of the history, technology, science (or lack of it), etc., can be tied to noah's sons – who did and who didn't do what.

And it doesn't mean you can't be successful (even satan may lead you), even without Jesus (or just being in america), but we have to live with the lot in life that we are given (where we are born, noah's sons, etc.), and we will be limited without Jesus, no matter what we try (and the unrest and riots and unhappiness and evil, hate, stealing, etc. will go on until we do, anywhere in the world, and satan is behind them all – with all his masks on, hiding, but you can see how he behaves, mainly against God and His word – that will give him away). And we will believe all the other beliefs, etc. in the world that have no proof – like you think the bible doesn't. And God will let it continue, if we don't go to Him and share His truth – go to Jesus.

Spend your time learning and sharing Jesus – His truth (in His word, with the Holy Spirit helping you), not going against others of noah's sons, with power, etc. (but that is all we are left with, when we don't go to Jesus and His truth).

And it even takes energy to steal, riot, destroy, etc. – use that energy for good, to help others, build, etc., and satan leads that (destruction, death, etc.), so we need to go to Jesus (**john 10:7-11**). And if you have energy to play sports, party, even goof off, etc. then you have energy (and time) to work, build, fix, clean your home, neighborhood, etc. Help others fix and mend things, etc., instead of rioting, spraying graffiti, etc. – don't destroy, build. Do the right thing, and go to Jesus to lead you. To what Jesus wants – find that out. Change our attitude and behavior, with Him.

But until we all go to Jesus, we will continue to do evil in this world. And God will punish and end this world someday. We are not good or righteous by being good, but by Jesus saving us and getting the Holy Spirit (**titus 3:4-7**). Ask Jesus into your life now.

Not sure you can do any of the things that God wants (what the bible says) without Jesus (**john 15:5**, all of **john 15** is good) – at least not good things (and keep failing).

People can do some things in this life and suffer the consequences – for you or others, or you can go to Jesus and be good to yourself and others. And there won't be peace without Jesus – no Jesus, no peace, so know Jesus and know peace (for israel, or america, the world, people, etc. – **john 16:33; john 17:15**) – and Jesus did not pray for the world, but for His own (we that truly believe Him – are saved, and the truth of His word – **john 17:6-10**). Even though it is nice that people try to right wrongs (may help a little), but won't really without Jesus and His word and follow it, and is the only answer – but we need to know the truth and share it. And we can all help each other (but also help yourself), not hurt each other – as well as we need to go to Jesus first. With all the differences and separations of man (through noah's sons, etc.), we all can and need to go to Jesus, and is the only way to solve them – Jesus will and can bring us all together, so choose Him – for now and after this life.

That's what will change this world and life, of all of the things that we complain about – He will help you. Don't depend on man (**jer. 17:5-10**) to solve your problems, but God, or you'll keep failing – go to Jesus for help (or satan will keep controlling man, and blinding you – **2 cor. 4:1-6**), so learn to help, but with Jesus and His word (the truth). And at least knowing where you are going when you die (or if in the rapture), in this evil world. And there is not much time left for this life (if it is your death or the end), or this world. So go to Jesus now, and see the difference. You can see in this world – you don't know when you will die – any time.

And the reason america can handle all of these people and differences, is because of Jesus and why He made america (and why we all got here, no matter how we got here – getting away from your old, and maybe bad, country and life) but going away from Him (as man is trying to do – with satan, and his groups, fooling man, **2 cor. 11:13-15**, and will divide man and nations – to destroy both without God, but should hopefully bring man to God, then unite all through Jesus), and if it continues it will destroy america (then the end comes – the rapture first, **1 cor. 15:50-55; 1 thess. 4:13-18**). You can live on this earth and function without Jesus (especially in america), but not very well, and won't get along. With Jesus is the only way to love and help others and break down the separations and differences that God put here – after the flood, with noah's three sons (so we would go to Him), and solve these problems (**john 15**). There are very few countries (and not as big or as populated) in the world (england, and south africa a little, maybe canada a little, possibly germany, some in south america, etc.), that have as diverse a group of people as america has or as prosperous, etc. (God made it that way – but to go to Jesus), because of Jesus and His truth. Some countries have more diversity in the last 100 years or so, with technology, etc., but mainly have their own – the same (one of noah's sons). The other countries have mostly the same people (not as diverse – not all of noah's sons, at least not many), because of the borders and languages (from the tower of babel – **gen. 11**, that God made – **acts 17:24-28**) – italians in italy, swedes in sweden, russians in russia, chinese in china, etc. (although the jews, after Jesus died, and mainly after the temple destroyed in 70ad, did scatter to most of the countries of the world – **gen. 9:27**), even these countries still have problems (because man is evil), but not the same kind of problems (some countries don't have the same kind of prejudice – not like america – not as big, or diverse – as many of noah's sons, which causes most of the prejudice, etc.), and why God made the world this way after the flood – so God wouldn't have to destroy the whole world again all at once, since the whole world (since the tower of babel) doesn't get the same level of evil at the same time (like it did before the flood), because today they believe different evil things (and cultures, language, appearance, etc. – countries that border each other may have eventually mixed a little, but not right away – and still today are separated, with a few people moving, some wars, etc.) and are controlled better with these differences and separations and beliefs from each other around the world (still controlled and led by satan – but separated, and usually don't get along), and bond a little (between themselves – their own group, nation, etc.), as He has done all throughout history, since the flood (as He did in sodom and gomorrah, **gen. 19**, for example, He did not kill everyone on earth again, just those in these two cities, and got the righteous out of there – like the rapture will be – and like lot and his family, only four people, and just like with the flood with noah, only eight people – the few – they go first, to safety, then destruction comes – it will be just like the rapture). These countries need to get the truth of Jesus and His word – not the things they think are true – or they will continue to struggle, until they do. Go to Jesus and be ready to go.

God separated us all – so we have to go to Him to straighten it out – in each country. But we are not going to get along with the world – nations, no matter what we do – all of noah's sons won't until we all go to Jesus and His word, and it has to be the truth – not satan's lies that are here (in all of the world). People coming from mexico and farther south, are mainly ham, but some japheth, too – a mixture, and all need to know the truth of Jesus and right now they don't (they believe a false belief), and why they struggle (as other countries do), and all seem to want to come to america (because that belief is hurting them – keeps them struggling, etc.). And people shouldn't come into a country illegally – not even america, or you are a criminal and should be treated as one (and some countries send all of their criminals to another country, and use women and children to accomplish that) – all have known of Jesus and need to go to Him, but know the truth, because satan tells lies in all countries, and go to Jesus yourself (and get the Holy Spirit), not anyone else – no need for a church, leader, etc. (but if you can find a good church – especially in america – go to that one, but there are too many false ones). Anyone trying to get into america should be taught about the truth of Jesus while they wait – mainly border crossings, etc. – whatever facilities they have – teach Jesus, but the truth and take care of the children, etc. and have to have some order and protection for america, too – you can't hurt the people of the country they are going to – there has to be rules and laws (and punishments, etc.) – especially for sinful people (that we all are) – and all need to follow the laws (and what they are for). And they can learn of the truth of Jesus, and even to the point of sending them back to their country to share the truth of Jesus and make their country better, and worth staying in – they become missionaries, etc.

It's too bad people use children – sometimes their own for their personal need – being selfish, like immigrants do getting in america, and they are used for evil. This is still an evil world – man is – satan leading, and we still need the truth of Jesus.

God will punish or harm people for doing the wrong thing (including what happened in sodom – **gen. 19**, and with noah's son, ham – **gen. 9**, and how man was before the flood – **gen. 6**, and even today people go away from Him and how He made us – **rom. 1:18-32**, like men with men and women with women, etc. – almost having man to be in control of man – making up ideas, truths, etc. – but really satan is – like a god, maybe even worshipped, but disregarding anything of God – God knows what is best or what is bad for us – and those people sharing this evil way of life with others, against the true God, and His truth, His word, separating man even more, by giving them up to these feelings, desires, etc., although not everyone will do this) – which isn't good for you (or others), but are trapped in our own desires (satan leading), without God. They can change by going to Jesus (and even keep it from happening), and live a different life than they lead (and some have, and some think you can't – but Jesus can). Don't be stuck in your life – don't listen to man (satan) – go to Jesus and change.

Sometimes books and movies and people, celebrities, etc. put some people and groups on a pedestal and are idolized, etc. – making it look like a great life (especially without and against Jesus and His word) – families may do the same. Take people off a pedestal – especially when they don't belong there – Jesus only, tell the truth, and change who you are and what you think is good.

Don't look up to or follow someone because they are good at something – but just what they believe in, and how they live their life. All the people that man looks up to in this world has problems – don't follow them, follow Jesus.

People, especially children, need to stop idolizing (led by satan) athletes, actors, musicians, politicians, celebrities, etc. (some people living a life through satan – like gods), so you can have less problems – go to Jesus – worship God – the true God and the truth of His word. But these same people could help, if they would go to Jesus – a few do. And find who God wants you to be and to be with – and help others get out, too.

And man may do the same to help people (by following God and His truth – His word), but it is for man to go to Him (God comes to us, and is waiting – through Jesus), because God knows what's best and right for man (since man is evil – and satan controls man, cleverly, etc., without Jesus).

Just like advertisers, companies, etc. that try to find ways of getting people to buy their products – luring, lying, etc., just to make it look better than it is – to believe it is the best or the right way, etc. – satan does the same thing in this world (away from God's ways) – tempting, even with false churches, etc. Away from the truth – God's truth.

We need to do unto others – to help others – even just your family, friends, etc. (especially with our differences, but all have to help themselves do the right, best things, too), but help and change is only with Jesus, because the help without Jesus is useless (no matter what it is, or where it is in the world, because people still die after you help them – with their physical and mental, etc. needs). The reason for all of the problems (and to solve them or trying to), is to share Jesus with others, but is a waste of time without Jesus – He is the answer and the purpose, and satan makes you think you (ego, pride, etc.), man, can solve problems without God (and His word).

The big test is in america (toughest mission field in the world – too many false christians in false churches – all think they are going to heaven) – and God uses it to share Jesus with the world (and the reason why we stay here – and not die yet, after we are saved – is to share Jesus – and His word – the truth of it – even though our real home is in heaven, and we are strangers here – **philip. 3:20**). Everyone in these false churches (even religions, etc.) – and there are many – think they are saved and going to heaven (going to church, being baptized, reading, charities, rituals, symbols, jewelry, idols, being nice, helping, etc.) – but they are not – spread the news to those you know (**matt. 7:13-23**). We need to know we are saved and going to heaven – get truly saved now (get the Holy Spirit from Jesus only now, and be ready). It's like getting (or someone giving you – a gift) a plane ticket (the Holy Spirit – gift from Jesus - salvation), then two months later you go on your flight, or getting a wedding invitation and the wedding is not until a few months later – you have your ticket or invitation (the Holy Spirit – it is free), and are ready to go (to heaven) whenever that is – so Jesus keeps us here to grow and learn and share Him and His word – but the truth, to the world. Jesus' salvation is a gift – you don't earn it or pay for it – it is free, just accept it – like a free ticket for a flight that goes later. Go to Him and ask Him and follow Him (and His word, and be led by Him) and wait for the time we will be with Him. This world is not our final home (we all die) – so stop worrying about it here – trying to make it here, and start worrying about what is after this world (then see what God does with you here, and where He puts you). Get your plane ticket first (salvation by Jesus – sealed with the Holy Spirit – **eph. 1:12-14**), then later the flight will leave (die or the rapture) for heaven to be with Jesus. So not being in (or being ready to go to) heaven should be your concern. And that is only with Jesus. Then He will help you help others properly – truthfully.

Absent from the body to be with Jesus, and to die is gain (**2 cor. 5:1-10; philip. 1:21**). But do what Jesus wants you to do here.

This world will be better when you know where you are going after this – with the truth of, and with, Jesus. Then share Him – but the truth.

God will protect you and help you do that (**john 17**), if you will follow Him (Jesus and His word), and do His will. And He helps man protect, too (**rom. 13**), if we go to Him, because we need to know we are protected and taken care of and need for people to do that (wherever we live) – so people don't do violence, etc. to you, so don't listen to those that think protection (police, fireman, etc. – all are not perfect, and neither are you – even some leaders, hospitals, etc.) is bad (it's like God – it's good power, and they are here for emergencies, accidents, injuries, even sports, wars, etc. we have in this evil world that man runs, really satan), but they all have to be with God in mind (with Jesus – that is what is missing – the real 'missing link' – the Holy Spirit in our soul), otherwise they can get away from what they are here for (they are not all doing things right either – and neither do you). We need protection (we all do, but especially women and children), and don't let those (that follow satan, and man – those that are trying to get into this country to do harm, evil, etc.) run this world. Don't let them set a bad example – live your life so others can live a better life, too (stop taking, and living an evil life – you get what you deserve), don't put yourself (or others) in that position. But a life with Jesus and what He wants for us. And it doesn't matter who you are (rich, poor, black, white, etc.), if you lie, get away with something; force others to lie, with money or threats (death, harm, etc.), then it is wrong – no one gets off, God will see to that. And you get relieved when you admit what you did, and forgive, love, help, etc. – so feel better, change, grow, etc. with Jesus. All can go to Jesus to change – then share Him. And get our original life, when God created us – adam – to have this good life with God in your life (with the Holy Spirit).

Think of others, not just yourself (especially if you want others to consider or think of you – treat you right).

But it takes time, but at least start, with Jesus.

Without Jesus you won't have life (**1 john 5:12**). It is what we are here for – to share Jesus – the truth – then you can make a difference in people's lives.

And don't honor evil (what man does) – no matter how people die or struggle in their life, and we all know what is right or wrong (you or they will suffer the consequences of the life we lead – especially against God and His word), and we all know of Jesus (**john 1:9-12;**

rom. 1:18-25). Even if you forgive someone, they may have to suffer the consequences of their actions – jail, fines, punishment, struggles, etc., but hopefully they will go to Jesus.

And talk of Jesus, not of yourself – but His truths, and ways (His word). Don't be selfish, etc. – the way we are born, and don't think of and talk about yourself – your life, etc. Jesus (and the truth of His word) is who we need to share and talk about. Store up treasures in heaven – people you help to get to know Jesus and His truth (**matt. 6:19-21**).

Share Jesus and His word with all – the truth, and keep praying, and they have to want to change, or they will end up destroying themselves or others (or both), and suffer (the only way some people will learn – and learn from others, what to do and what not to do). And try to help those that want to be helped – that humble themselves (especially going to Jesus), and want to live a good life (and don't stop trying) – but not help (materially, etc.) those that are faking like they want help (and are just taking advantage of you and living an evil life – family or otherwise) – and not using their money wisely, not working, taking drugs, alcohol, evil, etc. But keep praying and sharing Jesus.

Some people may change as they grow and learn (and do some good things, etc.), also with life experiences (but not all do learn or change), as well as their life may get better with work, financial, family, etc., but not all change even with that (we are evil, no matter what we have or do, etc., without Jesus).

You can do many things in this evil world, but not all are good or safe for you – like can you run across a busy highway with heavy traffic moving fast, etc. – and think you will not be hurt? Some things are not as dangerous, but will be bad for you (it is not a good idea to be free to do anything). We are all free to do what we want in this world – but not all is good for us. We will suffer until we learn this. God made this world that way, and we need to go to Him to be safe (for you and others). Think about what you do and stop things in your life that are not good for you or others. And you think you would, but you won't always know (not thinking straight, caring, etc.) without Jesus.

Once you accept that people are evil – born that way – including you – you will try to live a life that will not put you (or others) in a bad, dangerous position. Jesus wants to help you with this.

And find out how to live your life here without hurting yourself or others – Jesus is best for you – mentally and physically, etc., but mainly spiritually. Then be ready for heaven (for anything).

Why go to everyone and everything, but God? – Jesus is the answer; don't waste your time going to man (or yourself – or satan) and his ideas and programs, etc. Why not go to Jesus? – at least you will know where you are going when you die, and don't worry about dying (only without Jesus) – go to Jesus. Have you gone to Him yet? Know you are truly saved? Ask Him – to give the Holy Spirit and change you, and follow Him (and not satan – know the truth).

Struggle if you have to, but do the right and best things – the truth (don't give into evil or satan), do what God wants – going to Jesus, He will help with all. And change the separations (for good reasons) He put there (and we made worse, by not going to Him). He wants you to realize that – shared by others.

No matter what you believe, you are going against someone (**matt. 7:3**) – go to God (and His word – to Jesus), not against Him.

Jesus created us all (He is the Creator – **john 1:1-5; col. 1:13-20**), and over the years there have been some changes as He came to us in many different ways – including with the jews, who are still His people, even though today they don't believe in Him or follow Him (and why they have had problems over the years, by not following

God, before and after Jesus came here, even though at first Jesus was separate from all except jews, Jesus came for the jews only – **matt. 10:5-8; matt. 15:22-**24**; acts 2:36; acts 11:19**, not gentiles, until the jews rejected Him), but they are still protected (even if He uses america to do that, which is really Jesus). Jesus separates (**matt. 25:31-33** – what God the Father says to do). The jews (and today even Christians – **2 cor. 6:14-18**), are a separate called out people (**lev. 20:24-26; 1 kings 8:53**), but all can become a Christian (but not all are, that say they are – **matt. 7:13-24**).

So the jews had a separation from people of the world (gentiles – the rest of the world), and they couldn't be with gentiles – to eat, go to their homes, to marry, etc. (even though God used the gentiles to control the jews at times, when they didn't listen to God, a punishment – like how it was when Jesus was here with the romans). Kind of like what has happened in other countries, but that is what God wanted (and set up, especially after the flood with noah's three sons – **gen. 9:27**), and God still wanted the jews to go to Him, not against Him, and hope that others (gentiles) would see their God and His power (and they did at times, but the gentiles judgment was mostly – at that time – before Jesus died and rose – by how they lived their lives and with their own laws, if they – the gentiles, followed the rules, etc. in their own tribe, family, village, society, etc., **rom. 2:1-16**, would they have followed God? – no excuse, **rom. 1:17-32**), it was to eventually have man (jews and gentiles) all be one with Him (Jesus – **eph. 2:11-22**), and it will not happen any other way (and if we go against Jesus and His word – even america will fail). To eventually build His church (true Christians – not a building, denomination, etc.). But trust God to do the right, fair thing with those that didn't hear of Jesus (or the jews, etc.) back then (but we all have heard of Jesus today – no excuse). So Jesus came here for the jews first, then later with the gentiles – He is the shepherd of all, and will lay down His life (**john 10:6-18**) for them (which He did for all), but not for two or more churches, etc. (believing what they want – look at all of the denominations – adding and taking away from the truth), just one church (not a building, etc.) – the people (all true believers, like we should be today – the truth of His word) – after He died and rose – to be one truth. The jews (as a nation) didn't know God or follow God (for sure when Jesus was here – otherwise they would have all followed Jesus), the leaders just tried to look righteous, and in power – looking like they followed laws, but making others do it – hypocrites, just like some of today's leaders (**john 8:52-59**).

Even jonah was prejudice (not wanting to go to nineveh, and preach to the gentiles – **jonah 1**) – so jews against gentiles (God separating), but also gentiles against jews, even today – and all being the same against God – all satan led.

And when Jesus was here, He was going to take power away from the jewish leaders (that had power over the people – jews), from their selfish desires, etc. (who were trying to follow the bible – old testament, laws, etc., but without God, and why the romans were ruling them, because God allowed it), and Jesus was trying to show them the truth (and why God sent Him here, because the jews, leaders, were not following or listening to the prophets – **matt. 21:33-46**, and is also talking about the Christians and america today), so they rejected Him (killed Him – but He died for all of us, and needed to, no matter how tough it was to do). Even after His death they could have believe in Him. And He will come back for the jews (in the tribulation). And satan (leading the world over the years – before and after Jesus) wouldn't be against (or hate) the jews so much (especially those that live around the jews – israel, today), if they weren't God's people – even though they need Jesus and will be with Him some day. And Christians (and america) are hated today (even by some that live here), because Jesus was (and is) hated (**matt. 10:16-28; mark 13:12-13; luke 21:10-19; john 15:17-26**), but He will protect you (as He did others in the past, like daniel's friends – **dan. 3**, and daniel – **dan. 6**, etc. – **1 cor. 2:9**), if you go to Him (and if you die, you know where you will go – heaven, a true Christian's true home). Jesus had His earthly ministry with the disciples for the jews, but the jews, as a nation, rejected Him and killed Him (and the jews salvation is on hold until the tribulation – still coming – and soon). So after Jesus died and rose, He went to the gentiles, first with peter doing it (**acts 10 and 11; gal. 1; gal. 2:6-10**) – and he not wanting to (showing that Jesus is for all nations that believe – **acts 10:34-35**). And eventually the risen Jesus went to saul (paul) to do it, and after paul got saved (**acts 9**), and who has the true gospel and the truth for salvation that the risen Jesus gave him (**rom. 2:16; rom. 16:25; 1 cor. 15:1-4**), and for Christian living – in His books (**romans to philemon**). So go to paul, not peter (even he couldn't understand paul – **2 pet. 3:14-18**) – since Jesus earthly ministry had to die (like Him), then grow (**john 12:23-26**) with paul and the truth the risen Jesus gave him – having paul's ministry with the risen Jesus and the true Christians today.

So eventually God had paul go to the gentiles – with the secrets and mysteries, etc. (and God does keep secrets – **deut. 29:29** – until the right time – His time), that Jesus told paul, and had him write and share the truth to all for salvation (**rom. 2:16**; **rom. 16:25-27**). So we need to share and tell the truth to all.

We can inspire people – with truth, so tell the truth (especially of God's word), even if it is offensive (even if people hate you – care what God thinks of you, not man), but don't offend just to hurt, get back, etc. at people – just tell the truth (and know the truth) and work hard, and is best with Jesus. Because no matter what you believe, all are going to offend someone – so do right, best and learn and grow (grow up) – people will get used to it (and so will you). Live it. Share Jesus caringly, nicely, truthfully – so people can know and change from their beliefs – sharing the truth in love (**eph. 4:14-16**). And pray for them.

You should rather want to be attacked by satan or man (and hated by him), than be attacked by Jesus (and hated by Him) – even though He loves you and is waiting for you to go to Him. Be with Jesus and have Him love you by preaching the hard truth of His word, and He will help you through it – but it better be the truth. What would you do to lose your life and live (**matt. 16:24-26**)?

So Jesus was hated and so will you be – and He offended people (**matt. 11:6; matt. 15:12; matt. 26:33; mark 6:3; john 16:1-3**) – and we will, too. Tell the truth – even to your own family, etc. – and children need to learn young (if they can believe in the easter bunny and santa, they can believe in Jesus – and He is the only one that is real), because Jesus sends not peace, but a sword (**matt. 10:34-39**) – He separates (to become one with Him – with the truth, and what is best for us, God loves us). And it better be the truth – learn it and know it.

And try to be peaceful, as much as you can, but share the truth (but you have to know the truth first), in love (**eph. 4:14-16**) – even Jesus' own mother, and family, had to be saved by Him (they needed to believe who He is). Don't be ashamed of Jesus and the truth of His word or He will deny you (**matt. 10:33; matt. 16:24-26; rom. 1:16**), and have an answer for what you believe in (**1 pet. 3:14-16**). Learn it – know the truth, not a church, denomination, etc.

The problems in this world will give you a chance to share Him – some you overcame (you can relate to others with the same problems) – with Him helping you.

We all have been warned. Jesus is coming back with His sword (His word), and it will destroy some, and others it won't – which will it be for you? The sword (His word) won't hurt those that are His (other than to divide the word rightly and know the truth of His word – read it, study the bible) – we all have a choice. Just like when the jews were in egypt (the first passover – **exo. 12**), and God sent death around egypt (like a fog, etc.), and those that were His (had blood of the lamb on their doorposts – obeyed), did not have the first born killed. And also like lot in sodom, and like noah and the flood, they were saved and protected – God helps and warns what is coming – listen and follow. All are separated. But be together with Jesus.

Before the flood, you could be in the presence of the Lord or not – you had your choice (like satan and the fallen angels did in heaven – they made their choice and will eventually end up in the lake of fire), but since abraham, righteous jews went to abraham's bosom, and were waiting for Jesus – **matt. 27:50-53; luke 16:22-23; eph. 4:8-10**, those that were there, went with Him, and are not there anymore – no place like that now – no purgatory – like a false church teaches (and in abraham's bosom – separated in hades – across from abraham, was the rich man – in torment, who wanted out, but couldn't and wanted someone from the dead, sent to tell his family about that place – **luke 16:14-31**), and now it is Jesus (who came back and has told us all) – only Him that we need to all go through (**john 14:6; 1 tim. 2:3-6; heb. 1:1-3**), and the truth of His word, since He died and rose for us all. And there is no reincarnation, etc. either (all false lies from satan) – only death (**rom. 6:23**), we die once physically (**heb. 9:27**), then we either go to heaven or hell.

God, the Father, even separated from Jesus when He was on the cross, and why Jesus didn't want to do it (die on the cross with the weight of all mankind's sins – He did it voluntarily for us, willingly laying down His life, but there were other times He got out of situations where they – the jewish leaders, wanted to kill him, but weren't able to – it wasn't time yet, **john 10:31-39**). And if there was another way (to 'take this cup away' – **matt. 26:36-44; mark 14:32-36; gal. 1:1-5; 1 john 2:1-6**), Jesus wanted God the Father to do it, because that was going to be the first time that the Father and the Son were apart from each other (they existing forever) for eternity (God turning His back on Jesus and separating themselves for even a short time – for our sins, not His sins, and God not wanting to look at sin, and that was what was going to be so painful for Jesus) – it was not the dying on the cross, or the physical abuse (as bad as that was), it was that separation from God (losing a spiritual connection they had that was deeper than even man can know – as close as man can come to that feeling is losing a child or spouse, etc. – a truly loved one, but even stronger than that – and the closest that man may have felt that is when God had abraham, having to trust God, kill, or sacrifice, isaac – his only son, that he loved, **gen. 22**, knowing that separation, as God did with Jesus, to know what God, the Father, and the Son felt, but times 100 more – we can't fully know the pain). If you know you wouldn't want to give up your child (separated for any reason – they're lost, even kidnapped, etc.) – you love them too much – you will know as a mother or father that you wouldn't want to – you then would know how God, the Father, felt about Jesus – no excuse for you not to go to Jesus. You don't know fully how much Jesus went through for you (when He didn't have to do that – but He did that for us, sinners, evil – **john 15:13; rom. 5:6-8**). But we will know how good that will be when we are with Him in heaven for eternity, and we won't have to be separated ever again. So don't die without Him – you or others you know (but you have to be saved – with the truth, and the Holy Spirit, that only the risen Jesus can give you). Go to Him before you die.

And the example of isaac, and abraham about to sacrifice isaac – is about Jesus – and the sacrifice of the ram, and the shedding of blood for sins (that the jews did since then, mainly in the temple to God, for their sins). And jacob – who is israel – came from isaac, and is the birth of the jews – like Jesus came from the jews and God (the Holy Spirit). And moses was told of a Prophet coming (**deut. 18:15-22**) – who was Jesus – and moses knew Jesus (**heb. 11:23-29**). They all knew of Jesus.

There has to be a payment for the sin (and evil) we have in ourselves (in man – all born with it), and that we caused (from adam – man – we are all connected to him and sinful), because God is a just and holy God, and there needs to be a payment for wrong (and that is what Jesus death and sacrifice was for evil man – our sins). We also have to be punished and need to protect others from evil man – so there is payment for that while man is here. But we all could have been (and can be) saved – if you would just go to Jesus. Go and pray to Him now.

And however God judges those in the past (since adam), and those we don't always know are saved (who have died – those young or old) since then (even today – your family, friends, etc. – whatever they believed apart from the real truth of Jesus and His word) – just know that God will be fair and just with them all (He will be fair with people – including small children, that have died without Jesus – but it is possible that the parents of the children that have died young, will be judged by whether the parents were saved or not – so get saved – go to Jesus). But know that we all have to go to Jesus to be saved before we die.

There are those that have had terrible circumstances about their death, etc. – it's nice to know how someone died, and who may have killed them, and even find their body, etc. – for people (family, friends, etc.) to know (closure), and for punishment, etc. for who did it. God knows all of this. But it is best that whoever died or how they did, that they knew Jesus before this terrible thing happened. Have everyone be ready to go – because you never know when it will happen. Share Jesus, while we all have time. Don't wait – for you or for others.

So do not worry about those that have died (some who may be in hell), just those that are still alive (including yourself) – share the truth (get out of those false churches, religions, beliefs, etc., and help those you love, too). So you can't pray for or to anyone that is dead – all satanic, superstitious, etc. (false churches, religions, etc.). Get to know (be saved by) Jesus (get the Holy Spirit) before you die. Worry about those that may die without Jesus, not those that are truly saved. And we will not remember those that we love (or others), that are not in heaven, if we make it there (**rev. 21:3-5**) – so worry only about those that are still alive.

Don't follow those that are not saved, even family, etc. to hell – learn true salvation – pray to God the Father, through Jesus (**1 tim. 2:3-6**) – no one or anything else, and get the Holy Spirit.

And what He wants today is with Jesus – to show His power and truth, and help others to follow Him, and all can if they want (all can be – **rom. 10:13**), just go to Him now and pray and ask Him (get the Holy Spirit – **eph.1:12-14; eph. 4:26-32**, and that is the only sin that will not be forgiven – refusing the Holy Spirit, **matt.12:31-32**, then you will be saved – no rituals, traditions, church, baptisms, or even tongues, etc. will save you, just the Holy Spirit – **2 tim. 1:13-14**). Not even crosses will help you (they are fine, but not for salvation, etc.), or any other symbol – beads, idols, leaders, saints, etc., that we may carry around or even use to pray with or pray to – all is satanic – in false churches, religions, etc. – just Jesus and His truth of His word – not even signs and visions, angels, etc. (**matt. 12:38-40**) – after Jesus' death and resurrection (and the bible completed – the **book of revelation** written) – anything other than Jesus only would really be satanic. But whatever it is, it has to be from Jesus and to believe in Jesus and His word – no others to follow (don't let false beliefs, churches, cults, etc. lead you – really satan is). The last days we will see things happening (**matt. 24**), but we always need to be ready with Jesus (saved with the Holy Spirit, and be ready to go – and with the truth of His word), so no matter what happens, we will win (we don't have to worry about these things that happen). We need a revival of the fittest – not survival of the fittest – the 'missing link' is the Holy Spirit. We need God's word, and to be with Jesus (**john**

14:23) – the truth of it – getting as many people saved as possible, at all times.

So man doesn't have to sacrifice animals (not anymore) or sacrifice humans – almost like abortions today (never should have, even though people have died – mainly their own choice, for a cause that is right and good in this world, **rom. 5:6-8**) to make things right with God (or with and to the gods that people believe – mainly satan), because God sacrificed His Son for us (for our sins) – He did the sacrifice, once and for all – **john 3:16** (for us to go to the next world – to go to heaven, and eternity), so we don't have to make the payment (or any self-punishment that some churches want, etc.) – which is death and hell – just go to and believe in Jesus (and His word) – He shed His blood for us (**1 cor. 15:50**) – and get the Holy Spirit. Jesus laid His life for you (His love for us) – if you would go to Him (**john 15:13-14**). Follow Him, and His truth, and go to heaven, but we have to ask Jesus.

Even people for this country (america) sacrificed, died, struggled, etc. at the beginning (and throughout to today) of this country – like Jesus did, but be sure you are truly saved. And is one of the most loving things you can do, if it is necessary and for good (**john 15:13**).

Believe the truth, and share it – don't mislead and send people to hell (**matt. 23:13-15**). Pray like this to ask what you want to God the Father (**matt. 6:5-15**, and the real Lord's prayer is this – **john 17**) – but His will be done, and the only prayer that a non-Christian (or a false Christian, etc.) can pray to God is to ask Jesus into your life and repent and know the truth (**matt. 18:19-20; john 14:6 rom. 10:8-13; 1 tim. 2:3-6**), or He will not hear (and always His will **– isa. 1:15; jer. 7:15-16; jer. 11:14, luke 11:2**, and for man to know Jesus, is His will, and even Jesus does the Father's will – **matt. 26:38-44**). And if you pray for something, God may send someone to share the truth of salvation and Jesus (whether you think you are saved or not – but from His word, the truth) – and you may think you don't need to hear, but you do (like someone floating in the water, and are crying out – praying, but haven't drowned yet, and someone throws you a life preserver, and you say no). We are here for Him (and He will help us). So pray to Him (through Jesus) only (**1 tim. 2:3-6**) – and keep reading and learning the truth of His word – and the light will turn on – seeing things are the truth. Go to Jesus, and make sure you know the truth.

Because satan (and his demons – fallen angels) will hear your prayer (or things you say and do) and is always around, and will use it against you (**job 1:6-12; rev. 12:10**), just like when people are around when you think you say things in private – they hear (like when you were young and have a secret that only you and one other person know – no one else would know, then you get older) – then satan (or fallen angels – demons) can use those things, because he (demons) was around when you said that in private, but you didn't see him (so don't believe psychics, mediums, talking to the dead, etc. – satan can share things, etc.) – all are evil (and are against God and His truth) – and connected to satan, evil. There are no ghosts (no dead people floating around – relatives, etc. – only angels – the evil ones that are fallen angels – demons or spirits, trying to fool you). we all go to either heaven or hell (**matt. 10:28; 2 cor. 5:6-8**), after our body dies (**heb. 9:27**) – our souls in one or the other place. Jesus talks of spirits – demons, possessions, etc. (**matt. 12:43-45; luke 24:36-39**). And without Jesus we are all condemned to hell (**john 3:17-21**). Go to Jesus for heaven. No one can get you to heaven – except you go to Jesus yourself (no church, leader, lifestyle, group, etc.). But satan wants you to not know this, and keep letting him tell you lies, and run your life.

So don't call on or invite satan in (or he will ruin you – he is real), or any other gods, prophets, angels, etc. – trying to connect to the dead, etc. with witchcraft, mediums, astrology, voodoo, new age, etc., even sorcery – drugs, pharmaceuticals, etc. and even religions, etc. – like we see today so much (and will hurt man in the end times – now, **rev. 18:23-24**). Even your belief in the things of this world (ideas, groups, opinions, etc.) will connect you to satan, and you won't even know it (all without Jesus' truth). And satan does have power to cause problems for man (especially if you call on him, try to connect, etc.) – don't let it continue in your life – go to Jesus, and be free. Without Jesus, you are with satan.

Ask Jesus only into your life (and read His word) – with the Holy Spirit. Only God's prophets (in His word – the bible, and the Holy Spirit), are truthful – with the truth of His word. And Jesus (with the Holy Spirit) is the only one that came from heaven and went back up again (**john 3:12-13**), and knows the truth. Even though satan has power – he is evil (and destined for hell – and the lake of fire) and against God and His word – don't follow satan. And satan (and fallen angels – demons) didn't and can't go back to heaven. Learn the truth.

Some people in the world are possessed by demons (with all kinds of evil beliefs in this world) – not following the truth of Jesus, but trying to contact satan in their belief (opinions, desires, attitude, etc.) of this world – and even may look or act like a Christian. Don't believe or follow these false, evil beliefs of satan (that man follows and tries to share with others).

If you are not truly saved (with Jesus – getting the Holy Spirit), and you happen to be around religions, beliefs, cults, etc. (spells, witchcraft, etc.) or those people – those that are false beliefs – not with the true God – Jesus, then those groups, with satan (satan is real), and their evil ways can affect you – even though you don't believe what they do. Know who you are hanging out with – you don't need more problems. Go to Jesus to get healed – saved. And God will help you here.

So cast out satan, demons, etc. to heal, etc. – whether it's a person, nation, etc. by the Spirit of God – the Holy Spirit in the name of Jesus only. Know it is the true God doing this – no one else – say it is from Jesus – the truth (of His word), and we will see His power, otherwise we will not (**matt. 12:28; matt. 17:18-20**). Then follow Him, and the truth of His word.

That's why God wrote the bible, came here (Jesus), etc., because all of these evil things are here – He wants us to know. He wants you to know the evil and the good – the difference – and we should know after adam and eve sinned with the tree of good and evil. And what happens when we go to evil (satan), and not to God – it is the world we live in now, after sin (which is man's fault – adam – even we would do the same). Know who to go to and not to go to for help and truth – go to Jesus. Don't be fooled by satan (demons, etc.).

Angels are not used or prevalent – at least not to be seen, just to help when needed (since Jesus died and rose), the last is with peter – mainly in **acts 12** (otherwise just the word, angel, is used), and some in the **book of revelation**, so john could write that book – probably around 70ad (which is all in the future, may even see some things today) – mainly from the risen Jesus. We are to go to and be led to Jesus and His word – nothing needs to be new, after Jesus died and rose, and bible completed – the **book of revelation** is the last book (go to Him to get the Holy Spirit and be saved). So basically after paul started preaching and john got done with the book of revelation (and the temple destroyed in 70ad) are we to just go to Jesus (and the truth of His word) – angels are not needed to help (although if they help we will not know or see them) – for sure not to call on them or worship them – just to Jesus, the Head of us (**col. 2:18-19**). If there are angels, and they are seen today – they are from satan (demons). Good angels are not seen today (**heb. 13:2**). Don't worship or talk to angels, etc. (**col. 2:17-19**). God doesn't need to use angels to share the truth of Jesus, but man is used to share Jesus – just the truth of Him and His word, and the reason we are here after salvation, otherwise satan and demons (fallen angels) will mislead man. So don't trust angels, or go to, or call on them, or believe the things you think are from them – unless all that is said or heard, is that you go to Jesus and get the Holy Spirit, then learn the truth of His word – the bible. No other revelations, etc. (or any other beliefs, etc.) are needed. And the reason that Jesus said that the only sign given and needed will be of jonah (**matt. 12:38-42**) – Jesus dying and rising for us – for our sins. And why there are so many false churches and are sharing lies, etc. – beware (**gal. 1:6-10**). Go to Jesus only (and the truth of His word – not traditions, rituals, etc.)

God may use angels to help you, but you will not see them, or really know they did help – so no angels, especially since Jesus, died and rose (and the **book of revelation** written), because satan (with his angels – demons) came here to stop Jesus, and His message, etc. ever since (**rev. 12**).

Angels (including satan) didn't create (but were created by God), and they don't have anything to do with how things work here (except for misleading us – like satan does) – only God – the Father, the Son, and the Holy Spirit, does. So don't follow them or call on them. God uses them.

So don't try to pray to angels, man, a dead person, saints, etc. (like some false churches do), or you will get satan (or a fallen angel – demon, who will lie, hurt, etc. – trying to destroy God's work, like before the flood, **gen. 6**) – angels were (and are) to minister to man (those that go to God, like the angels ministered to Jesus when He was here – **matt. 4:11**), so after the flood and after God developed the jews (from **gen. 17** on – and adam or noah was not a jew), at that time the angels only went to the jews (along with the Holy Spirit at times) – so the top angels – gabriel, michael (and lucifer – satan, who left heaven – kicked out by God at the beginning – on the eighth day, to tempt adam and eve, and is now destined for the lake of fire – as well as those who follow him, and not Jesus, and His truth) – mainly those two angels (michael and gabriel) were for the jews only, and no one else – no other people or group. And today – since Jesus died and rose (basically the last 2,000 years), all people (the whole earth) have to go through Jesus (**1 tim. 2:3-6; heb. 1:1-3**), not through angels (gabriel, michael, or any angel, etc. for the last 2,000 years) and that's it, just Jesus only (and the Holy Spirit with His word – the truth) – even the jews need to go to Jesus (but they haven't, the nation hasn't – except some individual ones – and israel, as a nation, won't until the tribulation, coming soon). If any angel talks to you today, it is satan or demons (fallen angels), but whatever is said by anyone (any being, angel, person, etc.) for the truth – it will and should lead to Jesus and His word (the bible). So no angel, etc. (they may help you without letting you know they were there) will tell you anything else (just Jesus and His word) since Jesus died and rose (the last 2,000 years). No religions or false churches can (all are from satan – who can become an angel of light, like saying he is gabriel, etc., fooling people with lies, etc. – **2 cor. 11:13-15** – those people, nations, etc. were fooled by satan – and satan is good at fooling people, but they need to know the truth). And gabriel came to mary and said Jesus was the King of the Jews, and the Son of God (**luke 1:26-38**). And most beliefs, religions, etc. believe in the bible – at least up to abraham (**gen. 17**). And the flood, noah, etc. Don't believe man and their beliefs (can't prove their beliefs – satan leading with truth mixed with lies) – just Jesus and His word (who proved who He was – God). And satan filling you with pride to think you know the truth and others don't – all of those false churches and religions in the world (and those born into that belief – it's not their fault, but they need to learn and know the truth). Go to Jesus and know the truth.

And on a side note, when gabriel went to daniel, he flew from heaven where God is – so angels can fly swiftly – maybe the speed of light (maybe how we will move, when we are in heaven, with Jesus – for eternity). Read the prayer that daniel prayed and see how long it was, and you can see how quick gabriel flew to daniel – starting from the beginning of the prayer to daniel by the time he was done (**dan. 9**). So if gabriel flew from heaven – it says he flew swiftly – **dan. 9:21** (and heaven should be millions and millions of miles away) – possibly at the speed of light, at least – 186,282 miles per second, or faster, (and multiply it times the length of time of daniel's prayer) – it is millions of miles (and what we might be able to do in heaven – and why we can handle fast speeds here already – cars, planes, spaceships, etc.).

And even though the stars and space, etc. are far away now (millions of light-years), they were all made instantly – no evolution (no millions or billions of years needed) – then God spread the stars, etc. out after creating them on the fourth day of creation (**gen. 1:14-19; isa. 42:5; isa. 45:12; jer. 10:12; jer. 32:17; jer. 51:15**) – to where they are today in outer space (and have been there since the beginning – at creation). They didn't start or evolve out that far – no evolution – don't listen to man (satan) – even the planets, and the sun (which is a star), that are near us in our galaxy, were left here for us, but the rest were put out in space by God, after they were created – only 6,000 years ago. It is satan that starts all of these false beliefs and man follows.

So gabriel (angel of the Lord) is (was) for jews (for God's people), and Jesus – no one else – no other people, and he (gabriel, angels, etc.) did nothing after Jesus died and rose (except what God wants – helping, and sharing Jesus' truth from the bible), and Jesus is the Son of God, according to gabriel (**luke 1**), so anyone, after Jesus died and rose (starting about 2,000 years ago), was lied to by satan (posing as some other angel – gabriel, etc.) – who (satan) can turn himself into an angel of light (a world in sheep's clothing – **matt. 7:13-16**), and fool man (**2 cor. 11:13-15**) – talk to people, etc., and where these false churches, and religions, beliefs, etc. come from. It is Jesus only who all must go to and through (**heb. 1:1-3; 1 tim. 2:3-6**), and anyone (being, angel, man, etc.) can only lead you to Jesus and His word (the bible – no other books, etc.), and His truth only – no one (or anything) else, but Jesus. Jesus is the Light of the world. All things that come after that (bible completed – **the book of revelation**) will lead you to Jesus and His word – the truth of the bible – nothing else. So don't call on anything or anyone else – no angel, etc. – just Jesus. Only go to and hear of Jesus for the last 2,000 years – no other belief – or it is from satan (and his lies). And we have only been here for about 6,000 years, and mainly close to 4,000 years since the flood (from noah and his sons) – God's plan for us (which includes Jesus – God, coming here to save us).

And God will have you win over satan – if you keep going to Him (**rom. 16:17-20**), through Jesus only (and His word). Know the truth. Look into the truth.

So it continues – Jesus against satan (who man fights with – **eph. 6**), not these manmade groups that we see in the world and on the news (that man follows) – satan doesn't want you to know it is him behind all of these things – the masks he wears (groups and ideas, and beliefs, the leaders, etc.). And man tries to control satan (inside man, leading man, his effects on our life, etc.) with drugs, programs, desires, etc. (**gal. 5:19-21**), but doesn't work and it only takes a few (or one) to cause harm to many (ever been in traffic behind an accident – one person can cause problems for many in this world), or one to help others – like Jesus is one person (and is best) for good – they all need to go to Jesus (to fight satan's hold on the world and man), not philosophies, drugs (legal or illegal), etc., or they are wasting their time. And some people don't hide behind any groups (although there are some false christians), and just say they don't like Christians, and that is what is going on – satan against God (and His word), like at the tower of babel (you can see ham, through nimrod, with satan's help, trying to disrupt the world against God again – look at the world and even america). The way the world is going today (and if america keeps going against God and His word) satan will run this world more as one (all non-believers), and the end will come (with nimrod – ham, again, **gen. 11**), and satan (the anti-christ) ruling the world (**rev. 11 through 13**), all against God. A one world order.

And if you want to get away from being connected to ham (or any of noah's sons) and the evil he does in you (with satan), then go to Jesus and not be connected to ham (or man) anymore – or to any other of the sons of noah – japheth or shem.

Besides separation in heaven or hell (there may be different levels in hell – **psalm 86:13; matt. 11:23-24**, but all are separated from God), there is also the rapture of true Christians (can happen at any time – and the people left behind – non-believers, may even say it's ufos, aliens, etc. that took them – a deception by satan – there is nothing – no beings, aliens, etc., in space, except satan and demons) – so they that go (in the rapture) and all others (non-Christians, false Christians, religions, etc.) stay behind on earth (which is another separation – of believers – going, and non-believers – staying – similar to the flood, when the righteous went in the ark – taken out, and also in sodom and gomorrah – the righteous were taken out, before the wrath, destruction, etc.) – and this will happen right before the tribulation (**matt. 24; book of revelation**), if you are alive (didn't die yet), and you didn't go up to Jesus in the rapture (**1 cor. 15:50-55; 1 thess. 4:13-18**), you will have a second chance (because you will now know that any true Christian was telling you the truth about Jesus and His word, before the rapture) to be saved, and there may be many that are saved (**matt. 24:22; rev. 7:9-17**), even though those may be persecuted, beheaded, etc. (**rev. 13:15; rev. 20:4**) – so go to Jesus now (because you may not make it to the rapture to find this out). And it is satan that beheads people – physically and spiritually – groups (religions, false churches, etc.) do that (behead) – that follow him – like you saw with john the baptist – beheaded by herod (**matt. 14:6-11**), and have seen in the world in the past and today by groups, religions, beliefs, etc. (that satan leads), and will see in the future – in the tribulation. It also is done by false churches – especially spiritually (by putting themselves in place of Jesus here) – by diminishing Jesus and His truth, and having a church and it's leaders to take Jesus' place (putting themselves and satan and their false beliefs, in place of the truth of the bible) – beheading the church (it is Jesus who is the real Head of the church – no one else here on earth, in any of the false churches or religions, etc. – not peter, etc. – he is not a pope, and not a need for one – and peter was never in rome – **acts 18:2** – plus he was married, etc. – **luke 4:38-39**), and no one else in heaven – only Jesus – Who we are to get saved by and follow (and get the Holy Spirit from Him only). The church is the body and without the Head (Jesus), the body (church – true believers) dies – the truth is needed. Too many false churches (old or new).

The rapture could happen at any time (no one knows the day or hour, but God, the Father – and we shouldn't set dates, etc. – although the time is near) – but it may come between now to 2030 (2,000 years from around Jesus' death with 365-day years), otherwise it could be closer to 2035 or later (with 360-day years from when the temple was destroyed – 70ad) – God's years are 360-day years (and even today, with 365-day years, there are 150 days, like before the flood – between February 17 – second month, to July 17 – seventh month – **gen 7:11, 24; gen. 8:4**). So the months will be 30-day months (360-day years) in the last seven years (of the 490 years of daniel – **dan. 9:24-27**) the tribulation (after the rapture) – **rev. 11:2-3; rev. 12:6, 14; rev. 13:5**, as it was before the flood – **gen. 7:11, 24; gen. 8:4**. Jesus died about 30ad, and the temple destroyed in 70ad – so 2,000 years later – after His death, or after the temple destroyed (and at that time – in between 30ad to 70ad, He could have come back for the jews, as a nation – and today still will come back soon for them – **zech. 14; acts 1:1-12** – to the mount of olives or olivet). So Jesus will come for us – the truly saved (before the tribulation – the rapture) – maybe using 360 day years, instead of 365 day years. We do know from the information that God gave us in the bible (**gen. 5**), how many years from creation to the flood, and in **gen. 10 and 11 and 12**, to abram – and from abraham to Jesus is about 2,000 years (42 generations – **matt. 1:17**) and from Jesus' death and resurrection to today, is about 2,000 years – all adding up to 6,000 years (like the six day creation) and then the 1,000 year reign of Jesus, after the tribulation, and satan will be bound for that 1,000 years (like the seventh day of rest after creation – **gen. 2:1-3**) – so we know the numbers are similar to that (Jesus will be back around the 6,000 year mark). All adding up to 7,000 years – so no millions of years, etc. Do the math and see (with the numbers God gives us in the bible).

Regardless, it will be soon. God wants us to know what He did and how long, etc. – so we can believe. Jesus says things will happen before the end (**matt. 24**), and they are happening. Go to Jesus now and be saved – get the Holy Spirit.

If it is the end, God will take care of you – if you are with Him (Jesus – with the Holy Spirit). Keep sharing Jesus – don't hide, hurt, etc. – just keep reading His word and learning the truth and sharing Jesus until He comes – if you are truly with Him.

Be with Jesus – no matter when, or what happens in this world (before you die). And we need to be sharing the truth of Jesus with all in the world. And be ready – looking up.

The world – schools, families, beliefs, nations, medical, health, etc. are not sharing the truth, so people don't cope or get better or can't even be happy, etc. (and even want to end their lives, because of this evil world). Stand up against that (for your family, friends, nation, etc.) – go to Jesus and His truth (the bible) to live your life, the way God intended us to. Stand up for Jesus and the truth, not for any man, or person on this earth. The only time some people think of Jesus or God, is when they swear (and why use their name?) – you don't hear devil damn, or satan damn, etc. (or any other name of a god or leader, etc. of these false churches or religions in the world), just Jesus or God's name in vain (and even if you do, you can be forgiven – **matt. 12:32** – but you can't be forgiven for not getting the Holy Spirit here from Jesus and following Him – **mark 3:28-29**) – why people take their name in vain, is because They are real and the truth (and you feel something when you say it, whether good or bad).

Jesus matters, not man – then with Jesus we all can stand (and kneel). Go to Him and learn it, so you can share it. Jesus is the answer. Stop trying to go around that. We all matter to Jesus – just go to Him.

Being with Jesus will help man be caring and deal with others better, but what God wants and His way – through His word as truth. You will be a better person (better parent, husband, wife, friend, worker, neighbor, citizen, leader, policeman, teacher, coach, politician, etc.) with Jesus and make better decisions and help people better, even with all the differences we have (but He will make us one, and get along and do what's best for each other – **rom. 12**). God gave us things in this life to help us (even before we go to Him) to help us understand Him and possibly help man stay together and live for something – like family, friends, interests, even work, etc., but that's not enough, even though it is good, and those are here in this world, or it would be worse here, so it is nice having life, hope, faith, and especially love (but it better be with Him – **1 cor. 13**). And God put true Christians in positions in this life to help others – in all walks of life.

What God separated – only He can put together (unite, etc.), man cannot, and it is only with Jesus. We all have to go to Him, let Him rule. Whatever is separated can only be put back together by God, and whatever is put back together by God (through Jesus), cannot be separated by man, **rom. 8:38-39** (like marriage, but only by God, and man should not separate – **matt. 19:4-6; mark 10:6-9**). Get connected back to God, with the Holy Spirit.

It has to be with His truth (His word – the bible) and His way (not man's), then it will turn out the way God wants, which is best for us (like He originally wanted it at creation with adam and eve), if we would just go to Jesus (and get the Holy Spirit – that will teach you the truth of His word, **john 14:26; 1 cor. 2:9-16**). And He will take down all of the barriers and separations that are there now. But on our own, we will only help very little now.

Christianity is simple – a narrow way – through Jesus only, to get the Holy Spirit and eventually to know the truth of His word – the bible – history, science, etc. And satan wants to put lies in the truth in many ways for man to not understand – go to Jesus.

Look at the world through the eyes of God – His word – the bible – the truth for everything with the Holy Spirit teaching.

Are you a Christian? You need to be born again (**john 3**) – with the Holy Spirit through Jesus. Pray (**luke 6:12**), alone with God (as well as with others), through Jesus only (to no other being or person, dead or alive, etc., otherwise it is satan – **1 tim. 2:3-6**). And know His truth of His word (not what religions, most churches, leaders, etc. say). Listen to Him only (**matt. 17:5**), and with His word. Believe Him (**john 3:6**), and in Him. Obey Him (**john 8:12**), especially His word – the truth of it. Love Him (**mark 12:30**). Share Him (**matt. 28:19**), with the world (we all can do that – not just true churches and ministries, etc.). Serve Him (**john 12:26**) – doing His will, through Jesus and His word. Then we may have to suffer (and sacrifice, etc.) for Him (**philip. 1:29**) – not for things we want, but what He wants. Then that will be best for us. And do good things. He will give us what we need (**matt. 6:33**).

We are all from noah's three sons, whether we like it or not and have to accept who we are (and the differences, and separations, the punishments, and how God made us from those three sons – **gen. 9 through 11**) and wherever we are in this world (rich, poor, man, woman, black, white, bond, free, etc.), we can all go to Jesus to change that (and be free and be one). No other way. Or it (suffering, bad things, death, hate, etc.) will happen again and again (choose – heaven or hell). You choose for yourself. But get away from being connected to man – to adam, and noah's sons – which leads to hell.

You can't do any of this that is written in this book – at least not very good, without Jesus (and the Holy Spirit). Find out yourself in His word. There are many more things to say, and share, but it all comes down to going to Jesus and His word.

And we can't love like we should without Him in our lives.

So get away from man (adam, noah's sons), and get connected to God, the Father, only through Jesus with the Holy Spirit (**rom. 10:8-18**). Don't be without Jesus and His truth, and then share Him and His truth, with all you know. If you don't share Jesus and His word (don't need to share a church or leader, etc.), you may not be a true Christian. Get the Holy Spirit.

So that we all can be one and get along – not separated any more. Don't try it any other way. Stop trying to be God – satan making you believe that. Man (who is really led by satan) cannot do it.

Jesus loves us, so we can love ourselves and others – the right way. Go to God. Humble ourselves – stop trying to go against what God put in place, or we will stay separated. Connect to God – through Jesus. And get away from the connection to man – including noah's sons, and adam.

Keep praying, always, to God, the Father, through Jesus only – in His name (**john 14:6; 1 tim. 2:3-6**). Salvation in only Him.

So only with the Lord Jesus Christ and His word (with the Holy Spirit – get Him to be saved, and He will teach you His word and truth) – and only with the truth of Him and His word, can we be one on this earth – eventually in heaven, forever. Heaven and earth will pass away, but His word – truth is forever (**matt. 24:35**). If you keep reading, seeing the truth – look in the world – you can see and figure out more things that we need to do (**john 21:25**). Showing us that we need to go to Jesus and His word.

All (of noah's sons) one with Jesus, the way it was to be from the beginning when God created everything (from adam) – including us to be with Him – through Jesus (and the Holy Spirit). No other way (**john 14:6**).

www.ingramcontent.com/pod-product-compliance
Lightning Source LLC
Chambersburg PA
CBHW021601120626
46545CB00001B/10
* 9 7 9 8 8 9 1 1 4 0 9 4 3 *